EVOLUTION OF GOD

HOW THE CHRIST-LIKE GOD REVEALED HIMSELF TO MANKIND

LEONARDO WOLFE

ISBN 978-1-959182-14-6 (paperback)
ISBN 978-1-959182-15-3 (hardcover)
ISBN 978-1-959182-16-0 (digital)

Library of Congress Control Number: 2021901112

Copyright © 2022 by L.C. Wolfe

LEONARDO (a pen name for L.C. Wolfe)

All rights reserved. No part of this publication may be reproduced, distributed, or transmitted in any form or by any means, including photocopying, recording, or other electronic or mechanical methods without the prior written permission of the publisher. For permission requests, solicit the publisher via the address below.

Leonardo Wolfe

2701 Magnolia Springs Dr.
Apartment 253
Lexington KY 40511

1 859 576 8588
Printed in the United States of America

Special Acknowledgements

Many sources contributed to this book and most are acknowledged internally through endnotes for quotes and unique ideas as is customary in literature. Others are cited below for their special recognition as either extended quotations or as non-textual copyrighted material used with permission from the copyright holders. Their generosity is deeply appreciated.

Portrait of Dr. Carl Sagan by permission from artist Murphy Elliot (murphyelliot@hotmail.com)

Quotations (extended) from C.S. Lewis, "Mere Christianity", © 1942… 1953 with permission from C.S Lewis Company, London, UK

Quotations (extended) from Leslie Weatherhead, "The Will of God" with permission from Abingdon Press, Nashville, Tn

Sallman's "Head of Christ", c 1968, 1941 with permission from Warner Press, Anderson Indiana

Two panels from Charles Schulz' Peanut Series: PEANUTS © 1960, 1965, Peanuts Worldwide LLC, Dis. By ANDREWS MCMEEL SYNDICATION.

Acknowledgement of Intellectual Sources and Influences

THE TITLE "*EVOLUTION OF GOD*" IS NOT NEW OR original with this work, and in some ways, is not an accurate description of the contents of this book. Though this **Evolution of God** shares the title, in whole or part, with several previous scholarly works, and is enriched and influenced by these earlier works, our purpose and scope are neither derivative nor overlapping. But credit to and appreciation for these earlier books is necessary, for they are all top-notch scholars and intellectually challenging, and would be recommended reading for anyone who has a serious interest in the idea of God, how we arrived at such an idea and where does such an idea fit into our own "reality." Dozens of books and articles have helped shape this present *Evolution of Go*d over several years of preparation, but four are mentioned here for special appreciation and acknowledgement.

A massive, heroic book with *nearly* the same title as this present work, *The Evolution of God*, was published in 2009 by Robert Wright. It was recognized as a well-deserved finalist in 2010 for the Pulitzer Prize. Professor Wright follows the emerging idea of God from the Stone Age to modern time, using history, archaeology, theology and evolutionary science. Though Professor Wright labels himself "an unbeliever" his written works are considered by other scholars as "religion friendly." He holds that "gods arose as illusions" invented by mankind, but at the same time, he thinks it is an excellent thing for others to believe in God. Since he advocates belief largely for secular and social purposes, Wright insists that religions evolve in the direction that he considers most conducive to social harmony and global peace. He traces the **idea** of god from primitive animism to polytheism to monotheism and on to modern religious manifestations. He shows how the idea of god, or religion, provided a positive influence on human evolution and the creation of sustainable societies. He does not argue for the reality of the god or gods being worshiped, but contends that the evolving of the idea progressed in positive evolutionary steps, positive in the overall effects upon human culture. In this sweeping narrative that takes us from the Stone Age to the Information Age, Robert Wright unveils an astonishing discovery: there is a hidden pattern that the great monotheistic faiths have followed as they have evolved—a consistent moral trend upward over the history of mankind, a kind of moral evolution.

One hundred years earlier, in 1909, Phillip Gulley published ***The Evolution of Faith: How God Is Creating a Better Christianity.*** Gulley's book is a "believer's" review of the historical changes and development of faith in the Christian era, arguing that the trend of the changes in human understanding and practice of faith over time has been part of God's plan, "progressive revelation." It is a significant, prescient book in that Gulley advocates many of the ideas underlying this present work: progressive revelation, evolution as God's tool rather than His nemesis, breaking out of the rigid dictation and inerrancy view of the Bible, and the embrace of science rather than fear of science. Like Gulley, our goal and hope here is for the opening the way for a Christian Faith grateful for scientific knowledge, comfortable with people of other faiths and people of no faith, thus, a Christianity that looks more like Jesus and less like a religion.

The Evolution of the Idea of God by Grant Allen, was also published in 1909, by the Rational Press Association, a group of liberal American philosophers and free thinkers. Subtitled, "An Inquiry into the Origins of Religion," Allen describes his work as an attempt to bridge between two competing views of how religion developed: "humanists" and "animists", roughly comparable to this present book's focus on science and religion. Professor Grant is not presenting an apologetic for Christianity, and maintains a neutral, scientific search for the truth. His book is helpful in its wide scope of research, including not only written and archaeological evidence, but also the study of "savages, present and past." It is laudable that this book was written well before he had access to a wealth of archaeological and anthropological knowledge now available

Edward Caird (1835-1908) was a Scottish philosopher, the younger brother of the famous theologian John Caird. He was invited to give the prestigious Gifford Lecture the University of St Andrews for the sessions 1890–1891. The Gifford Lectures are an annual series of lectures which were established by the will of Adam Lord Gifford, established to "promote and diffuse the study of natural theology in the widest sense of the term—in other words, the knowledge of God." His lectures were published in 1893 as a book on the philosophy of religion entitled **The Evolution of Religion.** This treatise, which was widely acclaimed as a masterpiece, enhanced his reputation and led an invitation to return to give the 1901-1902 Gifford Lectures. These later lectures were published under the title **The Evolution of Theology in the Greek Philosophers.** His seminal work **The Evolution of Religion**, early in the Darwinian era, dug deeply into the same philosophical and scientific questions explored here. But, whereas Professor Caird dealt with the origin of the idea of God as part of his larger quest for the origin of religion in humans, the priority is reversed in this book.

Though some of the previous works cited above bear similar titles, and there are scores of other books dealing with the history of religion, none deal with the same content and approach as this current work. Here we look at the search for God as the central focus, the essential core around which specific religious practices would arise. Our quest is to discover (or speculate) how the first humans came to experience an awakening sense of a spiritual domain, an invisible reality, alongside their physical and material world. This may be seen as a "chicken or egg" question. Whether the idea of a god or gods came first, or perhaps some form of religious rituals preceded it is probably beyond our knowing. But as an organizing principle, the search for the birth of the earliest idea of a "god" in humans, and the subsequent development of that idea, provides a rich and fruitful field of endeavor. The premise of this book is that the earliest human concepts of God evolved over the millennia, from the most primitive animism to the present, richly endowed portrait of **Father God** presented by Jesus of Nazareth. This change over time we have labeled "evolution", and we try to demonstrate that change was gradual improvement, based on brain development, moving ever upward in human history toward a final or highest form of the *God-idea* as it is possible to imagine.

Contents

Special Acknowledgements iii
Acknowledgement of Intellectual Sources and Influences v
Preface xi
Dedication xix
Introduction xxiii

Chapter 1:   The War Between Science and Religion 1
Chapter 2:   But What About the Bible? 11
Chapter 3:   Then What About Science? 43
Chapter 4:   The Brain Game 64
Chapter 5:   Brain, Mind and Soul 106
Chapter 6:   Thinking, Language and Belief 151
Chapter 7:   The Ascent of Mankind 170
Chapter 8:   The Birth of God 195
Chapter 9:   Some Kind of God 235
Chapter 10: God is Great... God is Good 249
Chapter 11: Jesus, The Perfect Image of God 301
Chapter 12: A Christ-Like God 321
Chapter 13: God's Image in Us 341
Chapter 14: Animals and Other People 352
Chapter 15: Being Fully Human 373
Chapter 16: Freedom and Free Will 410

Chapter 17: Sin, Evil and Guilt.. 423
Chapter 18: Salvation and Redemption 448
Chapter 19: What is Real? 480
Chapter 20: Belief vs Knowing... 497
Chapter 21: Decisions and Choices... 517

End Notes 539
Sources for Chapter Epigrams 549

Preface

THIS IS A BOOK ABOUT GOD, A PARTICULAR AND SPEcific vision and version of God: the Christian God. This is more of a theological apologetic work than a scientific study, though every relevant field of science has been diligently searched for the evidence, clues or insight related to the central premise. That central theme is contained in a verse in the Christian Bible: *"On many past occasions and in many different ways, God spoke to our fathers through the prophets. But in these last days He has spoken to us by His Son."* (Hebrews 1:1) This is the simple proclamation of Christianity: God was revealed, fully and clearly, in Jesus Christ. In the centuries and millennia in the past God exposed/unveiled bits and pieces of Himself as the human mind developed and was able to grasp. Thus, gradual revelation of God was advanced through fits and starts, bits and pieces, moving inch by inch, insight by insight, culminating in the full, finished and final revelation of Himself the New Testament proclaims. The invisible God became visible in the person of Jesus of Nazareth; the spiritual Being became a human being. *"The Word became flesh and made His dwelling among us. We have seen His glory, the glory of the one and only Son from the Father, full of grace and truth."* (John 1:14) Jesus said of Himself, *"Anyone who has seen me has seen the Father."* (John 14:9) *"The Son is the image of the invisible God..."* (Colossians 1:15) *"For God was pleased to have all His fullness dwell in Him"* (Colossians 1:19) *"For in Christ all the fullness of the Deity lives in bodily form."* (Colossians 2:9) *"No one has ever seen God, but the one and only Son, who is himself God and is in closest relationship with the Father, has made him known."* (John 1:18) *"That which was from the beginning, which we have heard, which we have seen with our eyes, which we looked upon and have touched with our hands, concerning the word of life—the life was made manifest, and we have seen it, and testify to it and proclaim to you the eternal life, which was with the Father and was made manifest to us."* (I John 1:1-2) That is the claim laid out in the original Christian apologia, the New Testament, connecting with and building on the earlier body of revelations we call the Old Testament. Jesus had this strange claim about how the new revelation of God fit the older: *"Do not think that I have come to abolish the Law or the Prophets; I have not come to abolish them but to fulfill them"* (Matthew 5:17)

Apologetics is a word that is often misunderstood, as if it means 'apologizing' for one's faith. The word, however, derives its meaning from the Greek *apologia*, meaning a 'reasoned defense.' The word "apologetic" thus means "reasoned arguments or writings in justification of something, typically a theory or religious doctrine." It is probably hubris to claim a work to be an apologetic before the work is presented and tested intellectually. However, the intention of this work is to give a reasoned and rational idea of God which is scientifically relevant and comprehensively connected to the broad scope of human learning and fields of study. The author is not a scientist, and no claim is made herein that the propositions presented are scientifically derived or validated. Apparent connections observed in history, physics, religion, biology, psychology, and numerous other sources are noted and where patterns seem to exist, speculations and hypotheses are proposed. For example, the fact that the human brain structure has three layers (reptilian, mammalian, and neocortex) seems logically connected to Freud's map of the mind in three layers (id, ego and superego). The reptilian brain was the first brain, and it serves still to instinctually promote survival (fight or flight), to regulate breathing, heart rate, and to stimulate sexual arousal to assure reproduction. To the author, this seems very similar to the Id as Freud defined it.

Likewise, the higher functions of the human brain are largely associated with the neocortex, the primary location of reason, logic, planning and moral judgment. That brain function seems quite close to Freud's "superego," the inner supervisor or parent telling us what is right and wrong. Of course, the middle brain formation, the mammalian or limbic, is largely involved in emotions, feelings, pleasure, social skills and value judgment. This brain function certainly seems like the ego Freud defined, the conscious and unconscious elements of our "self", our identity. This proposed connection is not a scientific assertion, and is not backed by any new personal research findings. It may be seen as "pop science," scientific-like ideas such as appear in popular magazines (*Popular Science, Discovery, Popular Mechanics*, etc.) This brain/ego speculation may be true, but it must be tested, researched, and argued in scholarly journals and conferences, all activities beyond the author's skill (and pay-grade!) Optimistically, this example and the many such observations and patterns discussed in this book will be challenged with the scientific method, viewed as theories or hypotheses brought up for consideration.

Extensive references are given in the text (e.g., [12]) for follow up and further study of sources used; the notes themselves are "Endnotes" rather than "Footnotes" and are located at the end of Chapter 21. This is not a "scholarly" book in the academic sense, attempting to communicate with interested average readers more than with professors and researchers, but everyone is encouraged to delve into some part of this wide-ranging content and learn more for yourself.

There are complications in trying to address two very different audiences in this book, people who already believe in God but are suspicious of science, and people who are science-oriented but suspicious of God or gods. Both groups are viewed very positively by the author, who finds himself firmly in both camps. For the sake of simplicity, the religiously oriented will be called **Believers** here, and the others will be called **Skeptics**. "Skeptic" is chosen as a positive label in recognition and appreciation for the fact that all true scientists have to be skeptical as their mindset, their set-point, their default position. Just as Missouri is called the "show me" state and Missourians are supposedly hard to convince, so scientists say "show me the evidence, give me the numbers." Avoiding jumping to false conclusions is a good practice for both scientists and religious people. As discussed later, "doubt" is frightening to Believers, but shouldn't be, for reasons that will be explained. As will be argued in several chapters of this book, "uncertainty" is viewed by the author as a virtue in every walk of life.

Scientists and academic professionals will notice that the terms B.C. and A.D. are used here rather than the recent most common designations for dividing history, B.C.E and CE. Traditionally B.C. was used to designate the period "before Christ" and the A.D. (*anno Domini* – "year of the Lord") were used in the Julian and Gregorian calendars. In the last 50 years the older terms have yielded in many scientific publications to the B.C.E ("before common era") and CE ("common era"). This seems to be a totally unnecessary attempt at political correctness, shying away from any religious connotation. The time in each reference is the same and is tacitly tied to the supposed birth of Jesus (which was probably 4 B.C. in actuality) So B.C. and A.D. are used here to honor tradition and in recognition that most lay people are familiar with these older traditional terms.

Another "peculiarity" some will notice in this book is the use of capital letters in all references to God or Jesus: *He* rather than *he*. This is just a stylistic preference of an 83-year-old educated in a long-ago time in the Bible-belt South. For the same reasons all the references to the Judeo-Christian God use the masculine pronoun; this is not a sexist choice because God does not have a gender. Because "Father" is the favorite metaphor used to describe and personalize God in the Bible, made especially real and attractive by Jesus, the tradition of "He" is followed here for consistency. We could as easily go with the "Mother" image of God since so much of God's character and actions are gentle and nurturing like a good mother. Even Jesus sounded like a mother when He saw His beloved Jerusalem before Him, the city which has killed other prophets of God and would soon crucify Him: ***"O Jerusalem! Jerusalem! How often I have longed to gather your children together, as a hen gathers her chicks under her wings, but you were not willing."*** (Matthew 23:37, *New King James*) **Jesus** was Himself the perfect image of God and so He showed strength and courage as well as love and compassion, just as His father did. We can be like God in many ways, but we are gender bound (male, female, transsexual or other) and our gender identity affects our view of life. Jesus was born as a male, but that does not give "maleness" some extra value or convey any authority over "females." Most of us have a hard time imagining a Being without some gender (which is true of God) so thinking of God as an ideal, perfect Father is just a shorthand way of visualizing the invisible. If you are more comfortable calling God "she" or imagining a strong, wise Mother, feel free to do so. Some publishers have edited Bibles to eliminate gender references so as to not offend women, but it seems contrived and unnecessary. Just as we say "Mankind" without any malevolent intent, understanding that "Mankind" includes both male and female (and "undecided.")

For the non-theist or Skeptic, the apologetic goal of this book is **not conversion** to some specific faith or religion, but to make the IDEA of God reasonably plausible, based on scientific thought and good evidence, and to the degree possible, make this particular Christian God attractive and satisfying AS AN IDEA. The Skeptic may still not believe in gods, but perhaps can accept the proposition "**If there was a god**, this 'Jesus-like God' described here would be a **pretty good God**."

For the Believers--Christian or others, the goal of this apologetic is to provide a convincing case for the complete acceptance of science as not only compatible with the nature of the Christian God, but as absolutely necessary for an intellectually mature and defensible vision of God in a modern world. This objective is to equip the Believer to present their belief in God in the most effective way; God has not had very good "public relations representatives" in the past. In this work, questions of evolution and creation, the validity of the Biblical documents, and the multitude of intersections of science and faith will be thoroughly and transparently examined. The potential for harmony and mutuality between science and faith will be presented, an apologetic for a traditional Christian faith which is scientifically informed. Perhaps the greatest danger to an intellectually secure Christian faith is an old, entrenched, extended cultural battle with science or semi-science. That is an unnecessary battle. *If something is scientifically true, the Christian God is not surprised—in fact, it is God's laws that science is discovering.* Science has always eventually corrected its mistakes with better science. We only must insist that we have **good** science. Faith has no need to fear the truth, in science or elsewhere. **Any God who can be threatened by science is too small to worship. A small God is not worth defending.**

Christians are required to speak up for God, to explain Him reasonably to those who don't know Him: "*But in your hearts revere Christ as Lord. Always be prepared to give an answer ("apologia") to everyone who asks you to give the reason for the hope that you have.*

But do this with gentleness and respect, keeping a clear conscience." (1 Peter 3:15-16)

Readers will notice that quite a lot of scripture is quoted, usually in bold type to set it apart from the rest of the text. The vast majority of Biblical references are from the New International Version (NIV) and others are identified in the citation. The quotations will be familiar to many Believers, and it is important that Believers see **this book is not an attack on Christianity or the Bible**. Skeptics may find the scriptural references too "preachy" and not useful to them. The biblical passages are not cited as "proof" for non-believers, not really presented as evidence to bolster the theistic arguments. However, Skeptics are urged to read the cited passages as evidence that religion has wrestled with life's big problems, that Believers have faced the difficult questions, and have at least some rational bases for their beliefs. The ideas collected and packaged in this book are not new, and not actually strange to Bible scholars. Christians have explored and debated these issues for nearly two thousand years, and while these ideas will continue to be hashed out among Believers, it is hoped that this particular way of looking at and connecting science and traditional beliefs will advance understanding of a Jesus-like God, and understanding of others with different opinions. Mutual respect is a good basis for conversation.

Religious readers will notice and probably view with suspicion, the frequent resort to scientific studies and a heavy dose of "secular" quotations. This is not a science book, although it is partly about science. Believers need not feel intimidated, for the author is not a scientist, but rather has nearly 60 years in the fields of social work and Christian ministry. Science is praised in this book, but not idolized. Science has discovered so much of how the universe works and is governed, and all humanity is vastly better off today than 100 years ago because of science and technology. It is true that scientific technology is sometimes used for destruction and greed, but that is a human problem, not a scientific one. Chemistry can make compounds that cure or prevent disease; chemistry can mix other compounds to poison and exterminate whole populations. Remember, God made all those ingredients, and so they are "good." It is not science that make them harmful...it is us; people like us with our character flaws. But science has one supremely wonderful quality: **humility**. (*Please quit snorting and laughing!*) Scientists sometimes are arrogant, conceited and disgustingly sure of their superiority. But **science** itself is not vain, blind or haughty, for science is **skeptical**. Real science is based on a process that assumes that truth is tentative, that absolute certainty is impossible, and that "we may be wrong!" Science can and has given us some really convincing "nearly certain" truths or theories, and science remembers history and knows that the "nearly certain" finding today may be disproved decisively next year. And science is structured so that every true scientist looks at the official evidence of someone's research like an Inspector Cousteau or a Sherlock Holmes: they suspect an error and they pursue it with passion. Science is not always right, but as a field of endeavor, it almost always corrects itself. Only the most perfect theory survives, and even the "perfect theories" have been overturned. Believers should approach Skeptics with this mindset: they are probably rational and logical, and they have reasons for their skepticism. **Listen. Listen. Listen.**

Dedication

*It is significant that Carl Sagan (cited frequently here) gave the 1985 Gifford Lectures in Scotland, and published the content in one of his many books, **Varieties of Scientific Experience.** Carl Sagan was the inspiration and energizing spark for this present book. It would be unprofessional and presumptuous to admit that the author loves Dr. Sagan, whom he never met, but it would be the truth. The author is deeply indebted to Dr. Sagan, not so much for the content here as the spirit and attitude he demonstrated. It is inconceivable that Carl Sagan has evaporated into nothingness, my own religious doctrines aside, and it is a fond hope that our meeting will still take place somewhere beyond Time.

Major Concepts Presented in this Book

1. Believing is a **choice** made from possible alternatives based on the evidence accepted, in material physical science **and also** in non-material metaphysics
2. Believing is **not knowing**, for it is making a mental choice in the absence of certainty
3. Certainty is not possible in either science or theology; there are only degrees of certainty or confidence in the truth or reality of a proposition or theory
4. Logically, either there IS a God or there IS NOT a God, there being no third viable option
5. A rational argument can be made for believing in a GOD who created the universe and all things
6. This God has **gradually** revealed or made Himself known to humans over time immemorial
7. The evolving **human brain's** limited capacity was the **primary factor** constraining this revelation of God. The human brain was and is the means of communication between God and mankind
8. Human understanding of God was **progressive and incremental** as brain capacity evolved
9. This progressive understanding of God was universal in humans over time, not identical in all peoples and places, yet always developing in the same direction (toward monotheism)
10. The variety of human understandings of God presently exhibited worldwide represents the **differing evolutionary stages of humanity's concepts of God**, with multitudes of religions and cultural practices, but relatively few significantly different concepts of God
11. Darwinian Evolution is **not incompatible** with the biblical Creation by God and informed believers can become comfortable with this scientific explanation, recognizing that **anything** that is true is already known by God, and He created the laws of nature as well as the content of nature. Science seeks to explain WHAT and HOW while theology seeks to explain WHO and WHY. Evolution is widely accepted as

scientific truth, though like all science, it is subject to further revision. By acknowledging that the **Bible is not a book of science**, and that Science is not a study of God, believers can accept that God **could have** used evolution if He wished, and still be the Creator

12. This evolution of the concept of God was not Darwinian evolution (natural selection by gene based reproductive advantage) but by social, emotional and intellectual **usefulness.** Newer theories and ideas gained credibility, and the most elegant or probable are selected. This process is **much like science,** which proceeds from vague early guesses (hypotheses) to support from experience to verification and testing against other explanations. The "best" explanations of the natural and/or supernatural survive because they are satisfying and useful at the time; over time, competing ideas may replace earlier views by their greater "believability," just as in science

13. Anthropologists have identified a common set of stages of **evolving religious practices** from our earliest ancestors, apparently universal and culturally transmitted. Existing primitive tribes still living isolated from modern culture offer insight into prehistoric, Stone Age theology and religion, essentially peering back in time

14. Religious practice is a human creation in response to the practitioner's concept of God or gods; the focus of this book is on theology (god-study), not on religious practices

15. The Bible's Old Testament is a record of a specific ancient people's search for God, and is best viewed as a spiritual diary or personal journal of some 50 or 60 individuals in various stages of theological and moral development

16. The Old Testament is a theological book accurately reflecting the religious experience and understanding of the human authors, but is not book of science, geography or cosmology, or even primarily a book of history. Old Testament science (2500 years before Galileo), like Old Testament theology, is rudimentary or primitive compared to modern thought

17. The Old Testament gives an evolving, progressive picture of God, reflecting some of the most profane ideas of God, but

also some of the deepest, most profound understandings of God ever attained by any people of any time. Retrospectively, we can discern which picture of God is more congruent with what Jesus taught about His Father, and which images of God are human misunderstandings and mistaken theology

18. The New Testament is the continuation of the record of the ancient Hebrew's search for God, a trustworthy account of the intervention of God into human history through the physical, verifiable birth of Jesus of Nazareth, in the Roman province of Judah, about 4 or 5 B.C.
19. This Jesus claimed to be the embodiment of God in a human life, come to reveal clearly to all mankind the God they had been seeking—a God portrayed primarily as a loving Father, both supremely **Good** and **Great** and totally invested in the well-being of every individual human
20. Jesus is the full, complete, sufficient revelation of GOD, the final stage of the Evolution of God, and He is the perfect pattern by which all theology can be measured or evaluated, by means of His life and His teaching

Introduction

There is a God-shaped vacuum in every heart
BLAISE PASCAL

THE EMBERS OF THE BIG FIRE WERE GLOWING steadily, while streams of sparks followed one another in a brief dance toward the evening sky. Like a parade of tiny glowing birds, each launching on their own timing, one after the other, sometimes intertwining in their flight, along with whiffs of smoke, each having a moment of brightness and then fading away quickly and disappearing. The dozen or so people sitting around this campfire are quiet, totally still, staring together at the same warm, comforting fire, silently sharing, but somehow solitarily, alone in their inner world. Their minds are traveling on vastly different journeys, deep in reverie, thoughts and feelings unencumbered by words. Like the escaping sparks of the fire, these inner lights are real, and they give pleasure, but they slip our grasp, but something remains.

As the evening sky darkens, the once hidden stars begin to reveal themselves. Unlike the sun and the moon which are so sure and trustworthy, these tiny lights in the night are a mystery, a fascinating view which hides and teases, sometimes here and sometimes elsewhere, playing a game with our eyes and our minds, defying our attempts to understand. We first see that bright white star blink on, and then there are two or three more coming into view over there, and then we see faintly the dozens and dozens of dimmer lights joining the early comers, and we finally perceive whole patches of the darkening sky shining as a sheet of stars, clustered and united in their display.

Perhaps the placid scene described above happened in Rhode Island one summer evening last year, as something similar occurred hundreds of times in many other back yards, and in many other times, with many other similar human beings with many other similar brains and inner thoughts. But, for a moment, let us imagine this scene was duplicated on a grassy savanna in Africa, and that it was not just a year or so ago, but a hundred centuries ago, or a hundred millennia into our deep past. Certainly, there were people very much like you and me on that long-ago savanna in 120,000 B.C. Their brains were virtually the same size as ours (maybe even larger). Probably, they thought about the same kind of things in their quiet times as we do today. Though we find it hard to grasp, even 100,000 years ago, there were Homo sapiens, very much like us in most ways, sitting around community campfires. And even though it disturbs our stereotypes, those early relatives of ours were probably thinking about life and death, about fear and doubts, about love and joy and compassion and suspicion and trust. Some around that ancient fire were probably just as smart as any of us, and some of them were probably "a few fries short of a Happy Meal" like some of us. They were like us. Some of them were geniuses, creating tools and controlling fire and producing wondrous sculptures and works of art on cave walls, beautiful expressions of mind and talent comparable to our Rembrandt's and Van Gogh's.

Troubled as we are by the thought that we are descendants from ancient animals like orangutans, apes and chimpanzees, the evidence for this kind of evolution is compelling. Bible believing Christians and other religious readers may abandon us at this point, but it is not necessary, as will unfold in later discussions. The Evolution of God embraces both the Biblical account and the Darwinian account, with some appropriate intellectual reservations for both. Stay with me, Bible lovers, for the Biblical God is bigger than any box in which we have enclosed Him, and your faith is not endangered here.

Genetically, we are 97% identical to the present tree dwelling relatives in the jungle and zoo. Our evolutionary advance over them is only about 3% at the genome level, and that 3% probably took close to a million years to reach the "human" stage (homo-erectus, homo-habilis, homo-sapiens, etc.). What difference does that 3% make between our animal cousins and us? When did the first Adam become "a living soul," first gain the capacity for consciousness and self-awareness, to begin vaguely glimpsing the mysteries of mortality and morality?

Was there a "Eureka" moment, a flash of insight that marked the transition from animal to man? Did some long-ago ancestor awaken to see the world, the environment, the group of companions around him, with fresh eyes and thoughts? Was he alone, or did others of his generation begin to have these same thoughts, these same glimpses of realities beyond trees and skies and saber-toothed tigers and frightening noises in the darkness? With rudimentary language, did the First Adam share his thoughts with his spouse or his children, or the elders of the clan? Were there new arguments around the clan campfire about life and death, about unseen beings that might be all around them? Were there accounts of dreams that seemed to bring back some loved one who had died and been buried, but not forgotten yet by the survivors? Was that misty image actually the dead person returning in a dream? Was there some meaning or warning in this vision in the night? Somehow, some time, somewhere, such thoughts and discussions took place, and from these imagined new adventures of the mind we developed, over long eons, the mental concepts that became religion.

The world of the spirit was a much later part of our evolution than our understanding of the physical world. The physical world's demands on living creatures were the engine that drove evolution over the millions of years before we arrived. Those who adapted to the demands for food, shelter and safety survived and produced off-spring like themselves. Those individuals and groups that failed to adapt to the climate, the food and water supply, or the encounter with predators did not survive, and their lineage died with them genetically. Darwin theorized that subtle, random changes occurred in each species, and some of these mutations gave a survival advantage, and this advantage was passed down genetically to subsequent generations. Some such random changes were detrimental to adaptation to the physical demands of the environment, and so some species did not survive and went extinct. But the evidence in paleontology and archaeology and many other branches of science convinces us that early humans began to live and function in both the visible material world and the invisible immaterial world. Early on we find them preparing the bodies of their dead for burial, often with ocher body paint, and sometimes tools or personal possessions, clearly believing that the physical death was not the final stage.

So we begin, seeking to understand as well as we can, how our species came to believe in spirits and gods and, after 200,000 years or so, we came to believe in a benevolent Creator and universal God who has a vested interest in the fragile humans occupying this small planet.

Chapter 1

THE WAR BETWEEN SCIENCE AND RELIGION

*"Uncertainty is an uncomfortable position.
But certainty is an absurd one"*
VOLTAIRE

THERE IS A WIDESPREAD BELIEF AMONG AMERICAN evangelicals and other conservative Christians that there is an active and insidious "War against Christians", or a political "Attack on the Church." Annually, this war is reflected in public dispute about greetings of "Happy Holidays" replacing and disparaging "Merry Christmas." Replacing CHRISTmas with Xmas is another battlefield. Government rules about discrimination in public places brings heated disputes about homosexuality or gay marriage, or other touch points such as abortion, tax exemption for churches, or political advocacy by ministers, all seen as an anti-religion campaign, a part of "cultural wars."

But beyond these social or political skirmishes, the "war of Science on Faith" is seen by some as the Church's Gettysburg or the Normandy beach attack on Christianity. Atheists have become more vocal and visible in the media and in print, and it appears that most scientists identify themselves as agnostic or atheistic. This list includes such famous scientists as Carl Sagan, Neil deGrasse, Albert Einstein,

Christopher Hitchens, Richard Dawkins, Stephen Hawking, Steven Weinberg, Edward O. Wilson and many others. There is some ambivalence among such scientists, some preferring to call themselves agnostic rather than atheist, because "atheist" implies more certainty than they can claim. Agnostic means "I **don't know** if there is a god", while Atheist means "I'm sure there is **no** god." Since science is reluctant to claim certainty beyond a doubt in regard to atoms, light, gravity, black holes, and other phenomena, agnosticism seems more professionally appropriate.

If we look back a few hundred years atheism was very much a minority position. Most scientists in the late Middle Ages and the Renaissance were church men, some even clerics in the Catholic Church. Several had financial support in their research from religious leaders. But eventually, the findings of the new sciences clashed with the religious dogma, and some scientists either hid their ideas or bowed to the church authorities. The rare atheist would have been ostracized by society and possibly even killed (as in burned at the stake, depending on how far back you go). Fast forward to the present, and atheism is far more common and respectable, and in some circles is even the dominant view. Thus, our culture is divided by science and religion. Some segments of society are totally persuaded that science is the truth and savior, while a substantial portion of Americans are suspicious of science, even to the point of being "science deniers" on claims of global warming, vaccines, and racial differences. We even still have a few who still doubt the "moon landing" and insist the earth is flat (It seems unbelievable but in 2018 a "flat earther" launched his own rocket nearly 200 miles up to prove that the earth is flat.)

The Church's War on Science

It was inevitable that the guardians of the literal and inerrant Bible would condemn the new ideas of the scientists of the Late Middle Ages (15th and 16th centuries) and the beginning of the Renaissance in Europe. This period is sometimes labeled "The Age of Discovery." ***Columbus*** sailed to the Americas in 1492, and ***Vasco da Gama's*** exploration began in 1381; ***John Wycliffe*** translated the Bible into English in 1415; ***Jan Hus*** was burned at the stake *in 1415;* ***Galileo*** saw the stars through his new telescope in 1564; in 1439 ***Johannes Gutenberg's*** printing press made books available; **Leonardo da Vinci** (1452 -1519) was a scientist, inventor, painter, architect and more, truly a great "Renaissance man." It seemed that the age of science would change the world, and challenge the old culture, and it did.

Believers need to face the truth about the war with science: *religion started the fight*. When Galileo put out his scientific ideas about the earth and the sun, the Church (Catholic church had the power in this case) condemned his ideas loudly and threateningly. He was forced to recant—to deny what he had discovered or burn at the stake. He argued that the Sun is stationary in relation to the earth, and that the earth orbited the Sun. Over a hundred-year period the Church executed dozens, maybe hundreds, for teaching ideas that contradicted the Bible as the Church interpreted it. Most of these were scientists, and many were philosophers or clerics with so-called "heretical" beliefs. Sadly, most of these early scientists being persecuted were devout Christians themselves, and this was certainly the case of the targeted clergymen who translated the Bible into the language of the common people. So, it is not surprising that today's scientists generally have negative attitudes toward the Church or religion, and that science as a field seems to have contempt for religion, and ridicules anti-science believers who reject evolution, argue for a 6000-year-old earth, and exalt Intelligent Design instead of natural selection. We Christians started this alleged war long ago, and the damage we did is still with us. The wounds of that battle are still remembered, as philosopher Robert Anton Wilson reminds us:

> Every fact of science was once damned. Every invention was considered impossible. Every discovery was a nervous shock to some orthodoxy. Every artistic innovation was denounced as fraud and folly. The entire web of culture and 'progress,' everything on earth that is man-made and not given to us by nature, is the concrete manifestation of some man's refusal to bow to Authority. We would own no more, know no more, and be no more than the first apelike hominids if it were not for the rebellious, the recalcitrant, and the intransigent. As Oscar Wilde truly said, 'Disobedience was man's Original Virtue.'[2]

The Creation Conflict

The scientific explanation for the creation of humans seems to many Christians to be absolutely and totally incompatible with, and contrary to, the Biblical version. The millions of years' time frame for evolution of the human species stands in bold contrast to the seven-day account in Genesis 1 (actually 6 days of creation by God and one day of rest). If the Bible is taken literally and true, there seems to be no way that the scientific theory can be accepted. According to the Darwinian theory of evolution, various species of apes and monkeys gradually changed and adapted to their new environmental challenges, coming down from trees to walk upright on the savannas of Africa. New species branched off from their simian cousins, hominids in which the best suited survived and reproduced, while the less adapted perished. The evolved individuals produced more offspring and survived as a species, while the less adapted gradually declined and faded from the human gene pool.

The Bible, on the other hand, has God first creating the earth and shaping it instantly by spoken command, and then He created the light of day and the darkness of night—all on the first day. It was on the sixth day that God said, ***"Then God said, "Let us make mankind in our image, in our likeness...So God created mankind in his own image, in the image of God he created the male and female he created them."*** (Genesis 1:26-27). Using Biblical chronology (the Old Testament list of Jewish genealogical data) Catholic Bishop James Usher in 1650 calculated that the earth is only about 6000 years old, with Creation dated to October 22, 4004 B.C., about sunset. Many Christians believe that calculation even today, though his research may have some methodological deficiencies.

Can the scientific and the Biblical accounts be reconciled? Can they both be true? One way some Christians have attempted to harmonize the religious view and the scientific view is to interpret the Biblical account critically and analytically. They recognize, for example, that the Hebrew word ***yom,*** translated "day," can have a variety of meanings, including an indefinite period of time. Thus, some have suggested that these six days might then be equated with the billions of years claimed by geologists. Another approach is to reinterpret the genealogy, noting that there are many gaps between the "begats", and that in ancient cultures "father" can also signify "grandfather" or "forefather", thus allowing a much longer possible period of time recorded in Genesis. Another way of getting around the scientific evidence for the age of the earth and universe is argue that God **could** have created the universe instantly but make it **appear older** than it really is, "planting" fossils and geological patterns to "fool" us. Such an argument is not theologically impossible, but it appears to be thin and desperate rationalization. All these reconciliation attempts appear pitifully weak to most objective scholars, seen as trying to bend or adjust the evidence to fit our precious pre-existing conclusions. It is very hard for Skeptics to rethink and revise their materialistic, naturalistic world view in order to consider the possibility of a Spiritual dimension, just as it is very difficult for Believers to consider any other way of looking at the Bible than the literal and perfect Word of God they were taught to revere.

The problem with the traditional literal interpretation of the Bible as the inerrant truth inspired directly by God is that it hinders scientists from coming to the Christian faith, and it creates untenable conflict for Christian youth who encounter secular science in school. The six-day creation 6000 years ago runs up against geological and archaeological evidence unearthed in the last 100 years, finds which seem to be hundreds of thousands, or even millions of years old. To reject the radiocarbon dating and clinging to the traditional literal Biblical account makes the Christian student look foolish and ignorant. Our young believers are unnecessarily damaged by having to choose between science and faith.

Some Christians have made peace with science, as reflected in this quote from Quora, an internet blog encouraging progressive opinion and discourse, often relating to science and religion:

> I'm a Christian. I believe that science is a gift from God, given to us so that we can learn more about His creation. I believe that if science tells us that the earth is at least 4.0310 billion years old, then there is no reason for us not to believe it. I believe that Christians who limit themselves to a strict,

4000-year-old view of the Earth are limiting themselves by declaring that they understand God better than God understands them. I believe a lot of Christians need to open their minds up to greater possibilities.[3]

Science is not likely to make some new discovery in the future that suggests or proves that the methods of dating fossils and hominid skeletons is faulty, or that radiocarbon dating gives dramatically false readings. We're not going to read that some of the other laboratory testing procedures we use in dating antiquities is being revised, due to a mathematical mistake twenty years ago. The age of the earth is never going to be revised by science to 6000 years or 10,000 or 50,000: the science has been proven sound to the degree of certainty that is claimed in science. So, for the Bible believer, the adjustment to reality must come from the religious side. We will offer a plausible way of understanding the Bible in Chapter 2 that does not require denying scientific truth or surrender by either side.

Science Fights Back

Though Religion took the first shots in the War and won many skirmishes in the 14th and 15th centuries, the tide of history and facts was on the side of Science. As the Renaissance swept over Europe and Asia Science fought back effectively and decisively. The printing press made the Bible available to almost everyone, cutting the Church's monopoly in religious truth. Education grew more widespread because of the increased opportunities to read, not only Bibles but political and scientific writing. The genie was out of the bottle, and science showed its potential benefit to the common people. Medical care became more "scientific", serfdom became more unacceptable, improvements in sanitation and farming made life better because of science. Gradually science and technology seemed to offer more hope to common people than the extravagant and profligate religious leaders who lived and worshiped in opulent castles and cathedrals. Some scientists were burned, but science continued and eventually prevailed, for in our modern society, more people look to science and technology for hope of a better life than look to the religious promises proffered. In Europe the "church" is barely a public player in the lives of people; in the United States the replacement of religion with science is not so complete, but opinion polls show that most people believe in prayer and God, but not in church or other religious institutions. America is still a very religious society compared to most other countries, but the decline in church attendance and financial support is undeniable. So, how did Science "win" the war?

The Monkey Trial and the Bible

In July 1925 the state of Tennessee charged John Thomas Scopes, a substitute high school teacher, with violating a state law prohibiting the teaching of evolution. This trial was in many ways as sensational as the OJ Simpson trial in 1994 in Los Angeles. The small town of Dayton, Tennessee was the setting, and the public trial featured three-time presidential candidate Williams Jennings Bryan for the prosecution, and equally famous attorney Clarence Darrow for the defense. Scopes was found guilty and fined $100, but the verdict was later overturned on a technicality. This show trial was, in many ways, seen as the Gettysburg of the "War Between Science and Religion." This was before TV, but the national publicity familiarized America with the ongoing Fundamentalist-Modernist debate in religious circles.

One strain of Protestant Christianity in the 1900's was strongly conservative, arguing for the inerrant truth of the Bible, the strict literal interpretation of the Genesis story, miracles, and rigid rules for Christian behavior (especially for women). A more liberal strain of religious thought had come to America from European theologians who were dissecting and analyzing the Bible in what was called "Biblical Criticism." These new-thinking religious leaders in America argued that Science and the Bible did not have to be in mortal battle, and they offered a less rigid and less authoritarian way of interpreting the Bible. Something approximating a "pitched battle" engulfed Protestant America.

"Fundamentalism" was a reaction against the liberalization of some religious groups who seemed to be abandoning traditional Christianity's teachings about the Bible, Jesus, the Virgin Birth, Miracles, the Atonement, and a version of the second coming of Jesus and the Millennium (a supposed thousand-year rule of Christ on earth when He returns). These essential teachings were put into printed booklets and thousands were distributed beginning in 1910. The battle within Christianity was part of the reason Science won and religion lost the battle for the hearts of the people. Main line denominations split over these issues and today there are over 350 separate protestant groups or denominations, still identifiable as "liberal" or "conservative," reflecting openness to science versus opposition to much of science.

The Attack on the Bible

Evidence-based Skeptics charge that the Bible is "inaccurate history, filled with conflicting ideas, is scientifically wrong, is not supported by empirical facts, and no proof exists to substantiate that any of its characters actually existed." That is just one of the milder denunciations. The "science" of the Bible is challenged because the Biblical writers thought the Earth was the center of the Universe and everything else revolved around our home. The ideas about the shape of the earth in the Old Testament are primitive: a flat earth with four corners. There are some cases where two passages may differ or conflict, which makes it seem to Skeptics that one or both are wrong. This criticism of the Bible is sometimes called "cherry-picking," picking out a few parts to represent the whole orchard. But were we to read a compilation of works on medicine from writers over a period of 2000 years, we would certainly use the best of the works and ignore the rest. We would not throw out the entire collection because it tells of a leader named Jephthah who sacrificed his young daughter because he thought he was bound to keep his foolish vow to God, or the story about God slaughtering the disobedient Israelites by poisonous snakes, and a hundred other Old Testament stories of the wrath of God being carried out. "What kind of god is THAT?" they ask. It is a good question, a fair question, deserving of a reasonable answer. We will try to address the questions about the Bible in **Chapter 2 What About the Bible?** along with many other questions about God throughout the book. Mutual understanding between the contenders may make a truce possible, for Science and Religion are not "natural enemies."

A Word of Caution for Believers

Because this book is a Christian apologetic, partially an attempt to "defend the faith," to explain the Christian God to scientists, Skeptics or non-believers, it is crucial that unsuspecting Believers not be harmed or offended in their faith because of what is written. These believers should **be assured that the author of this book is a committed believer in the Bible, both Old and New Testaments, and loves and reveres them as the "Word of God."** The following chapter will deal extensively in the issues of Bible authorship, transmission, literary forms, translations and interpretations. Some may be disturbed at first by the fact that the arguments given in this book are not the standard, traditional "divine dictation" approach, the all or nothing mentality. Others may be troubled by the concession to Skeptics and critics that the Bible is not a book of science, world history, astronomy, economics, or geography. The Bible does not claim to be any of these, just as it is not a cookbook, a math book, or a guidebook for any other extraneous things. The Bible is God's way of revealing His nature and His plan for mankind, how fifty or more seekers experienced God and passed on their understandings of Him to us.

The Bible is about God—He is the primary subject, not the people and events that are reported as part of the context of how God made Himself known to imperfect people over several centuries. In a real sense, the Bible is a spiritual diary kept by our forefathers as they struggled to understand more and more about God and His will for the world. Science and all those other disciplines are NOT about God, and the Bible is NOT about those scientific fields of study. They are essentially non-overlapping fields of study. This concept by highly respected scientist / philosopher Steven Ray Gould will be elaborated in a later section. But for now, believers, keep your faith as we attempt to explain this trust in the Bible in ways that are understandable and palatable to the skeptical scientific mind. We can concede the historical and scientific errors which critics point out, misguided ideas by Bible characters as they grew in wisdom and knowledge. We don't need to defend their unscientific guesses about a flat, four-cornered earth, or the Sun that circled the earth, or the occasional mixing up of names of kings or cities or other such insignificant details. It is the revelation of God that we hold sacred, and the Biblical theology is perfectly safe from scientific critics.

Chapter 2

BUT WHAT ABOUT THE BIBLE?

"Most people are bothered by those passages of Scripture they do not understand, but the passages that bother me are those I do understand"
MARK TWAIN

MARK TWAIN WAS BEING WITTY IN HIS ANALYSIS OF the bible as reported above, but was reflecting a common understanding that the Bible is beyond understanding for the common folks. In his time in the late 1800's there was an abundance of traveling preachers in every country town, and a proliferation of new denominations to fit every religious taste. Not unexpectedly there were almost as many interpretations of the King James Bible (then the only widely recognized version) as there were personal copies of the Holy Book. Eventually there came to be more than 350 separate groups of Christ followers, usually based on one or two doctrines or beliefs, each able to "prove" their correctness by a Bible verse or two. It has been observed by the critics of religion that the Bible can be used to **prove anything** if you cherry pick a few verses, mix and match them, and ignore the original context. Here is an example: Combine Matthew 27:5 "So Judas threw the money into the temple and left. Then he went away and hanged himself." With "Jesus said, "Go and do likewise." (Luke 10:37).

In the hands of a serious Bible student, we can create or discover doctrines and commands that will fool some of the people, sometimes a mob of people. This is reminiscent of the Greek mathematician (287-212 BC) who invented the fulcrum and lever system "Give me a lever and a place to stand and I will **move the earth**."

This chapter is intended to give Skeptics a general but accurate understanding of what the Bible means to Believers, and how they use it. We also intend to present to Bible Believers a fresh, non-traditional perspective on the Bible, re-framing the way we look at the Book. This cartoon has two men looking at a number painted on the floor, standing on opposite sides: "It's a 9" says one; "No, it's a 6" the other claims. Looking at anything from different perspectives is instructive. Considering the other point of view challenges "the way it's always been." It is hoped that such a new way of looking at the Bible will enable believers to more effectively defend the Bible in the face of the many scientific challenges to its validity, without compromising their own trust in their sacred scriptures.

What's It All About?

The Bible is about God and about the revelation of Himself over several centuries, and it contains a **spiritual diary** of our forefathers as they struggled to understand more and more about God and His will for the world. Science and all those other disciplines are NOT about God, and the Bible is NOT about those scientific fields of study. They are essentially non-overlapping fields of study. This concept by highly respected scientist/ philosopher Steven Ray Gould will be **elaborated in a later section**. But for now, Believers, keep your faith as we attempt to explain this trust in the Bible in ways that are understandable and palatable to the skeptical scientific mind. We can concede the historical and scientific errors which critics point out, even misguided ideas by Bible characters as they grew in wisdom and knowledge. We don't need to defend their unscientific guesses about a flat, four-cornered earth, or the Sun that circled the earth, or the occasional mixing up of names of kings or cities or other such insignificant details. It is **the revelation of God that we hold sacred**, and our Biblical theology can be perfectly safe from scientific critics. *"In the past God spoke to our ancestors through the prophets at many times and in various ways, but in these last days he has spoken to us by his Son...the radiance of God's glory and the exact representation of his being."* (Hebrews 1:1) That God revealed by Jesus is safe here, and lifted up and glorified shamelessly. Jesus is the centerpiece of this book as He is in the **Good Book.**

Evidence-based Skeptics charge that the Bible is "inaccurate history, filled with conflicting ideas, is scientifically wrong, is not supported by empirical facts, and no proof exists to substantiate that any of its characters actually existed." That is just one of the *milder* denunciations. Defenders of the Bible must try to explain why the Almighty was so vicious and destructive in the stories about Jericho, Jephthah's young daughter, slaughtering of the disobedient Israelites by poisonous snakes, and a hundred other Old Testament stories of the wrath of God being carried out. **"What kind of god is THAT?"** they ask. It is a good question, a fair question, deserving of a reasonable answer; answering such tough questions is the objective of this book.

How Should We View the Bible?

What is the key to presenting the Bible as the "word of God" while accommodating the scientific and scholarly evidence that some things stated in the Bible are incorrect or inaccurate? To claim that the Bible is inerrant, infallible and absolutely true in every way is to close the door to the educated and informed modern person. Exposure to science and philosophy has persuaded them that the Bible is not perfect in **every way**, maybe not in any **relevant way**. There can be no enlightened discussion about God with such people if our only basis for arguing is an ancient work of fiction and poetry and some bits of history that is full of information **that can't be true, in a scientific sense.**

The Bible is the most printed book in the world, according to many reports, still selling more copies than any other work, in English and in dozens of other languages. About six billion Bibles have been printed and distributed, compared to 800 million for Chairman Mao's *Little Red Book,* or *Tale of Two Cities* with 200 million published. Of course, Bibles printed and sold does not mean Bibles read. In reality, many believers <u>revere</u> their Bible, but <u>read</u> it seldom. A melancholy old country song laments Biblical neglect; *"Dust on the Bible, dust on the Holy Word"* reveals a self-critical truth which evangelicals acknowledge: everybody "talking Bible" in church is not necessarily studying the Bible seriously. Sometimes the most adamant defender of the Bible is arguing from tradition rather than a thorough, intellectually serious study of the Bible.

Traditionally a reference to the Bible means both the Old Testament of Judaism and the New Testament of Christians, bound into one book. For most Christians, the Bible is the sacred text book of the Faith, the authoritative source book for all doctrine and practices down through 20 centuries. There have been other respected books valued and read by Christians, but none has been accepted as sacred in the same way as the Bible. Some Bible believers have adopted other religious documents as supplements, and some, such as the Book of Mormon, have come to be regarded as equally authoritative for the Latter-Day Saints (Mormons). Of course, the Old Testament is the primary Jewish holy book, but Judaism also accepts the **Mishna** and the **Talmud** as authoritative for their faith. They do not accept the New Testament as divinely inspired or relevant to their religion. Islam accepts the Old Testament as an important historical document, but the **al Qur'an** is the authoritative book of their faith.

The Claim for Authority

Christians cite II Timothy 3:15-17 (**KJV**) as the definitive credential for the Bible: "***All scripture is given by inspiration of God, and is profitable for doctrine, for reproof, for correction, for instruction in righteousness: That the man of God may be perfect, thoroughly furnished unto all good works.***" This quote (from the 1611 King James Version) is the touchstone of the faith Christians have in the Bible. It is the "Word of God" in some miraculous way. Some believe that every word and every punctuation mark in the Bible was given directly by God to chosen humans, and that it has been preserved and passed on through the centuries to us, intact and pure in every way. Others view the origin of the Bible as coming from God, but with somewhat more flexibility in the pen and ink process, and also in the preservation and transmission of the sacred words to our time. Skeptics often start here at the point of "inspiration" as a vulnerable breech for questioning the Bible's value. The "direct dictation" theory of the Bible is an easy target, and it is simple for these critics to find lots of flaws, logical conflicts, and many counter arguments to an infallible Bible. This theory and several other versions of Biblical inspiration are discussed below.

It should be noted that the "scripture" Paul refers to in his letter to Timothy is the Old Testament; there was no New Testament as of yet. Also, in the verses preceding this quote, Paul makes clear that Timothy has known the holy scriptures since his youth, that is, the Jewish Bible. Another note is that "inspiration" is the translation in the King James and other versions, but most newer translations use the phrase "God breathed" to describe its creation. This may be a more accurate translation of the Greek word Paul used, perhaps reflecting the Genesis account whereby God *breathed into Adam and he became a living soul.* So, Christians believe, the Bible became a *living Word.* Paul later carries this further: **"*For the word of God is alive and active. Sharper than any double-edged sword, it penetrates even to dividing soul and spirit, joints and marrow; it judges the thoughts and attitudes of the heart.*"** (Hebrews 4:12) The Bible is considered by many Christians to be "alive and active" not just a static collection of words or letters on thin paper.

It's Alive!

For true Believers, the Bible is **alive** in the sense that it conveys to the reader fresh insight, application to current circumstances, **inspiring** the reader as if it was a direct, one on one contact with God. Thus, inspiration means not only the God-breathed revelation to the ancient saint or prophet, but also the God enabled capacity to be continually up-to-date in some miraculous way. Just as God breathed into the mud-Adam the Breath of Life, so God still breathes life into the Bible for the seeker of truth. For the Bible believer, the ink symbols on the page come to life, speaking meaning to the reader at some deeper level. Consider how discovering an old letter from your youthful sweetheart **means** more than the dead words—it touches the heart and emotions, almost as if the Loved One was present and now speaking aloud. Christians find in their Bible an old love letter from God, and repeated reading never gets boring, for it reveals something new, something not noticed or understood earlier. This "mystical" type of experience does not happen every time, nor to every reader, but many devout Christians seem to get better at this receptive mind-set with practice and patience. Theologians attribute such experiences to the Holy Spirit, God's presence in the world today, just as Jesus was God's presence in Galilee and Judea in the First Century, bringing the message, the Good News, to that world and now to ours.

Christians have almost universally accepted the 66 books which the early church finally selected and approved from the scores of valued books circulating in the first two centuries of Christianity. This approved group is called the "canon", (Greek κανών) meaning "rule" or "measuring stick". After much debate, and with pressure from the Roman Emperor Constantine, the Christian Bible was made official about 367 AD. Another group of 15 books, the Apocrypha, are included in most Roman Catholic bibles, revered but not equal to the other 66 books. Eastern Orthodox churches include some of the Apocrypha. Besides these "canonical" differences, there are other serious differences among Christians about the very nature of the Bible, about the forms of inspiration, and finally, about interpretation of meanings. But still **All scripture is inspired by God** is on the believers' banner, the solid core of Christian belief.

What Does Inspiration Mean?

While all Christians accept some notion of the Bible as "inspired," modern religious scholars make a distinction in theories or types of inspiration of the Bible. The question is "**How does God convey His**

truth to humans?" Three basic approaches to inspiration are most often cited by Christian authors and historians. There are many more "theories" of inspiration, speculation about how God communicates, but most are variations of the three most popular described below: Dictation theory, Verbal plenary theory, and Dynamic theory.

Dictation theory: God dictated the books of the Bible word by word as if the biblical authors were dictating machines; The **dictation theory** of inspiration sees God as the author of Scripture and the individual human agents as secretaries or amanuenses taking dictation. God spoke, and man wrote it down, much like a court reporter. Dictation theory naturally holds that what God said was accurately written down and has been preserved to our time, and thus the Bible is **inerrant,** free of error. This view has some biblical support, since we know there are portions of Scripture in which God essentially says, "Write this down" (e.g., Jeremiah 30:2), but not all Scripture was created that way. The first five books, the Pentateuch, is essentially a chronicle of the Jewish people prior to settling in the Promised Land. While Moses is honored as the primary author, much of the Pentateuch probably existed in earlier records of the Hebrew tribes, before the Exodus. Moses could not be an eyewitness to the stories in Genesis, but he may be the one who compiled these oral or written histories, and incorporated them into his creation of the nation of Israel. Giving them a history and a set of laws allowed Moses to shape the descendants of Jacob, the twelve nomadic tribes, into a *sometime* unified people. Though supremely important and very close to God, Moses probably did not write down the Pentateuch word for word as God dictated to him. Without Moses' rescue of the Hebrews there would be no Pentateuch.

A quote from the 19th-century biblical scholar John William Burgon illustrates the <u>extreme</u> dictation view:

> The Bible is none other than the voice of Him that sitteth upon the Throne! Every Book of it, every Chapter of it, every Verse of it, every word of it, every syllable of it, (where are we to stop?) every letter of it, is the direct utterance of the Most High![4]

Luke states in the preamble to his gospel that he performed detailed research into the events of the life of Jesus before writing, including some earlier written or oral accounts (Luke 1:1–4). Many of the prophetic books read like journals of the prophets' lives, with messages from God as just a part of the overall story. It is hard to defend this theory of inspiration to Skeptics, since there are so many parts of the Bible that fail the "word for word" standard of perfect God-talk, and so many stories which clearly are based on a less than "Jesus" understanding of God. Besides those difficulties with dictation theory, the very idea that God picked out and dictated every single word and all the punctuation wreaks havoc with the idea of humans having a "free will." It is much more believable that God gave the basic ideas and His faithful human servant put those thoughts into his own language and style. Though much of the Bible is beautiful and inspiring, it is dangerous to blame God for every word and punctuation mark.

Verbal plenary inspiration: This view gives a greater role to the human writers of the Bible, while maintaining a belief that God preserved the integrity of the words of the Bible. The effect of inspiration was to move the authors so as to produce the words God wanted ("verbal") and was full and complete in every respect ("plenary"), though not necessarily word for word. In this view the human writers' individual backgrounds, life experiences, personal traits, and literary styles were authentically theirs, but they have been prepared and equipped by God for use as His special instruments in conveying His message. The theory is sometimes called simply "verbal inspiration" with less emphasis on the "full and complete" aspect. This theory of biblical inspiration seems in some ways similar to more primitive religions studied by anthropologists, where one tribal member is considered "inspired", seeming to be under the control of a supernatural spirit. This "shaman" or "medicine man" falls into a trance, or has a "spell" in which he may act and speak in strange, unnatural ways, presumably receiving some divine message for the tribe.

Dynamic inspiration: This is the most modern theory, more favored by liberal theologians and the "neo-orthodox" movement, modernists who sought to uphold traditional doctrines while adapting or reframing the ancient beliefs for the modern culture. By this theory, the **thoughts** contained in the Bible are inspired, but the words used were left to the individual writers. The Neo-orthodox doctrine of inspiration views the Bible as "the *word* of God" but not "the *words* of God". It is only when one reads the text that it becomes the word of God to the reader. This view is a reaction to the more conservative Dictation and Verbal Plenary theories, de-emphasizing the idea of textual inerrancy. Giants among Bible scholars **Karl Barth** (1886-1968) and **Emil Brunner** (1889-1966) pioneered this approach, and it was popularized by American theologians **Reinhold Niebuhr**, and **Paul Tillich.** This more flexible view of inspiration is feared by the more traditional and conservative religious groups, seeing it as the first step on a "slippery slope," leading inevitably to a very weak theology of "divine inspiration," leaving God out almost entirely. Many modern, younger Christians, however, have found this view more rational and defensible. For them, defending **every word** of the Bible as **dictated** and **inerrant** is perhaps an **unnecessary burden** in explaining and defending the idea of God as represented by Jesus.

Is It All or Nothing?

Without the security of an inerrant Bible, directly dictated by God, how can we choose what part is God and what part is human? A reasonable question. This concern is sometimes called 'cherry-picking' the Bible, picking out the passages you agree with and ignoring "pesky" passages that bother you. It requires more of the reader and more guidance from the Holy Spirit, but we can reasonably discern what "sounds like Jesus" and what doesn't. If we read a 200-year-old book about medicine we would not be surprised if some of the medical advice was wrong (based on modern science) and some parts can be valuable. Or suppose we had an 18th century compilation of history we would certainly use the best of the works and ignore the rest. We would not throw out the entire collection because of the varying quality, or the occasional misinformation. It would not have to be inerrant to be useful.

Neither must we accept the Bible as inerrant in all things in order to accept the Good News of Jesus. The God who gave us our Bible also gives us the minds and judgment to recognize portrayals of God which are consistent with what Jesus taught us about God, and we can recognize those passages which seem to be out of character with the Jesus/God, contradicting His teachings about His Father. Using all we can understand from the latest and best revelation of God (Jesus) we can distinguish the Old Testament passages which glorify the Father of Jesus, and those which mistakenly vilify Him and attribute godless acts and demonic demands to their *misunderstood God*. We have the mental and spiritual equipment to learn from and enjoy much of the Old Testament without getting tangled up in passages which are clearly the work of humans still trying to find and understand who God is and what does He want, misled by their limited experience and their constant exposure to pagan gods of their culture.

> **It is Jesus who is rightly called The WORD*and it is never okay to quote the Old Testament to endorse something that Jesus clearly forbids, or abrogate anything Jesus demands.**
> **(John 1:1)*

Rightly Dividing the Word of God

Admittedly, this is putting a heavy burden on us as the arbiters of what parts of the Old Testament are close to what God wanted us to know about Himself, and what other parts are the products of sincere but mistaken guesses of godly authors whose insight was inadequate and incomplete. Fortunately, we have the Truth we call Jesus as the standard by which all theology can be judged, and we have God's Holy Spirit always with us to guide us into all truth, to guide us so we can *"rightly dividing the Word of God"* (Timothy 2:15 **KJV**) as Paul charged Timothy to do through study and prayer. Just because not every word in the Old Testament is exactly what God intended does not mean that none of the Old Testament can be trusted as the Word of God. The compiled Bible we so revere **does not claim** every word is God's word: that is an impossible standard created by some of our sincere Christian brothers trying to help God by "idolizing" the Holy Bible. Idol worship is treacherous even if the Idol is leather covered, has red letters for Jesus' words, and has gilded page edges. Brennan Manning calls it *"bibliolatry"*:

BUT WHAT ABOUT THE BIBLE?

Group Bible Study

I am deeply distressed by what I can only call in our Christian culture the idolatry of the Scriptures. For many Christians, the Bible is not a pointer to God but God himself. In a word – bibliolatry. God cannot be confined to a leather-bound book. I develop a nasty rash around people who speak as if mere scrutiny of its pages will reveal precisely how God thinks and precisely what God wants.

The four Gospels are the key to knowing Jesus. But conversely, Jesus is the key to knowing the meaning of the gospel – and of the Bible as a whole. Instead of remaining content with the bare letter, we should pass on to the more profound mysteries that are available only through intimate and heartfelt knowledge of Jesus.[5]

Theories Are Working Tools

Theories of inspiration are, after all, **theories**, speculations about how the Bible is an authentic message from God to Man, providing the foundation and boundaries for our theology. Absolute certainty is not possible or necessary. One can hold any of these theories of inspiration, or some combination, and find guidance, assurance and comfort in the words of their Bible. Theologian Benjamin Warfield helpfully views inspiration poetically.

> As light that passes through the colored glass of a cathedral window, we are told, is light from heaven, but is stained by the tints of the glass through which it passes; so any word of God which is passed through the mind and soul of a man must come out discolored by the personality through which it is given, and just to that degree ceases to be the pure word of God. But what if this personality has itself been formed by God into precisely the personality it is, for the express purpose of communicating to the word given through it just the coloring which it gives it? [6]

For Christians the Bible is the product of Godly men, receiving God-sent messages, preserved and protected by God's superintending guidance, and delivered to receptive hearts in every age, minds prepared and equipped by God, and finally made personal and relevant to the life of Believers. When it works, when we are truly there, our spiritual eyes are opened and the Light comes on. This human-God connection is beautifully described in a favorite Christian hymn: "*Break Thou the Bread of Life*" with lyrics by Mary Artemisia Lathbury:

> *Oh, send Thy Spirit, Lord, Now unto me,*
> *That He may touch my eyes, And make me see;*
> *Show me the truth concealed Within Thy Word,*
> *And in Thy Book revealed I see the Lord.* [7]

"Seeing the Lord" in some mystical form is perhaps the only true test for inspiration of the Bible: sensing His presence, knowing Him more personally, more intimately than before. The purpose of the Bible is to reveal Jesus, to meet Him, to enjoy His presence and love.

What Can We Believe?

If an adult reads in science texts that the earth travels around the Sun, this information conflicts with the traditional, common-sense observation that the Sun moves from sunrise in the east to sunset in the west. He also remembers the Biblical account of Joshua praying for the sun to stop moving and stand still so he and his army would have time to slaughter the enemy: *"So the sun stood still, and the moon stopped, till the nation avenged itself on its enemies, as it is written in the Book of Jashar. "The sun stopped in the middle of the sky and delayed going down about a full day..."* (Joshua 10:13) The evidence in support of a geocentric model is overwhelming here. Joshua commanded the sun to stand still. He did not order the earth to cease rotating nor did he qualify his statement with the divine knowledge that the sun was merely made to appear stationary. The sun was commanded to stand still because it is the sun that moves around the earth. Other Biblical writers also believed that the earth was stationary, and never moved: *"Yet their voice goes out into all the earth, their words to the ends of the world. In the heavens God has pitched a tent for the sun. It is like a bridegroom coming out of his chamber, like a champion rejoicing to run his course. It rises at one end of the heavens and makes its circuit to the other; nothing is deprived of its warmth."* (Psalms 19:4-6)

Two additional poetic verses demonstrate this ancient earth-centric belief: *"The sun rises and the sun sets, and hurries back to where it rises."* (Ecclesiastes 1:5) Again: *"Say among the nations, 'The Lord reigns.' The world is firmly established, it cannot be moved..."* (Psalms 96:10.) Earth centered theology, geo-centric beliefs, were firmly established in the ancient poet's mind: *"Tremble before him, all the earth! The world is firmly established; it cannot be moved."* 1 Chronicles 16:30) Biblical writers got the solar science wrong (**BUT SO WHAT? EVERYONE ELSE DID TOO,** until Copernicus 2000 years later!)

Facing this scientific claim, the Bible Believer may say, "I don't care what scientists say! The Bible says the earth stands still and the Sun and Moon move around us—and I believe the Bible, every page, every sentence, every word!" Very many Christians accept the "infallibility" doctrine, perhaps reasoning that "if one part of the Bible is not literally true, how can I believe any of it?"

Apples and Oranges: Competing Sources of Truth

Such a losing conflict between faith and science is unnecessary, as many modern scientists and modern theologians have come to understand. One greatly respected scientist-philosopher, Steven Ray Gould, argues that science and religion each represent different areas of inquiry, fact vs. values, non-competing and non-overlapping. In a 1997 essay **"Non-Overlapping Magisteria"** for Natural History magazine, and later in his book Rocks of Ages (1999), Gould put forward what he described as "a blessedly simple and entirely conventional resolution to the supposed conflict between science and religion." Science and religion each has its own domain, or "magisterium", its own legitimate teaching authority, over which each form of teaching holds the appropriate tools for meaningful discourse and resolution.

Science tries to document the factual character of the natural world, and to develop theories that coordinate and explain these facts. Religion, on the other hand, operates in the equally important, but utterly different, realm of human purposes, meanings, and values—subjects that the factual domain of science might illuminate, but can never resolve. "These two magisteria do not overlap, nor do they encompass all inquiry (consider, for example, the magisterium of art and the meaning of beauty.") [8]

Gould emphasized the legitimacy of each field of endeavor only within its appropriate area of inquiry: "*If religion can no longer dictate the nature of factual conclusions residing properly within the magisterium of science, then scientists cannot claim higher insight into moral truth from any superior knowledge of the world's empirical constitution.*" Not every scientist nor every theologian agrees with Gould's "separation of powers" solution, but many find his solution to be satisfying and defensible. For example, to use Biblical quotes to teach a science lesson is to strain and overburden the religious doc-

BUT WHAT ABOUT THE BIBLE?

ument. Likewise, for science to make proclamations about morality, the soul, or other purely spiritual matters is to overstep the legitimate boundaries of their domain.

Complementing Rather Than Competing

"Religion and science go together. As I've said before, science without religion is lame and religion without science is blind. They are interdependent and have a common goal—the search for truth."

A. Einstein

There is much that people of science and people of religion can learn from each other, as long as each avoids making truth claims for the other field. An easy example is the Creation: "In the beginning, God created the heavens and the earth" is the Biblical explanation. Science says "Everything in the universe was created in the Big Bang" some 14 billion years ago." Science focuses on the "how", and has no answer for the "who", while religion focuses on the "who", and has no real information on the "how". The religionist can say, "God created everything", and the scientist need not argue the point since there is no way to prove the answer with the tools of science. The thoughtful theologian can concede that God **could** have created the world and the universe instantly, or He **might** have created it over millions of years; He has the power, and we can't prove the how or when. Likewise, the religionist can postulate from scriptures the WHY of creation (for the benefit of humankind), and the true scientist avoids the question as irrelevant to his field of inquiry. It is only when the religionist uses his faith to deny evidence that is clearly in the scientific domain that conflict and problems arise, or when science denies or disputes teachings that are clearly in the spiritual or religious magisterium. Like blind men describing an elephant (poem quoted complete in **Chapter 8**) each description of "parts" is both right and yet totally incomplete. The "Big Picture" needs observations from both Science and Faith in order to be more nearly complete.

Each area of knowledge and authority is valid in its area of expertise, but only when seen together are the truths elevated to Truth. A committed Christian or any person of faith is complete only when they can see and accept the truth of science as well as the truth of scriptures. To deny established science is to limit God, to argue that God could not do His work in any way other than what we have believed. A Christian does not have to accept every claim of science, just as scientists question new ideas, but to reject science just because it IS science is to be voluntarily blind. Our own interpretation of the Bible can become our "holy word" that we own and trust, convinced that we know the mind of God, rather than holding an appropriate reverence and humility toward the original intended message. A god that has to measure up to our interpretations and our predetermined conclusions, who must work only in the ways that make sense to us, **is a god too small.**

The Bible Is a Book of Truth: Religious Truth

So, what can Christians believe about the Bible and its inspiration? Making the Bible be the be-all and end-all for all truth in all domains, is a burden it cannot bear, and should not. Many Christians have come to see that the Bible is a book of religious truth, not a book of science or mathematics or geology or chemistry or astronomy. It sometimes reflects the nascent science of relatively primitive nomadic tribal people four thousand years ago, fifteen centuries before the dawn of science in ancient Greece and Rome, long before Pythagoras, Aristotle, Eratosthenes, Thales, Ptolemy, Hippocrates and Archimedes and the hundreds of others began to create science as we know it. It is unreasonable to expect that Abraham or Moses understood that the earth is round, and that it rotates or circumnavigates the sun. They knew the Sun was not a god, and they knew the moon was not a goddess, and so they had advanced beyond many of their neighboring people. They knew about the stars, and observed the movement of a few planets, but they had no concept of what they actually were nor how vastly distant these lights were placed. Still, they came to believe that whatever these lights were, God had made them, as He had the sun and moon, the mountains and all else. That was a spiritual truth, not a scientific claim, and so those ancient Hebrew minds had taken a leap beyond most other people on earth, another step in the evolution of the idea of God.

Some Believers may not be able to accept this view of the Bible and its authority. Some may think it is heresy to say that some of the ideas in the Bible are scientifically in error. The earth is not flat, it does not have four corners, the sun does not circle the earth, nor are there four or more giant pillars holding the earth steady. For those ancient people, these were good guesses, but not accurate. This does not deny or denigrate the "inspiration" of this book or these passages, for it is the best they could receive from the Source of All Knowledge, for it was as far as their brains had developed and could possibly comprehend. We can appreciate how right they were about **who** created the earth, while forgiving them for not understanding that our planet is a 25,000-mile circumference round rock covered with dirt and water, barreling along at thousands of miles an hour around a huge, relatively stationary super-hot star we call the Sun. We didn't really understand these things until five or six centuries ago, not until enlightened by such scientists as Galileo and Copernicus, who were devout Christians. The religious leaders of their day condemned these new ideas and persecuted the "heretics." (See **Chapter 1 The War Between Science and Religion.**") Even today, we still have many among us who think the earth is flat, and that the sun orbits us, and that the moon walk was a fake.

The key to treating the Bible with appropriate reverence and respect is to read it only for the spiritual and religious meanings, and not to read it for geography, or astronomy or forecasting the future. The Bible can honestly be regarded as infallible in the realm of spiritual and religious knowledge, when taken as a whole and respecting the progressive growth of understanding that is recorded there. As the Bible says "In various ways God has spoken to us in the **past**, and **now** He has spoken to us through His Son" (Hebrews 1:1) The **past** and **now**, a change in our understanding God over time, the incomplete and imperfect finally becoming the full and complete revelation of God. The full revelation in Jesus is the end of the process by which God spoke to this group of people over thousands of years, their newer understandings replacing earlier, less complete glimpses of God. Like seeing through a semi-opaque cloudy window, or over a foggy meadow, things become more understandable and clearer as the cloud or fog clears away. What we saw dimly in 2000 B.C., now becomes clearer and more distinct. Our guesses and imaginings about God and His nature become more certain and credible, the pieces begin to fit together and the total picture makes more sense.

A Spiritual Diary

Diary keeping

Let us propose that the Bible should be looked as a **diary**, an ongoing recording of the experiences of a people, the reflections of many individuals over the centuries as they wrestled with the idea of God and their efforts to decipher His ways and His will. We know that the Bible was in fact composed by dozens of individuals, living out their faith over hundreds of years, observing and experiencing drastic and dramatic events in their corporate history. The Old Testament, with its 39 books (in the Protestant version), credits as authors Moses, Joshua, Ruth, Samuel, David, Solomon, Ezra, Nehemiah and more than a dozen believe that the written Hebrew documents were compiled and edited by many scribes, priests and royal historians at some point in Israel's history, either from older preserved documents or from verbal transmission, probably both. We know from anthropological studies of tribal people that ancient stories and histories have been safely and faithfully passed down by word of mouth from one generation to another for thousands of years. We know of African elders who today can recite from memory the genealogy and history of their tribe's people, and pass along in vivid detail the stories they learned from their predecessors.

Oral or spoken transmission seems suspect in the 21st century, and we don't put much trust in reports that have not been written down contemporaneously. We recognize the fallibility and fragility of witness' memories in court testimony, and most of us experience serious flaws in our own personal memories. So, how could the "word of God" be preserved and transmitted for centuries before it was written down? Many modern Islamic students memorize the entire Koran, and there are numerous reports of adults who have memorized the entire New Testament. These were not savants, but ordinary people who had the discipline to work on memorization. Apparently, our capacity for memorization is greater than our need for it, since we have everything in printed or digital format. People who lived before the advent of abundant paper and ink had a great incentive to use memory as a dependable record. Diary keeping is an art that has fallen into disuse in modern times, though it was a widespread practice in America from the founding fathers through the Civil War. Many diaries have been found and preserved from these earlier days, and almost without exception, they provide unique and amazing information and insight to modern readers. Diaries are still kept by modern Americans, often by those whose teen-age years brought stress and confusion, and "Dear Diary" became a friendly ear, a secret companion to be entrusted with our deepest thoughts and emotions. Some diaries are day by day historical accounts, with only an occasional expanded entry when something important was reported. Some diaries are more reflections of feelings and questions than merely historical accounts. Diaries are often so revealing that their discovery and exposure by someone else can be devastating and horrifying, an unforgivable invasion of privacy.

Israel's Diary Reveals and Exposes Truth

Israel's diary is very public and open, and it exposes the good, the bad and the ugly, with very little attempt to whitewash the truth about individuals and events. Adam and Eve are presented unvarnished in their sin and shame, Cain is exposed as a self-centered murderer, Noah is acknowledged as being a drunkard, Abraham is portrayed as a coward and a liar, David is shown as the epitome of a schemer, adulterer and murderer. The warts and misdeeds are detailed alongside the great, heroic aspects of their lives. As a diary, it reveals the feelings and interpretations about the experiences, often without much detail about factual questions of "who, when, where, etc."

One aspect of diaries kept over a long time is the possibility of tracking changes in the thinking and emotions of the subject. People who look back through their teen-age diaries later in life are often embarrassed to recall how "silly" or "foolish" or "pitiful" they appear now to grownup eyes. "How could I have thought that?" "What was I thinking?" "Oh, my...I was brain dead! That was so ridiculous!" Sometimes, however, the review of what used to be can reveal truths overlooked or forgotten. The diary account may resonate emotionally and uncover suppressed feelings that need to be faced now. The honest account at the time of writing is the best understanding at the time, the interpretation that was logical and justified based on what knowledge or experience was available. The original account may have factual flaws, but it very likely reflects accurately the inner truth as it was seen at that time.

This, we believe, is a valid comparison to Old Testament accounts: they were true reports of the feelings and understanding of those individuals in their time, even if we now question their conclusions.

Original vs Copy

As discussed above, the accuracy and authenticity of the text is a crucial first step to the understanding of any written document, especially ancient works. For the purposes of this Apology the issues around Biblical documents and texts is covered in some detail in **Chapter 11, Jesus— Perfect Image of God.** Suffice it to say for now that we have a reasonably trustworthy Greek text from which to work, a text which is much older and closer to the original writings than what was available four hundred years ago when the King James Bible ("Authorized", AD 1611) was published. For the New Testament we have many actual original parchment copies, texts held in Christian hands only 50 to 100 years after Jesus lived, not necessarily the original "autograph" (from Paul or Peter or Matthew, etc.) but clean copies of their originals only

10 or 15 years old. In contrast, the earliest documents we have from the hand of Homer, or Julius Caesar, or Plato are more than 1000 years later than the originals, copies of copies of copies. There is no serious doubt among modern Bible scholars that these writings from these ancient men are reasonably close to what they first penned. We have just as much reason, or more, to trust the received documents of the Bible as we do the other famous ancient works. For now, the question is how to **interpret** what we have in hand, our English Bible, available in many useful and scholarly translations from Hebrew and Greek.

Whose Interpretation?

The Bible is like every other important written document, for even when there is absolute agreement on which words are on the page, there can be, and often are, **differing interpretations.** The original text of the Bible is not available, and scholars have endless debates about which ancient documents are most accurate and authentic. In addition, the words that we do have are in Greek, Aramaic or Hebrew, words that must be translated into English or other modern languages. Translation is an art, not a science, and so which English words are closest to the Greek word's meaning is never absolutely certain. Further, these letters and words, ink on paper, are actually only **symbols of meaning,** the coded representations of the meaning in the **author's mind**. These written symbols must be deciphered and read, and then their intended meanings reconstructed in **our mind**. Communication is the process of transferring meaning from one mind to another, using such symbols or sounds. It is in this **transfer of meaning** between minds that problems occur, and this gap is where misunderstandings can happen. For every historic document like the Bible, we face three major obstacles: a **text** that is trustworthy and authentic, an accurate, careful **translation** to our language, and a correct **interpretation** of the original author's intended meaning.

For purposes of this book, and in the interest of conserving trees, we will focus on the third factor, the **interpretation** component and we will only briefly discuss textual transmission and translation. These two issues are well-covered in many other books, and they have been subjected to much credible scientific investigation. Scientists have recovered ancient parchments and codices of biblical material and have established empirically the origins and dates of most of the known manuscripts of the Old and New Testament. With the help of scientists, we have pushed back the document dates to less than 100 years from the original in some portions, and we have confidence that the copies we have are very accurate and true to the original autograph.

Likewise, in the case of translation, science drives the continual study of ancient Greek, Latin, Hebrew and Aramaic, the original languages in which the Old Testament and New Testament were first recorded. Theologians and Bible scholars are dependent on scientists who are experts in language form and usage, by careful examination of non-biblical documents and comparison with words used in the Biblical material. So, we have reason to trust the translations which come from those old manuscripts.

There are many dozens of translations of the New Testament, especially, some which are the product of committees of scholars, and some the product of one person. Most translations by groups of Bible scholars are attempts to do a *word for word* translation from Greek to English, as much as possible. There often are several English words which might approximate the meaning of the Greek word, and sometimes there is no good English word that is exactly right. Translations produced by a group of ecumenical scholars are considered most trustworthy and unbiased, often identified as "standard."

Many talented individuals have produced their own translations or versions of the New Testament, often very learned and scholarly individuals who try to make the Bible more readable, using modern language and idiom, often in simplified form. The translations by individuals are usually *thought for thought* rather than word for word, trying to capture the meaning by phrase or paragraph. These types of translations are usually labeled "paraphrases." Not all translations are equally good or accurate, of course, and individual translation risks individual interpretation biases creeping in, but the competition of the market and the healthy critique by other Bible scholars tend to maintain a respectable and useful version. The abundance of translations and versions enables readers to compare two or three different translations, often producing a more robust and rich understanding of the Bible. We return now to the question of **interpretation**, the why and the how.

Why Do We Need Interpretation?

To explain the need for and the importance of interpretation we turn to a non-Biblical example. The problem of **transfer of meaning** discussed above applies to the Constitution of the United States, written so many generations ago, but revered as the source of all law in the United States. While the Bible's original text is not available, and the exact words used are still debated, the Constitution's authenticity is not in question: we have the **actual words of the original document** signed on September 17, 1787 in Philadelphia. The words of the Constitution are in English, and so translation is not a big issue. But when we turn to the meaning of these word-symbols, there is still much room for interpretation. The Supreme Court is the final interpreter of our Constitution, and each of the nine Justices interprets the written text based on the particular judicial models they follow, and there are several such diverse frameworks for interpretation of this our greatest literary achievement. The two most prominent and broad models of judicial interpretation are described below; these labels are not exhaustive, and their use may vary among legal scholars. These two at least illustrate the concept of models of interpretation.

Originalist: Judges who prefer to rely on a strict adherence to the original words of the text, using only their plain, ordinary meanings, and following the founders' original intent so far as possible. This is a **strict constructionist** approach, taking what was written as being fixed and unchanging, except by amending the Constitution. What did it mean at the time it was written, as understood by ordinary people at the time? **Textualist** is another name for this general view.

Pragmatist, or Living Constitution is the claim that the Constitution is not fixed and static, bound to the 18th century America, but has a dynamic meaning, so constructed that it can adapt to changing times and problems. This view takes not only the original meaning but considers the broader context, and the evolution of contemporary society. Pragmatists consider factors such as judicial precedent (prior court decisions), the technological advances, and sometimes even consider "natural law."

The late Justice Antonin Scalia was a **strict constructionist** and an ardent **originalist** interpreter of the Constitution, believing that the words are to be read as they were first written, and that the Constitution must be understood and applied in accordance with the original meanings and intent of the founders when it was first adopted. This legal philosophy is the ideological opposite of the **non-originalist** or **living Constitution** positions of Justices Stephen Breyer and the late Ruth Ginsburg, who favor consideration of previous court rulings, contemporary societal norms, and fundamental natural law. This model of interpretation tries to determine how the original intent from colonial America 200 years ago would be applied today to contemporary problems and issues unknown to Jefferson, Madison, Adams, and the other framers of the Constitution. This model has brought rulings on **privacy, personhood, free speech, abortion, church/state relations**, and many other topics absent or unclear in the 1787 legal documents. Supreme Court interpretations of the Constitution have dramatically changed American society in the last 100 years. Interpretation is a very powerful, but very tricky business regarding the Constitution. This principal is perhaps even more true when applied to the Bible, for there are many models or theories of Biblical interpretation, and there is no one view approved by all Christians.

Models of Biblical Interpretation

Just as there are several judicial models guiding the interpretation of the Constitution, so there are models of Biblical interpretation which shape the results. The traditional or orthodox approach to understanding the Bible, and perhaps the most popular view, is the broad category ***Literal***, by which Believers take the words in the Bible as direct and simple, plain language meaning exactly what it says. The slogan for this approach would be "Says what it means and means what it says!" This might be compared to the "strict constructionist" view of the Constitution as described above. Another broad category of Bible interpretation might be called ***Figurative*** or sometimes *Allegorical*. Readers who approach the Bible in this mode are looking for deeper, more spiritual meaning than just the obvious, everyday definition of the words; they believe the Bible is MORE than just a written book, and has hidden messages that can be discovered only by very sincere and deeply spiritual readers. Some others who agree with this basic premise of hidden message apply that method to some parts of the

Bible, and regard other sections as being better understood literally. So, Mark would be largely be considered literal, while the Book of Revelation would be almost entirely figurative or allegorical. Within these two broad approaches to the meaning of the Bible there are numerous variations and mixtures.

LITERAL MEANING	FIGURATIVE MEANING
Strict, word for word	Hidden, spiritual message
Means what it says, and says what it means	Meaning for Original audience, but also message for us now
Little interpretation needed	Depends on our interpretation

Traditional Literal Interpretation

Believers who take the Bible pretty much at face value, who don't consider it some mystery message to be untangled or decoded, are in the vast majority among Christian groups. This doesn't necessarily mean absolutely literally (e.g., few would argue that the rivers really should 'clap their hands' as the Psalm 98:8 says). Literalists still debate the meaning of words and whether the grammatical construction should be read this way or that, but by and large they are not as dogmatic as the figurative interpreters. A traditional literalist can accept that some literary forms are to be understood differently, so that a parable or a poetic psalm may have both a plain and a nuanced meaning. Within this broad category of literalism, the serious Bible student and theologians follow a further strategy called the **historical-grammatical** method, which strives to find the meaning of the text by considering the cultural and historical background of the writer and the intended readers, in addition to the grammatical, syntactical and literary form being used. In this more diligent search for the meaning the goal is to answer these questions: What did the author intend to communicate? What was the purpose of writing this? Who was the author writing to or for, who was the intended audience? As can be seen this historical-grammatical approach tries to peel away prejudices and biases of modern readers and put ourselves back into the original historic environment. Notice, this is quite similar to the judicial philosophy of many Supreme Court justices—the "originalist" interpretation.

Strict Literal Interpretation

Literal interpretation in general takes the biblical texts at face value, their simplest, most obvious, and natural meaning, seldom search for hidden meaning or secret messages. Literal interpretation is a broad category with many possible variations and views of inspiration. Some models of this brand take a more conservative and "traditional" position, often associated with the belief in *verbal or plenary inspiration*. In this approach divine inspiration of the text means that not only the biblical message but also the individual words in which that message was delivered or written down were divinely chosen. In an extreme form this would imply that God dictated the message to the speaker's or writer's word by word; some even claim that the punctuation and spelling is divinely directed. This approach is hard to defend rationally to Skeptics for several reasons. For example, the rigid dictated theory doesn't take into account the change from Hebrew or Greek to Latin and then to 1611 English of King James. Words in 1611 don't always mean what they do in the 21st century. For example, *"For our conversation is in heaven; from whence also we look for the Saviour, the Lord Jesus Christ* (**Philippians 3:20**): "conversation" meant "life" or "behavior" to King James, not "talking" as it means to us. But most proponents of literal verbal inspiration don't hold such an extreme view, recognizing that many writers and many styles would require some flexibility. Traditional interpretations passed down generations are usually considered the best interpretations by believers in Biblical literalism.

Moral interpretation

Moral interpretation is necessitated by the belief that the Bible is the rule not only of faith but also of conduct. The Jewish teachers of the late pre-Christian and early Christian Era, who found "in the law the embodiment of knowledge and truth" (Romans 2:20), were faced with the necessity of adapting the requirements of the Pentateuchal codes (estimated to include over 600 "sins" or prohibitions) to the changed social conditions of the Hellenistic Age (3rd century B.C.–3rd century AD). For example, the Mosaic law defined carrying a bucket of water on the Sabbath as "work" and thus a sin. Jewish faithful adapted by means of a growing body of oral interpretation which enabled the conscientious Jew to know his duty in the manifold circumstances of daily life. If, for example, he wished to know whether this or that activity constituted "work" that was forbidden on the sabbath, the influential school of legal interpretation headed by the rabbi Hillel (late 1st century B.C. to early 1st century A.D.) supplied a list of 39 categories of activity that fell under the ban.

Allegorical Interpretation

Allegorical interpretation places on biblical texts a meaning that is **not obvious**, not the plain explanation. Literalist, of course, view allegorical proposals as something that was never intended by the original author, with rare exceptions. In the first two centuries of the Church many churchmen were considered heretics because they took the Old Testament literally, with the many stories appearing to portray God as a genocidal, angry and vengeful tyrant. Trying to reconcile that Old Testament understanding with the Jesus God led them to doubt the validity of the Old Testament as divine truth. Some even denied that the Yahweh of the Old Testament was even the same God as Jesus' Father. Thus, viewing much of the older scripture as allegorical and symbolic rather than the apparent literal description. Marcion and Celsius were condemned by the official church leaders and with their many followers were excommunicated or "black-balled" for their views. In those first few centuries as doctrine and select religious books were being debated, the allegorical interpretation was increasingly popular. Allegorizing, it seemed, was the only procedure compatible with a belief in the Bible as a uniform divine oracle. Law, history, prophecy, poetry, and even Jesus' parables yielded new meanings when allegorized. The story of Joshua's destruction of Jericho was a moral lesson about the wrath of God against sin, and the power of God to overcome evil; the legendary story of God taking revenge on a gang of boys who were making fun of a bald prophet by sending a hungry bear to eat them all—gory but symbolizing the danger of opposing God's servants and leaders. Each preacher could apply these difficult cases to some spiritual truth, making interesting and frightening sermons.

The clearly sensuous meaning of the Canticles (the Song of Solomon) could be seen as pornography if taken literally, but those bawdy words was gladly embraced when those scenes of physical affection and endearments were understood to be about God's love for His people, expressing the communion between God and the soul, or between Christ and the church. There are still readers who can reconcile themselves to the presence of a book such as Joshua in the canon only if it's battles can be understood as pointing to the warfare of Christians *"against the spiritual hosts of wickedness in the heavenly places"* (Ephesians 6:12). If we seek an allegorical meaning in the Gospel parables, such as *The Good Samaritan* (Luke 10:30-37) we can imagine an allegorical meaning for the thieves on the Jericho Road, the Priest and the Levite can represent the defective Jewish religion, the Samaritan's beast must mean something, and the same with the Inn, the Innkeeper, and the two pence paid for the injured man's care. An allegorical meaning can sound amazing and mysterious, but it would miss the actual meaning Jesus intended when He was asked "Who is my neighbor?" The plain message is: "Love your neighbor as yourself means help every other human being you have the power to help." Jesus nailed it down for the Pharisee: "Go and do likewise." (Luke 10:37) The allegorical version of these stories may be clever and amusing, but that might not be what was originally meant.

Typological Interpretation

Typology is a doctrine or theory concerning the relationship of the Old Testament to the New Testament. Events, persons, or statements in the Old Testament are seen as **types** pre-figuring or superseded by **antitypes**, events or aspects of Christ or his revelation described in the New Testament. Typology is somewhat similar to allegorical interpretation, perhaps even a subcategory of it. But rather than reinterpreting the meaning of the original story typological interpretation deals with specific details such as persons, objects, time, titles or events in the Old Testament are seen to set forth *at a deeper level* persons, objects, or events in the New. So, **Noah's Ark** (Genesis 6:14–22) is interpreted to typify the **church**, outside which there is no salvation; Isaac carrying the wood for the sacrifice (Gen. 22:6) typifies Jesus carrying the cross; Rahab's scarlet cord in the window (Joshua 2:18–21) prefigures the blood of Christ; and so on. These are not merely sermon illustrations but rather aspects of a hermeneutical theory that maintains that this further significance was designed (by God) from the beginning, and hidden or disguised. Traces of typology appear in the New Testament, as when Paul in Romans 5:14 calls **Adam** a "type" of the coming **Christ** (as the head of the old creation involved its members in the results of his disobedience, so the head of the new creation shares with its members the fruit of his obedience) or when in 1 Corinthians 10:11 he says that the Israelites' experiences in the wilderness wanderings befell them "typically," so as to warn his own converts of the peril of rebelling against God. The Fourth Evangelist stresses the analogy between the sacrificial Passover lamb of the Hebrews and Christ in his death (John 19). The writer of the Hebrews treats the priest-king of Salem, Melchizedek, who was involved with Abraham, as a type of Christ (Hebrews 7) without using the word "type." And the Levitical ritual of the Day of Atonement is seen as a model (though an imperfect one) of Christ's sacrificial ministry (Hebrews 9) As can be seen this method is flexible enough to create almost any connection one could imagine, and thus, we can find some wild and strange interpretations on today's TV and radio.

Historical-Grammatical Interpretation

It is likely that most Bible-believing Christians generally follow a method of interpretation known as the historical-grammatical approach. That is, we try to find the plain (literal) meaning of the words based on an understanding of the historical and cultural settings in which the book was written. We then follow standard rules of grammar, according to the book's particular genre (poetry, history, sermon, parable, instruction, etc.), to arrive at an interpretation. We seek to perform careful interpretation or **exegesis**—that is, to "read out of" the text what the author intended it to mean. This is in contrast to **eisegesis**, which occurs when someone "reads into" the text his own ideas—what the reader wants the text to mean. This method of interpretation can be described in **W**'s (**WHO, WHEN, WHERE, WHY** and **WHAT?**) discussed in detail below.

We Believers have been known to look for "proof texts" or specific verses that prove what we believe, and it is an easy game to play for the Biblically literate (or to mislead the uninformed). Instead, exegesis is finding the AIM (**A**uthor's **I**ntended **M**eaning) of the passage because its true meaning is determined by the sender of the message, not the recipient. This approach is useful because it offers an internal system of "checks and balances" to make sure one is on the right track, anchored in something more reliable than opinion. With the Historical-Grammatical approach it is harder, but not impossible, to bend scriptures to suit one's whim or weird theology.

Truth Is Always Found in Context

You may have heard someone say that a particular verse has been pulled out of context, and Believers are sometimes guilty of this to prove a point; likewise, Skeptics or critics of Scripture often take verses out of context when they attack the Bible. The reason is that they can make the Bible "say" just about anything if they do not provide the context. For example, the critic might ask, "Did you know that the Bible says, **'There is no God'?**" Using this quote as a "trump card" he may triumphantly proclaim that **THIS** proves atheism, "For you say that your Bible is true in every way." Can it be true? Does the Bible say "there is no God?" How do Believers handle such a startling quote? We look at the context, which in this case is Psalms 14:1 and also Psalm 53:1. There we read the whole verse: *"The fool says in his heart, 'There is no God.' They are corrupt, and their ways are vile; there is no one who does good."* (Psalm 53:1) So, it's true that the Bible states, "*There is no God,*" but it attributes these words to a foolish person, and is not teaching atheism. So, let's just start with the most basic question. What does a text mean? The answer to this question is that a text means what the author intended it to mean. Only rarely does a person write something with a hidden message, some mysterious secret code to be deciphered. For a simple example, if you wrote a letter to your mother with some statements in it that are unclear, a little ambiguous, then what does the letter mean? Does it mean what you intended it to mean or how the readers interpret it? Of course, it means what you intended it to mean, even if readers misunderstood. It is true that some Believers see the Bible as a secret message hidden from the unbelievers, a bunch of coded revelations that can only be understood by clever detective work. Such an un-anchored approach to the Bible cannot provide a rational and logical answer to the meaning, for it can be whatever you imagine. **The true meaning of a text resides in the authorial intent** of the text. This leads us to the first primary and fundamental principle of interpreting the Bible: Ask of the text: **Who** said this, **to whom, when** and **why?**

These four W questions are stock and trade of journalists and historians, and work well for examining the meaning of a Bible verse or chapter. For example, the much-abused final book in the Bible, **The Revelation of John** was written first to Christians enduring severe persecution by the Roman Empire, a time when Christians were sometimes burned in the Colosseum for entertainment of the crowds because they would not renounce Christ and accept the Emperor as a god. The atmosphere in 90 A.D. was comparable to what Christians faced in China under Communism, and what North Korea is like in our time—oppression and execution. So, knowing this historical fact, it is easy to say that the book was written by a revered Christian leader (Probably John) to persecuted Christians to encourage them and guide them in trusting that God will prevail and that persecution will pass: God is able and will bring peace and justice again. "Wait patiently on the Lord." (Psalm 127:14 New Living Translation) That is the plain and simple interpretation of this mysterious book, with vivid and terrifying word pictures to depict the battle between good and evil. Is that the only interpretation? No, it is possible to see Revelation as a prophetic book predicting the distant future; rather than seeing it written to 1st Century Christians we can find in its mysterious text clues to our time, now, or to our future dark days when Satan rules the world for a while. Whether Revelation warns us about Hitler, or Stalin or some world dictator who is coming soon, we cannot know. We have espoused the view here that the Bible is not a book of predictions, science or sociology, but is best loved as the story of how God found people and people found God. If the Bible has a secret message, this book in your hands has no magic key to unlock it's supposed secrets.

*Looking back over the years, I realize the
Bible isn't magic, but it is corrective;
it isn't an answer book, it is a living book; it
isn't a fix-it book, it is relationship book.
When I confront God's word,
I am confronted; when I read God's word, it reads
me; when I seek God's presence, He seeks me.*

MIKE YACONELLI[10]

Chapter 3

THEN WHAT ABOUT SCIENCE?

"Science is a way of thinking. It is more than a body of knowledge"
CARL SAGAN

FOR MANY PEOPLE SCIENCE AND RELIGION ARE MORtal enemies, a zero-sum battle for "truth"; in fact, they share one important common base: certainty is not possible. True science always reserves the possibility that the current theory or law **may** be wrong or incomplete. The scientific method involves careful observation, formulating a theory explaining those observations, predicting results from the application of the theory, experimenting or testing the theory rigorously by "falsification", and then replication of the experiment by other scientists. (Note: "falsification" means trying to prove that the proposed answer is **wrong**, a process driven by competition among scientists for their own fame and recognition.) Once a theory has been supported by the findings (not disproved) it is considered "generally accepted", "proven" or "established", but always subject to further testing in which new data evidence may later weaken or throw into question the original theory. That is **good science.**

Truth and Doubt

Religion is often portrayed as being the bastion of "truth", a haven of certainty in a world of doubt and confusion. Religious leaders are expected to be absolutely confident in their beliefs and doctrines, and to stalwartly defend those truths with vigor and clarity; an "uncertain" minister is not going to gain many followers. Much of the claim for certainty and confidence comes from a belief that the Bible is a divinely given revelation from God, and that it is Truth itself. The most conservative Christians hold to such a strong conviction that they claim the Bible is "inerrant," is correct in every aspect, "every jot and tittle," to use a biblical rubric. Interestingly, this quaint phrase is related to the tiny pen strokes and small dots of Hebrew letters, minute elements that distinguish one letter from another very similar in appearance. Jesus uses these tiny details to assure the skeptical Jews that He was not altering the Torah: *"For truly I tell you, until heaven and earth disappear, not the smallest letter, not the least stroke of a pen, will by any means disappear from the Law until everything is accomplished."* (Matthew 5:18). So, some Christians insist that nothing can be added or removed from the sacred text: it is perfect in every respect. Some fight new translations as "changing God's Word" (meaning The King James)

This level of certainty sustains the faith of many, but hinders discussions with nonbelievers. Is it possible to have a secure faith in the Bible without being viewed as "close minded" by those who trust in science for truth? The question of "inerrancy" and the dependability of the Bible as an all-purpose, all-time guide to truth was discussed extensively in **Chapter 2: What About the Bible?** outlining a path which, it is hoped, both the religious and the non-religious can travel, side by side even if not hand in hand.

Certainty Is Two-Edged Sword

Certainty is a pleasant condition for the human mind, comfortable and relaxing; we don't have to be in the struggle for truth, for we have found it; we have "made up our mind." But certainty is a trap, even a "trap door" for thought, a jewel box with the lid tightly closed. We have captured the truth, and it is ours now. We might occasionally take it out of the box and admire it a bit, but we don't examine it or question it, for we don't want to damage it. Religious people often suffer from the "God in the Box" syndrome, holding tightly closed their concept of God in the protective crimson folds of their faith. If some new (contradictory) idea about God is encountered, their faith is secure because they know what is in "the Box." But it is not just religious folks who shelter and protect their version of the truth, for it is a plague even for Science and scientists.

As discussed before, Science is "self-correcting" because it has adopted a model of inquiry that fosters competition. For instance, somebody's grand theory about *dingbats* is published and dispersed in the scientific community. "Dingbat Theory" is debated in annual conferences, and counter-arguments are published in journals, and a dozen of other researchers report that their experiments did not support "Dingbats" or some fault is found in the data of the original "dingbat" research. Under ideal conditions, nothing goes unchallenged or disputed in the world of science, and the ideas that survive in some form are tentatively placed on the "widely accepted" shelf. But good scientists are rebels, and their default position is skepticism. "Dingbat" **may be true**, or it **may not**—we will await further evidence. Science has had many theories taken off the shelf and put in the trash bin over the years (discussed later), for every human endeavor is subject to imperfection. Skepticism is very good for scientific inquiry, but also presents an obstacle for scientists encountering religion. One harsh critic of scientists, William Batchelder Green complained:

> You say you will never believe in God until the fact of his existence is proved to you! Then you will never believe in him at all; for, in the face of positive knowledge, faith is no longer possible. Faith affirms in the presence of the unknown. If science should ever demonstrate the existence of God (which it never can) faith would become lost in sight, and men would no longer believe, but know. The reason why science is intrinsically incompetent to either prove or disprove the existence of God, is

simply this, that the subject-matter transcends the reach of scientific instruments and processes. The dispute is, therefore, not between faith and science, but between faith and unbelief. Unbelief is a disease, not of the human understanding, but of the human will, and is susceptible to cure.[11]

Calling "unbelief" a disease is a little strong, especially from the perspective of this book, which takes the more positive view that belief and unbelief are choices, decisions of the mind about the persuasiveness of the evidence. Some noteworthy scientists have said publicly that they "want to believe" in God and continuation of life after death, but they "could not." The intellectually honest inquirer may be open to belief, even seeking evidence to support that belief, but in the end their rational self concludes that "the evidence is lacking." As an advocate for belief in the Jesus/God, the hope is that persuasive evidence can be mustered that will tilt the scales toward belief, or more toward belief than unbelief. The quotation from Greene cited above does accurately state a major obstacle to scientists believing in religion: the instruments for measuring scientific phenomena are not suited for measuring religious phenomena, and so a searching scientist must find other tools or instruments to supplement their telescopes, microscopes, Bunsen burners and laboratory beakers. Those new tools are mental rather than material instruments. Actually, the additional mental tools required are not new to science: reason, logic, imagination and open mindedness are not "new" to science, but have perhaps been crowded out by numbers, data, measurements and unchallenged dogmas. Yes, science has its beliefs, doctrines and dogmas, the cumulative public confidence that science has the answers to everything. It is hard to stay humble when your profession is so highly regarded and has enjoyed so much proven success in making life better.

Crossing the Language Barrier

For people of faith to connect with people of science, it is important to understand what science is, and how it looks at things. Not all scientists are skeptics or unbelievers, but our language and our world views differ in fundamental ways, creating barriers to communication. For the non-scientist Believer, a short primer about science and the scientific method is given here, using a relevant historic example. This is not enough to make you a scientist, but it may help you to talk with and understand a scientist.

No scientist has created more conflict for Christians than Charles Darwin, wrongly viewed by many as a traitorous opponent of religion, a tool of the Devil, some might say. Many Believers consider his theory of Evolution by natural selection as the beginning of the hostility between science and religion. Though Darwin didn't actually initiate the conflict, he symbolizes it in many ways, serving as a "stereotype" of the villain to many Christians. By examining this man, his important works, and his scientific methods perhaps we can cast light on the "evolution problem," correct some popular misunderstandings, and illustrate how real science operates. From this case example we may be able to understand more clearly the difference between Believing and Knowing. The ordinary Believer can learn more from this section than the science practitioners and students who are already familiar with this pioneer of modern science. Science readers will probably see mistakes and challenge them.

Charles Darwin's Bombshell

Nothing excites more debate among religious people even today as the 170-year-old scientific theory popularly known as **Darwinian Evolution**. Charles Darwin, 1809-1882, was a British naturalist, geologist and biologist. Darwin's family tradition was nonconformist Unitarianism, and his baptism and boarding school were in the Church of England. When going to Cambridge to become an Anglican clergyman he did not doubt the literal truth of the Bible and in his early scientific career he remained a staunch "creationist." However, his interest in science diverted him from the ministry, and in 1831, at just 22 years old, Darwin set sail on a scientific expedition on a ship called the HMS Beagle. He was the naturalist on the voyage, essentially the "science officer." The focus of the expedition was on surveying and mapping, but it was his job to observe and collect specimens of plants, animals, rocks, and fossils wherever the expedition went ashore. He was very diligent in this endeavor, writing and sketching each day, keeping copious and detailed journals of all that he saw and learned from natives.

Darwin spent most of his time on land, examining and documenting a multitude of plant and animal life in South American and then throughout the south Pacific islands. He was puzzled by the geographical distribution of wildlife and fossils he collected on the voyage, noting how some species on one island was similar, but distinct in some significant way, from those on the next island. Yet all of the creatures and plants showed a marked relationship with those from the American continent he had just visited. The novel Galápagos species, Darwin reasoned, must have migrated, perhaps by accident, from Central and South America and then diverged from their ancestral stocks after arriving in the Galápagos. As he traveled from island to island, Darwin also encountered tantalizing evidence suggesting that evolution was proceeding independently on each island, producing what appeared to be new species. "Evolution" was not a new idea with Darwin, and the topic was hotly debated in British and European scientific circles, and the archaeological discovery of fossil evidence of prehuman ancestors in Africa and the Middle East was increasing in scope and acceptance by then.

Troubled Believer but Not an Atheist

A creationist when he visited the Galápagos Islands, Darwin still held the traditional belief that God had created each species separately and specifically for particular environments, and that while heredity played some part in changes in people over time, changes from one species to another was not possible. On the long voyage aboard the Beagle Darwin frequently expressed his Christian upbringing in his copious journals, and in his interactions with the Captain and crew. In his diary he wrote this:

> During these two years (i.e., October 1836 to January 1839) I was led to think much about religion. Whilst on board the Beagle I was quite orthodox, and I remember being heartily laughed at by several of the officers (though themselves orthodox) for quoting the Bible as an unanswerable authority on some point of morality. I suppose it was the novelty of the argument that amused them.

THEN WHAT ABOUT SCIENCE?

> But I had gradually come, by this time, to see that the Old Testament from its manifestly false history of the world, with the Tower of Babel, the rainbow as a sign, etc., etc., and from its attributing to God the feelings of a revengeful tyrant, was no more to be trusted than the sacred books of the Hindoos, (sic) or the beliefs of any barbarian.[12]

Darwin may have begun to have some religious doubts toward the end of this journey of discovery, but they appear to be questions about the accuracy of the Bible, not about the existence of God. Darwin did not become an atheist, but became a troubled believer struggling with religious dogmas and divisions, and with moral questions such as Evil being allowed to exist by a benevolent God. In 1879 he wrote *"I have never been an atheist in the sense of denying the existence of a God. – I think that generally ... an agnostic would be the most correct description of my state of mind."*[13] In fact, Darwin claimed to find in his amazing discoveries in nature the verification of divine creation rather than contradiction. He considered it *"absurd to doubt that a man might be an ardent theist and an evolutionist,"* essentially identifying himself as a theist in the mold of Thomas Jefferson and many intellectuals of that era. Theists believe in a Creator, but not in a personal, activist, history altering miracle-working God as taught in 19th century orthodox Christianity. He continued to attend his church for many years, probably a Skeptic, but because of his family he did not reject religion entirely.

No Rush to Judgment

It was only after Darwin returned to London in 1839 that he began to grasp the significance of the unique changes in the plants and animals he had observed over the five-year voyage. Evidence from the South American continent showed that species did not seem to be stable across either geographic space or the deep reaches of paleontologist time, and his conviction of "special creation" at a particular time was shaken. But the particularly compelling evidence of species change from the Galápagos Islands catapulted Darwin and natural science into the modern age. Note however, that his fully developed theory of evolution was not published until another 23 years had passed, 23 years of thinking, writing, discussion and debating with other scientists.

During those two decades of contemplating his own findings, Darwin was influenced by several other great scientists and scholars of the day. One of Darwin's teachers at Cambridge was the famous John Herschel (1792-1871), a scientist and mathematician who developed the early methods of scientific investigation, establishing an orderly relationship between observation and theory formation. He taught that nature was governed by laws that might be difficult to state mathematically, but could be understood by inductive reasoning and logic, a domain of natural philosophy. A logical explanation, a unified theory, could be reached by philosophical debate for any observed phenomenon, he argued. His *A preliminary discourse on the study of natural philosophy*, published early in 1831 became an authoritative statement with wide influence on science, particularly at Cambridge where it inspired student Charles Darwin to embrace scientific explanations rather than supernatural ones. His earlier attraction to William Paley's "natural theology"—an argument for a benevolent God based on intelligent design—gave way to the idea of "natural selection" rather than divine planning. Thus, Darwin became a modern scientist, trusting in observable, objective laws of nature rather than divine miracles. For a long time, he apparently believed in God, just not in the theology of the time.

One Key Opens the Door

Even more galvanizing for Darwin was in the work of Thomas Robert Malthus (1766-1834), English cleric and scholar, influential in the fields of political economy and demography. Malthus had earlier formulated the famous "doomsday" theory showing that because populations grow geometrically, while food supplies grow arithmetically, eventually the human race would starve. There would always be more mouths to feed than could be sustained in any existing environment. He predicted prophetically approximately when that cataclysm would occur. He observed that a normal increase in a nation's food supply improved the lives of the populous for a while, but it inevitably led to increase in population, which eventually outstrips the food supply needed. Though this Malthusian prophecy was disturbing, and not widely accepted, it did provide Darwin the missing key, the idea that allowed him to make sense of the evolution he had observed, an explanation he needed to produce a **unified theory of evolution.**

From Malthus' formula Darwin saw that the pressure of overpopulation would mean that some would starve, but some would survive by changing or adapting to the new conditions. With human deadly overpopulation, some would survive by moving to new territory; others might survive by conserving resources or finding ways to produce more food for their family. Those who did not change or adapt would perish eventually, he reasoned. From this insight Darwin developed the idea that the pressure of overpopulation would mean some would survive if they were in **some trait or quality better fitted than others who died**—thus assuring increasingly more of the adaptable population and eventual extinction of the unadaptable ones. This "selection" of survivors was **natural**, not divine, he realized.

The Resolution and the Revolution

After more than two decades of contemplating his discoveries, in 1859 Darwin published his earth-shaking book, **On the Origin of Species (by Means of Natural Selection).** It created a virtual bombshell in Victorian England and on the Continent, and arguably, ignited a world-wide revolution of scientific research amid a firestorm of controversy. As with Copernicus and Galileo, these new scientific theories were condemned by the religious leaders of the time, though Darwin did not face arrest or burning at the stake like some of his predecessors. He was, however, greatly reviled and threatened by many of the churches and clergy of his day; that animosity is still alive and flourishing in twenty-first century America. Darwin's name is probably mentioned in modern American pulpits more often than Satan; some clerics seem to consider these two names as synonymous.

Some historians say Darwin later lost his faith in God in grief over the death of his young daughter. Whether that tragedy destroyed his faith entirely or forever, we cannot know, but such loss is often blamed on God, and it is hard to explain how a "good" God would allow such a terrible outcome. We cannot judge this great scientist's spiritual condition, but we have judged in earlier sections the nature of the God Darwin tried to believe in, a loving Father who understands grief and doubt, and who has compassion on all the "poor in spirit" and "those who mourn" as Jesus taught in the Beatitudes:

> *"Blessed are the poor in spirit,*
> *for theirs is the kingdom of heaven.*
> *Blessed are those who mourn,*
> *for they will be comforted."*
>
> (Matthew 5:3-4)

From this overview of the experience of Charles Darwin we can better understand the struggle of the mind and heart of scientists, not only the intellectual effort involved in putting together a multitude of first-hand observations into a coherent pattern, but the spiritual and emotional stress thoughtful humans go through to reconcile old beliefs with new understandings. Darwin planned to be a Christian minister in his early life, perhaps to please his family, and his exposure to scientific thinking and challenges to his inherited faith pushed him into a new career path. It was a gradual process by which he advanced in science and declined in religious fervor. It is very likely that every agnostic in our society has taken the same gradual loss of religious certainty in their exposure to modern science and modern philosophy. Most people are not eager to throw off their youthful faith in a dramatic "unconversion." The decay of faith is, for most people, a prolonged journey. So, Believers should not assume that all Skeptics are hostile to religion or faith, for many will, in fact, be former believers, maybe even struggling to believe.

The other important point in Darwin's story is how difficult it is to make logical sense out of a plethora of facts and observations accumulated over some years. Most readers will have worked puzzles of one sort or another, and will have experienced the "missing piece syndrome," the missing information or data or word or jigsaw piece which solves the puzzle once it is found and put into place. Science is a puzzle solving enterprise, and a researcher may "know" that there is a "picture" here somewhere, some vaguely perceived idea which eludes discovery for years. Scientists test this idea, and then the other, ruling somethings out and something in, until finally it works: we find the answer, we see the whole and not just random parts. And, in the end, the solution may turn out to be wrong or incomplete when exposed to the harsh inspection by other scientists. Both science and religion are searches for truth, using different tools and different means for validation, and both require honesty and hard work.

The conflict between science and religion did not begin in 1859 with Darwin's **Origin of Species,** or his later book**, The Descent of Man.** Christians and other Believers need to honestly acknowledge that our religious ancestors persecuted the scientists of the Renaissance of the 15th and 16th centuries, as reviewed in **Chapter 1 "The War Between Science and Religion."** The "war" continues today in many ways, but to some degree Science has declared victory and ignores the ineffective shots some Christian leaders continue to fire off on TV or in books. Much of the shadow boxing is being done by sincere religious people who are poorly informed about modern science. This book is aimed at Believers who are willing to learn enough about their supposed "enemy" to engage in dialogue with scientists or mere laymen who had a good science education in school and appreciate the importance of science today. A brief primer of science follows to help bridge the communication gap.

Basic Science Primer

Science is **naturalistic** and **empirical**. Science starts with the philosophy or world view that the universe is entirely physical or material, and natural laws can describe all that is real. Non-physical, spiritual or supernatural things or laws are not necessary to explain reality. Science is limited to what can be observed, measured or weighed, things or laws that can be stated in numbers. Only what can be measured and verified is accepted as **real**. Science does not necessarily deny the existence of the non-physical, spiritual or ethereal realm, but dismisses or disregards discussion of such ideas because they cannot be measured or verified. Some scientists, however, **do totally reject the idea of a supernatural realm**, a "reality" that cannot be observed by the senses or measured in physical terms. Such confident rejections are technically not "good" science, because pure science remains open always to additional evidence, and a closed mind is always a travesty, whether it is a scientific or a religious mind. Absolute certainty may be enticing, but it is the deceptive **song of the Sirens** of mythology. Like Odysseus in Homer's **Odyssey**, modern scientists must bind themselves to the safety of true scientific methods in order to avoid the fatal allure of professional over-confidence. Those safe principles follow briefly.

Naturalistic Science Is the Dominant Model

Naturalism is the philosophical principal in science that all phenomena, effects and causes are natural, and not the result of any supernatural or metaphysical activity. For the purpose of investigation and inquiry, it is presumed that the natural world, physical reality, is a closed system, unaffected and uninfluenced by any non-material events, forces or entities. Everything can be explained by natural laws, without resorting to some supernatural explanation. "Supernatural" simply means *beyond* or *above* physical laws of the universe. We may not currently be able to explain **everything** through the natural laws we understand, but this is seen as just requiring more research and study. This obviously is antithetical to a religious world view of gods, demons, miracles, and other supernatural realities.

Empirical Science Demands Data

Empirical means that all knowledge must be based on observation or experience alone, capable of being seen, heard, smelled, or measured by more than one person; truth is evidence based, data based, usually translated to numbers. Non-measurable, non-empirical phenomena are dismissed as irrelevant. For science to accept something as truth it must be perceived by normal human senses, perceived and measured by more than one person, and verified by other competent scientists. Things that only occur once to one person or group are NOT real, unless they can be replicated under the right conditions by other objective observers. So, a group of five people in Idaho may report mysterious objects and lights in the sky or on the ground, but the event never is repeated, and scientific or forensic evidence is not found to support the story, or the evidence is suspicious. The five Idahoans may be stalwart citizens, including teachers and lawmen, but the report is not empirically established. It may indeed be true and factual, but it is not acceptable to science. The evidence is not there or is not convincing, and science is very much evidence based.

The idea behind this principle is that natural causes can be investigated directly through scientific method, whereas supernatural causes cannot, and hence presuming that an event has a supernatural cause halts further investigation. For instance, if a disease is caused by microbes, we can learn more about how microbes interact with the body and how the immune system can be activated to destroy them, or how the transmission of microbes can be contained. But if a disease is caused by demons, we can learn nothing more about how to stop it, since demons are considered supernatural beings who are not bound or constrained by the laws of nature. For science, all natural causes or events are subject to the regular laws of nature. Some other fields of study, such as history, also operate on this principle, that there is a **natural explanation** for all events, explainable by known laws of nature.

Skepticism

Skepticism is the third essential principle of science: the assumption that nothing is absolutely and eternally **certain**. Scientists, like all other human inquirers, have made **mistakes**, have **jumped to conclusions prematurely**, or **been fooled or deceived.** Lots of scientific knowledge from 1800 is no longer viewed as true, having been disproved or displaced by better science. History has its many false reports and incorrect information which had to be retracted and rewritten by later evidence. Science and history are evidence based, but do not necessarily claim that supernatural causes do not or cannot exist, because true science is skeptical—certainty is a trap avoided by knowledgeable scholars. Some scientists have violated this principle of skepticism regarding religion and other claims of supernatural realities, maybe in reaction to some assertive religionists who claim absolute and universal certainty in their claims for spiritual or supernatural knowledge or powers. Such clashes of fields exist, but there is no conceptual conflict between practicing science or history and believing in the supernatural. The two world-views can co-exist, and already do for many people who can accept uncertainty and open mindedness.

Both science and religion are searching for a **grand unifying theory of everything**, a way of holding all that is true together in some compatible, comprehensive and integrated explanation or theory. For science it is usually physics that is most clearly seeking for the final, perfect set of natural laws that can explain everything (light, energy, magnetism, dark holes, expanding universe, and everything else.) The late Stephen Hawkins was reportedly working on "a theory of everything," and Einstein spread out an astounding collection of theories that almost explained everything. But new findings are always coming along, requiring old unifying theories to be adjusted or rethought. Science hopes to someday be able to understand every natural law in the universe and how they fit together. But we are not there yet. In the same way, religion has always been seeking a grand, overarching theology, a unifying theory of all the spiritual realm of life, a way of explaining God, creation, evil, sin, human nature, and all the rest. It is not enough for either science or religion to have a collection of truths: the ultimate goal is a package that is Truth, the answer or explanation for everything. The Mind of Man is searching for meaning, and that encompasses all realms and realities experienced by humans, from the dawn of mankind till now. The human brain is hard-wired to search for patterns, to discover meaningful connection; likewise, Science formalizes that demand for evidence, facts, data, some quantifiable measurements.

Are We Talking Prose or Poetry?

In common usage we distinguish between two types of writing or communication: prose and poetry. In literature this is a crucial distinction, for these two forms operate in entirely different ways. This gulf is illustrated in a quote often attributed to Governor Mario Cuomo: "*You campaign in poetry. You govern in prose.*" His long political career taught him that a candidate promotes idealistic, noble ideas, worthy dreams of possible futures while seeking an office, but having been elected, must govern in hard reality, nuts and bolts, limited finances and competing interests. Campaign promises give way to practical realities, such as the necessity to persuade legislators and special interest groups to support ideas they did not originate, and the democratic limits on power that require compromises. Poetry and prose are similar in that both are used to communicate meaning, and both use the same basic vocabulary. Both usually follow the same grammatical rules (though poetry is less strict in syntax).

THEN WHAT ABOUT SCIENCE?

Prose is able to carry a large and complex message (a text, book, lecture, treatise, etc.) while poetry often seeks to convey a focused message, a deeper meaning in contrast with breadth of knowledge which prose conveys. Prose is heavy in facts, while poetry is aimed at feelings, seeking to invoke some emotional response. Prose is usually more concrete and direct, whereas poetry is often abstract or obscure on first reading. Prose is written in sentences and paragraphs, following standard rules and structure, while poetry is written in lines and verses, sometimes repetitive for effect. Poetry sometimes rhymes, but not always; poetry normally has an identifiable metrical pattern or structure which work better when read aloud. Prose may use some of the literary tools of comparison and contrast, but poetry resorts to metaphor and simile frequently to convey abstract or emotional meaning. The prose writer might say "The moon is in the third quarter tonight, somewhat blue because of the hazy atmosphere." The poet might write, "The moon is a blue sliver of silky night gown, parading leisurely across the darkened stage." Fact is the goal of prose, but feeling is the poet's hope. Poetry often ends up being sung, becoming the lyrics to a song, heightening the effect on the brain of the hearers. Prose is usually considered more mundane and ordinary, and is the preferred means of writing in newspapers, magazines and encyclopedias, while poetry is considered more of an art form, a creative and expressive skill with language.

It is proposed here that **Scientists** primarily view the world in **prose**, while **Believers** typically see and understand the world in **poetry**. This is a gross over-generalization, of course, but please permit us to use this generalization to suggest *possible tendencies* of thought pattern. Prose thinking is practical, no nonsense, mostly black and white, measurable and verifiable. Poetic thinking is idealistic, prospective, descriptive and comparative, more visual than rational. People may be born with tendencies toward these differing ways of communicating, or they could be molded in those directions by their education or their social environment; we know that musical talent reflects a more poetic mindset in development and that musical proficiency can be attributed to both genetics and environment. Musicians appear to think differently from bankers and doctors, at least in general mind set, and portrait painters probably see the world differently from house painters.

Are We of *Two Minds*?

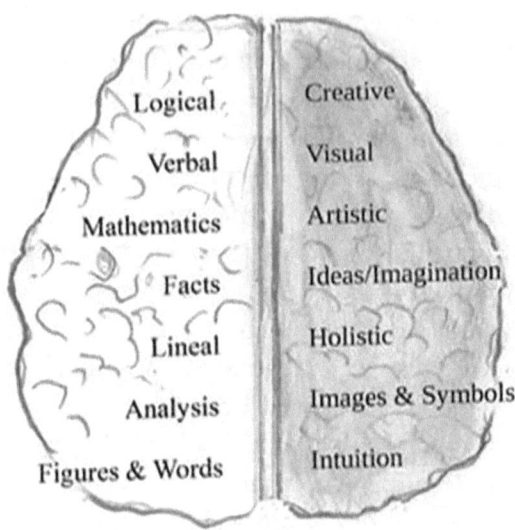

"Split Brain"

These contrasting ways of seeing the world may be related to the phenomenon of the "split brain" in humans, the two prominent cerebral hemispheres separated by the "medial longitudinal fissure", but connected by the "corpus callosum." According to conventional wisdom, people have a dominant side of the brain which strongly influences their thinking style, special abilities and their "handedness." We know that the brain is "cross wired" with the left side of the brain primarily controlling the right side of the body, and the right brain controlling the left side functions. Most recent scientific studies have cast doubt on the overall conventional "split brain" wisdom of the past, and they show that the brain wiring and control is much more complicated than a simple left-brain, right-brain organization. However, the evidence still supports the general concept of hemispheric specialization, but respects the amazing ability of the brain to adapt, to modify specific areas for a different function, to compensate a loss in one area by an increased nerve circuitry to another location. Some startling research will be discussed in **Chapter 4: The Brain Game,** giving more details about this disputed idea. Several studies seem to substantiate the older theory: several cases are cited of profound brain injury causing disabilities that seem clearly left-brain/right-brain connected; other amazing research cited involved patients who have had their corpus callosum severed surgically, and then displaying a stark left-right function. So, though the older so called "myth" of strict left-side right-side specialization has some shortcomings, the basic concepts are still worth considering briefly and simply. This is still a disputed area of science.

There are several versions of right-left specialization, some more general and some quite neurologically specific. Those who are right-brained are supposed to be *intuitive* and *creative* free thinkers. They are "qualitative," big-picture thinkers who experience the world in terms that are descriptive or subjective. Left-brained people tend to be more "quantitative" and analytical. They pay attention to details and are ruled by logic. Neurologically it appears the specialized neural wiring activates parts of the left-brain for data, while parts of the right side are activated more to stimulation that is visual, spatial, emotional and metaphorical. The implication is that our left side is wired to look at things in a scientific way, and the right side typically sees the abstract, the metaphorical, the visual, the spiritual, the awe inspiring, the mysterious, the beautiful and the wonderful. The left side deals mostly with facts, while the right side focuses on ideas and images. This theoretical division is reversed for those who are predominantly "lefties:" they typically are "right brained" while the majority right handers are usually "left brained."

Metaphors, Similes and Other Figures of Speech

Science books and articles can be very well written and interesting, and many are literary works in the commercial world. But scientists are not often praised for their writing skills and their beautiful words, but are mostly judged on the factual, trustworthy, and usefulness of their books and articles. Almost no scientist is invited to a "reading" of their work in a civic center or a public library. Their work focuses on being true instead of beautiful. A rogue science writer might use a simple metaphor once in a while, but likely will be criticized for doing so, and omitting it in the next edition. Religious writing, on the other hand, is very often written to be attractive and thought provoking, reaching for the "heart" of the reader more than for the mind. Metaphors and similes and other literary forms are the *modus operandi* of religious literature, from sermons to theological books, from prayers to public rituals such as funerals and weddings. "Spicing up" the message with pretty words is highly valued in religious circles, and Believers are moved still by the beauty of the King James Version of the Bible, with all the "thees" and "thous" and the Shakespeare-like phrases and quaint words from the 17th century. Other Bibles of the hundreds of versions available now are more academically "correct" translations of Greek and Hebrew words, but none is as artistically satisfying to many people as the familiar old English words of the King James.

The language of the Bible is a mixture of prose and poetry, of course, and readers need to attend to which form of writing is being read. Poetic passages such as all the Psalms, Proverbs, Job, Ecclesiastes and Song of Solomon are recognized as poetic books, but also most of the prophets (Isaiah, Jeremiah, Amos, Hosea, Joel, Job and Jonah, etc.) are predominantly poetry of the Hebrew type. Job and Jonah are actually epic poem-stories in the same sphere with Homer's Iliad and Odyssey (though shorter). Many of the 150 psalms were actually lyrics from songs sung in Israel's worship, and Psalm 119 is a clever and beautiful **acrostic** poem. It has 176 verses divided into 22 stanzas of 8 verses each, one stanza for each of the 22 letters that make up the Hebrew alphabet. The first verse of each stanza in the original Hebrew begins with the same letter. Other Psalms have similar patterns, reflecting exceptional literary skill, poetic genius even in translation.

Figures of Speech in The Bible

It is not surprising that the Bible is full of metaphorical and other literary techniques. A metaphor is a figure of speech that describes an object or action in a way that isn't literally true, but helps explain an idea or make a comparison. "Life is a carousel" is a musical metaphor equating life with a frenzied merry-go-round. A simile is another type of comparison "Life is like a box of chocolates," indicating a similarity between two things. Jesus was a master story teller and used many colorful figures of speech (both metaphors and similes). All of His 46 or so parables in Matthew, Mark and Luke, plus a dozen extended stories in John are analogies by which Jesus compared a familiar physical reality to an unfamiliar spiritual reality. A parable acts like an extended analogy which directs your gaze away from "what it is" (reality) to enable you to see "what it is like" (analogy), sometimes described as using an "earthly example to describe a heavenly truth." Jesus' story of the prodigal son (Luke 15:11-32) uses a human father-son conflict to point to the spiritual truth that God is a forgiving Father. A parable is a disarming form of indirect communication designed to make you look one way—to a Sower seeding a field—in order to grasp a meaning elsewhere—differing responses to God's word.

In an Old Testament example, the prophet Nathan tells David about a rich man who killed a poor man's beloved sheep instead of one of his own hundreds of sheep. David is incensed at the story (reality), and threatens the villainous man—until he realizes that **he is the man**. Nathan's story is just like (analogy) David's own recent murder of Uriah, husband of his pregnant mistress, Bathsheba (2 Samuel 12:1-7). To read all the Bible literally is to miss a great deal of its truth. For example, Jesus said it would be as hard for a rich man to be saved as it would be for a camel to go through the "eye of a needle." (Matthew 19) That absurd picture in the mind made a stunning impression about the dangers of riches corrupting people, and is intended to be silly instead of "true" in order to make the message memorable. Jesus told the story of the Good Samaritan, a very lovely story about loving our neighbor, (Luke 22:25-37) but we shouldn't call Jesus a fraud just because He (probably) made up a good fictitious story to illustrate His point. Dozens of His parables are creative short stories from His imagination, not historical accounts or news items. They are **true** but not factual or literal.

A Variety of Modes of Thinking

Besides the possible language division into prose and poetry, it is also widely recognized that humans think and communicate in more than one mode, and a dozen or so modes have been proposed. A small sample of the many taxonomies about thinking includes: *convergent* vs. *divergent* thinking, *inductive* vs. *deductive* reasoning, *vertical* vs. *horizontal* vs. *lateral* thinking, and *focused* vs. *diffused* modes. These modes, plus many more in the literature, all seem to follow a similar pattern of two or more radically different modes of thought, each of which is most useful for specific problems and are subject to our choices of our thinking strategy. Let us examine just one for now, the **convergent vs. divergent modes,** to understand the basic concept that our thinking style influences our belief system.

Joy Paul Guilford coined the term "convergent thought" to describe a thinking process seeking to find a single, standard answer to a problem, such as "2 plus 2" or "true or false" questions. The "right answer" is the important issue, not the creative way or method used to discover the answer. Logic is the standard for convergent thinking, whereas imagination is the driver for "divergent thinking" which is a thought process or method used to generate creative ideas by exploring many possible solutions. Convergent thinking produces the one answer which has been accepted as correct, whereas divergent thinking produces many possible or potential ideas to be evaluated. Brainstorming is a familiar method of divergent thinking, a structured gathering of spontaneous ideas from several people with all criticism withheld or deferred until the end. Convergent thinking is often used to complement divergent thinking, subjecting the multiple potential solutions to analysis and questioning, applying "critical thinking," which is another name sometimes used for convergent thinking.[14]

It is suggested here that **scientific** thought is primarily a **convergent** mode, while religious or **spiritual** thinking tends toward the **divergent** model. Certainly, science uses divergent approaches in trying out several possible hypotheses to explain some phenomena, and teams of scientists probably "brain storm" occasionally for new ideas. But it is also clear that science, perhaps more than religion, is looking for a single right or correct answer which corresponds to known rules and physical laws. Science, more than religion, relies on mathematical properties to get measurable results and to "prove" findings. Religion, on the other hand, seldom uses math or physics for religious questions, and is more likely to turn to group processes and group decision-making as the validation for the religious answer. Scientific conclusions are usually considered settled and "proven" at the end of the process, whereas religious questions are often seen as "open ended" subject to more thought and discussion.

THEN WHAT ABOUT SCIENCE?

Thinking in The Fast Lane

An interesting new way of looking at how we think has been proposed by noted psychologist Danny Kahneman in a book entitled **Thinking, Fast and Slow.**[15] His research has suggested that there two distinct systems of thought in the human mind, systems reflecting evolutionary development. The first is labeled System 1, which Kahneman describes as "fast, reflexive, intuitive and automatic." He says it is the primitive part of thinking that evolved in our ancient ancestors to survive in a dangerous world. It was necessary to react quickly in order to avoid being eaten, and this early mode of thinking did not require a lot of pondering and wondering, operating below the conscious level. It was more than just instinct, since it is based on prior learning and experience, and involved a kind of rehearsed response to a perceived threat. System 2, according to Kahneman, is "slow, rational and deliberate." This is the part of thinking that we consciously operate by observation, analysis, logic and decision making. System 2, the product of more evolution and brain development, is able to act as the executive, overriding rash or irrational decisions made in the System 1 panic button mode. Kahneman believes that modern humans still have both these systems, and that we sometimes fail to use System 2 to control and manage our more primitive impulses and thus to act irrationally.

The terms Kahneman uses, "fast" and "slow" are relative, of course, because all brain activity, of which thinking is a part, is **very fast**—electrical impulses measured in milliseconds. As we look in the next chapter focusing on the brain, it will become clear that humans are fascinating compound organisms, with parts from early evolutionary systems interplaying with developments that occurred later in the evolution process, both in body and brain. You may notice as you read further how the idea of two systems of thinking, one "fast, reflexive, intuitive and automatic" and the other "slow, rational and deliberate" seem to fit the pattern of superego, ego and id of Freud and similar analyses of the inner life of humans proposed by many modern scholars. That we humans are composed of distinctly different components is beyond dispute; whether the various observations reveal a **larger pattern** is debatable.

Chapter 4

THE BRAIN GAME

"The chief function of the body is to carry the brain around"
THOMAS A. EDISON

Edison's quote above seems a bit harsh in dismissing the rest of the body as a mere transport vehicle for the human brain. Certainly, the body is much more than merely a carriage for life and mind and personhood and the hundreds of other bodily components which are integrally connected to what it means to be human—to be an "us" or a "me." Science tells us that the whole human nervous system works together, and it's not just the three-pound organ in our skull that defines us. Though this book takes a more general and simplified view of the brain than a science text, it acknowledges that there is so much more neurological information available and needed to give a more complete understanding of the brain. The generalizations (such as the three-brain model and the "split brain" phenomena) are, we believe, **true** and helpful for this discussion, but are **not the complete science** of the brain. Much more knowledge about the marvelous brain will be discovered by science over time, but for now we will work with introductory level material and encourage readers to explore science books for a more advanced or "graduate level" understanding of the brain.

As suggested in the ***Preface/Introduction,*** the evolution of the idea of God parallels the evolution of the human brain; the concept of gods came after some mental capacities gradually became operational, and subsequent ideas about God progressively evolved over many millennia. The development or evolution of the brain is the central player in the evolution of humans, vastly more important than bipedalism or opposable thumbs or the growth of a larger "voice box." It is the human brain that distinguishes mankind from all other species on earth, including the closest relatives, the chimpanzees and apes. All animals have brains, but not all brains are created equal. We know from paleontology that the earliest hominids had brains that were smaller and less developed than later hominids who were our ancestors, and the modern human brain is larger and more complex than the brains of the early humans who moved out of Africa and into Asia, Europe and most other corners of the earth. Interestingly, the Neanderthals living in Europe until perhaps 30,000 years ago probably had a slightly larger, heavier brain than we do. But sadly, our big-brained, brawny, red-headed cousins went extinct some 28,000 to 30,000 years ago, though some of their DNA, as much as 4%, is still in the human genome of many current populations. Understanding the biology and physiology/function of present-day human brains is the absolute requirement for discovering how God came into the picture.

Why Study the Brain?

It may seem odd to include a major portion on brain physiology in a theological apology. It may seem even more inappropriate since it is acknowledged the author is not a neurologist or even a scientist of any kind, and so has no expertise on brain structure. What is presented here is based on the science of others who are experts, and whose research has shaped our understanding over the last quarter of a century; that science is changing as science should, and so what is presented here speculatively may not hold up under future examination. ***It is hoped that the ideas presented here will stimulate others to do the rigid study and experimentation suggested by this work.*** Left brain-right brain theories, once so very clear and exciting have now been challenged, but that issue is discussed later in this chapter, and partially defended. Likewise, the earlier clarity about the "three-brain" model has grown less clear and more complicated. The "three-brain" theory is central to the theories advanced in this book, and so the usefulness of the theory will be thoroughly explored here. The "science" presented here is best viewed as being at the early "hunch" or "speculation" stage. All science, good or bad, has such an "ah-ha" birth in someone's mind. In the author's mind, the science and the theology presented in this book seem to fit together beautifully, and allow many conflicts between science and religion to be resolved rationally.

On the other side, this book's positive advocacy for the evolution of the human brain may be troubling to religious Believers who have been taught that God created Adam and Eve as completely developed and fully functioning human beings at a specific point in history. Such readers are urged to "suspend disbelief" for a time to consider how much more marvelous the creation of our wonderful brain appears when one begins to understand how unbelievably complex and beautiful is this, arguably the *center piece of Creation*. In fact, we argue here, that **the brain is God's two-way communication system,** the divinely planned means by which we **know** God and **converse** with Him. It is with our brain that we experience God and form a relationship with Him, either of faith or doubt. Religion, we argue, is brain-based, and all **believing is a decision** made in our walkie-talkie brain. It is possible, we suggest here, that the physiology of the brain may provide a scientific basis for what Christianity calls "sainthood", and also an explanation for "original sin," what Paul calls our "carnal nature," (Romans 8:6) or "lust of the flesh" (I John 2:6) and what philosophers, poets and novelists have long called "the human condition." These controversial and theoretical ideas will be covered in detail later in this chapter.

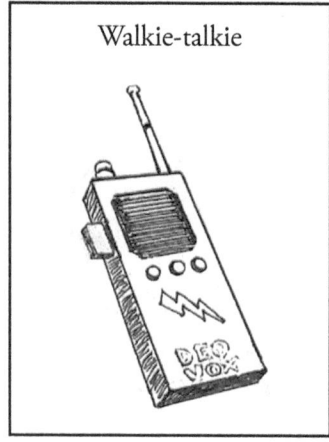
Walkie-talkie

Is Your Brain You?

Believers quite often speak of "knowing God in our heart", or having some concern or need "laid on our heart" by God. Many ancient people, including the people in the Bible, thought the beating heart was the life and soul of humans. For example, Jeremiah: "***The heart*** *is deceitful above all things and beyond cure. Who can understand it?"* (Jeremiah 17:9); and Jesus *"**But the things that come out of the mouth come from the heart, and these things defile a person. For out of the heart come evil ideas, murder, adultery, sexual immorality, theft, false testimony, slander.**"* (Matthew 15:18). Thanks to science we now know that **it is the brain** which is the organ of thought and mind, the seat of our personality, our consciousness, our soul. We still use "heart" metaphorically and poetically, but we "know in our hearts" (*borrowing Senator Barry Goldwater's campaign slogan*) that our miraculous, marvelous brain is where we actually live, the source of all that makes each of us who we are as a person, the center of everything which makes us human. In a significant, but incomplete way, we can say "My brain is me."

We are totally amazed when we consider the stars and the planets, the sun and the moon, and our glimpse of the universe and the vastness of the cosmos, through a telescope or in pictures from the Hubble Telescope. And the more we learn (from science) the greater is the opportunity for the believer to experience genuine awe and worship. We are overwhelmed when scientists tell us there are more stars in the cosmos than there are grains of sand on earth, or mystify us about voracious "black holes".

But the cosmos is but a minor work of God when compared to God's crowning creation: Mankind, and our **amazing brain/mind**. The Genesis story clearly has the creation of Adam and Eve as the **final** stage of the work of God, the purpose for which the rest of was completed. This creation of Man from mud is the creation which received the heartiest "That's good" from the Creator, a Creator who was very pleased with all that He had wrought. Psalmist David grasped this unfolding wonder in song in Psalm 8:3-6:

> *"When I consider your heavens,*
>   *the work of your fingers,*
> *the moon and the stars,*
>   *which you have set in place,*
> *what is mankind that you are mindful of them,*
>   *human beings that you care for them?*
> *You have made them a little lower than the angels*

and crowned them with glory and honor.
You made them rulers over the works of your hands;
you put everything under their feet:

As Carl Sagan pointed out, this Psalm of David probably reflects human ARROGANCE, imagining ourselves to be the primary masterpiece of the Creator of the Universe. Skeptics might say *"If there was a God, a Creator, what interest would He have in this tiny little speck of rock and water, a mere pale blue dot in an infinite sea of galaxies, nebula, super novae, black holes, newborn stars and dying suns?"* Surely this is most foolish human self-centeredness imaginable. Yes, Dr. Sagan and Skeptics, we must plead guilty: to claim that **we** are "special" is haughty, prideful, self-centered, disdainful, supercilious, arrogant, conceited, pompous, condescending, smug, patronizing, imperious, proud, snobbish, snobby, scornful, sneering, uppity, snooty, blatant narcissism and so-on. None of these adjectives is pleasant nor complimentary to Christian theology, or to Christians, and it **is** pretty audacious to imagine that we, humans of Earth, are important to the Universe. Yet, the God who is the subject of this apologetic, the Jesus/God, **has**, we assert here, put His human creation as the central object of His attention and affection. The Christian claim is *"***For God so loved the world** (the world of humans) *that he gave his one and only Son, that whoever believes in him shall not perish but have eternal life."*. (John 3:16) Our skeptical scientific readers may be amused or scoffing at this claim, but we hope all readers continue on through the apparent flotsam and jetsam with an open minded (that is, a *scientific*) curiosity about where this argument may lead.

The Brain's Hunger for Knowing

The following content is not intended to be a comprehensive study of the human brain, for the brain is so marvelous and complex that a large library of books would not contain all that is already known and all that is yet to be understood. We look, however, at the basic structure and the essential functions of the fully developed human brain, to further the argument that the evolution of the brain was the mechanism by which God prepared to reveal Himself. The human brain, like no other animal brain, is specifically "wired" to seek and to perceive

MEANING, to sort the many sensory signals coming in and to find or develop a pattern, a tentative explanation. All brains, from worms to wombats perceive their environment and respond to it, but it appears that only humans ask WHY? Humans seek to put the pieces of perception together in some kind of pattern, to try to explain (to themselves at first) anything new or unfamiliar by linking the new to the old information they already have. Based on research at Cambridge University and elsewhere, the paragraph below is an example of our mind's ability and desire to see a recognizable pattern or create one. Can you read it?

"It deosn't mttaer in waht oredr the ltteers in a wrod are, the olny iprmoetnt tihng is taht the frist and lsat ltteer be at the rghit pclae. The rset can be a toatl mses and you can sitll raed it wouthit porbelm. Tihs is bcuseae the huamn mnid deos not raed ervey lteter by istlef, but the wrod as a wlohe."

(Above is original composition by Author, and it drove <u>Spell-Checker</u> bonkers!)

Let's imagine how this pattern recognition was useful for our ancient hominid ancestors on the plains of Africa some 100,000 years ago. You hear a rustle in the bushes, a faint noise that your ears have been tuned to hear, sharpened by evolution (the earlier relatives whose hearing was not so acute likely were eaten by prey.) You hear the sound, look in the direction of the rustling, and wonder "Is that a bear or a tiger? Or, is it just the wind blowing the grass?" Your life depends on your guess; does it sound like that sound you heard a few "suns" ago?" Your brain automatically revs up, your breathing is shallow, your muscles tense, ready to run or fight. Special organs activate at the alarm, flooding your body with some powerful juices (cortisone, adrenalin and insulin, your modern cousins have now discovered), and both your hearing and eyesight are sharper and more focused by this frightening noise. Some archaic humans in this situation acted on the assumption the danger is real, and ran for their lives. Some decide it was just the wind in the bushes, so they relax. Either guess can be wrong. The frightened *Homo erectus* may run to safety only to find out it was not really a dangerous animal; he may be embarrassed (if that ability has evolved yet). The other hominid, the "brave one," may be mistaken, and end his life that day as a tiger's lunch. Over time, the ability to "see" patterns helps make the hominids quicker to respond, and thus more likely to survive and pass on their "cautious" genes to the species. In those perilous times and circumstances, the advantage is to those who perceive patterns, whether real or imagined. There would have been a natural selection for those hominids who tended to believe that all patterns are real and potentially dangerous. *"Better safe than sorry"* may be the motto for all evolution.

Apparently, for the survival of the species, it has been beneficial for humans to come up with a quick explanation for observed phenomena. Pattern recognition is an essential part of intelligence, even though the pattern "recognized" may be false or non-existent. Neurologist Michael Shermer explains ***"The brain is a belief machine. From sensory data flowing in through the senses the brain naturally begins to look for and find patterns, and then infuses that pattern with meaning."***[16] Our marvelous brains evolved to connect the dots of our environment, to project *meaning* and *cause* onto the massive flood of information, trying to explain "why" (and maybe "who?") In the primitive brain of hominids long ago, and in the modern brain of *Homo sapiens* today, the patterns of meaning generated can become beliefs, explanations and assumptions which become our personal possessions, and which can firmly shape our understanding of reality, *semi-permanently*. It is natural for the human brain to have confidence in those beliefs, adding emotional color to them, and causing us to look for confirming evidence, and to overlook evidence which might contradict our original beliefs. It may be disconcerting to skeptical or non-believing readers, but several studies have shown that our brains apparently are wired to make it **easier to believe than to disbelieve.** However, despite our propensity to gullibility, it is our brain's **need** for a pattern, an answer, or an explanation which drives our **hunger to know.** Hominids have been curious from our earliest conscious thought, and it is this curiosity that has allowed our species to survive and advance toward "civilization."

The Desire to Know the Unknown

The human brain is a vehicle equipped to receive the multiple signals from the material environment, but it also perceives signals from some non-material sources. Our brain is flooded with sights, sounds, aromas, taste signals from our tongue and tactile sensations from every square inch of skin—our five "senses." But our brain also considers "feelings" and "hunches" and "intuition" which apparently have no biological center but are still taken seriously as part of the environment we are assessing. Whether we call these other non-physical signals "spiritual," "metaphysical" or "supernatural," the human brain is quite capable of accessing such "other worldly" content—and most people have experienced some such phenomenon. Inspiration, insight, creativity, imagination, revelation, thoughts, impressions, visions, ideas, hunches, or "ah ha!" moments—such are the types of knowledge which seem to come from realms beyond empirical science.

Many famous musicians give credit to such an "outside" source for a song which "just came to me." Some of these artists report that it was like taking dictation, writing as fast as they could, maybe on the back of a napkin, to capture the incoming words or melodies. Many scientists also have written about discoveries that appeared to come to them in the middle of the night, or while walking their dog. Many such creative insights are only partial breakthroughs, of course, providing some new clues that then must be worked out in the material world of the lab or the mathematical world of axioms, theorems, formulas and proofs. Most authors, mathematicians, inventors and ordinary people have had flashes of insight, receiving ideas which they cannot claim to have originated. Quite frequently those who have benefited from such sparks of creativity are humbled by the experience, counting it a "gift" unexpected and inexplicable. Many express a hope that it will happen again, but also a fear that it may not return.

This idea of receiving messages and inspiration from beyond ourselves is not new: Ancient Greece had a pantheon of minor goddesses who were believed to be the divine sources of knowledge and skills involved in poetry, music, dramas, myths, visual arts, science, geography and math, among many. The nine Muses were supposedly offspring of Zeus, the chief god, each talented in a specific art, and they bestowed their favor and inspiration on humans as they chose. They were usually invoked at the start of lyrical poems or dramas, and are prominent in the Homeric epics. We still use the Muse descriptor for inspiration in the world of art and literature. Several modern novelists, playwrights and musicians give credit for their successful creativity to "my muse." In some cases, such as Pablo Picasso and Woody Allen, the muse is a fascinating woman who inspires heroic artistic output, at least for a season. ***Muse*** is commonly used as a verb meaning "to think or meditate in silence, to ponder or ruminate on a subject or question, to be "deep in thought." Interestingly, *amuse, music* and *museum* are cognates of muse, linguistically linked (*museum* was a place where the Muses were worshiped). Thinking deeply, drawing on some untapped inner resource, is an attribute worth cultivating, a part of the process of becoming fully human, pursuing our personal potential.

Extra Natural Reception

Inspiration is not always there for us when we need it; even geniuses and very creative people do not always get the great new idea or insight. Do we summon our own inner thoughts and creativity, or, does the inspiration truly come from a mystical source, perhaps our Muse? Could the experience be merely a tapping into our own unconscious mind? Or, is there some spiritual process involved, some contact or communication with the Divine? Are our brains able to "tune in" to such resources the way we can turn the dial on a radio and tune-in distant stations?

satellite dish

Are such "revelations" the product of biology, of neurons and synapses, of molecules and material? There is no certainty among scientists, but virtually no one denies that such events happen, and very few who have had such "enlightenment" dismiss it as mere coincidence, chance or random firing of neurons. It seems reasonable to accept that new ideas come from somewhere, and the hypothesis we advance here is that "somewhere" is actually "someone" — a "higher power," the Great Spirit, or God. Creativity would logically emanate from a Creator, and so our theory is that the benevolent Jesus/God advocated here is the **source of good ideas.** The God who made mankind and oversaw the evolution of mankind from primate to fully developed humans is the One who gives us insights and revelations to further our search for knowledge. He wants us to know **everything.**

It is the firm claim of this book that *the human brain is the receiving equipment for communicating with God and the creative energy that emanates from the Creator*. Without a brain, or with a less well-developed brain, God could not have an encounter with us, could not befriend us, could not be known or understood. (Caveat: an omnipotent God probably *could have* found some other way other than the brain to enter into a relationship, but His choice of the brain has worked out marvelously.) It is argued here that the human brain, as it is now, is an effective, readily available, communication link between Creatures and Creator. Granted, some people may be better at listening to God and enjoying a close relationship with Him, but it is not a difference in capacity, but a difference in knowledge and skill. God as revealed by Jesus is actively seeking to engage with us, mind to Mind, using our ability to think to improve our communication skills, not just with Him, but also between ourselves. Later in this chapter we will report on research done by scientists observing in real time brain activity in people who were praying or meditating (common ways to communicate with God.) As those experiments show, people who are trying to communicate with God use specific parts of their brains: when "talking to God" their brain literally "lights up."

Many have claimed to receive messages from God or some divinity, and some have even claimed that the message was delivered by a voice, an audible human-like voice. Some of these people have been anointed as "saints" and some have been committed to insane asylums: the content of the messages was the primary determinant of being labeled "saint" or "sicko." Psychopaths and other troubled souls very often claim: "God told me to do it," the "It" being murder, suicide attempts, or other antisocial actions. Candidates for "sainthood" often say the same thing "God told me to do it" where the "It" was such positive things as giving up one's last food, or warning some leader against some foolish action, or even risking loss of life in order to help someone else. It has long been observed by psychologists and psychiatrists that some mental disorders often have a religious component, and some unresolved emotional conflicts are rooted in unhealthy early exposure to harsh, guilt-producing forms of religion. This religious component in some forms of mental illness led some scientists to blame "religion" for many of the illnesses of the mind, and to identify "religion" as a toxic element in society. It can be honestly argued that "bad" religion is harmful to individuals and society, distorted and demonic ideas about God which are still preached and advocated in our free society. It is the hope of this book that a healthy image of God can prosper and expand in our modern world, replacing and discrediting those versions of God that are indeed "toxic."

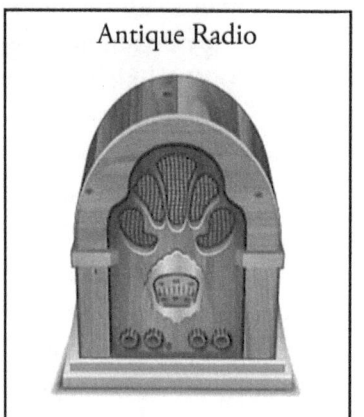
Antique Radio

If the brain is God's communication system with us, as we have suggested, it is important to know as much as possible in order to get the best signal we can, to so tune our minds that if God was speaking there, we would give Him our attention, much like the days of the Great Depression when families gathered closely around the old Crosley battery radio to hear every word of encouragement from their president, Franklin Delano Roosevelt. To miss his message because we have weak batteries, or our antenna is misdirected or our tuner was defective—that would have made the darkness of those days darker, the chill or fear more frigid. We propose that God loves all of us more than FDR loved the voters, and if there was a way to communicate hope and comfort, God would certainly find a way. Perhaps that damp, wrinkled three-pound mass of flesh and blood which we call our brain is His way to make contact.

Why Bother?

Since this is **not** a science book and **not** written by a scientist, why bother examining in some detail the actual physical structure of the brain? One answer is that the brain is such a wondrous and amazing bit of Creation that it is difficult **not** to talk about it, to sing its praise and glory in its potential. The second reason to get acquainted with this fleshly body part is that it seems to contain our Mind, our "us," even our spirit, bridging the gap between the natural and the supernatural. How the ethereal, the immaterial human spirit is able to arise from the tangible corporal mass of molecules, dendrites, neurons, water and fat is a mystery which we may not solve in this book, but it is a quest worth taking.

The Physical Structure of Our Brain

Neurology is the science field devoted to study of the brain and the nervous system, and the medical application of neurological science is perhaps the most demanding and respected. In common banter we retort "You don't have to be a brain surgeon to understand this," recognizing that working on the brain requires the highest scientific knowledge and skills. Neurologists must graduate from medical school, complete an internship, and receive three additional years in a neurology residency program (a total of at least eight years of preparation.) They treat brain tumors and cancers, brain trauma from injuries, and related other nervous system and spinal disorders. But neurologists also treat and manage a wide array of other serious ailments such as muscular dystrophy, seizures, Lou Gehrig's disease, Alzheimer's disease, encephalitis, strokes, multiple sclerosis, migraine headaches, and many other medical problems which haven't been explained by other medical specialties. Neurology studies the whole nervous system. All vertebrates have a nervous system consisting of two main parts: the central nervous system and the peripheral nervous system. The central nervous system includes the brain and spinal cord. The peripheral nervous system is a vast collection of nerves, which are enclosed bundles of the long fibers or axons, electronically connecting the brain to every other part of the body.

Before entering more serious and demanding discussion of the brain, a few "trivia" facts might help elevate the readers' appreciation for their brain.

- Our brains are about 73% water; even minimal dehydration degrades our attention, memory and other cognitive functions
- The typical brain weighs about three pounds; 60 % of the dry weight is fat, making the brain the fattiest organ in the body (so "fat head" is true)

- A normal brain comprises about 2% of the body's total weight, but uses 20% of the total energy and oxygen of the body
- The latest estimate is that our brains contain about 86 billion brain cells
- Each neuron in the brain can transmit 1000 nerve impulses per second, and can make tens of thousands of synaptic contacts with other neurons each second
- Our brain generates 12-25 watts of electricity, enough to light a small LED bulb

Mapping the Human Brain

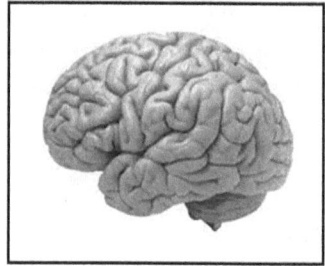

The brain and spinal cord together form the central nervous system. These vital structures are surrounded and protected by the bones of the skull and the vertebral column, perhaps providing extra protection congruent with the unique value of this stem. The functions which current science assigns to each discrete location are accepted for this discussion—relatively well established, but still under investigation and likely to change. Neurologists have enough reliable information about the location of major functions in the brain to know where to look if language is affected, or loss of balance is the issue, or vision problems. There are detailed "maps" which science has created to identify hundreds of separate functions associated with particular parts of the brain, including areas associated with reported spiritual or religious feelings, prayer, meditation, sense of awe, loss of time consciousness, and a pleasant sense of unity or "oneness" with the universe. A whole new field of brain study has developed based on these experimental findings, commonly called "**neurotheology**," The results of this "science of religion" will be examined later in this chapter. There is great debate in both science and theological circles about whether this apparent brain-related "religious" stimulation may be the physical "proof" of the reality of God or religion, empirical evidence about a spiritual side that makes us human.

Sometimes religious leaders have been tempted to rush in when some "gap" seems to have been found by science, claiming that gap is evidence of God. In 2012, scientists confirmed the detection of the long-sought **Higgs boson,** also known by its nickname the "God particle," at the Large Hadron Collider (LHC). This new particle seems to help give mass to all elementary particles that have mass, such as electrons and protons. Theists are tempted to claim and try to fill such findings or gaps with God, or prayer, or faith, or some other spiritual content. The debut and popularizing of the **"Big Bang"** theory of creation drew numerous theologians to equate this scientific theory with the Biblical Creation by God, refuting the idea of creation by random chance. The problem with religion filling in the "gaps" in science (and there are many) is that later advances in science often "fill" that imagined gap, pushing the religious explanation unceremoniously into the rubbish heap, at least in the minds of skeptics. We must be cautious not to build a case for God on an ever-moving scientific platform. Hence, the proposals here are introduced tentatively, not as established science, but as hypotheses or subjects inviting further thought, discussion and discovery.

The Other Trinity: A Three Brain Theory of Evolution

The human brain is actually three brains: the ***"reptilian brain"*** (brain stem) or Hindbrain, the ***"mammalian brain"*** or Mid-brain, and the ***"primate brain"*** or ***Neocortex***, sometimes also called Forebrain. Physically the human brain is composed of three distinct but overlapping and well-integrated parts, beginning with the bulb-like structure at the top of the spinal cord (**brain stem**), the larger, later, and more complex middle addition (**mid-brain** or Limbic system), and these are totally surrounded by the largest, latest and most complex brain part (**neocortex**). This *"triune brain theory"* is a widely accepted fact of science, though disputed by some, but research continues to more completely define exactly what each "brain" does. Even though the brain is actually a composite structure it is misleading to think of three separate brains, for by some miraculous process the brain components work together in amazing unity most of the time. Using the word "trinity" above referring to the brain is a "tongue in cheek" tease for Believers, but the human brain does appear to be a "three in one" phenomenon, though obviously not related to Christians' claim for the religious

Trinity (Father, Son, and Holy Spirit.) Such metaphors can obviously be pushed too far! We really don't want one of the Divine Trio to be associated with the "reptilian brain," for certain. *In the case of the brain as in other works of evolution, it appears that "nature" or God typically adds new forms and functions to older forms and functions, rather than starting all over each time.* This practice of conservative evolution is seen in many other species and even in other parts of the human body. We have several organs and systems that were apparently important earlier in our species but have become obsolete (such as appendix and wisdom teeth). These "vestiges" have been left in place but other parts have adapted to do their job. God (or Nature) seem to prefer not to "start from scratch" when evolving improvements.

The "three brain" theory presented here is disputed among scientists it must be pointed out. **Paul MacLean**[17] first proposed the idea of the "lizard brain" in 1957 as part of his triune brain concept, theorizing that the human brain supposedly consists of three sections, nested together based on their evolutionary age. He believed the neocortex, which he thought arose in primates, is the largest, outermost, and newest part of the human brain: It houses our conscious mind and handles learning, language, and abstract thought. MacLean thought the older, deeper limbic system—which mediates emotion and motivation—began in mammals. Finally, he traced the brainstem and basal ganglia back to primordial reptiles, theorizing that they controlled our reflexes, as well as our four major instincts as he so cleverly named them: to **fight, flee, feed,** and **fornicate**. (Author's note: *"Clever. Wish I had said that."*)

MacLean's ideas spread like wildfire in the science community and stirred both criticism and additional research. The triune brain theory soon became central to most people's understanding of our primordial ancestors' minds, including influential thinkers like Carl Sagan and Arthur Koestler. Even today, many people still think about the brain on MacLean's terms. But as enthusiasm grew in popular audiences, so did discontent among other scholars. Among other issues, critics claimed MacLean's groupings were too simplistic, and failed to account for birds, who display remarkable intelligence, despite possessing brains that are somewhat similar to lizards. Birds apparently did descend from a species of dinosaurs, according to recent science. However, all these issues amounted to academic disagreements, with little real evidence undermining MacLean's theories. Science is not convinced yet, but for our purposes in this book the idea seems to have a great deal of explanatory power—and so we accept it for now.

The brain seems clearly to be a work of evolution displayed in layers, much as the Grand Canyon displays the work of geological evolution over millennia in sequential layers from bottom up. It seems that the original model, the "reptilian brain" worked well for eons, serving the dinosaurs for millions of years, and still serving lizards, snakes and alligators in our day. But "nature" or God wanted something better and so added the mid-brain layer, the "mammalian" brain over other millions of years, and produced perfectly satisfactory mammalians to walk the land and climb the trees; that brain still serves them well today. But the upward "pull" or "push" of evolution or God called for some more advanced brain-power, and so the Neocortex or "primate" brain was gradually added to cover and coordinate the two earlier brain models, producing the equipment needed for Mankind to evolve.

	The Role Our Three Brains	
	Name	*Location*
Brain One	**Reptilian Brain**	**Brain stem and cerebellum**
		Survival instincts, control involuntary functions such as breathing, heart rate, blood pressure, etc.
Brain Two (old Mammalian Brain)	**Limbic System**	**Wrapped around brain One, includes amygdala and hippocampus**
		Emotions, feelings, relationships and memories
Brain Three ("Thinking" Brain)	**Neocortex**	**Outside surface (wrapped around brain two)**
		Executive functions, complex planning, logic, self-identity, language

There is enough agreement in neuroscience to sketch the broad outline of brain functions and locations: **survival** (reptilian brain), **emotions** (mammalian brain), and **executive** functions (primate brain.) Many may find the evidence for the evolution of the human brain more persuasive than other examples of scientific evolution or evidence from ancient fossils or dusty skeletons. The systematic change in the brain is undeniable, whether one accounts for this development by natural selection or by divine design. Brain evolution can easily be seen through the comparison of the brains of modern humans with other mammals and reptiles, where the similarity of the architecture of these brains is so obvious. Looking at diagrams or drawings of a human brain clearly shows that it is comprised of three overlapping parts, from the bulb-like structure at the top of the spinal column (*brain stem*) to the wrinkled, multi-folded gray matter that wraps around it (the *Neocortex*). The middle section (*limbic system*) hidden by surrounding brain matter was obviously added to the original brain stem as the second stage in the development of our brain. It all fits together like a Russian nesting doll. This threefold human brain is, of course, so integrated and interactive that it functions as one unit able to interface with the world of the outside environment as well as turn inward to access the world of feelings, thoughts, and imagination. The *neocortex* is the executive of this operation, while not always entirely in control of the emotional center (mammalian) or the instinct center (reptilian). Socrates famously taught "Know thyself", and one of the great battles of becoming "fully human" is fought in this triune brain field. We can often answer the question "What are you thinking?" and we sometimes, with more searching, can answer the question "What are you feeling?" To answer the question "What are your deepest urges or desires?" or "What really drives you?" may be beyond the normal awareness of most humans, perhaps discovered with help from a mental health expert or counselor.

The First Brain, The Reptilian Brain

The Reptilian brain is the oldest part of the human brain, almost identical to the brains of reptiles, now and for the last 500 million years. Our brain is built on this "reptilian" brain, one part of the entire central nervous system and brain complex. ***This fundamental concept*** *is likely repellent to non-science laymen and the religious reader. It seems odious to think of ourselves as having the brain of snakes, alligators, turtles, and dinosaurs in our skulls, but it is true; however, it's not as horrible as it seems, for evolution or God has made something wonderful out of that early reptilian model.* (Emphasis added). This original "brain" in reptiles operates primarily from built-in instincts, designed to preserve life by "fight or flight," a safety feature which does not require the thought and contemplation of the higher cortex humans have. Even in humans, this non-verbal, non-thinking lower brain is hyper-vigilant and rapid-response oriented. We can observe this reptilian brain sometimes when we are suddenly startled and frightened: we instinctively **act**, heart rate jumps up, adrenaline spurts through our muscles, our breathing is measured, and our concentration is raised to the highest level. When we act without thinking, it is probably our lower brain calling the shots.

All living creatures have basic functions that must be performed in order to sustain life. Those vital functions originate in this lowest, most primitive part of the brain and include such essentials as the involuntary or "autonomic" functions of breathing, heart-beat, blood pressure, muscle control, balance, regulation of body temperature, reproduction, and instinctual impulses such as "fight or flight." The "reptilian" brain still provides these basic elements necessary for human and animal life to exist; all the instinctual survival tools are in this part of our brain. Basic sexual impulses or the instinctual drive for reproduction originate in this basic brain, but to some degree the mammalian brain can control and override these strong drives, operating at a higher evolutionary, a more emotional/ social level, delaying gratification in favor of longer-termed benefits. Charm can *sometimes* substitute for the reptilian impulse to "grab" or be sexually aggressive. Some scholars identify the "subconscious" with this primitive brain, and science has demonstrated that some of the most destructive, irrational impulses arise from this lower brain. We will return to that controversial possibility later in this section.

It is not clear how much this basic primitive brain is influenced by the "mammalian" brain or the more developed Neocortex. Do instincts and basic urges of the reptilian brain override the instructions of the rational, thinking, reflective Neocortex? Can emotions aroused in the mammalian brain influence, for good or ill, the impulsive action of the lower brain, which is acting on "natural" urges? We don't know exactly how the "decision power" in human brains operates, but <u>it appears that there are conflicts</u> between these three components. All thoughtful people have experienced this type of dispute in our minds—a struggle to "do the right thing" when we are so sorely tempted to "do the wrong thing."

Our natural impulse when someone cuts in front of us in the line is to get angry (reptilian response), while our Neocortex tells us to "think. THINK!" Our rational self knows it would be predictably better if we just ignore this rude behavior ("Don't make an embarrassing scene," "It's not really important; you are next in line.") Still, our "darker angel" whispers, "Hit him! He's taken your spot." "Yell at him, tell him what a bone-head he is!" Your emotions are getting stirred up, and your face is turning red, and your breathing is getting fast and shallow. You may even clinch your fist in anger. Perhaps the more mature voice in your head says, "That guy is 6 feet 4 and all muscle. Don't be foolish enough to start a fight with him." The battle is on, a war in your mind, the struggle within your tripartite brain. Paul, the great New Testament theologian, had this fierce inner struggle:

> *"I do not understand what I do. For what I want to do I do not do, but what I hate I do. ... For I know that good itself does not dwell in me, that is, in my sinful nature. For I have the desire to do what is good, but I cannot carry it out. For I do not do the good I want to do, but the evil I do not want to do—this I keep on doing. Now if I do what I do not want to do, it is no longer I who do it, but it is sin living in me that does it."* (Romans 7:15-20)

THE BRAIN GAME

Divided Human Heart

Lucy, the little "psychiatrist" in the beloved Peanuts cartoons of Charles Schulz, is shown above explaining to the younger Linus about this inner battle. Schulz was a Christian artist who came to know the heart of man, to get a good grasp on the pull of our temptations and the weakness of our will in resisting. He frequently portrayed this war between our "better angels" and our "inner demons." Other artists and writers have captured this same inner struggle as between "the Dark Side" and "the Force", supposedly the good force operating in their Star Wars universe.

This reptilian brain controls body functions required for sustaining life including maintaining a suitable internal body temperature in response to the external environment. Reptiles are cold-blooded animals which are warmed by the daylight sun and conserve energy by restricting activities when it is dark, using the thermal environment rather than compensating for it as "warm blooded" animals such as humans do. Using environmental signals "warm blooded" animals actual produce more heat in the circulating blood, and produce sweating and "chill bumps" to overcome cold conditions. The reptiles' biological clock (controller) for their activity-rest cycle is located in the eye itself. This daylight/dark cycle appears in humans, called the **circadian** rhythm, driven by a "master clock" which consists of a group of nerve cells in the brain called the *suprachiasmatic nucleus*. This structure contains about 20,000 nerve cells and is located in the hypothalamus, an area of the brain just above where the optic nerves from the eyes cross. The body responds to light through the eyes but also through other groups of cells, a non-image forming system not related to vision, but does respond to light and affects our physiology, our mood and our behavior.

A circadian rhythm is any biological process that displays a natural cycle or oscillation of *about* 24 hours, with some influence by the environment (such as light and darkness). *Circadian* comes from the Latin circa, meaning "around" (or "approximately"), and diēm, meaning "day," Experiments in which humans were isolated in rooms with no sunlight exposure and had no clocks to keep track of time or day and night invariably showed that everyone has and displays a clear natural cycle of wakefulness and sleepiness, ranging from every 22 to 24 hours. These "about" 24-hour rhythms are driven by the internal circadian clock, and these cycles have been widely observed in plants, animals, fungi, and even bacteria. When it's dark at night, your eyes send a signal to the hypothalamus that it's time to feel tired. Your brain, in turn, sends a signal to your body to release melatonin, which makes your body tired. That's why your circadian rhythm tends to coincide with the cycle of daytime and nighttime (and why it's so hard for shift workers to sleep during the day and stay awake at night). People get *jet lag* when travel disrupts their circadian rhythms. When you pass through different time zones, your biological clocks will be different from the local time. For example, if you fly east from California to New York, you "lose" 3 hours. When you wake up at 7:00 a.m. on the east coast your biological clocks are still running on west coast time so you feel the way you might feel at 4:00 a.m. Your biological clocks will reset, but this often takes a few days and exposure to sunlight. This effect usually does not happen in east to west flights as the travel follows the sun, keeping time relatively in sync for you.

We know that almost all primates have the same kind of wake/sleep cycle as we do, and we assume this function was operational in the earliest hominids. Scientists call this pattern "diurnal" (active by day). But not all mammals follow this pattern, for a great many are "nocturnal" animals, doing their hunting and other activities in the night. A few animals operate only at twilight or dawn, neither "diurnal" nor "nocturnal." For the early ancestors of humanity what purpose would this circadian rhythm serve? What is the benefit of sleeping when it is dark and being alert when it is daytime?

Survival is the first need of all organisms and so the pattern of sleeping and waking probably has some survival value. We can speculate that early hominids like current apes are more vulnerable in the dark than in the daytime, because hominids did not have "night vision" which is enjoyed by tigers and lions and other predators of the night… so staying "home" in the tree nest or the cave and sleeping is a lot safer than wandering around in the wild outdoors. All animals need rest, and the circadian cycle makes such rest almost mandatory and automatic. At this level of evolution, behavior relating to survival of the species, such as sexual behavior, is instinctive and responses are automatic. Territory is acquired by force and defended. Might is right. In earliest childhood, the human mental state is controlled almost completely by the reptilian brain (along with the later evolved paleomammalian brain and the right hemisphere of the neocortex (the left hemisphere is underdeveloped in earliest childhood). The "reptilian" brain in humans is almost identical to the brains of current reptiles (snakes, turtles, alligators, etc.) and is likely was same in extinct reptiles such as the dinosaurs. It allows these less-complex animals to avoid danger, to find food and water, to mate and reproduce offspring. It does not "think" or "plan" in the human sense, but has built-in instincts required for survival. A somewhat strange example illustrates the effect of this first brain: there is a striking correlation between penile and clitoral erection during dream states, even in young children. Both boys and girls show signs of being sexually aroused. Why? It is unlikely to be sexual related dreams in the very young. It probably is an unconscious instinctual reflex. It is believed that in the reptilian brain sex, aggression and territoriality are essentially the same instinct, all related to survival. Many of the actions we label "impulsive" or "capricious" in children (and many adults) may be stimulated by the instinctual drives of the reptilian brain and not controlled by the more rational mammalian and primate minds. The child who hits another child sitting in the wrong seat "knows" the rule: NO HITTING. But in the heat of the moment, the "territorial" instinct overcomes the "Please the teacher" tendency. The ability of our higher brains controlling our original brain can be inhibited by tiredness, unrelated stress, or even by hunger or thirst. We don't always "act our self" and this battle between the instincts of the reptilian brain and the more civilized mammalian and primate brains is probably in play on those occasions.

This oldest brain can "learn" to some degree by what researchers call "conditioning." If a young frog hears a twig break, and seconds later a predator appears, the frog may connect the two events, and become "conditioned" to hiding as soon as the "snap" is heard. That is the simplest learning, called "classical conditioning" (see Pavlov). A more complicated learning is illustrated by the frog which bites a prickly thistle and experiences pain and discomfort; after several such lessons, the frog learns to behave in a way to avoid the pain. This process is called "operant conditioning" and B.F. Skinner proved that almost any kind of living organism can "learn" this way. The human "reptilian brain" is wired by nature to respond to most situations by pure instinct, but can and does learn some behaviors by conditioning. Some destructive impulses which may arise in this lower brain can be altered by therapists through one or other of these types of conditioning. Some addictions or phobias can be treated successfully by behavior modification therapy, either by the negative consequences being made unpleasant, or by positive reinforcement when a desired behavior occurs. This suggests that instinctual behavior arising in the reptilian brain can be modified even if not extinguished.

As discussed below, reptilian brain impulses can be restrained by influence of the mammalian brain and the higher functions of the Primate Brain. The degree of control exercised over the reptilian tendencies varies in individuals at the intersection of "will" and "want," where the rational thinking upper brain suggests a particular course of action but where the urge to fulfill basic drives overwhelms that rational choice. A person "knows" rationally that they should not eat that piece of cake because of the 300 calories and the fat that would be added to their backside, but the "want" or "desire" pushed up by the reptilian brain is so...SO...SO VERY STRONG it seems irresistible—and the chocolate cake disappears. We all have experienced this kind of inner battle, and that mischievous little devil in our reptilian brain often wins the battle. The "want" we call appetite is conflated with the survival need for food, and the need to survive can easily overcome the desire to be skinny. Even our metabolism fights our rational desire to lose weight, for when we cut back on food in a strict diet, the body somehow predicts an imminent famine and fears starvation—so it slows our metabolism and conserves fat.

The Second Brain – The Mammalian/Limbic Brain

The second component, the "mammalian brain" or "Limbic system" is the same form found in all mammalians (cats, dogs, horses, elephants, humans, etc.). Various writers use other terms such as the paleomammalian complex, or the mid brain. This part of the brain is unique to mammals though some scientists think rudimentary forms of the limbic system may be present in some birds and a few other non-mammals; this is still unsettled but it is clear that mammals have the fully operational second level of brain we are discussing. According to some scientists the limbic system of this mammalian brain is the center of emotion and learning. It is speculated that it developed very early in mammalian evolution to regulate the motivations and emotions that we now associate with feeding, reproduction, and attachment behaviors related to breast feeding and "mothering." It seems that the limbic system evaluates everything as either agreeable (pleasure) or disagreeable (pain/distress). Survival is often dependent on the avoidance of pain (as in injury) and the repetition of pleasure (as in sexual activity).

In humans this mammalian brain" adds the functions of "feelings," emotions, long-term memories, habits, attachment, bonding, regulation of hormones, sensations of hunger and thirst and much more. These same functions are present to some degree in all the animals we love. As discussed later, it is possible that some animal species, at least four, may also have some degree of the functions of the most highly developed "brain," the neocortex, thus "thinking" as well as "feeling." **(See Chapter 14 "Animals and Other People").** It does not seem sacrilegious to this author/believer to contemplate that the God of the Universe may have "built" humans on the earlier brains He developed for the pet Green Iguana and the ferocious Crocodile, or the mammals that fascinate us such as the Chimpanzees and the Silver Back Gorilla. They are not our brothers, but they have the same

Creator, and though they are not humans, they still are beautiful, marvelous, amazing fellow living creatures. God was just as pleased with these "lower" animals He made on Day Six as He was with the humans He created later that same day. (See Genesis 1:24-26.) Perhaps animals were His first prototypes, a trial run. After all, some pundits claim, didn't God make Woman second in order to improve the on His first try— Man?

The mammalian brain contains the **amygdala** and **hypothalamus**, two very important components still being explored by neuroscientists.[18] They perform some amazing feats, probably many yet undiscovered. Although we often refer to it in the singular, there are two *amygdalae*—one in each cerebral hemisphere. The amygdala has become best known for its role in fear processing. When we are exposed to a fearful stimulus, information about that stimulus is immediately sent to the amygdala, which can then send signals to areas of the brain like the hypothalamus to trigger a "fight-or-flight" response (e.g., increased heart rate and respiration to prepare for action). Metaphorically, it is like a security checkpoint at the airport. The **amygdala** scans for any threat or danger. If the amygdala identifies the data as safe and non-threatening, it authorizes admittance to the neocortex. The neocortex apparently integrates this new experience with existing data stored in memory. This hyper alert system can create emotional or mental problems in humans, creating excessive and debilitating anxiety if it malfunctions. Persons who have experienced great, frightening trauma can be helped to recover emotionally by a professional or even a group of friends who validate the horrible experience and provide comfort and social support. It is likely that some psychotropic drugs may act on the amygdala to relieve anxiety.

What happens when the amygdala sounds the alarm? Other parts of the brain are activated, specifically the **thalamus** which is also in the limbic brain. This activation can incite one of three alarm responses, driven by the lower reptilian brain: 1) the fight response, 2) the flight response, or the 3) freeze response. When these alarm responses are activated, the body will protectively and automatically respond according to the instructions of the brain. The heart rate increases, adrenalin shoots into the veins, breathing gets shallow and muscles tense. Vision can become more acute and hearing more sensitive. All these responses are automatic. Even after the danger has passed, the thalamus remains on high alert, activating the same responses if any hint of the original danger is sensed. This response makes perfect sense for early hominids: in the wild, predators often return with reinforcements!

The limbic/mammalian brain apparently does not have any concept of time. Past, present, and future are all one and the same, according to science. This might explain why your dog (a mammal) may greet you as though you've been gone for 30 years, instead of 30 minutes. This phenomenon also helps to explain why traumatized people can seem stuck in the past. For them, something that happened 50 years ago feels as though it is happening right now. To the mammalian brain, where these crossed wires and balls of tangle are housed, 50 years ago is today. When we talk about traumatized people being "stuck," it's as though wires got all tangled up and stuck in the limbic brain, and it was never equipped for long-term storage of memories with emotions attached.

The Third Brain – The Primate/Neocortex Brain

The neocortex is that part of the cerebral cortex (maybe 90% of it) that is the modern, most newly evolved part—thus, the "neo" prefix; it located at the front of the brain, between the temples. The cerebral cortex is the entire outer top part of all mammalian brains (the part that looks especially wrinkled in all humans). This large outer layer of the brain, the cerebrum, is a thick layer composed of **grey matter** which envelopes most of the earlier and older brain and amounts to about 80 to 85 per cent of the total human brain mass. Underneath the gray matter of the cortex lies white **matter**, made up largely of insulated nerve fibers running to and from the cortex. This most recently evolved part of the human brain, the Neocortex, is alternately cited in the science literature as the "primate brain" or the "Human brain" or even the "New Mammalian brain."

A deep furrow divides the cerebrum into two halves, known as the left and right hemispheres. The two hemispheres look quite symmetrical, almost identical, yet it has been shown that each side functions slightly different from the other. Traditionally, the right hemisphere is associated with creativity and the left hemispheres is associated with logic abilities. Some specific functions are associated with one side, such as language in the left and visual-spatial ability in the right. The corpus callosum is a bundle of axons which connects these two hemispheres. (*See more about the **Split Brain** later in this chapter.*) The brain is "cross wired" —that is the left hemisphere is primarily in control of the right side of the body, while the right hemisphere controls the left side of the body. So, typically, a "left-handed" person has a dominant right brain hemisphere. About 80% of people are right-handed, so the left brain is dominant in most people.

The neocortex is the most complex and highly developed part of the human brain in terms of its organization and number of layers. The scientific details are so expansive and complicated (*vertical columns, horizontal layers, sulci grooves and gyra ridges for example*) that this overview will only briefly highlight the most significant information. Much is known, and much is yet to learn, but what we know is awe-inspiring. Only mammals have some form of neocortex, but many small mammals, such as rodents have relatively smooth brains, whereas primates have deep grooves and ridges, the wrinkles so noticeable in pictures of human brains such as included here. These thousands of folds increase the brain surface (as much as 500 percent) without greatly expanding the size of the brain. If our brain was not wrinkled and folded our skulls would need to be twice as large as now! It is likely that the "little green men from Mars" of popular fiction have smooth brains, since their heads almost always are pictured as very large. Strangely it appears that the human brain is smaller today than it was ten centuries ago, but has a great deal more efficient mental power because of wrinkles.

Our **third brain** is the center for all the higher functions which distinguish us from other mammals, and is primarily responsible for sensory perception, motor command and control, spatial reasoning, logic and conscious thought, vision, hearing, touch, the sense of balance, movement, emotional responses and every other feat of cognition. We have learned much about the neocortex organization from the medical reports of brain injury. One report cited a patient who lost color sight in an accident (became "color blind"), while retaining other visual functions. It was speculated that the specific cortical area injured was responsible for "color vision. Some patients suffer partial wounds in the brain caused by accidents, war, strokes, cancers, and if the neocortex is hurt, the patients may lose various cognitive abilities such as speech capabilities, space recognition, eyesight, motor control, socialized behavior and so on. What happens depends on which part of the highly organized neocortex loses its function. We also know that certain abilities such as color recognition developed in the human brain but not in most other species.

The Other Divided Brain—The Lobes

It can't be emphasized enough that the **brain is ONE**, all the parts functioning as a whole, the whole being more than all the parts in function. One final review of the organizational complexity of the human brain briefly focuses on the "Lobes." Lobes are found in other organs as well as the brain: for example, the lungs, the liver and the kidney have identifiable sections or divisions called "lobes." Though in the brain there are no clear visible boundaries and borders marking them, the cerebrum is divided into four functional areas, or lobes. These are the **Frontal Lobe**- associated with reasoning, planning, parts of speech, movement, emotions, and problem solving; the **Parietal Lobe**- associated with movement, orientation, recognition, perception of stimuli; the **Occipital Lobe**- associated with visual processing; and the **Temporal Lobe**- associated with perception and recognition of auditory stimuli, memory, and speech. Injuries to one of these lobes usually creates a predictable problem which neurosurgeons then try to repair and restore. For example, a severe blow to the back of the head would likely injure the Occipital Lobe and cause blindness or visual impairment; a bullet into the Temporal Lobe would very likely affect speech and hearing. Fortunately (with God or Nature helping) damaged lobes appear able to adapt with therapy, or another lobe may compensate and take over a lost function.

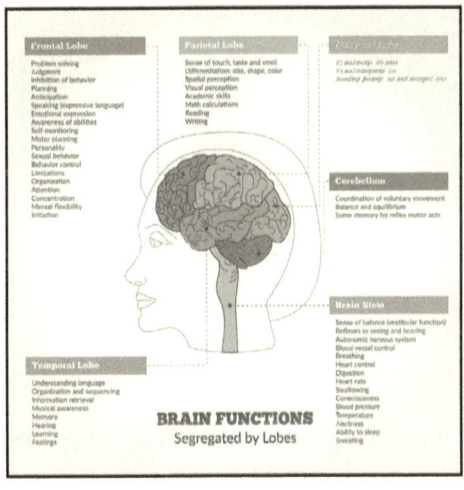

BRAIN FUNCTIONS
Segregated by Lobes

In a later section we will further examine the startling capacities which human brains may possess but which are accidentally revealed in head and brain injuries, abilities such as amazing art, music or memory.

Comparative Embryology

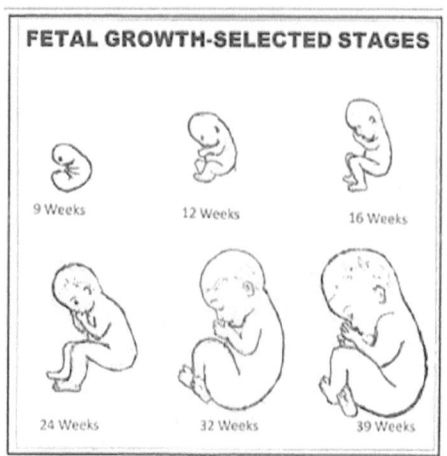

It seems abundantly clear that the human brain is an amazing piece of work, the apex of Creation and evolution. The preeminent importance of the brain was extensively discussed earlier, so now let's look at another sign. An interesting chart shown here suggests that the evolution of the human species brain may be prefigured in the brain development of the prenatal-human. Starting as the union of sperm and egg, the future human child goes through amazing changes in the 39 weeks of gestation, and the development of the fetal brain is the most fascinating of all the organs and parts. This observation is not to offer any scientific proof for embryological development being connected to the evolution of species. Observing the developing human we must be impressed with the tremendous investment of the fetus in building the upper brain, the neocortex, which so soon overwhelms and covers the earlier parts of the brain. Could this similarity between stages of embryonic development and phases of species evolution be a clue left by God, or a recapitulation in a small "nine-month movie" sped up to show us how evolution proceeded over many millions of years to produce us?

In the nineteenth century German zoologist Ernst Haeckel (1832-1919) proposed an unusual new idea; he called it "Biogenetic Law" but the popular name became *recapitulation theory* (meaning "repeating or paralleling something else"). Science no longer accepts this theory; his catchy motto is still in use: **"Ontogeny recapitulates phylogeny."** Haeckel's hypothesis was that the development of an animal embryo, from fertilization to gestation or hatching (ontogeny), goes through stages resembling successive stages in the evolution of the animal's remote ancestors (phylogeny). The chart suggests a disconcerting idea: humans and many other mammals look surprisingly alike at the earliest stages of fetal development. Comparative embryology charts often include reptilians and other animals as well as mammals, and the similarities are present for about half of the gestation period. The human takes about 39 weeks for the whole process while other embryos are on a much faster cycle. Haeckel created embryo drawings that scientists consider oversimplified and inaccurate. **Even though this theory is now considered largely discredited, visual comparison of embryos remains a powerful demonstration that all animals appear to be related.** This observable fact that human and animal embryos look very similar at first may be disturbing to some, for it might imply that we are just animals, just like other animals, with a few adjustments toward the end of development. Another interpretation is that it actually shows how God (or evolution) uses previously successful models as platforms for newer, better equipped animals, perhaps for a greater role in Creation, on the way to hominids like us.

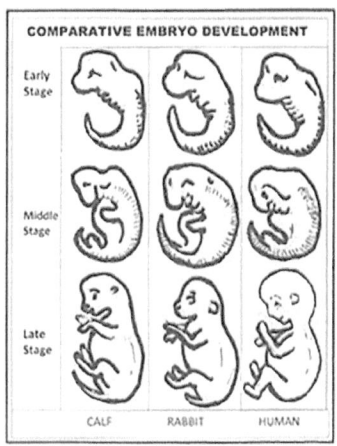

Haeckel's theory is no longer respected by scientists, but it may still have usefulness in trying to understand evolution. A serious difficulty in comparing traits between species rests on the fact that homologous or similar structures not present in the adult organism often do appear in some stage of embryonic development. In this way, the embryo might serve as a microcosm for evolution, passing through many of the stages of evolution to produce the current state of the organism. Species that bear little resemblance in their adult form may have strikingly similar embryonic stages. For example, in humans, the embryo passes through a stage in which it has gill structures like those of the fish from which all terrestrial animals evolved. For a large portion of its development the human embryo also possesses a tail, much like those of our close primate relatives. This tail is usually reabsorbed before birth, but occasionally children are born with the ancestral structure intact.

Tails and even gills could be considered homologous traits between humans and primates or humans and fish, even though they are not present in the adult organism. Some other of these formerly useful parts continue into adult life; such leftovers are called "vestiges" or "vestigial organs." Some examples of human vestigiality are the appendix, tailbone, wisdom teeth, muscles in the ear, goose bumps, the infant's ability to swim safely and naturally under water for several minutes until the epiglottis is fully developed, and the *palmar grasp reflex* by which babies up to about four months can support their full weight gripping something. (Surviving under water was useful for the child floating in the womb, and the powerful grip was useful for baby monkeys holding to mom's fur.)

We move on now to the "centerpiece" of the human brain, the ineffable wonder of **consciousness.**

Consciousness: The "Pearl of Great Price"

Explaining the nature of consciousness is one of the most challenging and most important areas of inquiry for philosophy and for science, an endeavor that stretches back as far as writing evolved to be literature. Long before Greek philosophers spent their days discussing mind, matter and morals men had become story tellers, and story tellers such as Homer were exploring, through their characters and their plots, what makes us human. Even long before the first word of men was written, people undoubtedly came to experience and think about being conscious, having some kind of private inner dialogue, and sensing that others of his kind also had this inner voice and self-awareness. This recognition is called "theory of mind" by scholars, the stage of mental development observed in children at age 3 or 4, and apparently achieved by some adult animals. (Note: see **Chapter 14, Animals and Other People"** for an extensive review of animal/human connections, and **Chapter 15, "Being Fully Human"** for further discussion of "theory of mind.")

Modern science is actively researching "consciousness" and "mind" through the fields of psychology, neuroscience, cognitive science and even computer science exploring artificial intelligence. Philosophy has specialty branches such a "Philosophy of Mind," "Aesthetics" and "Ethics" which often deal with the mind and questions of reality and knowledge. The study of consciousness is hampered by the lack of a universal (or even general) definition of consciousness. Scientists and philosophers may be using the same words, but actually may be looking at different phenomena. The workings of our inner life are mysterious and fascinating, and it has been the quest of many brilliant students since Socrates gave us the ultimate imperative: "Know Thyself." Actually, **knowing yourself** is perhaps the ultimate answer science and philosophy will finally agree on, though voluminous literature has already been created to dissect "consciousness" and to examine it from every philosophical and scientific position known to Mankind. Some scientists simply acknowledge that consciousness may **still be beyond our grasp** to understand and validate with theories and testing as we do on other subjects. In a chapter in the book *The Neural Correlates of Consciousness* Richard Frackowiak and seven other neuroscientists write:

> We have no idea how consciousness emerges from the physical activity of the brain and we do not know whether consciousness can emerge from non-biological systems, such as computers... At this point the reader will expect to find a careful and precise definition of consciousness. You will be disappointed. Consciousness has not yet become a scientific term that can be defined in this way. Currently we all use the term consciousness in many different and often ambiguous ways. Precise definitions of different aspects of consciousness will emerge ... but to make precise definitions at this stage is premature.[19]

Circling the Field

We have encountered a lot of scientific and religious terms that may not be familiar to all readers, and many more such words lie ahead of us. Sometimes we can grasp complicated, enormous concepts by looking at other related terms we more commonly use referring to a subject. Meanings evolve in actual normal language usage, perhaps vague or ambiguous alone, but cumulatively descriptive, even as the *Seven Blind Men of Hindustan* experienced an elephant. (See **Chapter 8** for details.) Just to keep as much clarity as possible the following related vocabulary words are straight from freshman psychology text books.

Awareness: the state or ability to perceive, to feel, or to be conscious of events, objects, or sensory patterns. In this level of consciousness, sense data can be confirmed by an observer without necessarily implying understanding. In biological psychology, awareness is defined as a human's or an animal's perception and cognitive reaction to a condition or event.

Self-awareness: the capacity for introspection and the ability to recognize oneself as an individual separate from the environment and other individuals. Sometimes uses "mirror test."

Self-consciousness: an acute sense of self-awareness. It is a preoccupation with oneself, as opposed to the philosophical state of self-awareness, which is the awareness that one exists as an individual being; shyness or sense of social inadequacy, or even shame (for example, having a visible birth mark).

Sentience: the ability to be aware (feel, perceive, or be conscious) of one's surroundings or to have subjective experiences. Sentience is a minimalistic way of defining consciousness, which is otherwise commonly used to collectively describe sentience plus other characteristics of the mind.

Sapience: Sometimes defined as wisdom, but the fundamental element is thinking, reasoning logically and intelligently (or wisely). Animals are **sentient** as are humans, but they are not "thinkers" in the same sense of weighing alternatives and exercising judgment.

THE BRAIN GAME

Medical Measures of Consciousness

The Glasgow Coma Scale (GCS) is the most common scoring system used to describe the level of consciousness in a person following a traumatic brain injury. Used by experienced clinicians it helps gauge the severity of an acute brain injury. The test is simple, reliable, and correlates well with clinical outcomes following severe brain injury. The test measures three functions: eyes open, verbal response, and motor response. The basic parameters of this tool are presented below.

Eye Opening (E)	Verbal Response (V)	Motor Response (M)
4 = spontaneous	5 = orientated	6 = obeys command
3 = to sound	4 = confused	5 = localizing
2 = to pressure	3 = words, but not coherent	4 = normal flexion
1 = none	2 = sounds, but no words	3 = abnormal flexion
	1 = none	2 = extension
		1 = none

Original chart by Author from several public sources

Clinicians use this scale to rate the best eye-opening response, the best verbal response, and the best motor response an individual makes. The final GCS score or grade is the sum of these numbers. Some readings are listed as "Not Testable" if no clear response is detected. The standardization of defining consciousness medically is making rare the horrendous stories of people in comas for years and being labeled "Vegetative State" only to finally arouse and report that they had known all that had gone on and been said even though they could not respond or communicate during that time.

Science and Consciousness

It's tricky to come up with a rigorous scientific definition of consciousness which enjoys a broad consensus. On the other hand, we are all familiar with what consciousness is. Put simply, for a conscious organism, there is '**something it is like**' to be that organism. This difficult concept comes from the American philosopher in a paper published in 1974 *"What is it like to be a bat?"* is a paper by American philosopher Thomas Nagel, first published in The Philosophical Review in October 1974, and later in Nagel's *Mortal Questions* (1979)[20]. In it, Nagel argues that **materialist theories of mind omit the essential component of consciousness, namely that there is something that it is (or feels) like to be a particular, conscious thing.** He argues that an organism has conscious mental states, "if and only if there is something that it is like to be that organism—something it is like for the organism to be itself." Put another way, consciousness is lost when falling into a dreamless sleep (or undergoing general anesthesia), and it is what returns the next morning on waking up (or coming around). We know at that moment that we are who we were before—we recognize our familiar self has returned, even if we are a bit confused at first; our initial trepidation relaxes as we get fully awake and self-aware again.

More generally, consciousness implies a continuous (but interruptible) stream of phenomenal senses or experiences – a technicolor, multimodal, fully immersive and wholly personalized movie, playing to an audience of one. Though there is not universal agreement, the majority of scholars do seem to accept consciousness as a given, something "real" but non-material, and we all seek to understand its relationship to the material world of science. How does a non-material "consciousness arise from a material body or brain?" Currently two major theories dominate the field of inquiry. The first way to understand consciousness is the **neurological approach**, focusing on the electrical activity of the cerebellum, the reticular activating system, the amygdule, the thalamus, the hypothalamus and the hippocampus. The key to consciousness lies in the brain activity, these scientists believe, somewhere in the electrochemical interactions within the brain. The second approach starts with a more **psychological approach**, observing and analyzing consciousness itself, similar and sometimes in partnership with the philosophers who have searched for the answer for centuries.

The most influential modern physical theories of consciousness are based on neuroscience, relying on data from electronic and sophisticated imaging equipment to observed the brain under controlled and rigorous laboratory conditions. Respected theories proposed by neuroscientists such as Gerald Edelman and Antonio Damasio, and by philosophers such as Daniel Dennett, seek to explain consciousness in terms of neural events occurring within the brain. They are trying to locate the specific brain site or sites which seem to facilitate consciousness, and to determine combinations and cross-communication of multiple brain areas which seem to be activated.

Recently, researchers discovered a brain area that acts as a kind of on-off switch for the brain, a region called the *claustrum*. This small, oddly shaped extremely thin sheet of neurons is situated just below the insular lobe of the cortex, the hidden lobe which can only be seen by a surgeon if other parts of the cortex are pulled aside. Most, if not all, mammals have a claustrum, but, oddly enough, no one can yet definitely say what the claustrum does or why it's important. When Christof Koch and his associates electrically stimulated this area, the female seizure patient became unconscious instantly; she regained consciousness instantly after stimulation ceased. The claustrum apparently is directly connected in some way to consciousness. In fact, Koch and Francis Crick, the late molecular biologist and Nobel Prize recipient who helped discover the mysterious double-helix structure of DNA, had previously hypothesized that this region might integrate information across different parts of the brain, like the conductor of a symphony. The claustrum appears to have a vast array of neural connections spread through the entire brain, supporting the idea that this strange element may be the grand central station for all the sensory information coming to the brain along with memories of all previous experiences of the person, somehow weaving a sense of reality we call consciousness.[21]

But looking for neural or behavioral connections to consciousness isn't enough, Koch said. For example, such connections don't explain why the cerebellum, the part of the brain at the back of the skull that coordinates muscle activity, doesn't give rise to consciousness, while the cerebral cortex (the brain's outermost layer) does. This is counter-intuitive because the cerebellum contains more neurons than the cerebral cortex. Some research is focusing on neurological disorders which impact consciousness as a way of finding more about what causes consciousness and unconsciousness. The most severe consciousness disorders include "comas," the "vegetative state" and the "minimally conscious state."

A **coma** is a deep state of unconsciousness in which a patient is alive but unable to move or respond to his or her environment. Coma may occur as a complication of an underlying illness, or as a result of injuries, such as brain injury. Usually brain waves are detectable, and if these brain waves cease the patient is considered "brain dead." Such "brain dead" persons may continue to have heart beat and respiration (with or without assistance) but are not expected to ever recover (some have existed in this condition for twenty years or more.) A person who shows clear but minimal or inconsistent awareness is classified as being in a **minimally conscious** state. They may have periods where they can communicate or respond to commands, such as moving a finger when asked or even talking, but usually sink again to unconsciousness. Some patients such as this recover from this state after months or even years.

Persistent vegetative state is a state of severe unconsciousness in which the person is unaware of his or her surroundings and incapable of voluntary movement. It is diagnosed if the unconscious person has been that way for six months or more. With a persistent vegetative state, someone may progress to wakefulness cycles but with no higher brain function. In persistent vegetative state there is breathing, circulation, and sleep-wake cycles. A rare but terrifying loss of consciousness is called "Locked-in syndrome" in which the person is totally paralyzed except for the eye muscles, yet remains awake and alert and with a normal mind. The terrifying part is that there are occasional reports of a patient being in a deep coma, a vegetative state, for many years and suddenly one day they wake up. Some of these patients report that they remained aware of their surroundings the entire time, but could not signal to others "Hey! I'm still here!" Some have compared this to an astronaut stranded on a space vehicle, drifting endlessly and aimlessly, able to hear the messages from the Earth station but unable to send any response because the radio has failed.

A more common example of unconsciousness is the **medically induced coma** which hospitals use to put patients to "sleep" during surgery, or on some occasions, longer periods of anesthesia to protect an injured brain from permanent damage due to swelling. Medically induced comas are tightly controlled and monitored to assure the lowest proper dosage so that consciousness can be restored within an hour or two after surgery. Again, some horror stories are published about patients who were anesthetized and unable to communicate that they still were feeling the pain of the surgery. Such cases are rare, but it is another way to get insight into what consciousness and unconsciousness are.

Being conscious means that you know it is you who is experiencing something, not observing someone else's experience. When we sense the outer world of our environment by seeing, hearing, touching, etc., we are aware that it is we who are looking or hearing, it feels like we are a thing, inside our skull, looking out on the world through the eyeball openings. It feels like you are the only one on earth to experience this precise scene, probably correct. This awareness of your own experience, awareness that you are the one experiencing it, this is consciousness. Sentience (the ability to feel, perceive, or to experience subjectivity) is not the same as self-awareness (being aware of oneself as an individual). The mirror test is sometimes considered to be an operational test for self-awareness, the ability to recognize that the image in the mirror is themselves and touching the paint spot on their face as an indicator of self-awareness. Several animals that have passed this test are considered to have a beginning concept of "self" like human children at about 18 months old. (This is discussed in some detail in **Chapter 14 "Animals and Other People."**)

Developing the Sense of Consciousness

So far as science has been able to determine, babies are not born with a sense of consciousness, and the emergence of the awareness of their "selves" as separate from the environment is a normal stage of child development. As the well-known infant researcher Daniel Stern notes:

> Prior to the age of eighteen months, infants do not seem to know that what they are seeing in a mirror is their own reflection. After eighteen months, they do. This can be shown by surreptitiously marking infants' faces with rouge, so that they are unaware that the mark has been placed. When younger infants see their reflections, they point to the mir-

ror and not to themselves. After the age of eighteen months or so, they touch the rouge on their own faces instead of just pointing to the mirror.[22]

The child's knowledge about the self continues to develop as the child grows. Infants apparently cannot clearly distinguish themselves from their environment, thinking that everything and everyone in their life is part of their comfort and care system. By two years of age, the infant becomes aware of his or her gender as a boy or a girl. At age four, the child's self-descriptions are likely to be based on physical features, such as hair color, and by about age six, the child is able to understand basic emotions and the concepts of traits, being able to make statements such as "I am a good boy." According to Jean Piaget, the Swiss psychologist known for his pioneering work on child development work, the egocentric child assumes that other people see, hear, and feel exactly the same as the child does. Tests involving dolls at different positions relative to another object or scene (or similar point of view exercises) show that children younger than four could not visualize the doll's view as different from his own; children four or five could accurately identify the "other's" point of view as much as 80% of the time. Experts say this means that younger children are still egocentric, able to understand only their own view or perspective.

> **90 percent of a child's brain development is before the age of 5**

Another developmental milestone is understanding what others are thinking (***theory of mind***); tests of this ability indicate that recognition that other people have minds like their own, and can attribute knowledge and feelings to the other person by around four years old. Up to the ages 4 or 5 years, the child believes that almost everything is alive and has a purpose (animism), so life, thoughts and feelings are attributed to teddy bears, dolls and even toy trucks. This misconception fades away gradually, with some residue up to school age and beyond. Interestingly, this early attribution of personhood to things which are inanimate is also a cultural marker for primitive religious beliefs—the stage of "animism." This may be another indicator of a pattern in human species development being recapitulated in our individual human development (that the pattern we follow in our mental development as individuals is somehow a reflection of what our early hominid ancestors experienced over hundreds of thousands of years of evolution and species change.

By the time children are in grade school, they have learned that they are unique individuals, and they can think about and analyze their own behavior. They also begin to show awareness of the social situation—they understand that other people are looking at and judging them the same way that they are looking at and judging others. Part of what is developing in children as they grow is the fundamental cognitive part of the self, known as the self-concept. The self-concept is a mental package that contains knowledge about us, including our beliefs, our personality traits, physical characteristics, abilities, values, goals, and roles, as well as the knowledge that we exist as individuals. Self-concept is largely influenced by **what we believe** other people think about us. Our early social environment is a powerful force in shaping us and shaping our image of ourselves. Damage to our self-image and self-esteem in childhood and adolescence is extremely difficult to overcome in later life.[23]

Throughout childhood and adolescence, the self-concept becomes more abstract and complex and is organized into a variety of different cognitive aspects of the self, known as self-schemas. A schema is a pattern or model which the mind creates as a shortcut for classifying or organizing information about a subject or person. For example, older children come to think of themselves as "smart student," "pretty," "talented," or "dumb" and "clumsy" to give a few examples. Everything that happens to the child is fitted into the pre-made schema; a child spills their milk and say or think "I'm a klutz, just like I thought (or was told). Challenging the negative schema is very difficult and long term: "No, you are not a "klutz" or clumsy—you just spilled your milk, and it was an accident. That's all! Children have self-schemas about their progress in school, their appearance, their skills at sports and other activities, and many other aspects. In turn, these self-schemas direct and inform their processing of self-relevant information (Harter, 1999), much as we saw schemas in general affecting our social cognition.

Consciousness and the Inner Life

We have not solved the mystery of consciousness and our wonderful brain, though we have surveyed a large field of scientific and philosophic theories and ideas. We know what consciousness is like (for us) for we have had a lifetime of experience with being mentally awake and active (conscious) and being helpless and inert, unconscious and out of touch with either our outer environment or our inner life. In our sleep we are usually not totally unconscious, are easily awakened, and are frequently dreaming (another part of our "inner life" we observe but do not control or direct.) Those of us who have been anesthetized by a medical doctor to spare us the pain and fear of surgery know what it is like to "lose" consciousness and to regain it gradually in the recovery room. In less than five seconds we are gone to that unknown place where thinking and feeling and moving are stopped for us. Our return to some consciousness typically is more gradual: first hearing a nurse urging you to wake up, then feeling a hand on your arm as a loved one calls your name, a fuzzy visual scene greets you when you open your eyes, and you begin to get the scene before you into focus. You try to speak hesitantly and haltingly, and your move your arm or leg or turn your head carefully to be sure "you" are there. Finally, you are "awake" but not really alert for a few more hours. But you have come back to where you were, come back from who knows where to who you were, and with some relief, find that the "you" is still the same as before. You are your "self" again.

Later, your mind may turn back to that experience of being "gone," being "out like a light." You may think about "What if?" "What if I didn't wake up?" It is possible that it could have happened; it has happened to others on rare occasions, even some of your friends who went to surgery but never came back. "What is that like?" "Is that what death would be like?" Thoughts like that are perfectly normal, of course, though we avoid them when we can. But unconsciousness reminds us of our mortality, our fragility, our "temporariness." After that experience many people have a greater appreciation for the normal state we enjoy—being alive and awake, and aware and thinking and feeling...life is good, very good when you are experiencing it, when you are conscious. Life seems more like a gift now than an achievement, for you had no control over your awakening from surgery. We come into life without any control over our conception and birth and we gradually develop our mind and our self and our position in the world, our personality and our hopes and dreams. Hopefully readers have all grown up being happy to be "you," liking your "self." Many people do not enjoy that blessing, that gift of a good self-image, good self-esteem. How blessed are those love themselves tenderly and mercifully; how sad are those who, deep down in the basement of the mind are disappointed and angry at themselves. The former condition is what God intends for us; the latter is the tragic outcome God weeps over and that He ceaselessly seeks to repair for all His creation, for all of us who are conscious. If you've got a brain and you are mentally awake, God is ringing your "bell" and wanting to talk with you. He's there in your mind, maybe behind some clutter and piles of trash, but He is there in the brain He prepared long ago, with you in mind.

Perhaps your image of God is not an attractive one, maybe even a hateful and vengeful God, or even a god that is just an illusion, a cosmic April Fool joke. Imagining a God who knows you and is calling your number may not seem particularly pleasurable. But stay tuned for **Chapter 9**, "**Some Kind of God**", **Chapter 10**, "**God Is Great, God is Good**" and **Chapter 11, "Jesus—The Perfect Image of God."** It is hoped that having the God of Jesus spread out before you will arouse a hope, a wish that it all could be true—that there could be such a God who loves you right now, just as you are. You might even come to believe that He can help you find joy and contentment in the world of "you." As the Bible tell us: ***"God is love. Whoever lives in love lives in God, and God in them…... We love because he*** (God) ***first loved us."*** (I John 4:16, 19)

But for now, we turn to **Chapter 5 "Brain, Mind and Soul"**, a follow-up to this chapter probing the non-physical and philosophical aspects of the Brain as well as Extraordinary brains.

Chapter 5

BRAIN, MIND AND SOUL

"I simply believe that some part of the human Self or Soul is not subject to the laws of space and time."

CARL JUNG

THE PREVIOUS CHAPTER, "THE BRAIN GAME", focused on the physical and functional aspects of the human brain, laying out the case that our brain evolved over the history of our species to do more than brains of any other species or animals. While some animal brains are much more capable than we imagined in the past, and some even allow "self-awareness" in ten or more proven cases, still, so far as we know, no other kind of brain has yet been able to contemplate things that are not physical or material. Humans can imagine things that never were and envision ideas and objects never previously thought of, able to describe things never seen. Only humans, so far as science has yet discovered, can anticipate some future and have some usable concept of tomorrow and yesterday. All brains can remember in some way or form, but remembering and reliving and reinterpreting the past seems to be only for human brains. We are blessed with the advanced skill of planning or intending something in the future, and we are doomed because we are the only animals who can "worry" about what has not happened.

Though several animals such as elephants, chimpanzees and black birds can recognize themselves in a mirror and comprehend that they are separate and different from that image, it is only humans with their marvelous brains who have learned to worry about how they look, what others think about them, and to consider what it is like to die. Imagining your "self" with all the knowledge, experiences, fears and hopes, dreams and ambitions—that is a consequential and unique achievement of mankind; but to imagine what it is like after your certain death is perhaps even more challenging for our brains. But we do imagine it, and dread it, and are perplexed about it. We don't want to think about "non-existence" or any such philosophical conundrum, and we try to hide it away deep in our brain's storage bin, but we can't avoid this primordial fear slipping past our mental guards once in a while.

Most brain activity in humans and other animals is about staying alive by dealing with the real, physical world we inhabit, but the human brain has evolved to perceive and try to understand the immaterial world, the realm that is outside the natural world of our sight, hearing, touch, smell or taste. Whether the "out there" is real or not, we humans are drawn universally and inevitably to contemplate the "super-natural," the "spirit" world, the nagging urge to believe that there is more to life than molecules and muscle and electro-chemical reactions. Something in us longs for another place, another "home" we almost remember. In this book we argue that it is God, the Jesus-like God, Who made us like that, and Who created our brain and the resulting mind to communicate and commune with Him.

The Mystifying Brain

Science has been studying and exploring the human brain for centuries, and we have an astounding body of knowledge. But what we know is probably only a fraction of what we still must learn, say the most expert researchers in neurology. Ancient people are known to have explored living human brains by drilling holes in the skulls, as shown in skeletal remains uncovered by archaeologists in Egypt, South America, and Europe. Apparently, these "operations" called "trepanning" were attempts to treat some disease or injury. We know that some of the "patients" survived these primitive surgeries, for their skulls show new growth after the treatment, evidence of some recovery, probably in only a few cases. Greek physicians such as Gales and Hippocrates had some appreciation for the brain, and identified some brain disorders and diseases back in the dawn of medical science. But clearly, most prehistoric people did not know the function of the brain, and often considered the heart as much more important. The heart and other organs were preserved in Egyptian mummies, but not the brain.

While not understanding the brain, some prehistoric peoples had apparently concluded that the head of an enemy was somehow critical to that person, and so decapitation became fairly common in primitive cultures of the distant past; this gruesome trophy still is sought by some aboriginals discovered in the last two centuries. In the jungles of Africa and the Amazon, as well as in sunny South Sea islands, "head hunters" still ply their trade on occasions, untouched or unaffected by modern culture. It is very unlikely that the collection and preservation of the head was a recognition of the importance of the brain contained therein—for in almost every case, the brain was discarded and only the bony skull was kept, sometimes displayed on a post or tree in a public place. Some skillful head hunters learned how to "shrink" the captured heads, producing grizzly totems which still terrify outside explorers. Modern anthropologists who have lived with and studied isolated hunter-gatherer Stone Age tribes believe that these preserved heads represent the "spirit" of the dead person, separated from the body and life, but still real in some sense. They seem to be holding the "soul" or the essence of their enemy captive, maybe preventing them from entry into some after-life. It is reported that visitors to these Stone Age tribes found the natives very suspicious of cameras, and many refused to have their picture taken. It appears they believe the camera has "captured" their soul which was a fearful prospect for them.

There are other societies which have preserved some part of their ancestors (skull, or even the preserved body) as an object of worship, sometimes kept on display in the home, and sometimes enshrined in a special section of the family residence. Some ancient people and some primitive tribes still isolated believe that these ancestors potentially have influence with the spirit world, and may protect their descendants. Some activity or ceremony likely celebrated the departed relative, including perhaps food or other gifts left at the altar. Ancestor worship is found in the early development of many ancient cultures, including ancient Israel.

The Soul Is an Ancient Concept

People have been believing in a "soul" or "spirit" as separate from "body" for many centuries, probably all the way back to at least *Homo neanderthal* and possibly as early as *Homo erectus* since we have evidence that these human ancestors buried their dead respectfully and sometimes even left food or tools for use in the "afterlife." Some of the smartest and wisest people who ever lived, the Greek philosophers of 400-500 B.C., certainly believed firmly in an immortal soul (or spirit) and a mortal body, a belief we now call "dualism." Plato reports Socrates' view in the **Republic** "Haven't you realized that our soul is immortal and never destroyed?" And later Socrates asks "What is it that, when present in a body, makes it living? —A soul."[24] Socrates and many others of the great philosophers of the ancient world accepted the "soul" as a real "thing" even though they knew it was not physical or material. Ancient Greek beliefs were varied and evolved over time. Pythagoras held that the soul was of divine origin and existed before and after death. The early Christian philosophers and theologians adopted this Greek concept of the soul's immortality and believed the soul is created by God and infused into the body at conception. Jewish theology struggled with the concept of "soul" as we discuss in some detail later, eventually adopting a "light" version of the Greek concept.

It is difficult to describe the soul in any way that doesn't make it sound like what we usually mean by the *mind*. It is easy to see how this confusion develops for we can trace some "fuzziness" in the teachings of Socrates, Aristotle and Plato, especially because knowledge and the mind were so highly regarded, and an attractive afterlife was not yet anticipated. Many people seem to be talking about the mind when they discuss immortality—the fundamental quality hoped for is ongoing consciousness, the important characteristics of what they mean by "mind." It is clear that the term "soul" carries a more theological connotation than "mind" or "consciousness in most discussions, but that doesn't necessarily mean that the words "soul" and "mind" refer to entirely different things. An eternal soul without a mind is not as appealing as a soul that can still think, feel and learn. Most people don't have a real problem with the Greek "dualism" of *body* and *soul,* but don't want to lose their mind in eternity.

Has Medicine Found the Soul?

The many reported stories of "near death experiences" in recent history gives some support to the richer version of life after death. Several popular books have been written about hundreds of patients who seemed to die on the operating table or in some other setting, people medically "dead" according to the doctors. Many, but not all of these patients seem to have very similar experiences according to interviews. The idea of floating gracefully in some kind of tunnel toward a distant light is a component of most of the cases. Almost all described a sense of peace and calm, a feeling of joy and love flooding over them. The story sometimes includes "hovering" above the doctors working on their dying body, clearly looking down from above the scene and sometimes remembering things that were said or done after they left their body. Many of the patients recall approaching a bright light at the end of the tunnel, and seeing either an angel or God welcoming them; many also mentioned seeing dead parents and relatives who had gone on long ago, again welcoming and beckoning them "home."

Not all the out of body experiences end happily: somewhat fewer public reports have been about those who experience "hell" instead of a heavenly light. These terrifying accounts are not as detailed as the others, but commonly described horrifying fear and distress, a sense of condemnation and shame, a feeling of "falling" rather than "flying." Rather than welcoming lights and family members these bad scenarios often feature taunting demons and hostile people from the past, cursing and blaming the poor deceased patient. All of the cases obviously come from patients who returned to life—all of the stories are from people who "died" and "recovered." All the "happy" stories appear to end in a very similar way: somebody (God or Jesus, etc.) intervenes and says something like "***Go back—it is not your time yet.***" These so called "out of body experiences" have convinced many that this is empirical proof of the "after-life" but many scientists raise serious objections. Some have pointed out that there are many logical explanations not requiring supernatural involvement—such as a chemical deterioration in the brain causing hallucinations, "imagination" fueled by the patients' beliefs and the public reports that they had read about. Some scientists have even conducted experiments under tight control to show that starving the brain of oxygen (a common element) is known to induce imaginary memories and hallucinations similar to the popularly reported incidents. The issue of reports from the "formerly dead" is not settled in the scientific and medical world, but many religious believers are totally impressed and claim that their biblical faith in immortality and heaven are thereby validated (by science, no less!) But another reported fact brings even more hope for the Believers: A large majority of those patients who reported these "out of body experiences" claim their life has been changed radically and permanently. Almost all say they no longer have any fear of death (since they have been there, done that.) But even more importantly, many of those returned to life have become more compassionate, more tolerant and patient with others, and vastly more generous of their time and resources on behalf of others. Many reports of such "conversion" experiences have been verified by friends and family who say *"He is a different person!"* or *"She is not the same woman I used to know...everything is changed, for the better. I like her a lot better now!"*

Becoming A Living Soul

A common theme uniting the world's religions is the basic distinction between two realms or categories: body/spirit, earthly/heavenly, human/ divine, body/soul. A more comprehensive discussion of "soul" is found in **Chapter 15 "Being Fully Human"** and for now we will only briefly address this critical subject. The soul, the animating force which makes humans alive, is one of the most interesting words in the Hebrew language: *"neshama"* (הנשמה). This word contains a fascinating secret. *"Neshama"* is derived from the verb *"nasham"* (נשם) which means "to breathe." What is the justification for this connection? Is it because our soul allows us to breathe? No, although breathing is one of the necessities of living, just as is a heartbeat and other bodily functions. There is a theological connection between soul and life.

The Bible story of Adam has God forming his body from the dirt, or mud, into the shape of a human, a lifeless mud-man. Then God infused the mud-man's nostrils with "the breath of life," and the man took his first breath as a living being. ***"Then the LORD God formed*** *a man from the dust of the ground and breathed into his nostrils the breath of life, and the man became a living being."* (Genesis 2:7) Earlier English translations have "became a living **soul**." The original Old Testament Hebrew verb here is *"nasham"* (נשם) which means "to breathe." The Hebrew noun here, *"neshama"* (הנשמה) is translated "living being/soul." It is significant that the noun *"neshama"* is a derivative of the verb nasham," showing that these ancient Hebrew writers connected the divine input to the creation of the soul or spirit, as well as the physical body. *"Ruach"* is the most common Hebrew word for "breath" and the New Testament Greek uses *"pneuma"* where the Old Testament has *"ruach."* And in New Testament Greek, *"pneuma"* is used for both "breath" and "spirit." ***"When you take away their breath, they die and return to the dust."*** (Psalm 104:29) ***"If it were his intention and he withdrew his spirit and breath, all mankind would perish"*** (Job 34:14-15). ***"You are God. You turn man back into dust and say, 'Return, O children of men.'"*** (Psalm 90:3) and ***"The body returns to dust and the spirit goes back to God who gave it."*** (Ecclesiastes 12:7). It is clear that the Biblical authors equated breathing and living. The departure of the breath is the departure of life, they reasoned: the physical body is the container of human life and spirit, and the empty body is discarded.

The Breath of Life

Prior to the 16th century medical science still considered breathing as the usual proof of life; when a person stopped breathing, they were presumed dead. Unfortunately, medical history is haunted by the likelihood that many people were buried alive by mistake when no breathing was detected. Feathers were sometimes used to detect faint breath, hoping that an unseen breath would disturb the light feather held near the mouth or nose. Mirrors were also used to check the body for a moist fog, a clouding of the mirror indicating that there was still life. Drowned individuals were sometimes rescued and helped to breathe again by early versions of first aid, and the return of breathing usually resulted in the return of life. It was logical for people to equate breathing with life just from observation, and the euphemism "breathed his last" meant "he died" in common language.

With the invention of the stethoscope in 1816 by French physician René Laennec the diagnosis of death could be more accurately confirmed by the absence of a heartbeat. This first "stethoscope" was simply a rolled-up sheet of heavy paper, pressed to the ear of the physician and the chest of the patient. Laennec reportedly invented the stethoscope specifically to deal with his own discomfort in listening for a heartbeat by the usual method of placing his ear directly on a woman's chest. The modern stethoscope, iconic symbol of doctors everywhere now, evolved from that simple cardboard tool. From that time until the twentieth century this provided a reasonably clear sign of life, or proof of death by absence of a heartbeat.

Brain Death to the Rescue

The use of the heart beat or pulse to determine life or death was a great improvement for the medical practitioners of the nineteenth century, most of whom lacked "professional" medical training. Fewer premature burials took place, and patients regarded medicine and doctors with more respect because it became more scientific. With the dramatic advances in medical science since 1900, more medical practice was being guided by research, and more precise measurements and data collection was demanded. The definition of death became a major dispute within science, and the ethical issues raised by "life and death" decisions were troubling. No premature burials were reported now, but a troubling number of cases were reported of a "dead" patient "coming back to life" either spontaneously or with extreme resuscitation efforts. In some cases, the heart that has stopped beating can begin to beat again, maybe after a delay of 5 or 6 minutes or longer. Even in a modern hospital today, the highest drama often comes when the lead surgeon looks up at the operating room clock and says solemnly: "The time of death is 2:47 pm." The efforts to save that patient officially end; death has been decided. In that modern hospital the doctor has numerous sets of data to inform his decision: the heart monitor "flat lines", the blood pressure drops drastically, the patient has stopped breathing, and the brain waves pictured on the monitor fade away. The brain is now dead according to the expensive technology.

The concept of brain death had been widely accepted by the late nineteenth century, but the technology for measuring brain activity was not yet available. Consequently, the adoption of "brain death" as the definitive measure was not formally adopted until 1968 after a decisive study and report by Harvard Medical School. Advances in science made resuscitation possible, and people previously considered dead such as drowning victims had their respiration restored: breathing was restoration of life in many cases, but some of those revived had irreparable brain damage, leaving them alive but in a vegetative state for years. Ongoing fear of premature burial still made science search for more certainty, and discovery of the brain's electrical waves and the invention of equipment which could effectively detect and monitor these pulses all led to defining death as "cessation of all brain activity," or "irreversible coma." This more scientifically certain definition of death was incorporated into laws, and helped resolve such societal issues as capital punishment, and the controversial cases of maintaining patients on life-support equipment for years, even against their wishes.

Organ transplants became more likely to succeed because of the speedier determination of brain death, allowing "fresh" organs to be retrieved without the fear of removing a liver or a heart from a still-living patient. Not all mysteries of the wonderful brain are solved yet, including the debate over whether brain dead patients may still have some level of consciousness, maybe hearing still, for several minutes after brain waves disappear. The reports of an occasional, very rare case of some "brain dead" patient reviving to some semblance of normality after months or years in a coma still clouds the issue and invokes fear in doctors. Evidence is conflicting. Research continues. Answers will come.

The Mind-Body Problem

Science, like philosophy, has never had a conclusive explanation for "thinking," nor for "mind," though philosophers have been debating such subjects for centuries. Science has more recently focused on this field through psychology and neuroscience; now computer scientists working on artificial intelligence are also studying human thinking, trying to reproduce thinking in machines. The purely materialistic theories of science argue that the explanation lies in the biology of the brain: thinking is in the neurons and synapses and the random firing of electrical impulses, along with chemical agents activated by these minute electrical charges. Recent study and research, supplemented by modern equipment such as MRI's, CAT scans, have revealed amazing new insights about thinking. We can now identify which part of the brain is involved in language and speech, vision and perception, problem solving, long term and short-term memory, mood and attitude, pleasure and fear, among many. We now know where mathematical activity is activated, what brain area is activated by art and music, and can even observe in real time brain activity associated with meditation and prayer in test subjects. Though science is generally committed to a material, physical explanation of thinking and mind, not every scientist agrees.

Most philosophers and theologians (ancient and modern) still find much more satisfaction and intellectual congruence in metaphysical explanations for mind and thinking. To them, the mind seems to require a supernatural or divine involvement rather than a random electro-chemical answer. "*The brain is not a meat computer,*" says neurologist Michael Egnor,[25] who thus dramatically challenges the concept of a material mind in which thinking and all mental activity are explained as physical effects created within the biological brain. Not surprisingly, this present book espouses Egnor's view, following the theories of Plato and Aristotle and almost all philosophers prior to the eighteenth century: the mind and the body are separate entities, symbiotically connected but each with a separate identity.

Perhaps the mind-body dispute is just an issue of semantics: perhaps we are using different names for the same phenomenon. There are many more words in common discussion of such questions. Brain and Mind are generally spoken of as separate things. Self, soul, spirit and heart appear in such discussions and printed material, and the Bible is notoriously unclear about the differences. For example, in the New Testament Jesus quotes an Old Testament command known to Jews as the Shema: "***Hear, O Israel: The Lord our God, the Lord is one. Love the Lord your God with all your heart and with all your soul and with all your strength.***" (Deuteronomy 6:4-5) In Matthew 22:37 we read: ***Jesus replied: "'Love the Lord your God with all your heart and with all your soul and with all your mind.*'"** There is a subtle difference also in the parallel passage in Luke 10:27: '***Love the Lord your God with all your heart and with all your soul and with*** *all your __strength__ and with all your __mind__.*'" Jesus adds "mind" to the Shema in both quotations, adds "strength" back in the second version. The intent of all three passages is clear: Love God with everything you have, your whole being, your whole self. Mind, Heart, Soul, Spirit, Self, Person, Persona, Personality, Ego, I, Me, Oneself, Character, Inner Being, Identity—are these many words for the same thing? It is clear that many of the terms cited above are referring to the same non-material "thing." Like the Blind Men of Indostan describing an elephant, cited elsewhere, philosophers and religious writers are operating from different perspectives, and thus apply different names to the same object. Let us try to reduce the verbal muddiness.

First, You "Gotta" Have HEART

"Heart" is a common metaphor used for millennia in most languages and cultures: "He broke my heart," "Have a heart, Brother, and help me out," "The heart is deceitful about all things," "She has a mother's heart," "Never give up, never give up: that's the heart of it really," "Follow your own heart," "The judge had a change of heart about the defendant," "It takes a lot of heart to keep fighting," "David was a man after God's own heart" and "Man looks on the outward appearance, but God looks on the heart." Each of these uses of "heart" are slightly different, but we recognize that there is a common thread running through them all: they all reference the center-piece of our identity, who we really are as a unique person. Up until the mid-1950's in our society the sound of the physical heart was the signal of life: if your heart stops beating, YOU are gone, your life has exited. Primitive cultures so seriously regarded the heart as life-itself that they tore the beating heart out of a victim's chest, having captured everything that made up that individual, they apparently thought. The "heart" then is a metaphor for the life I live in a material body—everything I am, myself, my consciousness, Me, my person. This dualistic view of mind and body says "I am Me, but I have a body." There is a person living in my body, a person who thinks, dreams, plans, imagines, fears, hurts, hopes, and loves, and that person is ME! I AM!" Or, as the Neil Diamond lyric proclaims: "I AM, I said! To no one there."

Believers may be troubled by the previous paragraph, especially the last "I AM!" for that is the name God gave to identify himself to Moses at the burning bush. ***"Tell the people I AM has sent you."*** (Exodus 3:14) This has a deep theological meaning for Believers, pointing to the eternal existence of God and His independence of time. Jesus repeated this mysterious name about Himself: ***"before Abraham was born, I am!"*** (John 8:58) Other translations read "I Am" to indicate a name. Both Testaments appear to teach that past and present are one to Him (See extended discussion of "God and time" in **Chapter 10**). In Christian theology God IS a "person" with the same qualities that define humans as "persons," with the difference that GOD NEEDS NO BODY. Christians take hope in this description of God as a "person" independent of a physical framework to believe that our "person" will continue on when our mortality claims our body. This is not suggesting some Eastern religious philosophy of disembodied souls eventually merging again into the great cosmic "All Soul" in which paradise is total loss of "self." Rather, what is suggested here is that WE are everlasting souls or spirits or minds who have grown into a spiritual being which is like God and is prepared to share His eternal home forever when we finish with, and discard, our material bodies. Little is revealed about in what form we will exist, but the Bible gives this encouraging idea: ***"Dear friends, now we are children of God, and what we will be has not yet been made known. But we know that when Christ appears, we shall be like him, for we shall see him as he is."*** (I John 3:2)

This is the great Christian hope of some meaningful life after the death of our physical body, perhaps one like the versatile "resurrection body" in which Jesus appeared after His crucifixion. We can't be certain, but the best guess is that we will be happy with whatever we are, and it will be a "heavenly" life, regardless of the paving on the streets or the jewels on the door. We will be home.

What Then Is the Soul?

"Soul" is most often used in religious conversations, and the Bible has a great deal to say about this particular element of humans, but "soul" or its linguistic equivalent has also been used by philosophers such as Socrates, Plato and Aristotle and all their successors for nearly 3000 years. In the Greek spoken by Plato the word translated as "soul" is ψυχή (psyche). Plato and all of his later followers were dualists, believing that humans possess both a body and a soul, with the soul being immortal. But Plato went further, dividing the soul/ψυχή into three parts: logical (thinking), spiritual (spirited, emotional), and appetite (erotic pleasure, carnality, concupiscence). He identified various nationalities or ethnic groups which seem to reflect predominantly one or the other of these qualities of the soul. Naturally, he sees his fellow Athenians as the logical, thinking type soul, and views the Phoenicians and Egyptians as mostly crude, greedy and lustful types. In retrospect it seems that Plato's "soul division" is probably referring to what we would call "temperament" or "character" or "personality" rather than fixed types of the deeper, immortal, essential element we consider "soul." Psychology generally deals with these unique variations in human personality, while philosophy and theology deal with the metaphysical entity we call "soul." Thus, we won't follow Plato in his *subdivision* of soul, but find persuasive his *distinction* of the soul from the body, and the *permanence* of the soul in some kind of afterlife, the incorporeal essence of a living being. It is mildly interesting to observe that Plato's tripartite soul in 340 B.C. is similar in pattern to the twentieth century Sigmund Freud's three level model of the personality, or the "psyche": superego, ego, and id next to Plato's three: logic, feelings, and lust. Were they perhaps observing the same phenomena in human nature? (For further discussion of this proposed connection please see **Chapter 15 "Being Fully Human"**)

Though there are a number of Hebrew and Greek words which are sometimes translated "soul" in the Bible, it must be admitted that the Bible does not present a clear and definitive doctrine of the soul. For example, the Hebrew word *nephesh*, is translated as "soul" in some passages and "breath" or "breath of life"" in others. Genesis 2:7 says "The LORD God formed man of the dust of the ground, and breathed into his nostrils the breath (*neshemah*) of life; and man became a living soul (*nephesh*). The Hebrew word "nephesh" is translated as "soul" 475 times in the King James Version, and as "life" 117 times, depending on context. Numbers vary by version or translation, such as King James, New International Version, or Revised Standard. The corresponding word is *"psyche"* in the New Testament Greek's (ψυχή) it is translated as "soul" 58 times and 40 times as "life." A few passages in both Testaments translate these words as "mind" or "heart." No consistent label for "soul" is seen. The biblical writers were all trying to understand the immortal, non-physical part of mankind, and no real consensus was reached; that is still the case with modern scholars and writers.

It may be confusing to review the variations in translating the many biblical words associated with soul, but in reality, the differences are not theologically significant, for reasons explained below. It is clear from the first "soul word" used in Genesis 2:7 that Adam was made out of dust or mud but was not alive until God "breathed the breath of life" into him. At that point, according to this account, the living body that had been only clay, now was given a "soul." Life and soul are apparently similar or the same in this early theology. Throughout the Old Testament people who died are spoken of as "giving up the *nephesh*" much as we say "He breathed his last." Genesis 5:5 simply says **"Altogether, Adam lived a total of 930 years, and then he died."** Nothing is said about his soul or his life after death, or anything about Heaven or Hell. This same silence applies to much of the Old Testament, suggesting that the early Hebrews had not yet developed a cogent theology of life after death.

By the time of Abraham, we read: **"Then Abraham breathed his last and died at a good old age, an old man and full of years; and he was gathered to his people"**. (Genesis 25:8). Other passages use the term "gathered to his fathers." The one strange exception describes Adam's great-great- great-great grandson, Enoch. Of Enoch we read: **"Altogether, Enoch lived a total of 365 years. Enoch walked faithfully with God; then he was no more, because God took him away."** (Genesis 5:23-24). It seems that Enoch, at least, may have been supernaturally spirited away and taken to be with God as a reward for being such a good, faithful man. This may reflect the Hebrew's first inkling of a life after death.

It is probably unnerving for Believers to face the likelihood that a theology of life after death was an evolving doctrine, primitive and bare for the first Israelites, unsettled, just as it was for their ancient neighbors and contemporary cultures in 1200 B.C. In fact, Babylonians and Egyptians were ahead of Israel in a concept of an "after world." The Egyptians had developed a complex theology of life after death, and their grand monuments, the pyramids, were testimony to that belief. True, they primarily viewed the afterlife, with its rewards and punishments, to be for their royal family rather than for the commoner. Stretching further back in history we can reasonably infer that Neanderthals and our earlier ancestors had a belief in life after death. By 80,000 years ago primitive humans buried their dead with bright red body decorations, tools and even food to use in the after-world. The chosen people of God, however, were late in coming to that belief (See **Chapter 8, "The Birth of God"** for a more detailed discussion of the Hebrew people's slowly evolving faith and beliefs.)

The Jewish After-Life

Though the belief in an after-life is found in the Psalms and some of the Prophets, the Hebrew view of the soul and life and death was not what Plato and the Greek philosophers taught. And further, we will assert here, the Old Testament belief about immortality is not what New Testament Christians came to believe, and is not what today's orthodox Christians believe. Consider at this passage from Ecclesiastes (9:4-6) a generally pessimistic book in the Old Testament, full of beauty but not so great on hope:

> *Anyone who is among the living has hope—*
>   *even a live dog is better off than a dead lion!*
> *For the living know that they will die,*
>   *but the dead know nothing;*
> *they have no further reward,*
>   *and even their name is forgotten.*
> *Their love, their hate*
>   *and their jealousy have long since vanished;*
> *never again will they have a part*
>   *in anything that happens under the sun.*

As will be discussed in a later chapter the Israelite vision of an after-life is a cold, dark and permanent place for all souls, good or bad. It is true that some such visionaries as the shepherd boy David speak of their hope to "dwell in the House of the Lord forever" but most common people probably believed that a place called Sheol awaited them at death. "Sheol" occurs sixty-five times throughout the Old Testament; it is an obscure, shadowy, gloomy place of existence, life after death, perhaps, but certainly not a desirable place. Except for continued consciousness the dead enjoyed no amenities. Sheol is, in many ways, closer to the Greek Hades than the Christian vision of Hell. It certainly is not Heaven.

Several other Old Testament passages seem to suggest existence after death. David comforted himself with the knowledge that he would see his dead child once again: ***"Can I bring him back again? I will go to him, but he will not return to me."*** (II Samuel 12:23). Earlier David seemed to hope for more: ***"But God will ransom my soul from the power of Sheol, for he will receive me."*** (Psalm 49:15 **RSV**) And there is the strange story of the dead prophet Samuel being summoned from Sheol by the Witch of Endor at King Saul's request:

> ***"Then the woman asked, "Whom shall I bring up for you?" "Bring up Samuel," he said. When the woman saw Samuel, she cried out at the top of her voice...What do you see?" The woman said, "I see a ghostly figure coming <u>up out of the earth</u>." "What does he look like?" he asked. "An old man wearing a robe is coming up," she said. Then Saul knew it was Samuel, and he bowed down and prostrated himself with his face to the ground. Samuel said to Saul, "Why have you <u>disturbed me by bringing me up</u>?"*** (1 Samuel 28:11-15).
> (Emphasis added by author)

This is a rudimentary belief in the continuation of the soul's existence and personal identity, but it was not much of a future to look forward to in 1000 B.C. Israel. But like other beliefs, it evolved over time as God was more clearly understood. By the time between Testaments (about 400 B.C. to birth of Jesus), the Jewish people had undergone national destruction and restoration, occupation and oppression, and exposure to Persian and Greek religious thought. The new idea of a bodily resurrection at some future time of judgment was incorporated, along with a developing idea of punishment and reward after death. The Hebrew theology did not draw a clear distinction between body and soul as the Greek philosophers had and envisioned a resurrection of the righteous in their original body (or maybe an improved immortal body). To many of these rabbinic Jews their version of a heaven was a full restoration of the happy days of David's kingdom on earth in some future idyllic time, "the Day of the Lord." When Jesus came preaching the advent of a "Kingdom of God" many Jews assumed, incorrectly, that He was proclaiming David's Kingdom and the rescue of Israel from political occupation and oppression. They held a victory parade for Jesus on Sunday, were disappointed, and so on Friday they crucified Him.

New Testament Theology of The Afterlife

But fret not, Dear Believers: The Bible does clearly teach a firm and strong theology of immortality of the soul and the continuation after death of a conscious existence for both the good and bad. But to find that theological revelation, we have to rely mostly on the teachings of Jesus and the Apostles in the New Testament since the Old Testament is ambiguous and conflicted on the subject. By Jesus' time the belief in life after death, resurrection, and heaven and hell were widely established. The Sadducees, one of the dominant religious/political parties in first century Judea, strongly denied the idea of resurrection and any kind of eternal existence, and so they vigorously opposed Jesus and His teachings. Ironically, it was the hyper-religious party called Pharisees who did believe in these doctrines that Jesus taught—but they plagued Jesus night and day and ultimately had Him killed. Jesus, of course, made it absolutely clear that the soul continues after death, and that the believers would enjoy paradise with God for all eternity. "***What good will it be for someone to gain the whole world, yet forfeit their soul? Or what can anyone give in exchange for their soul?***" (Matthew 16:26) Another time in a parable Jesus tells of a foolish rich man: "***But God said to him, 'You fool! This very night your life (ψυχή) will be demanded from you. Then who will get what you have prepared for yourself?'***" (Luke 12:20) Some versions use "soul" to translate *psyche*, and some use "life," apparently for the same idea.

Believers should feel no shame because some parts of our Bible had not yet come to fully understand this hope of everlasting life that we have ourselves received. As with other areas, the unfolding of Gods' revelation was gradually received step by step, a little light now, and more light in the future, until finally the true Light came in the flesh in Jesus. Jesus not only taught life after death, but He demonstrated it in the Resurrection. In the conversation with the sisters of the dead Lazarus we see their existing belief (a future mass resurrection) and the further light Jesus now gave to them.

"Lord," Martha said to Jesus, "if you had been here, my brother would not have died. But I know that even now God will give you whatever you ask." Jesus said to her, "Your brother will rise again." Martha answered, "I know he will rise again in the resurrection at the last day." Jesus said to her, "I am the resurrection and the life. The one who believes in me will live, even though they die; and whoever lives by believing in me will never die. Do you believe this?" "Yes, Lord," she replied, "I believe that you are the Messiah, the Son of God." (John 11:21-27)

This teaching moment by Jesus may be a little confusing. Is Jesus saying that those who believe in Him will "never die" physically? But He inserts the phrase "even though they die" so what does that mean? Jesus often spoke of "eternal life" which usually means "living forever" (*outside of time*) and it is sometimes translated "Everlasting life." But putting His whole message in the larger context it is clear that Jesus is **not** talking about physical life or death (which He did not promise to eradicate), not a quantity of life but about a quality of life; He offers a life that is full and complete in the way God planned. He is talking about that "new life" in another passage: *"**Very truly I tell you, whoever hears my word and believes him who sent me has eternal life and will not be judged but has crossed over from death to life.**"* (John 5:24) Jesus is making the magnificent promise that those who accept His offer of forgiveness and fellowship will not have to worry about **Judgment Day** (a big and dreaded concept in Judaism of His day). According to Jesus in these passages, we who identify ourselves with Him in trust and become "believers" are given a kind of "pass" into eternity: we don't have to "pass Go" or collect 200 condemnations, but we go directly from life to Life Eternal. Other parts of the New Testament echo that same concept, that Jesus has "**taken away the sting of Death**" —that is Sin (1 Corinthians 15:56) and so physical death is not used as a punishment and the Judge has already closed the case against us stamped as "Forgiven" or "Paid." No fine, no punishment, no probation, no fear of surprise. We are "Home Free" because

Jesus settled our case "out of court" on the Cross. That's the comforting promise Christians believe.

A Proposed Common Terminology

After this extensive survey of the meanings attached to the traditional metaphysical terms for the non-physical, non-carnal part of humans inhabiting the physical body, it is time to simply state what they mean in this book. This is not so cavalier as in *Alice in Wonderland*, where Humpty Dumpty scornfully asserts "When I use a word it means **just what I choose it to mean** – neither more nor less." Very convenient but not very helpful in communication. No such claim is made for all time that our choice of "Soul" is the single best, most encompassing word available to absorb *heart, spirit, psyche, self* and other such words. For the sake of clarity, "soul" will be used herein to identify the part of us which we argue survives our physical death and continues our personal, sentient, conscious existence forever. This is one premise of the larger argument about what it means to be human. Many Believers will be more comfortable using "spirit" rather than "soul" and some theologians will continue to argue that the Biblical "soul" is NOT the same as the "spirit" or other terms used in Scripture. There is no necessity for unanimity in this discussion and the proposals in this book are suggestive, not infallible proclamations. Notice that we have not included "mind" nor "consciousness" in this definition of soul. We will attempt to provide a logical connection between mind, consciousness and soul in the next sections.

"Mind" and "Consciousness" share some of the attributes of soul, though the argument has been made that these are distinct and separate entities. Briefly stated, "mind" and "consciousness" are treated here as **add-ons**, the product of the brain, experience, learning and other content that is unique to each individual, and are significant parts of what makes us a "person", an "I" or a "me." We propose that these two elements of who we are become integrated into our spiritual identity, our pre-existing "soul," a soul that is given to all humans at the initiation of life. Under this theory the soul is a gift from God, "pre-installed" as it were, and our consciousness and our mind are created over time by our physical brain. This concept of the soul is obviously close to the somewhat unfashionable "tabula rasa" theory of mind, and in contrast to the

Platonic view of the soul. Plato saw the human psyche as an entity that preexisted somewhere in the heavens, before being sent down to join a body here on Earth. Plato considered everything in this world to be an imperfect representation of its perfect eternal Form or Idea. Aristotle split with his teacher on this, and is considered the father of the tabula rasa concept, espousing the theory that the mind is like a blank tablet on which humans "write" their mind. He wrote:

> Haven't we already disposed of the difficulty about interaction involving a common element, when we said that **mind is in a sense potentially whatever is thinkable, though actually it is nothing until it has thought?** What it thinks must be in it just as characters may be said to be on a writing-tablet on which as yet nothing stands written: this is exactly what happens with mind.[26] (Emphasis Added)

Seventeenth century English philosopher John Locke and eighteenth-century Swiss philosopher Jean-Jacques Rousseau brought the *tabula rasa* ("blank slate") idea to modern times. As Locke theorized, *tabula rasa* meant that the mind of the individual was blank at birth, and he put great emphasis on the premise that individuals had free will, the ability to author their own soul and mind. He argued that all individuals are free to define the content of their character—their own unique self, but retained their basic identity as a member of the human species, an identity which cannot be altered.

Borrowing a modified version of this *tabula rasa* concept from Locke and others, and for the overall purposes of this book, we consider the human soul to be our personal journal, mostly blank, presented to us by God at the beginning of our life. "*Ensoulment*" (a traditional Jewish concept) is the spark of life our bodies receive at some stage of development, and functions as the passport for our existence, for our complete journey through our life on earth. We speculate that this innate life/soul is a spiritual entity, in the same way that God is spirit (non-physical), a soul immortal but mutable, changing and developing as we live our earthly life. We are able to shape our souls as we choose, having been given an unfettered moral free will as our inheritance from God. We are filled with "potential," capable of almost any option for our life story. We nurture and develop our soul by our consciousness and our mind. What we experience, what we think, what we choose with our mind determines the shape and quality of our soul. In this theory, the soul is created by God, and with our physical brain we create our non-physical mind and consciousness. Our soul, our mind and our consciousness, being non-material entities, do not cease to exist when our body and our brain are dead. Our souls are infused with <u>who we are</u> and <u>what we have experienced</u>, the essence of our identity which goes on eternally, both conscious and mindful. At least metaphorically, we return to God with what we have made of ourselves.

Mind Over Matter

As with the terminology discussed above relating to "soul" we need to get as clear as possible what we mean when we talk about Mind. We need to first get clear about what most folks mean when they use the term ***the mind***. What, exactly, are they referring to? Whatever its nature, it is generally agreed that mind is that capability which enables humans to have subjective awareness (recognizing your separate identity), to perceive and react to our external environment, to form intentions or decisions to act, to have consciousness, to think thoughts and to experience our emotions. Science has studied the mind since the pre-Socratic philosophers of Greece, and in modern time through the fields of psychology, psychiatry and neurology, among others. The final answer has not yet emerged and so there are hundreds of variations in explaining the mind. In common conversation we are totally unclear: we "have a mind to do." we "make up our minds," "change our mind," "are of two minds" (undecided), and even "lose our minds." Further, we ask "Do you mind?" answer "I don't mind," or we warn our children to "mind" the teacher (be obedient). It has been extraordinarily difficult for our society to decide exactly what we mean by "mind."

One of the common understandings among most of us is that our mind is private, and that what we think in that sanctuary, what we say to ourselves in that inner conversation, is secret. We get fascinated by performers who claim to be "mind readers" but we know (or hope) that it is some kind of trickery: it almost certainly is always fake, according to the best science. One of the Bible teachings that can be disturbing is that God knows our thoughts, our minds: "***You have searched me,***

Lord, and you know me. You know when I sit and when I rise; you perceive my thoughts from afar. You discern my going out and my lying down; you are familiar with all my ways. Before a word is on my tongue you, Lord, you know it completely." (Psalm 139:1-4) "*I the Lord search the heart and examine the mind, to reward each person according to their conduct, according to what their deeds deserve.*" (Jeremiah 17:10). Jesus is credited with this divine insight as well: "***Jesus knew their thoughts and said to them...***" (Matthew 12:25) and "***Knowing their thoughts, Jesus said, "Why do you entertain evil thoughts in your hearts?*"** (Matthew 9:4) Believing that your mind, your thoughts, are known by God can be a comfort if you have been unjustly accused or misunderstood by society: "At least God knows I am innocent!" But having your deep inner thoughts exposed to God is also terrifying if you secretly harbor hate, deception, or misdeeds you thought were hidden.

One of the most horrifying events in any person's life is being exposed, being confronted with some shameful guilty secret. In many Christian groups this terrifying sense of guilt is called "conviction," becoming aware that God knows your soul and is judging you in unfavorable or harsh condemnation. In orthodox Christianity, and especially in the evangelical brand, this "conviction" is seen as the work of the Holy Spirit (more about this subject later) who is actively and operationally involved in speaking to the "lost sinner" in their innermost mind, activating their conscience, "nagging" them about right and wrong, and creating spiritual dissatisfaction and emotional unrest. The mission of the Holy Spirit is to do in our time what Jesus did in His earthly life: appealing to, and inviting everyone to come to the loving relationship offered by the loving Father, helping men face their own helplessness in trying to be good or righteous on their own, and turning from self-help to God-help in living the "good life," the "abundant life" as children of God. This doctrine is totally in harmony with a central premise of this book: God uses our brain as His communication system with us. The evolution of our brain over time to the stage at which it could generate the "mind" and "consciousness" enables us to "speak" to God and to "hear" from Him to whatever degree we allow it. God seeks to get us to follow Him through conversation rather than coercion. "***Come, let us reason together*" says the Lord.**" (Isaiah 1:18 **KJV**).

Mind Beyond Matter

We have advocated here for a dualistic view of humans: we are both body and soul: a material mortal body inhabited by a non-material immortal soul. Historically, there is also the clear link between dualism and a belief in immortality, and so any discussion of immortality is naturally more theological than scientific. Strict materialists do not recognize a spiritual or non-material realm or reality, and so immortality is difficult for strict materialists to accept. If the conscious mind is not physical, it seems more plausible to believe in the possibility of life after bodily death. On the other hand, if conscious mental activity is identical with brain activity, then it would seem that when all brain activity ceases, so do all conscious experiences and thus any possibility of immortality. What do those who believe in life after death envision? Most Believers expect the continuation of one's conscious thoughts, memories, experiences, and one's own person or self. Though Believers sing and talk rapturously about the glorious heaven "above" and wax eloquent about streets of gold, and pearly gates, most recognize that such hyperbole as found in the last book of the Bible, Revelations, is metaphorical exaggeration. Who wants to walk on slick gold streets, anyway? Most Christians don't seriously focus on great food, dazzling jewels, lovely landscapes, or wonderful golf courses in the after-life. It is true that some brands of Islam promise a harem of beautiful virgins for some (men only), but neither the Koran nor the Bible gave them that idea. Thinking of heaven as some kind of ritzy resort with all the amenities is approximately what popular culture often expresses, but that is not a Biblical idea.

Our freed souls will be us, in some important ways, with our own identities and our individualities. We apparently will recognize each other in heaven, according to Jesus and early Christians, but we may not be in the same relationships we had in life. Jesus taught clearly, if not definitively, that there will be no marriage in heaven: the Pharisees posed a "trick" question about a widow who married her oldest brother-in-law as was the tradition, and six brothers-in-law died. His enemies asked, "In heaven, whose wife will she be?" And Jesus said to them, "*Jesus replied, "The people of this age marry and are given in marriage. But those who are considered worthy of taking part in the age to come and in the resurrection from the dead will neither marry nor be given in marriage, and they can no longer die; for they are like the angels. They are God's children, since they are children of the resurrection."* (Luke 20:34-36) Again *"At the resurrection they will neither marry, nor are given in marriage; they will be like the angels of God in heaven.* (Matthew 22:30) Sorry to disappoint some who were starting to like the idea of life after death: it looks like marriage (and sex apparently) are not part of the heavenly realms. But then neither will there be bosses and workers, or kings and servants, bullies and victims, politicians and constituents, landlords and renters, or rich people and poor people. We will be somehow like angels who serve God now.

Relationships are tools of earth-life, not needed in the after-life. Status or positions will not exist between people in that place of perfect freedom. Apparently only one relationship will exist in heaven: the love relationship between Our Heavenly Father and we His beloved children. Will there be any other love? Will there be friendships and fellowship among us living souls? We don't know, other than the knowledge that "God is love" and that our early goal was unconditional love for each other. It is reasonable to speculate that loving God and loving our neighbor as one's self will still be the standard in the hereafter as it has been in our earth-life. Feelings and emotions are a part of who we are now, and it is likely that we will continue to enjoy positive feelings and emotions in our paradise, but we will not be plagued by the negative feelings and emotions of our earthly life, such as anger, fear, resentment, hate, shame, jealousy, or any of the other promptings of our darker side, the promptings of our older reptilian brain. (Note: this "reptilian brain" reference is to a much longer discussion of brain evolution in the previous **Chapter 4 "The Brain Game"** in case you skipped it.)

Extraordinary Brains

We have previously looked at normal, typical brains in prehistoric hominids and in modern humans, generalizing the form and function of the human brain as it evolved over the millions of years as seen in fossil records. Most of the changes in our species have involved successively larger brains and more complex brain structure as the species evolved. Brain development allowed improved tools, nutrition, shelter, communication, social behavior, and ultimately survival in challenging environments. But now we turn to **abnormal** brains studied in our time, to examine the amazing variation which is possible in the "standard" brain, both for good and ill. We will consider the surprising ability of the human brain to continue to function after it has been severely damaged, or partly missing due to a birth defect. We will also review the phenomena of some brains that can do "superhuman" tasks impossible for us "normal" mortals.

In the previous chapter we have looked at the opportunistic "experimental" evidence of the brain's division of labor, how it organizes and specializes specific areas of the brain for discrete functions. Studying someone who has lost part of their brain by accident or trauma overcomes the usual ethical problem of intentionally damaging a healthy human brain in an experiment the way we do with non-humans such as rats, dogs and chimps. In these cases of abnormal brain, we are looking at what effect is produced by taking something away. What could we learn by researching the effect of adding something to the brain? Of course, we still have ethical restrictions on adding chemicals such as LSD or heroin into the living human brain in the laboratory under controlled scientific protocol. Such brain experiments have been done: the Nazi's conducted thousands of such repulsive experiments on both children and adult Jews. And even more reprehensible morally is that our country has performed such dangerous human experiments in our not-too-distant past (often related to military scientific research).

We need not detail such past failures of our society for they are gruesome and shameful, and they have finally been made illegal under any circumstances. But we do have available ethical and verifiable examples of people whose brains are extraordinary and amazing, with **added abilities** that far exceed the brains of any of the rest of us. Let's see what we can learn about our own ordinary evolutionary brain from these extraordinary brains reported in the literature, brains that are so different from normal brains due to injury, disease or unknown congenital differences at birth. We will consider how and why some humans are geniuses, some are exceptionally talented in art, music, math and memory and other unusual abilities, while most of us are *adequate* in brain function, but *not remarkable*.

Normal Brain – Profoundly Damaged

We start with those whose brains were likely "normal" until some accident or illness altered their brains in various ways. The most famous example, still used in medical school curriculum, is **Phineas Gage.** Gage (1823–1860) was an American railroad construction foreman remembered for his improbable survival of an accident in which a large iron rod was driven completely through his head, destroying much of his brain's left frontal lobe. We have scientific observation and study from the day of his accident until he died three decades later. We know the reported effects on his personality and behavior over the remaining 12 years of his life, effects sufficiently profound (for a time at least) that friends saw him as "no longer Gage." Prior to the accident Phineas Gage was, according to the town doctor, John Martyn Harlow, *"a perfectly healthy, strong and active young man, twenty-five years of age, nervo-bilious temperament, five feet six inches in height, average weight one hundred and fifty pounds, possessing an iron will as well as an iron frame; muscular system unusually well developed—having had scarcely a day's illness from his childhood to the date of injury."*[27]

In a small town in Vermont in November 1848 at about 4:30 pm Gage was preparing an explosive to blast away rock to make way for a train rail to be laid. He was tamping the explosive powder into a small hole previously drilled, a normal procedure in construction. He was using a three-foot iron bar known as a tamping iron, quite heavy. For some reason the iron rod and the rock created a spark, igniting the explosive. The tamping iron shot from the hole, through the left side of Gage's head just above his jaw, passed behind his left eye through the left side of his brain and exited completely through the top of his skull. Reports from the scene say the heavy iron rod landed 80 feet away from the injured man. Gage

was thrown onto his back and had some convulsive arm and leg movements, but within a few minutes he spoke and was able to walk with a little assistance. Later that day Dr. Edward Williams came to his lodging to find Gage sitting on the front porch. Amazingly, Gage jokingly announced "Doctor, here is business enough for you." Dr. Williams later wrote about that day:

> I first noticed the wound upon the head before I alighted from my carriage… the pulsations of the brain being very distinct. …The top of the head appeared somewhat like an inverted funnel, as if some wedge-shaped body had passed from below upward. Mr. Gage, during the time I was examining this wound, was relating the manner in which he was injured to the bystanders. I did not believe Mr. Gage's statement at that time, but thought he was deceived. Mr. Gage persisted in saying that the bar went through his head. Mr. G. got up and vomited; the effort of vomiting pressed out about half a teacupful of the brain [through the exit hole at the top of the skull], which fell upon the floor.[28]

Somehow, Phineas survived the injury, and remarkably tried to return to work about twelve days later. Despite his own optimism, Gage's convalescence was long, difficult, and uneven. Though recognizing his mother and uncle on the morning after the accident, the next day "lost control of his mind, and became decidedly delirious," the medical report says. For several weeks he alternated between alert improvement to semi-comatose spells lasting days. No one expected Gage to survive.[29]

But Gage did not die as it had been expected. One of the doctors observed that the wounds were **"truly terrific; but the patient bore his sufferings with the most heroic firmness. He recognized me at once, and said he hoped he was not much hurt. He seemed to be perfectly conscious."**[30] A month after the accident Phineas Cage was "walking up and down stairs, and about the house, into the piazza," the doctor noted. After a few more weeks Gage seemed better in every way and appeared to be recovering, and insisted on going to visit his parents in New Hampshire. There he gradually began doing some little jobs around the farm, working half a day in plowing and planting. His mother reported that Phineas' memory was somewhat impaired, and he was not as "outgoing" as he had been, but in many ways appeared normal, in spite of profound brain damage.

Phineas Gage lived a simple but unpredictable life the next twenty-five years, variously working as a horseman and stage carriage driver, some carnival exhibitions as a strange oddity, and finally went to Chili in 1852 where he worked several years in stable work, caring for horses, and driving passenger carriages. Eventually he began having seizures again and lost his job. He traveled to California where he stayed with relatives; his health deteriorated and he died there in 1860. The original doctor who had seen him the day of the accident was able to get Cage' skull exhumed and sent to him for study. Gage's story is known by nearly every neurological student in medical schools today. Phineas Gage influenced 19th-century discussion about the mind and brain, particularly debate on cerebral localization, and was perhaps the first case to suggest the brain's role in determining personality and that damage to specific parts of the brain might induce specific personality changes. Prior to this case it was universally believed that serious loss of brain volume meant certain loss of most human abilities and qualities. A report of Gage's physical and mental condition shortly before his death implies that his most serious mental changes were temporary, a few years, and that in later life he was far more functional, and socially far better adapted, than in the years immediately following his accident. We have learned much more since Gage, and neurologists know a great deal more now about the plasticity and ability of the brain to rejuvenate itself to some degree. It seems a brain missing much of its mass is still able to function in at least some cases.

Is Half a Brain Enough?

A newspaper in July 2009 reported the case of a 10-year-old German girl born with "half-a-brain" because the right side of her brain did not develop in the womb. Despite lacking one hemisphere, the girl has normal psychological function and is perfectly capable of living a normal and fulfilling life. She is witty, charming and intelligent the paper reported. The girl's underdeveloped brain was discovered when, aged three, she underwent an MRI scan after suffering seizures of brief involuntary twitching on her left side. Apart from the seizures, which were successfully treated and a slight weakness on her left side (hemiparesis), the girl had a normal developmental and medical history, attending regular school and taking part in activities such as roller-skating.

Scientists were most amazed to find that the child has both fields of vision in one eye, scientists said, perceiving through one eye what normally requires two eyes providing separate images. This is the only known case in the world of a person so equipped. University of Glasgow researchers used Functional Magnetic Resonance Imaging (fMRI) to reveal how the girl's brain had rewired itself in order to process information from the right and left visual fields in spite of her not having a whole brain. Visual information is gathered by the retina at the back of the eye and images are inverted when they pass through the lens of the pupil. Normally the left and right fields of vision are processed and mapped by opposite sides of the brain, but scans on the German girl showed that retinal nerve fibers that should go to the right hemisphere of the brain diverted to the left. They also found that within the visual cortex of the left hemisphere, which creates an internal map of the right field of vision, 'islands' had been formed within it to specifically deal with, and map out, the left visual field in the absence of the right hemisphere.

The Specialized Brain—The Savant

The term 'idiot savant' was introduced in 1887 by Langdon Down, a London physician, in reference to 'feebleminded' children (the unfortunate old label) who had special and sometimes remarkable "faculties." Among these were exceptional powers of calculation, drawing, mechanical aptitude, and, above all, of remembering, playing, and sometimes composing music. **Savant** is a word originally associated with very learned people, especially scientists: *Savant* comes from Latin *sapere* ("to be wise") by way of Middle French, where *savant* is the present participle of *savoir*, meaning "to know." Until the 19th century it was one of the highest titles of recognition by the intellectual elite. Strangely, the word came to be connected to a rare category of disabled people who also have an extraordinary "island of genius" such as a massive memory, math competence off the scale, or exceptional musical expertise. In the previous century such one-trick geniuses were given derogatory labels such as "Idiot" and "Feeble Minded." Scientists began studying these amazing feats of memory and adopted the term "Idiot Savant" to capture the unusual combination of mental deficits with some extraordinary ability.

Almost all such known "idiot savant" cases were considered "mentally disabled" and usually not functioning very well in society. In the early 20th century, the "idiot" label was dropped for social equality purposes, but also because these exceptional people were successful "geniuses" in some special field. What they lacked in mental and behavioral skills they more than compensated by astounding abilities absent in almost everyone else—abilities to memorize phone books, name the day of the week for date in any month or year in history, or play piano better than Mozart or paint better pictures than Raphael. Some who may not be able to dress themselves nevertheless may be able to draw detailed sketches of an entire city block after one short observation—including every window, door or sign.

One of the earliest savants to be reported scientifically was in a 1783 German publication—**Jedediah Buxton.** Buxton was described as a "lightning fast" calculator. One reported demonstration of his genius was answering the question "How many minutes has a man lived who is 70 year, 17 days and 12 hours old?" Nearly instantly he gave the correct answer of 2210500800 seconds, even correcting for the 17 leap years included. The case of Blind Tom, an American slave who exhibited prodigious musical powers from an early age, attracted worldwide attention in the 1860s.

While still rare, we now know that there are a lot more savants than we knew about fifty years ago, because we have recognized autism as a fairly common brain disorder and as many as one in ten autistic people are also savants. Professionals now use the preferred term "savant syndrome" since it is considered a continuum of symptoms, as we eventually recognized autism to be a syndrome rather than a single disability. The new name was "Asperger's Syndrome" until 2013 when it became part of one umbrella diagnosis of *autism spectrum*. Many autistic children are very bright but seriously disabled in social and relationship skills. Sometimes autism is mixed with mental deficits or low intellect, but sometimes it is also connected with a "savant syndrome" involving one great power of memory, music, math, art, and others.

The movie *"Rainmaker"* starring Dustin Hoffman is an accurate portrayal of a savant with unbelievable memory recall, disabled in many ways but exceptional in others. **Kim Peek** was arguably the most well-known savant through the popular movie *Rain Man* based on his life; Dustin Hoffman won the Best Actor Academy Award for his portrayal of this savant. Peek was born on November 11, 1951 with an enlarged head (*encephalocele*), a malformed cerebellum, and an absence of a *corpus callosum* and both the anterior and posterior *commissures*. He was able to memorize over 9,000 books, and information from approximately 15 subject areas. These include: world/American history, sports, geography, movies, actors and actresses, the Bible, church history, literature, classical music, area codes/zip codes of the United States, television stations serving these areas, and step by step directions within any major U.S. city. Despite these abilities, he had an IQ of only 87, was diagnosed as autistic, was unable to button his shirt, and had difficulties performing everyday tasks such as bathing and brushing his teeth.

Peek has been studied rather extensively, but neurologists have yet to link the missing structures of his brain and his greatly increased mental abilities. Science has discovered the reason for his amazing ability to read books so rapidly: he was able to split his vision so that each eye reads a different page, allowing him to read two pages at a time. He also had developed language areas in both hemispheres, something very uncommon even in surgically split-brain patients. Language is processed in areas of the temporal lobe, most commonly on the left side of the head, and involves a contralateral (opposite side) transfer of information before the brain can process what is being read. In Peek's case, there was no transfer ability—this is what led to his development of language centers in each hemisphere. Many believe this is the reason behind his extremely fast reading capabilities, much as if he had two brains for reading. Though Peek did not have the corpus colostomy surgery to divide the two hemispheres he is considered a *natural* split-brain patient. Peek died in 2009.

This type of case, with its unique features, is very helpful to neurologists trying to understand the functions of the two hemispheres and the working of the connecting tissue of the corpus callosum. Science learns much from things that work right but even more from things that operate differently, hoping to find ways to make all brains better and capable of tasks we cannot yet imagine.

The Enhanced Brain – The "Acquired Savant"

Savant originally meant "wise man" or "sage", people who were extraordinary thinkers and gifted with insight and wisdom about life and philosophy: the familiar cartoon of a pilgrim climbing a rugged mountain and asking the "guru" sitting there "Master, what is the meaning of life?" Such respected and revered people were believed to be divinely inspired and gifted, or may have gained wisdom through intense study or meditation. Now the common usage of "savant" is about a rare category of people born with some extraordinary skill or ability untaught and unlearned, while severely limited in ordinary social or intellectual abilities. Kim Peek, discussed above, was a savant at birth. But not all savants are savants from birth, some having some experience in childhood or adulthood which **caused them to be savants**. Let us call them "acquired savants," a category of miraculous people greatly different from Kim Peek and other such typical savants. After more research science dropped the negative label and now attaches the specific superiority, such as "musical savant" or "mathematical savant."

A savant with the pseudonym "**Martin**" illustrates this effect. Apparently, Martin had been normal at birth, but contracted meningitis at age 3, causing seizures and spastic weakness in his limbs and voice. The illness also apparently affected his intelligence and personality, rendering him impulsive and socially inept. He could not keep up with his classmates in elementary school and was taken out of school and kept at home. For many years he was able to live independently, doing simple and unskilled work as an adult, until serious illness required admission to a nursing home when he was 61. There he was observed and studied by medical professionals. For, in spite of his physical and mental problems, "Martin" developed unusual musical abilities. As a child he had always been fascinated by music, listening to it for hours on end, and people noticed that he would listen intently and then sing the melodies he had heard, or play them on the piano. With his spastic limbs and unpredictable voice Martin was not a great musician at first, but he was encouraged in his efforts by his father—who was a professional opera singer. In later life he had a fairly normal though barren life; his only pleasure, it was said, was to sing in church choirs. Though Martin possessed exceptional musical talent, he could not be a solo singer with his hoarse, spastic voice.

Along with his musical abilities Martin also developed an astounding memory. Once he finally was fitted for glasses to correct his limited vision at about age 8, he became an avid reader, retaining everything he read with accuracy, though not always understanding what he read. This great reading memory, like his musical memory, was found to be <u>auditory</u>: whatever he read he processed as sound. Some savants have "photographic memories, but Martin had "phonographic memory."

According to the doctor who met him at the nursing home in 1984, Martin reported that he knew more than two thousand operas, as well as the Messiah, the Christmas Oratorio, and all of Bach's cantatas. To test his amazing claim the doctor brought several dozen of the musical scores he had mentioned, and was amazed and unbelieving at first: Martin knew all the music. The doctor later wrote:

> I found I was unable to fault him. And it was not just the melodies that he remembered. He had learned, from listening to performances, what every instrument played, what every voice sang. When I played him a piece by Debussy that he had never heard, he was able to repeat it, almost f lawlessly, on the piano. He then transposed it into different keys and extemporized on it a little, in a Debussyan way. He could grasp the rules and the conventions of any music he heard, even if it was unfamiliar or not to his taste. **This was musicianship of a high order, in a man who was otherwise so mentally impoverished.**[32]

What could account for Martins musical prowess? Was it his highly skilled musical father, perhaps genetically giving Martin this skill? He was born into and grew to adolescence a musical environment which may have influenced him. Or was it that his very poor visual skill encouraged his brain to pour effort and resources into strengthening his auditory and musical skills to an extraordinary degree? For his first three years Martin was nearly blind and so naturally he used his auditory abilities more than in a normal situation to learn and orient himself. Darold Treffert, author of *Extraordinary People* notes that more than one third of all musical savants are blind or seriously visually impaired.[33] This connection is embodied in a scientific theory of savantism which suggests this very principle: one serious defect or weakness can trigger the human brain to over-develop some other ability to compensate the shortfall.

Another possible answer for this savant phenomenon is less intuitive, but possible. Perhaps some yet unknown aspect of meningitis, while destroying some of his cortical controls and mental capacity, at the same time unleashed and stimulated some dormant savant power that was present, freeing the new superpower to manifest itself. Is it possible that most human brains are hiding vast reservoirs of **high-octane brain power** which evolution or God have not needed to activate? We don't know the answers yet about why some brains develop "super power" in one area, and often puny powers otherwise. If one brain can create and play music without training, why can't others do it? If one person's brain can be equipped to remember and recall accurately every word in the Bible, is it possible for the rest of us? What can our brains do under the best circumstances? **What is possible** for us, for mankind?

The Extra-Enabled Brain

We coined the label "Extra-enabled" to describe ordinary people who seem to have one or two abilities that distinguish them from their peers. Some of these are born with special skills not found in most people, such as those who "hear colors" or have "photographic memory" or have total recall of every minute detail of what they have seen, heard or read. A few such extraordinary people have what is now labeled *autobiographical memory*, able to accurately remember **every** day of their lives in great detail, down to what they had for lunch on a specific date five years ago. These are "normal" people living normal lives, and the discovery of their special ability may not happen or be recognized in childhood.

Due to copyright laws, no photos of Wiltshire's amazing artwork can be shown here. His work can be seen on many sites on the internet, and a movie about his work has been created, Billions of Windows. He continues to draw cityscapes and landmarks in every country, and is able to function successfully socially and financially with only minimum help.

These unusual "gifts" are not just natural "talents" for art or music or some other genetically related exceptional endowment, for "talented people" are relatively common in a large population. A "talented" person is usually thought of as one who has **more** of some ability than average, more "natural" ability (such as art, music, poetry, etc.), ability that others may develop with training and practice. We accept the fact that IQ varies across the whole spectrum of people, with most people fitting in the middle of a Bell curve and the rest falling somewhere on the two extremes. It is probably "normal" in a population to have some "geniuses" and some "intellectually disabled" (or the more politically correct label "differently-abled brains.") We have a similar understanding that exceptional talent also is widely distributed in the population, and that some people with "natural ability" can further develop their endowment to the *expert* or *professional level*. Our study here is about people who possess the superior level without training or practice. These are those we suggest have brains that are "extra-enabled."

Stephen Wiltshire was born in London, England, in 1974 to Caribbean parents; his father, Colvin, was a native of Barbados, and his mother, Geneva, is a native of St. Lucia. He is known for his ability to draw from memory a landscape after seeing it just once. His work has gained worldwide popularity. He was even invited to be a member of the order of the British empire. He has appeared on many TV shows and in a movie, and has a world-wide following in the art world. Wiltshire was apparently normal at birth, but was mute throughout. At the age of three, he was diagnosed with autism. The same year, his father died in a motorbike accident.

At the age of five, Wiltshire was sent to Queensmill School in London where he expressed interest in drawing. His early illustrations depicted animals and cars; he is still extremely interested in American cars and is said to have an encyclopedic knowledge of them. When he was about seven, Wiltshire became fascinated with sketching landmark

London buildings. After being shown a book of photos depicting the devastation wrought by earthquakes, he began to create detailed architectural drawings of imaginary cityscapes.

He began to communicate through his art for he remained mute, drawing pictures of what he wanted. The instructors at Queensmill School would deal with his lack of verbal communication skills by temporarily taking away his art supplies so that he would be forced to learn to ask for them. Stephen responded by making sounds and eventually uttered his first word— "paper." His teachers encouraged his drawing, and with their aid Wiltshire learned to speak fully at the age of nine. His great artistic skill and photographic memory became widely known, and his sketches and drawings began to bring substantial prices. He has frequently taken helicopter rides over London, Paris, Montreal, New York and Chicago, and will then draw the landscape that he saw with accuracy and immense detail, right down to the exact number of windows in a building. He has had several exhibitions of his own work in museums and galleries in England and Europe. He has his own permanent gallery in London.

His work can be seen on many sites on the internet, and a movie about his work has been created, <u>Billions of Windows</u>. He continues to draw cityscapes and landmarks in every country, and is able to function successfully socially and financially with only minimum help.

Harold Whitmore Williams was born in Auckland in 1876. He described "an explosion" in his brain' at age seven, and apparently that event led to his new extraordinary ability for learning languages, an ability which grew to an extraordinary degree. His amazing capacity to learn new languages can be verified by the fact that in his lifespan of 52 years, he could speak more than 58 languages including English and Old Irish. He knew every language of Austrian Empire Hungarian, Czech, Albanian, Serbian, Rumanian, Swedish, Basque, Turkish, Mandarin Chinese, Japanese, Tagalog, Coptic, Egyptian, Hittite, and other dialects. No scientific study is reported about Williams so we don't know what the neurological event was in his case—possibly a stroke. But according to available information he was relatively normal throughout his adult life, other than having this prodigious ability with language. There have been reports of other people who were exceptionally gifted with languages, some who seemed to just be talented, and some who acquired the enhanced ability from injury of illness. We know that language acquisition is usually related to a narrow developmental stage in children from 2 to about 15 years of age during which most people can easily learn and speak a new language, while adults appear to have lost something in their brain development which makes new languages possible, but difficult. The case if Harold Whitmore seems to be a reversal of that pattern, his language facility operating as it does in children.

The Injured Brain – Accidental Genius

An accident left Derek Amato with a severe concussion and a surprising new ability to play the piano. At age 39 the salesman from Colorado was visiting friends in his hometown of Sioux Falls and he and two buddies were swimming and "horsing around" with a football. Derek jumped into the pool head first while trying to catch a football thrown by his friend; he fumbled and his head slammed into the pool's concrete floor with bone-jarring force. He surfaced and was pulled out of the pool, holding his injured head. But to his surprise, he did not lose consciousness nor seem to be seriously hurt. He was conscious and able to speak.

His friends drove Amato to his mother's home and she immediately took him to the emergency room, where doctors diagnosed Amato with a severe concussion. They sent him home with instructions to be awakened every few hours. He drifted in and out of consciousness the first few hours, and the brain damage began to become clear within a week or so. He lost 35 % of his hearing in one ear, had severe headaches, and noticeable memory loss. But the most dramatic effect of the trauma appeared just four days after his accident. Amato awoke hazy after near-continuous sleep and headed over to his friend's house. Amato spotted a cheap electric keyboard in a corner and without thinking he rose from his chair and sat in front of it. He had never played the piano—never had the slightest inclination to. Now his fingers seemed to find the keys by instinct and, to his astonishment, ripple across them. His right hand started low, climbing in lyrical chains of triads, skipping across melodic intervals and arpeggios, landing on the high notes, then starting low again and building back up. His left hand followed close behind, laying down bass, picking out harmony. Derek Amato sped up, slowed down, let pensive tones hang in the air, then resolved them into rich chords as if he had been playing for years. When Amato finally looked up, his old friend's eyes were filled with tears. Amato played for six hours, leaving his stunned friend's house early the next morning with an unshakable feeling of wonder.

Again, we ask: Where did this musical ability come from? Had it always been there and was simply not activated until the concussion? In his case he gained a savant-like ability and did not appear to lose any significant other function in exchange. Another theory is that the blow to his head altered his sensory filters so that it could not ignore the individual notes and details as previously, allowing him to perceive input he previously would have screened out. Our brains are selective, we know, for if every sight, sound, smell and taste around us flooded into our consciousness constantly we would be driven mad.

Remodeled Brains —Some Other Examples

A 10-year-old boy is knocked unconscious by a baseball. Following that traumatic blow, he suddenly could do calendar calculations. He can also remember the weather, along with other autobiographical details of his daily life, from that time forward. An elderly woman who had never painted before becomes a prodigious artist after a particular type of dementia process begins and progresses. Another elderly patient with dementia has a similar sudden epiphany of ability, but this time in music. A 56-year-old builder, who had no particular prior interest or skills in art, abruptly, for the first time in his life, becomes a poet, a painter and a sculptor following a stroke that he miraculously survived. An 8-year-old boy begins calendar calculating after a left hemispherectomy for intractable seizures. These are examples of what some call the "acquired" savant, but a better description might be "accidental genius." Most official savants have lost some important functions and display some other extreme capacity. People who were previously "normal" until an accident or illness changes their brain in some astounding way, some additional touch of genius in art, music, memory or other ability.

Is it possible such dormant potential resides in all of us, unknown and untapped? We are left with the mystery, and with the optimism that many brains may very well have comparable hidden abilities or touch of genius which we might someday unlock. Perhaps we will find a better method than slamming our skulls against solid concrete. We can hope to someday build or unleash a better brain that could be helpful in facing the next 500 years or so of Mankind.

The Mixed-Up Brain—Synesthesia

We end this exploration of unusual brains with the strange brain condition known as synesthesia.

Synesthesia is a perceptual phenomenon in which stimulation of one sensory or cognitive pathway leads to automatic, involuntary experiences in a second sensory or cognitive pathway. The sensation of sound, for example, may be perceived as color or smell. The term is derived from ancient Greek: the "syn" (σύν means "together" and aesthesia (αἴσθησις) means "sensation." Synesthesia can be any two sensations mixed or crossed in the brain's perception areas: sound-color, or color-taste, or taste-sound or sound-touch. It is not known if there are any cases of triple or quadruple mixes. People who are synesthetes report this is a lifelong experience which they often did not know was "strange" when they were young. They assume that everyone "hears" colors. One well known musician/composer who is a synesthete is **Billy Joel**; he hears music as colors, and "sees" words in color. Seeing is not exactly the correct description—he associates words in different colors in his mind.

I would say the softer, more intimate songs — there's 'Lullaby' (Goodnight My Angel), 'And So It Goes,' 'Vienna' and another called, 'Summer, Highland Falls' — when I think of different types of melodies, which are slower or softer, I think in terms of blues or greens... When I [see] a particularly vivid color, it's usually a strong melodic, strong rhythmic pattern that emerges at the same time. When I think of these songs, I think of vivid reds, oranges and golds. Certain lyrics in some songs I've written, I have to follow a vowel color. A strong vowel ending, like an A or an E or an I, I associate with a very blue or a very vivid green...I think reds I associate more with consonants, a T or a P or an S. It's a harder sound. These [letters] are what I associate with reds and oranges.[34]

Billy Joel has the specific form of synesthesia which science labeled **Chromesthesia,** where sounds are perceived as colors (Chromo means "color"). Some other famous musicians who share this condition are **Pharrell Williams, Dev Hynes. Lady Gaga,** and **Tori Amos.**

Another common form of synesthesia, known as **grapheme-color** synesthesia or color-graphemic synesthesia, involves letters or numbers perceived as specific colors (for example, 2 is "seen" as red, and 6 might always be purple). Most people display some rudimentary form of this phenomenon when choosing colors for a room: some colors are perceived as "cool" and other colors are seen as "warm." Many people find some colors "soothing" (pale yellow, for example) while other colors would never be used in a bedroom because they are "stimulating" (such as bright red.)

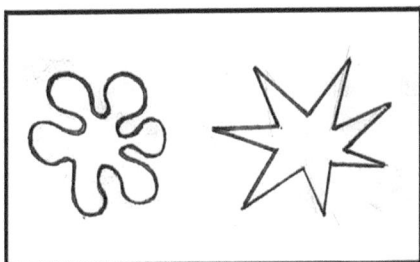

An interesting connection found in the brain is association of specific words with emotions or some specific meaning. Psychologists use a test called the "*Bouba – Kiki Effect*" to determine if shapes have certain "sounds" to people, regardless of what language people speak? For example, does every person associate certain physical characteristics, like sharpness and roundness, with certain sounds? Subjects are shown these two "made up" words shown at the left (Bouba and Kiki) and are asked which one seems soft and which one seems hard. Nearly everyone tested in various experiments identify "Bouba" as soft and rounded, and identify "Kiki" as sharp and pointy. The psychologist then uses these fake words to see if the labels are applied to pictures or drawings of other common words. Almost all the participants picked the same images as *Bouba* (soft) and identified other objects as *Kiki* (sharp). This connection was found in all the languages tested and in all age groups—some degree of associating certain sounds with specific abstract concepts. Is this an evolutionary product from our earliest attempts at language? Was proto-language "shaped" by shapes or textures?

Things in the environment of *Homo erectus* needed names in order to communicate with others, and so sharp things like "knife" or "scraper" would have "hard" sounds, and smooth or rounded objects such as "rock" or "cloud" would prompt softer sounds. Even before true language was possible, grunts and other sounds may have indicated some abstract meaning. Even in our own Latin/English alphabet the letters can be seen as "sharp" or "rounded" (for example "E" and "K" are angular and sharp pointed, and "O" and "B" are softer visually and in pronunciation. One plausible theory is that "hard" sounds are made by our mouth shaped tighter and angular, and soft sounds are shaped by more open and rounded lips. This apparently universal connection of a sound with a concept is another example of "cross-wired" senses in our brains.

Another vivid example is the "phantom limb" phenomenon; it is quite common for some person whose arm or leg has been amputated to continue to "feel" pain or sensation in the missing part. Soldiers injured in combat are often troubled by this strange cross-wiring or persistence of memory and need physical and psychological therapy to control this real pain; it is not "imaginary" for the brain and the nervous system are producing the full effect of pain though the signals prompting the feeling of pain may be subjective rather than objective.

Although often termed a "neurological condition," synesthesia is not listed in either the DSM-IV or the ICD since it most often does not interfere with normal daily functioning. Indeed, most synesthetes report that their experiences are neutral or even pleasant. **Like perfect pitch** (another superior ability) **synesthesia is simply a difference in perceptual experience.** Some people are "tone deaf" and can't match a tone they hear; many people have the ability to hear tones fairly accurately and imitate them in singing a tune; some very few musicians naturally can identify and duplicate any musical tone (e.g., A flat minor, or G sharp major, etc.) It appears that people are born with perfect pitch though training and practice may be needed to perfect this gift. What is it about the brain that allows some people to function on a very high level musically, but most of us are limited to "singing in the shower?"

The Aspirational Brain – What Might We Become?

It has been alluded to several times in this chapter that the human brain may have a better future if we don't destroy our bodies or our planet. We can see clearly how far we have come as a species since our great ancestors such as *Homo habilis, Homo erectus* and *Homo neanderthalensis*. Our brains improved in form and function over millions of years; is it unreasonable to suppose we might develop yet further in our brain capacity? Is evolution finished, or has God said "That's good… enough." We know that part of our mental improvements in the last 50,000 years can be attributed to better nutrition, better medical care, better shelters and somewhat better cultural structure. We are fighting for our life in the area of brain disorders such as Alzheimer's disease, mental illness and MS, and we are chronically optimistic that science will save us from these dread wasters.

But if we live longer and eat better and exercise and floss our teeth, will we be better humans in 2120 than we are today? We don't know. We have presented in this chapter evidence that the brain is capable of doing magnitudes of wonderful accomplishments that elude us now, except for a few. Those few we have described above demonstrate that some brains can and do perform super operations of math, art, music, memory and creativity. It seems logical to argue that if some brains can perform mathematical miracles in an individual, it is likely that that same capacity is included in most brains, dormant or latent, but still available. If an accident to some brains can unlock some artistic skills in some people, that same superior artistic ability may be present in most other brains, waiting to be activated. We are blessed in most cases with an adequate memory, but some people have brains that can memorize and reproduce massive written or oral material; if some brains can have super memory, why not all brains?

From the standpoint of classical evolution, Mankind **may not need** to improve our brains. In many ways *Homo sapiens* has mastered the environment, adapted to all the challenging conditions, and is relatively secure in the continuation of the species. From a Darwinian perspective, the "fittest have survived" and natural selection may be still improving the "gene pool" in some ways, but we pretty much have all we need now. We don't really **need** beautiful paintings and sculptures to survive; they are pretty and interesting, but art is an evolutionary luxury. Right? The same can be said of music—we enjoy it and it can move our emotions, but music does not help our species to survive in any physical and tangible way, does it? A good memory is certainly useful to all of us, but being able to memorize the entire Seattle phone book is not very useful; memorizing the first 10,000 decimals of "Pi" is very impressive, but who needs that? Is there any need for brain improvement if such improvement were possible? Better brains next century might enhance species survival through science and maybe political skills but no matter how super brains we produce our species is capable of destroying ourselves through the flaws in human nature, our tendency toward selfishness, greed, hunger for power, and our craving for pleasure and our avoidance of discomfort. Where we **really need** better brain-power is in the realm of the spirit, the qualities of character which actually **make us human.** We could really use a lot more people who are **fully human**, fully developed morally and socially, people who become "actualized" to their full potential, more men and women who act on the highest universal principles and ideals and are able to transcend norms and rules and answer to a strong inner conscience. Moral development is one of the possible outcomes of a better brain in our future.

Evolution probably is not as active in shaping us as it was with the first hominids two million years ago or more, for we are OK now from an evolutionary perspective. But God, the Creator and Father of Jesus, still has plans for us, and a more capable and effective brain is part of His tool box. Since we are able to communicate and fellowship with our Creator through our brains and minds, God certainly wants us to have better equipment. His stated goal for Mankind is summarized by the Apostle Paul:

> ***So Christ himself gave the apostles, the prophets, the evangelists, the pastors and teachers, to equip his people for works of service, so that the body of Christ may be built up until we all reach unity in the faith and in the knowledge of the Son of God and become mature, attaining to the whole <u>measure of the fullness of Christ</u>.***
>
> ***Then we will no longer be infants, tossed back and forth by the waves, and blown here and there by every wind of teaching and by the cunning and craftiness of people in their deceitful scheming. Instead, speaking the truth in love, we will grow to become in every respect the mature body of him who is the head, that is, Christ.*** (Ephesians 4:11-15)

Believers don't always understand that the plans of God are for all people, that God actually does "so love the world" — the whole world, the good, bad and ugly. So, the passage from the New Testament is usually seen as God's plan for the Church, for the Christ-followers. But we assert here that the God revealed by Jesus takes a much more universal view—He is not willing to have some blessed and some damned, and so His plan of growing up spiritually, becoming more like Jesus in every way, is meant for all humans everywhere. Paul does mention various church leaders such as pastors and evangelists, for building up the Church is part of His outreach plan. But from a fully Christian perspective, all who believe in God are expected to be servants, to work with God to further His plans on earth. And so, this passage has a universal appeal to work for a better world, a world of peace and harmony, compassion and empathy for each other, living in unity and mutual support. That goal of God is not just for a few million "Christians" but for all the atheists, agnostics, skeptics, Buddhists, Muslims and Jews, and any other belief system men may now embrace. This is not a "pie in the sky" dream and is not a plan for "heaven on earth." God may be kind but He is not ignorant: earth will never be completely like heaven or paradise—but we can hope to make it less like Hell in important ways. For science and religion to find a way to peaceful cooperation would be a step toward the light; for Christians and physicists to honor and respect each other, for Darwinists and Creationists to sit down together would be carrying out the will of God, His plan for His hominids on this *small pale blue dot* in the vast universe.

Chapter 6

THINKING, LANGUAGE AND BELIEF

*"Too often we enjoy the comfort of opinion
without the discomfort of thought"*

JOHN F. KENNEDY, 35TH US PRESIDENT

EIGHTEENTH CENTURY FRENCH PHILOSOPHER RENÉ Descartes famously wrote: "I think, therefore I am" ("Cogito ergo sum" in Latin). Descartes reasoned there must be a thinking entity (in this case the self) for there to be a thought. Thinking was convincing proof to him that he actually existed, and his "self" was not just some illusion or imagination. Existence is the most fundamental question in philosophy, the "ontology" branch, the foundation for knowing. Thinking about thinking is a good place to start understanding our brain and its' miraculous off-spring, our mind.

Thinking About Thinking

What is thinking? A seemingly easy question is actually quite a puzzle for philosophers and scientists of today, and it was the subject of discussion in the Athenian forum among such wise men as Socrates, Plato, Aristotle, and most other philosopher/scientists we know about. Did you have a thought as you began this chapter, or as you read the first few lines? As this section was being written the author was pondering, with some uncertainty, how to approach the elusive subject of what goes on in the human brain, and whether a physical, material brain could host such a non-physical, non-material entity as a "thought." While pondering, certain thoughts and words presented themselves and directed fingers to push specific keys in a habitual sequence, now viewed on the computer screen. From whence come these thoughts? How can the three-pound lump of gray matter in your skull create and express ideas and sensations that are somehow your own thoughts, that are somehow "you." It simply stretches credulity to believe our brilliant thoughts simply arise electro-chemically in that wet, soft bundle of billions of cells, neurons, axons, dendrites, acting with trillions of electrical connections. After all, from a materialist's perspective, our wonderful brain is mostly water, and has more fat than any other organ. Can a fat-head or a wet-head really think great, original thoughts? Or even nonsensical thoughts?

It is generally agreed that thinking is a function of our mind, and the view of this book is that our mind is generated by our brain. Our "minds" have thoughts, and we all think, but it is not easy to pin-point exactly what that means. We think "thoughts" and thoughts are always about something, but thoughts are not material entities in themselves. I may think about an elephant, but my thought is not an elephant—it is non-material representation of a material, physical thing, an elephant. An elephant is not about something else—it is just an elephant. A rock is just a rock, but if I think of a rock my thought is not a real rock, a physical rock—it is just a mental image of a rock. There is a clear distinction between thoughts (non-physical) and objects in the external environment I observe which are physical, and have a material reality (following the most common-sense philosophy, Realism, that what we perceive is real, objective, and actually exists independent of our minds.) To answer the old philosophical query: *"If a tree falls in the forest and there is no one to hear it, does it make a sound?"* Yes, there is sound if a tree crashes in the woods, even if there is no one there to hear it. That is Realism: things exist outside our mind, not projections from our mind.

Thoughts may also be about non-material subjects such as beliefs, memories, or even other thoughts we have thought. Thoughts may be able to imagine a thing which doesn't exist yet, but which might be created. Thoughts are the tools which we use to understand reality, to analyze and organize what we have perceived, to formulate plans or ways to respond to what we have sensed. Thoughts may sometimes seem to just be random, free-floating ideas which arrive unbidden, but it is possible that our conscious awareness may not be the whole story. In a later section the idea of the "unconscious mind" will be examined, the idea that there is a part of our mind which is normally below the threshold of our awareness. A similar term "subconscious mind" is sometimes used, probably referring to the same phenomenon in a less "clinical" way. At least for all our conscious thinking, thoughts are intentional, according to most psychologists and philosophers, current and ancient, going back at least to Plato.

Intentional Thinking

This theory of intentionality or thoughts directed toward an object or end, i.e., thinking for a purpose, is not really new, but it was reinstated to prominence by Franz Brentano, a 19th century philosopher.

> Every mental phenomenon is characterized by what the Scholastics of the Middle Ages called the intentional (or mental) inexistence of an object, and what we might call, though not wholly unambiguously, reference to a content, direction toward an object (which is not to be understood here as meaning a thing), or immanent objectivity. Every mental phenomenon includes something as object within itself...[35]

According to this theory, thinking is work, meaningful and goal directed, drawing on all our hopes, dreams, beliefs, desires, or memories to imagine a new condition or state of affairs.

In essence thinking is problem-solving, managing the present perceived realities of our environment and planning a new or more desirable outcome. Reality is a collection of objects that we personally sense, and knowledge is our accurate awareness of reality, thoughts that correspond to reality. Learning is the acquisition of new, reality-based knowledge and the adaptation or integration of that new knowledge into our total understanding of reality: our own schema about how all reality fits together. This process of coming to grips with external reality is most easily seen in the mental development of young children, from the first perception of a newborn baby (usually mother's face) through the organization of all the many perceived realities into a pattern ("schema" is Piaget's term, discussed elsewhere in this chapter). All of our conscious life is devoted to this acquisition of knowledge (corresponding to reality) and the incorporation of that knowledge into our minds. With greater knowledge that is accurate we gain the increasing ability to think useful thoughts, directing those thoughts toward our intended outcome.

Rational, goal-directed thoughts are not all that enter our minds, of course. "Day dreams" are largely regarded as wasted time, drifting along in our thought stream; sometimes that assessment is accurate, but sometimes our minds in "neutral" may be more useful and productive than we give them credit. A variety of mental states are possible, and conditions called "reverie" or "meditation" or "mindfulness" may be versions of "day dreams" but which are better appreciated. Those who experience these "relaxed" states of mind often get emotional benefit, reporting that they feel more "at peace" or "in harmony" with their world, sometimes sensing a more positive view of themselves and their self-worth. Also, it is widely believed by "folk philosophers" (and some scientists) that such relaxed mental states seem to allow memories to surface which we had labored unsuccessfully to recall by our "thinking." Thinking "too hard" say many, often blocks the memory for which you are searching. It is unclear whether this resistance of our memory to "pushing too hard" is a verifiable scientific truth, but it would be doable research. The psychological and even physical value of such quieted mental states is clearly proven in many scientific and medical research studies.

The Language of Thought

Multilingual people are often asked "What language do you **think** in?" Frenchmen who also have a good grasp of English, or English speakers who learn Spanish, cannot always give a quick answer. In some cases, those proficient in several languages indicate that they switch back and forth in a given conversation, but most frequently it appears that the "first language," their native tongue, is their most common language of thought. Introspection seems to convince most of us that we think in "words" and those words are the same as our spoken language. But several modern philosophers and linguists have disputed that common-sense idea that Frenchmen think in French and Englishmen think in English. They point out that human infants have not learned a language yet, but they are apparently born with the ability to think; what is the form or structure of <u>their</u> thinking?

These scholars argue that there is an innate type of language in all humans, dubbed "mentalese," a framework which allows children to add content and learn specific rules of syntax from their social environment—the family conversations they hear and learn to imitate. Syntax refers to the rules governing the order of words, the ways in which a complex language is used to make sense. The normal pattern in English is subject-verb-object, such as "Jesus spoke parables." The meaning is changed when the order is shifted, e.g., **Spoke parables Jesus**, or **Parables spoke Jesus**. Note that **Parables Jesus Spoke** uses the same three words, but the sentence meaning is changed entirely. Sometimes writers change syntactic order just for variety and interest, which is easily understood to mean the same as the original. The syntax, the "rules" usually determine the meaning of sentences or phrases as much as does the definition of the individual words chosen. This theory says that we inherit the basic rules, and we learn the words (vocabulary) of our first language to be arranged to convey our intended meaning.

Learning from Autism

As we explored in the previous chapter, we can learn much from brains that are different, unusual or even damaged. Autism is a serious neurological disorder which affects communication and social interaction, apparently a developmental disorder in the brain, usually diagnosed by age two. Children who are autistic do not learn to talk and communicate as toddlers, often have very limited interests in the environment, and tend to do endless repetitive behaviors. Forming relationships is very difficult for these children, almost never looking others in the eye or acknowledging the presence of others. Autism is an older name for this problem and it is now labeled "autism spectrum disorder" (ASD) because we now recognize that there is wide variation in the type and severity of symptoms people experience. ASD affects all ethnic, racial, and economic groups and is life-long. No cure is yet available but there are treatments and services which can greatly improve a person's ability to function in ways that seem to be close to "normal." But we know that the underlying brain disorder continues even after a person has learned to overcome many of the overt autistic behaviors.

One autistic person, **Temple Grandin,** has won recognition and even fame in academics and science. She has a PhD, is a college professor, an author and a respected animal activist. Her passion against animal cruelty and her invention of a humane enclosure for cattle has earned her many awards and speaking engagements. Because she has managed to "work around" the disabling aspects of autism and function socially in the broader society, she is able to reveal what autism is like, what happens in her head. Here are a few insights from her writings and interviews. She starts with a childhood memory:

> I can remember the frustration of not being able to talk. I knew what I wanted to say, but I could not get the words out, so I would just scream.[36]

Temple Grandin was fortunate enough to get early and continual support, training and one-to-one treatment to overcome her deficits. Through special education classes and gentle encouragement, she learned to "act" like other children in most ways; it was not natural or easy to do.

> Let's get into talking about how autism is similar to animal behavior. The thing is I don't think in a language, and animals don't think in a language. It's sensory based thinking, thinking in pictures, thinking in smells, thinking in touches. It's putting these sensory based memories into categories.[37]

It is very interesting and instructive how she sounds like an observer of herself, her condition and the needs of society:

> Mild autism can give you a genius like Einstein. If you have severe autism, you could remain non-verbal. You don't want people to be on the severe end of the spectrum. ***But if you got rid of all the autism genetics, you wouldn't have science or art.*** All you would have is a bunch of social 'yak yaks.'[38] (Emphasis added)

Finally, she gives us a window on the mind and thinking—a first-hand account of her thinking:

> I'm a visual thinker, not a language-based thinker. My brain is like Google Images. My mind sort of works like a search engine. You ask me something, and I start seeing pictures. Language for me narrates the pictures in my mind. When I work on designing livestock equipment, I can test run that equipment in my head like 3-D virtual reality. In fact, when I was in college, I used to think that everybody was able to do that.[39]

From the introspective research of Professor Temple Grandin, we know that some people think in pictures and concepts and not in words as we would have guessed. Her language is different from the normal brain, and though she managed to master verbal communication and writing, she still is thinking in a different language, a visual language.

How Does Our Language Develop?

We know how children learn our language because we have observed our children doing it, a little bit at a time. Some of us may even remember vaguely when and how we started "talking." We know that the earliest "babbling" of babies is the start of language, and we adults compete to see who can detect what the baby is saying: "Is that da-da? It sounded like that to me." "Mom ma" was her first word, the proud mother says. The endless noise of these young children seems enjoyable to them, and they will keep up their practice when you really want quiet. But we know that those babblings become recognizable attempts to actually say some—pointing at a cup and whining "Wawa wa" and we reward the attempt with water and praise, getting first one word in their vocabulary and then another. Children learn to imitate sounds they hear in their family, and so they eventually talk the same language and style as their parents or siblings. We can describe the process, but what is actually happening to the child? How is the brain changing or developing to add this new skill? Philosophers and scientists have been studying these questions for a long time, and though not every question has been answered we still know a great deal about the acquisition of language now, and possibly how our hominid ancestors came to speak.

The idea of a kind of universal "built-in" language platform was developed a half-century ago by the American linguist, philosopher, cognitive scientist, historian, political activist, and social critic, **Noam Chomsky**. Chomsky is still alive at this time and very influential in intellectual circle, probably more famous for his political views than his seminal work in linguistics. In 1957 he published a slim volume based on his PhD thesis: *Syntactic Structures*.[40] He argued that language is not a matter of learned behavior (as B.F. Skinner and other behaviorists believed) but language depends on some innate rules in the brain, a structure or platform built in on which human language was built. These natural rules in the brain were later called "universal grammar," rules common to all humans. "Syntax" is the common name for this rule structure, and is distinguished from the "vocabulary" or the actual collection of words we know and use.

Chomsky noted that there is a tremendous gap between the limited linguistic exposure children have as children and the virtually unlimited and rich linguistic knowledge they attain over time. Although children may be exposed to only a moderate subset of the available syntactic variations in their first language, somehow, they acquire the ability to understand and produce an infinite number of sentences, including the ability to make up sentences they have never heard before. They learn new vocabulary words all through life, but the way those words are structured in language is at predetermined, he says, "hard-wired" in our brains, probably genetically.

Chomsky reasoned that the primary language data the child experiences must be supplemented by some innate linguistic capacity, a **universal capacity he labeled "language acquisition device"** or LAD (as scientists tend to use in journals). This capacity might be seen as a "universal grammar," a human brain development that is missing in non-human species so far as we know. Humans are the only species with a clearly recognized spoken language, though research is continuing on whales and orcas and some other animals who vocalize in ways that resemble a form of communication among themselves. Apparently, only evolving humans gained the physical equipment (specific genes, voice box, vocal box, an agile tongue, and vocal cords) which make spoken language possible, and that evolutionary gift, combined with the evolved brain capacity for LAD, endowed us with the ability to use spoken language, the wonderful "gift of gab" which we so enjoy and generously employ.

Thinking in Pictures

A rare case from the medical literature gives us suggestive evidence that pictorial thinking has its own power independent of language. In a striking case study, in 1998 the psychologist Nicholas Humphrey at the University of Cambridge revealed the remarkable similarities between cave painting styles at Chauvet and the drawings of a 20th-century autistic girl named Nadia. Nadia's case raises the possibility that painting and drawing, far from being the preserve of the fully modern mind, might have preceded language altogether. Nadia was born in 1967 in Nottingham in England, and suffered from severe developmental disability. At age six, she still could not speak, had physical impairments, and many social incapacities. But even with these substantial deficits, Nadia could draw pictures with great accuracy and expression as early as age three.[41]

Humphrey noticed something vaguely familiar in his patient's art work. When he placed Nadia's toddler drawings next to the images from Chauvet and other prehistoric cave art, he noticed striking similarities in the rendering of animals such as horses and elephants. The drawings, separated by 40,000 years, seemed to be in the same fluid style, minimalist lines and colors, contour lines of the creatures are very much alike, and the way in which the figures are reiterated and overlaid on top of each other are remarkable. Nadia's drawings might fraudulently pass for *Cro-Magnon* cave paintings enough to fool many art dealers. How did she learn this style? It is possible that Homo sapiens of 40,000 years ago were graphically literate before they were verbally literate. Was communication in pictures and visual symbols before it was spoken? Graphic simulation, even today, is just as a tool of communication as verbal language: both are kinds of knowledge and skills.

We cannot place too much confidence in anecdotal data, but Nadia's case should at least provoke some skepticism about the notion that Upper Paleolithic peoples had modern minds with symbolic language. If Nadia was so good with pictorial representation, while lacking the foundation of linguistic symbolism, then it is possible that Homo sapiens of 40,000 years ago were graphically literate before they were verbally literate—used pictures before words. An even stronger interpretation is that Nadia was pictorially sophisticated because she had little to no conceptual/linguistic distraction in her mind. Without the alienating aspects of linguistic symbols, Nadia might have been more perceptually sensitive – leading to greater accuracy and expression in her drawing. Nadia made meaning very effectively without propositional tools. Our recent ancestors could also have had impressive non-linguistic minds – perhaps always in imagination mode. Image-thinking could have had a complementary evolutionary pathway, alongside language, or could have evolved earlier from natural selection helping tool-making capacities and body adornment as a way of communicating. Transmitting meaning is language, with pictures or sounds.

Theories of Language Still Unsettled

Not every scientist or philosopher agrees with Chomsky and his many followers, citing the widely different syntax formats found in the thousands of languages humans have used. There are clearly exceptions to the universality of a specific syntactical pattern shared by all human brains. Some of the primitive languages of isolated tribes today do not follow the most common ideas about nouns and verbs, about plurals and combinations, or even the basic subject-object distinction.

However, there are some compelling findings which do support the Chomsky theory. We will briefly outline that evidence.

One widely accepted hypothesis is that there is a *"critical period"* in child development when learning to read is most viable: before a certain age most children cannot learn to read, and after a certain age if a child has not been exposed to words and reading, it becomes extremely difficult for them to ever achieve this. Educators have been aware of and using this "critical period" idea for many years, working with pre-kindergarten 2-4-year-olds to learn some letters and corresponding sounds, to recognize that books contain stories to read, that books are read from left to right and from top to bottom, and other such preparation for reading. By the age or 4 or 5 most children can identify letters of the alphabet and can recognize simple words. Many people have an almost magic experience at this stage, where the black marks called letters stop looking like "chicken scratches" and they suddenly can see words and can string the easy words together, and joyfully, they can "read." "See, I CAN READ!" There is a moment (or day) when they could not see the pattern on the page, and another moment later when it suddenly makes sense. Something happens in the child's brain and the change is permanent, unless some catastrophic brain injury or disease damages the brain. It is truly magical evidence of the wonders of which the human brain is capable. We know our brain is "wired" to find patterns and meaning, and that this drive dates back to our earliest direct human ancestors

Another recognized reality is that while adults *can* learn a second language, it is almost always with much *more difficulty* than for pre-adolescents; adults learning a new language may become proficient if they work hard, but almost without exception, adults who learn a second language cannot escape having an accent that betrays their nativity. On the other hand, children who are exposed to a second language while living in the new culture, easily get proficient in that new language, and "speak like a native." Children of missionaries in China, Brazil, Japan and other places have *mastered* their adopted language while their parents always fall short of full and authentic fluency without strange accents. This supports the idea that a young brain is wired to acquire language, and an older brain loses that facility to some degree.

Feral Children and Language

A unique bit of evidence about language development involves deaf and feral children who have not been exposed to language in their infancy or childhood. Deaf children, of course, cannot hear the spoken language and so are not able to incorporate spoken words into mental content. Deaf children who are taught American Sign Language (ASL) can acquire language skills comparable to non-deaf children, IF the ASL was introduced in their first two years or so; unfortunately, most children learn ASL in school, after age 6 or so. Studies show that early learning children performed much better than later learners, especially after puberty. This supports the theory that the brain has a critical but limited period designed for language acquisition, and after that period of brain development the mastery of language is hindered.

Feral children are those who have been tragically deprived of social contact and interaction, often children who have allegedly been brought up from infancy "in the wild" such as some verified cases of children living with animals like packs of wolves and groups of monkeys. Stories of such wild children have been told for many centuries, such as the familiar tale of the founders of ancient Rome. They were said to have been raised by a female wolf who nursed and protected them after they had been abandoned in the woods. The famous Tarzan story is another such child lost in the jungle and raised by apes and taught to do fantastic feats of gymnastics in the trees. Many such stories are probably myths or misunderstandings, but at least a dozen children have been studied and written about. Documented studies showed

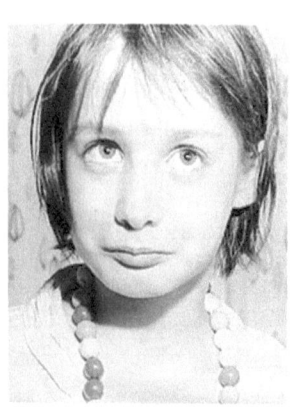

that these feral children who were returned to civilization as teenagers were never able to acquire normal language skills, no matter how rich and helpful their new environment was. Many of these children reverted to animal like eating, growling and walking on all fours at every opportunity. Some feral children are not raised by wild animals, but by seriously mentally ill parents, and these horrendous crimes usually produce the same permanently primitive behavior.

A classic example is "Genie" a victim of gross child abuse and neglect. From birth to age 13 when she was discovered, "Genie" was kept in isolation, strapped to a potty chair and forced to wear diapers. She was never spoken to or heard language, and when finally taken into a clinical environment, she was completely without any language, other than grunts, moans and screams. After seven years in a very rich educational environment (hospital) she was able to use a few basic words, but never learned to talk intelligibly. Another such child, "Isabelle" was incarcerated and isolated with her deaf mother until age six, when she was rescued. She had no language skills at the time of her rescue, but unlike "Genie" she quickly acquired normal language abilities through a special training program. The difference, it appears, is that "Genie" was past the critical time in brain development to acquire language, and "Isabelle" at age six, was still within the critical period.

It appears that science has not yet made a full and final finding about the nature of language acquisition in all its complexities, but has made considerable progress which will surely be expanded by ongoing research. Recently some neurological research has suggested that if a critical brain development period does exist, it may be due at least partially to the delayed development of the prefrontal cortex in human children. This pattern of prefrontal development is unique to humans among similar mammalian (and primate) species, and may explain why humans—and not chimpanzees—are so adept at learning language. The provable difference in brains of humans and our animal cousins may finally substantiate that spoken language and written language are distinct human characteristics, and may inform us whether animals "think" in the same way as humans, or if their mental activity is non-linguistic and non-symbolic. We will continue to struggle to understand our own mental activities in the meantime, hypothesizing and theorizing as the that it means to "think" and whether God can communicate with our minds using our native language, His specialized "spiritual language" or perhaps with emotion-based content, or maybe we get our messages from Him through imagery, or even in some other yet unidentified system of "speaking."

How and When Did Hominids Speak?

Noam Chomsky, famous linguist, is a prominent proponent of *discontinuity theory* of human development (*human development occurs in distinct age-related stages, starting and stopping rather than continuously.*) He argues that a single chance mutation occurred in one individual perhaps as late as 100,000 years ago, installing the faculty for language (a component of the mid-brain) in "perfect" or "near-perfect" form. [42] This brain capacity plus the physical changes in the vocal cord structure would both be required for genuine spoken language. A majority of linguistic scholars disagree with Chomsky on time frame and the single mutation theory, seeing language as mostly innate, but it must have evolved in the usual gradual way. Many scholars place the time range for the evolution of language and/ or its anatomical prerequisites back as far as 2.3 to 2.4 million years ago, about the point of the phylogenic divergence of *Homo* to the emergence of full behavioral modernity some 50,000–150,000 years ago. Detecting language use from the fossil records is problematic, though primitive skulls reveal brain size and sometimes even suggest some specific brain structures such as the Broca area associated with speech. Few dispute that *Australopithecus* probably lacked vocal communication significantly more sophisticated than that of great apes in general, but scholarly opinions vary as to the developments since the appearance of *Homo* two million years ago. Estimates of this kind are not universally accepted, but jointly considering genetic, archaeological, paleontological and much other evidence indicates that language probably emerged somewhere in sub-Saharan Africa during the Middle Stone Age, roughly contemporaneous with the emergence of the *Homo sapiens* species.

Hand and Sign Language

There is another kind of language humans use today, and it is quite likely that our most distant Homo relatives made use of it: **gestures.** It is not just Italians who comedians portray as "talking" with their hands, and as the joke goes, "would be totally mute if you tied their hands!" Almost everyone uses gestures and body language to communicate, and many people (the deaf, for example) use hand signals exclusively and very effectively. It is not likely that *Homo habilis* came up with "Stone Age Sign Language" similar to modern "American Sign Language" but it is a sure bet that they communicated to some degree with their hands and face, at least. We observe the development of language in our children and can see the progression from gesturing and other body language, to gesturing to supplement beginning oral word testing (pointing and saying "drink") on to the mastery of spoken communication first, with a gesture or other sign for emphasis (for example, "want cookie" supplemented with an impatient scowl or even a foot-stomp.) It seems quite clear that human communication evolved through similar stages as our hominid ancestors worked cooperatively and needed more complicated messages understood.

It is not hard to imagine a hunting party of such hominids, stealthily and slowly approaching a herd of deer. The first person sees some movement in the woods up ahead, and points silently in that direction ("Look there" is communicated). Maybe a finger to the lips means "Shh, be quiet." Another waves his arm and points to his mate and himself and then toward the left side of the prospective deer ("He and I will go around that side" is his meaning.") Why would oral communication mostly replace the gesture among humans? Again, we can imagine that hominids found themselves out of sight of each other, so hand gestures were useless, and so vocalization in the form of shouts or warning sounds were needed. The use of gestures is largely ineffective in the dark as well, so sound took its place. It seems obvious that this kind of gesturing, supplemented with grunts and other vocal sounds is a very plausible way language developed. In fact, that is precisely what Darwin, the Father of Evolution had predicted:

> ***I cannot doubt that language owes its origin to the imitation and modification, aided by signs and gestures, of various natural sounds, the voices of other animals, and man's own instinctive cries.***[43]

Animals communicate with us and with each other, with very limited vocal ability and with brains which are also limited. Animal vocal signals are, for the most part, intrinsically reliable. When a cat purrs, the signal constitutes direct evidence of the animal's contented state. We trust the signal, not because the cat is inclined to be honest, but because it just cannot fake that sound. Primate vocal calls may be slightly more manipulable, but they remain reliable for the same reason—because they are hard to fake. Apes and monkeys are not constrained by the human protocols of honesty and trust. Monkeys and apes often attempt to deceive each other, while at the same time remaining constantly on guard against falling victim to deception themselves, according to observers in the wild. Some have theorized that primate resistance to deception has hindered the evolution of language among them because words are easier to deceive than the actions that can be seen and verified. Nevertheless, primates can and do communicate with hand gestures as well as vocalizations, quite effectively letting their wishes or their anger be known.

Sound with Meaning?

The traditional conception of language came from Aristotle's description: "sound with meaning." His sound-meaning connection has been the dominant paradigm for centuries. Modern theory postulates two stages: the *internal* (I-language creating conceptual and intentional content) and the *external* (sounds, signs or some other physical expression of the internal thought). Thought becomes language. Not all scholars agree with Chomsky's theory about an innate linguistic framework, especially when it is applied to the language of thought, the inner language we all use. Granted, it would be most helpful if we did think it before we speak the thought. Some point out that not all thought is verbal—not always consisting of words. Introspection suggests that at least some of our thoughts may be pictures or images rather than words or even some more ethereal form such as "feelings." We know that a **smell** can provoke a very powerful memory which we may have a hard time describing because it does not seem to be either words or pictures. Smell seems to have a more direct contact with the brain in such cases. It may be physiological—our nose and olfactory glands are only millimeters from our brain.

One conclusion that appears to emerge with considerable force is that Aristotle's maxim should be inverted: "Language is sound with meaning" he wrote, but it may be that *"language is meaning with sound,"* an entirely different perspective. The core of language appears to be a system of thought, with externalization a secondary process, vocalizing after thinking. It might be that "I think, therefore I speak" is the new paradigm challenging Descartes' famous premise.

Linguistics and Perception

Language is clearly a tool of communication, the mechanism for transferring thought from one mind to another mind or minds. Language relies on "meaning" or shared ideas about what words mean. We all laugh at the "misunderstandings" that form the primary plot of comedy shows (i.e., "I Love Lucy," "All in The Family" and "Bewitched.") Misunderstandings is a pregnant term, for *failure to communicate* is a major problem for mankind. We know that people understand messages sent with words and terms with which they are familiar, and listening to someone using unfamiliar words and phrases is always confusing. The unfamiliar words may be a different language (French or Russian) or it may just be the specialized language common among scientists or lawyers or even clergymen. A language foreign to the listener will need to be translated (a familiar word substituted for a strange word.) Or, if the words are in the native tongue but modified by professional *"cant,"* (jargon, e.g., "legalese") the ordinary layman is left confused. The scientist might be speaking about "biogenics" or the lawyer may be describing "voir dire" while the theologian is preaching about "transubstantiation." Their respective colleagues may understand what was said since they share a similar vocabulary, but to the non-professionals it will be totally mystifying. Words reflect specific meanings, and those meanings are reflections of perceptions and beliefs already held by the thinker/speaker.

Linguistics, the study of language's inner workings, provides us with some concepts and technical vocabulary that are also useful for thinking about religion, because language and religion are both mental constructs, non-physical realities helping us to make sense of the world around us. Each provides categories with which to organize the way we think about life: singulars and plurals, nouns and verbs, right and wrong, sinners and the saved. Studies have found that when there are no words for a concept in a language, people have a very hard time believing the truthfulness of thoughts associated with those concepts and may not be able to perform tasks which require that information. Eskimos may have 50 different words for "snow" while Polynesian natives have none. Trying to explain snow to tropical islanders is nearly impossible, and trying to convince Icelanders to worship by dancing in grass skirts is a hard sell. There is no existing framework on which to "hang" such new ideas.

Language is so much a part of who we are that it can actually shape the way we think and act. To have a word for something makes it believable, but the absence of the word makes it almost impossible to act upon. Behavioral economist Keith Chen notes that language structure can even impact your ability to save, increase wealth, and maximize business. He notes that a simple sentence such as "It rain tomorrow," versus "It will rain tomorrow" makes a difference in how we perceive time, accepting it resolutely or anticipating and planning to use time. Research has shown that people who are "time conscious" are more likely to succeed financially than those who are more *laissez-faire* about time.[44]

Language and Belief

If I can't say it, can I believe it? If I can't express it in words, can it be true or real? If I believe it, do I really need a word for that belief? Beliefs are often described as mental representations that have propositional structure, which means they can be characterized in terms of sentences. They permit rational inference such that we can use sets of beliefs about the world to infer new things about the world, and have truth value such that our beliefs are either true or not. Given the parallel structure between belief and language, perhaps it shouldn't be surprising that some people think that it is impossible to have belief without language. Language and belief both appear to have a structure using strings of words allowing us to think things and communicate them. Beliefs usually can be put into words, strings of words that have our intended meaning. As discussed earlier, our thinking may not be in our mother tongue, but might be non-linguistic understandings that we "feel" or "sense" or some other method. We externalize them by putting words together to represent what we think/believe. We may sometimes have "thoughts" or "beliefs" which we cannot translate into language, experiential "knowing" for which we have no vocabulary.

The problem of religious language considers whether it is possible to talk about God meaningfully if the traditional conceptions of God as being incorporeal, infinite, and timeless, are accepted. In the language of materialism those traditional conceptions of God are not understandable for God is said to be invisible, unmeasurable, everywhere but no place specific. In the materialistic mind-set there is no place to "hang" such concepts, no drawer or shelf to store such ideas. So, religious language has the potential to be meaningless to the non-religious. Speakers of religious language must accept that their "native tongue" is a foreign language to science thinkers, and either use a different vocabulary or find a way to connect religious concepts to existing materialistic concepts. The latter is one of the goals of this book, and another whole chapter (**Chapter 20 Belief vs Knowing**) tries to bridge the vocabulary gap.

Thomas Aquinas argued that statements about God are analogous to human experience, putting spiritual concepts into familiar common vocabulary. Jesus did this with parables, explaining "the Kingdom of God" as like a farmer, or a merchant. An analogous term is normally univocal (has one meaning) but sometimes has other familiar meanings as well. He proposed that those godly qualities which resemble human qualities are described analogously, with reference to human terms; for example, when God is described as good, it does not mean that God is good in human terms, but that human goodness is used as a reference to describe God's goodness, not a one-to-one correlation but using a familiar idea, goodness, as the starting point for vastly superior version of goodness. In this book we have intentionally employed this approach, advocating for a God who is like a wonderful father (a familiar human image) enlarged to an infinite degree. Portraying God as "like Jesus" is the same technique—picturing the Jesus that many people already admire and showing that He is the finite visible manifestation of the infinite, invisible and all loving Heavenly Father. This is acknowledged apologetically as "anthropomorphic description" using human experience or qualities in order to explain or elucidate some other complex and unfamiliar entity.

Chapter 7

THE ASCENT OF MANKIND

"This is one small step for a man, one giant leap for mankind"
NEIL ARMSTRONG

PICTURED RIGHT ARE THE FOOTPRINTS OF REAL PEOple, your ancestors from more than 200,000 years ago, hominids on the way to being us. Their footprint looks like ours, yours. They walked like you, probably loved and cared for each other as you do, cried and died as we all do. They were our distant relatives, thousands of generations back in our family tree. All we have to remember them by are a few skulls, skeletons, hip bones, maybe just a jaw with teeth like ours. Here and there we find some of their hand tools, artwork, and a rare footprint here or there. Some paleontologists believe that the group whose footprints were miraculously preserved in Tanzania are the oldest such

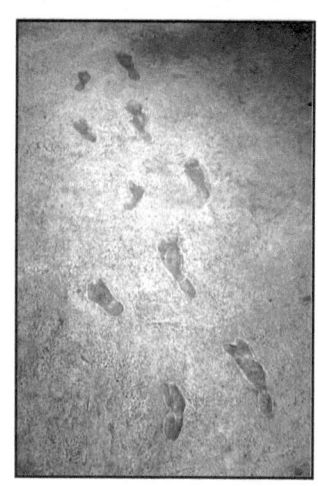

Ancient human footprints

markers from our past, and possible were left by a male, a smaller female, and probably a child, maybe a family. Other footprints were later found, indicating a larger group of proto-people. But from them, so long ago, we became who we are now.

And So, We Began

From the first climb down the tree to walk upright on the jungle floor to the first footstep of Neil Armstrong planted on the powdery surface of the moon Man has progressed inch by inch up the ladder of Humanity. Relentlessly, evolution has marched "upward" toward what we are and what we may yet become. Over a few million years our ancestors changed and adapted to the challenges, but also many promising species came and went to extinction, while our own species, Homo sapiens, has so far managed to survive. It is not clear whether we will survive in the future, for we have continued to foul our beautiful "nest" with dirty air, polluted streams and oceans, and we play with ghastly weapons of mass destruction like little boys with a pack of firecrackers on the Fourth of July. Looking back, it is indisputable that Mankind has made a lot of progress since 1 million B.C. at least material and physical progress; looking ahead, we anticipate that our future as a species will only get better and brighter, if we don't do something cosmically foolish with our scientific prowess. From our dear, departed *Homo habilis* to *Homo sapiens* on the moon, we humans have made a lot of progress, sometimes with retreats into dark ages, but eventually continue advancing ever upward and onward like a moth attracted to a candle. Thus, in hopes of progress the title of this chapter is optimistically **The Ascent of Mankind.**

Charles Darwin's 1859 blockbuster book *The Origin of Species* turned the Western world upside down, making "evolution" a household word. Though he was vilified by many for the idea that human beings were somehow the descendants of apes, he actually intentionally avoided discussion of human evolution because, as he said, "the subject is too surrounded with prejudices." The world was not yet ready, he reasoned, and so it was not until 1871 that he produced the companion book, *The Descent of Man*. This book did firmly put apes in our family tree, and made it clear that all races are part of one family, that racial and other such differences were invented by society. He proposed a new theory of sexual selection, a form of biological adaptation distinct from, yet interconnected with, natural selection: rather than "the survival of the fittest" by random genetic mutation, Darwin proposed "sexual selection" as the method of evolution, where the females made choices among competing males for procreation. The theory is that a female choosing a mate consciously or unconsciously picked a male she believed was the "healthiest" or "strongest" prospective father of her children. The "best" male specimens produced the most offspring, thus promoting the improvement of the gene pool over eons of time. In the animal world, Darwin had observed, males of each species had their courting ritual, with gorillas pounding on their chests in masculine display, while birds such as peacocks spread their beautiful feathers and danced their seductive dance to impress the intended female mate. Among some animals, at least, survival of the **fittest** becomes survival of the **cutest**. Humans may be in this category.

Darwinian evolution does not assert that humans are descended from apes or other simians, but that we share a common ancestor in our family tree. Understanding that difference may make evolution a little less insulting to Christians and other Believers. Science has not yet identified that ancient common ancestor but does have evidence that the split into the homo branch and the simian branch occurred several million years ago.

It is significant for the purposes of this book that the simian branch still is very much as it was at that great separation, while the homo branch has evolved upward, ever upward in terms of brain capacity and environmental adaptation. environment. Though we still share a great percentage of DNA with our simian "cousins" (up to 97 %) there is no real comparison in the developmental progress between the two branches. Apes look pretty much the way they have for a million years, and live their lives in very nearly the same way now as then; homo sapiens, on the other hand are geometrically changed in their appearance and in their capabilities over those million years. There can be a valid argument that people are not all that improved from our *Neanderthal* or *homo erectus* ancestors: sure, we can drive cars and they could not, and we can microwave our lunch at work, which they could not do. But, are we happier or more at peace with our environment? Are we improved in our dealings with each other, or with the "others" around us? How much better are we than the chimpanzees living in the wild protected from human "society?" We can move a lot faster in our planes and trains, but do we enjoy life and tranquility and leisure as much as our less-evolved ancestors and cousins? It is debatable. Still, objectively and materially, we are much improved over our earlier "models:" we live longer, stay healthier more often, we battle each other with words and ideas more than with rocks and sticks (most of the time), and we have largely mastered our environment rather than just adapting to it. This latter is probably an illusion, for we are frequently reminded of our essential puny powers by hurricanes, tsunamis', tornados, forest fires, earthquakes and floods. In spite of our weaknesses, we still are an **advanced civilization.**

The Way Science Classifies Us

Scientific Classification of Humans

Kingdom:	Animalia
Phylum:	Chordata
Class:	Mammalia
Order:	Primates
Suborder:	Haplorrhini
Infraorder:	Simiiformes
Parvorder:	Catarrhini
Superfamily:	Hominoidea
Family:	Hominidae
Genus:	Homo
Species:	H. sapiens

Since science has the privilege of naming the categories of living things on Earth, and traditionally has created descriptive names in Latin, it seems appropriate to review the basic lexicon scientists use to classify our section of nature and to define the words used in discussion evolution. Attention should be paid to the many similarities of these official scientific names—often only one letter distinguishes one category from another (for example: ***Hominidae, hominid, hominin, and hominine.***) Science majors will probably already know these categories, but many religious Believers may not be as familiar. If interested, many on-line sites (such as Wikipedia or Google) can provide extensive information. Humans are thus classified by science as ***Animalia-Mammalia -Primate- Hominidae-Homo Sapiens***. Quite an interesting family to which we belong. The Swedish botanist Carl Linnaeus (1707-1778) ushered in a new era of taxonomy which was very elegant and logical, replacing numerous earlier attempts to classify all living and non-living things. Changes still are occurring in this field, though the Linnaean system is still the solid foundation on which science continues to build classifications. Binomial nomenclature is used to name an organism, with the first word, beginning with a capital, is the *genus* of the organism and the second word, beginning with a lower-case letter, is the *species* of the organism. The name must be in italics and in Latin, which was the major language of arts and sciences in the 18th century. The scientific name is often abbreviated in scientific writings, where the genus is shortened to only its first letter followed by a period. In our example on the prior page, Homo habilis would be shortened to H. habilis. Our *Kingdom*, Animalia, includes thousands of types of animals, all of which share, at some time during their lives, a hollow nerve chord and a notochord, a flexible rod between the nerve cord and the digestive track. Thousands of animals have the beginning components of spinal cords and so are all part of the same *Phylum* chordata with us.

What Do Ancient Footprints and Hand Prints Tell Us?

Ancient human handprints

Seeing well preserved human footprints from hundreds of thousands of years ago had a much greater emotional impact on this writer than the dozens of prehistoric skulls and bones observed at the Natural History Museum in Washington DC. Looking at hand prints from a dozen or more of our extroverted relatives from forty or sixty centuries past makes it all seem **so real**. These hominids, of whatever species, were **people:** living, struggling, giggling people leaving their mark on the world like a group of teenagers of our own times. In some ways, viewing these artifacts is akin to finding a tree on our old homestead, the tree where we carved our name, maybe even with a sweetheart's name in a crude heart. Seeing again what we once created floods our memories and our heartstrings, because these are our marks, proof of our existence. It is hoped that readers of this chapter will be moved in a similar way with the realization that fossils and tools and broken pieces of pottery are proof that somebody, some real, conscious person was here, lived a full life, had joys and sorrows, and eventually died—all so long ago that we cannot wrap our minds around all this. *Neanderthals* were people; *homo erectus* individuals were people: *Homo habilis* men and women were people. These species and those even more primitive may not have been able to do all that today's humans can do; we are not sure when speech developed, or when exactly those ancient ones could build and control fire; it is unclear how far back in our family tree we have to go to find any type of religious activities. But whatever deficits they may have had, these were humans in the scientific sense. (We will address the scientific requisites and markers for the "human label" later in this chapter.)

Before the discovery of the Laetoli footprints in Tanzania (pictured at the beginning of this chapter) there was much debate as to which developed first in the human evolutionary time line: a larger brain or bipedalism (habitually walking upright on two feet). The discovery of these footprints settled the issue, proving that the Laetoli hominids were fully bipedal long before the evolution of the modern human brain, and were bipedal close to a million years before the earliest known stone tools were made. Some analysts have noted in their assessment that the middle trail bears "telltale signs that suggest whoever left the prints was burdened on one side. We can easily imagine that a female was carrying an infant on her hip, and that she and her toddler and male companion were a primitive family traveling together, perhaps in search of shelter or food. This cannot be proven, of course, but we know there are prints from one adult male, one adult female and a child, with foot prints which seem exactly like our own today.

What may be the earliest known footprints of our own species (Homo) have been found on the slope of Roccamonfina volcano in Italy, called Devil's Trail by local Italians. The three sets of footprints and a hand print surviving in hardened volcanic ash were made about 325,000 years ago presumably by early archaic humans, likely *Homo heidelbergensis*. *H. heidelbergensis* are believed to be hominid predecessors of the *Homo neanderthalenis* species in Europe, and probably co-existed with other early human groups for thousands of years. These early humans were hunter-gatherers, and they worked together in coordinated groups. Their several tools were fashioned from stone and wood but they were effective hunters. They were "big game hunters" literally, for male *heidelbergensis* were tall and strong, reaching 5 feet 9 inches and weighing an average of 150 pounds. They probably we able to kill an occasional mammoth, deer and other such prey. They likely also scavenged some leftovers from victims of wolves and big cats. The footprints demonstrate that these hominids habitually walked upright, not the alternating knuckle walk of apes and chimpanzees. The feet do not have the extended grasping big toe like apes, so useful in climbing, and so it appears they had permanently left the trees for upright travel on the ground. The arch of the foot revealed in these preserved tracks show evidence that these early hominids had arched feet (flexible sole of the foot) typical of modern humans. The toe patterns reveal an opposable big. toe so useful in climbing, but absent in modern humans. It appears that these bipedal walkers still were tree climbers, perhaps nesting in the safer trees at night, walking on the ground in daytime. These ancient foot prints are very much like those of modern humans, but significantly different from chimps and apes and other non-bipeds then and now. These hominids seem to have moved in a leisurely stroll judging by the length of their stride, approximating our own casual walking pace. However, we know they could run: another set of hominid prints preserved in Australia from the distant past shows a very long stride, believed by scientists to show a male running as fast as a modern Olympic sprinter (possibly running for his life.)

The footprints themselves were an unlikely discovery because all the conditions of the environment had to be favorable to preservation. These footprints were made in ancient mud which was then covered by silt from a neighboring river. This preserved them for millennia until very recently when the rock was eroded clear by the tide. Other sets of footprints found were serendipitously covered by ash or lava from a nearby volcano. Under normal conditions footprints in sand or mud disappear with a heavy rain, so finding any ancient footprints is a God-send for archaeologists and paleontologists who use modern technology to photograph, scan with lasers, map and chart them at their natural site. The surroundings often enable these scientists to date the fragile artifacts by materials found near the fossil record. The level of terrain or depth of the "dig" can help establish how long ago such footprints were created; bones and other artifacts found at a site can be dated to a probably range of a few hundred years by carbon testing and other proven laboratory methods which have been invented in the last hundred years.

Our Family Album

Many people enjoy an occasion perusal of old photographs which have been preserved for many decades, with black and white pictures of Grandpa Harper, who lived in Missouri until age 1, and other faded photos of forgotten cousins and aunts. We try to imagine what life was like for them, dressed in those furry long dresses and flowered bonnets; in the background is a small, humble house, and we are told by our older relatives that these people, our ancestors, were "pioneers," settlers on homesteads they carved out of the wilderness. Photos of family members we actually saw in our childhood bring back some wispy memories, some forgotten events or conversation, and can even relive a forty-year-old smell recalled as fresh as today. We know we are connected to the long-ago people, that somehow, they "produced" us and our immediate family members, that metaphorically, their blood flows in our veins...we are "family."

We don't have photographs of our older ancestors—-the Neanderthals, the early *Homo sapiens*, the *Homo erectus*, the *homo habilis* or the *Australopithecus afarensis*. But thanks to a century of archaeological and paleontological work we have hundreds of skulls and fossilized examples of virtually every type of human. We have nearly complete skeletons of some species, and partial skeletons of others, and in some cases, only have a partial skull or a pelvic bone. Using the forensic technology developed by law enforcement agencies, we can make those empty skulls and those bare bones "come alive" in museum displays such as the Smithsonian's Natural History Museum. Just as FBI experts can cover a murder victim's skull with clay and plaster, and with a little paint and imagination, produce a realistic human face that can be recognized and identified. The "Story of Mankind" display at the Smithsonian has life-sized models of a dozen or more of our ancient ancestors, hauntingly lifelike in an appropriate environmental setting.

These models of our distant relatives are not flattering nor handsome, and seeing them "in person" can be startling for a first-time observer. Those Smithsonian images are copyrighted by the artist who created them, and expensive, so we present here reconstructions by the author using imagination and reviewing hundreds of other artists' attempt to reconstruct primitive hominids. We can't be sure, but the Smithsonian reconstructions are probably very close to a real portrayal, for every feature has been researched and cross-verified by the experts who dug up the bones. The author's drawings are not so scientifically accurate, but the eyes of all five species are the same, portraying the "humanness" or personhood, while changing the externals such as brows, noses, facial hair, etc. So, now let's meet your very ancient ancestors from nearly a million years ago, as portrayed by several paleontologist/artists who have created life-sized models of many species, a few shown here.

Homo Habilis ("handy man") lived in Eastern and Southern Africa as long ago as 2.4 million years, scientists tell us, and probably became extinct some 1.6 million years ago. This species is considered one of the earliest members of the genus Homo, a classification in which most experts place modern humans, *Homo sapiens,* as well as several other species of extinct early humans, including *H. erectus, H. heidelbergensis, H. neanderthalensis,* and an early form of Homo sapiens called Cro-Magnon. *Homo habilis,* our ancient ancestor had a larger brain case, a smaller face and smaller teeth than the earlier hominid species such as *Homo australopithecus* and *Australopithecus africanus,* and other species considered by experts as anatomically closer to apes than to modern humans, sometimes given labels such as "archaic" or "proto-human" species. *Homo habilis* was given the "handy man" label (Latin: *habilis*) in the belief that this species was the first stone tool-maker; we now know that guess was wrong, for tool making has now been found in several older species. *Habilis* tools did became much more advanced than those achieved by the earlier species, including highly skilled "flaking" techniques to produce very sharp cutting tools and weapons.

H. habilis was short (from 3.5 to 4.5 feet), weighed about 70 pounds, and had disproportionately long arms compared to modern humans; however. Their smaller face was more human-like, less protruding than *australopithecines* from which the species is thought to have descended. *H. habilis* had a cranial capacity slightly less than half of the size of modern human, but his brain was still much larger than the earlier proto-human, and larger than the brains of modern apes and chimpanzees. The "handy man" had very human-like feet and hands that suggest an ability to manipulate small objects and tools routinely and skillfully; we have some evidence that they sometimes built simple, temporary shelters.

They were likely scavengers rather than genuine "hunter-gatherers" based on finding few large animal bones in their archaeological sites. They likely worked in groups of a dozen or so, it is believed, and there were probably more nomadic rather than having settled or permanent living sites. They probably could not make or control fire, but likely used naturally occurring fires caused by lightening to begin cooking meat (They probably learned about cooking from the scavenged animal parts that had been burned by a forest fire.) It is a tribute to their courage if they intentionally approached a natural fire and carried a burning limb back to their camp, for they were undoubtedly afraid of fire as animals are. Their teeth were suited for a variety of food, including vegetation, fruit, nuts and small animals.

Homo habilis was the first species whose skulls exhibit an enlarged Broca's and Wernicke's brain formations, two features now associated with speech and reason. However, their voice box was not large and not positioned for vocalization like we are, so if they spoke at all it would have most likely been simple sounds and calls such as is exhibited in modern apes and chimpanzees. Though they may not have had an actual language with a vocabulary and syntax, they certainly could communicate with gestures, grunts and other signs, for they worked and hunted together, a sure sign of some form of communication.

This first of our anatomically "look-alike" ancestors are considered "successful" since it survived about a million years, compared to

Homo sapiens' record of about 400,000 years, so far. They were clearly coexistent with several less successful species who went extinct, but since we don't yet have viable DNA samples, we don't know whether there was any inter-species contact or interbreeding. Genetic material may be found eventually and we may find some *habilis* in our genome.

Homo Erectus ("upright man") is usually regarded as the first of the Homo genus to have more than a passing resemblance to modern humans and are the oldest species whose body proportions closely match modern humans, with relatively elongated legs and shorter arms as compared to the size of the torso. These modern features are considered adaptations to a life lived on the ground, indicating the loss of earlier tree-climbing skills, and lending them the "upright" label.  With their improved anatomy they could walk and probably run for great distances. They were relatively big, on average, from 4.5 feet up to 6 feet, and they weighed up to 150 pounds. Their brain was significantly larger than their contemporaries or the earlier species, but still about 25 percent smaller than ours, on average.

Early *Homo erectus* first appeared in East Africa around two million years ago. *Erectus* is generally considered to have been the first species to have expanded beyond Africa, spreading over two or more continents. By 1.8 million years ago, the species had migrated to modern-day Georgia, at the border between Eastern Europe and Western Asia; it is not certain whether they reached eastern Europe. Firm evidence has been found that shows *H. erectus* inhabited a large cave in Zhoukoudian, China, leaving human remains, ancient hearths, charcoal, charred (cooked) animal bones, and lots of seeds (probably part of their diet). *H. erectus* was the first to use controlled fire to cook and the first to make hand axes with shaped stone and wood handles. At two other sites we have evidence that *H. erectus* controlled fire by 1.5 million years ago, able to start fires with flint, and use it for cooking, warmth and protection from animals. Larger gender difference in size indicates male domination and influences the social structure of the species. Most of the recovered *erectus* fossils show a relatively small size difference between males and females, and thus, suggesting a more egalitarian relationship in mating partners and a more favorable environment for care taking of the young. Archaeologists have found evidence on fossil bones that children and the frail elderly of the *H. erectus* group were kept alive, even when injured. This, and evidence of careful and ritualistic burial of children and the elderly suggests the budding of a caring and protective "society" which has common values beyond survival. In such small steps, Humanity advances.

By 143,000 years ago this amazing ancient ancestor went extinct, but had survived longer than any other human species, as much as nine times as long as our own Homo sapiens species has been around. That is a notable achievement, reflecting the great advancements they made toward becoming fully human: we owe them our admiration and gratitude.

Homo Heidelbergensis lived in Africa, Europe and Asia 700,000 years ago, and probably went extinct about 200,000 years ago. Their name comes from the German pit where their first fossil record was found. This early human species still had a large brow ridge we know from the many skulls found, but it had a larger brain and a flatter face and wider nose than other early proto-human species such as *Australopithecus afarensis* and *Homo habilis*. Heidelbergensis was the first human species to live in colder climates, and their short, wide body likely was an adaptation to help conserve heat, and their wider nostrils were helpful in warming the frigid air of the north. Males averaged 5 ft 9 inches and weighted about 136 pounds; females stood about 5 ft 2 inches and weighed about 112 lbs. These ancient ancestors controlled and used fire, and many of their campsites have been excavated with animal and human bones and skulls in abundance. This species was the first to build actual shelters, simple dwellings of wood and rock. They were the first to make and use wooden spears, and with that new weapon they were the first early humans to routinely hunt large animals. They likely lived as "hunter-gatherers" whose diet included both fruit, vegetables and meat. Increased access to meat protein is what scientists believe helped them develop bigger and better brains, and the stamina to live and prosper in such wide-ranging environments.

We do not know if Homo heidelbergensis had language, and if so, what kind. They did not leave any images or marking that would indicate communication skills. We know they had the basic brain structures that are needed (Broca's and Wernicke's areas) and their voice box was lower and large enough for vocalizing. It is not likely that they had a formal language with a large vocabulary and syntax rules, but there can be no doubt that they found ways to communicate effectively in order to achieve coordinated activities and surviving so long on the way to being fully human, to gradually becoming more like us.

Homo Neanderthalenis—commonly called Neanderthals ("th" is silent) is an extinct species of human with the closest biological relationship to modern humans. Their DNA is just 0.12 % different from modern humans, geneticists found, and up to 4% of modern human DNA is directly from our *Homo neanderthal* ancestors (excepting African populations).

The Neanderthal are believed to have existed from about 600,000 ago, and survived to 30,000 years ago or possibly a bit later. Neanderthals lived throughout Europe and southwest to Central Asia. Archaeological sites for this species have been found in Belgium, Croatia, France, Italy, Hungary, Israel, Czech Republic, Crimea, Uzbekistan, Iraq, Greece, Netherlands, and Siberia. Neanderthals had most of the physical features of modern humans, and likely would fit in with the crowd in a modern city. *(An American insurance company used actors made up like Neanderthals and wearing modern clothes, with the slogan "**Even A Caveman Can Understand This**".)* Sorry for the insult, Cousins. You deserve more respect.

Neanderthals made and used a diverse set of sophisticated tools for hunting and butchering, tools also used for preparing animal skins for clothing. They used controlled fire, lived in shelters, made and wore simple clothing, and were skilled hunters of large animals, such as deer and bison. Their varied diet also included native vegetation and fruits as well as meat. We believe they wore ornamental objects such as shells with some symbolic meaning attached to them, and probably decorated their fair skin with colored "paint" they created from plants and minerals. Though it is still disputed, some of the cave paintings in Europe, originally attributed to *Homo sapiens*, are very likely actually the work of *Neanderthals*. These disputed paintings are deeper in caves than the others, and though they are not as well drawn or sophisticated as the amazing art done by *Homo sapiens* on other cave walls in France, Spain and Germany, they are still easily recognized drawings of animals and objects. We don't know for certain that they had language, though the large size and complex nature of their brains and the presence of the Broca's and Wernicke's brain features make it possible. They had human like voice box structures and one of the critical gene factors associated with speech is in their genome. It is highly likely that they spoke and communicated successfully since so many of their survival strategies and techniques required teamwork, cooperation and coordination. They left no written records so far as we know but their art work indicates the capacity for symbolic thought, a critical part of language.

Though they likely clustered with others in a clan or small group, they also formed and maintained nuclear families and took care of their children for a much longer childhood than apes or chimpanzees do today. Male and female roles were very likely established, with males as the hunter/gatherer and the females as the care-takers of the children and disabled. Discoveries of elderly or deformed Neanderthal skeletons suggest that they took care of their sick and those who could not care for themselves. Skeletal analysis shows that some serious injuries had been survived, and that the victim had lived years longer with help from others. Though sometimes still disputed, there is an abundance of evidence that they intentionally buried their dead with offerings such as tools, colorful stones and maybe even flowers. There is some indication that they placed "grave markers" at the site, maybe a simple pile of rocks to remember the dead, and also to keep animals from digging up the body of the deceased. Other, earlier species also seemed to bury their dead at least some of the time, but the Neanderthals appear to have ritualized and routinized this burial practice. Anthropologists and paleontologists consider this practice of caring for the dead as evidence that these ancient humans had some kind of belief in "life after death," perhaps an early stage of developing a primitive religion.

Scientific study indicates that the Neanderthal brain was similar to the modern human brain of infants, but by adulthood, *Neanderthal* brains became slightly larger, on average, than ours. They were almost certainly physically stronger than modern humans, with a large, robust, stocky body size, with the males averaging 5 ft 5 inches and weighing 143 pounds, and females standing 5 ft 1 inch in height and weighing in at 119 pounds average.

We know that *Neandertals* and *Homo sapiens* were living at the same time in Europe for a thousand years or more, and that they occasionally interbred and produced "hybrid" children who survived to adulthood. Scientists say a substantial percent of *Neanderthal* DNA has survived in modern humans, most notably seen in the skin, hair and diseases of modern people. Modern genetics has now shown that all extant human groups (excepting Africans) have up to 4 % neanderthal genes in their genome. DNA experts have suggested that the gene for red hair is a gift of the *Neanderthals* to the world, and that blue eyes may also be part of our inheritance from our "most nearly human" relative. *Neanderthals* might not fare well in an American beauty pageant, but most of us have a few relatives at our family reunions who are a bit hard to look at. Some of us might even lose a beauty contest to some "above average" *neanderthal* individual; we know for certain that we would lose to them in a wrestling match.

Neanderthals lived before and during the last great **ice age** in some of the most challenging and unforgiving environments ever inhabited by humans. Their survival during tens of thousands of years of the last glaciation is a remarkable testament to human adaptation.

Some recent archeological evidence suggests Neanderthal may have lived as late as 28,000 years ago in Gibraltar before going extinct. We don't know what brought this admirable species to an end, but two major theories seem plausible: they may have been exterminated by the more numerous *Homo sapiens* who came to their lands with more lethal weapons such as bow and arrow; or they may have been gradually absorbed into the *Homo sapiens* gene pool through interbreeding. A third possible explanation is a combination of those two: many were killed in battle or by new diseases brought by the homo sapiens, and many more were incorporated into the stronger *Homo sapiens* culture. When a population drops below a certain threshold of healthy adults (perhaps a thousand), extinction is inevitable. It is possible that a final clan of ten or fifteen individuals may have been the last survivors, and then one day it came down to a single lonely person in the cave, the **Last of the Neanderthals.**

Cro-Magnon is not a species name the way *Homo erectus* is, in modern scientific classifications, but because their discovery was before many other species, and because they are not precisely descendants of Neanderthal of Homo sapiens, they often get treated as a separate species. The distinctions between Cro-Magnon and later Homo sapiens are somewhat vague and subject to dispute. Archaeologists recognized early on that the new fossils were not *neanderthalenis*, and first thought they were entirely different from the more advanced *Homo sapiens*. After further study of additional fossils and professional arguments among themselves, they changed their minds, as good scientists do. Now the name "Cro-Magnon" is seldom used by scientists, who usually opt instead for "Anatomically Modern Humans." people who lived in our world at the end of the last ice age (ca. 40,000-10,000 years ago). Many scientists now consider Cro-Magnon to be a very closely related branch of *Homo sapiens*, probably direct ancestors though classifications are fluid in science because new discoveries are always coming along. We are profiling Cro-Magnon here separately from *Homo sapiens* because some distinctive features and achievements are associated with them that seem to be from a slightly earlier stage of the modern species, *Homo sapiens*. Because the *neanderthal*, Cro-Magnons and *Homo sapiens* shared the same time and space for about 10,000 years, it seems likely that they learned from each other and evolved by **cultural change** more than through the **genetic change** of evolution's "natural selection" mechanism.

Cro-Magnons were anatomically modern (physically like us), straight limbed and tall compared to their contemporaries, the Neanderthals. They were, on average, 5'5" to 5'7" inches tall and weighed about 140-150 pounds. They had a more robust, athletic physique than modern *homo sapiens*, a useful adaptation for survival in the sometimes-harsh winter weather. The Cro-Magnons had fairly rounded skulls, with wide faces, robust mandibles, blunted chins and narrow noses, considerably different in appearance from the Neanderthals they encountered. Their fossil skulls show a distinctive rectangular eye socket, which scientists find similar to the modern Ainu people who are indigenous to Japan. The Ainu are probably the original occupants of Japan, but they are racially and culturally different from modern Japanese and have successfully resisted assimilation into Japanese society. This distinctive facial feature has led some scientists to conclude there is a direct biological connection between Cro-Magnons and the Ainu: many also see the same direct lineage reflected in Native Americans who have this same feature. It is believed the Native Americans migrated from Asia across to Alaska during one of the Ice Ages as early as 15,000 years ago. There does seem to be a visible similarity between the three widely separated groups suggesting some common ancestry. Theoretically, Cro-Magnons may have crossed from Asia to Japan in some way, creating genetic pools in China and Japan; their Chinese relatives then migrated to the New World with the same genetic signature. It is speculation, but very interesting speculation.

The Cro-Magnons had the voice apparatus of modern humans and they undoubtedly could speak. Their brain capacity was about 1600 cc, a bit larger than the average European or American. Their long leg bones are slightly different from the Neanderthal, leading some to speculate that they were transitioning from long distance hunting and gathering to a more settled lifestyle, even possibly the beginnings of agriculture. No fossil evidence has yet been found to support this, and development of agriculture has traditionally been dated much later, @10,000 B.C. The flint tools the Cro-Magnon created are associated with a technology credited to the Aurignacian culture which perfected the flint spears and knives with thin, very sharp edges, a difficult technique that eluded many species. They also excelled in working skillfully with bones and antlers for effective tools. Evidence has been found indicating the Cro-Magnons spun, dyed, and knotted flax fibers for weaving baskets, sewing clothes, and fastening flint blades to wooden spears. They pierced bones, shells and animal teeth to make body ornaments, and created some of the famous cave paintings in Europe. By far one of their most astonishing capabilities is shown many artifacts such as the **Venus of Willendorf,** a beautiful carving depicting a graphic 11.1-centimeter-tall female figure. This "Venus" was created about 30,000 B.C. Anthropologists believed it to be a totem for entreating fertility and fecundity; other such figurines have been found in ancient sites in many parts of the earth, and probably can be seen as an early religious symbol, perhaps a belief in some form of deity. Some are primitive carvings, but some, such as this Venus of Willendorf, have intricate fine detail (even appearing to have braided hair). Obviously, the large mammary glands and the broad hips of these many "Venus figures" indicate that child birth and child rearing were valued highly by the Cro-Magnons. Slim figures have not always been the gold standard for human beauty, especially in ancient times. Primitive men apparently thought "plump" is beautiful and healthy.

Like some other early humans, the Cro-Magnons were primarily "big game" hunters utilizing group strategy to kill mammoth, bears, horses and reindeer. They hunted with spears and javelins, and may have had "spear throwers" such as modem Aborigines use which multiply the power and distance of the spear. This new technology was a real advantage in approaching dangerous big animals, where close encounters are not advisable. It is possible, but not certain, that the Cro-Magnon may have followed the herds of big animals in migration, making semi-permanent hunting camps rather than establishing permanent settlements. Some remains of huts made from mammoth bones, tree limbs and animal skins have been found, supporting the idea of a nomadic life style. Some other Cro-Magnon sites show more sturdy dwelling structures of stone, wood and animal hides, possibly a settlement. Cro-Magnon, *neanderthalensis*, *Homo sapiens* and other human ancestors shared our planet for several thousand years and in numerous locations. As the result of new genetic studies, we know that another, newly discovered early Asian human currently called "Denisovan" coexisted with Cro-Magnon, *Homo sapiens* and *Homo neanderthalensis*, and possibly all these species met and interbred to some degree. Genetically, part of all of these may live on in our own human genome. We know very little for now about the Denisovans, a prospective new species found in Siberia, identified on the basis of very few bones or artifacts, but enough to know they were early human whose place on the family tree is still being research. Because they are possibly another part of our family, we will briefly sketch what science can tell us about them.

The Denisovans or Denisovan hominids is an extinct species or subspecies of archaic humans in the genus Homo, found only recently but apparently are a significant species. Its taxonomic status is still unsettled, and it currently has been given temporary tentative species or subspecies names: *Homo denisova, Homo altaiensis, Homo sapiens denisova*, or possibly even some variation of *Homo sapiens*. The sparse remains of one or more Denisovan individuals were found in 2010 in a cave in Siberia, near China, a cave that has also been inhabited by Neanderthals and modern humans. Since that first discovery a few years ago, DNA from the bone fragments have been sampled and the species is clearly a new and different type. Other archaeological sites in Europe and Africa are being actively explored in hopes of supplementing the few fragments extracted, so new information about the Denisovans will be published by the time this book is read. Their DNA genetic data matches much of modern human genes, and is associated with dark skin, brown hair and brown eyes, according to genetic scientists. From DNA from a finger and a few teeth, scientists have found their genetic imprint from Siberia to Southeast Asia, with 3-5 % of the DNA of Melanesians, Aboriginal Australians and Papua New Guineans is derived from Denisovans. These ancient ancestors "got around" a lot, it appears, and may even have traversed some part of the Pacific Ocean 80,000 years ago, as indicated by their genetic footprints. Denisovans appear to have become extinct about 40,000 years ago. Not much else is known about their lives, their achievements, their social structure or their place in our family tree. There may be other such ancestors yet to be discovered.

Homo Sapiens ("wise man"). We modern humans, *Homo sapiens*, are but a single twig on a branch of the evolutionary tree that reaches back some seven million years, to when we split from our closest living relatives, the chimpanzees and bonobos. The larger branch of which we are a part, the genus Homo, reaches back perhaps two million years, with several now extinct species that preceded us, the *H. sapiens*. Tracing a direct line of our ancestry back along this branch is difficult because the fossil record is a patchy mosaic of incomplete skeletons, scattered bones and partial skulls. Very few early humans died at the right time and place for their remains to be preserved. Entire species probably became extinct without leaving a single toe bone for us to dig up in the dozens of places we are now looking. Of all the archaic or proto-human species which have been discovered, we are not quite sure yet which ones may be ancient cousins, and which might be our great, great, great, great, great grandparents. We know they were our relatives, but just don't yet know everyone's place in our family tree.

The fossil record between two and three million years ago, when our oldest Homo ancestors emerged, is particularly sparse, archaeologists tell us, making this one of the least understood parts of human evolution. Our earliest Homo ancestors lived in Africa, and likely descended from *Australopithecus afarensis*, best known for the famous "Lucy" fossil found in Ethiopia in 1974. Lucy is a 3.2-million-year-old, nearly complete female fossil whose discovery was heralded in newspapers and magazines around the world. Pictures of her reconstructed face and torso made her as famous for a while as any movie star. It was unbelievable that this small human-like creature lived over three million years ago. Supposedly this famous old lady was named "Lucy" by the archaeologists who found her because the Beatles song, "Lucy in the Sky with Diamonds" was playing on the camp radio when she was found.

We have covered several of these early human species above, and so we turn now to ourselves: human beings of the species *Homo sapiens*. Sadly, we are the only ones left. Most of the other hominid species that existed on the earth became extinct during the many climactic changes, ice ages, droughts and volcanic eruptions, but *Homo sapiens* managed to survive (perhaps why the species name "wise man" was given). Luck may have played a part in our survival, or perhaps divine assistance; most scientists would probably take the same position as this book: **it was actually the brain** that evolved and developed in our species that made the difference, and makes the difference now. Modern humans have very large brains, which vary in size from population to population and between males and females, but the average size is approximately 1400 cubic centimeters. Housing this bigger brain involved the reorganization of the skull into what is thought of as "modern" — a thin-walled, high vaulted skull with a flat and near vertical forehead. Modern human faces show much less of the heavy brow ridges and prognathism (protruding upper jaw or lower jaw, giving a "monkey face") found in many other early humans. Our jaws are also less prominent and not as strong as our earlier ancestors, with smaller teeth, the effect of evolution adjusting us to our softer, more varied modern diet.

During a time of dramatic climate change some 300,000 years ago, *Homo sapiens* evolved in Africa. Like other early humans which were living at this time, they gathered and hunted food, and evolved behaviors that helped them respond to the challenges of survival in unstable environments. Scientists sometimes use the term "anatomically modern *Homo sapiens*" to refer to members of our own species who lived during prehistoric times. Anatomically, modern humans can generally be characterized by the lighter build of their skeletons and taller stature compared to earlier humans. The name *Homo sapiens* was applied in 1758 by the father of modern biological classification, Carolus Linnaeus. It had long been known that human beings physically resemble the primates more closely than any other known living organisms, but at the time it was a daring act to classify human beings within the same framework used for the rest of nature. Linnaeus, who was concerned exclusively with similarities in bodily structure, faced only the problem of distinguishing *H. sapiens* from apes (gorillas, chimpanzees, orangutans, and gibbons), which differ from humans in numerous bodily as well as cognitive features. (Charles Darwin's landmark book on evolution, *On the Origin of Species*, would not come until 101 years later.) Since Linnaeus's time, a large fossil record has been discovered, providing a much more complicated cast of characters to classify. This record contains numerous extinct species that are much more closely related to humans than to today's apes and that were presumably more similar to *H. sapiens* behaviorally as well. Following the ancestors of modern human beings into the distant past raises the question of what is meant by the word human. *H. sapiens* is human by definition, whereas apes are not. But what of the extinct members of the human tribe who were clearly not *H. sapiens* but were nonetheless very much like them? There is no definitive answer to this question. Although human evolution might be said to involve all those species which are more closely related to *H. sapiens* than to apes, the adjective human is usually applied only to *H. sapiens* and other members of the genus Homo (e.g., H. erectus, H. habilis). Behaviorally, only *H. sapiens* can be said to be "fully human," but even the definition of *H. sapiens* is a matter of active, long-standing debate. **Chapter 15, Being Fully Human** has a lengthy discussion of this very question.

Some paleoanthropologists want to extend the span of this species far, far back into time to include many anatomically distinctive fossils, and naming and assigning classification to newly discovered fossils is similar to a competitive sport. A majority of paleoanthropologists, wishing to unify the study of hominids into line with that of other mammals, prefer to assign to *H. sapiens* only those fossil forms that fall within the anatomic spectrum of the species as it exists today. In this narrow sense, *H. sapiens* is very recent, having originated in Africa more than 315,000 years ago. Since we are members of the *Homo sapiens* family under discussion, it is not necessary to describe in great detail what milestones we passed, what lifestyles and social structures we developed, or many of the other interesting details described for *H. erectus, H. habilis*, etc. (For those interested in the details a Timeline covering 200,000 years or more is easily available on the Internet by searching for "human evolution" or "human ancestors" or "hominid species."

Our last species competitor died out about 28,000 to 30,000 years ago, and we have access to the beginnings of written history some 8,000 years ago: so, we probably know a great deal about how *H. sapiens* progressed over that 20,000 or so years. Writing probably developed much earlier in human history than written records show, for we know that numbers and counting preceded alphabets, with evidence of numerical communication dating back to 8000 B.C. We even have some very old bones and rocks which have notches or marks that appear to be an early form of "book keeping," some of our Stone Age relatives keeping track of something 20,000 years ago. We know that some form of writing developed independently at least five times in human history in Mesopotamia, Egypt, the Indus valley, China and Meso-America. We pick up our own written story around 3500 B.C., our ancient narrative kept in wedge shaped cuneiform marks on wet clay tablets in Sumner and Babylon (now Iraq), and in the picturesque hieroglyphics of Egypt.

We have spread over all the earth (so far, only camping in Antarctica) and developed hundreds of different ways of living our lives. We have some *Homo sapiens* who fly space ships, and we have some *Homo sapiens* who are still hunter-gathers like our *Homo erectus* and *Homo habilis* ancestors from over 100,000 years ago. We speak perhaps 6000 languages, and we practice a hundred religions, and we kill each other, and we can and do marry and have beautiful children who combine two or more racial types. We perhaps are only a little arrogant imagining we have conquered Earth, for we are *Homo sapiens*, "Masters of the Universe." Human evolution, it appears, has consistently been a process of trial and error. Historically, we have considered this process as, more or less, a direct series of ongoing improvements within a single line of heritage, species after species of Homo, progress which eventually culminated in the burnished "perfection" of *H. sapiens*. As flattering to the modern human ego as this picture may be, evidently it is quite wrong. Instead, human evolution throughout its long history seems to have been a matter of experimentation, with new species being constantly spawned and thrown into the ecological arena to compete and, more often than not, become extinct. Viewed this way, *H. sapiens* is simply the last surviving twig on a vast and intricately branching bush, rather than the sole occupant of a summit that has been laboriously climbed and, by extension, somehow earned, somehow deserved.

This Is Us, We Are Family - The survivors: Homo sapiens

Chapter 8

THE BIRTH OF GOD

"Whatever you think God is, know he is more than that."
(IBN ATA ALLAH (SUFI SCHOLAR)

THE IDEA OF GOD IS ALMOST UNIVERSAL NOW, AND apparently has endured in the human mind since the dawn of consciousness. Some idea of divinity is found in every known culture and civilization of the historical past, and every society known today has some form of god or gods. The idea of God is different for everyone to some degree, and often is different for one person at various times. Our experience of the divine is deeply personal, often beyond our ability to describe with words. Our experience of the supernatural is often profoundly influential on how we live, what we believe and who we become. Ideas of God shape cultures and civilizations as well as individuals.

Varieties of Perspectives

We all know from experience that people observing the same object or scene can have very different views about what they see. The same is true of all our senses—we perceive external reality in widely diverse ways: a sound is identified by one listener as a gunshot, while another hears a car backfiring; a smell is clearly the odor of gasoline says one nose, while another nose is sure it is turpentine that is wafting in the air. Who is right? Who is wrong? We often disagree based on the same evidence. This is one reason "eye witness" testimony is viewed skeptically by law enforcement officers, for witnesses so often contradict each other. There are identifiable reasons why people have divergent perceptions, some related to preconceptions or prejudices held, and whatever the reason, it is a fact that our senses can be fooled. Optical illusions and professional illusionists mislead us all the time, and everyone remembers being deceived by our own eyes. "Seeing is believing" we like to say, but it is not always so. Though we humans are so much alike, we each perceive our own unique reality, which is why we have so many interesting arguments among ourselves. But sometimes it is not a simple question of "right" or "wrong" perceptions, for sometimes divergent views can both be right, or can both be wrong, as illustrated in the fable **The Blind Men of Indostan,** in this poetic version by *John Godfrey Saxe:*

It was six men of Indostan, to learning much inclined, who went to see the elephant (Though all of them were blind), that each by observation, might satisfy his mind.

The first approached the elephant, and, happening to fall, against his broad and sturdy side, at once began to bawl: 'God bless me! but the elephant, is nothing but a wall!

The second feeling of the tusk, cried: 'Ho! what have we here, so very round and smooth and sharp? To me tis mighty clear, this wonder of an elephant, is very like a spear!'

The third approached the animal, and, happening to take, the squirming trunk within his hands, 'I see,' quoth he, the elephant is very like a snake!'

The fourth reached out his eager hand, and felt about the knee: 'What most this wondrous beast is like, is mighty plain,' quoth he;
'Tis clear enough the elephant is very like a tree.'

The fifth, who chanced to touch the ear, Said; 'E'en the blindest man can tell what this resembles most; Deny the fact who can, This marvel of an elephant, is very like a fan!'

The sixth no sooner had begun, about the beast to grope, then, seizing on the swinging tail, that fell within his scope, 'I see,' quothe he, 'the elephant is very like a rope!'

And so, these men of Indostan, disputed loud and long, each in his own opinion, exceeding stiff and strong, Though each was partly in the right, and all were in the wrong!

So, oft in theologic wars, the disputants, I ween, tread on in utter ignorance of what each other mean, and prate about the elephant, not one of them has seen![45]

The Blind Men and the Elephant tale is significant for this book because it illustrates how God has been so misunderstood. Probably everyone has their own unique experience with deity, religion or some kind of "spiritual" feelings at some point in life. That personal contact with some supernatural phenomenon often seems real and complete, leading us to feel we have grasped and understand the whole elephant when we have only felt the elephant's trunk, or maybe the ear. Just as the six blind men each had very different views of what an "elephant" is like, so humans have always had divergent ideas about God or gods. The problem is not that there exist a lot of Gods, but that every person "sees" a **portion** of divinity rather than comprehending the **whole**. We argue here that there is only one God just as there was only one elephant, but like the Blind Men, we create our own "reality" from a sample because we have limitations in conceiving the fullness of God. As Paul said, "*Now we see but a dim reflection as in a mirror; then we shall see face to face. Now I know in part; then I shall know fully, even as I am fully known.*" (I Corinthians 13:12) This expression of religious short sightedness or incompleteness of revelation is not reflected in much of what theologians and ministers teach; more often the claim implied is that "This is the Truth" about a particular doctrine or system of theology. But Christians, like natural scientists, ought to recognize that we ought to reserve some mental space for "undecided" or "undiscovered." **We know in part, at least for now.**

We Humans Are Not "Fool Proof"

Everyone is fallible, and sensory perceptions can fool the sharpest mind. We all have a limited view of reality, and our brains conspire to fill in the pieces we cannot see from our vantage point. Our minds play tricks with us in all sorts of ways, from "photo shopped" pictures we wrongly believe to be authentic to the merchandising technique of placing expensive merchandise at eye level and making the package colors scream "Look at me." Magicians specialize in creating an illusion, leading us to focus on one place while the action is elsewhere. Political propaganda makes a deluge of semi-false claims against an opponent, and we are misled into thinking we know a great deal about the other candidate, while we actually know only slices and patches of the whole, molding our perception into a distorted and exaggerated conclusion. Talk show radio pundits accumulate millions of followers by appearing to be absolute certain, "right more than 97.6% of the time," gaining cult-like loyalty through shameless self-promotion and arrogance. People are impressed with people who "know all the answers" because we are brain-wired to look for answers, to make sense of our world.

Even regarding the Christian God, some people's experience points to a harsh "God of justice and holiness" while others see a kinder "God of mercy and love." The evolution of God is the evolution of our **understanding the whole** (so far as our brain is able to grasp). Once, long ago, we humans thought the Sun was a god to be placated; later we imagined a god who was like a cosmic King, a superior god ruling over many lesser gods. Whatever our view of God became in the past, we created myths, rituals and ceremonies to keep in his favor: these are our religions, a human institution designed to worship and satisfy our version of the divine. A multitude of possible gods leads to a lot of different religions.

Varieties of Religions

There exists an astounding variety of **religions** in the modern world, numbering in the thousands, all of them organized attempts to worship some vision of their deity. **Religion, as used here, is this human response to a god or gods, a structured or ritualistic way of pleasing (or appeasing) the divine power they now recognize.** Religions are group functions, binding people with similar beliefs and understandings about their view of their god or gods. A religion with only one adherent may be possible, but not much can be learned from that singularity. Though a lot can be learned by studying all the variety of religions, that is not the purpose of this work. **This is a study of God,** and the variety of god-types that can be explored is more limited and more manageable, while the varieties of religions is almost limitless. How did the idea of a supernatural divine Being or a non-material force come to the earliest self-conscious hominid ancestors of our species? How and why did those earliest ideas change and develop, and how did those changing ideas get passed on through the thousands of generations that have passed? Did God evolve like the alligator or the pine tree? Or did we evolve in mental capacity?

ANIMISM————->>————million years————->>————*JESUS/GOD*

The question this chapter seeks to answer is how did the human race move from the most primitive type of **animism** (attributing life and power to inanimate objects such as rivers, trees, lightening, the moon, mountains, clouds, etc.) through multiple stages identified by paleontologists to the present **Father-God of Jesus?** How did we advance from the earliest beliefs in the "tree spirit" or the "river spirit" who were regarded with fear and awe because they may be hostile, to the idea of a single, all-powerful Creator of everything who is also actively and lovingly engaged in a relationship with all mankind? How did we develop beyond the fear and superstition of ancient minds to reach the high mark of divinity—a God who is like a perfect father in His concern for every human, who wants only what is ultimately good for us, and wants us to grow to our fullest potential?

Can We Possibly Know?

It is acknowledged that trying to determine the ideas and beliefs of primitive humans is more difficult than learning about their religious practices and activities. Beliefs and thoughts don't leave fossils or other artifacts buried in the jungles of Africa or the caves of Europe. But there is good and increasing evidence from archaeology, anthropology, paleontology, and other earth sciences about how hominids such as *Homo habilis, Homo erectus, Australopithecines, Neanderthals, and Homo sapiens* lived, and some of the religious practices they followed. Using the findings from a century and a half of digging and analyzing, we can reasonably infer their understanding of the supernatural based on what they left behind. This is not direct evidence in the case of our most ancient ancestors, but, coupled with modern extensive study of isolated tribes living today in South America and Africa and South East Asia, hunter-gatherers still living in the Stone Age, we can formulate a credible picture of what human life was like 50,000 or more years ago. We can also theorize some stages of theological development in our species by observing our children in their normal development from birth through adolescence. As explained earlier, the stages of individual human development we can observe now seem to be a model or pattern which might apply to the development of our species. For example, at one stage of childhood, most children believe that the moon is following them or watching them, their toys can talk, and their teddy bears are alive. In children we call this imagination, and in the history of religions we call this belief "animism," about which more is discussed below.

There is widespread agreement among leading anthropologists, paleontologists and philosophers that the dawning of our consciousness—our self-awareness and our recognition that others also having thoughts, intentions and feelings—brought with it the awareness of **mortality**. Humans can anticipate their eventual death, but animals do not, so far as we know now. The dread of dying is a persistent specter in adult humans now and it was inevitably troubling to our early human predecessors. John Shelby Sprong, an Episcopal theologian observes: *"I admire our ancestors, whoever they were. I think the first self-conscious person must have shaken in his boots. Because as he becomes self-conscious, he's no longer part of nature. He sees himself against nature. He looks at the vastness of the universe and it looks hostile."*[46]

Consciousness and the Inner Life

The first ideas about God probably grew out of the dawn of consciousness in hominids, the ability of the developing brain cortex to recognize its own identity, and to realize that the others like him were also separate beings, and each had a mind like his with their own self-awareness. Self-awareness is not the totality of consciousness, but it is an essential marker of humanness, and it is made possible by the evolving hominid brain. (A more detailed discussion of Consciousness is found in **Chapter 15: Being Fully Human**, and the crucial place of brain development in experiencing God is in **Chapter 4: The Brain Game**)

Whenever that critical ability arrived, 100,000 or 150,000 or a million years ago, the first glimmering of ideas about God probably involved some vague, ethereal fear, a suspicion that "something" is "out there," real but unseen, something or someone whose intentions are unknown. Primates had these fears and vigilance long before their descendants attained self-awareness, knowing instinctively that danger lurked around them, potential danger behind every tree or bolder. But pre-conscious primates like apes and chimps do not look at such threats with superstition—they fear the saber tooth tiger or the cave bear for what they are—predators seeking to eat them. But with the proto-human's better brain came *imagination,* the new ability to fear things not visible. This may sound like paranoia, but it was a healthy response to a world and environment so often hostile. Tigers and bears were imagined to be intentionally stalking the prey because of hunger or instinct, but with thoughtful plotting, the early human believed: "Bear not just hunting for supper—Bear has picked me on purpose."

Having developed self-consciousness in themselves, they may have assumed that the rest of the world was equally self-conscious.

They began to believe that the rocks, mountains, rivers, sun, moon, trees, land animals, birds, fires and even mountains might be alive and conscious, perhaps each animated by a different "spirit." These spirit-inhabited elements prominent in their environment were viewed as potential enemies or friends, with unknown intentions. Again, Bishop Sprong: *"Those animating spirits might be benevolent or demonic, but in either case they were assumed to be personal, to have selfhood, to be in charge of their particular area of life, to be capable of responding to human need and to be in possession of supernatural power."*[47]

The First Hint of God: Animism

Fear of these unknown powers was the logical first response, which over time could have morphed into awe and then respect as they attempted to appease these unseen forces. We know that fear, awe, and respect are still stages in the development of religious ideas, as seen in modern children and in existing hunter-gatherer tribes that have been studied while uncontaminated by modern civilization. The experts such as anthropologists, paleontologists and ethnographers have labeled this most primitive concept of God or the first type of religion "**animism.**" (See below for further discussion of several existing isolated hunter-gather tribes, essentially still living in the Stone Age).

Animism is the belief that all things are "animated," and have a spirit or soul, including animals, rivers, trees, mountains, moon, wind and storms. "Anima" is the Latin word for "soul" or "spirit," animating or giving life to creatures and objects. The object or animal is regarded as being alive, having feelings, intentions, and usually, a voice. At one early stage of development most children believe in animism: they think the moon is watching them or following them; their teddy bears or other dolls are "alive" and tell them things, feel pain and loneliness, and have other human-like qualities. Anyone raising children or teaching toddlers know this stage and how real it is to the child. This animistic belief is usually gone by age five. (**Author's note**: This child development example is cited as another way in which normal human development stages are similar, possibly related, to theoretical stages in species development, a concept extensively discussed in **Chapter 15: Being Fully Human**)

Though most anthropologists identify *Animism* as the first religion in hunter-gatherer societies of the early Stone Age, some have observed that it **still** typically found in the isolated extant hunter-gatherer societies researchers have studied in remote jungles and polar regions of the world; animism is not completely extinct. The Greeks and Romans were not "animists" in the primitive sense, but some among them revered and worshiped inanimate objects (such as statues or idols) and special locations (such as a "sacred forest" or a religious shrine such as Delphi, the ancient sanctuary home of the legendary Oracle of Delphi). Most Greeks and Romans did not attribute soul or spirit to the inanimate objects or imagine them as having feelings, intention and personality.

Animism is a natural response to a very human need, the urge to find out "cause" in their environment, for lots of things happen we can observe, and there must be a reason, a "cause" or as scientists' term it, an **agent.** Young humans of today begin to think in causal terms by age two in most cases, quizzical about why the toy fell off the tray, or how did that stuffed rabbit disappear? The belief that everything has a cause is apparently part of our brain's "hard wiring" and it certainly was present in the ancient hominids who became our human ancestor. Primitive man observed something moving, or heard some noise, or smelled some odor—and the natural response is "What was THAT?" Long before science would answer most of those questions these very early humans concluded that "things" all around us are alive in some way, trees and rocks and rivers, and the moon and stars all had the power to make things happen. Just as the hominid knew that he could cause things to happen, he also believed that most of the things in the forests, rivers and mountains had such power to act harm or help him: they were *animated* or alive, he believed. With growing imaginations, the Stone Age people invented "spirits" and "ghosts" in a vast unseen world all around them. It did not take a lot of imagination to fear these unknown and unpredictable spirits of their environment; were they angry? Were they friendly? Who can know what the spirits want? Over time and improvement of **their** still-small brain, two important cognitive tools developed: **agent detection** and **theory of mind.**

Agent detection is a deeply imbedded cognitive process by which humans and animals decide whether to ignore, fight, flee, pursue, or engage when encountering an agent (this being anything the animal or person believes acts with intent). For humans, agents include living people and their spirits after death, along with spirits and gods in nature believed to have a will and powers that can help or harm us. When an agent is detected, theory of mind (the ability to attribute mental states such as beliefs, desires, and knowledge to oneself and others) immediately comes into play by inferring how the agent is likely to respond. A primitive human happens upon another human, a stranger suddenly appears in the woods. The two humans cautiously and carefully look for clues about the other's intent. "He has a rock in his hand" one thinks to himself, "That could be trouble." Both silently observe "body language" and the facial expressions. If they have evolved to having a "theory of mind" they will act on the assumption that the other person is thinking and feeling just like I am." A friendly looking smile on one face may reassure the other that no harm is intended. The fact that the other person has stood still probably shows that he is not aggressive, not looking for a fight. So, with mutual recognition of "mind" in the other, they can trust their instinct and make a friendly gesture—maybe raising a hand or waving; maybe dropping the rock and displaying the empty, non-threatening hands (the origin of the handshake?).

And so, for Stone Age people and even more ancient early humans, spirits caused everything that happened on earth or in imaginary spiritual realms. Spirits caused rain to fall, rivers to flow, sun to shine, fruit to grow, herds to migrate, and enemies to invade. People invented myths for explaining the minds of those spirits, who craved gifts, respect, obedience, and adulation just like people in authority. They prayed to the spirits to nurture, defend, and not harm them. They offered sacrifices because that's what powerful people, and hence what spirits desire. Steven Mithen, Professor of Archaeology at UK's University of Reading explains: "*Upper Paleolithic period hunters were living in a landscape full of symbolic meanings. For them there are not two worlds of persons (society) and things (nature), but just one world–saturated with personal powers and embracing both human beings, the animals and plants on which they depend, and the landscape in which they move.*"[48]

Primitive men almost certainly attributed human like qualities to the objects of nature and to animals in a full-fledged animism, and they developed rituals intended to please the "spirit" and avoid harmful consequences. Believing in such spirit inhabited objects naturally led to the idea of leaving a sacrificial animal or other gift for the "spirit" at the foot of a "sacred" mountain, on the banks of scary rivers, beneath that special tree or wherever they imagined the spirit would accept it. Those who had already developed some language likely "sang" and danced and chanted "prayers" to please or appease the troubled "spirit," even like we have seen in documentaries about African tribes. Modern scholars agree that "animism" was the most primitive religion, the clan or tribe revering/fearing invisible supernatural beings living in natural objects. Obviously, the identity and disposition of these spirit-possessed objects varied from tribe to tribe and from century to centuries, and stories or legends were developed to pass along these beliefs to children and grandchildren.

Many older readers may have grown up in homes where the elders passed along "superstitions" such as ***it's bad luck if a black cat crosses your path***, or ***break a mirror brings 7 years of bad luck***, or ***a bird coming down the chimney into the house means a death in the family***. Our grandparents probably really believed these aphorisms passed down from generations past, and doubters could not convince them otherwise. These are not specifically animism, though attributing bad luck to black cats or black birds is pretty close. All these reflect some suspicion that someone or something may be threatening harm if we are not careful. Early "spirit" fear in our ancient ancestors is not hard to imagine.

Biblical Animism

By the time the Old Testament was put into written form many of the earlier practices had been cast aside, and animism in its pure form is not prominent in the stories. The burning bush from Exodus 3:2-5 and Deuteronomy 33:16 are possible references to the animistic idea that God inhabited a bush (an unusual bush that kept burning). Moses is told to take off his shoes before approaching the bush for ***"It is holy ground."*** That sounds animistic, but didn't result in Moses worshiping bushes later in Exodus.

2 Samuel 5:23-24 is cited as a remnant of animism as David listens to a signal from some trees nearby, suggesting God is in those trees: ***"As soon as you hear the sound of marching in the tops of the***

poplar trees, move quickly, because that will mean the Lord has gone out in front of you to strike the Philistine army." In both these cases the apparent presence of God in a bush and a grove of trees is temporary, and neither of these inanimate objects is later an object of worship in Israel. Trees have been such objects of worship, in Israel and in most earlier civilizations. The Greeks and Romans had sacred groves which were connected with divine guidance, and the Hebrew tribes fell into a tree-worshiping cult several times.

Another less convincing incident is the story of Jacob stopping for the night and sleeping on the ground with a stone for a pillow. He has his famous "ladder to heaven" dream. *"When Jacob awoke from his sleep, he thought, "Surely the Lord is in this place, and I was not aware of it." He was afraid and said, "How awesome is this place! This is none other than the house of God; this is the gate of heaven." Early the next morning Jacob took the stone he had placed under his head and set it up as a pillar and poured oil on top of it. He called that place Bethel."* (Genesis 28:16) Bethel features prominently later in Israel as a place of worship. He sets up his pillow stone as a marker, but it seems he is consecrating the location as a dwelling place for God rather than the stone. Sacred stones were objects of worship by Israel's neighboring nations, so some animistic ideas were current in their mind. Some scholars consider the "cloud by day, pillar of fire by night" which led the Hebrews in the Exodus as animistic objects. They were clearly regarded as symbolizing God's direction, but again, these objects ceased to be useful and were not later worshiped as God-animated objects. The Hebrew tribes had at times "holy mountains" and "holy places" they revered, but do not seem to think of these inanimate objects as tying YHWH to specific places; He came and went as He pleased. The gold covered wood box called the "Ark of the Covenant" is a special case where it seems Moses and the other Israelites believed God was actually present on a semi-permanent basis; we will examine it in a later section which deals with "totems"

Many of the myths from the Babylonians, Vikings, Greeks, and Romans include animated animals who are active, intentional characters in the stories, often speaking, plotting and scheming like humans. The famous Greek storyteller Aesop left us hundreds of wonderful "fables" with animals who are intelligent and vocal, characters who teach a moral lesson. Everyone probably remembers tales such as "The Boy Who Cried Wolf," "The Hare and The Turtle," "The Lion and The Mouse" and "The Fox and the Grapes." These fables are not "animism" in the religious sense, but simply use talking animals as a vehicle for telling a story with a lesson. Native Americans in pre-colonial times apparently used this technique of talking animals to entertain and educate the young, as well as conveying their history and origins as a people. ***Hiawatha*** is the most famous such American Indian thanks to the poem by Henry Wadsworth Longfellow. His fictionalized Hiawatha communicates with talking animals, trees, rivers and other objects of nature, and these talking animals, plants and things are friends and helpers for the brave warrior, but they are not worshiped in the fashion of animism. American Indians revered and respected nature and the environment "religiously," but they mostly were monotheistic, worshiping one god, "The Great Spirit." Some Native American tribes also had "totems" such as the eagle, the bear or the wolf as emblems of tribal identity, and while taking pride in their tribal identity and revering their tribal emblem they did not regard it as a living spirit or divinity in an animistic fashion. Likewise, they frequently identified individuals with animal names such as "Red Fox" or "Brave Eagle," either as a name based on the child's personality or as a parental hope for the qualities associated with the name.

Portable Gods: Totemism

Totemism is usually considered the second stage in the evolution of religion, though as illustrated above the line between one stage and the next is not sharply drawn. A totem (a word derived from the Ojibwe tribe's "***doodem***") is a sacred object created by people to represent a spirit being identified with a particular group of people, such as a family, a clan or tribe. It is often emblematic of that group of connected people, representing their identity, and providing divine protection over the unit of believers. A totem can also be a more portable, individual or family token of protection, such as the sacred object or a symbol that serves as an emblem of a group of people. A totem may be adopted by a family, a clan, or a tribe, those who share a belief in the totem's power and benefit. One such popular totem survives today: the "lucky rabbit's foot," carried in modern suit coat pockets into tall skyscrapers and offices.

Other totems still with us include lucky coins, lucky shirts, and other such objects viewed with a mild bit of superstition. Most such totem carriers don't have a rational argument for the hope that their totem will bring them luck, but continue to carry it "just in case." In biblical times a similar case of a "lucky" totem is Moses' rod, a wooden walking stick which he had brought from Egypt in the Exodus and which he used to part the Red Sea. In battle, the army of Israelites came to trust in having Moses raise his lucky staff in the air during the fight; they seemed to be victorious as long as Moses held up the stick, but be defeated when he tired and put his arm down. The solution: men were appointed to hold Moses' arm and lucky rod up for him when he got weary. That is a clear belief in the value of a totem. (Exodus 17:8-15) Many other lucky totems are mentioned in the Old Testament.

The creation of "totem poles" among indigenous natives of Alaska and the north west coast might be seen as a variation of animism, objects used to depict spiritual reverence, family legends, sacred beings and culturally important animals, people, or historical events. Some ornately decorated totem poles seem to symbolize characters and events in native myths, and some likely depict supernatural beings such as **The Thunderbird**. Many tribes have variations on this legendary powerful divine being believed to control the upper world and compete with some other supernatural beings for the underwater world of horned snakes and other demons. Some legends have the Thunderbird "throwing lightening" and using weather as a show of magical powers. Totem poles and the stone or wooden idols of many cultures, including the ancient Hebrews, are considered an evolution of religion beyond animism, an advance from fearing unknown and unpredictable divinities in trees and rocks to more specific ideas of particular gods with names and histories. These man-made objects came to represent supernatural beings, but were usually not regarded as alive or possessing a spirit or soul, and so are more like "totemism" than "animism." The gods or goddesses represented by totems and idols had well-developed myths and legends about the divine being worshiped, and the physical symbol is a focused reminder of the "real" god, who probably lives elsewhere.

An interesting legend appears in one of the books which were not accepted into the Old Testament canon: ***Bel and the Dragon.*** This story is supposedly an additional chapter 14 in the canonical Daniel of the Old Testament, and involves the biblical Daniel and the Persian king Cyrus. Cyrus taunts his trusted friend Daniel about the reality of the idol/god of Persia, Bel, citing evidence that these idol/gods actually eat and drink each day from the offerings laid before them by worshipers. Daniel scoffs those idols are just clay covered with bronze, and are not alive. Daniel challenges the idol worship by quietly sprinkling ashes around the temple by Bel's statue, and then showing the king the many footprints on the temple floor the next morning. Daniel shows that it is a group of priests entering the temple through secret door who are actually consuming the food, not their "god" Bel. Naturally, the king in wrath has all the priests and their families slain, and rewards Daniel for his cleverness. This is an effective legend by which the Israelites fought persistent idol worship, especially Baal, as the Canaanites' called Bel, enticing their people for generations. Baal, Ashtoreth, Chemosh and Dagan and some lesser false gods of the neighboring nations were strong competitors against YAWEH for the affection and devotion of the twelve tribes that came to Canaan to claim their "promised land."

The Strange Case of the Ark of The Covenant

It is challenging to know how to classify the major object of worship in the Bible: The **Ark of the Covenant** which the Israelites created and carried throughout the 40-year exodus from Egypt was certainly worshiped and revered, but **was it an idol**? About a year after exiting Egypt, Moses had this gold-covered wooden chest built to the specifications God gave him. It was made of a particular type of wood, and measured 2 ½ cubits in length, 1 ½ cubits wide and 1 ½ cubits high (approximately 52x31x31 inches). A gold laden lid covered the chest, and two golden "cherubim" were positioned on the lid, facing each other with wings outspread over the Ark. Inside the sacred chest were placed the two stone tablets of the Ten Commandments, a golden bowl of the miracle food mana, Aaron's magic rod, and probably the patriarch Joseph's bones.

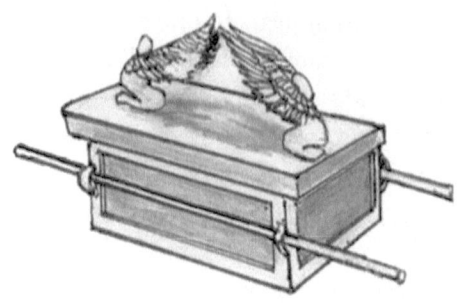

Ark of Covenant

The Bible shows clearly that the people believed that God/Yahweh was present in the Ark, or more particularly, in the space between the two cherubim. The Ark was kept in the tent-tabernacle during the Exodus, hidden from sight of all but a priest. It was carried on the journey to the Holy Land by four priests by long wooden rods inserted into golden rings on both sides of the Ark. It was kept covered as it traveled, and it seemed to possess amazing power to inflict God's wrath on any who touched it, even accidentally. It enabled the tribes to cross the Jordan river into the Holy Land by dividing the river and holding back the water the moment the priests who carried it stepped into the river. Several hundred years later, during David's kingship, the Ark was lost to the Philistines who captured it in battle and placed it as a trophy in their god Dagon's temple. The Ark is said to have wreaked havoc on Dagan's statue and the temple, so magically mischievous that the Philistines returned the Ark to Israel. Eventually, David's son Solomon built a magnificent temple in Jerusalem and the Ark was placed in the Holy of Holies deep within the temple. There, behind a large curtain, the High Priest would enter once a year to sprinkle a blood-offering on the Ark, a day of Atonement for the sins of the people. When Jerusalem and the Temple were destroyed by the Babylonians in 586 B.C. the Ark disappeared forever. The hit movie, "Indiana Jones and the Ark of the Covenant" portrays the rediscovery of the lost Ark, with extravagant and violent special effects revealing the awesome power of the Ark, or the wrath of the Jehovah God who occupied it. Stories appear every month or so in modern media about the search for the Lost Ark, and the teasing tales of supposed sightings.

What did the Ark mean to the ancient Israelites? It is undeniable that they thought God was actually physically present in or upon the Ark, an occasional display of God's glory, or *shekinah*. The word shekinah does not appear in the Bible, but the concept clearly does. Later Jewish rabbis coined this expression, a form of a Hebrew word that literally means "he caused to dwell," signifying that it was a divine visitation of the presence or dwelling of the Lord God on this earth. To Moses and the Hebrew tribes, it was God who appeared to them in the "pillar of cloud by day and a pillar of fire by night" (Exodus 13:22-23) After the construction of the Ark of the Covenant it was believed that the real and visible present of the Lord was in that sacred box, or appeared as a dazzling light between the two cherubim on top. It appears that they continued their belief in the actual, real presence of Jehovah physically located in the temple, in the Ark. For them, this was not a symbolic object like a wooden or golden idol of the surrounding peoples, but was revered as God Himself in some way. Later, their poets and prophets understood and explained that God cannot be contained in a box or a building, because He is everywhere, "omnipresent." Still later, they came to understand that God "dwells in our hearts" closer than a brother or life itself. Fifteen centuries after the Ark was built for God's dwelling place, the New Testament apostle Paul reflects the evolution that has taken place in our concept of God, that God dwells in us, not in a box or a temple:

> *"(S)o that Christ may <u>dwell</u> in your hearts through faith. And I pray that you, being rooted and established in love, may have power, together with all the Lord's holy people, to grasp how wide and long and high and deep is the love of Christ, and to know this love that surpasses knowledge— that you may be filled to the measure of all the fullness of God."* (Ephesians 3:17-19)

Idol Worship in The Bible

The Bible does not hide the fact that our Biblical ancestors were attracted to idols and idol worship. The Old Testament mentions several people who possessed *teraphim*, or household idols. These images were used as talismans to bring a blessing upon the household. Two women married to Hebrew men of kept family idols—Rachel and Michal. In the story of Jacob working many years for his prospective father-in-law Laban in order to marry Laban's daughter Rachael, Jacob eventually took his two wives and other family members and livestock and fled. Laban caught up with the tribe and accused Jacob of stealing his "family gods" or small idols or totems. Rachael was the culprit heisting the Laban family idols, for reasons not given (Genesis 31:32). Even as far back as Abraham, father of the Hebrews, the Bible says his father, Terah, had an idol-making business in the Babylonian city of Ur. One legend (not in the Bible) says a young Abraham slipped into his father's shop one night and decimated the stock of sacred statues. However, it seems likely that some such small idols were included in the luggage of the large family tribe of Abraham which left Ur of the Chaldees on the journey to their "promised land."

It is no surprise to Believers that the ancient Hebrew people had idols and followed the cult of the divinity the physical objects represented. The most memorable idol was the **Golden Calf** formed by the disgruntled people who exited Egypt with Moses (Exodus 32:4). While Moses was away on the mountain receiving the Ten Commandments the restless Israelites, aided by Moses' brother Aaron, threw their gold jewelry into a big fire and "lo, out came a golden calf" as Aaron explained. Thousands of tribal members were dancing and singing worshipfully to the golden idol when Moses returned. In his anger at the unfaithfulness of his people, Moses threw down the two stone tablets, *breaking all the commandments at one time.* The second of those commandments was: **"You shall have no other gods before me. You shall not make for yourself an image in the form of anything in heaven above or on the earth beneath or in the waters below. You shall not bow down to them or worship them; for I, the Lord your God, am a jealous God, punishing the children for the sin of the parents to the third and fourth generation of those who hate me, but showing love to a thousand generations of those who love me and keep my commandments"** (Exodus 20:3-4) (Emphasis added)

Throughout the Old Testament that Second Commandment seemed the hardest to follow, for we find the Israelites slipping back into idol worship time after time, unable to resist the many tribal gods worshiped by the existing people of Canaan when the Hebrew tribes invaded under Joshua. Perhaps they found it easier to worship an idol they could see than God who was invisible. Repeatedly, their prophets or priests would rebuke their faithlessness, and their enemies would attack them, but still the idols came back quietly but surely. YHWH, the invisible God, had a centuries long struggle against the "visible" idol gods of Canaan: *Ashtoreth, Baal, Chemosh* and *Dagon*.

The Attraction of Visible Pagan Gods

Ashtoreth (also called Astarte) was a goddess of fertility and maternity, and apparently involved sexual activity as a part of worship (a pretty attractive evangelistic method.) It was this goddess who was worshiped by many of Solomon's 700 wives which helped bring the wisest King to ruin. Ashtoreth was represented by a limbless tree trunk planted in the ground, usually carved into a symbolic representation of the goddess. Because of the association with carved trees, the places of Ashtaroth worship were commonly called "groves," and the Hebrew word "Asherah" (plural, "asherim") could refer either to the goddess or to a grove of trees. One of King Manasseh's evil deeds was that he **"took the carved Ashtaroth pole he had made and put it in the temple"** (2 Kings 21:7) Anthropologists and historians consider the Ashtaroth poles as phallic symbols, a common fertility emblem widely used in many ancient cultures, and still sometimes used in modern times.

Baal, (also called Bel) was the supreme god among the Canaanites in many forms, but often as a sun god or storm god. He was a fertility god (sometimes considered the husband of Ashtoreth) who supposedly made earth bear crops and women bear children. Rites involved with Baal worship included cult prostitution and sometimes human sacrifice. Baal was a most prominent and persistent enemy of the Hebrew's Yahweh throughout the Old Testament. The most famous of these conflicts is the "trial by fire" between the prophet Elijah and the 400 prophets of

Baal at Mount Carmel recounted in First Kings 18:20-40). In one of the most dramatic stories in the Bible the persecuted man of God, the prophet Elijah, challenged the Baal priests to a contest: ***"Then you call on the name of your god, and I will call on the name of the Lord. The god who answers by fire—he is God."*** (vs. 24) Elijah prepared a stone altar with wood to burn the sacrificial bull he had prepared, and the prophets of Baal did the same; neither was to light the fire. Elijah has the Baal priests go first, and they pray and dance, crying and yelling from morning till evening, even cutting themselves in order to get Baal to answer. After five- or six-hours Elijah began to taunt them: "Perhaps your god is asleep...Yell louder." or "Maybe your god has gone on a journey...pray more fervently." As twilight approached the old prophet of Yahweh stepped up to his rough altar and slain bull; he ordered the bull, the altar and the firewood to be deluged with water from four large jars, several times, drenching the area with water running into a ditch. Then Elijah prayed, and a great fire came down from the heavens, consumed all of the bull, the wood, the stones of the altar, and dried up all the water in the ditch. Big Finale! Trial by Fire! ***"When all the people saw this, they fell prostrate and cried, "The Lord—he is God! The Lord—he is God!!"*** (I Kings 18:39)

Chemosh was a fish-like idol, the national god of the neighboring Moabites and probably of the Ammonites also. Chemosh was regarded like Baal in supremacy, and it maybe were simply different names for the same god. Chemosh worship was never as influential in Israel as some of the previously mentioned, but unfortunately, Chemosh worship was introduced into Israelite culture by King Solomon, whose many wives from other cultures turned his heart to other gods (1 Kings 11:4–7). The Bible records Chemosh demanding human sacrifice: in the days of Judah's King Jehoram, the king of Moab faced military defeat, and the Moabite ruler ***"took his firstborn son, who was to succeed him as king, and offered him as a sacrifice on the city wall"*** (2 Kings 3:27). The cult of Chemosh was eventually destroyed in Judah (the surviving kingdom) during the seventh century B.C. religious reformation and revival led by King Josiah (c. 649–609 B.C.).

Dagon first appears in extant records about 2500 B.C. in Mesopotamian "Mari texts" with a slightly different spelling as Dagan. The famous "Code of Hammurabi" created by the Babylonian King

THE BIRTH OF GOD

Hammurabi (c. 1810 1750 B.C.) begin by calling himself "the subduer" of the settlements along the Euphrates with the help of Dagan, his creator." Dagan or Dagon appears in many ancient near-east cultures before we encounter him in Canaan in the Old Testament. This god of the neighboring Philistines is represented in statues/idols as having the body of a fish and human head and hands. The great Hebrew hero, Sampson, frustrated and aggravated the Philistines for many years, but this super-strong man was betrayed by Delilah and was captured and tortured by the Philistines in revenge. In the end, Sampson destroyed himself and many of his Philistine enemies by bringing down the huge temple of Dagon. (Judges 16:27-30) The threat of the Philistines did not die with Sampson. In a later battle they captured the sacred Ark of the Covenant and placed it in their temple next to Dagon's statue. According to 1 Samuel 5:1-5, the next day Dagon's statue was toppled to the floor. They set it upright, and the next morning it was again on the floor, with the head and hands broken off. Later, the Philistines put King Saul's armor in their temple and hung his severed head in the temple of Dagon. The Ark kept deviling the Philistines as they moved it from one place to another, and each location experienced great misery and suffering. They finally brought the Ark back to Israel to rid themselves of the troublesome "god of Israel." (Judges 6:13-16)

The God of Israel and The Development of Judaism

The examination of the religion and the idea of God that developed in the Semitic tribes that eventually became Israel is potentially troubling to those who hold the Bible as a sacred record. It is hoped that rather than challenging or damaging the faith of such believers, an objective and intellectually honest study can create a firmer, more comprehensive basis for belief. It is an indisputable fact that the Hebrew religion did not spring up full-grown and fully developed in one momentous day, or in one generation. The fact that Judaism changed over time should not disturb us, for we know and appreciate that over many centuries the **final outcome became the Jewish faith** of Jesus, His disciples and Paul, the apostle to the world, and to us today.

We recognize that individuals develop their religious faith a step at a time, with the earlier ideas and beliefs somewhat child-like, but growing in depth and complexity over the years, even over a lifetime.

Today's children have religious beliefs and faith at a tender age, but their early ideas of God and "being good" are often pretty silly, even funny. But they grow and change and their concept of God evolves into a fairly orthodox idea of Jesus and Moses and Abraham, as they are exposed to Bible stories in church or Sunday School. As Paul confessed *"When I was a child, I spoke like a child, I thought like a child, I reasoned like a child. When I became a man, I put the ways of childhood behind me."* (I Corinthians 13:11) Some people never get much further than their childhood theology, but most adults mature in their understanding of religion and faith, often drifting toward something close to Biblical teachings. Just as human children grow up and grow out of some earlier misconceptions of God, so has Humanity grown up over the centuries: **"In the past our ancestors... but now we..."** (Hebrews 1:1) is how the early Christians positioned themselves and their "new covenant" through Jesus—a final point along the continuum from Abraham, Moses, Isaiah and their other forefathers. Just so, Israel was a child being led by a patient God, a child learning slowly and fitfully, often falling back into heathen thoughts and practices. But in time, these ancient Hebrew wanderers would bring to the world the One and only God, the righteous and holy God who created the world and all that is in it, the God who is mercy and love, and who seeks to give us an abundant and perfected life in fellowship with Himself. We can acknowledge that the science of the early Israelites was primitive and wrong, by today's standards, but we are not scandalized by their faulty science, because we know that the first "real" science was still 800 years in the future. If we can overlook their primitive science, we should be just as compassionate and non-judgmental about their early, primitive theology.

Culture Influenced the Hebrew Tribes

The nomadic Semitic tribes who migrated from the ancient Sumerian civilization in the fertile crescent were exposed to and were influenced by many religions, with multiple gods, and a rich trove of ancient legends and myths about the ancient gods. In their "promised land", they lived among heathen tribes and cultures: Canaanites, Philistines, Phoenicians and numerous other smaller groups. All these city-states had multiple gods, and those neighboring gods were believed to require ritual genocide of enemies, human sacrifices, even their own children to appease these tyrannical heathen gods. The gods were placated by blood, they thought, and the wrath of these tribal gods was terrifying. It is not surprising that our early ancestors at first also thought their God demanded mass murder of enemies, and required human sacrifice, even their own children. Their distorted and limited early understanding of God is not a reason to overlook or reject the underlying Biblical spiritual message. The fact that this compiled diary of the Jewish religion contains such gross misunderstandings (foolishness) confirms that this is a reliable diary, an accurate account of what they thought and did, the "good, the bad and the ugly", imperfect pilgrims, warts and all. We can learn from what they got wrong as well as what they got right. **And they got a lot right** in spite of their heathen culture.

The familiar term "An Eye for An Eye" (sometimes adding "A Tooth for A Tooth") was one of Israel's laws given by Moses. We consider this a primitive and bloody principle of justice, and American law has moved past the simple "tit for tat" model still common elsewhere in the world. As primitive as "eye for an eye" sounds, it was an **improvement** over the Code of Hammurabi (1754 B.C.) which shaped all middle-eastern civilizations at the time Israel was established. Under the older law the victim of an assault or physical harm was allowed to retaliate with **more severe punishment** against the perpetrator, perhaps taking an arm or a foot in addition to the "eye for eye" rule. A revengeful victim was allowed to impose almost any penalty against their enemy, including death for serious injury. This may seem a minor improvement in tribal law, but it was accompanied by many other legal liberalizations. Treating the stranger or foreign alien with kindness and mercy was a huge step beyond their neighboring tribes; the "jubilee" rule was and is unique to ancient Israel: every seven years all debts were to be forgiven, and every 50 years, all property reverted to its original family ownership. This was a huge social value which the ancient Hebrews practiced but not even America has adopted; capitalism almost inevitably gives us winners and losers, and there are no "give backs" in our laws and traditions.

The Hebrew religion gave us monotheism; it gave us the concept of rule by law; it gave us the concept that the Divine works its purpose on human history through human events; it gave us the concept of the covenant, that the one God of the universe has established a special relationship with a specific band of humans, chosen to carry his "light to the Gentiles." (Isaiah 49:6) They got the ***chosen*** part a bit wrong, mistaking God's favor as favoritism, thinking that being the people of God meant they were His **only** people in a privileged position. It took Jesus' final revelation of a universal God rather than a Jewish God for the picture to be clear—that "God so loved the **world**" (John 3:16) —all people. Even then, Peter and the other early church leaders still were in some confusion about Jewishness. It was Paul who fought for and preached the new vision that Gentiles were the children of God as much as Jews, and that all the barriers of race, gender, social or economic standing, all human divisions, rituals or customs are irrelevant to God.

Ancient Israel Shaped Our History

The Old Testament vision of God has had an enormous effect on human culture and history, giving birth to the three "Abrahamic Faiths." **Judaism, Christianity,** and **Islam** all claim the same ancestor Abraham, and value the same Old Testament. Today, **about two thirds of all religious adherents on earth** are members of this one great Abrahamic tradition. Beyond dispute, this tremendous force in human history was born and evolved within a wandering nomadic tribe of Semites who became Israel. We can't know with absolute certainty how the primitive desert people came to their earliest thoughts about God, but we know it was a rocky and twisting road. Through archaeology, anthropology, history, and other scholarly pursuits, coupled with a thorough study and analysis of the Hebrew scriptures, we can sketch the basic outlines of religious development with some confidence. We know that major historical events such as the Exodus had profound effect on Israel, and many identifiable cultural and geographic changes helped shape the beliefs and practices of the Hebrew people. Many of these specific influences can be identified historically, and the interaction of Israel with the rise and fall of many great civilizations can be traced with some accuracy.

We know, for example, that the Babylonian captivity (586 B.C.) made indelible marks on Judaism, and several new ideas from Persian and Babylonian religions were incorporated when Israel was restored to their homeland. Scholars believe that it was this catastrophic destruction and displacement of Israel by Babylon's Nebuchadnezzar II which led the Jewish religious leaders to compile and edit the wealth of oral and written documents which had been passed down generation to generation. It was this group of priests and scribes who assured that there would be a written record that would survive even if the nation perished. This compilation became our Old Testament, we believe. Much as Abigail Adams rescued and preserved Washington's portrait as the British arsonists attacked the White House, these remaining Jewish custodians rushed in ahead of the enemy, and prevented the final loss of the story of these people. Let us review some of the most significant influence and changes which were directly incorporated into Western Civilization culture and remain because of Israel and its God.

Abraham To Moses-The Formative Years (@ 2000-1400 B.C.)

We begin, not with Adam or Noah, but with Abraham, the "father of three world religions" according to most historians. The creation and flood stories in Genesis prior to Abraham are shared in some form by all the ancient civilizations such as the Sumer, Babylon, Egypt, Indus Valley and Minoan, all before 2000 BC. Israel's unique story begins about 2000 BC with Abram (later renamed "Abraham" by God) in the city of Ur in the Babylonian empire. Beginning with the family patriarch, Abraham, the "family" became a "tribe" and then several "tribes" and in a gradual and fractured way these desert wanderers and shepherds became a "people." Abraham's family and servants were probably less than a hundred individuals when they left Babylonia and moved to the land known as Canaan, a land already occupied for two millennia, and home to several advanced cultures, including the inventors of the alphabet—the sea faring Phoneticians, and the occupants of the oldest city in history, dating back to around 8000 B.C. The new people, later called "Hebrews," lived among the Canaanites relatively peacefully for many years, buying some land, raising sheep, and staying separate from the indigenous neighbors. The "conquest" of the land and its possession which God had promised Abraham did not take place for some 500 years, and included a long interruption as captives in Egypt. The stories of Abraham's children, grandchildren and great grandchildren includes some of the most interesting and well-known tales, and readers are encouraged to read these amazing accounts in the Bible, specifically chapters 11-50 of Genesis. The details are fascinating and worth the effort to read them. Only a brief outline of the main characters is included here, revealing the "big picture" of how history moves under God's direction, even with the human's "free will" and frequent divergence from God's original plan.

Abraham lived a long and prosperous life in Canaan with his wife Sarah, and his promised son, Isaac, succeeded him as the Patriarch of the family. Ishmael, the son of Abraham and Sarah's impatience, was alienated from Isaac and the family, and generally regarded as the ancestor of the Arab people. Isaac was ready for marriage and Abraham sent a servant back to Babylonia to recruit a suitable wife from the relatives who had stayed behind. Isaac and Rebekah had twin sons, Esau and Jacob, boys exactly opposite from each other. Jacob, the younger by two minutes, tricks Esau and gets the aging Isaac to designate him his successor. Chapters 26-36 are mostly about Jacob's many exploits and encounters with God, and God changes Jacob's name to Israel, the eventual name of the nation from then to now.

Jacob has twelve sons by three wives, including his favorite son, Joseph. The rest of Genesis is largely the story of Joseph, his betrayal by his jealous brothers, his captivity in Egypt, and his eventual rise to power as the chief assistant to the Pharaoh. This is one of the most compelling stories in the Bible. The upshot of the plot is that Joseph's entire family moves to Egypt under Joseph's protection, including Jacob and the eleven brothers who sold Joseph into slavery. Jacob's sons became the "Twelve Tribes of Israel" and the sojourn in Egypt lasted some 400 years, during which the Hebrews went from "honored guests" to "slaves" to the Egyptian pharaoh (for Joseph had long been forgotten in Egypt). The tribes grew greatly in numbers, perhaps a million eventually, and occupied their own portion of Egypt where they apparently continued Abraham's religion. The birth and miraculous rescue of Moses turns the page of history for the Abrahamic descendants, and the escape of the whole group from Egypt, the "Exodus" was led by Moses, the dominant figure in the rest of the story of Israel.

Historians are not agreed on the exact date of the Exodus, and some scholars question whether it actually happened. The suggested date of about 1400 B.C. is supported by many Bible scholars, and there is some archaeological and written evidence supporting the event and this date. The research is still active on this question, including trying to find Egyptian references to the Hebrews. There is not overwhelming archaeological support for the Exodus described in Genesis, but there is enough to see that **something earthshaking** happened in Hebrew history for the clear results and the influence of the Mosaic story and the Mosaic law is undeniable. Something changed the nomadic Semitic tribes who wandered the deserts of the Middle East for hundreds of years into the effective militia which invaded Canaan and set up permanent settlement and control of most of the land. These people have forever looked back upon this Exodus event as the proof of God's work: **"Remember how I brought you out of Egypt"** (Exodus 20:2) is written and read and engraved on Jewish hearts forever. We can reasonably accept the basic story that a man named Moses actually existed and led the Israelites out of Egypt and created a religious and social structure for the large collection of tribes, legal and ceremonial rules that are still followed today by Jewish people. There may have been more than one exodus from Egypt, and their story may be different from what we have, but the end result is the same: Israel conquered their "promised land" and successfully maintained their identity as a "people of the Covenant" (between God and Abraham and then God and Moses) for several centuries.

The Covenant Relationship – Old and New

The revolutionary concept of a sacred "covenant" between a holy God and a chosen nation gave form and substance to their theology. In fourth millennium, B.C. Mesopotamia, kings and their conquered vassal states often entered into a "covenant", a kind of political contract, providing protection for the defeated peoples, and loyalty, fealty and tribute for the ruler. Israel took that idea and entered into such a covenant with their God, beginning with Abraham and renewed by Moses. They came to accept that their holy God loved them and blessed them, and in return they would be His people, obedient and faithful to Him. They came to interpret their many defeats and suffering as being the consequence of their own failures, a justified punishment for their national sins. Time and time again, through the thousand years after

Moses had led them out of Egypt and slavery, they violated the covenant, wandered off into idol worship, and eventually returning to a faithful relationship with Yahweh. By the time of their greatest tragedy, the Babylonian captivity (from 586 B.C. to 639 B.C.) they were able to refine and promote what became Judaism, the Jewish faith, with written compilations of their history and their laws, together elevated to The Law, the *Torah*. Their greatest moral teachings came from enlightened prophets and poets who brought a high and holy vision of God which sustained the faith through the next five hundred years leading up to the birth of the Messiah, Jesus of Nazareth.

Age of The Patriarchs (@1950-1300 B.C.)

For the most part, the people surrounding the Hebrews hardly noticed these newcomers for much of Hebrew history. The Hebrews themselves don't actually appear in written history until the reign of Marniptah, king of Egypt from about 1224-1211 B.C. The son of Ramses I (1290-1224 B.C.), generally taken to be the king of Egypt at the time of the Hebrew exodus, undertakes a military campaign in Asia in 1220 B.C. An account of the campaign inscribed in granite, lists all the conquered peoples mentions **Habiru** or **Apiru** as a tribe "now living in Canaan."[49] Most scholars believe these were the Hebrews.

Before this point, the only history is the Hebrews we have are written by the Hebrews themselves, in Genesis 12-50. In the Hebrew account of their own history, they trace their origins back to a single individual, Abraham, who came originally from Mesopotamia, the "cradle of civilizations" in the ancient world. The period of history from Abraham until the Exodus from Egypt, about 500 years, is traditionally called "The Age of the Patriarchs" (**Abraham, Isaac, Jacob** (who was renamed *"Israel"*) and **Joseph** who became a powerful Egyptian official. *Patriarch* means "Father-ruler" which is the accurate description of the nomadic tribes of that period; the senior male of the clan was in absolute total command over all the sons, daughters, grandchildren and slaves who lived together in the sheep herding open land. Abram (later renamed "Abraham" by God) was such a clan/tribal leader over as many as 300 or more members. The eldest son usually succeeded the father, and other sons often would leave to establish their own family, usually granted some of the herd and slaves. The book of

THE BIRTH OF GOD

Genesis is the story of this Patriarchal age after the Flood and until the whole nation is trapped in Egypt several centuries later.

The first and most revered of the Patriarch was Abraham, a Semite living in Haran, a city in northern Mesopotamia; Semites were a race of nomadic people believed to descend from Noah's oldest son, Shem; Greek and Latin had no "h" sound so "Shem" became "Sem." Abram's father, Terah, originated in Ur the great ancient city in southern Mesopotamia (today's Iraq). He was a maker and seller of idols used by most families, and probably he and Abram and most others worshipped many gods, with the "moon" goddess especially popular in Ur. The family migrated north to Haran where Terah dies, and Abram becomes clan leader—a very prosperous clan with many sheep, cattle and property. Suddenly, from out of the blue it seems, Abram hears God's call:

> ***The Lord ("Elohim") had said to Abram, "Go from your country, your people and your father's household to the land I will show you. "I will make you into a great nation, and I will bless you; I will make your name great, and you will be a blessing. I will bless those who bless you, and whoever curses you I will curse; and all peoples on earth will be blessed through you."*** (Genesis 12:1-3)

So, Abram went, as the Lord had told him, taking all his extended family, all his possessions, and set out to the west, not knowing yet where he was being sent. Abram, now named Abraham, was already 75 years old, his wife Sarah was also old, childless and barren. The Bible counts this single decision, this step of blind faith in the voice of God, as the obedience which was counted as **righteousness**. God had, for some reason unknown, chosen Abraham to be the father and founder of a chosen nation, the Hebrew people who would descend from Abraham and his barren wife. We do not know whether this old Semitic man had ever encountered this Elohim/God before, or if he connected this God with the ancient tales he had heard of Creation, Fall, Flood, Ark and rainbow. We only know, he heard and he obeyed, and God was pleased with him. Because of Abraham's faithful obedience, he is considered the father of Judaism, Islam and Christianity.

The "Chosen" People

The "election" of the Hebrews by God is a mystery for which no answer is sufficient. We know that the whole context makes this "chosen people" responsible for bringing God's blessings to all mankind, not just the Jews: *"and all peoples on earth will be blessed through you."* (Genesis 12:3) Abraham was promised (and commissioned). Over the following eighteen centuries after Abraham his people wandered in and out of God's plans, were enslaved thrice and very nearly obliterated twice. It is almost unbelievable that these rebellious, slow-learning desert dwellers could have survived, or even more unbelievable, why He put up with them. Yet somehow, they still were the conduit for the *Incarnation*, the final great revelation of God in His Son, Jesus of Nazareth. The story of how the descendants of a man from the ancient civilization of Babylonia and Chaldea in the Mesopotamian crescent came through history to produce a religious faith in the 21st Century which inspires and guides several billion people worldwide, a faith that at its best worships a God who looks at us as His children and loves us without limit, whether or not we love Him...how that happened is a drama worthy of any mystery novel or Superhero movie of today. We will only review the highlights of that history here, while encouraging both Skeptics and Believers to dig deeper and savor the greatest story in history...for it is His story, God's patient persistence in making Himself fully known.

The Period of the Judges (@ 1400-1000 B.C.)

The military conquest of much of Canaan was led by Joshua, the successor to Moses (who had not been permitted to see the final success). The very large army was able to subdue a large part of the country, and the twelve tribes were allotted specific territories as their heritage. Some tribes took the hill country and some took the plains, and eventually the unified army was abandoned, and tribal rule was instituted in each territory. One telling biblical passage describes it this way: *"In those days Israel had no king; everyone did as they saw fit."* (Judges 17:6) The 400 years in that new land was much like our own American frontier west, without established legal authority and leadership. The tribes administered their own laws and justice, with the tribal leaders chosen by lineage and seniority.

When something arose that was beyond tribal impact, such as attack by some neighboring nation, the tribes were sometimes called to arms for unified effort, with some participating and some declining. An *ad hoc* leader would emerge under direction from Yahweh, and somehow the authority for leading the whole nation for a temporary assignment was recognized by the tribes. These special assignment leaders were called "judges" but the term meant "General" more than "Judge." Conveniently, these stories of a dozen or so such leaders are found in the Book of Judges in the Bible.

A famous example is **Gideon**, a wheat farmer minding his business and hiding from the marauding Midianites is visited by an angel telling him he is to lead the nation to punish these enemies. Gideon is reluctant, but eventually is convinced that the call is from God, and gathers a large army for battle. Strangely, God tells Gideon to get rid of most of the army, whittling it down to just 300. Those 300 employ a clever tactic using oil lamps, trumpets and loud shouting to frighten the sleeping Midianites with what they thought were thousands of attackers. The terrified Midianites were so confused they killed each other, and the rest ran for their lives. After this great victory Israel had several years of peace and tranquility and Gideon was treated as a wise man and consulted in disputes, fulfilling the more traditional role of a "judge."

The story of the period of Judges is accurately encapsulated in two or three verses surrounding this tale of Gideon: Judges 6:1 "The Israelites did evil in the eyes of the Lord, and for seven years he gave them into the hands of the Midianites." Enter Gideon. Big victory. But then "*No sooner had Gideon died than the Israelites again prostituted themselves to the Baals. They set up Baal-Berith as their god and did not remember the Lord their God, who had rescued them from the hands of all their enemies on every side. They also failed to show any loyalty to the family of Jerub-Baal (that is, Gideon) in spite of all the good things he had done for them.*" (Judges 8:33) This is the pattern repeated over and over again during this period of these people "chosen by God." Forty years of peace, during which they drift away in idol worship and other sin. Finally, God sends a leader, they are rescued and return to Yahweh worship, and enjoy peace for another

40 years. The pattern of sin, salvation, forgetting, sinning and rescue occurs in all the stories of **Othniel, Deborah, Ehud, Sampson** and the rest.

How Judaism Changed from Many Gods to One God

The evolution of the Yahwist religion during these 400 years after Joshua was discussed in substantial detail previously in this chapter under the topics **Biblical Animism, Idol Worship in The Bible, Portable Gods: Totemism** and **The Attraction of Visible Pagan Gods.** Those sections point out that Judaism evolved through the same stages as other religions from prehistoric time, and the "seasoned" religion pictured in the Old Testament did not fall perfect and complete from heaven or Sinai, but it was *polytheistic* for a while, *monolatristic* sometimes, *henotheistic* before finally and fully *monotheistic*. The traces are still there in the Old Testament, remnants of religious development that cast off earlier, now useless residue. Polytheism is belief in many gods; monolatrism is acceptance of many gods but worship of particular one; henotheism accepts many gods but worships one who is highest or chief, a council of gods or a pantheon of gods such as in ancient Greece. Of course, monotheism is the claim that there are not several gods but only One God: not "God above all gods" or "God among all gods" but **THE ONE AND ONLY GOD**.

All these theological forms were believed and followed by our religious ancestors, the Hebrew people. *It is no disgrace that our forebearers changed their earlier beliefs, and that understandings of God reflect what we are able to comprehend at any stage*. Everything we know now is an improved, more complete version of something we "knew" when we were young. That is growth and development, and we should not be disconcerted that the Bible accurately records what people once believed and also what they now believe. We look at the latest as the highest or best, and it is clear that the Bible's ultimate conclusion is **THERE IS ONLY ONE GOD.** For us it means that there are not any other gods, big or small, and there never were. God the Creator is and has always been God, and has no competitors. Judaism gave us this wonderful, solid truth after they struggled with the idea for centuries. We have received it as their contribution to the world, and particularly to those who seek or those who believe.

The Impact of The Babylonian Captivity

Within the constraints of this book, we cannot do justice to the great historical event that had the most impact on Judaism—the seventy years spent in captivity in Babylonia/Persia. To extend this chapter to any details about that critical period is to risk weariness and boredom, plus several more trees. So, in the interest of ecology, we will only briefly describe this era. The Kingdom of David lasted through the reign of his son Solomon, but after Solomon's death the Kingdom became "kingdoms." The disputed succession of Solomon's son, Rehoboam, around 930 B.C., led to rebellion and establishment of the Kingdom of Israel in the North (ten tribes), and the Kingdom of Judah in the south, including David's capital, Jerusalem. The biblical account reports that the country split into two kingdoms: The Kingdom of Israel (including the cities of Shechem and Samaria) in the north and the Kingdom of Judah (with Jerusalem) in the south. This split produced a catastrophic two centuries of decline with successions of a few good and many evil kings in each nation.

In 721 B.C. the northern kingdom was invaded and destroyed forever by the new world power, Assyria. Judah was smaller and not as powerful militarily or financially, but it lasted longer, until 586 B.C. when the Neo-Babylonians destroyed Judah, its capital Jerusalem, and the temple and forcefully resettled most Judeans in Babylon. Though the kingdom of Judah was gone and the Temple was gone, Judean scribes and priests preserved the most prominent biblical literature and religious traditions from certain destruction during and after the Babylonian exile. When the Persian king Cyrus conquered the Neo-Babylonians in 539 B.C.E., he secured the periphery of his empire by allowing his Jewish subjects to return home. Although some Judeans stayed in Mesopotamia, those who returned rebuilt Jerusalem, the temple, and Judean society. Judah was the only Israel from then on, and the focus of the Old Testament is on the fate of the Kingdom of Judah. The fate of the ten tribes of the Kingdom of Israel is uncertain, and subject to some questionable speculations. "The Lost Tribes of Israel" makes a good mystery and Joseph Smith, the founder of Mormonism, claimed they resettled in Central America. It is likely they gradually dispersed to other areas or blended in with the Canaanite society around them. At the time of Jesus, the

Samaritans were seen as unfaithful remnants of the northern kingdom, Israelites who escaped the Assyrian slaughter and then intermarried with non-Jewish people of Canaan, no longer pure Jews.

Two important effects of the political destruction and forced exile were **1**: *the compilation and editing of the Old Testament* and **2**: *the influence of Persian religious ideas on Judaism.* The first effect has already been mentioned in earlier sections, and these facts are disturbing to some Believers. We modern people don't have much confidence in "word of mouth" history—we trust written documents as safer and more accurate; however, before the invention of paper in almost **all history** was preserved and passed down by respected elders in tribes and clans, and this oral tradition continues in many areas of Africa and the Amazon. We may be reassured by noting that the <u>Odyssey</u> and the <u>Iliad</u> (required high school reading) were two lengthy, epic poems attributed to a wandering Greek minstrel named Homer—and they were **not written down** until hundreds of years after the poet had died. Passing history from generation in oral form is a reliable and respected tool used by most of our species for many thousand years.

The many oral traditions and the many assorted written documents that were part of Judaism were saved and codified because the fall of the Kingdom of Judah threatened to destroy all of the rich treasury the priests and prophets and poets had produced over the centuries. It fell to the priests and temple officers to preserve these priceless documents and records and the recording by Hebrew scribes any remaining oral traditions, history and songs. By the time the Exile had ended seventy years later the Old Testament canon for the Mosaic Torah and the majority of the other books was largely established. Old records and stories were combined into some order, preserving everything possible even when some of it might be duplication or even contradiction. Of course, some of the later prophets and some historical books were produced after the Exile and were added to the sacred book in later years. This collection and preservation of sacred texts seems to have ended with the "last" prophet Malachi, about 400 B.C.

The second major effect of the Exile was the accretion of some "new" theology to Judaism. At the time the Persian Empire overthrew the Babylonians, many of the Persians practiced Zoroastrianism, an old monotheistic religion that worshiped a deity named Ahura-Mazda.

Zoroastrianism went beyond Israel's monolatrism insisting that only one god exists. Prior to the Exile the mention of "other gods" was still common. Whether the concept came to Judaism through Zoroastrians or not, the teaching — known as monotheism — is now the central tenet of Judaism. Other Zoroastrian concepts, including the idea of divine war with evil (the Devil), heaven, hell, angels, and a day of judgment may have been originally introduced to the Jewish community in Babylonia. Scholars are not certain that these elements came from Persia, but textual analysis suggests these were introduced later, post-exile.

The Exile and the destruction of Jerusalem and the magnificent Temple of Solomon forced several other changes on Jewish religious practice. With the Temple gone the central religious act of offering sacrifice to God in the holy place was impossible, and the traditional worship activities in the Temple were in the past. In Babylon the Hebrew captives devised a new way to worship, the Synagogue. This institution was created wherever ten or more male Jews could congregate, and reading of the Torah and other scriptures became the new form of worship. Songs and chants replaced the trumpets and cymbals and other musical instruments of the old Temple worship, and eventually teaching and preaching were part of synagogue life. In time the synagogue became the public school for boys to learn to read the scriptures, and perhaps other educational activities. By Jesus' time there was a new Temple in Israel, but the synagogue remained a stable local place of worship and Jewish life. The synagogue was "portable" and so Jews carried their worship system as they spread over the whole Roman world.

Jeremiah was an outspoken prophet in Judea before the destruction of Jerusalem, and had spent years warning kings and citizens that God's displeasure with their idolatry, greed and injustice was going to fall on them soon. Needless to say, Jeremiah was not popular. Nevertheless, he preached God's message faithfully and forcefully, and his teaching advanced the theology of Israel significantly. From Jeremiah the exclusiveness of monotheism was proclaimed definitively, and the concept of religion being about the inner person, the heart, and not on externals such as ritual and ceremonies. Jeremiah firmly teaches that religion is inward, a matter of heart, not depending on ritual or ceremony: ***"This is the covenant I will make with the people of***

Israel after that time," declares the Lord. "I will put my law in their minds and write it on their hearts. I will be their God, and they will be my people." (Jeremiah 31:33)

Not only is Jeremiah plowing new theological ground by his emphasis on personal, intimate religion or "heart-felt" religion, but also introduces the idea of a **new covenant**," a covenant between God and individuals, not on stone tablets or scrolls but in their heart or soul. This is a huge advance over the covenants with Noah, Abraham and Moses which were promises and agreements between God and groups of people. Under Jeremiah's inspiration the idea of sin became a personal responsibility and not just a family or tribe or nation sinning. Finally, Jeremiah is the first to broach the idea that God is seeking not just a covenant of heart with individual responsibility, nor just a nation of law and justice, but the new idea of God's openness to including Gentiles, to teaching them:

> *Lord, my strength and my fortress, my refuge in time of distress, to you the nations* ("Gentiles") *will come from the ends of the earth and say,*
> *"Our ancestors possessed nothing but false gods, worthless idols that did them no good.*
> *Do people make their own gods? Yes, but they are not gods!"*
> *"Therefore, I will teach them—this time I will teach them my power and might.*
> *Then they will know that my name is the Lord.*
> (Jeremiah 16:19-21)

After the return from Exile the new brand of Jewish prophets began to reveal more and more of the great love and compassion and concern for the poor and needy. Chapter 1 of Isaiah confronts the sad spiritual condition of Judah with these astonishing, stinging words:

> *"The multitude of your sacrifices—what are they to me?" says the Lord.*
> *"I have more than enough of burnt offerings, of rams and the fat of fattened animals;*

> *I have no pleasure in the blood of bulls and lambs and goats.*
> *When you come to appear before me, who has asked this of you, this trampling of my courts?*
> *Stop bringing meaningless offerings! Your incense is detestable to me.*
> *New Moons, Sabbaths and convocations—I cannot bear your worthless assemblies.*
> *Your New Moon feasts and your appointed festivals I hate with all my being.*
> *They have become a burden to me; I am weary of bearing them. When you spread out your hands in prayer, I hide my eyes from you;*
> *even when you offer many prayers, I am not listening. Your hands are full of blood! Wash and make yourselves clean.*
> *Take your evil deeds out of my sight; stop doing wrong. Learn to do right; seek justice. Defend the oppressed.*
> *Take up the cause of the fatherless; plead the case of the widow."* (Isaiah 1:1, 12, 15-16)

Another great 7th century prophet, the shepherd prophet Amos says this:

> *I hate, I despise your religious festivals;*
> *your assemblies are a stench to me.*
> *Even though you bring me burnt offerings and grain offerings,*
> *I will not accept them.*
> *Though you bring choice fellowship offerings,*
> *I will have no regard for them.*
> *Away with the noise of your songs!*
> *I will not listen to the music of your harps.*
> *But let justice roll on like a river,*
> *righteousness like a never-failing stream!* (Amos 5:21-24)

And even the great poet of the Psalms chimes in:

> *Sacrifice and offering you did not desire—but my ears you have opened—burnt offerings and sin offerings you did not require. Then I said, "Here I am, I have come—it is written about me in the scroll. I desire to do your will, my God; your law is within my heart.* (Psalm 40:6-8)

The Old Testament prophets of the seventh and eighth century before Jesus prepared the way for the ultimate understanding of God, advancing the Jewish theology beyond a tribal God to a God of all Mankind, from a God who they thought could be appeased by animal sacrifice to a God who seeks a personal relationship with individuals, not just a nation or a race of tribe. These amateur preachers from all walks of life, sometimes reluctantly, received revelation from God and communicated that message to the people of Israel even when it was unwelcomed and often dangerous. They were not the stereotypical "fortune tellers" or "soothsayers" common in ancient times, for they were spiritual visionaries: they could see sin and evil in society and recognize that a day of accounting was coming, that God was patient but not derelict in His duties. These *ad hoc* mouthpieces for God were not academic theologians or Bible scholars, but they were able to see what God is like in practice and to see what God wanted for His Creation. Through them, God became more visible.

Jesus Builds on The Old Testament Prophets

Jesus stands in continuity with these prophets, advancing a new understanding of God by what He said and what He did. He took as His identity the most iconic vision in the Old Testament, the **Suffering Servant** in Isaiah. To the disappointment of the first century Jews (and to His disciples) Jesus did not take on the role of the "Conquering Messiah" who would restore David's throne politically and militarily; instead, He said "*Come to Me, all you who are weary and burdened, and I will give you rest. Take My yoke upon you and learn from Me; for I am gentle and humble in heart, and you will find rest for your souls.*" (Matthew 11:28-29) Rather than offering a sword, Jesus offers a "yoke," the agricultural device joining two oxen together to do heavy work. To the Jewish nation occupied by the Roman army, the "yoke" was a symbol of oppression, a powerful "dog whistle" as we say in our own political times. The most revealing description of Himself was in His "declaration" in His home synagogue at the beginning of His ministry at 30 years of age:

> *He went to Nazareth, where he had been brought up, and on the Sabbath day he went into the synagogue, as was his custom. He stood up to read, and the scroll of the prophet Isaiah was handed to him. Unrolling it, he found the place where it is written:*
> *"The Spirit of the Lord is on me,*
> *because he has anointed me*
> *to proclaim good news to the poor.*
> *He has sent me to proclaim freedom for the prisoners*
> *and recovery of sight for the blind,*
> *to set the oppressed free,*
> *to proclaim the year of the Lord's favor."*
> *Then he rolled up the scroll, gave it back to the attendant and sat down. The eyes of everyone in the synagogue were fastened on him. He began by saying to them, "Today this scripture is fulfilled in your hearing."* (Luke 4:16-21)

It was no accident or coincidence that Jesus read this passage from Isaiah 61:1-2. Jesus took the large synagogue scroll and unrolled it to this specific passage; He definitively and deliberately took this Old Testament prophet's promise and made it His platform, His purpose in coming to Earth.

Not surprisingly, some of the observers were astonished that He was so well educated and eloquent; others were skeptical, saying "Isn't this Joseph's son? A local boy? Who does He think He is?"

Who is Jesus?

**That is the question, the central question,
the question this book seeks to answer,
or to encourage readers to answer for themselves.**

Albert Schweitzer, the great theologian, musician, doctor and humanitarian penned these haunting words about the mystery of Jesus, really coming to see Him in some way. His answer here is somewhat mystical, reflecting the spiritual perception required where physical perception fails.

*He comes to us as one unknown, without a name,
as of old, by the lakeside, He came to those who knew Him not.
He speaks to us the same word: 'follow thou me!'
and sets us to the tasks which He has to fulfill for our time.
He commands.
And to those who obey Him, whether they be wise or simple, He will reveal Himself in the toils, the conflicts, the sufferings which they shall pass through in His fellowship,
and, as an ineffable mystery,
they shall learn in their own experience, who He is.*[50]

Chapter 9

SOME KIND OF GOD

"God don't make no mistakes, that's how He got to be God."
ARCHIE BUNKER

EVEN THOUGH BELIEF IN SOME KIND OF DIVINITY OR spiritual being is nearly universal among virtually all human groups, and such belief has existed throughout recorded history, not every **individual** shares that belief. In historical times some people have been **atheists** (from Greek "*without gods*")), who believe affirmatively that "there is no god." Others have been **agnostics**, (Greek "*without knowledge*") who **doubt** the existence of god or gods. These are often individuals who have searched for evidence or proof that meets scientific standards, but finding none, vote "undecided." Agnostics are not necessarily neutral about the question of "god", but are usually seen as "skeptics", perhaps leaning more toward doubt than belief. Charles Darwin, the father of "atheistic evolution" according to many Christians, was, in fact, only a biblical skeptic, a doubter, but he continued an active church life until his death. Skeptics or agnostics are much more numerous than confirmed atheists, and their group includes many famous modern scientists and philosophers, such as Bertrand Russell and Carl Sagan. Russell, an influential English philosopher and author was often labeled "atheist", but in an interview in 1958 he said, "Agnostic would be a better term" for his beliefs about God.[51]

Scientists Looking for God

Carl Sagan, the great American astronomer, cosmologist, astrophysicist, prolific author, and science popularizer on the TV program *Cosmos* was often mislabeled "atheist". He himself, in numerous interviews and broadcasts, denies the label. "I don't know if there is a god," he would say, "And so, I cannot have the certainty of an atheist." In broadcast interviews late in his life, he spoke of wishing he could believe, particularly to believe in life after death. He commented on what a waste it  was if such great minds as his parents were simply lost in the darkness of death. As he faced his own death from an incurable disease in the prime of his life, he bravely and valiantly continued his work without rancor or bitterness. Throughout his life he sincerely struggled to find evidence to support such beliefs and was observably sad that he could not. With his immense accumulation of knowledge in virtually every field of science, and with a remarkable grasp of philosophical and religious thought, Sagan seemed sincerely disappointed in one of those final interviews. Though he wanted to believe that life was not simply lost at death, and that something more than the visible, measurable physical world existed, he could not satisfy his brilliant questioning mind. It was a lovely dream, he concluded, but probably just wishful thinking.[52]

Carl Sagan represents the highest challenge for the Christian apologist, for his knowledge was so vast and all encompassing, and his search for truth so pure and true, and yet he could not accept a Christian God or any other supernatural being. Like all truly competent scientists, he left the question open, unproved and unresolved, waiting for additional evidence. All experimental science operates on the principles of observation, asking questions, forming a hypothesis, testing the hypothesis experimentally to predict a logical outcome, thereby confirming or refuting or modifying the hypothesis. But modern science is totally "materialistic" or "empirical," accepting as real only that which can be seen, measured, weighed, or otherwise observed by other scientists. Scientific reality is only what the five human senses can detect. Since God is admittedly "non-material", materialistic science cannot identify, measure, or quantify God (or any "spiritual" element). A spirit being cannot be seen, heard, smelled, tasted or tactically felt. So, how would one go about describing God to a person who acknowledges only physical, material subjects?

Can We Prove the Existence of God?

The traditional approach to "proving" the existence of God is to use philosophical, logically consistent arguments instead of trying to provide physical, empirical evidence. In practice, however, almost all the historic philosophical arguments for God's existence **use** observable material data, citing the existing natural world and the laws of nature as evidence for an intelligent actor beyond or outside of nature.

The argument that the existence of God can be known to all based on observation of nature was made by the Greek philosophers, and is cited by the Christian apologist, Paul. Speaking in the public forum in Athens about 60 A.D., he noted that the Greeks were a very religious people, for among the many deities honored with statues in the city, the Greeks even had one labeled "Unknown God." The Greeks instinctively knew about God. "*(S)ince what may be known about God is plain to them, because God has made it plain to them. For since the creation of the world God's invisible qualities—his eternal power and divine nature—have been clearly seen, being understood from what has been made, so that people are without excuse. For although they knew God, they neither glorified him as God nor gave thanks to him...*" (Romans 1:19-21)

The Western tradition of philosophical discussion about the existence of God began with Plato and Aristotle, who made arguments that would now be categorized as **cosmological** (the existence of the world or universe is strong evidence for the existence of a God who created it). Another interesting argument for God's existence is credited to Anselm of Canterbury, known as an **ontological** proof (*by definition.*) Anselm said, God is "*that than which nothing greater can be thought.*" Anselm defined God as the greatest conceivable being, a conception in the mind, the "supremely perfect being." Since nothing greater can be conceptualized, that Greatest must be God. Thomas Aquinas and Rene Descartes each proposed other versions of the cosmological argument, and Immanuel Kant made a strong argument for God based on the "existence of good." These ancient arguments are instructive and well worth further reading and consideration. Obviously, there have been many critics of these arguments, and many modern counter-arguments have been advanced by scientists such as Stephen Hawking, Francis Collins, Lawrence M. Krauss, Richard Dawkins, and John Lennox, as well as philosophers including Richard Swinburne, Alvin Plantinga, William Lane Craig, Rebecca Goldstein, David Bentley Hart and Sam Harris.

Plausible but Not Certain

For the purposes of this current work, we will not rely on the traditional arguments for the existence of God, but will propose that a belief in God is a plausible option comparable to the choice scientists make in tentatively accepting (*believing*) a new theory based on available data. Neither science nor religion can provide indisputable "proof" for their beliefs, there being no absolute **certainty** in life.

The question of the existence of God can be logically stated: "Either there IS a God", or "There is NOT a God." There are no logical choices beyond these two statements. There have been numerous "proofs" of God offered by philosophers and theologians, but they are really just arguments for the existence of God, not really "proofs." All serious modern thinkers will likely conclude that we cannot "prove" nor "disprove" the existence of God. Atheists view the data to be stronger for the "No", agnostics see the evidence as being about equal on both sides, and thus a "Maybe" while theists see the "Yes" side as having the most convincing evidence.

A similar dichotomy applies to scientific analysis, though the pure science is always neutral or "maybe" on theories proposed. Science, in general is skeptical, always seeks to "falsify" the existing theories, to provide evidence that the theory is wrong or incomplete, and thus science is largely self-correcting. Certainty is feared and it can be fatal for scientific progress. Religion has no such restraint. Doubt is generally feared by religion, typically resisted as theological skepticism, or "lack of faith." For many religious leaders, "faith" means something near to certainty, whether about God or orthodox doctrines. In common religious discourse, "faith" comes close to being quantifiable, with some people regarded as having little faith, or weak faith, and the more saintly having great faith, a huge amount of faith.

As we will discuss later, this popular view of "faith" is not Biblical, and the more astute believers base faith on "**who**," rather than "**how much**." And seasoned religious practitioners don't claim certainty in their beliefs, open to new understanding, and they tend to express "confidence" rather than dogmatic, absolute certainty. "Confidence" means "satisfied" or "comfortable" to the religious, much in the same way that "confidence" in science means a percentage of certainty, as in "The results of the experiment yield a 95% confidence interval." In laymen's language, this means there is a 95% probability that this result would be the same if the survey had a larger sample, or the experiment were repeated many times, and so this finding is "almost certainly accurate." Probably. In science and in faith, "probably" is a reasonable standard.

Scientists follow the scientific method, within which theories must be verifiable by physical evidence and experiments. On that basis, the existence of God, for which empirical evidence cannot be tested, is incompatible with science. The Catholic Church maintains that knowledge of the existence of God is the "natural light of human reason," Many modern theologians acknowledge that belief in the existence of God may not be amenable to scientific demonstration or refutation, but rests on faith alone. Atheism concludes that lack of empirical evidence proves that no divinity exists in reality. Some other religions such as Buddhism, don't concern themselves with the existence of gods at all, while religions such as Jainism reject the possibility or need for a deity.

Some Kinda God

Back in the early 1960's the Presbyterian Church in American hired a comedian to develop some radio advertisements to get people thinking about God and church. Stan Freberg was famous for his wacky comical stories and was a very successful advertising producer. You may remember an ad he created for a prune company with this slogan: "First the pits, and next the wrinkles." For the 1-minute church radio ads, Freberg used the same wit with a twist. In one commercial, a secular-type says he can't make it to church because "this Sunday I'm playing golf." Paraphrasing Freberg, we hear him ask "What about next Sunday?". "Uh, I, I promised to take the kids to the beach." Freberg: "Well, how about two weeks from Sunday?" "Oh, I never plan that far ahead. Two weeks. Why, **the world could blow up by then.**" There's a meaningful pause and Freberg comes back softly with, "*That's right.*" A chorus then swings into a catchy jingle that concludes, "***Where'd you get the idea that you can make it all by yourself? Doesn't it get a little lonely sometimes out there on a limb without HIM? It's a great life, but it could be greater. Why try and go it alone? The blessings you lose may be your own.***"[53]

Another one-minute message had a "hippy-dippy sounding" man commenting on a poster just being tacked up on a bulletin board (remember, this was back in the 60's). Again, paraphrasing "You make this poster, Dude?" Freberg's voice says, "Sure did." "Yeah? *Far Out man,* I dig those wild and wacky colors!" "Yep, bright colors, just trying to get people to stop a minute and read the message." "Message? Like, what's the message, Dude?" Freberg reads the poster, "***God so loves the world He gave His only son***" There's a pause as the "hippy" ponders:

"Weird, Man... gave His **only** son?" "Yep, gave Him to be crucified, killed on a cross" Freberg pauses, the hippy looks puzzled and the young man mumbled "...uh. God let people **kill** His Boy?" **Come on!** What kind of God is that, Man? What kinda God would do something wacky like that? **Why would He do that?**" Quietly Freberg speaks. "Like it says here, **Because He loves up.** Loves everybody. Even loves the people that killed Him." "**Nah... *now*** I know you're kidding, Man. Ha! Fat chance! Loving those dudes that killed Him? **No way!**" Freberg pauses, and then quietly "He even loves **you.**" The young man is taken aback, and draws back for a clearer look at Freberg: **"Me? Really?"** (*long pause*) **Huh? WOW, that's some kinda God!**"

Maybe It's the Wrong God

Some versions of God are so warped and toxic that no rational person would accept the idea of such a god. Even among the ancient Greeks, the pantheon of gods worshiped by the common people was seen as corrupt and unworthy by the philosopher giants who have so influenced human thought for 2500 years, Socrates, Plato, Aristotle, and many other ancient philosophers rejected the pantheon of Gods (Jupiter, Zeus, Mars, etc.) because their legendary behavior was more vile and depraved than the humans they supposedly ruled. As the poet-sage Xenophanes complained, and Plato after him: **"Homer and Hesiod have ascribed to the gods everything that is a shame and a reproach amongst men, stealing and committing adultery and deceiving each other."**[54] These forward-thinking men of old doubted the reality of god because they were so repulsed by the portraits of the gods described in popular Greek legend, poems and dramas." Do we have a better selection of "gods" in our culture than the Athenians had? Almost nobody believes in Zeus, Poseidon, Apollo, Hermes and Aphrodite anymore. If we set aside the many non-Christian sects and religions in the world, do Christians, Muslims and Jews have several choices listed on their God-menu? It is widely acknowledged that there is only **one** God recognized by the three Abrahamic religions, maybe with different names (Allah, Yahweh, God/ Jesus) but most Believers can accept that all are the same God. It might come as a surprise to Believers that their God actually has a great deal of competition. There are many popular images of God in American media, many portrayals of the Deity which differ from the Biblical norm, and might be considered "imitations," fakes, or pseudo-gods.

God Needs Better Publicity

The God of the popular media such as movies, plays, and magazines vary from an old white-haired man (George Burns or Morgan Freeman), to a smack-talking Black woman (Whoopie Goldberg), a profane, snippy, grumpy but hilarious little man (*Monty Python and Holy Grail*), a wizened black slave known as "De Lawd" (Rex Ingram) and as a beautiful female Christian singer (Alanis Morissette). God often appears as Jesus (theologically correct), and while many such Jesus players are rugged, robust young white men, bearded and buff, usually very solemn and subdued, but always gentle and kind (think of *Jesus Christ Superstar* and *Godspell*), in one TV series Jesus is a Black ghetto messiah, disturbingly like His Ghetto brothers in speech and behavior. Some popular portrayals of Jesus emphasize the pitiful suffering, stoic, mutilated and bloody "Man of Sorrows" (such as *The Passion* movie). Perhaps most startling of all was the 2017 film *The Shack* in which Father God is an elderly Black woman, and the Holy Spirit is an Asian young woman; Jesus is "normal" in this film, strong, gentle, muscular white man.[55]

There are obviously many images and conceptions of God available in the culture apart from those that are presented by religious groups. The secular presentation of God is sometimes an attractive, likable character capturing some of what Jesus portrayed, sometimes a lot more likable than the "Biblical" God preached on street corners by "high dollar" TV evangelists. A central premise of this apology is that God would have more followers if He had a better press secretary, or switched advertising agencies. God has gotten a bad rap, misrepresented by both His friends and His enemies. Many surveys have shown that a majority of American's polled have a distorted, misshapen image of God (as compared to the image of Jesus which we hold here to be the gold standard). Atheists most clearly describe a god (that they don't believe in) who is harsh, petulant, condemning, demanding, unjust, nasty, AND ENDLESS ADDITIONAL ANTI-GOD qualities. Where did the atheists get such a horrible picture of God? Paraphrasing a military term and *Pogo* comic strip, "*We have met the enemy, and **it is US!***" We believers are probably the source of most of the bad publicity about God. Believers have been hamstrung by a loyalty to the Old Testament hammered into their minds by generations of preachers and teachers who offer no options: you either believe the Bible, word for word, or you don't believe the Bible at all (and it is made clear what will happen to you if you don't believe the Bible—and it "ain't pretty.")

Which God Do You Reject?

The problem agnostics and atheists have with God may not be **existential**, but **descriptive**. The God they are looking at is a distortion, a red herring, and incomplete or flawed God, a phony caricature of God. Caricatures of God can be funny, and sometimes very instructive. A creative minister/comedian, Rev. Curt Curtinger, produced an excellent video some years ago called *GodViews*, in which he performs a half-dozen five-minute skits portraying common, but distorted, visions of God.[56] The first is "**The Sheriff**", wherein Curtinger imagines God as being a typical western lawman, big hat, gold badge on his shirt, riding toward the audience on a black horse. He stops at fence and pulls out a little black book and a pen, a bit menacing looking down from his mount. Paraphrasing here, Curtinger portrays the "God character" speaking in a southern drawl *"Howdy there. I guess you know who I am, yeah...I'm God, and you been breaking my laws. You don't need to tell me your names, 'cause I have got 'em all right here, right in my little black book. I've been a'watching you, watching with my All-Seeing Eye. I been checking every breath that you take, every move you make, every vow you break, I been watching you."* He goes on to read from his little book about the various laws and ordinances they have violated (e.g., Statute 147.2, and Ordinance 124, part B), and he insinuates that they are going to have to pay the penalty, pointing his finger, *"down below, if you know what I mean. Ain't that right, Guilt? Yeh, that's right. My old horse here is Guilt."* As he rides off, we notice the black horse has a big "**GUILT**" name tattooed on his haunch. A lot of people have such an image of God, a vengeful supervisor hoping to catch us doing wrong, many of them misled by having that kind of a father—harsh, critical and impossible to please.

Another skit imagines "God" as being like a super-attentive and accommodating servant in formal wear, with clipboard in hand and a tea towel draped just so over his arm. He speaks with a British accent appropriate to his role as a **"Butler."** Minister/Actor Curtinger greets a visitor with surprise; looking at his clipboard he comments that the man's last visit was Easter. Like a stereotyped TV butler, he fawns and smiles graciously at the visitor, and offers him all the amenities of the house, plus a new red sports car, while expressing hope that the man will come again soon. He is SO EAGER TO PLEASE. Thus, we have portrayed a milquetoast, "namby-pamby" version of God so popular today: "Ask God and you can get anything you want." (Especially if you send in a love offering to our TV ministry). Curtinger uses these facetious, satirical scenes to show how many people actually think of God, including a **"Party Host,"** a tottering **"Old Man,"** and a profane, overworked **"Mechanic"** trying to fix everything. This is a very effective counter-attack on the false and distorted images of God that are common in our culture. Others could be easily imagined in this fake God lineup: The Tyrant, The Magic Lamp, The Wimp, or The Inattentive Father figure. It is said that *imitation is the sincerest form of flattery*, but God is not flattered by our silly misconceptions.

John Bertram Phillips ("J. B.") was an English Bible scholar, translator, author and clergyman serving in London during World War II, when England was under attack nightly from German rockets. He is most noted for his version of The New Testament in Modern English which he created as a way to minister to the young people he knew as Vicar of the Church of the Good Shepherd in a declining area of London. This fresh new way of reading the Bible was an attempt to put the biblical message in the common language, the kind spoken in London pubs and streets. His first work was *Letters to Young Churches*, a colloquial translation of Paul's letters. Later he published his version of Acts and finally the entire New Testament. These have been immensely popular in America since being released, but Phillips had a difficult time finding a willing British publisher. Happily, another famous Christian of that era, established author C.S. Lewis, helped get the works published. (More about Lewis later). But it is J.B. Phillips' other book that is most relevant to our own inquiry here: *Your God Is Too Small: A Guide for Believers and Skeptics Alike* (1953)

A Good Father Image of God

Phillips' point is that belief in God is not an abstraction, but is totally defined by "What kind of God?" It is reasonable to reject belief in a god that demands sacrifice of your child in order to appease him, and it is optimistically reasonable to believe that real God would be like a good father: loving, kind, merciful, forgiving, sacrificial, interested, involved, persistent, dependable, and so on. Even if we did not have a good father, we know what a good father is like in our culture, and though no earthly father is comparable to the divine Father in perfection, we can see enough to know what we seek in our God. Whether one believes in such a God or not, IF there were a God, we would want that kind of deity. And in our honest search for such belief, we can see that "small" gods, "inadequate" gods, "destructive" gods are not really in the contest for belief. He argues rather persuasively that "if there IS a God, it must be a good God if we are to believe. He observed:

> **Most people believe in some kind of God.** It's quite difficult really to believe that all the wonders of the universe which science is gradually revealing

to us were not designed by Someone.58 (Emphasis added)[58]

But many people find it very hard to believe in God as a Person who is interested in the world and in the people to whom he has given life and the power to think. Terrible things happen in the world, like wars and concentration camps, and they can't help asking themselves, "Why doesn't God do something about it?" And then they see wicked people apparently getting away with their wickedness and decent-living people suffering quite undeservedly. So, they conclude that although there probably is a God, he is a long way off and doesn't trouble to interfere with the problems of this planet. He may be "at home" in his own inaccessible heaven, but apparently, he's not "at home" to us poor mortals who sometimes long for the reassurance that he cares about us.

Phillips presents a list of 13 "unreal Gods" which he believes are destructive: popular misconceptions about the "real God" Phillips espouses, a "constructive God." The destructive list includes "Resident Policeman," "Parental Hangover," "Grand Old Man," "Meek and Mild," "Heavenly Bosom," "God in a Box," "Managing Director" and "Pale Galilean." He describes each of these inadequate views of God in some detail, pointing out how such misunderstandings arose, and why they are not sufficient for faith— they are "Too Small" in his terms.

Systematically, Phillips shows how each of these inadequate, small gods is false and destructive to real faith. The first is the conscience, which he labels "**Resident Policeman.**" To many people, conscience is almost all that they have by way of knowledge of God. This still, small voice which makes them feel guilty and unhappy before, during, or after doing something wrong, is God speaking to them, so they believe. It is this which, to some extent at least, controls their conduct. It is this which impels them to shoulder the irksome duty and choose the harder path. No serious advocate of a real adult religion would deny the function of conscience, or deny that its voice may at least give some inkling of the moral order that lies behind the obvious world in which we live. Yet to make conscience into God is a highly dangerous thing to do. For one thing, conscience is by no means an infallible guide; and for another it is extremely unlikely that we shall ever be moved to worship, love, and serve a nagging inner voice that at worst spoils our pleasure and at best keeps us rather negatively on the path of virtue.

It is obviously impossible for an adult to worship the conception of God that exists in the mind of a child of Sunday-school age, unless he is prepared to deny his own experience of life. If, by a great effort of will, he does do this he will always be secretly afraid lest some new truth may expose the juvenility of his faith. With such a limited image it will only be by great effort that one can serve, much less serve such a God who is really too small to command his adult loyalty and cooperation.

> It often appears to those outside the Churches that this is precisely the attitude of Christian people. If they are not strenuously defending an outgrown conception of God, then they are cherishing a hot-house God who could only exist between the pages of the Bible or inside the four walls of a Church. Therefore, to join in with the worship of a Church would be to become a party to a piece of mass-hypocrisy and to buy a sense of security at the price of the sense of truth, and many men of goodwill will not consent to such a transaction.[59]

Conscience can be so easily perverted or morbidly developed in the sensitive person, and so easily ignored and silenced by the insensitive, that it makes a very unsatisfactory god. For while it is probably true that every normal person has an embryo moral sense by which he can distinguish right from wrong, the development, non-development, or perversion of that sense is largely a question of upbringing, training, and propaganda. Surely, neither the hectically over-developed nor the falsely-trained, nor the moribund conscience can ever be regarded as God, or even part of Him. For if this is accepted, God can be made to appear to the sensitive an over-exacting **tyrant**, and to the insensitive a comfortable accommodating "**Voice Within**" which would never interfere with a man's pleasure.

In two other "inadequate gods" Phillips recognizes that the "Father" analogy used by Jesus can be distorted by our experience with earthly fathers who are uncaring, unjust, tyrannical, conceited, feckless, cruel, or even over indulgent and disengaged. The "**Parental**

Hangover" and the "**Grand Old Man**" distortions deal with the defective models of parents that form the basis for some "small" images of God. Bad fathers (too harsh or too weak) might damage our image of God, and our deepest, earliest psychological imprint may be the parental superego which we fear and hate, but whose nagging, condemning voice we can't easily escape. But still, we know what "ought" to be in spite of what "was or has been." A **good** father is, we believe, a universal longing, a positive model imprinted on our deepest consciousness, a natural instinct, probably a product of evolution.

A noted radio and TV minister, Joyce Meyer, followed faithfully by many Evangelicals, makes a telling comparison:

> We don't think there's something wrong with one-year-old children because they can't walk perfectly. They fall down frequently, but we pick them up, love them, bandage them if necessary, and keep working with them. Surely our heavenly Father can do even more for us than we do for our children. [60]

The image of God as *Father* is found in the Old Testament, though it was not the most prominent vision of Yahweh in the earliest Hebrew thought. God is sometimes thought of as a *Patriarch*" who leads his family and servants with a firm hand, sometimes compassionate and sometimes harsh. Some passages portray God as a *Warrior* defending His people. Then for some time the idea of God as *King* held sway, incorporating the majesty and power of earthly rulers along with the occasional tyrannical king. The later prophets tendered the idea of God as the Father of Israel using love and discipline to manage his rowdy children. For example, throughout the Old Testament, God is declared to be a "***compassionate and gracious God, slow to anger, abounding in love and faithfulness***," (Exodus 34:6; Numbers 14:18; Deuteronomy 4:31; Nehemiah 9:17; Psalm 86:5, 15; 108:4; 145:8; Joel 2:13). Yet in the New Testament, God's loving-kindness and mercy are manifested even more fully through the fact that "***God so loved the world that he gave his one and only Son, that whoever believes in him shall not perish but have eternal life***" (John 3:16). Throughout the Old Testament, we also see God dealing with Israel the same way a loving father deals with a child. When they willfully sinned against

Him and began to worship idols, God would punish them. Yet, each time He would deliver them once they had repented of their idolatry. This is much the same way God deals with Christians in the New Testament. For example, Hebrews 12:6 tells us that ***"the Lord disciplines those he loves, and he punishes everyone he accepts as a son."***

It was Jesus who finally and completely revealed the Father to us, the wonderful image of God as our Heavenly Father, our father just as He was Jesus' father. We are portrayed not just as servants of God, or friends of God, but children of God. And even more difficult to grasp, the New Testament even has the audacity to speak of ourselves as brothers of the Son, "joint heirs" with Jesus: ***"Now if we are children, then we are heirs—heirs of God and co-heirs with Christ, if indeed we share in his sufferings in order that we may also share in his glory."*** (Romans 8:17) This is an elevation of the human race that boggles the mind, but it appears to be the way God views us: not as renegades but as His children. It is theologically true what the hymn says:

> *My Father is rich in houses and lands,*
> *He holdeth the wealth of the world in His hands!*
> *Of rubies and diamonds, of silver and gold,*
> *His coffers are full, He has riches untold.*
> ***I'm a child of the King***[61] (emphasis added)

Chapter 10

GOD IS GREAT...
GOD IS GOOD

*God is Great, God is Good; Let us thank Him for our food.
By His hands we all are fed, Give us Lord our Daily Bread.
AMEN.*

THIS SIMPLE CHILDHOOD PRAYER HAS BEEN REPEATED at mealtimes in American homes for many decades, and many of the readers will undoubtedly recognize it. Perhaps it was a ritual passed on from grandparents to parents to their children, memorized and quickly repeated by the youngest child, or rotated among several siblings. It may have even been a competitive privilege claimed by the fastest or loudest young prayer warrior. As with most repetitive or ritualized activities, it's meaning and significance faded for most of us who learned it by rote at a young age. And yet, this little mealtime prayer contains all the theology needed to grasp the essential understanding of the Christian God, the picture revealed in Jesus of Nazareth. In fact, the first line, six words contain all the theology we really need. **God is great. God is good.** That's the basic outline that this apology seeks to explain and defend. The other three lines in this simple prayer describe **religion**: how we should respond to God—recognizing with gratitude His provision and providence, what He does for us.

A theological apology or defense such as this book must not only deal with God's existence, but also with His nature. A great many people believe in the existence of a Creator, a "Higher Power", or a "Man Upstairs" but may have a warped or distorted view of what their God is like. Many of these misshapen images of God are repugnant or scary, in many ways unsavory. We deal with some of these misguided concepts of divinity in a later section, as we compare them with the much more attractive Jesus-God. But looking at the most basic characteristics of possible gods begins with two fundamental attributes: *transcendence and immanence.*

Transcendence and Immanence

These theological terms are actually two quite simple ideas: (1) Is God far away, removed from us, uninvolved in human life: <u>transcendent</u>? or (2) Is God close to us, ever present and actively involved with us: <u>immanent</u>? Even among orthodox believers this distinction is rather arguable and generates entirely different doctrines about what God is like and what He does. The Bible allows both ideas: – *"For my thoughts are not your thoughts, neither are your ways my ways," declares the LORD. "As the heavens are higher than the earth, so are my ways higher than your ways and my thoughts than your thoughts."* (Isaiah 55:8-9) contrasted with *"You have searched me, Lord, and you know me. You know when I sit and when I rise; you perceive my thoughts from afar. You discern my going out and my lying down; you are familiar with all my ways."* (Psalm 139:1-3) Jesus described the Heavenly Father in very involved, intimate terms: *"Are not five sparrows sold for two pennies? Yet not one of them is forgotten by God. Indeed, the very hairs of your head are all numbered. Don't be afraid; you are worth more than many sparrows.* (Luke 12:6-7) One of Jesus' titles is *"Emmanuel,"* which means "God with us," and the birth of Jesus is referred to theologically as "incarnation," meaning "God in human flesh," the ultimate in immanence.

In another poignant passage Jesus is looking out over Jerusalem and laments: *"Jerusalem, Jerusalem, you who kill the prophets and stone those sent to you, how often I have longed to gather your children together, as a hen gathers her chicks under her wings, and you were not willing.!"* (Matthew 23:37) Jesus certainly taught that God is just and righteous, and will be our ultimate Judge. ***"Then he will say to those on his left, 'Depart from me, you who are cursed, into the eternal fire prepared for the devil and his angels."*** (Matthew 25:41) There is judgement, but far more often, and most clearly, Jesus spoke of His Father's supreme goodness. Certainly, God is Great, but Jesus' message was heavily weighted toward God is Good, showing the Father's infinite Goodness. He made this comparison to human fathers: ***"Which of you, if his son asks for bread, will give him a stone? Or if he asks for a fish, will give him a snake? So, if you who are evil know how to give good gifts to your children, how much more will your Father in heaven give good things to those who ask Him!"*** (Matthew 7:9-11) Even flawed humans know what a good earthly father is like, but God is **so very much more** loving and devoted to our well-being than the very best human father who ever lived.

Near or Far: A Balanced Theology

The Bible, taken as a whole, presents a balanced understanding, a God who is so far beyond us that He inspires awe, fear and wonder, and yet a God who is so enamored with us that He attends to every breath we take, every thought, every fear we have. The God revealed in Jesus Christ is **both** transcendent and immanent: Ruler of all creation, and attentive, protective Father of every human. He controls numberless galaxies, and also watches over His children tirelessly and patiently.

Christian groups which emphasize the absolute sovereignty of a *transcendent* God and His undefiled holiness are following the tradition and theology of John Calvin, one prominent leader of the Protestant Reformation of the 16th century. Calvinists view God as so high and holy that He cannot be touched or moved by our faults or sorrows. The famous sermon by the Puritan pastor Jonathon Edwards ***"Sinners in the Hands of an Angry God"*** gives a vivid, horrifying view of that kind of God—a God holding doomed sinners over the fires of Hell like a spider on a thin strand of web. It is said that this sermon caused the grown men and women to sob and cry out in prayer. That brand of Christianity rejects the idea of "free will" in responding to God, leading to a doctrine of **predestination**: God alone chooses who will be saved, and His will is righteous. Some Calvinists even teach a gruesome "double predestination" where God alone determines, in advance, who goes to heaven and also who goes to Hell. Our destiny is pre-determined before we are born. This is clearly a "deterministic" world view, a philosophical position also held by many modern scientists and philosophers. Such scholars consider the idea of human "free will" as an illusion, and all that exists and happens is determined, not by God, but by the inviolable laws of nature. (See **Chapter 16, Freedom and Free Will** for a different view). A less hostile version of a transcendent God was popular with Deists such as early American political leaders Thomas Jefferson and Thomas Paine: they viewed God as transcendent, majestic and righteous, creating everything, but He only set it in motion like a watch maker winding a clock and starting it ticking. He has now retired to His distant throne, watching with limited interest but no direct involvement. That is a totally "Transcendent God."

The other strand of theological positioning is *Immanence*, which sees God in more personal, intimate terms, believing in a God who wants an individual one-to-one relationship with His beloved creatures, and who is actively involved in our earthly life. He is invisible but close to us, hearing our hearts and minds and guiding us in our choices. He gave humans "free will" and honors that freedom, allowing us to ignore or reject Him, or to love and serve Him. Only love and devotion given *voluntarily* is genuine, and God wants "friends" rather than "marionettes". This kind of Father-child relationship is what Jesus taught and demonstrated, and it is the promise of the Gospel, a relationship free of fear and trepidation, living in God's love and approval, and responding to that love by seeking to become more like Him in every way possible. The parable of the Prodigal Son told by Jesus illustrates that kind of involved God, a father who doesn't wait for the wayward, "lost" son to arrive home, but instead runs to meet him with forgiveness and restoration (Luke 15:11-31). A transcendent version of this story would probably have the Prodigal sneak into the barn, eventually getting the courage to go upstairs and knock on the door of his father, an angry father who only grudgingly allows the culprit to stay. A reluctant father is a model of "transcendence," and a "running to meet him" father is a model of "immanence." Jesus showed us that God seeks us, woos us, even pursues us in love unbounded.

The **Incarnation** is the perfect example of "immanence." God came to earth as a baby, Jesus. Jesus became one of us, became a man, with all the pain and pleasure of humanness. He lived and worked in a hot and dusty land under brutal occupation by Rome. He faced every human challenge, dealt with every temptation and emotion, experienced love and betrayal, sorrow and loss. Finally, He was tortured and killed, He died in public scorn and humiliation. From first to last, He saw it out, lived like us. This was no God from afar, aloof, unconcerned about our plight. "**He became like us so that we might become like he is**," as 2nd century church leader, Athanasius put it.[62] Paul explained this concept to the Greek scholars in Athens:

> *"The God who made the world and everything in it is the Lord of heaven and earth and does not live in temples built by human hands. And he is not served by human hands, as if he needed anything. Rather, he himself gives everyone life and breath and everything else. From one man he made all the nations, that they should inhabit the whole earth; and he marked out their appointed times in history and the boundaries of their lands. God did this so that they would seek him and perhaps reach out for him and find him, though he is not far from any one of us.28 'For in him we live and move and have our being.' As some of your own poets have said, 'We are his offspring."* (Acts 17:24-28)

To be sure, the Old Testament of the Jews, the Koran of the Muslims, and the New Testament of the Christians all essentially agree: God is **Omnipotent** (all powerful), **Omniscient** (all knowing, wise), **Omnipresent** (everywhere), and **Eternal** (no beginning and no end, everlasting). There is also basic agreement in the three Abrahamic faiths that God is also Holy, Just, Merciful, Forgiving, Loving, and other benevolent attributes. The initial four qualities listed above are related to the Greatness of God, while the other qualities are related to the Goodness of God. So, for now, we focus on the Greatness of God, and what that means for this exploration, beginning with the concept of a "timeless God."

The Eternal God

The central thesis of this apologetic is that the final, highest and most complete conception of God is the image revealed in Jesus Christ, and that this pinnacle of revelation was an evolutionary process, a gradual progressive understanding over eons of time. **Chapter 11** is devoted to making the case that the revelation of God demonstrated by Jesus is, in fact, the best possible God humans can conceive. Any serious study of the Biblical God usually starts with the previously listed categorical statements about the nature of God—what defines that particular deity (omnipotent, omniscient, omnipresent, and eternal). However, for this book's stated apologetic purposes, we need to start with the fourth attribute, ETERNAL: that is, God's relationship to **time**.

The Bible, both Old and New Testaments, clearly and consistently describes an "eternal God." David, the psalmist, living about 1000 B.C. wrote *"Before the mountains were born or you brought forth the whole world, from everlasting to everlasting you are God."* (Psalm 90:2). *"For this God is our God for ever and ever; he will be our guide even to the end."* (Psalm 48:14) Isaiah, the greatest of Hebrew prophets, living about 700 B.C. wrote *"This is what the Lord says—Israel's King and Redeemer, the Lord Almighty: 'I am the first and I am the last; apart from me there is no God.'"* (Isaiah 44:6) Paul, the great Christian world missionary, wrote around 50 A.D. *"Now to the King eternal, immortal, invisible, the only God, be honor and glory for ever and ever. Amen".* (1 Timothy 1:17) John, the last surviving of Jesus' disciples, in about 90 A.D. proclaimed *"And he swore by him who lives for ever and ever, who created the heavens and all that is in them, the earth and all that is in it, and the sea and all that is in it, and said, '"There will be no more delay!"'* (Revelation 10:6).

Consider the implications of the idea that God is **eternal**, *outside* of time, independent and unaffected by the passage of the hours and days and years that sweep us all along. This God created the world and everything that exists, and before He created all that exists, there was nothing but God. Before the Big Bang, God was already there. Of course, saying "before" is using the concept of time, which had not been created, so, technically, there is no "**before** the Big Bang". Or, as

Genesis 1:1 puts it, *"**In the beginning, God created....**"* There was no **before** the beginning. Not coincidentally, the Gospel of John also says *"**In the beginning was the Word, and the Word was with God, and the Word was God. He was with God in the beginning. Through him all things were made; without him nothing was made that has been made.**"* (John 1:1-2) Not only does John argue for a Creator before all time, but he also proclaims that Jesus, the **Word**, as part of the God-head, was there before all time. Jesus himself proclaimed this mysterious idea in these words invoking the same title God shared with Moses at the burning bush: *"**Before Abraham was, I AM**"* (John 8:58 **KJV**, *with emphasis added here; the Greek has no upper and lower case in manuscripts*). Jesus claims to be outside of time and sequence. This eternal "now-ness" is proclaimed in Hebrews 13:8 *"**Jesus Christ is the same yesterday and today and forever.**"*

To think about a God who is outside of time, not bound or influenced by is to open our minds to some amazing ideas, and to lay the foundation for logical answers to some puzzling theological questions. "Does God know the future? Does He know what will happen to me next year?" "Will dead believers have to wait in the grave a long time before they go to Heaven?" "If God already knows whether I will be going to Heaven or Hell, what choice do I have? Does it make any difference how I live if He already knows what the outcome will be?" "If God knows the future, can the future be changed?" Before further addressing how God's relation to time explains so much that has confused and bothered believers and skeptics alike, let us turn to Stephen Hawkins to start our examination in some depth this wonderful, mysterious thing called "time."

> Since events before the Big Bang have no observational consequences, one may as well cut them out of the theory, and say that time began at the Big Bang. Events before the Big Bang, are simply not defined, because there's no way one could measure what happened at them. ... the Big Bang is a beginning that is required by the dynamical laws that govern the universe. It is therefore intrinsic to the universe, and is not imposed on it from outside. [63]

It's About TIME

Time is one of the great inventions of the human mind, and though it provides a platform by which we can understand our lives, *Time itself* is not clearly understood. What is time? Is it material, since it can be measured? Is it metaphysical, supernatural, since we cannot see it or control its flow? Is it cyclical, endlessly repeating itself, or is it relentlessly horizontal and progressive, moving from past to present to future? Popular culture sometimes comes up with an astute saying such as **"Time is what keeps everything from happening at once."** This insightful quote is repeated widely and in varying forms, claimed by many but unverified as to the original source. Another version is proposed: **"God created time to keep everything from happening at once."**

This is pretty good theology, for in fact, God did create time when He created the universe. Nothing existed before Creation, or before the "Big Bang" and everything existed after the Creation/Big Bang, including Time. The first words in the Bible are time-based: "In the beginning" (**before time**) and when God acted, "God created" (**time began**). That story of creation unfolds day by day, through a six-day period, followed by "rest" for the Creator. Much talk and ink have been expended arguing whether the Genesis day was an ordinary 24-hour period, or whether "day" could mean any period of time, since it was God's work day. The Hebrew word *yom* translated into the English "day" can mean either a 24-hour day, or an indefinite long period of time, depending on the context. It takes some serious mental gymnastics to argue that these six days were normal earth days (solar days), for the Sun and Moon were not created until day four (Genesis 1:14-19). It seems safer to consider these first "days" as undefined periods of time, what we might call eons or epochs, or even "geological periods" as science might suggest. Even if the Bible must not be taken literally in every instance, as this present book suggests, still this Creation story can be enjoyed as a wonderful spiritual, metaphorical truth about **Who** was the Creator, rather than **How** or **When** He created. Claiming that God is the Creator is an unassailable statement of faith because it is a valid option to the question "How was the Universe formed?" Other valid options may include "the Big Bang" or the "multiverse", but no options are scientifically **provable** with the information we now have.

Much of religious thought about "eternal" has been rooted in a "hereafter", a time after time has ended. "Eternity", the promised future for believers, is from Latin (<u>aeternus</u>) for "timeless" or "no beginning and no end" or "outside or beyond time." Time is limited and limiting, enclosing every human's existence, but eternity is viewed as an escape from time, a permanent "present", a never ending "now." This concept is very difficult for time-bound creatures such as ourselves to understand, or even accept, but it is Biblical, and it is also scientific. **Time** is a potential common ground for science and theology.

> The Moving Finger writes; and having writ,
> Moves on: nor all thy Piety nor Wit
> Shall lure it back to cancel half a Line, Nor all thy
> Tears wash out a Word of it.
> —Omar Khayyám[64]

"*Tempus fugit*" is one of a handful of Latin phrases that most people know, but in Latin or English, virtually everyone is aware of the awful truth it states: **"time flies."** Time. What is it? Is Time the great "Moving Finger" of Omar Khayyam, a fact for all creation, a rule governing all aspects of the cosmos, seen and unseen? Or can it be that <u>time is an illusion</u> as many scientists believe? Without a doubt, time does work its will on every human life (and to all life, so far as we know). ***"There is a time... to be born, and a time to die"*** as the Biblical book of Proverbs (3:1-2) reminds us. As discussed elsewhere in this book, this awareness that there is a "time to die" marks a significant difference in the evolution of humans. It is argued by many psychologists, paleontologists and philosophers that this shadow of our eventual death, the recognition of mortality, marks the true beginning of "humanness," a kind of psychological and intellectual dividing line between pre-humans and true humans. So far as we know, no other animal anticipates mortality or worries about it as humans do, though all creatures cling to life and fight to avoid death. This survival instinct is likely built into the reptilian brain of all vertebrates, but higher brain development and function allows humans to foresee their own demise, and to suffer anxiety from that knowledge. Some animals, such as elephants, appear to mourn their dead relatives, but we are not able to determine whether individual elephants ever anticipate their own future death.

For humans, realizing our ultimate mortality can be a blessing or a curse. Under the best circumstances, accepting that one's life is limited and passing inescapably can motivate and energize us to make the best of every day, being present and purposeful in accomplishing important outcomes. But for many of us, this knowledge of our mortality makes time seem to be our enemy, the thief who steals our precious life from us. Dread of a diminishing future can easily spoil the pleasure of our present. Either of these perspectives is tenable, but one enriches life and the other deadens it. The quality of life may be largely determined by this perspective.

Science and Time

Manipulating time is a familiar theme to science fiction writers, including "time travel" to the past or to the future, bending time, or repeating time, time dilation, chrono warp, hyperspace bubbles, and "warp" speed, to name a few. Hundreds of movies and television plots rely on tricks with time. Theoretical physicists such as Albert Einstein, Max Planck, Werner Heisenberg, and Stephen Hawkins have given us such concepts as the curvature of space, relativity, and a "space-time continuum" where time is considered a fourth dimension (mathematically integrated with the original three spatial dimensions: (length, width, depth.) The general theory of relativity demonstrated that time is flexible when observed from platforms moving at different velocities and directions. We now know in practice that objects and people in space flight age at a slightly different rate from corresponding objects on earth. At a velocity approaching the speed of light it is theorized that a human would virtually stop aging, relative to earth time. Generally, scientists agree that nothing can exceed the speed of light.

Time means a lot to ordinary humans. But what is time to a rock? Or to a river? Certainly, time affects all material things, living and inanimate, combining with natural forces to wear and move and shape, and sometimes to destroy all things. It is the natural laws that operate in the universe, and science has given us a good grasp on the effect and the measurement of time. What once looked to ancient humans like valleys and mountains created by some violent clash of supernatural monsters, now we see as the handiwork of mighty earthquakes or colliding continental plates, or the patient work of a river, a stream of water that, in a million years or so, carves grand canyons and verdant valleys into the landscape. That much time is unimaginable to most of us, as the world of science has discovered the vast distances in the solar system and beyond, so vast that we must speak of "light years" of distance rather than the miles or meters we can ordinarily comprehend.

Light years combines time with a physical constant (the speed of light), making measurements more manageable among the astrophysicists and astronomers and cosmologists of the scientific community—a shortcut way to communicate big things. The speed of light is about 186,000 miles a second, and there are a lot of seconds in an earth year (the standard used), so the actual mileage for an object that is one light year from earth is about **5.88 trillion miles.** Scientists like to be precise, so a light year is exactly 5,878,625,373,183.6 miles in common terms that light can travel in 365.25 earth days. And, just to make it even more impressive: the closest star to Earth, other than the sun, is Alpha Centauri some 4.4 light-years away. The twinkle we see tonight left that closest star over four years ago. With our satellite telescope, the Hubble, we have been able to see and photograph galaxies of millions of stars that are hundreds of light years away from us. To think about such vast distances in terms of time is beyond the ability of most human minds to even consider, much less understand.

Why Take the Time?

Why this long excursion into the mysterious element we call "time"? Part of the reason for this review of the place of *time* in the scientific world view is to stagger the imagination of the Believers, to open the mind of the non-science religious reader to the massive extent of God's creation, the astounding scope of distance and time in the Cosmos. It is mind-numbing to encounter claims of scientists who speak in terms of hundreds of millions of years for the age of the planet, or the billions of years back in time to the "Big Bang", the beginning of creation. Most lay people have some trouble truly grasping the import of looking back 300 years to the beginning of America, or 400 years to the arrival of the Mayflower at Plymouth Rock. To conservative Christians, it is fairly easy to accept the idea that Creation was 6000 years ago, based on the calculations of Bishop James Ussher who in 1650 published his tracing the generations listed in Genesis back to October 23, 4004 BC. Many Christians accept this date as fact, the so called "Young Earther Creationists." We are familiar with the span of time between our own birth and the birth of our grandfather, or even our great grandfather—100 years, maybe 150. We can mentally manage parcels of time, but are swamped by the infinity of time and space. We cannot understand evolution if we cannot grasp the vast amount of time creation of our world has taken. The formation of our world of rocks and air and water, the forests and mountains, the living things on earth—all that we have—has taken more than 4 billion years by scientific estimate. If our "work schedule" for God allows only 6000 years, there is no possibility for the small accidental evolutionary changes to occur, no time for the long, patient process of some beneficial changes aiding survival of some species, eventually, over thousands of generations, naturally selecting and creating the current human genome.

A Vast God for The Vast Universe

The other reason for this extensive exploration of this mystery we call "time" is to lay the foundation for defining how God relates to time, drawing on the thinking of the most forward-looking scientists and **science fiction writers**. It may seem contradictory to suggest that fiction could inform us in any way about either science or theology. However, it is the nature of technological advances in history that amazing ideas created by great science fiction writers have foreshadowed the actual development of the imagined product in reality (usually some years later). Remember Dick Tracy's wristwatch phone from the 1930's and 40's? And the space ships dreamed up for Flash Gordon became reality in the Saturn 5 rocket which flew men to the moon 50 years later. Through the popular **Star Trek** TV series Gene Rodenberry created in 1966 most of our society became familiar with holodecks, warp speed, black holes, phasers, replicators, and a thousand other glimpses of the future. We learned a lot of "science" from Star Wars movies, and the multitude of space dramas that have followed, perhaps some "science" that is wrong or improbable, but still an education of the culture. Other popular science programs were scrupulously scientific: **Cosmos,** with Carl Sagan, was a monumental contribution to the increased influence and respect which science gained in the last 30 years. Science is our hope, many believe.

Can Believers, overwhelmed with evidence of the vastness of creation as revealed by science, ever hope to converse with the modern millions who are "science savvy," including our sons and daughters? Can the religious mind be open to the "big picture" of God's creation which science has discovered, the incredible size, distance, complexity and beauty of the universe? We must. Somehow, we must be in that discussion. We dare not offer or defend a "small" God to the skeptical world.

Looking through the lens of science at such cosmic wonders arouses a multitude of confusing feelings in all who view them: amazement, awe, astonishment, doubt, fear, apprehension, humility, excitement, or "brain-numbness". Some scientists have been encouraged in their belief in a Creator, and others have seen these same images as verification that everything is material—only matter and energy—which follow the same laws of physics they have identified on this planet. And what about "believers"? Does the unbelievable vastness of the Cosmos make them praise their Creator with even more appreciation and awe, or does it terrify them with a threat of crushing their spiritual beliefs? Noted astrophysicist Carl Sagan challenges believers by his questions here:

> How is it that hardly any major religion has looked at science and concluded, "This is better than we thought! The Universe is much bigger than our prophets said, grander, more subtle, more elegant?" Instead, they say, **"No, no, no! My god is a little god, and I want him to stay that way."** A religion, old or new, that stressed the magnificence of the Universe as revealed by modern science might be able to draw forth reserves of reverence and awe barely tapped by the conventional faiths.[65]

A small God, an "earth God", is not adequate to be the God of the Universe, not for Skeptics, and not for Believers. If God is real, He must be **even greater** than we have understood, even greater than our visionaries in poetry and song have proclaimed. Some of our religious hymns try to lift our imagination above the mundane. **How Great Thou Art** is an example:

> O Lord my God, When I in awesome wonder,
> Consider all the worlds Thy Hands have made;
> I see the stars, I hear the rolling thunder,
> Thy power throughout the universe displayed.[66]

Another hymn reaches beyond our earth-bound picture of God: **God of Wonders:**

> Lord of all creation, Of the water, earth and sky
> The Heavens are Your Tabernacle, Glory to the Lord on high
> God of wonders, beyond our galaxy, You are holy, holy
> The universe declares Your majesty…[67]

For modern believers, as it was with our ancient Hebrew forefathers, we find poetry and music to be an easier vehicle than prose for expressing our deepest thoughts, our highest aspirations, our most intimate emotions about God. Some would attribute this this to "left brain-right brain" differences, and that possibility is given some credence and is explored in another chapter of this book.

Omnipresence: Where Is God?

Finally, what about God's omnipresence? How can this be so? How can God be everywhere at once? As long as God is unbound by time and space there is no contradiction. Not only has God created all things, but also his presence is necessary to sustain them in being, just as the presence of hydrogen atoms is necessary to sustain water in being. God is **present** to all beings, but He is **not all beings** (that's pantheism). He is present to all things, and the existence of all things is dependent on his presence, just as the caller of a square dance is present to the dancers on the floor and the existence of the square dance depends on the mind (and voice) of the caller. If the "caller" stops, the dance stops.

With the rise of quantum physics in the last century to current prominence in science, the quandary of matter being in two places at once is now tenable. Experiments continue but there seems to be evidence that a molecule can be in either the form of waves of energy, or act as particles, and at the subatomic level of protons and quarks a lot of mysterious things can happen. Science previously believed that matter only contained particles, and light only existed in waves. More recently, quantum physicists have found that light can act like a particle, bending around corners or bouncing off walls. And matter can behave as a wave, such as electrons moving in waves around a neutron. Most startling was the next discovery: simply observing particles actually changes their behavior. Electrons have been shown to behave as waves, though apparently only **when no one is watching**. It is believed that subatomic elements respond to the expectation of observers. At the scale of atoms and electrons, many of the equations of classical mechanics, which describe how things move at everyday sizes and speeds, cease to be useful. In classical mechanics, objects exist in a specific place at a specific time. However, in quantum mechanics, objects instead exist in a haze of probability; they have a certain chance of being at point A, another chance of being at point B and so on. This "haze" was first identified by Werner Heisenberg in 1927, and called *"The Heisenberg Uncertainty Principle."*[68] He showed that there was a limit to how precisely the properties of electrons could be known or predicted. A proton could be seen at a specific point, but that precise location made the speed uncertain, and vice versa. Matter and light did not seem to follow the traditional physical laws. Superposition—the notion that tiny objects can exist in multiple places or states simultaneously—has become a cornerstone of quantum physics. For decades researchers have stalled at this apparent impasse. They cannot say exactly what a superposition is without looking at it; but if they try to look at it, it disappears. The science involved is obviously more complicated than this brief description, but the general outline is accurate (for now).

Quantum physics is certainly way beyond the scope of this book and way beyond the capacity of the elderly author to really understand. It is cited, however, because it seems to be approaching the concept of "omnipresence" or at least "multi-presence" as a reality in nature. This does not explain how God can be everywhere as theologians argue, but it makes the idea seem less far-fetched. We don't want to fall into the fallacy of "God in the gaps" for science is the master of uncertainty, and science will add more to our understanding of the nature of physical reality, bit by bit, probably forever. However, even while citing this oddity of science, it is not the answer to how God can be omnipresent, being everywhere at once. What follows is an argument based on the mysterious concept of "time."

Time Means Nothing to God

Time controls all that we are, all that we can do, all that we can become. Our little lives are marked with a very small dash between two dates: 1938-2021, the brief lifetime of a person like us. Time may be in control of the creation, **but time does not control the Creator**. Time has no meaning for theology, for God is "timeless" as Christians understand God. The God who created time (for our benefit) can and does sometimes cross that boundary, entering time and history. The Creation itself was a divine step into time, when God acted in a linear order (first, second, etc.), when there was a start and a finish, the passage of time. Then the Creator returned to the realm of "eternity," the timeless observation post from which He oversaw His world unfold. Only rarely, God would intervene into time with divine help such as parting of the Red Sea, and the provision of manna to the Hebrews seeking the promised land. God was, and is, both *immanent (present with us)* and *transcendent (beyond us),* as He chooses.

Consider the following chart created to visualize and illustrate the concept of "time" as a bubble in "eternity, a type of "space-time distortion," to use Star Trek speak, permeable to God's intervention and to mortal humans' soul or spirit exiting time at death to a conscious, permanent existence with God. "Time Shall Be No More" we proclaim in our hymns.

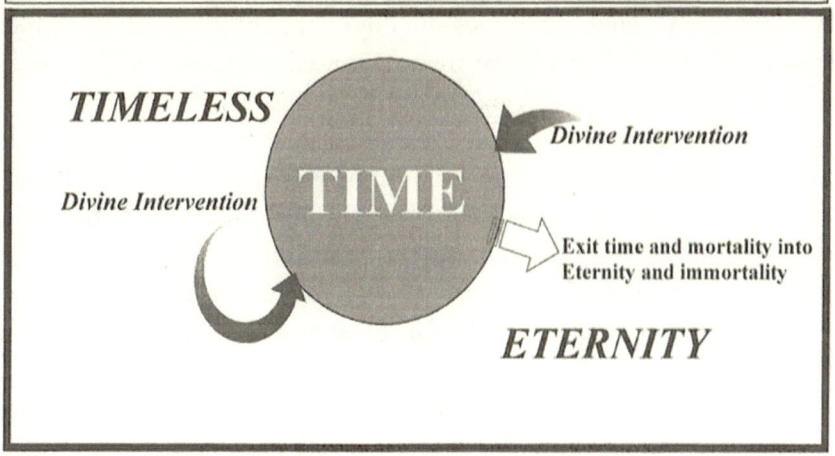

Chart illustrating the concept of **time as a bubble in eternity**, a type of "space-time distortion" permeable to God's intervention and to mortal humans' soul or spirit exiting time at death to a conscious, permanent existence with God

Imagine for a moment that you are watching *Star Trek the Next Generation,* or just reading some work by science fiction author Ray Bradbury. You get acquainted with SPACE-TIME continuum, Black Holes, Worm holes, "bending time" and so forth. In the REAL UNIVERSE as in the Fictional TV shows, space and time are clearly interlocked and even interchangeable in some remarkable ways. No further astrophysics lesson now, but imagine a "bubble" within limitless time and space, a bubble in which time operates because there are creatures in that bubble who experience time. Outside that bubble, time doesn't exist, is irrelevant, and has no influence on God. God **created** the earth in a specific space and time, a place for His big plan for creating Man. The world He created had a beginning and has an end, as do all the living creatures He planted here. From a theoretical and philosophical perspective, God is <u>outside</u> of time and we are <u>inside</u>. For a while, according to Genesis (chapters 1-3) God entered the earth-time-space on a regular basis to fellowship with Adam and Eve, His prize creation. After the humans disobeyed God, they were sent out of the Garden of Eden, and God did not come to visit as before. God is still the Creator and Master of all that goes on in time, but He largely lets the "game" play out as humans will and decide, giving us the freedom to follow God's wishes, or follow our own. On rare occasions, this theory continues, God steps back into Time on our planet, and "intervenes." Miracles are recorded in abundance in the Bible, and attributed to God, which is probably correct (directly or indirectly). Why God intervenes sometimes and does not at others is not known to this author. He is God and we are not, so we have to accept that God's ways are sometimes mysterious to our little minds.

Then one great day God intervened in a big, gigantic way: He came to earth, came into time, God in the Flesh, the fully human Jesus Christ. For three decades, God dwelt among us and we beheld His glory (I John 1:14). Paul gives us the beautiful verbal picture of that cosmic event: ***Christ Jesus…who, though he was in the form of God, did not count equality with God a thing to be grasped, but emptied himself, taking the form of a servant, born in the likeness of men. And being found in human form, he humbled himself by becoming obedient to the point of death, even death on a cross.*** (Philippians 2:5-8) In some way we cannot explain scientifically, God became a man, Jesus of Nazareth, in a specific time in human history (about 4 B.C. to 30 A.D.) lived and died within the bonds and limitations of time. He was, in that life, subjected to the same laws of nature as other men. Gravity pulled on Him, cuts made Him bleed, He slept and ate and drank to sustain His physical body. He laughed and cried, He worked and sweat; He peed and pooped; His body was just like ours, *only likely a lot healthier since He walked several miles a day.*

You know the story—ultimately Jesus was killed by those He came to rescue, dying on a Roman cross in a horrible, painful death. But God was not dead, and Jesus returned to life after a few days, and revealed Himself and His salvation to the remaining disciples, God had, through Jesus, torn down the wall of sinfulness Adam and Eve had built between man and God, and now fellowship, peace with God and renewal of our live is available to everyone who will accept it. When He was finished, Jesus left our time and returned to Eternity where, He has promised, we will be joining Him forever. We only have to die.

Jesus broke the Spector of Death with His Resurrection, making it possible for believing humans to finally conquer the ancient fear of death, the gnawing dread of impending mortality. We have confidence now that Death is not the END, but it is only the EXIT. To leave time (our living) is to go into Eternity, and there/then we can be with our Creator forever, time without end— "for time shall be no more" (Revelation 10:6 *King James*). We don't know what Eternity with God will be like, though we can guess it will be pretty nice since God loves us so much. It won't be wine and bagels or "wild, wild women" but we will probably be very satisfied. It will be Heavenly.

Though the greatest thinkers of the Old Testament and New Testament had not even a faint grasp of what modern science has discovered about time (e.g., Einstein, relativity, space-time continuum, etc.), still, they could somehow imagine that the God who created everything must have been **before** all the things He created. The Creator must precede the creation, they reasoned. What later philosophers conceived as "The First Cause", the shepherds, farmers and the scribes of the nomadic tribes of Israel 3000 years ago described in poetry, stories and songs of awe and amazement. It is worth citing again how David, the outdoors shepherd boy developed his wonderment and reverence, inspired by nature, and the great insight which came to him: *When I consider your heavens, the work of your fingers... what is mankind, that you are mindful of them* (and me)? (Psalm 8:3-5)

What Difference Does It Make?

What are the implications of a timeless God, a God not affected by time? If it is true, as argued above, that God is outside of time in some great cosmic sense, what does that mean for humans, especially humans trying to find meaning and purpose in life through religion? The idea of a "timeless God" is not new, of course, at least to theologians and biblical scholars: most laymen probably have never seriously considered the issue. Many theologians, and the ancient philosophers before them, have put forward the "timeless God" concept based on the many relevant scriptures. The traditional, orthodox view has been that God is timeless in the sense of being outside time altogether; that is, He exists but does not exist at any point in time and He does not experience temporal succession. Any theistic view of the world includes some notion of how God is related to the structures of the universe, including space and time. It appears that many modern theologians and philosophers have moved away from this idea in recent years, questioning the position of Plato, Philo, Augustine, Anselm and Thomas Aquinas on this theological position. Many philosophers today see God as *temporal but everlasting*; that is, God's existence did not begin in time, nor will his existence ever cease in time, but He **still acts in real time**. Current Baptist theologian Roger Olson argues against the traditional "timeless God" view as not being found in the Bible, and offers this insight into the history of a "timeless God:"

Under pressure from Greek ontology (Plato, Aristotle, et. al. through Medieval Catholic theologians) traditional "classical theism" has generally agreed that the God of Abraham, Isaac and Jacob (the Yahweh of the Bible) is somehow (i.e., differently expressed) "outside of time" such that temporal sequence, the passage of past into present into future (or future into present into past) is known to God but not experienced by God. Put in other words, for this classical theistic view, God's eternity means (in relation to time) "simultaneity with all times." In other words, in this view...God exists in an "eternal now." For him, our future has already happened. This is not just a claim about God's foreknowledge; it is a claim about God's being. It is not merely epistemological (knowledge); it is ontological (being, itself).[69]

For starters, if God is outside of time, there are no "yesterdays" or "tomorrows" from His perspective; "Yesterday, today and tomorrow" are the same to Him: *"Jesus Christ is the same yesterday and today and forever."* (Hebrews 13:8) This Biblical teaching is about the eternal sameness of Jesus, but it is theologically the same as saying "**God is the same forever.**" "*I the LORD do not change. So, you, the descendants of Jacob, are not destroyed.*" (Malachi 3:6) "*Every good and perfect gift is from above, coming down from the Father of the heavenly lights, who does not change...*" (James 1:17) "*God is not human, that he should lie, not a human being, that he should change his mind.*" (Numbers 23:19) This latter verse is sometimes translated (as it is in the King James Version) "that he should **repent**", admit that He made a mistake. If God is outside of time, then He has **no past**, and if He has no past, there can be nothing to change, nothing to regret or to repent of. Change requires time, and time's effect on humans and all material objects is clear to us: we change because we have a past, and we have a **present** which affords us the opportunity to change our mind, change our beliefs, change our behavior, change our direction. "We **were** (**then**), but we **are** (**now**)." God doesn't have those blanks on His resume. The implication from this concept is that

God is absolutely **dependable**, His plans and His promises are certain: He will not change His mind **no matter what we do.** Humans cannot change God; the created cannot change the Creator.

Aside from the scriptural support given to this idea above, there is a logical proposition that verifies the immutable, unchanging nature of God. If God had decided to do X last year, and we pray, cry, or offer sacrifices, and we persuade Him to change His mind to do Z instead of X, then either X or Z is wrong, is bad, or is a mistake. Either God's first choice was good, or His second choice was good, but it cannot be both, logically.

The argument advanced here upholds an image of a God who is steady, firm, consistent, predictable and always the same: right and good. However, this argument creates a serious problem for our theology of prayer. The traditional idea of prayer among most religions of the world is based on the possibility that God can be persuaded to do something for us that probably will not happen unless something changes. Whether it is a plea to stop the growth of cancer cells in our mother, or to gain a promotion by gaining the favor and approval of our unfriendly boss, we are seeking to alter the laws of nature or the course of history. Can God grant these requests? Yes, He is the Lord of all Creation, and so He has the power; either request is a "piece of cake" for the Almighty. But, **should He intervene?** The problems with answering "yes" to this question are *staggering*, the implications *monumental.*

Can We Change God's Mind?

If prayer (or any other means of persuasion) can change God's mind, that would open up the arena for an Olympic level of theological competition, for that idea creates more questions than answers. Does God change His mind only if the *person praying* is a stalwart, upright Christian (or Buddhist, etc.)? Is there a big sign on the Pearly Gates or the Prayer Room: **"Only True Believers Need Apply"**? Perhaps the secret to successful prayer is in *quantity*: ten people praying for the request is better than one, and a hundred praying hands carry more weight than 50. Maybe it is the *position* of the petitioner: down on your knees is more effective than standing, or prostrating yourself on the floor is superior to sitting in a pew. Could it be the *location*? Is praying in a church or temple or mosque more pleasing to God than the prayers in the woods, or on the subway? Ah ha! "Faith" is the answer: "***O Ye of little faith…If you have faith as big as a mustard seed, you can….***" (Matthew 17:20) To succeed in God-changing prayer, then, requires the needy person to believe—really BELIEVE. If you have any doubt, forget it! God will not listen. Then there is the bargain hunter who prays to God and tries to make a **deal**: "I will quit drinking, God, if you will help me just this once. I'll even give my next year's tax refund to the church. OK?" Is good prayer mostly just "The Art of the Deal?"

The good God revealed by Jesus: GOD DOES ANSWER PRAYER because He loves us and intends the very best for us, always. He will not ignore your many prayers like a politician dumping your letters or emails to his office. He hears, and He responds, always. Does He always say "Yes"? He cannot give a "Yes" if you ask for something not good for you. "***Which of you, if your son asks for bread, will give him a stone? Or if he asks for a fish, will give him a snake?***" (Matthew 7:9-10) The alternate request is also clear: if you ask for a snake, a good father will give you a fish instead: the good father doesn't ignore the request, but neither does he put his child in danger by saying "Yes."

Considering what we recognize about "good fathers" — the very highest ideal of parenting that we can imagine—we know that good fathers must answer a childish request with "No" sometimes. "No" is an answer, even if it is not the answer we desired. Good fathers sometimes, but not always, may explain: "No, because…." Experts on parenting advise against such defensive explanations for young children: explanations may suggest to the child that there is an argument that can be won by attacking the explanation, and often produce a tantrum to try to get a "Yes" instead of the "No." Parents of earlier times were comfortable saying "No, just because I said so!" This explanation asserts the rightful authority of the parent, and doesn't falsely suggest the parent might be persuaded to change his mind. "Tough love" often is closer to true love than "wishy-washy" parenting.

There is another answer to prayer, as there is in child-parent exchanges: "**Not now**." This is not a magic formula that good fathers can use to avoid rebellion or "conniption fits," for it is seen as a "No" most of the time. But with wise parents, as with an all-wise good God, a delay in granting the request can be in the child's best interest, and what is not safe now might be safe at a later time. For example, a 15-year-old asks Dad to buy him a car, and Dad says "No, not now." The good father is looking ahead to the later time when the son has learned to drive safely and has gotten a license. Or, the wise father may be delaying the dangerous privilege until the son has been completely cured of drug or alcohol addiction, or until other evidence of maturity are demonstrated. The same "No, not now" answer would be wise and good if the request was for a gun, or a trip to Mexico with some unsavory companions. Weak or broken parents may say "Yes" just to get some peace and quiet, but good parents never harm or allow harm to their children in order to serve their own interests or sanity. Thus, a good God, a Jesus-like God, would have to say "No, not now" to us on occasion, and we can learn to wait, trusting in the Father's wisdom and love.

So, the Heavenly Father revealed by Jesus answers **all** prayers: "Yes", "No", or "Not now." In your childhood you may have successfully argued with a parent's answer, getting them to change their mind, but you cannot win an argument with the good God, no matter what you do. No tantrum is loud enough, no sobbing is pitiful enough, no deal is sweet enough to change God's mind. A god that you can control with your prayers or persistence is not worth having. Read that again:

A GOD THAT YOU CAN CONTROL WITH YOUR PRAYERS OR PERSISTENCE IS NOT WORTH HAVING!

If your god is not powerful enough to resist your control, he/she is not powerful enough to help you. He is not a Genie in a bottle (or Bible) who appears to magically grant your wish(es) in a puff of smoke. The "real" Jesus/God is our Lord, not our Servant. **Any other God is too small**.

Time is the great *enabler of possibility* for those of us living in it: if there were only the now, then even if you could think about what could have been, no possibility could ever become actuality: change is possible only through time, and only through change can the *possible* become the *actual*. As we will discuss later, the "will of God" is for change, not of Himself but for us to change, to improve, to fulfill our potential, to become what He created us to be. God created time for us, His human children, so that we can grow and develop. We can see how development is programmed into every new human baby, a series of stages and milestones that move us from "cooing" and "booing" to full, mature adulthood, equipped to not only make our own life meaningful, but also able to improve the lives of others. **We have time to grow,** a loving gift from God our Father. Yet time is also the death of all possibility. Time inevitably moves us along toward an ending, our own final destiny, death. We have millions of "now's", but the "now's" of time run out eventually. Every day the possibility of what we could be, what we could have been, shrinks a little, and as we hurtle toward death, the horizon closes in on us, and our opportunities for growth diminish as the end approaches. We have time enough to become what God planned, but only a finite amount. And then, we exit time into the timeless sphere of our Creator, where there will be no more change because there is no time.

But What About All the Answered Prayers in the Bible?

What then, the Believer may ask, about the many biblical examples of God answering prayers instantly and miraculously? What about the stories where God seems to change His mind and withhold His wrath or judgment due to some special prayers or special people praying? King Hezekiah became gravely ill, and God sent Isaiah the prophet to tell Hezekiah that he was about to die. Hezekiah, who had been a good king, prayed and cried to be spared; God sent Isaiah back with a revised answer: God gave the king 15 more years of life. (2 Kings 20) Did God change His mind? Hezekiah did die, but not so soon. When Jonah got out of the big fish that had swallowed him, he decided to obey God and preach damnation to the wicked city of Nineveh. He gave them the message that God was going to destroy the city because of their evil ways, and then sat down on a hillside to watch the destruction. But amazingly, the Ninevites repented and turned to God (Jonah must have been a terrific preacher!), and "***When God saw what they did and how they turned from their evil ways, he relented and did not bring on them the destruction he had threatened.***" (Jonah 3:10) Jonah had seated himself nearby to watch the great city obliterated, and he was **not pleased** that God "changed" His mind. The circumstances changed (the people repented) and so the new circumstance called for a different answer—mercy. That little vignette gives us an important clue: if we change as God wills, our good God answers based on our "now" and not our "then." Changing our mind and heart is not a bargain to change God's mind: it is obeying God and seeking His will. This may seem like a "cop out" answer but notice that our change, freely made, gives God something new to work with in helping us grow and develop as He planned. More about how God works within the scope of *our free will* is covered in **Chapter 16, Freedom and Free Will.**

The Old Testament writers believed that God sometimes "repents" or admits a mistake: *"I regret that I made Saul king, for he has turned back from following me, and has not carried out my commands."* (I Samuel 15:11). Earlier, before the Flood, we read this:

> *"The Lord saw how great the wickedness of the human race had become on the earth, and that every inclination of the thoughts of the human heart was only evil all the time. The Lord regretted that he had made human beings on the earth, and his heart was deeply troubled. So, the Lord said, "I will wipe from the face of the earth the human race I have created—and with them the animals, the birds and the creatures that move along the ground—for I regret that I have made them.""* (Genesis 6:5-7)

After God led the Hebrews out of slavery in Egypt, they were rebellious and disobedient. God told Moses He was tired of their wickedness, and He was going to destroy them all. Moses pleaded with God to spare them and have mercy. *"Then the LORD relented and did not bring on his people the disaster he had threatened."* (Exodus 32:14)

Such passages as these from the Old Testament are difficult to reconcile with either the theology of an omniscient God, or of a God who is like Jesus in perfect goodness. As we have argued earlier in this chapter, if God is all-knowing, it is logically impossible for Him to regret or repent, for that would require that **He had been wrong**. If God is not omniscient, then there are things God does not know; if He does not have all knowledge and wisdom, then God can be surprised, even outwitted. If God does not know **everything,** then the *laws of physics,* then the *laws of "nature"* may be news to Him. If God is not all knowing, then Newton or Einstein or Neil Armstrong or the Wright brothers or Neil Armstrong, might have surprised Him! Try to imagine such a scene with a "cartoonish" deity getting surprised by the Wright Brothers at Kittyhawk: *"Heh! Peter come quick. Look at those Wright Brothers there in Kittyhawk. Wait a minute! Hold on! That can't be true—people can't fly! Can they Peter?"* Of course, such an ill-informed God is no god at all, a "god too small." In addition, as we pointed out in an earlier section that God could not make a mistake or commit an error which He later realized, because there is **no earlier or later** for God: He is outside of time and sequential events. Regrets require a past. Changing your mind requires time for a "then" and "now."

Did the Old Testament God Change?

So, what can we do with Biblical passages that contradict what we believe has been fully revealed in Jesus? Is the Old Testament God a different one from the New Testament God revealed by Jesus, as some early Christians such as Marcion believed? Earlier we addressed the issue of some mistaken science found in the Old Testament; they were wrong about the sun orbiting the earth, about the shape of the earth, confused about the "canopy structure" of the sky, and ignorant about the actual location of the stars and planets in relation to the earth. Like everyone else in their time, they made bad guesses and some scientific errors because all of "science" was at a primitive stage 3000 years ago. We can easily make allowances for their scientific naivete because of their lack of experience, their deficit of information. Just so, we must also make sympathetic allowances for their *incomplete theology,* their understanding of God was only beginning to take shape, and evolved for more than a thousand years. They made preliminary guesses about YHWH which they later revised, realizing that their earlier visions of God were misguided. We know that a modern child has a distorted vision of God at age three or four, a mistaken belief that God is constantly, invisibly watching them in order to punish their misdeeds. In another year or two the developing child can grasp a healthier, friendlier image of God, more like a protector than a predator. The early Israelites were like our little children, theologically and ethically immature.

When Israel Was a Child (Hosea 11:1)

The early Hebrews knew of historical events when God seemed to be acting, but their vision was still limited and conflicted. Their Mosaic understanding of God led them to believe God was changeable—just as all their neighboring nations believed: gods can be appeased or mollified. With the right kind of ritual and the appropriate sacrifice of animal or person, angry gods could be changed to more friendly deities. Prayer and promises were eventually substituted for blood offerings. Prayer can sometimes get Yahweh to change His plans, they believed, and their stories reflect that interpretation.

Just as we argued earlier, the Iron Age nomadic tribes of Israel were searching for a God among the hundreds of heathen gods in their culture, and their understanding of Yahweh, their ultimate One and Only God, evolved and changed over many generations. They had national experiences which proved to them that God had chosen to be their God, that they were "special" among all peoples, and that He had miraculously preserved them and led them to a "promised land." Without much political or theological organization in their first 400 years in Palestine, the vestiges of older, more brutal religious ideas and practices persisted, but were gradually reformed. Their theories about what this God Yahweh was like and what He demanded grew through trial and error (like all knowledge) and some of their earlier ideas of God were challenged by moral leaders who eventually were regarded as prophets—individuals who spoke for God. These wiser thinkers, along with the rudimentary priesthood that developed, helped to shape their theology to reflect a more humane, merciful and benevolent God, more like Jesus. **God didn't change, but Israel's understanding of Him changed over time.**

In short, the vicious and petulant God in some parts of the Old Testament is a distortion and a mistaken perception. They were probably right in following God when they were led into their "promised land" and they were probably hearing God correctly telling them how to defeat the walled city of Jericho in order to claim their new land. But they were surely following their tribal instincts and traditions when they slaughtered every living thing in the city: men, women, children, livestock. They thought YHWH had ordered this genocide, but that was not God's order. They were wrong. If we cannot imagine Jesus of Nazareth ordering that genocide, knowing what He was like, then we cannot, <u>must not</u>, attribute such heinous actions to His Father, God. Jephthah was a good man who thought keeping his promise to God was more important than his daughter's life (Judges 11), but Jephthah sacrificed her because he had foolishly promised God to sacrifice the first thing coming to meet him after a battle. Sadly, instead of his faithful dog, it was his own dear daughter who came. "A bad promise is better broken" we now advise. But this early Israelite kept his promise, for Jephthah was so terribly wrong about God, as we now know and understand. **But he couldn't know;** these Bronze Age tribes couldn't yet understand.

Living by The Law

These nomadic tribes in their "promised land" had an extensive, almost comprehensive set of Mosaic laws, some ceremonial, some dietary and hygienic, but scores of the rules were dealing with ordinary group life. For example, one of the 600+ biblical laws prescribed stoning to death a child who was disobedient, a law supposedly ordered by God. (Deuteronomy 21:20-21) That law might have assured better behaved teenagers in the desert (certainly fewer teenagers) but they were sadly wrong in their understanding of the Heavenly Father, the one we came to know through Jesus. ***"Observe the Sabbath, because it is holy to you. Anyone who desecrates it is to be put to death; those who do any work on that day must be cut off from their people."*** (Exodus 31:14) Having a day of rest each week is a wonderful thing, but killing neighbors for mowing their lawn on Sunday is surely not what God wants, at least not in America.

One of the realities of life is that our earlier versions of truth, our original understandings as children often prove to be wrong as we grow up. When we mature, we can see in retrospect that our views had been childish, misinformed, and even silly: becoming wiser means changing our minds. That is the story which the Old Testament actually gives us—an earlier and more primitive understanding of God, which then unfolds and expands over time. Some of the ancient ideas about God were wrong, we can now see, as we compare them to what Jesus revealed about God. It is foolish to treat misunderstandings as sacred truth just because they are recorded in the Bible. One of the great proofs of the accuracy and usefulness of the Old Testament is that it records what the people actually thought and did, whether good, bad or ugly. It has not been "sanitized" by later editors. We sometime excuse our foibles with *"It seemed like a good idea at the time."* The Old Testament is what the people thought was right at the time, unvarnished and raw. It is incumbent on today's Believers to discern the difference between human speculation and divine revelation. The key to discerning truth is Jesus: **What Would Jesus Do?**

Is This Blasphemy?

Some believers will consider the previous few paragraphs absolute "blasphemy," see them as denying the truth of these several Bible passages, thus denying the inspiration of the Old Testament entirely. Before grabbing your torches and pitch forks, dear Believers please consider: **Is it not even more blasphemous to attribute to God actions which are more like Satan's evil work than that of Jesus, or His Father?** Jesus Himself harshly condemned the Pharisees for accusing Jesus of being demon possessed, saying that the miracles Jesus did were from Satan and not from God. Giving God credit for the work of Satan or giving God the blame for Satan's deeds is called "blasphemy" by Jesus: *"Truly I tell you, people can be forgiven all their sins and every slander they utter, but whoever blasphemes against the Holy Spirit will never be forgiven; they are guilty of an eternal sin."* (Mark 3:28-29) This is the scariest verse in the Bible, the so-called **Unforgivable Sin**. Based on this passage above, all Believers should be very cautious in blaming God for the Old Testament atrocities, and you don't have to, because **there is another way to defend God,** a better way to guard and preserve His reputation among Skeptics!

We are advocating a more rational, realistic understanding of the Old Testament as an **evolving** attempt to know and serve God as they developed spiritually over the centuries, and incremental growth in their understanding. With this evolutionary view of the Old Testament, we can honorably relieve these sincere God-seekers of blame for sullying the image of God, and we can face a skeptical and doubting world with a more sympathetic and lovable God, a God like Jesus. We do not give up the spiritual truth of the forefathers of our faith by admitting that they got some things wrong at first. We no longer have to defend or explain a God who kills millions of sinners in the Flood, demands human sacrifices and inhuman treatment of slaves and women. We can just say "Their early theology was mistaken, but God led them step by step, from Moses through the poets and prophets, the Psalms of David and the forward-looking work of Isaiah, Amos and Hosea, through Jeremiah and Ezekiel and Joel…and "in the fullness of time" to the final revelation of God in Jesus of Nazareth, the "fullness of God in Christ." We can't cling to the obsolete and distorted image of God of our past if we hope to change the Skeptics' normal complaint from **"Who would believe in a god like that!"** to something like this: **"Hummm…a "*Good* God"?...** a god really **like Jesus?….** Now that's something to think about…**an intriguing idea."**

OK, So God Is Great, But Is He Omnipotent?

God is great almost by definition: a god who is only "Second Greatest" would not be worth much. "God is great" is unfortunately now more associated with the "*allahu akbar*" battle cry of Islamic jihadists than with praising Allah or Jehovah. It is significant though, that Islam has centered its statement of faith on this sentence for so much of what is debated about God/Allah/Yahweh is really encompassed in the question: **How great is God?** Is He all powerful, and all knowing? Is He unlimited in His control of all creation? Can He be everywhere at once, all the time, ever present now and in the past and future? Does He operate within the laws of nature, or does He act above and outside of all known laws of science, whatever He chooses? Is HE omnipotent as our theologians say? Omnipotent means "all powerful" but is God able to do **everything**? Can God make a two-sided triangle? Can He make a round square? Can God create a rock so heavy that even He cannot pick it up? The brief answer is that God can do everything that is **doable**, but not something which is **logically impossible**. Creating a round square is a logically impossible task. God can only do what is logically possible. *God cannot do something which is impossible by definition.* The great Christian apologist, C.S. Lewis wrestled with the question of God's omnipotence and the issue of human free will in his book, **The Problem of Pain**:

> His Omnipotence means power to do all that is intrinsically possible, not to do the intrinsically impossible. You may attribute miracles to Him, but not nonsense. There is no limit to His power. If you choose to say, 'God can give a creature free will and at the same time withhold free will from it,' you have not succeeded in saying anything about God: meaningless combinations of words do not suddenly acquire meaning simply because we prefix to them to two other words, 'God can.' It remains true that all things are possible with God: the intrinsic impossibilities are not things but non-entities.... nonsense remains nonsense even when we talk it about God.[70]

So, God cannot do that which is logically impossible, silly propositions. He cannot make 2 + 2 = 5. He cannot become evil, He cannot stop loving the world of people, He cannot lie, and He can't remember our sins when He forgives them. Who He is, His central nature and character cannot change, for He would no longer be God. Scriptures list several of these impossibilities: *"God is not a man, that he should lie, nor a son of man, that he should change his mind. Does he speak and then not act? Does he promise and not fulfill?"* (Numbers 23:19) Another: *"God did this so that, by two unchangeable things in which it is impossible for God to lie, we.... take hold of the hope offered to us may be greatly encouraged."* (Hebrews 6:18) Yes, some things are impossible for God. So, are these real limitations? Do they mean God is not actually omnipotent?

Notice that these impossibilities cited for God are about His character, WHO HE IS. God must always be God, must always be true, must always be righteous, must always be just, must always be good and can never do evil. The best and briefest definition of God is given in I John 4:8: "**GOD IS LOVE**" —that is WHO He IS.

"God is love" is more than a cute slogan for a T-shirt or a child's bracelet. Love is what defines God, what drives God, the force that led

Him to create us and to put up with our childish, selfish ways, our foibles and our failures about which He knows every detail. But ironically, God's love is the reason He cannot do some things, even though they are not hard to do nor logically impossible. He cannot do some things BECAUSE He loves us lavishly and extravagantly. Remember the old proverb: "**If you love something, let it go. If it returns, it's yours; if it doesn't, it wasn't yours. If you love someone, set them free. If they come back, they're yours; if they don't, they never were.**" God must approve of that sentiment, because that is what He did in creating humans. He loved us, but He did not make us love Him in return. He gave us the choice, not just in responding to Him, but in everything.

Humans Have Free Will

Scientists and philosophers debate this assertion, and the concept of "Free Will" has fallen out of favor with them for now, though it was a settled belief from the time of Socrates and Plato until our time. Many respected philosophers, scholars and scientists deny free will and mount significant arguments for "determinism," from atoms and molecules to genetics and DNA, from the formation of supernovas to the choosing of the next word in this sentence. According to determinism every event is simply the effect of previous effects, all future events are predetermined and unalterable. As a consequence, human freedom or real choice is an illusion, according to this point of view. But religion is almost exclusively based on belief in freedom of will, and thus human accountability for our choices and their behaviors. One strand of protestant theology, followers of Reformer John Knox, *is apparently* largely deterministic, teaching *predestination,* the belief that God decided in advance who would be "saved" and who would be "damned." This unhappy view of God obviously is not the view espoused in this book, for it is impossible to reconcile the God of Jesus with an idea of a god who makes all the choices for us, sets our destiny, making our own lives pointless. (See further discussion of "free will" in **Chapter 15, Being Fully Human**, and more extensively in **Chapter 16, Freedom and Free Will**). Theologian Don Richardson offers a useful perspective on free will and God's will:

... human free will implies God's prior decision not to tamper with the metaphysical base of that free will. It also implies man's ability to reject the persuasion God uses to influence that free will while leaving its metaphysical base intact! **Persuasion, not compulsion, is what even He must rely upon***! And persuasion, by its very definition, must be resistible!*[1] (Emphasis added)

God's Prime Directive

Fans of the science fiction **Star Trek** TV and movie series created by Gene Rodenberry will be familiar with the term *"Prime Directive."* Set many centuries into the future, the Star Trek adventurers traveled throughout the galaxy "exploring strange new worlds," but they were bound by the strict prohibition of interfering in any way with whatever new civilizations or species they encountered. Observe, study, interact with the aliens, but never act in any way that changes their development or their destiny: that was the Prime Directive established by the scientists and governors of the Federation who sent the Enterprise on its mission. This safeguard against contamination of other worlds and species with the science and culture of humans is like today's researchers who take great care visiting isolated tribes or regions not to carry any diseases or contaminants that might cause harm to the native population, nor to introduce technology that would alter their culture prematurely.

God apparently has imposed and followed His own Prime Directive in the evolving self-revelation to the human species. To understand this God which is portrayed in this book we must deal with how the Creator deals with time, and with human will. The question of human "free will" will be dealt with in a later chapter, but suffice it for now, to assert that sentient human beings HAVE FREE WILL, the real power to make choices in all domains of their life. **The God described here did not create us to be a race of robots or mar-**

ionettes. We are not inherently controlled or programmed to act a certain way, or to choose a predetermined path. Part of **God's Prime Directive** is that He will not impose His will on us, will not violate our freedom of self-determination. The question of Free Will has been the subject of philosophers for centuries, and the question is still as hotly debated today as it was when Plato and his peers discussed it 2500 years ago. A bit later, we will explore the necessity for human free-will and the crucial implications arising from a lack of divine control over human choices.

Drawing again on the familiar concepts of modern science fiction, we have some notion of space travel at "warp speed" and the concept of moving forward or backwards in time, sometimes finding and using "wormholes" as passages between universes and even history. Science has not yet achieved all these wonderful things in reality, but have gotten close enough in theory that such ideas are not ruled out as impossible. Though the Bible certainly acknowledges that God gave Adam and Eve free will, and thus to their descendants, the theology there is not as clear as in some science fiction stories, such as those dealing with artificial intelligence and creating human-like robots, androids, cyborgs or other automatons. If we can program these human-like machines to do anything we wish, to respond to our every command, to perform duties impossible or unpleasant for us—then we have true servants who we created and who depend on us for their continued existence. But, as the science fiction stories illustrate, we **cannot make our creatures love us.** Not even *like* us, or *appreciate* us, or *admire* us. They can only do what we taught them to do or programmed them to do; so, if we entered a "love" program into their digital brains, we might receive hugs, handshakes, even kisses. But not love. Anything they give to us is just what we gave them to do; so, in essence, we are loving ourselves through their mechanical operations. Would we feel loved? Would we be uplifted and happy with that "relationship?"

The Omnipotence of God—Is A Limited God Good Enough?

The "omnipotence" of God is almost the definition of God in most discussions. In philosophical terms if a proposed god was powerful but not **all-powerful**, then we would probably find some other entity is

more powerful. A second-most powerful god is not very interesting, and would not be very useful, would it? So, can a God who limits Himself regarding our "free will" still be powerful enough? How can God carry out His divine will for us if He doesn't force us to do what He wills? That is the dilemma we will try to deal with in this section. The following outline will guide our discussion, so you can see where our argument is headed. Some of these premises are discussed elsewhere in this book, and some will not be exhaustively explicated in this work, but hopefully with enough detail to suffice.

American philosopher Edgar Sheffield Brightman, in *The Finite God*, introduced the controversial concept of a limited, finite God as a way of accommodating the twin ideas of an infinitely Good God and an infinitely powerful God:

> The advance of modern thought has compelled us to modify our faith either in God's character or in his omnipotence. **We believe that it is far more reasonable to deny the absolute omnipotence of the power manifesting itself in the world than to deny its goodness. On our view, God is perfect in will, but not in achievement; perfect in power to derive good from all situations, but not in power to determine in detail what those situations will be.** It is not a question of the kind of God we should like to have. It is a question of the kind of God required by the facts.[72] (section in bold for added emphasis)

Omnipotence in the Bible

There is no argument that at least some of the Old Testament writers conceived of God as omnipotent, the one and only God and the creator and controller of the universe. Here are a few of the verses that seem to view God as omnipotent:

> ***"Is anything too hard for the LORD?"*** (Genesis 18:14)

> *"But will God really dwell on earth? The heavens, even the highest heaven, cannot contain you. How much less this temple I have built!"* (1 Kings 8:27)

> *"Yours, Lord, is the greatness and the power and the glory and the majesty and the splendor, for everything in heaven and earth is yours."* (1 Chronicles 29:11-12)

> *"I know that you can do all things; no purpose of yours can be thwarted."* (Job 42:2)

Let us concede the point that the Old Testament (at least by time of the Exile) views Yahweh as omnipotent, all powerful and all knowing. Much of the New Testament is likewise clearly in the "omnipotent camp" but is beginning to allow for the possibility that individuals can thwart the will of God, at least for their own lives. For example, Peter wrote **"The Lord...is not willing that any should perish (be condemned to Hell) but that all would come to repentance."** (II Peter 3:9 King James Version) Paul echoed this view to Timothy: **"This is good, and pleases God our Savior, who wants all people to be saved and to come to a knowledge of the truth."** (I Timothy 2:4) Some translations use "wishes" or "wills" but it is clear God does not intend or wish or will that any person slip out of His divine plan and protection. He is **not willing it,** but it seems to imply that **it nevertheless does happen**; some people reject God's love and suffer the consequences of their willful decision. As we have cited earlier, Jesus bemoans and grieves over the fact that His love for Jerusalem and her people is not returned: **"Jerusalem, Jerusalem, you who kill the prophets and stone those sent to you, how often I have longed to gather your children together, as a hen gathers her chicks under her wings, and you were not willing."** (Luke13:34) He was willing, but they were not, so, for the time, God's will <u>was not done</u>.

Perhaps the reader is already settled in their mind (either for or against "free will"), but let us take a brief consideration of four arguments:

Logical Contradictions: The evidence cited above shows that Biblical writers realized that God does not always get His will (at least at first), and the Old Testament also describes numerous occasions when God's will and intention were not carried out due to the sin and rebellion of the Jewish people. Over and over God's plans are not followed and He patiently comes up with another plan, patiently but also after letting bad consequences punish the disobedience. We have earlier discussed the many other exceptions to God's omnipotence—noting things that God **cannot do**, such as lie, or change, or cease to love His errant children. Obviously, God cannot do preposterous tricks such as creating a rock which is too heavy for Him to lift, or making weird math such as 2 + 2 = 5 or 7. So, there is room for the idea that God has limitations, things He cannot do because those things are not "godly" or consistent with His nature. That opening in omnipotence offers us a logical solution to the dilemma.

Humans Have Free Will: In Chapter 16 we will thoroughly explore the philosophical, psychological and biological reasons we humans all believe we are free to make actual choices. "All" may be open to challenge, for many people in the sciences argue for determinism and against the reality of our free will "illusion." But it is asserted here that at some point and at some level, every person has likely found that to "feel human" means to "feel free." We won't belabor this point here except to suggest that readers try this "**thought experiment**" introspectively: The next time you are hungry consider whether you wish you had a snack or some other quick food. Do you wish you had something to eat right now? Could you get up now and go get something in the kitchen (or somewhere)? Can you decide: **I will get the food!** *Will* you? Is anything hindering you from doing what you wish, what you decided, what you intended? Consider alternate futures: Imagine a world in which you **did** go get food. Now, try to imagine an alternate world in which you **did not** go to get food. Are both scenarios equally possible? Are you free to do either option "A" or option "B"? If you are convinced that you really did have a valid, doable choice and that you were the one who determined which option you took, then you probably think you have "free will." But are you free in only such trivial choices as discussed above? Is your freedom less free in larger issues such as marriage, or accepting a job, or calling your angry brother to apologize?

God <u>Gave</u> Us Our Free Will: If there is a God and He created human beings, then He probably could have made us different than we are, totally under His control by soft or harsh means, but clearly not free to be or do whatever we wish. God *could* have taken that route, *but did not*, for reasons we have outlined earlier in this chapters: If God forced us to love and obey Him, we would be robots or helpless automatons, forced to obey but unable to love. Love is an intentional act or relationship, a voluntary and personal choice to further the interest of the "other," rather than, or more than, our own "interests." Love is the opposite of "selfishness" –self-love—for love means valuing others as we value ourselves. **It is not a feeling** or emotion—it is an intention. Feelings may support or accompany that intention but love is an act of the will. The Golden rule is at its core a description of love: "***Do unto others as you would have them do unto you.***" (Luke 6:31) Love is doing. God had a choice in His Creation, control us or let us control ourselves—Fixed Will or Free Will. He may have regretted that fateful cosmic decision (He hasn't yet) but He decided to make us Free in our will, but still bound by all the other constraints and laws of nature. He did not abdicate His throne and His rule over all nature, and He did not just "wind up" the robots or flip our "on" switch and go off and forget us. He voluntarily ceded control of our minds, our thoughts and our wills for our lives, but did not proscribe His influence and persuasion and "wooing" of His children. He lets us choose, but He still has parental tools and methods to try to keep us from unwise and dangerous decisions. Those tools and methods are discussed below.

God's Plan and Goal for Us Is Love and Communion: The message of Jesus and his followers who wrote the New Testament is unanimous in the view that God has always had positive intentions and plans for all humans, though that understanding had to evolve over millennia. It is pretty clear that God had hopes and plans for Adam and Eve in the Garden of Eden, but those plans did not work out well. He had intended for them to live forever in a paradise where He would fellowship with them every day, a picture of peace and harmony between nature, Man and God. Did God **need** companionship? Was that the reason He created Adam? It is clear that God **wanted**

Adam to be there when He came to Eden "in the cool of the evening" as it is so sweetly put. We can say that God enjoyed fellowship with Adam and Eve, that face to face conversation to close each day. We don't know how many days or years that little evening appointment continued, but on some such twilight God was distressed that Adam and Eve were not at their regular walking path. They had sinned, had disobeyed their God-friend, and so they hid in the bushes. God wanted that relationship, and enjoyed it, but He did not **need** it or anything, for He did not lack anything, was not somehow incomplete. His want and wish were His love for His creation, His plan to give them the ability to become Fully Human, the best that they can be, fulfilling their potential. The Bible has many scriptures that convey this same idea of God, along with several stories illustrating that same intention. A few verses will be reviewed here as a sample, starting with the most quoted verse for many today, words given to Jeremiah to give to the captives in the Exile: **"For I know the plans I have for you," declares the Lord, "plans to prosper you and not to harm you, plans to give you hope and a future"** (Jeremiah 29:11). Though this was a promise to a specific group for their time it is not unreasonable to deduce that the promise applies to us as well. When our life is in shambles, off the track, wouldn't it be nice to believe that Someone really important has a plan for us, a plan for our happiness, for our fulfillment as humans? Wouldn't it be encouraging to discover that God loves you as if you were His only child? Believers have the evidence "in their believing" that God is like that, that when we stop running from Him, we begin getting to know Him in our own experience, becoming ever closer and more intimate in our relationship with Him, moving from being a fugitive to being a friend.

Long ago a fugitive from God named Augustine fought and ran and defied God for many debauched years though he had a good Christian mother. He is famous for the "tongue in cheek" prayer "Lord make me chaste—but not now." When finally, Augustine stopped running he became one of Christianity's great saints, and then wrote the beautiful prayer that concludes "*Thou hast made us for thyself, O Lord, and our heart is restless until it finds its rest in thee.*"[73] Augustine of Hippo recognized a "restlessness" in his inner being, and many scholars 1800 years later find this is true of most people. A more modern 17th century philosopher theologian, Blaise Paschal pictured human need in these words: *"There is a God-shaped vacuum in the heart of each man which cannot be satisfied by any created thing but only by God the Creator, made known through Jesus Christ."*[74]

Something Draws Us Back to Eden

Many theologians and philosophers have observed that we all seem to long for a *something* we can't quite name, some deep inner urge to connect with "a deeper reality" or "higher power," to have an inner peace. Many thinkers have suggested we are longing for something we have lost, something we vaguely remember which we miss in a strange way. Psychiatrists may say this is just an unconscious memory of the comfortable time in the womb which we miss when the outside world is not so pleasant. But some wise men say that Mankind is longing to return to Eden, to go back to some lost home, some mystical, maybe mythical, time and place where all was well and good, a remembrance of being loved and protected, a feeling of perfect peace inwardly and outwardly. Psychiatrist Scott Peck was a popular advocate for that kind of mystical primal longing to go back to Eden, in several books explaining the psychological and spiritual effects of this longing for Eden (really, longing for Eden's God), how some pathological illnesses are rooted in how this inner longing is managed.[75] His theories about human nature have influenced this author's views over the years, especially this concept of an empty place in the soul which requires a spiritual solution. This idea is beautifully stated in the prayer by St. Augustine above.

This is a compelling theory about human nature which scholars have been examining for hundreds of years in research on why religion seems to be so widely and persistently a factor in human lives, from the earliest *Homo sapiens* at least through today, from darkest jungles to frozen tundra: Humans seem to have a "need" or instinct for religion of some kind. These many studies and books may attribute the religious impulse to fear, evolutionary need for mutual cooperation, or as a tool of social organization. Scientists usually have viewed this phenomenon as a natural adaptation to increasing populations and to environmental changes rather than actual religious revelation. In that view, religion is just a useful means to an end—improving survival. In contrast, we support the view here that God created Mankind <u>for</u> Himself and <u>like</u>

Himself in spirit, and He implanted a fundamental urge or unconscious desire to be in harmony with the invisible but real spirit world and the God. The creature longs to know the one who created him, as children long to know their earthly fathers. We agree with Pascal: God intentionally left a "God-shaped" hole in our psyche, a longing and an emptiness that only God can fill.

God Is a Good, Conscientious Father

This preferred metaphor for God in this book may be getting tiresome for readers, but it is hoped that attaching some obscure and unseen entity called **God** to a universal known idea like "father" will make the nature of God plain and understandable. Good earthly fathers are invested in their children and evolution has conspired to build a "father instinct" into most human fathers (and many other animals, especially mammals). In addition to providing the sperm cell that generated the child, the biological sire almost always protects and nurtures his own progeny—because "parental love" has been instilled, or because evolution insists that genes be sent forward for the species to survive. The "father job" includes training and equipping one's children so they can survive, prosper and reproduce, sending the genes further down the gene stream. In animal fathers, helping the offspring to hunt for food and water and to avoid danger pretty much ends the "fatherhood" term. Chimpanzees grow in guarded care for a year or so and are fully functioning adult Chimps by year three. With human children, however, the "father-term" lasts much longer and is more demanding. Human fatherhood extends to socialization and acceptance of authority structure, and absorbing family values, plus usually substantial intellectual education, preparing for work and responsibility before entering society as a solo human being.

Earthly human fathers are not all "good" fathers, for one reason or another, and some fail miserably at this pivotal role. But in spite of an imperfect population, we can learn because we know what a good father is like. We know that beyond the basics of protecting the child from harm and providing the basic necessities, a good father does a great deal more, because the goal is not just survival, but full growth into a fully human individual. The ideal father helps the immature child grow and develop to meet their own potential, to help his child become "all he can be" to borrow an Army slogan. The most successful fathers raise children that are **better** than their parents, more capable and more fulfilled in their life. Human fathers balance the protection of their child to the perfection of their child—knowing that the child cannot grow or learn if he is shielded from every risk and disappointment. Good fathers let their toddlers fall as part of learning to walk. They may take measures to keep such falls from being bloody or bruising, but he must let the child learn by doing, and doing involves mistakes. God is like that dual purposed human father: He must allow us to learn from our mistakes and missteps, and so He cannot prevent every problem. But like the good earthly father, God will protect us from catastrophic and fatal dangers, just as the earthly father will interrupt the child's learning to walk if that child is walking into a dangerous city street. Both God and good fathers hold back while we are learning, but put out a strong hand when we are in mortal peril. The goal of parenting, like the role of God toward us is not to impose His will on our lives but to guide us toward what He created us to become. His will is best for us, but we must find that will for ourselves.

What Is God's Will?

Jesus urged His followers to trust in God's intention, His will, His plan, saying: "*So do not worry, saying, 'What shall we eat?' or 'What shall we drink?' or 'What shall we wear?' For the pagans run after all these things, and your heavenly Father knows that you need them*. (Emphasis added) *but seek first his kingdom and his righteousness, and all these things will be given to you as well.*" (Matthew 6:31-33) Some have mistakenly taken this as a promise that all our earthly needs will be provided, but we also know that He promised the same disciples "*In this world you will have troubles...*" (John 16:33) and going hungry and suffering persecution was promised as well. The promise is conditional, "Seeking first the kingdom of God" which means putting God's will and work ahead of everything else. It does not guarantee that believers will always have everything they want (which would be a nice fringe benefit) but means that every need will be met. Again, this is not a promise that the basic needs such as clean water, food and shelter will be provided to the faithful always, for we know that the faithful throughout history have suffered hunger and thirst and homelessness no matter how holy their lives. Neither does this reality mean that hunger and thirst, homelessness and sickness, pain and persecution are God's plan. Certainly, these plagues of human existence are NOT GOD'S WILL. Nobody gets cholera as part of God's "lesson plans."

God's plan is not just that we must endure hardship and suffering in order to go to heaven; His plan is for us to succeed in our work for Him here on earth: *"For we are God's handiwork (or perhaps "God's handyman")* **created** *in Christ Jesus* **to do good works***, which God prepared in advance for us to do."* (Ephesians 2:10) "Created…to do good works." One of the greatest honors God has bestowed on Mankind is *the chance to be His partner*, to work with Him toward having His "will be done on earth as it is in Heaven." In 1961 the late President John F. Kennedy called his country to duty, to great goals, to service, closing his Inaugural Address with this recognition: *"…let us go forth to lead the land we love, asking His blessing and His help, but knowing that here on earth God's work must truly be our own."*[76] That is His plan for us—doing God's work on earth. What a challenge!

So how can the God described here do what is good for us if He can't impose His will on us? He could, but He does not by His choice, for His goal for us is to grow to our highest potential, which we can do only by making the best choices in life. Computers and robots can "learn" scientists tell us, but they cannot "choose" or "will" some action. It appears so, but in reality, they can only do what they were set up or programmed to do. Scientists are working marvels in developing "artificial intelligence" ("A-I") but most theorists acknowledge that man-made devices cannot duplicate what human brains can do; they can imitate but not duplicate. (This is not universally held by all scientists, some expecting more from AI in the future.) We have scary novels and movies about smart machines taking over, enslaving the human race, but it is not a worry that should keep us awake at night (for now, at least). But God can do what humans can do—God can consider and decide and will and act. And by considering another way of framing the question of God's Will -vs- Our Will we will offer a proposed solution to the dilemma. It was most clearly explained by a British pastor serving in London during World War II in Leslie Weatherhead's small book, *The Will of God*.[77]

The Three Wills of God

Like many Christians Leslie Weatherhead had trouble explaining to his parishioners why "bad things happen to good people" as the problem is now framed. He tells of the struggle that drove him to find an answer that would satisfy his mind and his heart, reconciling a God who is good but allows evil. In opening chapter of *The Will of God* Weatherhead introduces the subject with true stories from his ministry where people were told "It was God's will" after terrible tragedies. An extended quote seems necessary in order to adequately convey Weatherhead's struggle and insight:

> I have a good friend whose dearly beloved wife recently died. When she was dead, he said, "Well, I must just accept it. It is the will of God." But he himself is a doctor, and for weeks he had been fighting for her life. He had called in the best specialists in London. He had used all the devices of modern science, all the inventive apparatus by which the energies of nature can be used to fight disease. Was he all that time fighting <u>against</u> the will of God? If she had recovered, would he not have called her recovery the will of God? Yet surely, we cannot have it both ways. The woman's recovery and the woman's death cannot equally be the will of God, in the sense of being his intention."
>
> Let me illustrate the confusion again. "My boy was killed ten days ago in one of the raids on Berlin," said a woman, "but I am trying to bow to the inscrutable will of God." But was that the will of God? I would have said it was the will of the enemy, Hitler, if you like, of the evil forces we were fighting. Are they then the same thing?"
>
> Here is a mother wringing her hands and weeping in anguish because her baby is dead. Her minister stands by her, longing to comfort her; but though

his presence and prayers may offer consolation, he knows only too well that when the storm is raging it is too late to talk about the anchor that should have been put down before the storm began. What I mean is that it is so important that we should try to think clearly before disaster falls upon us. If we do, then in spite of all our grief we have a philosophy of life that steadies us as an anchor steadies a ship. If we do not, the storm is so furious that little can be done until it is abated. If only the minister could have injected into the mind of the woman his own belief about God! But that, alas! Is impossible. In her anguish, this is what the woman said: "I suppose it is the will of God, <u>but if only the doctor had come in time, he could have saved my baby.</u>" You see the confusion of thought. If the doctor had come in time, would he have been able to outwit the will of God?

The matter came to me poignantly when I was in India. I was standing on the veranda of an Indian home darkened by bereavement. My Indian friend had lost his little son, the light of his eyes, in a cholera epidemic. At the far end of the veranda his little daughter, the only remaining child, slept in a cot covered with a mosquito net. We paced up and down, and I tried in my clumsy way to comfort and console him. But he said, "Well, padre, it is the will of God. That's all there is to it. It is the will of God."

Fortunately, I knew him well enough to be able to reply without being misunderstood, and I said something like this: "Supposing someone crept up the steps onto the veranda tonight, while you all slept, and deliberately put a wad of cotton soaked in cholera germ culture over your little girl's mouth as she lay in that cot there on the veranda. What would you think of that?"

"My God," he said, "(W)hat would I think about that? Nobody would do such a damnable thing. If he attempted it and I caught him...(pause), I would kill him with as little compunction as I would a snake and throw him over the veranda. What do you mean by suggesting such a thing?" [78]

    Weatherhead knew his friend was angered by this, but then he gently pointed out to the grieving father "You yourself accused God of doing just that!" The pastor confronted his Indian friend with the implication of his defective theology: a God who does or allows such awful things cannot be good. It is hard to defend a God who would do such a thing intentionally, no matter what other theological ideas we might propose to excuse it. It would be as unthinkable for God to act that way as it would for a perverse human; it would be "ungodly" by any measure. Thus, this cannot be the wish, the will, the intention of the God revealed by Jesus. There must be some other answer for the fact that horrible and unspeakable things happen to people, other than to say "It's God's will." To say "It's God's will" is to accuse God of things for which we would kill a human who did such things. That false accusation is actually called "blasphemy" in the New Testament, so we hear God blasphemed every day by good intentioned people blithely opining: "It _must_ be God's will."

    Weatherhead studied scripture and philosophy and his own experience, and eventually preached a series of five sermons in London in which he developed the concept "The Three Wills of God." It was very unique at that time (1947) but today many others have accepted or adapted their theology to this basic outline, for it has such strong explanatory powers for a difficult theological problem. The book is readily available today and readers are encouraged to read it for themselves, getting a much better grasp of this concept than can be sketched out in this chapter. Over the last sixty or seventy years, several Christian authors have agreed that God's Will has three parts, and their names for those three parts vary, but we will present Weatherhead's original names: God's **Intentional** Will, His **Circumstantial** Will, and His **Ultimate** Will.[79]

God's Intentional Will

Weatherhead started, as good pastors should, with a scripture: Romans 12:2 says: ***"Do not conform to the pattern of this world, but be transformed by the renewing of your mind. Then you will be able to test and approve what God's will is—his good, pleasing and perfect will.***" The older King James version uses "acceptable" instead of "pleasing." (**KJV**) There he saw Paul was using three different terms to describe God's will, not necessarily three different wills, but at least the concept of differing levels in practice. God's Intentional Will for humans is His original desire for all mankind, His ideal plan based on His nature, Goodness. Jesus introduces a parable in which the "good" shepherd leaves the 99 sheep who are safe and goes searching for the one which is lost. ***"In the same way your Father in heaven is not willing that any of these little ones should perish."*** (Matthew 18:14) God's original plan is that all His "sheep" (people) be safe and cared for. Peter reiterates this is God's intention in this verse: ***"The Lord….is patient toward us, not willing that any should perish, but that all should come to repentance.*** (2 Peter 3:9 **KJV**). If Adam and Eve and all their billions of descendants had followed God's original intention and plan, we'd probably all be enjoying paradise on earth. But, sadly…it didn't work out that way. They, and we, have all wandered off the path God had in mind.

God's Circumstantial Will

God's circumstantial or permissive will is God's plans within certain events, the circumstances of life (including evil), that God allows, or what God permits to happen and uses but does not devise. Meaning: it was never intended as a part of the original plan of God. It is not God's ideal. This is what God will accept, given our choices, good or bad, in particular circumstances, so as to not limit the free will He has given us. He accepts that some will be lost and never return to His love offered to them, but He doesn't give up easily. Undoubtedly, in the Biblical scenario, some people will go to Hell in spite of all God's efforts. But the Jesus/God presented in this book is like a good Father, and so it is not unreasonable to envision God, metaphorically, at least, stretched out on the edge of the pit of Hell, grasping the fingers of the sinners in desperate hope of pulling the beloved lost child back to safety. We can imagine that scene at the Grand Canyon with a heroic young father crying and trying to reach the upraised hand of his child, stretching and grasping for any way to save him. God is like that—maybe not in the physical, literal way but just as true and certain in the spiritual struggle of wills. God cannot always get His will but He never gives up.

Writers have given a number of illustrations of how God's Circumstantial Will is His working within our free will and our current condition, good or bad. One story is of a young man from a poor family who plans to become a doctor, and overcoming all odds, becomes a skilled surgeon. One night on a dark and rainy road he is hit by a drunk driver and he is severely injured. He recovers but his skilled hands have been mangled and reconstructed, so his surgery career is over. Was this God's will? No, it seems certain God planned what the young man planned, a valuable skill to save hundreds of lives. But was the drunk driver doing God's will? No, certainly this was not what God originally planned. Both the young doctor and God were caught in undesirable circumstances. But God still is active and has a revised plan, what we call God's Circumstantial Will. With God's help the young doctor became the director of a clinic for the poor in the city, caring for thousands of needy people and making the world a better place. He traded a surgical suite for a neighborhood free clinic, using what God had given him in a new but just as valuable way. Under the circumstances, God had an alternate plan to make something good out of something bad.

That divine ability is what Paul meant in the famous passage in Romans: *"And we know that in all things God works for the good of those who love him, who have been called according to his purpose."* (Romans 8:28 NIV) **Note**: this is one of those passages where some study is needed such as were discussed in **Chapter 2, What About the Bible?** Most Believers have grown up familiar with the passage as found in the King James Version (**KJV**): "*We know that all things work together for good for those who love God, who are called according to his purpose.*" The difference in the two versions is subtle, but significant. The older King James (1611) says "**all things work together…**" whereas the newer New International Version has "**in all things God works…**" If we believe everything works out OK in the end, we are fatalists. If we believe that God works things out in His time, we are theists (specifically Christian theists). Circumstances of life, so far as we have ever been able to determine, are not stacked in our favor. Everything that happens is **not good** by any theology or philosophy known to us. Bad things happen (disease, accidents, tornados, jobs lost, etc.) but God has a way to overcome those circumstances. It is like we are caught in a burning building and someone is there who knows a safe escape route. "Follow me," the rescuing fireman says. "Follow me" says the God who works for us in our troubled circumstances. "Emmanuel" is one of the titles for Jesus, meaning "God with us." That is our hope, whatever happens, God is with us, not just to watch, but to work for a way out. We will return to this idea of how God works for good later in this chapter.

God's Ultimate Will

This is how God achieves His Sovereign plans, given man's choices, be they good or bad, God's will can be delayed or diverted but cannot stopped. Perhaps a young boy might put rocks and sticks in a creek and maybe create a dam that causes the water to back up: he can slow the water, but he cannot stop it, for the water always finds its way to the sea. So, we can hinder God's will by disobeying Him, or may divert it by our bad choices in life, but God cannot be stopped. Repeating Job: "*I know you can do all things, and no purpose of yours can be thwarted.*" (Job 42: 2). *He works all things together for the good of those He called, who love Him* (Rom. 8:28). God works, within human free will, to put the pieces of our lives back together after we have broken them. This means He can ultimately accomplish His divine purpose in spite of our foolishness. Ultimately God will have the victory, though He may delay to give us one more chance to get on board. I can opt out of the Kingdom of God, but I cannot stop the Kingdom of God from succeeding. No circumstance in this world of suffering can ultimately keep God's will from happening. Paul, who was writing from a Roman cell awaiting his own beheading, wrote with joy and confidence about God's control: *"For I am convinced that neither death nor life, nei-*

ther angels nor demons, neither the present nor the future, nor any powers, neither height nor depth, nor anything else in all creation, will be able to separate us from the love of God that is in Christ Jesus our Lord. (Romans 8:38-39) **Death. Life. Angels. Demons. Present things. Future things. Powers. Height. Depth. Anything else in creation.** Nothing can defeat God's love and will. Nothing.

The real good news is that God can even use the evil circumstances of life to bring about the ultimate triumph of his will. The Cross of Christ is perhaps the best illustration of God adaptive will. Jesus came preaching the Gospel and inviting disciples to follow Him. He went everywhere teaching, preaching, healing and performing miracles, seeming to expect His message to be heard and believed. But in a short time, His crowds went from "Hallelujah" to "Crucify him." It seems that God's intentional will was to convert the lost sheep back to God, but they would not accept. Then the plan to crucify Jesus was brought to fruition, and it appears God accepted this as His circumstantial will, the best that could be made of a bad situation. Jesus clearly was not in immediate agreement to this Circumstantial Will, for He agonized in the Garden, praying till bloody sweat fell from His face. *"Take this cup from me" finally became "Nevertheless, not my will, but thine be done."* (Luke 22:42) It was not God intention that Jesus would be killed when He was sent to earth (so far as we can know) but once His message was rejected, a sacrificial death on the cross became the best available option for God. Jesus was crucified, died and was buried, but God was able to transform that horrible event into a victorious resurrection three days later. God's plan for the salvation of humanity was finalized, and the death of Jesus was the means by which God could lavish His forgiving Grace on the sinful world. Satan and Sin were broken, and salvation through Jesus began and God's ultimate goal and plan was implemented and accomplished.

Paul saw beyond the veil of history and God's plans to detect the cosmic purposes of God which were being fulfilled. He speaks of "predestined" several times, reflecting his awe of the Eternal All Mighty who created the world and rules in ultimate sovereignty through His workings in history; Paul is not denying free will here, but simply the mysterious way God can allow free will for us and still be the Sovereign Almighty God at the same time.

> *In love he predestined us for adoption to sonship through Jesus Christ, in accordance with his pleasure and will.... In him we have redemption through his blood, the forgiveness of sins, in accordance with the riches of God's grace that he lavished on us. With all wisdom and understanding, he <u>made known to us the mystery of his will</u> according to his good pleasure, which he purposed in Christ, to be put into effect when the times reach their fulfillment—to bring unity to all things in heaven and on earth under Christ.*
> (Ephesians 1:5-10) (Emphasis added)

Paul envisions the whole eternal cosmic plan of God as being the unification of all things, to bring all creation back under the rule of His Son, Jesus. He seems to mean by this the restoration of a right relationship between God and Man, the harmony and perfection of all physical creation, the integration and unity of the whole universe. This is Paul's attempt to describe a "Grand Theory of Everything" so desired by Stephen Hawking and the rest of our great scientists. We cannot be certain about what it all means, but we are encouraged to have faith and trust in the God who does know what it all means. It is fitting to finish this chapter by returning to the closing words of Leslie Weatherhead who has given us a template for better understanding God's will and ours.

> You see, even Jesus did not say, "I have explained the world. What he did say was, "I have overcome the world." And if we can only trust where we cannot see, walking in the light we have—which is often very much like hanging on in the dark—if we do faithfully that which we see to be the will of God in the circumstances which evil thrusts upon us, we can rest our minds in the assurance that circumstances which God allows, reacted to in faith and trust and courage, can never defeat the purposes which God ultimately intends.

So doing, we shall wrest from life something big and splendid. We shall find peace in our own hearts...And then one day—for this has been promised us—we shall look up into his face and understand...We can't understand any number of other tragedies and hardships that afflict our lives or the lives of others. We just can't grasp it.

But we can understand that our God is a God of love. He never wants to hurt us. His only intention is for the good of us all. We can understand that in the evil circumstances of this world, God wants us to respond creatively and positively, so that we can turn evil into good. And God will provide the resources to do just that. We can understand that in the end nothing can defeat the purposes of God. One day we will look into his face and all the questions and the heartaches and the pain and the frustration of this life will not matter anymore. It will all be good. It will all be God. And that's enough for now.[80]

Chapter 11

JESUS, THE PERFECT IMAGE OF GOD

As the print of the seal on the wax is the express image of the seal itself, so Christ is the express image – the perfect representation of God.
ST. AMBROSE

THERE ONCE WAS A MAN WHO LIVED IN PALESTINE IN the waning days of the nation of Israel. Jesus was a religious leader and teacher (not a formal "Rabbi") from age 30 to his death at 33. He lived in a land occupied by Roman soldiers and governors, and his life and teachings ran afoul of the Jewish religious establishment, and subsequently of the Roman provincial authority. We know from evidence that he actually was a real person, not just a myth, and we know some of the details of his life and his teachings from the writings and the memories of eyewitnesses and followers. Within 25 years of his death several written documents were already compiled and circulated describing what Jesus said and what he did. It is likely that the written accounts were based on an extensive oral tradition of "sayings", biographical and chronological notes remembered and compared by his followers. They had access to an oral treasure trove of memorable "stories" Jesus told, parables and allegories that captured the imagination of his audience of common folk. Thousands heard Him teach, and many remembered groups of sayings such as the Beatitudes, and concise but startling lessons on life: *"You have been told to love your neighbor and hate your enemy, But I tell you, love your enemies and pray for those who persecute you..."* (Matthew 5:42-43), *"So in everything, do to others what you would have them do to you, for this sums up the Law and the Prophets."* (Matthew 7:2)

It is the assertion of this book that to understand God in any reasonable way, we must look at Jesus, His life and His words. This central pillar of Christianity is based on the reports of Jesus own words, cited earlier: *"Anyone has seen me has seen the Father"* (John 14:9) and *"I and my Father are one."* (John 10:30) This singular Jewish teacher/preacher who lived in Israel about 4 B.C. to 29 A.D. has come to be worshiped as God by millions upon millions of people, spanning twenty centuries. His followers have been willing to suffer or even die for Him, willing to sacrifice all earthly goods and pleasures to serve His cause. What we know about Him comes mostly from the written record of His disciples and those who followed His teachings in the first 50 years of so of His death. Although we have elsewhere presented overwhelming evidence that the New Testament is an accurate and trustworthy historical document, many people are still skeptical that such "biased" records are believable. The New Testament is certainly not neutral about Jesus: *"Jesus did many other signs in the presence of the disciples, which are not written in this book. But these are written so that you may believe that Jesus is the Christ, the Son of God, and that by believing you may have life in his name."* (John 20:30-31)

Was Jesus a Real Person?

The authenticity and reliability of the New Testament has been widely accepted by modern scholars in broad terms, though critics still challenge some details, with some justification. In a later section we will make a more full-throated defense of the New Testament, arguing that it is a trustworthy report of the events surrounding Jesus of Nazareth by writers who had firsthand knowledge of the things they report. There are hundreds of other ancient non-biblical documents by Christians in the first and second century, many of which are comparable to the canonical books in the New Testament. These letters and treatises from very early Church leaders were obviously colored by their firm belief in Jesus, perhaps limiting their "scientific confidence level" for Skeptics. Seizing upon the notion that it is the Church's own approved Gospels which are the primary source of our information about Jesus, some Skeptics dismiss Him as only a fictional character created by some deluded people of the first century. There are, however several secular historical references to Jesus in Roman, Greek and Jewish sources. The extra-biblical references to Jesus cited below, while not being definitive, verifiable historical proof, do substantially corroborate the New Testament on several essential facts. It is true that these external references are sparse (five or six) and none are contemporary with Jesus' life, dating some 30 to 50 years after the Crucifixion. As skimpy as these written references may be, they are accepted by most historians as valid, tangible documents. The fact that every one of these external references to Jesus was written by a non-believer, even a hostile witness, shields these quotes from charges of "bias." We can say confidently that these records clearly substantiate the fact that a historical person named Jesus actually lived in the Roman province of Judea while Pontius Pilate was governor (A.D. 26-36), that this Jesus was executed by the Romans, and further, that this same Jesus, or "Cristos", had a vast number of loyal followers 50 years later spread throughout the Empire. We also learn that the Roman authorities were concerned about this Christian movement which would not "worship" the Emperor, but were otherwise regarded as good citizens. Let us now examine those "unbiased" historical accounts in some detail, from the most substantial and significant source to the less enlightening document.

Evidence for Jesus from Ancient Non-Christian Sources

Publius Cornelius Tacitus (A.D. 56-120) was a Roman senator and orator, probably the greatest Latin language historian of all time. Among his surviving works is *Germania,* about the Germanic tribes Rome conquered, *Historiae,* the definitive history of the Roman Empire from A.D. 69-96, and the later *Annals* (A.D. 116), dealing with the Empire from A.D. 14-68. In *Annals* Tacitus recounts the six-day Great Fire of Rome that burned much of the city in A.D. 64 during the reign of Roman Emperor Nero. It appears that the Great Fire was the work of the Emperor Nero, possibly to clear slums so he could use the land for his own building projects. (The story of Nero fiddling while Rome burned is probably fictitious.) Nero put the blame for the destructive fire on the new group of suspicious outsiders, the Christians, but the rumors still tarnished and angered Nero. Tacitus reports:

> But not all the relief that could come from man, not all the bounties that the prince could bestow, nor all the atonements which could be presented to the gods, availed to relieve Nero from the infamy of being believed to have ordered the Conflagration, the fire of Rome.
>
> Therefore, to scotch the rumour, Nero substituted as culprits, and punished with the utmost refinements of cruelty, a class of men, loathed for their vices, whom the crowd styled Christians *[Chrestianos]*. Christus, the founder of the name *[auctor nominis]*, had undergone the death penalty in the reign of Tiberius, by sentence of the procurator *[procuratorem]* Pontius Pilatus, and a pernicious superstition *[exitiabilis superstitio]* was checked for the moment, only to break out once more, not merely in Judea, the home of the disease, but in the capital itself, where all things horrible or shameful in the world collect and find a vogue. Accordingly, an arrest was first made of all who pleaded guilty; then, upon their information, an immense multitude was convicted, not so much of the crime of firing the city, as of hatred against mankind.[81]

What can we learn from this ancient (and rather unsympathetic) reference to Jesus and the early Christians? Notice, first, that Tacitus reports Christians derived their name from a historical person called Christus (from the Latin), or Christ. He is said to have "undergone the death penalty," obviously alluding to the Roman method of execution known as crucifixion. This is said to have occurred during the reign of Tiberius (14 A.D. to 37 A.D.) and by the sentence of Pontius Pilatus (26 A.D. to 36 A.D.) This confirms much of what the Gospels tell us about the death of Jesus. Tacitus also confirms that the number of these Christian followers of Christ in Rome was **immense** by 64 A.D., and that they were spread in large numbers all over the Roman Empire.

But what are we to make of Tacitus' rather enigmatic statement that Christ's death briefly checked "a most mischievous superstition," which subsequently arose not only in Judaea, but also in Rome? One suggestion is that Tacitus is bearing indirect testimony to the belief of the early church that the Christ who had been crucified had also risen from the grave. While this interpretation is speculative, it does help explain the unusually rapid growth of a religion based on the worship of a man who had been crucified as a criminal. It was no small band of Jewish believers, eleven Disciples and a few other unnamed followers—Christianity had exploded within 30 years, spread all over the Empire.

Pliny the Younger (A.D. 61-113) Another important source of evidence about Jesus and early Christianity can be found in the letters of Pliny the Younger to Emperor Trajan. Pliny was the Roman governor of Bithynia in Asia Minor (now part of Turkey). In one of his letters, dated around A.D. 112, he asks Trajan's advice about the appropriate way to conduct legal proceedings against those accused of being Christians. Pliny says that he needed to consult the emperor about this issue because a great multitude of every age, class, and sex stood accused of Christianity. At one point in his letter, Pliny relates some of the information he has learned about these Christians:

> They were in the habit of meeting on a certain fixed day before it was light, when they sang in alternate verses a hymn to Christ, as to a god, and bound themselves by a solemn oath, not to any wicked deeds, but never to commit any fraud, theft or adultery, never to falsify their word, nor deny a trust when they should be called upon to deliver it up; after which it was their custom to separate, and then reassemble to partake of food – but food of an ordinary and innocent kind.[82]

This passage provides us with a number of interesting insights into the beliefs and practices of early Christians. First, we see that Christians regularly met on a certain fixed day for worship. Second, their worship was directed to Christ, demonstrating that they firmly believed in His divinity. Furthermore, one scholar interprets Pliny's statement that hymns were sung to Christ, "as to a god", as a reference to the rather distinctive fact that, "unlike other gods who were worshiped, Christ was a person who had lived on earth." If this interpretation is correct, Pliny understood that Christians were worshiping an actual historical person as God! Of course, this agrees perfectly with the New Testament doctrine that Jesus was both God and man.

Not only does Pliny's letter help us understand what early Christians believed about Jesus' person, it also reveals the high esteem to which they held His teachings. For instance, Pliny notes that Christians "bound themselves by a solemn oath" not to violate various moral standards, which find their source in the ethical teachings of Jesus. In addition, Pliny's reference to the Christian custom of sharing a common meal likely alludes to their observance of communion and the "love feast." This interpretation helps explain the Christian claim that the meal was merely "food of an ordinary and innocent kind". They were attempting to counter the charge, sometimes made by non-Christians, of practicing "ritual cannibalism," perhaps sacrificing and eating a child in a gruesome ritual. The early Christians had to face and try to repudiate this and other such slanderous attacks on their religion. Interestingly, they were sometimes charged with "atheism" because they would not worship the Greek or Roman gods.

Gaius Suetonius Tranquillus (A.D. 69-122) was a popular Roman historian at about the same time as Tacitus and Pliny the Younger. He mentions early Christians and may refer to Jesus Christ in his work *Lives of the Twelve Caesars*. In his *The Life of Claudius*, we find the statement, "***As the Jews were making constant disturbances at the instigation of Chrestus, he expelled them from Rome.***" This may suggest that Jews and Christians were still in some fellowship, or that Rome did not yet know the difference. One passage in the biography of the Emperor Claudius Divus refers to agitations in the Roman Jewish community and the expulsion of Jews from Rome by Claudius during his reign (A.D. 41 to A.D. 54). This likely was the expulsion mentioned in the Acts of the Apostles (18:2), which brought the Christian couple, Aquilla and Priscilla, into contact*with Paul, with whom they partnered thereafter in the spreading of the Gospel.

In this context "Chresto" is mentioned. In *Nero 16* Suetonius lists various laws by Nero to maintain public order, including halting chariot races as the drivers were cheating and robbing and pantomime shows which frequently were scenes of brawls. Amongst these is punishment for Christians. He states:

> During his reign many abuses were severely punished and put down, and not a few new laws were made: a limit was set to expenditures; the public banquets were confined to a distribution of food; the sale of any kind of cooked viands in the taverns was forbidden, with the exception of pulse and vegetables, whereas before every sort of dainty was exposed for sale. Punishment was inflicted on the Christians, a class of men given to a new and mischievous superstition.[83]

Titus Flavius Josephus (37-100 A.D.) **Josephus**, whose Jewish name was Yosef ben Matityahu, was a Jewish scholar, historian, and possibly a priest, wrote three major books, including *The Antiquities of the Jews and History of the Jewish War.* The extant manuscripts of the writings of this first-century Roman/Jewish author include references to Jesus and the origins of Christianity. *Antiquities,* written about 93 A.D, includes two references to the biblical Jesus Christ in Books 18 and 20, and a reference to the biblical John the Baptist in Book 18. Modern scholars have largely acknowledged the authenticity of the reference in Book 20, Chapter 9, 1 of the *Antiquities* to the condemnation of one "James" by the Jewish Sanhedrin. ***"This James,"*** says Josephus, ***"was the brother of Jesus the so-called Christ."*** This reference to the condemnation of James and the following reference to the life, imprisonment and death of John the Baptist are also considered completely authentic, not altered by later Christian editors (who would have undoubtedly omitted the "so called" from the referenced to Christ.)

> Now some of the Jews thought that the destruction of Herod's army came from God, and that very justly, as a punishment of what he did against John, that was called the Baptist: for

> **Herod slew him, who was a good man.** Herod, who feared lest the great influence John had over the people might put it into his power and inclination to raise a rebellion... Accordingly he was sent a prisoner, out of Herod's suspicious temper, to Macherus, the castle I before mentioned, and was there put to death.[84] (emphasis added)

A number of variations exist between the statements by Josephus regarding the deaths of James and John the Baptist and the New Testament accounts, and generally these differences seem to disprove any later Christian editing, since they would have surely made Josephus agree with the New Testament if they were making changes. As interesting as these two brief references are, there is an earlier one, which is truly astonishing. In a section of *Antiquities* called the *"Testimonium Flavianum,"* (meaning "The Testimony of Flavias Josephus") the relevant portion is this:

> About this time there lived Jesus, a wise man, **if indeed one ought to call him a man**. For he was one who performed surprising deeds and was a teacher of such people as accept the truth gladly. He won over many Jews and many of the Greeks. He was the Messiah. And when, upon the accusation of the principal men among us, Pilate had condemned him to a cross, those who had first come to love him did not cease. He appeared to them spending a third day restored to life, for the prophets of God had foretold these things and a thousand other marvels about him. And the tribe of the Christians, so called after him, has still to this day not disappeared.[85] (Emphasis added)

Did Josephus really write this? Most scholars think the core of the passage originated with Josephus, but that it was later altered by a Christian editor, possibly between the third and fourth century A.D. But why do they think it was altered? Some question why none of the references in Antiquities have parallel passages in *The Jewish Wars* written 20 years earlier, but proof by absence is often dismissed. It may be that Josephus obtained new information or documents during those 20 years, and included the new material in *Antiquities*; historians typically keep researching and collecting more records for some future book. Josephus was not a Christian, and so some few passages look like what a Christian might add in later copies.

For example, the claim that Jesus *was a wise man* seems authentic, but the qualifying phrase, "if indeed one ought to call him a man," is suspect. It implies that Jesus was more than human, and it is quite unlikely that Josephus would have said that! It is also difficult to believe he would have flatly asserted that Jesus was the Christ, especially when he later refers to Jesus as "*the so-called*" Christ. The passage *He appeared to them spending a third day restored to life* is likely not what Jewish Josephus would have included, so it likely was added later by Christian scribes.

But even if we disregard the questionable parts of this passage, we are still left with a good deal of corroborating information from Josephus about the biblical Jesus. We read that he was a wise man who performed surprising feats. And although He was crucified under Pilate, Josephus affirms His followers continued their devotion and became known as Christians. When we combine these statements with Josephus' later reference to Jesus as "the so-called Christ," a rather detailed picture emerges which harmonizes quite well with the biblical record. It increasingly appears that the "biblical Jesus" and the "historical Jesus" are one and the same! Jesus was, without a logical doubt, a real, historical person who lived in a particular place and time, and had an observable, verifiable impact on a lot of people—affecting a whole world of people to one degree of the other.

A Real Man—He Lived and Died Among Us

We have more "contemporaneous" and "near contemporaneous" documentary evidence that Jesus lived than we do for such famous figures as Homer, Hippocrates, or even Julius Caesar. No doubt Homer was real, but existing written evidence is several hundred years after his death; similarly, though Julius Caesar was certainly a real person, the earliest existing documentation of his life is hundreds of years after the fact. Almost all famous ancients are known from copies of copies or copies of some original documents. Regarding Jesus, we have him mentioned in an actual papyrus document that dates to only 130 years after his death, during the lifetime of students of some of the original eye-witness disciples. This is like saying "I never met John F. Kennedy, but I learned a great deal from one of his close White House advisors who was my teacher in graduate school."

There are not very many people who lived more than 2000 years ago who are known to us by name. We know the kings and queens and the emperors and the military heroes, but ordinary men and women live and leave no lasting effect, no remembered name or words or deeds. People born on the edge of society, the poor, the unlearned, the rural farmer or shepherd, live and die in quiet solitude, important to those who loved them, but gone like a morning fog dispelled by the breeze. Readers of this book are not so inevitably destined to an "unremembered life," for these are much more public times, and modern men and women have much more opportunity to make an impact, to make a difference in your world, and even the possibility of being remembered by history and by future generations. Dealing with the subjects in this book perhaps may sensitize the readers in self-examination (Socrates taught us: *"The Unexamined Life is not worth living"* didn't he?) We think about God, the infinite universe, the brevity of our lives, and the uncertainty about meaning and purpose for living, and it surely is humbling, maybe even depressing.

We are a very, very, tiny speck of protoplasm, on a fragile little "pale blue dot" in a vast darkness, as Carl Sagan so beautifully led us to see. "What is mankind?" the Psalmist David asked, feeling so small under the limitless stars in the night on the hillside. Because David was addressing God his psalm gives an answer: *"What is man, that thou art mindful of him? and the son of man, that thou visitest him? For thou hast made him a little lower than the angels, and hast crowned him with glory and honor."* (Psalm 8:5-6 **KJV**) The answer David got by faith is that mankind is the object of God's affection, the centerpiece of His creation, and even though He attended to the sun and the moon and the stars, He also attends to us, mankind. To believe that we are important to the Creator, really important, is a marvelous gift, an insight that can't be proven, an assurance that we are loved that makes no sense except to our heart or mind or soul or spirit, whatever that inner "you" is called. It can be sensed, but it can't be seen. To *even begin* to believe that God is "there" and that He loves us as we are now is to begin to see what Jesus has done. "For God so loved the world (all of us) that He gave His one and only Son" so that everyone who believes Jesus will not perish (disappear forever) but will have eternal, unlimited life worth living." Only Jesus is able to show us that God.

Our Best Sources

It is from the first four books in the New Testament, Matthew, Mark, Luke and John, that we learn most of what Christians believe about the historic Jesus. The four "gospels", or "good news" books, are generally accepted as authentic and official and exclusive by Christians. There are extant copies of other "gospels" (e.g., *The Gospel of Thomas, The Gospel of Peter, The Gospel of Mary,* even *The Gospel of Judas),* and while these often are very old and are valuable archaeological finds, none are seen as authentic or canonical by Christian scholars. As many as 100 other such gospels are known by fragments of their work, or by mention in other early writings. Some of these circulated quite early in church history, and most were condemned as heretical by church leaders, labeled as "pseudo gospels" or fakes. The four accepted gospels were widely recognized and favored in the late first and early second century, when the first compilations of approved scriptures were being circulated. Origen, an early Christian theologian, listed 24 approved books about 225 AD. Other lists came quickly, and these four gospels, along with the other 23 books now in the New Testament were almost universally accepted as scripture. These 27 were "canonized" or made official by church leaders gathered from all of expanded Christendom in 393 A.D., at the urging of Roman emperor, Constantine, seeking unity in the empire, not necessarily doctrinal purity.

Matthew and John were among Jesus' first disciples and eyewitnesses; Mark was a young follower whose life intersected with Jesus at the upper room provided for the Last Supper. It is believed that Mark was afterward a disciple and traveling companion of Peter, and that Mark reflects Peter's remembrances and experience as an original disciple. Luke was a Greek physician, we believe, who became a disciple and helper for Paul, traveling with him on missionary journeys over much of the Roman empire, recording the events in great detail.

John, who identifies himself as the "beloved disciple" or "the disciple whom Jesus loved" (John 20:2) is very likely the brother of James, sons of Zebedee, two fishermen who were among the first disciples to leave all and follow Jesus. Interestingly, Jesus nicknames the two, "Sons of Thunder", which may reflect some rowdiness or exuberance these young men displayed (not otherwise discussed in the Bible). At the Last Supper, the final Passover meal Jesus shared with his twelve disciples, John is described*: "Now there was leaning on Jesus' bosom one of his disciples, whom Jesus loved."* (John 12:23)

One Jesus, Four Portraits

The four Gospels tell the story of Jesus in four different ways, each with a distinct emphasis and a particular audience. Matthew emphasizes the teachings of Jesus, with collections of sermons, stories, and lists of religious sayings, probably drawing on existing oral traditions widely circulated in Israel. Much of what Mark's earlier gospel presents is incorporated into Matthew's account. Matthew was a Jewish tax collector for the Romans before Jesus called him to follow, and his audience is the Jewish people. His Jesus looks like a Jewish rabbi, using rabbinical teaching style, quoting hundreds of Old Testament scriptures, giving proof that Jesus was the Jewish messiah the nation has long awaited.

Mark, the shortest gospel, has an activist Jesus, moving quickly and decisively about His mission, almost frantic in this account, punctuated by phrases such as "Immediately" and "quickly". Mark emphasized that Jesus is the Son of God, he puts much more attention on the miraculous acts of Jesus than on His teachings (though some parables and sayings are included). More than one third of this gospel centers on Jesus' final week, the climatic arrest, trial, death and resurrection of Jesus. Mark's Jesus is the "suffering servant", the one who will "*give His life as a ransom for many...*" (Mark 10:45) Tradition is that Peter's 30-year ministry of preaching and teaching was assisted by a young Mark, possibly also providing Peter with translation for Greek audiences. Over time, it is believed, Mark took notes and wrote down much of Peter's remembrances, recognizing that many of the original disciples were being executed, and Peter was likely to also soon be gone. The quick pace, the vivid descriptions, and the focus on the "Mighty works" of Jesus certainly could reflect the story as told by the impetuous and outspoken disciple, Simon Peter. Mark captures the haste and can-do spirit of Peter, and maybe some of his salty language and style.

Luke was not a disciple of Jesus, and never met Him in person so far as we know. He was a Greek physician, apparently, and became a disciple and a trusted companion to Paul, attending to Paul over many years, traveling with him in his four missionary journeys to all the Gentile world. Eventually Paul was arrested and taken to Rome for trial before the emperor (a right Paul had as a Roman citizen). Luke appears to have undertaken a carefully researched study of the life and teachings of Jesus and his disciples as a part of a legal brief defending Paul in a trial before the Emperor. He had access to Mark's gospel, and probably most of Matthew's content, supplemented with interviews and conversations with surviving people who had known Jesus and his work. Luke likely met Mary, the aging mother of Jesus, for his account has more details about her story than any other gospel. To complete his defense of Paul against his false accusers, Luke also wrote the companion book of Acts, recounting the spread of Christianity after the Jesus' death and resurrection, showing Paul as the leader of this peaceful religious movement in the Roman Empire.

These first three Gospels are clearly telling the same essential story, often having duplicate versions of the same stories or sayings. They each see Jesus in much the same way, and they are commonly labeled "**synoptic**" gospels, "**synoptic**" meaning "seeing together" in Greek. These synoptic gospels have so much in common that "parallels" have been published, with the corresponding passages from each of these gospels arranged in three parallel columns.

John's Reflective Gospel

John, author of the Fourth Gospel, probably the youngest of the original disciples, was the only one of the twelve to die a natural death, apparently living well into his 90's, according to church legends. These legends are not documentary history in the more scientific sense, but as is discussed in the **Chapter 2, What About the Bible?** ancient oral history has been shown to be fairly accurate reporting, and becomes "fixed" or settled when it is finally put in written form. The various oral traditions about the elderly John were transmitted in many extant letters from Christian bishops as early as 96 AD. At least one such Bishop, Polycarp, was personally taught and discipled by John. Some of these legends seem a bit far-fetched, such as the claim that John survived being put in boiling oil by the Roman persecutors. We can't be sure about the hot oil, but we know in fact that the 90-year-old John was persecuted by the Roman authorities and exiled in his last years to the island Patmos as an "enemy of the state."

John, who refers to himself as "the disciple whom Jesus loved (John 19:26), had before him the three synoptic gospels in writing by the time he began his own unique Gospel and probably had many of the letters of Paul. Instead of writing another chronological account of the life and teachings of Jesus, John pursues a more interpretive model. Having been so close to Jesus, and having lived so long, has contemplated for 60 years about **the meaning of Jesus**. John paints a picture of Jesus that lifts up His divinity and His universality through a series of about ten scenarios. He starts, not with the birth of the man Jesus, but rather goes back to the beginning...the Big Beginning, Creation. "In the beginning..." John starts, just as the Old Testament book of Genesis opens, "*In the beginning, God...*" John places the existence of Jesus before history: "*In the beginning was the Word, and the Word was with God, and the Word was God.*" (John 1:1) Having lived nearly a century in the Greco-Roman world, John was very culture in metropolitan Ephesus, a large city in the Roman province of Asia Minor (modern Turkey). In using the Greek concept of Logos ("word") John presents Jesus in terms familiar to the educated and enlightened people of his time.

John's Gospel is distinctly different from the "synoptics", both in style, format and purpose. Whereas the Synoptic Gospels are typically dated between 50 or 65 A.D., it seems likely John's Gospel was available in its present form about 90 or 95 A.D. All the other disciples are believed to have been martyred in the first three or four decades after Jesus. John, who refers to himself as "the disciple whom Jesus loved (John 19:26), had before him the three synoptic gospels in writing by the time he began his own unique Gospel and probably had many of the letters of Paul. Instead of writing another chronological account of the life and teachings of Jesus, John pursues a more interpretive model. Having been so close to Jesus, and having lived so long, he has contemplated for 60 years about **the meaning of Jesus**. John paints a picture of Jesus that lifts up His divinity and His universality through a series of about ten scenarios. John's Gospel has no Christmas story, no birth narrative for Jesus: he starts, not with the birth of the man Jesus, but rather goes back to the beginning...the Big Beginning, Creation. "In the beginning..." John starts, just as the Old Testament book of Genesis opens, "*In the beginning, God...*" John places the existence of Jesus before history: "*In the beginning was the Word, and the Word was with God, and the Word was God.*" (John 1:1) Having lived nearly a century in the Greco-Roman world, John was very familiar with culture in metropolitan Ephesus, a large city in the Roman province of Asia Minor (modern Turkey). In using the Greek concept of Logos ("word") John presents Jesus in terms familiar to the educated and enlightened people of his time. The Greek speaking world of John's day would immediately recognize this as a philosophical treatise, much in the intellectual style of the great Greek philosophers such as Plato, Aristotle and Philo.

John was written in the simple Koine Greek of that day, but he incorporates a number of "word plays", or clever turns of phrase that can have more than one meaning. For example, in John 3 Jesus is talking privately with a wealthy Jewish leader, Nicodemus. ""*Very truly I tell you, no one can see the kingdom of God unless they are born again*" (John 3:5) Jesus uses the Greek word, "*anothen*" which can mean either "again" or "from above." Nicodemus responds to the "again" translation, and is astounded by the idea of a grown man reentering his mother's womb and being "born again." Jesus seems to mean "from above" or "from God", cleverly meaning both ideas: "a new beginning, given by God. Then Jesus said "*The wind blows where it wishes, and you hear its sound, but you do not know where it comes from or where it goes. So it is with everyone who is born of the Spirit.*" (John 3:8) This is another word-play by Jesus: the Greek word "*pneuma*", can mean either "wind" or "spirit." Jesus then closes the teaching by explaining that the process He has in mind is a new beginning, a spiritual renewal, a gift of the Spirit of God. Such skillful word twists were not to confuse readers, but to intrigue and engage, to stimulate thought.

One final example is in the last chapter of this marvelous book, chapter 21. The resurrected Jesus appears on the bank of the lake where Peter and several other of the disciples were fishing in a boat near the shore. He has a fire going and they bake fish for breakfast. "***When they had finished eating, Jesus said to Simon Peter, "Simon, son of John, do you love me more than these?" "Yes, Lord," he said, "you know that I love you." Jesus said, "Feed my lambs." Again, Jesus said, "Simon, son of John, do you love me?" He answered, "Yes, Lord, you know that I love you." Jesus said, "Take care of my sheep."*** (John 21:15-16) *Jesus* uses the Greek word "*agape*", the word for the highest, most perfect love, God-like love. Peter answers, "I *phileo* you" meaning the friendship kind of love in Greek. Three times Jesus repeats the question, just as Peter had three times denied Jesus at the Praetorium. Peter uses the lesser word for love each time, and in the end, Jesus asks "Do you even *phileo* me?" That must have shamed Peter to the heart. John tells this touching story of how Jesus restored Peter as a disciple, with the added dramatic finesse with language that makes this Gospel so rich and compelling. Peter denied three times and Jesus tested him three times and commissioned him three times.

Millions Upon Millions Believed

It is agreed that these four Gospels contain the **bulk** of what we know about Jesus, supplemented with a few other details scattered in Paul's writings and the citations from Jewish and Roman historians cited earlier. Whether one accepts these Biblical documents and the secular mention of Jesus as authentic or accurate, it is still undeniable that millions of people now living, and millions who preceded us, believe in this Jesus and order their lives around Him. Belief is subjective, but the documented effects of this Jesus belief are overwhelmingly positive in the long scope of history. Certainly, there have been many fanatics who claimed the name of Jesus for their foul and awful actions, and such fanatics are active in our time. These perversions of Jesus' life and teachings are far outweighed in the daily lives of good, kind, generous, unselfish ordinary people in every place and time, those who do good in the name of Jesus, who act as nearly as possible as they believe Jesus would act. Millions today in every land and culture seek to "be like Christ," endeavoring day by day to have their lives shaped and molded to look more like Jesus' life. Unknown to many, Jesus is a trusted Friend to many more of our *Homo sapiens* tribe, a living Presence in their lives, invisible but invaluable.

One Solitary Life

He was born in an obscure village, the child of a peasant. He grew up in another village, where he worked in a carpenter shop until he was 30. Then, for three years, he was an itinerant preacher.

He never wrote a book. He never held an office. He never had a family or owned a home. He didn't go to college. He never lived in a big city. He never traveled 200 miles from the place where he was born. He did none of the things that usually accompany greatness. He had no credentials but himself.

He was only 33 when the tide of public opinion turned against him. His friends ran away. One of them denied him. He was turned over to his enemies and went through the mockery of a trial. He was nailed to a cross between two thieves. While he was dying, his executioners gambled for his garments, the only property he had on earth. When he was dead, he was laid in a borrowed grave, through the pity of a friend.

Twenty centuries have come and gone, and today he is the central figure of the human race. I am well within the mark when I say that all the armies that ever marched, all the navies that ever sailed, all the parliaments that ever sat, all the kings that ever reigned—put together—have not affected the life of man on this earth as much as that one, solitary life.[86]

More Than a Man

There is plenty of trustworthy evidence that a man named Jesus lived in Palestine approximately from 4 B.C. until 29 or 30 A.D; most of that evidence has been reviewed above. Christians believe that Jesus was a real flesh and blood man, but that He also was fully divine at the same time—a God-Man. The early Christians fought many theological battles over this combination concept, but eventually settled on the formula in the **Nicaean Creed** (325 A.D.) and slightly revised in 385 A.D.:

> *"We believe in one God, the Father Almighty, Maker of all things visible and invisible. And in one Lord Jesus Christ, the Son of God, begotten of the Father [the only-begotten; that is, of the essence of the Father, God of God,] Light of Light, very God of very God, begotten, not made, being of one substance with the Father; By whom all things were made [both in heaven and on earth]; Who for us men, and for our salvation, came down and was incarnate and was made man..."*
> (Complete versions included in many church hymnals)

The nature of Jesus was one of the heretical topics the Church resisted for three centuries: some said Jesus was God, but **only appeared to be a man**; others believed Jesus was a man but at some point in His life was elevated to divinity (not necessarily God); still others envisioned a Jesus who as a hybrid—half God half human. This identity struggle for early Christians was a hold-over from the Greek philosophy that considered human flesh and blood as inherently evil, and thus Jesus could not have been an actual (evil) mortal man. Some strange, complicated heresies made some trouble by suggesting a series of created beings or "emanations," a series of hierarchically descending radiations from the Godhead through intermediate stages to matter, with Jesus being the final physical version putting a healthy distance between the Holy God and the human Jesus, avoiding mixing pure

JESUS, THE PERFECT IMAGE OF GOD

Good with the impure human body. The Church creed tried to settle the issue forever by carefully selecting the Greek language's subtle words "*<u>begotten, not made</u>, being of <u>one substance</u> with the Father; <u>by whom all things were made</u>...*" to assert that Jesus was not created but was equal and coexistent with the Father, and He participated in the Creation with the Father. It is still difficult—probably impossible—to explain how Jesus could be completely God and completely man at the same time. One or the other seems understandable, but we have a hard time grasping the concept of 100 % God and 100 % human at the same time in one person.

One metaphor which satisfies the Author may not impress the readers: a gallon of water scooped from the Atlantic Ocean is the same as the Atlantic in substance though not in size. The bucket IS all Atlantic Ocean water, but it is NOT ALL of the Atlantic. Jesus was God, but not ALL OF GOD—He was an accurate and authentic representation of God, but took on the temporary limitation of His omnipotence to be in <u>one place for 33 years</u>. Jesus left eternity and entered time in a visible human form, while God the Father remained outside of time. Paul so beautifully describes this amazing idea in Philippians:

> *In your relationships with one another, have the same mindset as Christ Jesus:*
> *Who, being in very nature God, did not consider equality with God,*
> > *something to be used to his own advantage;*
> *rather, he made himself nothing by taking the very nature of a servant,*
> > *being made in human likeness.*
> *And being found in appearance as a man, he humbled himself*
> > *by becoming obedient to death—even death on a cross!*
> *Therefore, God exalted him to the highest place*
> > *and gave him the name that is above every name,*
> *that at the name of Jesus every knee should bow,*
> > *in heaven and on earth and under the earth,*

and every tongue acknowledge that Jesus Christ is Lord,
  to the glory of God, the Father. (Philippians 2:5-11)

More Than a Great Man

C.S. Lewis once believed that Jesus was a good man, even a great man, but certainly not God—there is no God he had decided. One day his mind was changed and he understood Jesus in a totally new way:

> I am trying here to prevent anyone saying the really foolish thing that people often say about Him: I'm ready to accept Jesus as a great moral teacher, but I don't accept his claim to be God. That is the one thing we must not say. ***A man who was merely a man and said the sort of things Jesus said would not be a great moral teacher. He would either be a lunatic—on the level with the man who says he is a poached egg—or else he would be the Devil of Hell.*** You must make your choice. Either this man was, and is, the Son of God, or else a madman or something worse. You can shut him up for a fool, you can spit at him and kill him as a demon or you can fall at his feet and call him Lord and God, but let us not come with any patronizing nonsense about his being a great human teacher. He has not left that open to us. He did not intend to. [87] (Emphasis added)

Chapter 12

A CHRIST-LIKE GOD

"God loves each of us as if there were only one of us"
AUGUSTINE

CHAPTER 10 **"GOD IS GREAT—GOD IS GOOD"** FOCUSED on the first part, "God is <u>great</u>," and Chapter 11 introduces the focus on "God is <u>good</u>" with "**Jesus, The Perfect Image of God.**" The bold assertion is made that "God is good— like Jesus." This chapter furthers the description of God's goodness by arguing that the Incarnation of Jesus, and His life and death on the Cross are the cosmic proof of the goodness of God. His gift of His Son was the eternal evidence of God's love for His earthly, human children. One of the basic tenants of this book is that atheists, agnostics and Skeptics don't believe in God largely because the God they have been exposed to is a horrible, no-good, nasty god. They are repulsed by the image or description of God that is preached on cable TV, written about in multitudes of books and magazines, and referenced by politicians cloaked in religious disguise. They have heard often about the so-called Jewish/ Christian god who destroyed the world once in a fit of anger, who ordered a hundred-year-old man to kill his only son as a sacrifice to a god, a god who ordered the slaughter of an entire city by killing every man, woman, child and animal, and who on another occasion gleefully drowned a whole Egyptian army, and sent thousands of poisonous snakes to kill the very people he was supposed to be rescuing from slavery. That is just part of the dirty resume of this god that has driven so many good people to not just doubt his existence, but to actively hate and despise him in absentia. Who could blame those who have been turned off by the kind of god described in the Old Testament? If that god was the real God then this book might as well have been about famous artists, or the impact of television on Bolivian children, or some other interesting subject rather than a defense or apology for that God. No rational person can successfully defend the defamed god described above, but fortunately, **that god doesn't exist**. But a real God does exist, we assert, and He is like Jesus, a visible snapshot of the invisible God that Jesus claimed as Father. If you see Jesus, you see the God of Creation and the Father of all mankind. That is the operating premise in this book. If you see the real God, you might love Him. He's so much better than His popular public image would suggest.

The Un-Christlike God

We can get a pretty good contrast between the "bad" god and the Good Jesus-God by listening to those who calls the hand of so-called Christians, such as TV comedian **Bill Maher's** stinging indictment:

> If you're a Christian that supports killing your enemy and torture, you have come up with a new name for yourself… 'Capping thy enemy' is not exactly what Jesus would do. For almost two thousand years, Christian have been lawyering the Bible to try to figure out how 'Love thy neighbor' can mean 'Hate thy neighbor.'
>
> Martin Luther King, Jr. gets to call himself a Christian because he actually practiced loving his enemies. And Ghandi was so *** Christian, he was Hindu…But if you're endorsing revenge, torture or war…you cannot say you're a follower of the guy who explicitly said, 'Love your enemy' and 'Do good to those who hate you…'

And not to put too fine a point on it, but nonviolence was kind of Jesus' trademark—kind of his big thing. To not follow that part is like joining Greenpeace and hating whales. There's interpreting, and there's just ignoring. It's just ignoring if you're for torture—as are more Evangelical Christians than any other religion. You're supposed to look at that figure of Christ on the Cross and think, 'how could a man suffering like that and forgive?'

I'm a non-Christian. Just like most Christians.

If you ignore every single thing Jesus commanded you to do, you're not a Christian—you're just auditing. You're not Christ's followers, you're just fans. And if you believe the earth was given to you to kick ***while gloating, you're not really a Christian--you're a Texan. 88

Rejecting the un-Christlike God

Bill Maher would not be considered a fan of Christianity and the Christian church, and he quite often is biting in his humorous take down of TV or radio preachers and politicians who wrap themselves in the religious robes or use the Bible for a weapon. He obviously hates something about religion. Is it God? Is it Jesus? It seems he actually is pretty impressed with Jesus, for he castigates the hypocrites who use Jesus' name but not His example or His teachings. In essence, this prominent critic of religion rejects any "unchrist-like God," any cheap substitute. He may not pretend to live up to Jesus' claims himself, but he can certainly tell the difference between the real and the fake. Of course, Maher is not the only secular person "whipping up" on those who take Jesus' name but bring shame and dishonor on His name with their lives. Mahatma Gandhi, the great Hindu saint of India reportedly said almost the same thing as Maher: **"I like your Christ, I do not like your Christians. Your Christians are so unlike your Christ."** Abraham Lincoln, who was reluctant to discuss his own faith had this wise observation according to some accounts: **"I care not much for a** *man's religion whose dog and cat are not the better for it."* It is both *sad* and *encouraging* to encounter such critiques of Christianity: sad, because it seems that Jesus' followers are His worst publicists; encouraging, because so many people know enough about Jesus that they can easily see a fake. Not everyone who admires Jesus as a man can accept Him as God incarnate, but at least Jesus has a pretty good reputation in our world. That's a good starting place.

Bradley Jersak published a marvelous book, *A More Christlike God: A More Beautiful Gospel,*[89] which further inspired and enriched this apology, this defense of God. Growing out of his own Christian struggle and his own pastoral ministry, Jersak spells out this antidote to the poison publicity God has gotten in our society: God is like Jesus, **exactly**, and Jesus is supremely **good**. It is not news that Jesus claimed identity with God the Father: *"He who has seen Me has seen the Father"* (JOHN 14:9) pretty much nails it down, Biblically. It seems clear that the solution to God's *bad* reputation with atheists and other Skeptics is to focus on Jesus, His life and His message.

The Good Life of Jesus the Man

It is our intent to introduce the reader to Jesus as a person, not as a theological concept. He was a real, physical man, one who laughed, cried, hurt, worried, loved, endured hatred and violence. He was a person in the flesh known intimately by his small group of disciples in sweat and tears, in trouble and triumph, walking long distances, sitting beside him, disciples who slept beside him outside on the ground, men who ate and drank with him, accompanied him to weddings and funerals. These friends fished and worked together, sometimes quarreled and argued with each other, and ultimately, one of them betrayed him, and others abandoned him to death. They never doubted that Jesus was a man, a human being with flesh and blood—a real living man; they never wondered if he was a spirit or a ghost, or an apparition. As one of them later wrote to counter the false teaching: *"That which was from the beginning, which we have heard, which we have seen with our eyes, which we have looked at and our hands have touched—this we proclaim concerning the Word of life."* (I John 1:1)

We will attempt to bring Jesus to life in a literary way, describing and explaining Him in both the very concrete, material, robust and earthy sense as well as the spiritual, mystical, mysterious and ethereal way He is experienced by many of His followers. His followers knew Him as a down- to-earth, tough, full-fledged man in those brief years He was physically present with them. In His flesh He was strong, charismatic, fearless and bold, but again was just as often soft and gentle, compassionate and full of love and kindness. He laughed with His friends, partied with sinners, and He cried for His friends and for His Jewish people who rejected Him. After three short years following Jesus, seeing Him killed and alive again, they came to know Him in a deeper, more intimate way, just as He promised in His parting hours with them: He would be with them forever.

One striking feature of the Gospel accounts is that they give us no description of Jesus's appearance. The only description in the Bible is a prophecy in Isaiah 53:2, usually thought to be speaking of the Messiah to come: *He grew up before him like a tender shoot, and like a root out of dry ground. He had no beauty or majesty to attract us to him, nothing in his appearance that we should desire him.* No modern reporter would fail to tell something about how Jesus looked, his height, his hairstyle and skin color, or how He was dressed. But not a word is recorded in recognized accounts.

Thus, we face this reality: our culture's image of Jesus has been most effectively created through art and poetry, from the Middle Ages through today. The most widely known portrait of Jesus in America (shown on the left) is this 1940 painting by Warner Sallman: a blue-eyed Caucasian with long flowing hair, a classic Greek nose (instead of the common Semitic hooked nose) and well-kept mustache and beard. Millions of color prints of "The Head of Christ" hang in homes of all classes around the world; this Jesus to many people. The Old Masters of Europe (Rembrandt, DaVinci, Raphael, Michelangelo, Verrocchio, etc.) typically had a similar feminine looking white Jesus, sometimes quite frail in appearance. The "meek and mild" Jesus of poetry is reflected in most of the traditional images of Jesus. He frequently seems to be in deep thought, off in some dreamy spiritual reverie. Such visible images had a profound impact on the modern mind, unconsciously imbedding the idea of Jesus as some weak, helpless sissy, ethereal and irrelevant. The Great hymn writer, Charles Wesley gave this word-picture of Jesus, "meek and mild" seeming a bit *weak* and *sissy* now:

> *Gentle Jesus, meek and mild,*
> *Look upon a little child;*
> *Pity my simplicity,*
> *Suffer me to come to Thee*[90]

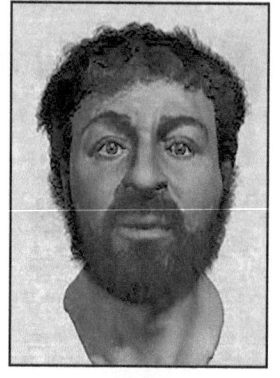

Recently forensic anthropologists in Britain, in collaboration with Israeli archaeologists using human skulls from Jesus' time made a reconstructed face of a dark skinned, sturdy man of ancient Palestine. The artistic rendering of their findings is shown at right. In truth, Jesus almost certainly looked like Palestinians today, since He was a "Palestinian Jew." Even the familiar weather-beaten face of the late Palestinian leader, Yasser Arafat may resemble Jesus more than the paintings by Rembrandt, DaVinci, or Michelangelo's works. In recent years several artistic portrayals of Jesus have been published in an attempt to give us a more realistic portrait of Jesus, maybe even a "mod-

ern Jesus" imagined like the one pictured at the left, a 21st century office. Another approach imagines Jesus as Oriental or African, giving interesting takes on the "Everyman" incarnation. Jesus was clearly no "meek and mild" Milquetoast-like "pale Galilean" such as what has been embedded in our collective Western consciousness. He was, by all Biblical accounts and implications, a strong, commanding man-among-men, followed and admired by a rag-tag collection of rough, tough, boisterous men, such as volatile Simon Peter and the brothers known as "Sons of Thunder."

Looking for An Easy Road?

One of the charges against religious people by the atheists is that we believe in a sugar daddy in the sky who will take us to heaven when we die. In other words, for all our talk of self-sacrifice and helping others and doing good–in fact it's simply self-interest. We're investing in a great big life insurance plan, "fire insurance" to be specific. We get a "Get Out of Hades Free" card for being religious. We pay in the good works and faith and love and all that good stuff and we get happiness and heaven and forgiveness and a chance to see Grandma and Grandpa and all our loved ones again.

This "sugar daddy" charge is true, honest Christians must admit: many nominal Christians hold this distorted, "cheap grace" form of religion, never really understanding or accepting the cost of following Jesus, the price of discipleship. Jesus made it abundantly clear to those who proposed to follow Him in His Palestinian ministry: *"Then Jesus said to his disciples, "Whoever wants to be my disciple must deny themselves and take up their cross and follow me. For whoever wants to save their life will lose it, but whoever loses their life for me will find it."* (Matthew 16:24-25). Significantly, all three of the synoptic gospels have this same warning to disciples: *Mark 8:34-35 and Luke 9:57-62.* John's Gospel doesn't mention the cross but describes the danger even more explicitly: *"In the world you will have troubles..."* (John 16:33) Some translate this as *tribulation*. Again, He warned: *"They will put you out of their synagogues. Indeed, the time is coming when anyone who kills you will think he is offering a service to God."* (John 16:1-3).

We often hear the secularist acknowledgment: "Jesus was a good man." As we have cited before, C.S. Lewis takes serious offense at this statement. Jesus was **not a good Man**, Lewis argued, for He boldly **claimed to be God**, and that leaves us three options:

1. Jesus was a liar; or
2. He was delusional, like someone claiming to be Napoleon or a boiled egg; *or*

3. He was who He said He was. **Good man is not an option**.

Lewis is right, of course: Jesus was **more** than a good man. But even those who reject Jesus as a religious leader, or reject His claim to be God incarnate, regard His life as a sterling example of what it means to be a good person, to be fully human, to be role model for how life could be lived.

Jesus Christ, the Person

Before looking at the teachings of Jesus about the Father, we can learn much about the Father by looking at what Jesus did and what he was like. "***In Him was the fullness of God revealed.***" (Colossians 2:9) The biographical story illustrates and confirms the teaching. His **life** was part and parcel of the **message**. The oldest and most divisive theological issue for Christianity is this: Was Jesus a human? Was He God? Or was He some hybrid? Logic in the first century looked at this issue the way logic does today: it is reasonable to select one of these options about Jesus since they are mutually self-excluding. That is how many modern Skeptics look at the question, and it was a 150 year long "dog fight" among the early church leaders before it was officially settled.

Many were persuaded that Jesus could not be a human in the same way we are human, for we are flawed and temporary, sinners by our very nature. So, Jesus could not be a befouled human. "He may have looked like a human but it was a disguise" the *Gnostics* said. Others accepted the idea that Jesus was a real human, and was God-filled, but was not God. "He prayed to his Father" they pointed out, "so how could he pray to himself if he was God?" Some theorized that Jesus was a real human being, but at some point, was "taken over" by God, temporarily replaced, a substitute Christ. Then there are others who say Jesus as "half-and-half," a unique mixture of human and divine operating at the same time in his earthly life; it was the divinity that did the miracle healings, and it was the human half who was crucified. Of course, all these speculations were renounced as heresy by the third century when Christianity was made "official" and "unified" by the Emperor Constantine. In several gatherings of the world's church leaders the theology was hammered out: Jesus was fully human and fully divine, no mixture and no separation. It was and is a "mystery" the church admitted, and including the Holy Spirit as a co-equal part of the unified Trinity made it even more difficult to explain.

We are fortunate in our lifetimes, the era of quantum physics and quarks and uncertainty principles that scientists are able to hold two or more conflicting concepts as true at some level of physical reality. We cannot explain the Trinity in any convincing way, though it is clearly taught in the New Testament, but we can vaguely grasp the idea that Jesus was fully human in the same way we are, but at the same time He was God in the flesh, God living as a human. "*The Word became flesh and made his dwelling among us. We have seen his glory, the glory of the one and only Son, who came from the Father, full of grace and truth.* (John 1:14). The 90-year-old John who wrote the previous verse recalled the thrill of seeing Jesus and spending three years with Him, and we repeat here his words about that experience: "*That which was from the beginning, which we have heard, which we have seen with our own eyes, which we have gazed upon and touched with our own hands—this is the Word of life.* (1 John 1:1) Those who saw Him, talked with Him, heard him, touched Him, even smelled Him—they were certain to their final day that Jesus was a man (more than a man, yes, but definitely a real, live human being.)

Jesus' own favorite title for Himself was "Son of Man," a phrase used more than 80 times in the Bible. It was an Aramaic phrase (His native tongue) a way of saying "a real man." When Jesus appeared to the surprise of the disciples after He had been crucified, He explicitly points out His body parts: "See my hands" and "See my wounded side; ghosts don't have hands and feet as I have." He then said, "By the way, what's for supper?" Certainly, ghosts or spirits don't eat and drink like Jesus did. **He was real.**

The Way Life Should Be Lived

Almost universally it is accepted that Jesus "*went about doing good,*" as the Bible observes; but then it adds "*and healing all who were under the power of the devil, because God was with him.*" (Acts 10:38) Some deny that such a person ever lived, that Jesus is a complete fictional character, but no serious claim has been lodged that He was a **bad** man, a trickster, a con-man working the Galilean crowd. According to the New Testament, Jesus spent three public years doing good things for others, especially favoring the poor and downtrodden, and was always kind, loving, generous, accepting, forgiving and every other quality we value in another human being. The New Testament claims, and it is standard Christian doctrine, that Jesus was **perfect, sinless**: *"He committed no sin, and no deceit was found in his mouth."* (I Peter 2:22)

Compared to the Jewish priests and high priests who were supposedly godly men, Jesus is holy: *"For we do not have a high priest who is unable to empathize with our weaknesses, but we have one who has been tempted in every way, just as we are—yet he did not sin.*" (Hebrew 4:15) Notice that the author of Hebrews heads off one anti-Messiah argument: Jesus was **like** us, no extraordinary advantage: He was **fully human** and was tempted by the same things that tempt us; we fall and He never did. That sinless life figures in the doctrine of Salvation (discussed in **Chapter 17 Sin, Evil and Guilt**) for Jesus' sinless life qualified Him to take our guilt and sins and offer His life as an acceptable sacrifice to pay for all our moral bankruptcies according to the Bible.

Yes, apart from the theology of Jesus, He did indeed do great and wonderful, even miraculous **good.** The four Gospels are largely reports of His goodness on display, and everywhere He went preaching and teaching, He also healed all kinds of sicknesses. People brought their lame, blind and diseased to Him, sometimes interrupting His sermon. Never does He say "Go away! Can't you see I'm busy?" No, He took the time, every time, to listen and touch and somehow a miracle took place, and the blind man sees his family for the first time, the crippled man runs around praising God, the deaf and the mute all respond to the goodness of Jesus demonstrated by His healing. Some thought that He just used this "so called" power to get a crowd and to impress them, but they were wrong. He almost always was stopped in His path by someone intruding, yelling from the sidelines or grabbing Him by the sleeve or the legs, or even being lowered from the roof in front of Him.

He always had compassion on the people, the Gospels tell us. He was visibly moved by their pain and suffering, and He gave them His precious time and attention. Jesus' great heart was moved by human need. He ached inside for the needy people. He had compassion for the faceless crowds who clamored for His help, seeing not a blur of nameless people but all separate individuals, each precious to God. His disciples sometimes saw only "losers" and "hapless" but Jesus saw the "lost" and "dying." ***"When he saw the crowds, he had compassion on them, because they were harassed and helpless, like sheep without a shepherd"*** (Matthew 9:36) On several occasions He told the healed person to keep their contact a secret, rather than "Go and tell everyone what I have done for you." In His conflict with the Pharisees who challenged Him on every hand, Jesus does occasionally refer to His miracle working as evidence that He has come in the name of God the Father, as He has claimed. Unfazed, these hypocritical religious leaders acknowledged that He had done powerful work but they attributed that power as coming from the Devil rather than the Father. Jesus reminded them that among His many healings were many cases of "casting out demons and devils;" He silenced them and infuriated them by pointing out that using *Satanic power* to cast out *Satan's demons* was not logical. He reminded them of the adage *"A house divided against itself will fall."* (Luke 11:17)

The Friend of Sinners

One of the activities of Jesus which drove His religious adversaries up the wall was "hanging out" with the worst sinners in town, the tax collectors and prostitutes and other unsavory characters. He even went to eat at the home of these known sinners, sometimes as the honored guest. They pretended to be scandalized, for it was unheard of for a Rabbi to eat with the riff-raff and scum of society—for example a scoundrel like the cheating chief tax collector, the wealthy Zacchaeus. And Jesus had to retrieve this sinner from out of a tree and invite Himself to dinner! **"All the people saw this and began to mutter, "He has gone to be the guest of a sinner."** (Luke 19:7) Jesus was so often found in the company of these disreputable or undesirable people that He earned His favorite nicknames: **Friend of Sinners**.

Friend of Sinners is one of the 134 names and titles of Christ in the Bible but from the perspective of this book it is the most beautiful one, the most descriptive one, the nicest kind of insult. Jesus went about doing good, a holy man, without a doubt, but He was apparently especially **fond of sinners.** He did not fear being tainted or polluted by these sinner friends, and He felt no discomfort in their presence. This personal quality reminds us of an ironic lyric sung by pop singer Billy Joel: ***"I'd rather laugh with the sinners than cry with the saints; the sinners are much more fun."***[1] Jesus was not hanging out with sinners for fun or entertainment, of course, for He often made it clear: He came to rescue sinners and not "saints." And if you are "fishing for men" as He told His disciples they would do, it is best to go where the fish are swimming. Sinners need a Savior, Jesus was saying, but the so-called "righteous" Pharisees and their ilk apparently did not need Him, or at least, didn't realize it. He twice commented that it was for these outcasts that He came, and not the "religious" claimants: **"It is the sick that need a physician and not the healthy"** (Mark 2:17) He said in a taunting metaphor. That is an amazing characteristic of Jesus, an acting out of what had been said about Him in the Fourth Gospel: "God so loved the world…" (John 3:16) Jesus came into time and space because He loved the sinners of this small world, loved us all—the good, the bad and the ugly.

One of the greatest stories in the Bible illustrates the gentle, compassionate love of Jesus for the down and out, the condemned, the "losers." Here is John 8:2-11:

> *At dawn he appeared again in the temple courts, where all the people gathered around him, and he sat down to teach them. The teachers of the law and the Pharisees brought in a woman caught in adultery. They made her stand before the group and said to Jesus, "Teacher, this woman was caught in the act of adultery. In the Law Moses commanded us to stone such women. Now what do you say?" They were using this question as a trap, in order to have a basis for accusing him.*
>
> *But Jesus bent down and started to write on the ground with his finger. When they kept on questioning him, he straightened up and said to them, "Let any one of you who is without sin be the first to throw a stone at her." Again, he stooped down and wrote on the ground.*

> *At this, those who heard began to go away one at a time, the older ones first, until only Jesus was left, with the woman still standing there. Jesus straightened up and asked her, "Woman, where are they? Has no one condemned you?"*
>
> *"No one, sir," she said.*
>
> *Then neither do I condemn you," Jesus declared. "Go now and leave your life of sin."*

For the sake of transparency, it must be acknowledged that while this story is included in <u>many</u> old papyrus scrolls, some of the oldest manuscripts do not include this story. Critics say it was added by a later scribe, but for many centuries most Christians have accepted this passage as genuine because it sounds so clearly like the Jesus pictured elsewhere. Jesus was always loving and compassionate, not condemning in His other encounters with sinners, and He frequently sent them away with this same message: "I don't condemn you. Your sins are forgiven. Now go and sin no more." He was never hesitant to disapprove of sin and condemn it by name, but He never condemned the repentant sinner. Even those who walked away unrepentant were watched with love and sadness, not with hatred or spite. One of the most poignant encounters is with a young man identified as "rich young ruler" told in Mark 10:17-31:

> *As Jesus started on his way, a man ran up to him and fell on his knees before him. "Good teacher," he asked, "what must I do to inherit eternal life?" "Why do you call me good?" Jesus answered. "No one is good—except God alone. You know the commandments: 'You shall not murder, you shall not commit adultery, you shall not steal, you shall not give false testimony, you shall not defraud, honor your father and mother." "Teacher," he declared, "all these I have kept since I was a boy." <u>Jesus looked at him and loved him.</u> "One thing you lack," he said. "Go, sell everything you have*

> *and give to the poor, and you will have treasure in heaven. Then come, follow me." At this the man's face fell. He went away sad, because he had great wealth."*

Jesus did not condemn the young man or make some sarcastic remark, for Jesus obviously was sad as the young man walked away. He mused quietly, probably with a resigned sigh "How hard it is for the rich to accept salvation."

Perhaps the greatest demonstration of Jesus' unconditional love for sinners was just minutes before He drew His last breath on the Cross. The Romans had placed a convicted criminal on each side of Jesus on Golgotha" (Luke 23:32-43), called thieves, bandits or malefactors in various translations, but likely were Jewish rebels waging guerrilla warfare against the Roman occupiers. One of the bandits cursed the crowd and mocked Jesus, but the other acknowledged Jesus as an innocent man, and asked Him a small favor: "remember me." Philip Yancy has written a thoughtful description of this:

> Jesus forgave a thief dangling on a cross, knowing full well the thief had converted out of plain fear. That thief would never study the Bible, never attend synagogue or church, and never make amends to those he had wronged. He simply said "Jesus, remember me," and Jesus promised "Today you will be with me in Paradise." It was another shocking reminder that grace does not depend on what we have done for God but rather what God has done for us.[92]

Jesus Loved the Weak and Disadvantaged

Some of the favorite modern pictures of Jesus show Him with children crowding around Him, climbing on His lap or being held in His arms. That is such a representative snapshot of this Man among men—He was moved by the plight of the poor, the sick, the mistreated and the outcasts of society. His initial announcement of His ministry was read from the Prophet Isaiah in a passage cited earlier:

> *"The Spirit of the Sovereign LORD is on me, because the LORD has anointed me to proclaim good news to the poor. He has sent me to bind up the brokenhearted, to proclaim freedom for the captives and release from darkness for the prisoners"* (Isaiah 6:1)

This "platform" outlining Jesus' ministry goals seems to bear some resemblance to a modern liberal democratic candidate for President (free healthcare, prison reform, minimum wage, fight poverty, end to all kinds of discrimination, etc.) This is not to politicize Jesus, for He would not be a Democrat, Republican or Green Party in modern America. He surely would vote, but He certainly could not get elected in this country, or any other on earth. He was always ahead of the crowd, and He was always looking one way while the populace and the leaders were looking the other direction. John Fugelsang has described this "rebel" Jesus in startling terms:

> **JESUS was a radical, nonviolent revolutionary who hung around with lepers, hookers and crooks;**
> **He wasn't American and never spoke English;**
> **was anti-wealth, anti-death penalty; anti-public prayer.**
> **But He was never anti-gay, never mentioned abortion or birth control,**
> **never called the poor "lazy,"**
> **never justified torture,**
> **never fought for tax cuts for the wealthiest Nazarenes,**
> **never asked a leper for a co-pay.**
> **He was just a long-haired, brown-skinned homeless community organizing Middle Eastern Jew.**[93]

In Jesus's life we observe one of the most counter-intuitive and surprising combinations: truth and love so strong and so graciously balanced. He "spoke the truth in love" as we are urged to do, but so often we use truth as a hammer to hurt the person we are judging.

Then as now, people rejected and shamed those who held beliefs or practices judged to be wrong and immoral. But Jesus astonished everyone by being willing to eat with tax collectors, Jews who were collaborators with the occupying Roman imperial forces. This outraged those we might call the "Left," those zealous against oppression and injustice. But he also welcomed and ate with prostitutes (Matthew 21:31–32), which offended those promoting conservative, traditional morality on the "Right." Jesus deliberately and tenderly touched lepers (Luke 5:13), people who were considered physically and ceremonially contaminated but who were desperate for human contact. Yet he also ate repeatedly with Pharisees (Luke 7:36–50; 11:37–44; 14:1–4), showing that he was not bigoted toward the bigoted. He forgave the enemies who were crucifying him (Luke 23:34) the crucifixion spectators who jeered insults at time, and the friends who abandoned Him and let Him down in the hour of his greatest need (Matthew 26:40–43).

Jesus Was Humble and Gracious and Forgiving

Our perspective on humility can be radically changed if we will ponder and meditate on the greatest example of humility in history: Jesus Christ. By the very act of leaving heaven, coming to earth, and taking the form of man, he demonstrated an unfathomable humbling of himself. Paul recognized it:

> ...*he* (Jesus) *made himself nothing*
> *by taking the very nature of a servant,*
> *being made in human likeness.*
> *And being found in appearance as a man, he*
> *humbled himself*
> *by becoming obedient to death—*
> *even death on a cross!* (Philippians 2:7–8).

This beautiful passage was probably used as a worship chorus in the first century Christians and it reminded them that Jesus gave up Heaven for them, and then gave up His human life. Notice that it says Jesus **"made Himself nothing, taking the form of a servant."** The original Greek means **"He emptied Himself,"** and then reemphasizes the humility, "He **humbled** himself" to become a mortal human, accepting death on the cross. He remarked at His trial that He **could** have called an army "of twelve legions of angels," but He **would not**. (Matthew 26:53)

Throughout his life on earth, Jesus demonstrated a spirit of profound humility, and admonished these disciples to serve each other rather than trying to outdo each other. *"You know that the rulers of the Gentiles lord it over them, and their high officials exercise authority over them. Not so with you. Instead, whoever wants to become great among you must be your servant, and whoever wants to be first must be your slave—just as the Son of Man did not come to be served, but to serve...* (Matthew 20:25-28). On His last night with the disciples, He demonstrated it again: He took a towel and basin and washed their dirty feet, a job that a servant normally would do. He washed the feet of everyone, including Simon Peter who would deny Him in a few hours, and Judas, who had already betrayed Him.

> *"Do you understand what I have done for you?" he asked them. "You call me 'Teacher' and 'Lord,' and rightly so, for that is what I am. Now that I, your Lord and Teacher, have washed your feet, you also should wash one another's feet. I have set you an example that you should do as I have done for you."* (John 13:12–15)

After the Resurrection Jesus met the small band of disciples on a lake shore, early one morning as the men had been fishing all night in their boat. Eventually they recognized His voice as He called to them, and Simon Peter swam to the shore rather than help bring the boat to shore. After they had eaten the breakfast Jesus had prepare, Jesus turned to Simon Peter, the one who profanely denied knowing Jesus at Pilate's trial. "Peter, do you love me?" The details of this passage were covered in Chapter 11 and so do not need repeating here. The impact of this conversation between Jesus and Peter was that Peter was forgiven and accepted back into discipleship. Rather than condemning Peter for his faithless denials, Jesus lays His hand on the Big Fisherman's shoulder and commissions him "Feed My sheep", to shepherd the little band of disciples after Jesus was gone back to the Father. Graciously Jesus has restored the fallen disciple and appoints him to lead the little group now in Jesus' place. He didn't make Peter a "pope" but did designate him as the person responsible for what the disciples (and soon, their thousands of believers.) would face.

Jesus Did Wonders for People

It is easy to get caught up in the "Miracle Worker" image of Jesus, for He did indeed perform many "miracles" of healing during His short ministry, restoring sight to the blind, making lame men walk and jump, casting out "demons" tormenting some, gave smooth skin to lepers, and even raised two people from apparent death. We need to consider how the people of Jesus' time understood what was happening when Jesus healed diseases. Today, we understand the natural world to operate according to impersonal forces or "laws of nature." When someone experiences healing that cannot be explained according to our understanding of these laws, we might call it a miracle, understood to be God's "interfering" somehow with the laws of nature. People at the time of Jesus didn't conceive of the world in terms of impersonal laws. Rather, it was the will and purpose of God that supported and guaranteed the normal functioning of the world. Divine power was always at work in mysterious and unpredictable ways, they believed. The extraordinary—such as a sudden or unexpected healing—was considered a particular eruption of this always-present divine power rather than an interruption of the working of the cosmic machinery. Because of this, the word **miracle** as we use it today does not really reflect how ancient people understood the extraordinary happenings. We will not deal further here with whether these "miracles" were "real" and thus countermanded physical laws of nature, but only point out that those who were "healed" believed they has seen a miracle from God, and so did most of the on-lookers (other than the "religious" leaders.)

Jesus did dozens of healings and other unexplainable feats, and was widely known in the small little country He traversed. He had a "following" it is clear, some of which Jesus accused of just wanting to see something, or to get some of the food He fed to a crowd of 5000 one day. There were gawkers, but close reading shows that Jesus did not do these things for "show" or to try to get a crowd together—He almost always did the miracle because someone **needed** it. Jesus was moved by pain and suffering, and would often interrupt what He had been doing or where He was going because someone asked for help. He didn't turn anyone down so far as we know. In most of the healing cases reported in the Gospels Jesus addresses the **faith** and the **sin** of those seeking His help, and He calls the forgiveness of their sins (which He did) as more important than restoring their health. He could have led a popular "traveling show" and become rich by putting on a "healing show" but He did not seek fame for Himself, but Honor for His Father God. Satan tried to trick Jesus into doing "tricks" to impress the crowd, but Jesus resisted the temptation to glorify Himself. Jesus was not a **showman** but He used His good life to **show Man His Father.**

Jesus Was the Goodness of God Demonstrated

Jesus went about doing good as we have shown, and His love for His followers and those who rejected Him was abundantly clear in His life. He lived a life of goodness as a live demonstration of how much the Father loved all mankind. The most beloved Bible verses put into words what Jesus put into action: "**For** *God so loved the world that HE gave His one and only Son…*" (John 3:16) And even more clearly: "*But God demonstrates his own love for us in this: While we were still sinners, Christ died for us.*" (Romans 5:8)

    The life that Jesus lived and the death He endured are presented as proof that God is love. That is the reason He came, that is the reason He preached, and that is the reason He healed and comforted people in need. He illustrates what Christians sometimes quote to each other "*The way you live may be the only sermon a sinner will ever hear.*" Another slogan is similar: *"I'd rather see a sermon than hear one."* A third such reminder of the importance of our example: *"Preach the Gospel every day in every way you can. And, if necessary, use words,"*

The Good News Jesus Taught

The word "gospel" used in the New Testament means "good news" and it has some history. The Greek word translated "gospel" is εὐαγγέλιον (evangelion) from which we derive "evangelism," "evangelical" and "evangelistic." By the time Old English had absorbed Latin and German and other languages the term used was "gōdspel" from "gott" (meaning "good") and "spel" (meaning "news, a story.") The term "God Spell" or

"Godspell" is still used occasionally, more famously in a popular rock opera in the 1970's, a musical based on Matthew; it has been revived a number of times, as recently as 2012. The message which Jesus came preaching at age 30 was called "Good News" by the New Testament writers, and by Jesus Himself. *"After John was put in prison, Jesus went into Galilee, proclaiming the good news of God. "The time has come," he said. "The kingdom of God has come near. Repent and believe the good news!"* (Mark 1:14-15)

Chapter 13

GOD'S IMAGE IN US

*"I like your Christ, I do not like your Christians.
Your Christians are so unlike your Christ"*
MAHATMA GANDHI

THE QUOTATION ABOVE FROM THE GREAT INDIAN holy man, Mahatma Gandhi, is a stern rebuke to Christians who claim to be made in the "Image of God" (***Imago Dei*** in Latin). It must be admitted that Christians don't often measure up to that high standard of being like Jesus, ***"Who is the image of the invisible God"*** (Colossians 1:15). Gandhi had his theology correct: Christians are supposed to be like Jesus, and Jesus showed us God in Himself. To "be like Jesus" is the same as being "in the image of God." The "image of God" is a key concept in Christian theology, foundational to Christian thinking about human identity, human significance, bioethics, ecology and other topics. Many Christians see evolution as incompatible with the image of God. How could God's image bearers have evolved from simpler life forms? Doesn't image-bearing require miraculous creation of humans rather than shared ancestry with chimpanzees? And when in the evolutionary process did humans attain this image? These questions are tied to many other issues concerning human origins, including the soul, the Fall, and the historicity of Adam and Eve, but in this chapter, we will focus specifically on *the image of God.*

The phrase "image of God" does not appear many times in the Bible, but the importance of the concept is emphasized by its repetition in the Genesis creation account:

> *Then God said, "Let us make mankind <u>in our image</u>, in our likeness, so that they may rule over the fish in the sea and the birds in the sky, over the livestock and all the wild animals, and over all the creatures that move along the ground." So, God created mankind in his own image, <u>in the image of God</u> he created them; male and female he created them.* (Genesis 1:26-27)

The Unique Creation Story

Whether you consider the Genesis stories myth or historical facts there is no denying that the Genesis account envisioned a much more important and elevated position for humans than the ancient authors of Akkadia, Babylon and Central America. Many ancient civilizations have similar myths or stories of creation and the origin of Mankind. Those ancient people pictured divine creation of humans, it's true, but their many gods did not have benign intentions and their interactions and relationships with humans appear to be as brutal and harsh as slavery. A more detailed discussion of those ancient precursors to Genesis is found in **Chapter 8, The Birth of God.**

Here we have a story of <u>one</u> deity creating **one** human being (later expanded to a "set"), and the evident purpose of the creation of the first man was for companionship or fellowship with the Creator. It is true that God assigned Adam the job as *caretaker for the Garden of Eden*, but it was not an onerous task, not a punishment, at least until after the *Fall*. Take note especially in Genesis that God gave Adam some serious "perks" as well as the title of "gardener," permitting the Man to name all the animals, birds, fish and even crawling things, one by one as God brought them to him: *"And out of the ground the LORD God formed every beast of the field and every bird of the air, and He brought them to the man to see what he would name each one. And whatever the man called each living creature, that was its name."* (Genesis

2:19) **This is a truly amazing, heart-warming element** in this story: God treated Adam as a valued person, almost making him a co-worker. Not incidentally, the process by which men and women produce new humans is called "pro/creation," implying that making babies is a partnership in an ongoing creation, creating again with the Creator. Yet another beautiful touch in this ancient story: *"Then the man and his wife heard the sound of the LORD God as he was walking in the garden in the cool of the day..."* (Genesis 3:8) Though it is not spelled out explicitly, it appears that God habitually came each evening and walked with Adam and Eve in the garden. How long that beautiful ritual continued we can't tell, but the divine-human companionship ended when Adam and Eve sinned. In the rest of the verse quoted above, when God came for their daily walk, they hid from Him, for they were ashamed of their sin, their betrayal of God's friendship. **End of Paradise.**

"Image" Is Not Physical Similarity

It is pretty clear that "***Let us make mankind in our image, in our likeness***" is not referring to the physical appearance (an old white man with long hair and beard, as per Michelangelo) but is suggesting non-material similarities between the Creator and the created. For centuries Biblical scholars have speculated about what it means to be "in the image of God," often using the Latin "Imago Dei" in the formal discussions. There are perhaps as many explanations as there are scholars, but no real consensus exists in religious circles. A thorny question is eventually raised as part of the Darwinian argument: "How could humans have evolved and still be created in the "Image of God"? Was the first *Homo erectus* already "imago Dei?" Were the *Neanderthals* also "in God's image?" Let us explore some of the most popular ideas about the concept of Mankind bearing some resemblance to God, carrying in our humanness some mark or some qualities that link us to the Creator of the Universe. Some writers say the whole idea is appalling, that Mankind is in no way god-like, and that considering ourselves "in the image of God" is a delusion of grandeur. The affirmative theories fall into such categories as biological, genetic, intellectual/mental, moral, spiritual and philosophical.

The Old Testament, which is the source of this "imago Dei" idea, is firmly opposed to "images" in relation to Yahweh, with the first of the Ten Commandments containing this prohibition: ***"You shall not make for yourself an image in the form of anything in heaven above or on the earth beneath or in the waters below. You shall not bow down to them or worship them..."*** (Exodus 20:4-5) In the ancient cultures of Egypt and Canaan, people made images of their gods from metal and wood and set them up in local temples to worship. Scholars agree that in Egypt and other ancient people, the material idol was believed to be the true manifestation of the particular god of that people. It is clear that idol worship was a persistent problem for the Israelites occupying a land filled with idols of wood, stone and gold, in addition to seductive sexual practices in worship of these pagan idols. So, it was absolutely forbidden to have any "graven images" in the Hebrew tents or towns. While the Ten Commandments were still new, "hot off the press," the wandering Hebrews escaping from Egypt created and worshiped a Golden Calf while Moses was on the mountain with God. Needless to say, both God and Moses were "ticked off," and Moses broke all the Ten Commandments at once! Over and over again the Old Testament tribes are tempted and succumb to the worship of Baal, Ashtoreth, Chemosh, Dagon and miscellaneous other tribal gods, and they suffer defeats and occupation, finally turning away from idols and back to God, restored in their relationship with Yahweh, their protector.

Considering that making carved images of men, animals and gods was such an anathema, it is strange that the first story in the Old Testament involves "images" as a positive thing—humans in the "image of God." How did those early, or later, Hebrew story tellers come up with the revolutionary idea that their God, Yahweh, had put His own image or likeness on or in such faulty, unworthy beings as Man? Certainly, by the time they wrote this idea, they already knew humans were often vile, viscous and reprehensible by any standard; at first glance, no similarity to God is visible in the humans we know. It is agreed that some, a very few, **good** and **worthy** people exist, but those exceptions don't balance at all the vast majority of men and women who are sinners and reprobates. Could God's image be imprinted on some humans and not on others? Was the honor earned or was it a gift, maybe an inheritance?

It is disappointing to find that the rest of the Old Testament has very little to say about the divine image in the human race. The two passages cited previously (Genesis 1:26-27 and Genesis 9:4-5) are almost all the references made to the "image of God." We do have a brief rehearsal of these Genesis passages in David's oft-repeated poetry: *"(W)hat is mankind that you are mindful of them, human beings that you care for them? You have made them <u>a little lower than the angels</u>..."* (Psalm 8:4-5) The concepts of being honored by God, occupying a higher position in creation than all other creatures, and being overseers of God's creation are found here without the "image" reference.

Caretakers and Trustees

This passage makes it clear that part of being "in the Image of God" means that "ruling" over all the animals is a **stewardship** Mankind has been assigned: we are God's trustees of Creation, entrusted with the duty to take care of the animals God created. For those of us who find much in the Old Testament that is outdated and primitive, this biblical story is ecologically focused, a position that should make **PETA** proud. This passage, and several others, is a counterbalance for some of the "gruesome God" theology which unwittingly defames Jehovah. All animals belong to God and He loves all His creation, and like an elder brother, Mankind is responsible for the care and protection of those animals—in cooperation with the Creator. Among other things, being *in the image of God* means **loving what God loves,** representing God on earth.

That marvelous insight, that theology of shared care-taking, is not only modern: it is actually much further advanced than humans have achieved in our time. We have made laws protecting animals (mostly pets) from abuse or neglect; we have finally removed chimpanzees, apes, and other hominids from the test laboratories, activists such as **Greenpeace** are fighting daily to "save the whale" or "save the Rhino," we have shamed women into giving up their fashionable fur coats to some degree, we have campaigned against mistreatment in chicken cages and inhumane slaughter houses. Notice that our standard is **humane**, which is close to saying **"Treat animals like humans."** We are not quite as civilized as Hiawatha, who called the animals "Brother."

That image of God is wonderfully appealing, and we may advance to that image someday, for these ideas from the ancient past, voiced by simple shepherds, farmers and soldiers, reveals something about God that we can only partially understand. (More about this later).

God Made Us All Relatives

Humans don't like to be compared to other people or other things, especially to animals (i.e., "dirty dog", "pig", "snake in the grass," "louse" and "slug" are common epithets we use). Darwin hit a serious "sore spot" in 1859 by suggesting that mankind is descended from non-human animals which lived a million years ago. Religious people took great umbrage at the thought that humans are descended from "monkeys" through evolution. Actually, Darwin **did not** suggest humans descended from "monkeys," chimpanzees or apes. His work, later supported by archaeologists finding humanoid fossils, suggests that humans and apes we were each separately descended from some **common ancestor**. Humans went one way on the evolution tree, and the ape families went a different route of evolution. (We could say we are "cousins" to the simian species, but they are **not our brothers and sisters.** We may be relatives, we may even concede, but we're **not blood relatives** we insist.) But the Bible actually affirms we are **caretakers** of the earth itself, and of all on it that walks, crawls, swims or flies. We are the original "conservationists." The Bible is not entirely clear regarding treating animals as relatives, to say the least, and it certainly is true that the Old Testament worship involved the sacrificial death of animal. Bulls and sheep and birds were all appropriate for an offering for one's sins or for the nation's sins, and sometimes as a toke of thanks for something God had done. The connection is sometimes made that the animal is substituting for the person offering the sacrifice, and the ceremony probably included sprinkling the blood of the animal upon the person seeking God's favor. During the Exodus, the forty years wandering in the Sinai Peninsula, a goat would be chosen to represent the whole people, and their sins were symbolically and ceremonially laid upon the poor goat. The goat would not be slain in the normal sacrificial manner, but it would be cast out into the wilderness, carrying the imputed sins away from the camp: this animal was called the "scape goat" then, and the idea has entered our modern vocabulary—blaming someone else. The theological implications of the relationship in the Creation between people and animals is complex and has some significant application to modern society. This theology of animals will be examined in **Chapter 14, "Animals and Other People."**

The Biblical Teaching About *Imago Dei*

For centuries, theologians have discussed these and other passages, debating the meaning of the image of God. Being made in God's likeness is not a matter of our physical appearance, because humans don't all look the same. But to what does the image of God actually refer? Many ideas have been suggested over the centuries, producing a huge body of theological writing. While hard to summarize, we give a brief overview below of some common themes for the image of God. After developing this theological context, we'll consider how these ideas intersect with evolution.

Abilities: A traditional view of the Church is that the image of God refers to the human abilities that separate us from the animals. The simple answer was that we can talk, think, plan, decide, pray, feel empathy, worship, and do many other things which we believe animals cannot do. Often our motive is to distinguish humans from animals by showing that humans have unique abilities that make us special and superior to animals. Saint Augustine (354-430 AD) wrote something like this when he said *"Man's excellence consists in the fact that God made him to His own image by giving him an intellectual soul, which raises him above the beasts of the field."*[94]

However, scientific evidence is piling up that we humans have more in common with animals than was once thought. Genetic evidence shows that humans and chimpanzees share much of their DNA, up to 97% according to some scientists. Studies of animal behavior (particularly of chimps and other apes) show that animals not only laugh and cry and care for each other, but can learn sign language and even have basic reasoning ability. In fact, Christian neuroscientist Malcolm Jeeves writes that *"any attempt to set down a clear demarcation between the reasoning abilities of nonhuman primates and humans is found to have become blurred."*[95] Obviously, humans have a much larger brain capacity to reason than animals, but reasoning is not a *uniquely* human ability. As neuroscientists and animal behaviorists learn more about animals, they see how traits appear in a rudimentary form at a level similar to human children, things like communication and rationality. Experiments show that until about four years old a human child and a chimpanzee raised together will be at the same level on reasoning and other human abilities, but chimpanzees quickly fall behind the child after that time. Whether or not one accepts evolution, evidence from *living* humans and animals does not show a distinct difference in kinds of abilities (only degree). Elsewhere we have introduced Koko, the late and great gorilla who seemed more "human" than a lot of people who are well known. Human skills and abilities alone don't seem to define the image of God, the **imago dei**.

Another serious challenge for this unique human ability picture of the image of God is the place of people with mental disabilities. If a person is impaired in reasoning or language, are they bearing less of God's image? Are they failing to show His true likeness? The Christian answer to these questions is No! The Bible repeatedly teaches that God values all people, particularly those who are rejected by society or unable to care for themselves. In fact, the Old Testament points to image bearing quality as the reason that *all* human life is valuable:

> *And for your lifeblood I will surely demand an accounting. I will demand an accounting from every animal. And from each human being, too, I will demand an accounting for the life of another human being.*
> *"Whoever sheds human blood,* by *humans shall their blood be shed;*
> *for in the image of God has God made mankind."*
> (Genesis 9:5-6)

This is a major motivator for Christians who seek to protect the unborn, the poor, and the aged. Surely bearing God's image must mean something other than using our mental and physical abilities, being like God in terms of our spiritual qualities. Being in God's image means to "act like God" in some way uncertain, perhaps "acting in His stead" on some occasions—being the hands and feet of God through our love and compassion.

Relationship Capacity. Another common view is that the image of God refers to our capacity for a relationship with God. Following Thomas Aquinas' view of *"aptitude for understanding and loving God,"* the Catholic catechism says, *"Of all visible creatures only man is able to know and love his creator. ... he alone is called to share, by knowledge and love, in God's own life. It was for this end that he was created, and this is the fundamental reason for his dignity."*

Being in the image of God means humans are "persons" and not just something, "someone" because we are child of Someone, we call our "heavenly Father." Our value or worth is not our achievement but is the result of how God views us: we are important because we are important to God. As discussed in an earlier section, "we are restless until we find our rest in Him." It is our God-given capacity to have a personal relationship with the Creator that stamps us with the image of God; we can connect and commune with God because He designed us that way. The mark may be faint or even invisible to us as it was in the early stages of our species development and our brain reaching to consciousness; some humans today may not be able to retrieve this "image of God" in their mind or heart, due to disuse or neglect. But the Good News is that God is still working on reconnecting with the weak signal, the rescue beacon that continues to send out a signal, a weak "beep-beep" for someone who may be searching for you, or for Someone who is always searching for His lost children.

A Calling and Vocation. Many modern theologians and Old Testament scholars understand the *imago Dei* is not a certain set of capacities or features that distinguish humans from other animals, but instead as a "calling" or a "vocation" (means the same thing) to serve God by bearing His image as a witness to the world. Jesus was the **perfect** image of God, of course, perfectly manifesting God's presence and doing God's will in His life, death and resurrection. We cannot match that perfect image, but we are called to imitate Christ, to be like Him and to do His work on Earth. Paul wrote several passages about this goal of Christ-likeness: *"For me to live is Christ, and to die is gain."* (Philippians 1:21) and *"I have been crucified with Christ and I no longer live, but Christ lives in me."* (Galatians 2:19). Paul even alludes to this by citing his wounds: *"I bear on my body the marks of Jesus"* (Galatians

6:17) We have already discussed the work of God that is assigned to His followers, and the critical role our faithfulness in carrying out the Will of God plays in God's ability to accomplish His ultimate will on Earth while allowing Mankind to exercise our own human free will. In a related metaphor the New Testament pictures the "Church" as displaying the image of God in the world as part of our communal command to "Go into all the world...." to bear witness to God's Good News in Christ.

Being Image Bearers for God

As a result of our being made in the image of God, we have great privilege and great responsibility. It is unfortunate but true that some claiming to be Christians present an image that is not like Christ, and the task of representing God credibly is made harder by these bearers of a false image. But that being said, we must acknowledge **first** that every human is a fellow image bearer; all people, men and women, are created in the image of God and are equally valued in God's eyes, not just some elite leaders or priestly class: we all are image bearers if we identify as Believers. **Second**, we ourselves must be diligent in our pursuit of a true image of God in our lives. The work in shaping our lives to be like Christ is never complete on earth, but God is at work molding and shaping us to a closer likeness to Jesus, chipping away what is un-Christlike and adding on the finishing touches like a dedicated artist.

And **third,** as bearers of God's image on Earth, we must be always be careful caretakers of the World we occupy, the natural resources as well as the human resources. God has assigned to all Believers a role in making the planet better, healthier and more verdant every year, spiritual warriors for ecology, advocates for clean air and clean water, and for preservation of all animal species, some dozens of species which go extinct every year—forever gone. Of course, it is the humans which God values above the mountains and the oceans—the "world" is all the individuals, about 8 billion souls in our time. It is of interest to God that children are starving in North Korea and Africa, that disease is killing millions in poorer countries worldwide, that women are abused and bartered in many places and that young girls are sold into sex trafficking in every corner of poverty. God sees these things and cares; if we are to be *In The Image of God* we must see what God sees, love what God loves, and do what God can do with our hands, feet, mouths and money. Quoting President Kennedy once more with a wise prescription about how to live our lives:

> *With a good conscience our only sure reward, with history the final judge of our deeds, let us go forth to lead the land we love, asking His blessing and His help, but knowing that here on earth God's work must truly be our own.*[96]

Chapter 14

ANIMALS AND OTHER PEOPLE

"All animals are equal, but some animals are more equal than others"
GEORGE ORWELL

It should come as no surprise that many Christians and other Believers are uncomfortable with the idea that humans are animals. Uncomfortable is not the word, actually, it is more like **horrified** and ***aghast.***

It is not hard to picture a religious father learning that his 8-year-old son's public-school teacher has told the class today that they were "animals" because humans are all part of the animal kingdom; sputtering and enraged the father yells and jumps around greatly agitated. Perhaps slipping into a bit of profanity he threatens to drive immediately to the school and tell that teacher what he thinks about her "science." He clinches his fist and says "I'll show her what kind of animal I am—she'll learn a thing or two from this old man...this old daddy bear!" Mom tries to get him to calm down, but it is futile. He will not tolerate having his children taught "that humans are just animals, no better than pigs or horses, or even that old Border Collie on the couch." Catching his breath, he roared out "That's FOOLISH! That's pure **HEATHEN PROPOGANDA!** I won't stand for that!"

Not all religious people are blind-sided by such lessons in school, for the curriculum has included this classification system for a century or more. By the third-grade American children have learned that all living things are classified by science into several large groups based on very basic similarities and shared characteristics. The first classification is called "Kingdom", and within each Kingdom organisms are further divided into smaller groups who share more detailed similarities; this second level of classification is called "phylum." Here we leave the basic biological science class, without discussing the other five subdivisions: "classes", "orders", "genus" and "species." Those of us who were not science majors probably vaguely remember these lessons about "phylum" and "genus", and most of us probably never had occasion to use these terms in our day-to-day lives. For our purposes here let it suffice to point out that science identifies five distinct kingdoms of living things: Monera Kingdom, Protist Kingdom, Fungi Kingdom, Plant Kingdom, and Animal Kingdom. Let's count it as blessing that we humans were not assigned to the "fungi" or "plant" kingdoms; **animal kingdom** is not too bad, is it? *It has been reported, anonymously, that some apes and chimpanzees have taken* great offense *at being considered in the same classification as humans.*

Animals as People?

What can we learn from studying animals that can help us understand humans? Quite a lot, actually. Whether one believes in Darwinian evolution or not, the fact that animals exist and are alive cannot be overlooked. Without any resort to viewing apes as our distant cousins we can easily see that animals and humans share some characteristics such as breathing oxygen, male/female differences, sensitive to pain, need for food, seeing and smelling, walking and sleeping, and finally dying. We share a Kingdom and we share many similarities. We humans have always considered themselves superior to animals, and have often used that sense of superiority to dominate and subjugate any animals we can physically control. It is true, however, that early humans had a long history of "animism" where they considered all nature to be "alive" or have its own "spirit," including rivers, trees, mountains and animals. They regarded wild animals as dangerous threats to be appeased or avoided, but also as potential food and clothes as a "gift" from the animal spirit.

So, from the dawn of human self-awareness their relationship with the animals in their environment was more fear than fondness.

Modern man has tamed nearly every animal species to some degree, even far stronger animals such as elephants and horses. It is possible to "train" such dangerous beasts as tigers and lions, and many such animals are put through their routines in circuses and fairs across the nation. The highest rank for an animal is "pet", with the human master's benevolent term, "owner." Objectively, this is not much different from the *owner/slave relationship* which existed openly in our country until the last century and half. On the other extreme are the millions of dogs and cats in America who are pampered and treated as royalty, beloved companions who sometimes become surrogate children for the lonely. Several such "pets" have "inherited" great fortunes from their grateful owners/benefactors who set up lifetime trust funds for "Buffy" or "Phoofy."

Though deep devotion to pets is not uncommon, the official relationship is always that people "own" animals, and the owner's power over the animal is nearly unlimited. Only in the past hundred years has the concept of "animal rights" been raised, and society is struggling with issues of humane treatment for all animals. Elephants have been removed from circuses, chimpanzees have been released from laboratory testing, dolphins and whales have been rescued from show business captivity, and many advocates are fighting to return wild zoo animals back to the "wild" or some other more natural existence. The question of ethical treatment of animals will be discussed later in this chapter, and it may be more troublesome to readers than most of the other content presented. The more "human" an animal seems to be, the more conflicted we humans are about how to treat them.

How Do Humans Differ from Animals?

We have discussed earlier that "being human" still occasionally includes some very beastly and savage behaviors, and it is not uncommon for society to judge some people as being "animals," not in a good way! Certain medical conditions or injuries can cause people to act in many ways like animals: crawling on all fours, foaming at the mouth, barking or growling, and lapping up water or food with their mouths like a dog does. So called "feral children" provide another case study: these are infants who allegedly have been raised by a pack of animals (chimps, wolves, etc.) and who continue to be animal-like when returned to human care. Crouching in the corner, eyes filled with fear, biting or scratching those who approach them, tearing off their clothes, curling up in a fetal position to sleep, attempting to run away or escape—these and dozens of other *animal-like* behaviors have been seen in human beings. Are humans just civilized and trained animals at the core?

There have been many experimental studies comparing human children to very young chimpanzees, bonobos and orangutan, including some in which a family raised a chimp alongside their own toddler. Every effort was made to treat both human and chimp the same in terms of care, attention, affection, teaching, and discipline. In some such studies regular measurements of physical and mental ability were conducted and records kept carefully. The summarized results were that the chimpanzee was more physically advanced in the first several months, and did better on some cognitive tests than the human baby did at first. The chimpanzee advanced cognitively until about age four, whereas the child caught up and kept developing in mental and physical abilities far beyond even the adult chimp on various child development assessments designed by Piaget (object permanence, conservation, etc.) For example, a toy is shown to the child and the chimp, and then hidden under a blanket. Before 12 months of age neither child nor chimp can immediately find the toy, lacking the ability to realize that objects continue to exist when no longer seen; by sixteen months or so, both child and chimp understand the concept. Language begins to develop in the child about two years old, but the chimp never progresses past babbling or random noises. This seems to show that very closely related animals (97% DNA) have only a fixed and limited mental potential. Science describes this as a difference in **degree** but not a difference in **kind.** The animal has the same kind of intelligence, but to a lesser degree. Other such animal studies have shown that this difference in degree can be closed significantly in some animals.

Koko the Amazing Gorilla

Consider the case of **Koko**, a female western lowland gorilla, the so called "talking gorilla," known for having learned a large number of hand signs from a modified version of American Sign Language (ASL). Her instructor and caregiver, Dr. Francine Patterson, reported that Koko had an active vocabulary of more than 1,000 signs of what Patterson calls *Gorilla Sign Language* (GSL). Koko was not the first ape to learn sign language, but in her case Dr. Patterson exposed Koko to spoken English from the beginning, and reported that Koko **understood** 2000 words of spoken English and responded to them, when she chose to, in a very human-like fashion. In addition to what she was taught, Koko occasionally made up her own new words. For example, upon seeing a swan swimming for the first time, Koko signed "water-bird." Another time she invented the term "finger-bracelet" to describe a ring Dr. Patterson was wearing. She identifies herself as a "fine-gorilla-person." She was able to understand and create many such compound words and sentences, though not always with perfect syntax. Her communication was in many ways similar to the language of young children, messages understood by family members even when it was not precisely "good English." Because of copyright restrictions the gorilla shown here is not Koko, but very similar to her. Many actual photos and videos are available on line for those who want to see this amazing "animal," so nearly human.

Koko was born in the San Francisco Zoo and lived most of her life in Woodside, California, at The Gorilla Foundation's preserve in the Santa Cruz Mountains. Dr. Francine Patterson, a developmental psychologist, was essentially a mentor to Koko for over 40 years. Koko gained public attention upon a report of her having adopted a kitten as a pet and creating a name for him. Many people came to know Koko through the numerous internet-based YouTube short films, and a documentary Koko: A Talking Gorilla.[97] Koko amazed scientists in 2012, when she showed, she could learn to play the recorder (a simple flute). The feat revealed mental acuity but also, crucially, that at least some primates can learn to control their breathing and purse their lips to "blow", abilities beyond what was thought to be possible. Koko was considered by experts to be functioning developmentally approximately at the level of a young child; her IQ was judged to be in the 70-90 range.

Koko persuasively demonstrated that she feels emotions much like a human being. In her public appearances, she seemed to experience emotions like happiness, frustration and heartbreak, as well as a wicked little sense of humor. For her birthday one year she requested the usual things ("Good drink", "Sweet cereal") but she also asked for "cat." Three kittens were brought to her and she examined each one, then chose a gray male cat as her pet and cared for him as if he were her baby. She named him "All Ball." Later that year, the cat escaped and was hit by a car. When Patterson explained the cat had gone, Koko signed "bad-sad-bad" and "frown-cry-frown-sad." She sat quietly in a corner for several hours, apparently grieving. Later she was asked what happened and she signed "Cat, cry, have-sorry, Koko-love." Later, she was able to pick out two new kittens which became her surrogate babies.

Koko was befriended by several famous people who would visit and play with her, including TV's "Mr. Rogers" — Fred Rogers. The gentle man and the gregarious gorilla took an instant liking to each other, teasing and hugging each other and signing the word "love." The most amazing episode in Koko's life was her friendship with celebrity comedian Robin Williams. The YouTube video of their amazing first encounter, conversation and friendship bond is widely available on the Internet. Williams got into her apartment-like cage, and they wrestled and tickled each other (at her request). She took his glasses and wore them for a while, testing her vision with them. Koko caressed Williams and inspected his face, hands, and even pulled up his shirt. Several times Williams is shown laughing out loud, and Koko did the gorilla laugh with widely curled lips and squeals. Watching that one encounter will likely alter most people's perception of the animal/human relationship, for one is hard pressed to ever say again, "She's **just** an animal." When Williams died in 2014 Koko took it hard. Her keepers were not planning to tell Koko of her friend's death, but Koko overheard people talking quietly, and some on the phone talking about Williams. Koko directly asked Dr. Patterson in sign language "What's wrong?" She was then told the truth. Koko became very somber, her head bowed and her lip trembling, according to witnesses. She spent several hours in a corner away from the others, apparently mourning the loss of Robin Williams. Her "mourning" continued a few days.

Koko showed some signs of understanding death. After Koko had observed and showed interest in a gorilla skeleton in the compound, Dr. Patterson asked her "Is this alive or dead?" Koko signed "Dead, draped." Draped was Koko's sign for "covered up" as in buried. Patterson then asked, "Where do animals go when they die?" The gorilla said "A comfortable hole." The she signed a kiss, "good bye." Koko apparently even understood her own future death. Koko had slowed down her activity and seemed tired and sad. One day Dr. Patterson sat with her quietly; Koko looked directly at her caretaker and signed two words: one was "patient" and the other was "old." It was as if she were saying, "I'm getting old." Koko died in her sleep soon afterward and is buried in an honored spot at the compound.

Was Koko Just an Exception?

What can we make of such an amazing animal? Was Koko *almost* human? Was she a "person" in any sense of the word? Did she have a "mind?" Was she "thinking" in the same way humans think? Within the religious context of this book we ask, "Did Koko have a soul?" These are tough questions about which science is not yet ready to give definitive answers. Perhaps Koko was unique, an abnormally bright gorilla, an oddity in the animal kingdom. Certainly, we have exceptional people, oddities among us who are clearly smarter than average, or more talented than other people. Was Koko just the Einstein of the apes? It appears not. There are apparently many other bright stars in the animal kingdom, and not just in the hominid branch, or mammals, but also in some aquatic animals, some avian species and even some insects. None is as famous or as well documented as Koko, but apparently many of the skills we think make us humans are also demonstrated by the other animals we count as our inferiors.

As presented in earlier chapters of this book, **consciousness** is considered the fundamental distinction between humans and our non-human ancestors. The evolution of the brain eventually provided the new ability to be self-aware, to recognize one's self from other selves and the environment. Self-awareness is often used as a marker for being conscious, and until recently, only humans were believed to have that ability. It is true that most of the hundreds of living species on earth do not possess it. However, we now know that some animals, at least ten species, have been proven to have some measurable degree of self-awareness (one of the elements of consciousness). These self-aware animals can easily recognize themselves in a mirror (the original scientific method) while other animals, including very young humans, cannot. A classic case has a chimpanzee surreptitiously marked on the forehead with a small patch of red paint. The chimpanzee looks in a mirror, and notices the red paint; but instead of touching the red in the mirror, the self-aware animal touches his own forehead: he knows the image is a reflection of himself. The same test found that elephants can make the same distinction in a mirror test, and in other tests that have been developed. The current documented self-aware animals, besides humans, chimps and elephants includes: **Orangutans, Gorillas, Bottlenose Dolphins, Bonobos, Orcas, Rhesus Macaques,** and **European Magpies.** Recent research seems to establish that some insects display self-awareness in other forms of testing. The list of self-aware animals may not be complete, but we know that we have at least 9 or 10 non-human competitors in the self-awareness game. Let us briefly survey a few of these human-like animal acts while holding in abeyance the questions this discovery raises for humans.

The Other Self-Aware Animals

Primatologists are scientists who study the primate order of mammals, including lemurs, lorises, tarsiers, monkeys, apes and humans. Within these categories fall the more widely recognized gorillas, bonobos, chimpanzees and orangutans. The most famous primatologist is Jane Goodall, who in 1960, traveled to the forest at Gombe Stream in Tanzania where she lived among the animals for 55 years and her determination and skill allowed for her to observe behaviors of the chimpanzees that no other scientist had seen. An award-winning movie was made about her life with the chimpanzees in 2017, "Jane In the Shadow of Men." The 84-year-old Goodall is still an international activist on behalf of the animals of the world, quoted as saying: *"The least I can do is speak out for those who cannot speak for themselves."*[98]

All the animals listed above were considered "self-aware" by some version of the mirror test (able to recognize their own face as separate from the mirror by noticing and touching a paint spot on their head.) The normal response from most animals and young children is to touch the mirror, not realizing the mirror image was themselves. There are hundreds, probably thousands of stories about animal intelligence (some scientific studies, some personal anecdotes. For example, magpies are known for their ability to steal shiny objects and to hide away their "loot," a researcher reported, and "It's not too far-fetched that a master thief like a magpie has that perspective-taking ability." New Caledonian crows are able to learn how to make, and use a variety or tools and when given the choice, select ones that are appropriate for a particular task. This demonstrates their ability to learn from the past, and make decisions about what is required for the future.

There are a vast number of well documented research studies showing that many species of animals possess numerous "nearly human" abilities. Many of these established that the ten species listed above have "self-awareness" or the ability to know they are separate individuals from others, who have a sense of identity and can recognize that others of their species also are thinking, self-aware individuals like themselves. This is an important threshold for deciding when early hominids crossed that line into being humans—consciousness, self-awareness and understanding that others also have minds and identities. Scientists call this ability **"*theory of mind*."** Children reach this milestone around two years of age in normal circumstances. We could site many more scientific studies that show animal intelligence to be quite respectable, and some studies have even suggested that the IQ of a porpoise may be higher than the average human IQ. This is not conclusive, but we should probably avoid getting into a mental contest with *Flipper* of TV fame (OK, technically he was a dolphin, but still very smart.)

Rather than cite further scientific evidence of the human-like abilities of animals, we will present a few anecdotes reported by laymen who have lived with animals for years, their special pets. Nowadays, twice as many American households include pets as include children, and even mainstream religion is encountering even more challenging questions like "Do animals have souls?" We will address that in a later section of this chapter, but for now just contemplate the fact that some religious ministers have conducted animal weddings, funerals, and dedications for their parishioners who requested the blessing of their animal friends. Some congregations even have an annual ceremony to "Bless the Beasts" or some other catchy term, but very seriously extending their spiritual help to the community. These ritual blessing of the animals is often celebrated on or near October 4, the official feast day of St. Francis of Assisi, a Catholic Christian patron saint of animals.

Some Animal Stories You Won't Believe

The collection of anecdotes about animals included here is from the article "Seven of The Most Impressive Feats of Animal Intelligence"[99] though there are scores of other similar articles about amazing examples of animal intelligence and/or heroics. One tells about a musician who wanted to test some ideas about dolphins and whales he had been contemplating. Off the coast of Vancouver Island, he dropped a special submersible speaker overboard and played recordings he had of the animal's hornlike whistles and songs, sounds many had studied before and many believed they were actual language. He was pleased to get some responses from some whales. Some other musicians with him tried playing "people" music, and the dolphins and whales ignored the sounds. Then he played a recording of a Tibetan monk chanting religious prayers, and to his surprise the whales gathered around the speaker and just huddled silently, listening to the chanting. When pods of killer whales fall strangely silent to eavesdrop on a chanting Buddhist monk, what exactly are they responding to? Is it to the vibrations themselves, sounds and sensations either pleasing or baffling to their ears? Or are they hearing the resonance of something more intangible, some transcendent echo reflected back from deep within them? Were they moved emotionally in the way humans sometimes respond? Was this "soul" music to the whales and dolphins?

Alex the parrot is one of the most accomplished birds known to science. It is reported that recently Alex astounded researchers by demonstrating a rough understanding of the concept of **zero**, an abstract concept never understood by the greatest mathematicians of ancient Greece, and a concept that still is difficult for moderns to grasp. To test Alex the trainer laid out four groups of blocks: two blue, three green, four yellow and six orange. She then called out a number and asked Alex to identify the color of the pile with that many blocks. Alex refused to answer her, instead repeating the number "five" over and over. None of the colored piles had 5 blocks. Finally, the trainer said "OK, smarty, what color is five?" Alex quickly answered "None!" *A bird with a brain the size of a walnut had understood the "absence of quantity," something human children don't typically grasp until age three or four.* In another recent scientific discovery, it was found that bees can also understand the concept of zero, in a very clever but convincing experiment. Researchers trained bees to find a sugar water treat under the card with the lowest number of black dots, and then introduced a treat card with no black dots. The bees quickly learned to select the card with no dots, or zero, in order to get the reward. They somehow "figured out" the math concept that "nothing" can mean "something," the concept of zero. This same quite abstract "reasoning" has since been detected in a few other animals and insects.[100]

Can Animals Have Concern and Compassion?

Kenyan conservationist Daphne Sheldrick who has worked with elephants in the wild for many years says *"Each one is…a unique individual with its own unique personality. They can be happy or sad, volatile or placid. They display envy, jealousy, throw tantrums and are fiercely competitive, and they can develop hang-ups which are reflected in behavior. They grieve deeply for lost loved ones, even shedding tears and suffering depression. They have a sense of compassion that projects beyond their own kind and sometimes extends to others in distress."*[101] Other observers have reported elephants standing silent guard over their stillborn babies for days with their heads and ears sunk low. Other scientists report that elephants come together to "mourn" their dead in a kind of funeral ceremony. Another story from a hunter who claims he saw a grieving red fox bury the body of another who had been killed by a mountain lion: "***She would kick up dirt, stop, look at the carcass, and intentionally kick again. I observed this 'ritual' for about 20 minutes. A few hours later I went to see the carcass, and it was totally buried.***"[102]

One striking report in this compassion-like behavior concerns a bonobo female named **Kuni**, who found a wounded bird in her enclosure at Twycross Zoo, in England. Kuni picked up the bird, and when her keeper urged her to let it go, she climbed to the highest point of the highest tree, carefully unfolded the bird's wings and spread them wide open, one wing in each hand, before throwing it as hard as she could toward the barrier of the enclosure. When the bird fell short, Kuni climbed down and guarded it until the end of the day, when it flew to safety. Having seen birds in flight many times, she seemed to have a notion of what would be good for a bird, thus giving us an anthropoid illustration of the ability to "mentally change places" with another creature. What was the bonobo thinking? Why did she give assistance to an animal of a different species? We don't know, but it is thought provoking.

Animal Bravery and Heroism

No set of animal stories would be complete without the tales of heroic animals that saved human lives. Some of these are legendary. Eleven-year-old Anthony Melton's pet pig, **Priscilla**, made headlines in 1984 when she dove into a Houston Lake to save his life. Swimming out to the boy, who was in over his head and starting to panic, she towed him to shore with her leash. Unbelievable, but apparently true. In 1975, it was reported in newspapers that a woman shipwrecked off the Philippines was saved by a giant sea turtle that surfaced underneath her and carried her on its back for two full days until rescuers finally arrived. Again, this is hard to believe but was reliably reported in the media.

And finally, there is the story of an elderly Tennessee woman was rescued by her pet canary. Upon seeing her trip and fall unconscious, the bird proceeded to find its way out of her house, which it had never left before. It then traveled the length of several football fields to her niece's nearby home and pecked furiously against the windowpane until the niece realized something had happened. She went running to check up on her aunt and got medical assistance. Unfortunately, the heroic canary promptly collapsed and died from the effort, but the old woman's life was saved.

There are many such stories, not all verified, and probably the readers have some of their own. People who love and live with their pets often are certain the animals are nearly human, showing intelligence, emotions, playing tricks, smiling and pouting, and having an understanding of time and future plans (such as when the school bus comes in the afternoon bringing the young owner home.). This is not to say that all we have are anecdotes. Systematic studies have been conducted on so-called "consolation" behavior. Consolation is defined as friendly or reassuring behavior by a bystander toward a victim of aggression. For example, chimpanzee A attacks chimpanzee B, after which bystander chimp C comes over and embraces or grooms B. Based on hundreds of such observations, we know that consolation occurs regularly and exceeds baseline levels of contact. In other words, it is a demonstrable tendency that probably reflects empathy, since the objective of the consoler seems to be to alleviate the distress of the other. In fact, the usual effect of this kind of behavior is that it stops screaming, yelping, and other signs of distress. Animals can be quite humane and caring, like people; but like people, we know that animals cannot, or are not always nice to each other. Circumstances intervene for them as for us.

Empathy is fragile among us all. Among our close animal relatives, it is switched on by events within their community, such as a youngster in distress, but it is just as easily switched off with regards to outsiders or members of other species, such as prey. A chimpanzee who was gently grooming bugs from another chimp's back has also bashed in the skull of a live monkey by hitting it against a tree. Empathy is selective and flimsy. Bonobos are less brutal, but in their case, too, empathy needs to pass through several filters before it will be expressed. Often, the filters prevent expressions of empathy because no ape can afford feeling pity for all living things all the time. This applies equally to humans.

Our evolutionary background makes it hard to identify with outsiders. We've evolved to fear and hate our enemies, to ignore people we barely know, and to distrust anybody who doesn't look like us. Even if we are largely cooperative within our communities, we become almost a "different animal" in our treatment of strangers, mobbing together against "them." By "we" is meant all of us "animal-people," and "them" is any new arrival who speaks a different language, has a different skin color, or worships a different god than the rest of us. Like other animals, we can sometimes work up a violent frenzy.

The Biblical Position on Animals

As reviewed earlier the Old Testament account in Genesis has God creating all the animals of the air, land and sea before He created Man. In a quaint little twist God gives Adam the privilege of naming every living creature which God had made. We may wonder where Adam got such a vocabulary and how long it took to finish the job: *Scientists estimate there are about 8.7 million of animal species on earth, with about 6.5 million on land and 2.2 million in oceans. If we take only the animals which have spinal cords, the total number of such animals is about 60,000 different species (omitting all insects such as fleas and beetles). There are several hundred NEW animal species discovered or identified each year.*[103] That is a lot of names and a fair amount of time required. Again, rather charmingly, Adam is not happy. It seems that God had thought one of these many animals would become a companion for Adam, but Adam was hoping for something better. After God created Eve and presented her to Adam it is likely that he grinned and said, "Now THAT is more like it!" Admittedly that statement was not included in Genesis but it fits the story line quite well.

The Genesis account does make it clear that Adam (mankind) was commissioned with the duty to care for all the animals, to "have dominion over them" as the King James translation puts it. Dominion does not mean domination in the traditional sense—it implies "responsibility" and "stewardship" over the belongings of another: all animals belong to God and God appointed Man to take good care of them, as a landowner might hire someone to oversee his farm carefully and satisfactorily. The newer translations say of Man "*...that they may rule over the fish in the sea and the birds in the sky, over the livestock and all the wild animals, and over all the creatures that move along the ground.*" (Genesis 1:26) Some newer translations say "tame animals" instead of "cattle", probably more appropriate.

The Bible seems to indicate in Genesis that humans did not eat animals, and that Adam and Eve were vegetarians. **"Then God said, "I give you every seed-bearing plant on the face of the whole earth and every tree that has fruit with seed in it. They will be yours for food."** (Genesis 1:29). Animals are not on the menu! We do not find there the approval for killing animals for food, but it appears that after expulsion from Eden, the human family became farmers AND shepherds (Cain and Abel). It seems to simply pass unmentioned that post-Eden the practice of eating animals was the normal practice. Many groups of Protestants, such as the Adventists, consider the life in the Garden before the First Sin was God's original plan and His preference, and such groups practice total vegetarianism as a religious duty, obeying this prohibition against eating meat. Most Christians, however, do not practice meat-free diets for religious reasons, though there are many who live meat-free lives for their own health reasons, or out of respect for animals. It appears from science that meat-eating may not be the healthy diet which would extend and improve human life, and so we might guess that God, like any good father, would prefer we have a healthy diet and a healthy lifestyle. The counter argument from science, however, asserts that it was the eating of meat by the early hominids that allowed their brains to develop more effectively. The meat-eating early ancestors of *Homo sapiens* learned to use tools, make weapons, and eventually to kill and butcher large animals for food. The development of the use of fire led to cooking the meat, adding to the safety and the nutritional value of their animal kills.

We may yet, as a civilization and a species, return to a meat free diet for health reasons, but also possibly because we move toward thinking of animals as persons, near-humans with rights and respect. This may be the most difficult concept suggested in this book, that we may learn so much about animals that we cannot continue to treat them as "things" or "brutes." It may be a century or two in the future, but if we started to believe that all animals might be like Koko described earlier, if we understood more, such a change of view of animals would probably evoke the taboo of "cannibalism" which is so distasteful to humans. (Sorry, the pun just happened on its own, maybe "inspired?")

A Change of Plans?

After the Flood, Noah and the remaining seven humans were given new, revised instructions: *"But you must not eat meat that has its lifeblood still in it. And for your lifeblood I will surely demand an accounting. I will demand an accounting from every animal. And from each human being, too, I will demand an accounting for the life of another human being"* (Genesis 9:4-5) Based on this scripture and tradition Judaism has strict regulations for the preparation and consumption of meat, known as Kosher rules. Some animals were prohibited entirely, and some were acceptable if the "lifeblood" has been drained out completely. These are complex and extensive restrictions which are important to Jewish believers, but are not relevant in this work. But notice, that in addition to giving kosher laws, this passage reiterates Mankind's responsibility to protect and honor life, all life. God says He will "demand an accounting" for every animal and every human. Creation is His, and we humans are His partners in caring for it as He does: in God's way, or "in God's image."

While God apparently now has no religious qualms about Christians eating a juicy hamburger or a roasted turkey, it does not mean that God doesn't care about the animals (other than us). The evidence is quite striking in a very poignant illustration Jesus used: *"Are not two sparrows sold for a penny? Yet not one of them will fall to the ground outside your Father's care."* (Matthew 10:29) Some other translations have Father's *notice* for *care* here. Another example: *"Look at the birds of the air: They do not sow or reap or gather into barns—and yet your Heavenly Father feeds them. Are you not much more valuable than they?* (Matthew 6:26) The Bible makes it clear that **all life is precious to Him,** and Mankind is deputized to do God's work and will in the preservation of life. This is part of the Image of God, a compassion and respect for all life, human and non-human.

Are Animals Persons? Legal Issues

A grassroots movement has recently emerged in which a number of scientists, philosophers, ethicists and legal experts have rallied together in support of the idea that some nonhuman animals are persons and thus deserving of human-like legal protections. Their efforts have upended conventional notions of personhood by suggesting that humans aren't the only persons on the planet. So, what is a person, what do we mean exactly? An immediate challenge for animal personhood advocates is to formally define what they mean by a person—not an easy task. We humans automatically get to be called persons, and as a result, we've never really had to come up with formal definitions. Even the abortion debate hasn't settled the issue; 'personhood' is typically invoked when a fetus is viable outside the womb, but others insist that personhood begins much earlier—-at the first heartbeat, or the first brain waves, or even as early as the first eight cells that develop from fertilization. The legal implication is that defining when one becomes a "person" defines when one has human rights. If some animals were legally defined as "persons" they would be entitled to human rights and protections just as we are.

In recent decades the trend seems to be moving away from defining personhood as something one is simply born with by virtue of their species (*Homo sapiens*), but whether one has certain cognitive, psychological and emotional capacities. Some scientists have tried to list the positive attributes that define "person." One is bioethicist Joseph Fletcher who has compiled a list of 15 markers for being a "person" including self-awareness, self-control, a minimum level of intelligence, a sense of time (including a sense of the past and future), concern for others, curiosity, and so on. His list is very logical and supported by current scientific thinking, but it creates some problems for us. Based on his 15 attributes, many animals would be classified as "persons" BUT many humans would not. A person in a coma or vegetative state without brain activity would not be considered a person. A fetus or an unborn child would likely not qualify as a "person" based on Fletcher's list, nor would a profoundly disabled person: not all humans are persons, and not all persons are human, he would argue.[104]

An insightful essay by Aviva Rutkin, "When is an animal a person?" uses neuroscience to set the rules" focuses on the daunting question, "When is an animal a person?" It's surely an extremely important question and also a "hot" topic, as many people are working on achieving the legal status of "person" for nonhuman animals (animals). For example, attorney Steven Wise and people working with The Nonhuman Rights Project have been working to achieve legal personhood for chimpanzees, and a recent essay by philosopher Mark Rowlands called "Are animals persons?" concludes "personhood is widely distributed through the animal kingdom."[105] Concerning the legal efforts of Mr. Wise, we read:

> ... the non-profit *Nonhuman Rights Project* has drawn attention for its attempts to take legal action to free captive chimps – so far Hercules and Leo from a Long Island research lab and Kiko and Tommy from private ownership. A new documentary, *Unlocking the Cage*, chronicles the group's so-far-unsuccessful quest for what its president Stephen Wise describes as 'legal transubstantiation'. If the courts ever find in its favor, 'the non-human animal would come out of that courtroom looking the exact same, but her legal status would be forever changed', Wise said on the film.[106]

Animal rights groups such as **PETA** and **Greenpeace** have been advocating for decades for protection and rights for animals, especially endangered animals and animals used as research "guinea pigs" in laboratories. Public opinion does seem to be shifting toward giving animals at least some rights. Last year, a Gallup poll found that 32 per cent of people in the US believe that animals should receive the same rights as people – an eight-point rise since 2008. Organizations like **The Nonhuman Rights Project** focuses on legal action such as *habeas corpus*, to protect against unlawful imprisonment. The group wants captive chimps to be sent to a sanctuary, where they can live in a wilder and more open environment. Court actions are having mixed results, winning some freedom from torturous testing or experimentation, and relocating some 200 chimpanzees from research labs to an animal sanctuary.

Judging by Pain Instead of Brain

There seems to be another wave in the animal rights field that doesn't center on proving that some animals and some species are intelligent and sentient and self-aware (human-like) but concentrating on the idea that suffering means the same to a dog as to a human, that mistreatment and abuse is just as wrong for a tiger or an elephant as it is for a child or a disabled elderly woman.

Most animals are what we describe as 'sentient' - they can think, perceive their environment, and experience suffering and pleasure, although they may experience and understand these in diverse ways from humans. Animals are also 'conscious' just like people, that is, they have an awareness of things within themselves and their surroundings. All animals, indeed all living things that have been tested by science for response to "pain" have found that everything living feels pain. There are different levels of consciousness and so different levels of sensing pain, but all animals hurt when hit, and many can experience emotional pain such as feeling rejection or hate toward themselves.[107]

> It is not just **"DO ANIMALS THINK?"** But more importantly **"DO ANIMALS SUFFER PAIN?"**

An animal may not react in the same way when it is injured. Prey species like mice can be good at hiding their pain, especially when showing weakness may mean they could get eaten by an eagle! An animal may not be able to explain uncomfortable experiences to itself, thinking in the same way we do in a dental office. This means that they may feel more frightened and unsure about experiences, similar to how a child may react when it gets hurt. We may never be able to understand how an animal thinks, just like we may never be able to understand just how our friends or family think! But what is important to remember is that we are just one of many species, and many of these species of animals, just like us, are conscious, and are able to feel emotions and pain or pleasure, too. With our pets whom we see daily we can be fairly certain if they are in pain, are upset, are worried or frightened, or if they are happy and content, enjoying life and experiencing real pleasure. We don't know if every animal in the jungle, or every vertebrate on the planet is capable of experiencing pain and pleasure just like we do; we don't yet know how to draw the line between species that suffer and species that don't, but we humans are, on our good days, troubled by the thought that animals are equal in some way to us.

It appears that we are going through a cultural shift regarding animals, perhaps parallel to the cultural shift that finally led humans to renounce enslaving other humans and treating them like sub-humans. It took many centuries for that change in public morality, and a good deal of that civil rights revolution was the recognition of the pain and suffering of slaves. Even yet, over 150 years since Lincoln's great Emancipation Proclamation, true civil rights are not yet final. When we realized at some deeper level that "the slave is my brother" as the great Christmas hymn O Holy Night proclaims in verse 1 and 2:

> *The stars are brightly shining*
> *It is the night of our dear Savior's birth*
> **Long lay the world in sin and error pining**
> **'Til He appeared and the soul felt its worth**
> *A thrill of hope, the weary world rejoices*
> *For yonder breaks a new and glorious morn*
> **Chains shall He break, for the slave is our brother**
> And in His name all oppression shall cease
> Sweet hymns of joy in grateful chorus raise we
> Let all within us praise His holy name.[108] (Emphasis added)

Believing in a God like Jesus can be a life-altering experience, for it might challenge your thinking about such difficult topics as how we should treat animals. We all pretty much agree that humans should not ever cause any animal unnecessary pain, or any suffering just for human entertainment. We already know that and so have advanced as a society. But is there more? Does God require more of His "highest" creation? No answers are offered here, other than the "feeling" that history and culture are on the march toward a world where humans are the caretakers for God's animal menagerie and not the oppressors of our fellow animals who share the planet.

"We can judge the heart of a man by his treatment of animals"

Emmanuel Kant

Chapter 15

BEING FULLY HUMAN

"There is so much good in the worst of us, and so much bad in the best of us, that it ill behooves any of us to find fault with the rest of us."

JAMES TRUSLOW ADAMS

One of the central premises of the study of mankind is that something abides and endures among all the multitude of changes that evolution has brought to humans, something which is similar in important ways in both modern and prehistoric humans. For our purposes here, "human nature" is the term used to describe this phenomenon. This is not a new term in the human sciences, but it may be assigned a larger place in the present attempt to understand humanness.

How Did We Get Here?

More than a century of scholars and experts have extracted much evidence from careful study of animals in the wild, natural habitat, particularly apes, chimpanzees and other primates in the same anthropoid family as humans. Many scientists have devoted their lives to the study of the remaining isolated human tribes who have been unaffected by the wider culture, these living humans are believed to be essentially unchanged from primitive times, perhaps still living in the "stone age" culturally. These studies are fascinating windows into the way humans evolved, giving us growing insights into how we came to be humans, insights that inform theories and hypotheses that are part of science. Still, in science we recognize that absolute certainty is beyond us in our search to know what it was like to be *Homo habilis*, or *Homo erectus* or *Neanderthal*, or *Homo sapiens*. As in all science, we may be wrong or only partially right, and the next great excavation or archaeological dig may upend our present understanding of human evolution. Insight opens the doors, but humility warns us not to close any doors, minds, ideas or theories prematurely.

We cannot know empirically what human nature was like for the early *homo sapiens* or their homo predecessor species, but we can intelligently and logically postulate some ideas from available data in multiple disciplines. We can postulate certain commonalities true for all humans, ancient and modern such as death, a sense of mortality, child birth, sickness, fear, sadness, and formation of personal and intimate relationships. By our wealth of studies in psychology, sociology, and anthropology we already have a good understanding of what these common events in human life mean and do to us, and can reasonably project those findings back through time to our early hominid ancestors. Studies of human development by such scientists as Maslow, Erickson, Piaget and Kohlberg found the same results in a wide range of modern cultures, and so the stages they identified seemed to be independent of cultural influences, developmental patterns that seemed to be hard-wired in our genetics. We can also identify with some confidence the large cultural changes and progression of early humans, such as tool making, using fire, burial rituals, artistic expression, forming large cooperative social groups, and adopting agriculture and animal domestication in place of the previous hunter-gatherer way of life.

Humanness and Human Nature

Because this is a book about God (the idea) and the developing conceptualization of that idea in early and evolving human beings, the premise in this book is that the evolving human brain and the evolving idea of God are inherently intertwined. Thus, the question of "being human" is of vital interest here, the question of "*When and how did the evolving hominids* ***become*** *humans?"* That raises another question, *"How and when did the idea of a* ***spirit world*** *arise in those early hominid brains?"* Further we ask *"What is it to be* ***fully human?*** *and are we there now, the final version, the ultimate potential for what humanness means?"* A final question is raised herein: *"Can we* ***project our ideas about humanness*** *upon our image of God,"* since humans vary so greatly in behaviors and character, from admirable to despicable?" If we anthropomorphize God, as this book suggests we must, can we rationally imagine a God is who better than we are, better than the best humans? And if we can't imagine such a good God, is a lesser God worth discussing? Critics of religion often strike an effective blow with this assertion": **"God didn't create Man; Man created God."** One version of this pithy saying is attributed to George Weinberg: *"Man created God in his image: intolerant, sexist, homophobic and violent."*[109] Another non-believer, Eckhart Tolle wrote: *"Man Made 'God' in his own image. The eternal, the infinite, the unnamable was reduced to a mental idol that you had to believe in and worship as 'my god' or 'our god'."*[110] Other skeptics have pointed out that, *"If Man created God, he did a poor job."*

Despicable Gods

The ancient Greeks imagined a whole pantheon of gods (Zeus, Hera, Poseidon, Demeter, Athene, Hephaistos, Ares, Aphrodite, Apollon, Artemis, Hermes, Dionysus, and sometimes Hestia) and the Romans imagined similar gender paired gods, but with different names (Jupiter and Juno, Neptune and Minerva, Mars and Venus, Apollo and Diana, Vulcan and Vesta, and Mercury with Ceres.) These gods made for wonderful, exciting stories, myths and tales of the most trashy, corrupt and lascivious deeds and activities. Both Greek philosophers and Roman statesmen ridiculed these badly behaving deities and asserted that if humans behaved as the gods behave, we would banish them from our midst. So, attributing human qualities and behaviors to the gods is a risky business, and a horribly distorted God would result if the worst of humanity were attributed to Him. If our God is not better than us, what use would such a God be? Thus, we need to consider carefully what is the highest and best of what it means to be human, to be fully human.

Certainly, we mortals have imagined some horrible gods and spirits over the history of our species, and critics are spot on in rejecting any such wicked, despicable, abominable deity. But it is not necessary to imagine such a terrible god when other images of God are readily available to us—for example, the image of a "loving heavenly Father" revealed in the teachings and example of Jesus. Thinking of God as a "father" is to apply a known, visible human model to the Creator of the universe, a God we cannot see or fully comprehend. This, we acknowledge, is in fact anthropomorphic thinking, which this apology advocates.

Anthropomorphism is the attributing of human characteristics and purposes to inanimate objects, animals, plants, or other natural phenomena, or to a god. Most pet lovers engage is this practice of describing their dog or cat or pet pig as being almost human: "Fluffy looks at me with those big brown eyes and she knows exactly what I say" or "Charlie curls up next to me just like a child" or "I know Rotter gets lonely when I am gone, for he jumps around and barks with excitement when he sees me come in..." Scientists generally avoid any hint of this in their research and observations, regarding this as biased and flawed reasoning. Without a doubt this is a risky business—thinking about God as being somehow similar to us. It is, at the very least, audacious and brash. Using ourselves as the measure of the divine is so egocentric that it is *embarrassing to suggest it*. And yet, in trying with our limited and finite minds to understand the Creator of the Universe, with what else do we have to compare?

To What Shall We Compare God?

In normal conversation, when we are describing something, we most often start with a comparison—explaining something unknown by showing similarities to something known. For example, in trying to describe a rare animal only recently discovered, we say "It is like a bear, only much smaller, and it lives in trees and swings from limb to limb like a monkey." The human brain is wired to understand some new idea by comparing and contrasting it with ideas and images already stored in memory. So, for the purpose of this book, we try to find some beginning comprehension of the unseen deity by comparison with some being we can see—human beings. We will risk being anthropomorphic here. ("gasp!")

Such anthropomorphic attempts have yielded amazing visions of gods and goddesses from ancient times, but often these deities were like the worst, most profane humans imaginable, magnified by unlimited power and uncontrolled morality. Tying the image of God to human nature and behavior can yield a loving Father-God of Christianity, for some human fathers are wonderful and admirable. But there are also despicable, malicious people among us, so it is easy to imagine a god like Zeus, an all-powerful, devious, lustful philander who seeks only his own pleasure, and bound by no rules of morality in heaven or earth. Anthropomorphism can imagine any image of god that we choose. Christianity has chosen to believe in a God who is infinitely better than the best human being: a loving Father God, "Our Father, who art in Heaven..." This may be a false analogy, but it feels right to millions of Believers. If we were created in God's image, then to understand him to the limits of our ability, it seems reasonable to create the model of Him in our image.

The Bible certainly claims that God created Man in His own image, cited before in Genesis 1:27. Theologians have continued to parse and tease the meaning out of these words, and a good sized book store could not shelve all the books that have be and are still being written to explain what is meant by the "image of God." Almost universally, no theologian argues that God looks like a male human, though our artists have almost always painted or sculpted God as a very old, white bearded, robust white man. Michelangelo's Sistine Chapel contains perhaps the most widely recognized image of God of all time, portraying on the vaulted ceiling the creation of Adam. The muscular Ancient One, with flowing white beard and hair, reaches a creative finger out to touch the outstretched finger of a beautiful specimen of a man: Adam, blond, European, and naked.

The Problem with Human Nature

Many biblical scholars consider "in the image of God" to be referring to the spiritual being, the soul or spirit of humans, not the bodily appearance. Thus, humans are equipped by God to be like God and act like God in some yet unrealized way. The book of Genesis portrays this image in the original humans, Adam and Eve. These two humans enjoy companionship with God who apparently comes "in the cool of the evening" to walk with them in the Garden. They are precious to this Creator, who said of His creation, "That's good." This lovely unity with God is shattered by the willful decision of Adam and Eve to eat the forbidden fruit from a tree in the center of Eden, "the tree of knowledge of good and evil." Before their fall, these two humans ate freely from another favored tree, "the tree of life", and that apparently guaranteed them immortality, a permanent life in Paradise with God. Sin entered the human heart, this ancient story tells us, perhaps metaphorically, but still a true picture of humanity.

The two sinners are expelled from the garden and banished from their daily walk with God, specifically so that they cannot eat again from the "tree of life", and thus live forever. Somehow, their disobedience had broken something within them, the "image of God," according to this amazing story. Now they have a conscience, now they know right from wrong, and now they are responsible for their choices throughout their now limited life. "*In Adam's Fall, we sinned all*" is the famous Puritan alphabetic mantra written on primitive "horn books" and taught in the schools and churches of New England for many generations. "**Original sin**" is the theological term for this concept—that all descendants of Adam have inherited that "sin tendency," we are born sinners. Egocentric willfulness is who we are at the core, a part of our human nature, "I" becomes our name, our identity. This doctrine has been a part of Christian tradition from the earliest years, and is specifically taught by the author of half of the New Testament, Paul of Tarsus. Consider his complicated analysis here, (with emphasis and notes added)

> *Therefore, just as sin entered the world through one man* (ADAM), *and death through sin, and in this way death came to all people, because all sinned…For if the many died by the trespass of the one man* (ADAM), *how much more did God's grace and the gift that came by the grace of the one man,* (JESUS CHRIST) *overflow to the many!...For if, by the trespass of the one man,* (ADAM) *death reigned through that one man, how much more will those who receive God's abundant provision of grace and of the gift of righteousness reign in life through the one man, Jesus Christ! Consequently, just as one trespass resulted in condemnation for all people, so also one righteous act* (JESUS' SACRIFICE ON THE CROSS) *resulted in justification and life for all people.* (Romans 5:12-21, *edited for brevity*) Note: words in ALL CAPS for emphasis.

Paul is dealing with some complex theological reasoning here, and in the original Greek strings sentences together without catching his breath, so this passage may seem obtuse. The essence of his argument is that *somehow Adam represents the whole human race and human nature,* and due to his sin human nature is flawed for everyone. It is not a genetic argument, or a biological explanation, but posits a universal moral character flaw that every human being shares by virtue of being human, just as much of what defines "human" physically is two eyes, two arms, one heart, five toes and two ears. Just as all human beings are alike in some clear physical ways, so all humans share a common "nature", including a "moral nature." The common flaw in all humans has been identified by famous atheist, Richard Dawkins, in his book The Selfish Gene.[111] Though Dawkins does not consider his "so called" selfish gene to be a negative factor, he is addressing the same problem with human nature that others have explored for centuries, and which figures so prominently in this book. Dawkins tries to show the evolutionary advantage that selfishness provides, though he is not actually discussing a genetic entity, an actual human gene.

The Science of Selfishness

Richard Dawkins is a noted British ethologist, evolutionary biologist, and author of dozens of very influential books on biology, evolution, religion, pseudoscience and alternative medicine. He is a stern opponent of supernaturalism, creationism, organized religion, and belief in any deity. The Selfish Gene published in 1976 earned him immediate recognition as a serious scientist, and his 1982 book, *The Extended Phenotype* further developed his earlier work and popularized his theories. He later admitted that the "selfish gene" title was misleading, since he is not discussing traditional Darwinian gene mutation as the mechanism for evolution. He proposes a gene-centric model operating at the organism level, rather than at the individual gene level. Using this distinction to answer his critics he developed the theory of reciprocal altruism, whereby one organism provides a benefit to another organism in the expectation of future reciprocal benefit, rather than the Darwinian model of trying to pass on one's own genes directly and at any cost. Altruism and selfishness are normally opposites in common conversation, but Dawkins tries to show that even "altruistic acts" often are actually selfish behaviors in disguise (or maybe unconsciously motivated.)

Altruism of course is "unselfish concern for and aid to others," a highly praised but somewhat rare quality of humans. Dawkins, like many other religious critics, argues that almost all acts labeled as "altruistic" are, in fact, cleverly disguised acts of self-interest. Critics point out that many human acts of kindness and generosity can be explained by the "payoff" the altruist receives (recognition, praise, self-esteem), and in many cases the altruism results in reciprocal rewards ("I'll scratch your back, and you scratch mine.") Dawkins asserts that, even though the natural instinct for self-preservation and self-propagation is universal, humans learned that helping their close relatives furthers their instinctual goal of passing on genes to the next generation, because close relatives carry essentially the same genes as the altruist. His effort to explain altruism as a Darwinian card trick is not very persuasive, for such trickery is not easy to pull off, and, remember "***It's not nice to fool Mother Nature.***"

Dawkins, a brilliant scientist, also created a helpful new concept called the **meme** (the behavioral equivalent of a gene) as a way to theorize about how the Darwinian principles of natural selection might be extended beyond the realm of genes. The meme is a cultural carrier rather than a genetic carrier in evolution, Dawkins believes. Any idea or set of ideas that a group of people shared would be capable of replication and repetition across generations, through communication within and across other groups of humans. Though not as predictable or certain as the transmission of genetic codes by Darwinian natural selection, nevertheless, memes can convey cultural knowledge, beliefs and technologies that are the functional equivalent of genetic evolution. For example, one clan of early humans develops the use of sharp rocks attached to smooth stalks or poles, and improve their hunting success. This information is passed on from father to son, from generation to generation, and perhaps tribe to tribe, improving future humans through cultural transmission or cultural evolution. In time the cultural content is adapted, modified or replaced by new memes, new ideas and inventions. It is likely that religious ideas evolved in this manner, through cultural evolution, parallel with physical and mental evolution, with more complex brains permitting more complex thought, more human-like behaviors and relationships.[112]

There Is a Name for It

Dawkins is certainly not the first author to identify or acknowledge that something in all humans is inclined toward selfishness or it's manifestation in all kinds of "undesirable" behaviors. Besides the Biblical description quoted above, virtually every major philosopher from Plato to our time has noted our tendency toward evil competing with our desire to be good. The ancient Greek dramatists often had "hubris" as a flaw in the major character, a defect that eventually led to the downfall of the otherwise admirable character, such as Oedipus, Hercules and Achilles. ***Hubris*** is defined as "excessive pride or self-confidence," with synonyms such as arrogance, conceit, self-importance, egotism, or selfishness.

In a famous Greek myth, a youth named Narcissus falls in love with himself upon seeing his face in still water, and is so proud of his own beauty that he sits staring at his reflection until he starves to death. The myth gave name to "narcissism" in modern times as either a **personality disorder** of excessive vanity, self-absorption, and egotism, or a **mental illness** of extreme self-centeredness arising from failure to distinguish the self from external objects, unable to understand other people's feelings. Young babies are self-centered and self-absorbed as a natural stage of human development for the first several months, but progressively grow in awareness of other people and objects as distinct from themselves. It seems that adult narcissists have failed to advance beyond that egocentric stage, but ironically, they are often very "successful" and become political leaders because of their overwhelming self-confidence and their lack of guilt in bullying or treating people as "things," either as a useful object or as obstacles. One can even become president of a country by exuding unshakable self-confidence and unlimited ambition; such qualities may appeal to "normal" voters who feel insecure and uncertain of the future. Just as in the Greek tragedies, hubris may be admired for a while, but it has in it the seeds of destruction; unrestricted self-centeredness and selfishness is seen as an offense against the gods in Greek drama, and eventually the gods, or fate, or karma take vengeance. Many philosophers and theologians see in such ancient myths and stories the metaphor for human nature: we are all flawed by self-love, and the urge to be important. The ancient Greek philosophers and dramatists called this human failing *hubris* and the Bible calls it PRIDE. This universal human flaw is illustrated in the cartoon below.

"The Great Scientist" cartoon by author

Pride and Prejudice

The Bible describes the same human failure as "pride," as in "pride goes before a fall." This universal human flaw is viewed by both Old and New Testaments as rebellion or disregard for God, thinking of one's self as self-sufficient, able to live well without divine help. "Pull yourself by your bootstraps" is a popular motto reflecting this independence from God, this glorification of mankind (or at least of one's own self). The story of Adam and Eve is the story of "pride" for the Serpent was able to tempt Eve by promising **"For God knows that when you eat from it your eyes will be opened, and you will be like God, knowing good and evil."** (Genesis 3:5) Wanting to be "like God" was for Eve a desire to be independent, her own boss, to be in control of her life, to be important. According to the Bible, this desire of the human heart is a cosmic struggle between the Creator and the created. This theme is beautifully presented by the Jewish prophet Jeremiah:

> *This is the word that came to Jeremiah from the Lord: "Go down to the potter's house, and there I will give you my message." So, I went down to the potter's house, and I saw him working at the wheel. But the pot he was shaping from the clay was marred in his hands; so, the potter formed it into another pot, shaping it as seemed best to him.*
>
> *Then the word of the Lord came to me. He said, "Can I not do with you, Israel, as this potter does?" declares the Lord. "Like clay in the hand of the potter, so are you in my hand, Israel. (Jeremiah 18:1-6)*

This same metaphorical theme is followed by Paul in the New Testament:

> *But who are you, O man, to talk back to God? Shall what is formed say to Him who formed it, "Why have you made me like this?" Does not the potter have the right to make from the same lump of clay one vessel for special occasions and another for common use?* (Romans 9:20)

Anyone who has raised a son or daughter (or worked in a day care center) knows what this primal urge to be in control looks like, the demand for independence and the resistance of authority. Even two-year-olds seem "naturally" rebellious and self-assertive: **"No! Me do it!"** is part of a healthy, normal stage of growing, the first steps toward some ultimate "grown up" stage where we think we run our own life; we all probably had such a dream about when we would have no bosses telling us what to do and when to do it, a time when we imagine we are "our own person" making our own decisions, free at last. Humans need that innate drive for the species to survive, we couldn't evolve if we remained docile, dependent and servile children in adult bodies. Ambition may be a positive name for this inner motivator in human nature, like most human traits part of a continuum with too much or too little at the extremes. Ambition in the extreme can become tyranny, and little or no ambition can become sloth and helplessness. Even compassion in the extreme can become control and pandering, and too little compassion may lead to narcissism or socio-pathology. Human nature is a complicated and homogenized mixture, the "good, bad and ugly" abiding within all of us.

The Scientific Consensus: Something Is Wrong

Child psychologist Burton L. White, PhD, finds a "selfish" trait in children from birth, a trait that expresses itself in actions that are "blatantly selfish." Sociologist William Graham Sumner finds it a **"fact that everywhere one meets fraud, corruption, ignorance, selfishness, and all the other vices of human nature."** He enumerates "the vices and passions of human nature" as "cupidity, vindictiveness, lust, ambition, and vanity." Sumner finds such human nature to be universal: in all people, in all places, and in all stations in society.[113] Psychiatrist Thomas Anthony Harris, MD, on the basis of his "data at hand," observes "sin, or badness, or evil, or 'human nature', whatever we call the flaw in our species, is apparent in every person." Harris calls this condition "intrinsic badness" or "original sin."[114] *Original Sin* is not a critical, "must believe" doctrine in modern Christianity. While widely accepted as biblical, it is not regarded as relevant by many church groups. Most ordinary laymen in the church pews probably would not even be able to define "original sin" or identify the scriptural references. The concept of an inborn flaw or sin passed down to us from our most distant ancestor is hard to defend, and most modern theologians abandoned it long ago. The Bible is crystal clear that actual "sin" is a personal, willful, voluntary act (or a failure to act) that is contrary to God's will. The New Testament uses several Greek words translated as "sin." "***Hamartia***" ἁμαρτία means "to miss the mark," failure to live up to the Divine standard (I Corinthians 6:18). The word ***parabates*** means "transgression" "crossing a boundary." "trespassing" (Romans 5:14) ***Anomia***, meaning lawlessness, law breaking. (I Timothy 1:9) Sin can also be an omission, a failure to do what is right: ***"Therefore, to him who knows to do good and does not do it, to him it is sin."*** (James 4:17)

"Original sins or "inherited sin" are not choices, not intentional acts of a free will, and thus must seem unjust and unfair to non-believers. "**What kind of God would blame me for the sin of my great, great, great, great grandfather?**" Good question. Not Jesus, for certain. From at least the dawn of historical records, mankind has observed that something is wrong with us, something dark and wicked is part of human nature. Socrates examined the question of virtue, living a good life, and he concluded that moral ignorance was to blame for the fact that virtuous men were so scarce. Great, heroic men almost inevitably produce evil sons, he observed. Perhaps virtue was not something that could be learned. But if we look at this ancient doctrine as an attempt to explain why humans seem to have a congenital moral defect, it weakens the idea of responsibility for personal sin. It is difficult to portray sin as a personal act of disobedience for which a person is morally responsible (such as stealing), while also holding a person responsible for an inherited stain over which they never had control.

How Did We Become Human?

We know, from a scientific standpoint, that becoming human was not a startling event, an instant "turning on the light", a birth-experience type of sudden self-awareness. The change from the early, primitive hominids (*homo erectus, homo habilis,* etc.) was a gradual, evolutionary process spanning thousands and even hundreds of thousands of years. The development of physical abilities such as tool making, walking upright and cooperative hunting advanced our ancestors toward "humanness," but it is **only** when the hominid brain grew and evolved to a certain capacity that the central and fundamental human characteristic was even possible—**consciousness and self-identity**. Being human is a mental achievement rather than a physical achievement, more related to brain development than **physical** or **bodily** evolution.

In anthropology and paleontology, the stages of evolution arriving at "human" are defined in mostly physical measurements and attainments such as these: bipedalism (walking upright), opposable thumbs, brain size related to body size, possession of vocal cords and related throat structures making rudimentary speech possible, etc. Another approach is to measure achievements such as use of tools, control of fire, use of speech to communicate, cooperation in groups, providing extended child care, production of art and music, and ritualistic burial of the dead. Without these and many other evolutionary physical and cultural improvements, the brain would not have evolved in size and complexity, and so **the proposed central marker of humanness— "thinking"** —likely would have not been achieved. Without the advances in thinking, reasoning, and planning, Homo sapiens would likely have joined that trash-heap of history, **extinction**, along with *Neanderthal* and nine or ten other hominid species. Some extinctions might have been caused by unavoidable natural catastrophes (drought, volcanic eruption, asteroids, ice age, etc.). Disease may have extinguished a species, and possibly one species may have exterminated so many members of another hominid species that they went extinct. But certainly, to avoid extinction, it was the advance of human thinking which played the most significant role in the survival of our species until now. (Our self-label, *"Homo sapiens,"* or "wise man" rather immodestly pays homage to this superior mental prowess we think we possess).

Some Qualities That Made Us Human

In addition to having a better developed brain (not necessarily larger) there are other qualities that make us different from other mammals, including our closest relatives, the chimpanzees and apes. Some of these differences are **differences in kind** and others are **differences in degree.** For example, both dogs and humans have a nose and a sense of smell; the noses are very similar in kind (noses), but the dog's sense of smell is probably 1000 times better than ours (a difference in degree). Chimpanzees have a tail, but humans do not (other than a tiny vestige tale-bone), and so that is a difference in kind. Some animals have webbed toes which makes them great swimmers; humans can also swim, but we do not have webbed fingers or toes (normally) and that is a difference in kind. All animals have eyes of some type, but humans can see in color, and many animals only see black and white, we believe. That is a difference in degree of seeing.

But what about **mind**? Do other animals have minds like we do? If so, are their minds different from ours in some major way, or are the minds essentially the same but humans have a greater capacity and greater mental power? We know that all vertebrates have perception— the ability to see objects in their environment and respond to them (don't bump into trees, run from a predator, etc.). We also know that some mammals have memories just as humans do; who hasn't observed sleeping dogs acting out some previous experience, dreaming about a fight or a chase? Perception and memory are significant markers shared by humans and some animals. Perception is responding to the present, and memory deals with the past. Can animals imagine the future, as human minds can do? Can animals plan for the future they can imagine, as humans do. From all that is known at present, anticipating the future and acting to make that future reality is limited to humans and a **very few animals.** Experimental studies have found that some birds seem to anticipate a future event, and porpoises and elephants have shown evidence of this ability to imagine a future and act accordingly. The late, great gorilla, Koko, using sign language, seemed to have a mind quite similar to humans, using memory, imagination, planning, and conscious self-awareness. It thus appears, that animals have the potential for minds, but not the actuality of mind as humans experience it. It seems likely that evolution has produced brains that can generate minds, and that the human species advanced farther up that continuum than other species.

Moral Laws and Conscience

Just as physical laws are derived from an understanding of the **nature of material existence,** so **moral laws** are derived from an understanding of **human nature. Moral laws** are our attempt to describe to the best of our knowledge **what we as human beings should and shouldn't to do.** Human beings are, despite the anecdotal evidence, moral creatures: have a moral nature. We are born with an innate sense that there is a right and wrong, these categories are set but the content is only assigned as we grow. In some ways this may remind readers of John Locke's "tabula rasa" theory, the idea that we are born with a "blank slate" human nature, the mind at birth without rules. We propose here, however, that the "slate" is not blank, but is preset at birth with the categories of "right" and "wrong" in place. We are able to sense the difference in a rudimentary fashion, a sensitivity to "right" as our eyes are sensitive to light. C.S. Lewis has an enlightening discussion of this pre-set moral heritage; rather than trying to summarize his amazing insight, we have, with permission, included a longer section for its impact:[115]

The Law of Human Nature: Everyone has heard people quarrelling. Sometimes it sounds funny and sometimes it sounds merely unpleasant; but however it sounds, I believe we can learn something very important from listening to the kind of things they say. They say things like this: "How'd you like it if anyone did the same to you?"- "That's my seat, I was there first"- "Leave him alone, he isn't doing you any harm"- "Why should you shove in first?"- "Give me a bit of your orange, I gave you a bit of mine", "Come on, you promised." People say things like that every day, educated people as well as uneducated, and children as well as grown-ups.

Now what interests me about all these remarks is that the man who makes them is not merely saying that the other man's behaviour does not happen to please him. **He is appealing to some kind of standard of behaviour which he expects the other man to know about. And the other man very seldom replies: "To hell with your standard." Nearly always he tries to make out that what he has been doing does not really go against the standard, or that if it does there is some special excuse.** He pretends there is some special reason in this particular case why the person who took the seat first should not keep it, or that things were quite different when he was given the bit of orange, or that something has turned up which lets him off keeping his promise. It looks, in fact, very much as if both parties had in mind some kind of Law or Rule of fair play or decent behaviour or morality or whatever you like to call it, about which they really agreed. And they have. If they had not, they might, of course, fight like animals, but they could not quarrel in the human sense of the word. Quarrelling means trying to show that the other man is in the wrong. And there would be no sense in trying to do that unless you and he had some sort of agreement as to what Right and Wrong are; just as there would be no sense in saying that a footballer had committed a foul unless there was some agreement about the rules of football.

Now this Law or Rule about Right and Wrong used to be called the Law of Nature. Nowadays, when we talk of the "laws of nature" we usually mean things like gravitation, or heredity, or the laws of chemistry. But when the older thinkers called the Law of Right and Wrong "the Law of Nature," they really meant the Law of Human Nature. The idea was that, just as all bodies are governed by the law of gravitation and organisms by biological laws, so the creature called man also had his law-with this great difference, that a body could not choose whether it obeyed the law of gravitation or not, but a man could choose either to obey the Law of Human Nature or to disobey it.

We may put this in another way. Each man is at every moment subjected to several different sets of law but there is only one of these which he is free to disobey. As a body, he is subjected to gravitation and cannot disobey it; if you leave him unsupported in mid-air, he has no more choice about falling than a stone has. As an organism, he is subjected to various biological laws which he cannot disobey any more than an animal can. That is, he cannot disobey those laws which he shares with other things; but the law which is peculiar to his human nature, the law he does not share with animals or vegetables or inorganic things, is the one he can disobey if he chooses.

This law was called the Law of Nature because people thought that everyone knew it by nature and did not need to be taught it. They did not mean, of course, that you might not find an odd individual here and there who did not know it, just as you find a few people who are colour-blind or have no ear for a tune. But taking the race as a whole, they thought that the human idea of decent behaviour was obvious to everyone. **And I believe they were right.** If they were not, then all the things we said about the war were nonsense. What was the sense in saying the enemy were in the wrong unless Right is a real thing which the Nazis at bottom knew as well as we did and ought to have practised? If they had had no notion of what we mean by right, then, though we might still have had to fight them, we could no more have blamed them for that than for the colour of their hair.

I know that some people say the idea of a Law of Nature or decent behaviour known to all men is unsound, because different civilisations and different ages have had quite different moralities. But this is not true. There have been differences between their moralities, but these have never amounted to anything like a total difference. If anyone will take the trouble to compare the moral teaching of, say, the ancient Egyptians, Babylonians, Hindus, Chinese, Greeks and Romans, what will really strike him will be how very like they are to each other and to our own. Some of the evidence for this I have put together in the appendix of another book called *The Abolition of Man;* but for our present purpose I need only ask the reader to think what a totally different morality would mean. Think of a country where people were admired for running away in battle, or where a man felt proud of double-crossing all the people who had been kindest to him. You might just as well try to imagine a country where two and two made five.

Men have differed as regards what people you ought to be unselfish to, whether it was only your own family, or your fellow countrymen, or everyone. But they have always agreed that you ought not to put yourself first. Selfishness has never been admired. Men have differed as to whether you should have one wife or four. But they have always agreed that you must not simply have any woman you liked.

But the most remarkable thing is this: whenever you find a man who says he does not believe in a real Right and Wrong, you will find the same man going back on this a moment later. He may break his promise to you, but if you try breaking one to him, he will be complaining "It's not fair" before you can say Jack Robinson. A nation may say treaties do not matter, but then, next minute, they spoil their case by saying that the particular treaty they want to break was an unfair one. But if treaties do not matter, and if there is no such thing as Right and Wrong— in other words, if there is no Law of Nature— what is the difference between a fair treaty and an unfair one? Have they not let the cat out of the bag?

(Some lines in bold for emphasis by author)

Are We Blank Tablets?

This passage is so profound and so crucial to understanding human nature that reading it again would be well worth your time. As C. S. Lewis so ably argues, it seems there IS some kind of universal "moral law" embedded in human nature, some innate ability to recognize right and wrong. However, it seems that we are not born with a knowledge of **what** is right and wrong. That we have to work out for ourselves. We have the moral capacity, a conscience, but the **content** of conscience is largely cultural and learned. As an example, virtually every known human society labels "murder" as wrong, forbidden or taboo, but each society defines "who" can and cannot be killed with impunity. Enemies may be killed, when possible, but a kinsman may not be killed, according to one tribal code, and in our own culture it is allowable to execute a person convicted of some serious crime, but it is not legal to kill one's wife or child. The content of people's consciences differs, but everyone has some such inner guide, with the exception of some mentally deranged people or sociopaths.

John Locke's philosophy of empiricism saw human nature as a *tabula rasa,* "a blank slate" at birth, our minds free of any preexisting rules or "do's" and "don'ts." Locke believed that our sensory experiences in life added the data and formed the rules based on our environment, our culture. This is not accurate about the mind, we now know, for research with babies and children has demonstrated that much of the wiring is already established in our infant brain. We add and accommodate content and rules into existing mental structures in predictable stages. Locke's "tabula rasa" concept does seem to apply to morality and the development of a conscience. We can agree with Locke that our environment, our culture, shapes our lists of right and wrong behaviors, our own set of commandments and rules of human values. Our adult values and the content and strength of our conscience is not inevitably or irrevocably molded by our upbringing, but it is undeniable that "*As the twig is bent, so grows the tree.*"

Is Human Nature Natural?

Human nature refers to the distinguishing characteristics—including ways of thinking, feeling and acting—which humans tend to have naturally, independently of the influence of culture. The questions of what these characteristics are, how fixed they are, and what causes them are among the oldest and most important questions in western philosophy. These questions have significant implications in ethics, politics, and theology. This is partly because human nature can be regarded as both a source of norms of conduct or ways of life, as well as presenting obstacles or constraints on living a good life. The complex implications of such questions are also dealt with in art and literature, while the multiple branches of the humanities together form an important domain of inquiry into human nature and into the question of what it is to be human. All the most interesting plots in literature involve the kinks and twists of human nature, almost always struggling with good and bad or right and wrong.

The branches of contemporary science associated with the study of human nature include anthropology, sociology, socio-biology, archaeology, developmental psychology, and evolutionary psychology. In addition to these so called "soft" social science fields, the study of humans often calls for expertise from the so called "hard" natural sciences such as biology, comparative anatomy, neurology, genetics, geography, geology, ecology and climatology. Of course, philosophy, the ancient mother of all sciences, deals with the kinds of questions raised here about "what does it mean to be human, to be a person," and especially issues of morality, ethics and justice. The "nature versus nurture" debate is a broadly inclusive and well-known instance of a discussion about human nature in the natural sciences.

What then, does it mean to be human? All of the current population of Homo Sapiens is, by definition, human, somewhat over 7 billion people on planet earth. Though we "humans" don't always treat all of these people as if they were human (consider mass exterminations, genocide, wars, ethnic cleansings, massacres, etc.) such inhumane actions reflect our un-humanness, not the sub-humanness attributed to our victims. Some of the greatest acts of humanness occurred in the Holocaust, in the hiding of Jewish neighbors from the Gestapo, to the scores of men and women who lived and acted heroically within the death camps. Only a few of these great humans has been recognized, but it is undisputed that those were great human beings, examples of the highest and best that humans can become.

The Humanist Ideal

The nearly universal liberal ideal holds that every person is of equal and supreme value, regardless of race, language, gender, color, religion, mental and physical health, and many other qualities. We make our lists of factors that should **not be used** to discriminate, characteristics used to give either preference or exclusion regarding rights and privileges. In "modern" times (80 years ago) we have enshrined this idea in **The Universal Declaration of Human Rights**[116], a milestone document adopted by the three-year old United Nations in 1948. It sets out, for the first time by an international assembly, fundamental human rights to be universally advanced and protected. The Preamble begins:

> *Whereas recognition of the inherent dignity and of the equal and inalienable rights of all members of the human family is the foundation of freedom, justice and peace in the world"* and is followed by 30 specific articles.
> *Article 1. All human beings are born free and equal in dignity and rights. They are endowed with reason and conscience and should act towards one another in a spirit of brotherhood.*
> *Article 2. Everyone is entitled to all the rights and freedoms set forth in this Declaration, without distinction of any kind, such as race, colour, sex, language, religion, political or other opinion, national or social origin, property, birth or other status*

Yet, while we generally give homage to such beliefs in human rights and standards for humanness for everyone, still we are inclined in American society to define some people as unfit to live in society, or even unfit to live at all—based on their criminal acts. Capital punishment is still legal and relatively popular in the United States (though abandoned by most countries of the world). Regardless of what our posters say, we **don't** treat every human equally, or regard everyone as of equal value. We can comfortably talk about "good people" and "bad people", even labeling some as "evil." In our public policies we still regard some poor people as "unworthy" and others as the "worthy poor," though we don't use those terms in public any more. Still, our governmental approach toward the needy in our society is based on categorical determination: are they too sick to work, disabled or blind, mentally incapacitated, too old for employment? (**Worthy of help**). Or are they able bodied, capable of independence, intelligent enough to do some work? (**Unworthy**, not eligible, "lazy")

Espousing the essential equal worth of all human beings does not mean that all humans **are equal**, all pretty much the same. We can easily identify some people as taller than others, some as stronger or faster than others, and even some smarter than others. **We all are different**, and in our most civilized times, we appreciate and value variety and diversity. Scientifically, we know that cross-pollination and genetic mixing is as healthy for societies as it is for flowers and fruits. Racial intermarriage and cross-cultural mingling produce more handsome and better humans and ultimately better nations. Enlarging the gene pool is part of the great strategy of evolution. On our best days, we applaud it; on most days, we fear it.

Are we being crude and uneducated when we speak of individuals as "**good people**" or "a good man", and in contrast, label others of our species as "**bad people**" or "a bad person."? Are humans actually, objectively or theoretically arrayed along a continuum, on a scale from "goodness" through "inert" over to "bad" (or off the scale as "evil")? Consider the crude scale below. Could you place someone you know somewhere on this scale? What about a politician in the news? Or a foreign leader whose deeds you have read about? Where would you place yourself?

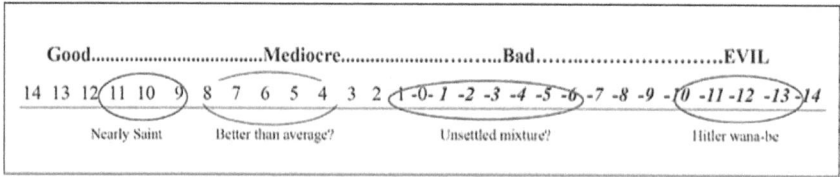

Before modern science gained general recognition, we had our human rating systems, and the history of mankind is the story of how we have separated ourselves into winners and losers, masters and servants, worthy and unworthy, holy and wicked. The strong or rich or fortunate defined the "others" as less than themselves and built societies around those differences. The "caste" system of India was the most clearly and rigidly ranking structure in the world, though some of the rigidity and inevitability of that ancient system has moderated now. The advent of psychology in the 19thcentury brought science and pseudo-science to the measurement of differences in humans, trying to determine the relative intelligence of individuals and groups. Some "pioneers" measured the size of the head or the pattern of bumps found thereon to determine personality, criminality, and moral character. There was a time when our society put labels on people to sort out the "others" from our "normal" selves; those labels are rejected by most people now and so negative or derogatory are considered crude and uneducated. Today our vocabulary is gradually moving to less and less distinctions in ability, more understanding that "differences" are just "different," not good or bad, normal or abnormal. Even labels about "age" can be used in a way that harms or offends some people. Using more modern scientific methods, questionnaires and mathematics, scholars proposed the IQ as the true "measure of man," an Intelligence Quotient based on intellectual ability compared to the wider population and age groupings. Decisions based on such things as IQ were used to determine fitness for military service, admission to schools and even jobs—to separate the "wheat from the chaff" (*using Jesus' words as a little nod to our Bible readers—Matthew 3:12*).

Modern science, moving beyond IQ, has developed more sophisticated measurements and tools to evaluate the fitness of a candidate for employment, military service, or for high security clearance. There is an ongoing debate as to the reliability of any such measures and evaluative conclusions to such testing. **Perhaps we may be missing a scientific benefit because we don't apply such modern tools to evaluate candidates for governor, senator, congressman or president—objectively weighing strengths and flaws to make a good choice.**

Human Development and Human Evolution

In the following section the theory is proposed that a universal model of how all humans develop (from conception through childhood to adulthood, and on to the end of life) provides a useful model for describing how the human species developed, predictably and sequentially, reflected in the stages of human evolution. Just as the child develops in predictable, sequential stages (unless some abnormality intervenes) we know there is a pattern built for that growing from conception to adult maturity. We are making here a bold attempt to show that there is a universality of physical, mental and moral progress in human beings entirely based on brain development and the related increase of cognition. This brain related development is certainly accepted by science—the idea that our individual physical and mental development proceeds in an orderly and sequential manner, unfolding according to the genetic pattern, orchestrated by the brain.

We argue here that the developing of the human brain followed a similar fixed and sequential pattern to the development of our species. The brain is the instrument for both models.

Let us use the model of **individual development** to compare to the **species development**, comparable stages found in humans, to corresponding passages in evolution of the brain in early humans. For example, a two-year-old of today might be comparable in brain power to the early *homo habilis* or *homo erectus*. Scientists have found that a mature chimpanzee is mentally on par with a 3 or 4-year-old human child. The human keeps on progressing mentally after four birthdays, while the chimp cannot advance much more as adults. *Homo habilis* may have progressed to the level of modern chimpanzees or further, but they were essentially "children" in terms of evolution. The further development toward humanness was made possible by bigger and better brains which eventually came by evolution.

The Science of Humanness: Abraham Maslow

Many scientists in the past 100 years have studied the differences in individuals based on developmental stages. **Abraham Maslow** in the early 20th Century studied human motivation—why do people respond as they do? He theorized that motivation was based on universal human needs, which he portrayed in a pyramid form (see chart below) Maslow argued that five critical needs drive all human behavior: **survival** or physiological needs, **safety** needs, **belonging** needs, **esteem** needs, and **self-actualization** needs. He proposed that the more basic needs must be satisfied before any of the higher needs become activated or motivate us. For example, survival or physiological needs (food, water, shelter, rest, etc.) dominate every person and supersede any other concerns. Survival depends on meeting these basic needs, and everything else will be sacrificed to meet those survival needs.[117]

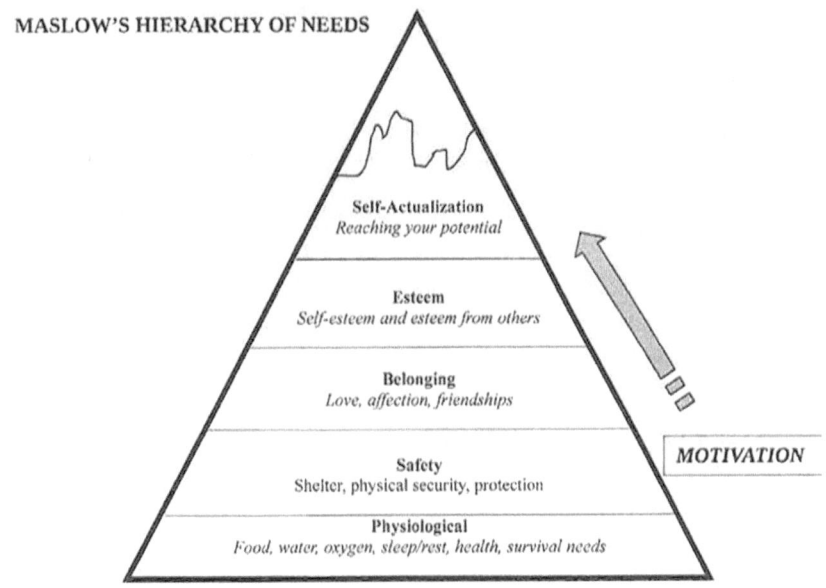

To illustrate by a primitive example: suppose an early human has escaped a killer lion on the Serengeti and has found temporary safety in a tree. What could motivate that man to leave his safe place while the lion was still around? Only physiological needs could overcome his safety needs, if the man is dying of thirst or is freezing or starving. He can be driven to risk his safety in order to meet his physiological needs. He may finally chance that the lion is asleep or has left, or he hopes to outrun the predator. The pattern applies up the scale to psychological needs for friendship, love, relationships, and a sense of belonging. If those needs are met, developing humans can be motivated to pursue even higher needs such as self-esteem, pride of accomplishment, recognition and prestige. For the rare individual who has succeeded in meeting all the four prior needs, the hope of fulfillment of one's full potential comes into play, the urge to be creative, to achieve self-satisfaction, to "be all one can be", or, as Maslow labels it, to reach "Self-Actualization."

Maslow's theory has been helpful to later students of humanness, to those who try to find what it means to be fully human, to be the best that we possibly can be as individuals. This hierarchy of needs has had its critics and also its descendants who have expanded and refined Maslow's ideas. But the concept of stages of human functioning based on the meeting of underlying universal needs is still a sound way to look at who we are and what we can become. We can recognize that some people in our world rise to the pinnacle of human nature, become "self-actualized", and stand out from the majority of struggling humanity still wrestling with physically surviving, or those who still search vainly for love or companionship, some sense of acceptance. Many of us, though good people, never quite get our needs for self-esteem and sense of accomplishment fully met; we live respectable lives, but we have an empty spot, a vague, unfulfilled dream of who we hoped to become.

Only A Few Reach Their Highest Potential

We see the relative few who rise above the rest, people who seem to have "gotten it together," who are comfortable "in their own skin", who are at peace with themselves and the world, who seem to be released from the limits that impede others, who perform at levels of excellence that cannot be fully explained by talent or hard work, or lucky breaks. Though we may not all agree on the names of such exemplary persons, living or dead (names such as Jesus, Gandhi, Martin Luther King, Jr., Mother Teresa, are often cited), the fact that we recognize this category is telling. We **know** what a great person is, even if we cannot precisely define such greatness. We know it is not intellect—there are a lot of very, very smart people, but not all geniuses are "nice" or uplifting to meet, or people we would enjoy having as a friend. We can name many successful, powerful, "important" people, but some of the VIP's are miserable human beings, and are not role models we seek for our own children. Being a great human being involves qualities which sound pretty Biblical: compassionate, caring, kind, patient, gentle, joyful or positive, faithful and trustworthy, even tempered or self-controlled, and just simply "good". The counter characteristics we almost universally dislike in people also guide us: those who are selfish, egotistical, harsh, pushy, manipulative, rude, demanding, dishonest, bitter, overly critical, hypocritical, or undependable. There are lists of such positive and negative human traits than run into the hundreds, so we are pretty confident about defining the "good human."

Lawrence Kohlberg and Moral Reasoning

Philosophers from Socrates and earlier thought a lot about what makes some people "good" and how can humans become "good" (what Socrates called "virtue") They struggled to define what they meant by "good" but there were enough examples of good people they could agree on that it was clear that some ideal existed in nature or in the universe which all men could recognize. It was something like Justice Blackburn's statement about pornography: "I can't define it but I know it when I see it." Socrates argued that "self-knowledge" was the key to morality, and lack of reason was behind all bad actions of men.

Reasoning is still a huge area of psychological interest and research. It is generally understood by psychologists and others in the human sciences that there are different levels of moral judgment and competence. The work of American psychologist **Lawrence Kohlberg** is probably the most influential in the science of morality and moral reasoning, though others have followed and modified his work a bit. He was greatly influenced by the work of Piaget and began researching moral development in the same way Piaget had studied child cognitive development. His research veered sharply away from the "behaviorism" of B.F. Skinner and others who had dominated psychology for years. Kohlberg's extensive study and interviews of hundreds of people of all ages and cultures convinced him that an innate framework for moral thought was part of the human brain at birth, and developed through distinct, predictable stages, similar to Piaget but going beyond the ages Piaget studied.[118]

Kohlberg's "Moral Development" theory says that moral reasoning, the basis for all ethical behavior, has six identifiable developmental stages, each more adequate at responding to moral dilemmas than its immediate predecessor. He used a series of carefully constructed moral dilemma scenarios to which he asked subjects to respond with a judgment of the right or moral decision. In a non-judgmental way he asked for the reasons for their choice; it was their reasons which revealed different levels of moral reasoning/development, and not the right or wrong answers. One such dilemma is the **Heinz Story**

A woman was on her deathbed. There was one drug that the doctors thought might save her. It was a form of radium that a druggist in the same town had recently discovered. The drug was expensive to make, but the druggist was charging ten times what the drug cost him to produce. He paid $200 for the radium and charged $2,000 for a small dose of the drug. The sick woman's husband, Heinz, went to everyone he knew to borrow the money, but he could only get together about $1,000 which is half of what it cost. He told the druggist that his wife was dying and asked him to sell it cheaper or let him pay later. But the druggist said: "No, I discovered the drug and I'm going to make money from it." So, Heinz got desperate and broke into the man's laboratory to steal the drug for his wife. **Should Heinz have broken into the laboratory to steal the drug for his wife? Why or why not?**[119]

After several years of research, he constructed the **model shown below**, listing six stages of moral reasoning grouped into three levels of two stages each. He labeled the three broad levels **pre-conventional**, **conventional** and **post-conventional,** much as Piaget had organized his findings. No firm ages are attached to the levels or stages, but generally the Pre-conventional level applies to infants and pre-school children (birth to 5), and Conventional applies to school-aged children (6-12). The Post-conventional level is attained only by a few teenagers and some adults Kohlberg found.

Kohlberg's Stages of Moral Development

POST CONVENTIONAL Shared standards, rights and obligations	Stage 6: Self-selection of Universal Principles Stage 5: Sense of democracy and relativity of rules
CONVENTIONAL Performing "normal" roles, acting "appropriately" (Good Boy)	Stage 4: Fulfilling duties and Upholding rules and laws Stage 3: Meeting the expectations of others for approval
PRECONVENTIONAL Values in external environment (other's control), not personally internalized	Stage 2: "Getting what you want" by trade offs or "deals" Stage 1: Punishment and avoidance of pain or displeasure

Like physical norms of development, the norms of moral development are pliable and are a range rather than a single point. Some adults never develop beyond stage 4, the "law and order" orientation; he found that stage 6, the stage of "universal principles" is reached by only a small percent of adults. He determined that the process of moral development was principally concerned with **justice**, and it continued throughout the individual's lifetime. He argued that the stages are sequential, with no person skipping; he also found that a retreat from a higher level to a lower one is very rare, and if it occurs it is likely the result of some severe physical or emotional trauma.

The familiar chart probably is sufficient to understanding this theory of moral development based on moral reasoning. Each stage represents an orientation, a general way of looking at life. Very young children, in Stage 1, mostly understand only punishment and reward—obeying to avoid pain. Parents often do not accept that younger children **are not capable** of understanding right and wrong in the abstract—and we actually teach them, inadvertently, that getting caught is bad, and so we train them to be sneaky and to lie if apprehended. School age boys and girls have moved beyond the punishment or reward motivation, and care much more about social approval, being liked, rather than punishment, typical of Stage 3 of this model. We know from experience that not very many human beings think on the level of Stage 6, the "Universal Principle" perspective which reflects an admirable maturity and wisdom found in our greatest cultural heroes such as Abraham Lincoln or Nelson Mandela.

The review of the theories about "Humanness" developed by two famous psychologists, Abraham Maslow and Lawrence Kohlberg has served to support the proposition that being a good human, or being "fully human" is not so much a religious function as it is a brain function—ways of thinking. It is not that religion does not play a part in morality and goodness, but it may not be the primary cause or originator. The most mature and intellectually satisfying forms of religion do not rely on fear of Hell or hope of Heaven as their primary message. Mature Christians, for example, move past an earlier focus on keeping commandments and obeying Biblical doctrine, and rise to the more gratifying experience of being totally accepted and loved by God and loving to please Him (rather than to appease Him or fear Him). Certainly, the Bible urges Believers to use their brains:

> *"Do not conform to the pattern of this world, but be transformed by the renewing of your mind. Then you will be able to test and approve what God's will is—his good, pleasing and perfect will..."* (Romans 12:2) Paul said essentially the same in Ephesians 4:23: *"...put off your former way of life, your old self, which is being corrupted by its deceitful desires; to be renewed in the spirit of your minds; and to put on the new self, created to be like God in true righteousness and holiness...."*

God, who created our brain and works with our mind, helps us grow spiritually by using our brain to think better and deeper. To illustrate one of the major propositions of this book (*that patterns of individual development may emulate patterns in species development*) consider the chart below which makes a side-by-side comparison of what we have asserted about the brain and what psychology asserts about our development as human beings. We place side by side for comparison the concepts of Lawrence Kohlberg and Abraham Maslow, which have been outlined earlier, adjacent to the related brain structure and function we have earlier described.

BRAIN STRUCTURE	KOHLBERG	MASLOW
Reptilian brain (instincts, *survival*)	*Pre-conventional moral reasoning* (Self-interest, avoiding pain)	*Physical Survival needs* Safety and Security
Mammalian brain (Social, emotions, relationships)	*Conventional moral reasoning* (Social approval, being "good" Obeying and conforming)	*Social Needs* (Love, Belonging Self-esteem)
NeoCortex (Higher-order brain functions sensory perception, cognition, generation of motor commands, spatial,	*Post-Conventional Moral Thought* (Transcendent Universal moral laws over legal rules, abstract notions of Justice, Personal Conscience driven moral decisions, Greater Good)	*Self-Actualizaton* (Achievement of full potential, inner peace, open minded, accepting of self and others, free from need for extensive reasoning and language)

The implication of this chart suggests that there is **some kind** of relationship between who we are in our brain and who we are as human beings involved in the world of other humans. This may be a totally wacky idea, a want-a-be theory by an amateur seeing connections where they don't exist. It may be that the role of the **reptilian brain** is not as significant as proposed in this book, that while it may have originated in the long-ago age of dinosaurs and giant lizards, it no longer makes humans feel or act like our reptilian predecessors on the planet. In the spirit of science and honest discourse, it is accepted that this hypothesis about the three-part brain may be outdated or simply dismissed decades ago based on real research and experimental studies. Even so, let's examine the evidence and see if it is just a big coincidence that the structure of the brain looks similar to models proposed by Maslow, Kohlberg, Freud, and other students of human behavior.

As discussed extensively in **Chapter 4, The Brain Game**, the human brain evolved in three iterations, with the original brain stem common to all reptiles such as frogs, lizards, snakes and dinosaurs. This original or first brain is labeled "Reptilian Brain" by many scientists, and though in humans it is nearly totally integrated and interconnected with the other parts of the brain, it still is the central actor in our basic survival needs (heart rate, respiration, blood pressure, body temperature, etc.) It is autonomic, operating on its own without much input from the rest of the brain. It acts reflexively rather than being controlled by the rational, thinking part of the brain. We know that the reptilian brain can continue to function keeping someone "alive" even though the person is "brain dead" and in a vegetative coma. The impulses of this original brain are directed toward protecting and preserving the life of the body, by any means necessary. It is inherently self-centered, concerned only for its own survival and functions. In Maslow's description of human motivation, the first and strongest factor are "Survival Needs" such as food, water, oxygen, rest and anything required for survival, staying alive. When our life is being threatened, we are concerned about surviving more than anything else; we will do anything necessary to escape with our life. This level of motivation is necessarily self-centered, saving ourselves trumps almost every other interest. Does that sound like the "Reptilian Brain" influencing us?

Moving on to Kohlberg we again see that the lowest level of moral reasoning is "What's in it for me?" This perspective is very normal and functional for newborns and young children, for they have to stay alive in order to rise to the other tasks of becoming a human. Moral reasoning in this first stage is very "primitive" thinking, focused on avoiding pain, avoiding punishment, avoiding being caught. Selfish children are "normal" for that reflects their brain development and thinking ability. Again, it seems to correspond to the "Reptilian Brain" influences, the "Me First" perspective.

The second stage of human brain evolution brought us the "Mammalian Brain" according to many scientists, the middle layer of brain atop the brain stem and surrounding it. This is the same model found in all mammals, a second layer of brain which evolved to deal with our social environment, the area of relationships, emotions, feelings, affection and maternal "instincts." Higher level mammals such as dogs and cats can interact with us in nearly "human" ways: they can show affection, display fear and anger, and can communicate with us on an emotional level. Virtually all mammals are capable of being our "pets" and companion, because our brain and their brain have a resonance as mammals.

Consider again, how the operation of the Mammalian Brain is similar to Maslovian and Kohlbergian models. What motivates and controls our behavior in Maslow's "Social Needs" levels is human contact and interaction, friendship, respect, love, and self-esteem—these are emotional needs, "feelings" and relationships are most important to us, and this seems very close to the major function of the human "Mammalian Brain." Compare this to Kohlberg's 3rd and 4th stage of moral reasoning: the middle "Conventional" perspective is social approval, being good, complying with societal rules, and so on, things most influenced by the Mammalian brain it appears. Remember, without the Mammalian brain we **could not be social animals** and we could not operate on the moral or behavioral levels which we consider more fully human.

Leaving Maslow and Kohlberg let us briefly try to connect brain development to some other popular theories of human behavior, ideas about being truly human. The most famous such theorist is Sigmund Freud, the creator of "psychoanalysis" over a century ago. According to Freud the problems plaguing his mentally disturbed patients arise from hidden, suppressed feelings and experiences held in our "unconscious minds." Like an iceberg the human mind has more content below the surface than is exposed above the surface, Freud believed; we push unpleasant, embarrassing or shameful thoughts and memories down into our unconscious for safe keeping, but some "leak" through or surface against our will and emerge as neuroses or other psychological or physical manifestations. Psychoanalysis is the process of recovering and rehabilitating those hidden "sins" which plague us until we face them and deal with them. According to Freud, our minds or personality structure involves three levels: **id, ego, and superego.**

The *Id,* usually pictured on the bottom, is the part of the mind housing our most primal instincts, the impulsive, unconscious part of us that seeks pleasure, demanding immediate gratification. According to Freud it is sexual desire that fuels the Id and drives the impulses; Freud also introduces the concept of "death instinct" as another suppressed fear which surreptitiously haunts our minds in unguarded moments, sharpening the drive for pleasure in the face of ultimate pain and loss. It does not stretch the imagination too far to see how the Id is comparable to the Reptilian Brain and reflects the same general perspective as Maslow's lower levels and Kohlberg's first stage of moral thought. Our biology outdoes our psychology and our theology in our immature stages of development.

The Superego, usually pictured at the top, is similar to what we call "conscience" and incorporates the moral norms of society and acts as the strict supervisor who upholds the rules of right and wrong, and tries to control the impulsive aggression of the Id. According to Freud the Superego forms at about age four or five, and at first represents the child's parents as a surrogate moral compass and a developing personal conscience. We have discussed before the innate ability to distinguish right from wrong and childhood is the time when the content is added by parental rules, school rules and society's rules. The position and operation of the Superego might be compared to the higher levels of achievement which both Maslow and Kohlberg envisioned: reaching for the ideal, one's highest potential, peace of mind, or self-actualization, *a la* Maslow; and living by higher, universal, transcendental principles that surpass legal rules and put the "Greater good" above one's personal needs. The two idealistic peaks of human hopes bear some resemblance to the Superego whose high standards are so difficult to reach, while still exerting an upward force toward growth and perfection— "Be the best you can be!"

The **Ego**, pictured at the middle level, is the mediator between the Id and the Superego, the rational conscious part of personality which tries to balance the conflicting demands of the Id and the Superego, cognizant of reality and consequences but tries to find some form of compromise to satisfy the desire for pleasure and the displeasure of the conscience. Freud sees our human psyche as a battleground, mostly below our level of awareness. This image was earlier shown in a Peanuts cartoon about the human heart (**page 83**) Freud considered the constant stress of competing demands on the Ego as the basis of much mental illness, even suggesting that "going insane" is a method for controlling the mental pain by abandoning ego control responsibilities.

Freudian theory is still widely used in psychiatry and counseling, though with hundreds of variations; the basic Ego, Id and Superego are still treated as universal human personality structure. It is not hard to see how the three levels of Freudian concepts fit with (or match) Maslow's levels of human motivation and Kohlberg's levels of moral reasoning. It may be just a coincidence or a stretch of the imagination, but it seems reflect some reality that crosses various disciplines and theories of human nature.

Does This Pattern Represent Reality?

The "three-layer" pattern followed by the three cited, and numerous other theorists with similar models, strongly suggests that they all came to see the structure of human nature or personality in approximately the same way. Internal conflicts within our psyche or brain seems to drive our behavior and other forces try to keep it under some control. It is not just the psychiatrists and psychologists who see humans this way (many do not), but the author of most of the New Testament, Paul the Apostle, certainly saw and felt his own inner struggle between good and evil *"I don't understand myself...I do the evil I don't want to do...and don't do what I want to do."* (Romans 7:15)) Does that diagnosis ring true for you? Is that the way we actually are?

*After all
We Are Only Human!*

Chapter 16

FREEDOM AND FREE WILL

> *"I have noticed even people who claim everything is predestined, and that we can do nothing to change it, look before they cross the road"*
> STEPHEN HAWKING

WHY DID YOU TURN TO THIS CHAPTER, THIS PAGE, at this time? Did you do it because you chose to do it, or were you compelled to take this action by some outside force? Did you consider doing something else with your time today, maybe write a letter? Did something prompt your thought about this book, maybe a memory of reading this book yesterday? Or, did it just seem to be a coincidence that you happened to notice this book on your desk, one of many books in view? And why did you pick up this book instead of the blue one, or the book with yellow post-it notes sticking out marking some section for attention? This little mental quiz illustrates the crux of the question of what is called "**Free Will**," and its polar opposite and counter-point concept of "**Determinism**."

The vast majority of modern scientists believe in "determinism" as a foundation for their work with the natural physical world. Most other people, including Believers, still hold to the conviction that humans have "choice" or "free will" at least to some degree. Until last century, virtually every philosopher from Plato on, every theologian and every scientist agreed that the power to consider options and make real choices was a fundamental difference separating humans from non-human animals. It is so intuitive, it is so reasonable to believe that we are exercising "free will" in our adult lives all the time, freely deciding what we want, what we think is best, what is right or moral. How could you not believe in "free will?" Yet, **science now says it is an illusion**: your actions, your future, all are the result of natural forces you cannot control, including genetics, biology, physics, culture, and all your prior actions. "Free will:" a reality or an illusion, or maybe a delusion? That is the big question.

Defining Our Terms: Will, Free Will, Determinism

Will is difficult to define as a singular, separate entity, for in the literature both ancient and modern the idea of will is almost always linked to "free" will, or to "will-power." For simplicity's sake let us define "will" as the capacity of human minds to make decisions and to form intentions. Science usually uses "volition" instead of "will" but the meaning is essentially the same. The mental process by which all humans become aware of some environmental circumstance or sensory data usually calls for response; in primitive times the early human was confronted with a potential danger (seeing or hearing a bear) and reflexively, or with analytical thought, a decision is made. The "thinking hominid" now quickly considers the options: run, hide or find a weapon; the option "be eaten by the bear" is a realistic choice, but it is an undesirable one (instinctively, a "reptilian brain instinct.) The decision is made in the mind to make a run for it: "I intend to run for my life" is the decision now becoming the intention. The "I intend" or "I will" is implemented by signals to the heart, lungs, legs and arms: MOVE! This, in simplistic terms, is what constitutes a "will," the forming of an "intention" to act on a decision between two or more choices. Fear, panic, curiosity or just lack of knowledge can interfere with the rational "will" and other internal and external factors can interfere with the operationalization of that intention or will. The decision maker may not be physically able to run for one reason or another, or there may be a physical obstacle in the escape route intended, or there may be another bear near the exit route, requiring still another decision (confront momma bear or baby bear?) The chain of events might look like this:

Awareness ->-Perception ->- Interpretation -> Decision/Choice ->- Intention/Will ->-Action.

Determinism would dismiss all of this *dangerous bear* scenario as simply a hominid operating on "instinct" or the natural reflex of "self-preservation." But **that** is an argument on "*what caused the hominid to run*?" rather than the internal mental process that actually occurred with viable alternatives for choice and the ability to make that choice. Was the hominid exercising "free will" or not? Was the outcome predetermined by some earlier action? Here it can get a bit silly. The strict determinist would propose that the bear was at that location because he was hungry and some berries were growing in that spot. The hominid had made an earlier decision to go into the woods to hunt for some food, and that earlier decision determined that he would meet the dangerous circumstance later. We could back-trace the hominids' string of previous decisions back to his first steps away from his nursing mother years ago, and that decision eventually led *ad infinitum* to this decision. That would be determinism, at least "soft" or "partial" determinism. "Hard determinism" is totally mechanistic, positing that every event is caused by some prior event, and that knowledge of present causal events would accurately predict future events. This is fairly easy to understand when the subject or event is physics: the effects of stars and planets and moons and gravity and "dark matter" and light—are phenomena strictly governed by physical laws; chance or randomness are discounted and causal relationships are clear and clean. But human thought, cognition, ideas and behavior are not simple physical realities and so the laws of physics may not be binding on them.

Free will is the ability to choose between different possible courses of action without external or internal constraint. When a conscious human encounters circumstances where preferences or choices are presented the process of considering the various alternatives is a mental process wherein options are possible. Suppose you encounter the dessert table at a banquet, and you observe two types of pie, three attractive cakes, and several bowls of assorted fruit. Your mouth is perhaps watering, for you normally very much enjoy desert. Some mental process goes on as you look at the alternatives; you generally prefer chocolate and so you exclude the lemon and coconut cream pies and focus on the cakes. One is covered with chocolate icing and the other two have white icing; the cakes have been cut and some of the pieces are missing, so you observe that the chocolate covered cake is actually white or vanilla inside, while one of the other cakes is chocolate inside and covered with vanilla icing. Which will you choose? You hesitate and imagine the tastes; finally, you choose the chocolate cake with vanilla icing, thinking that it will suit your taste better tonight. But wait. Something tugs at your mental coat tail, an inner voice of caution: "Remember, you are trying to lose weight." Call it conscience or reason or some internalized voice of your mother—you are conflicted. You want that cake, but you *shouldn't* consume that many unhealthy calories. More than a little disappointed, you reach for the fresh fruit and walk away from the desert table. You chose fruit, formed the intention to put some on your plate, and you did in fact follow your intention and took some fruit.

Was that fruit preordained for you? Did you really have a choice? Could you have actually made a different choice and eaten the chocolate cake instead? The likely answer is **"Yes"** you did have a real and unconstrained choice, and you could have just as freely chosen pie or fruit instead of cake. No waiter stopped you from getting the cake; no rule or law kept you from the desert table—it was legal and allowed. From a philosophical perspective, you were exercising "free will" on that occasion. The fact that something exerted pressure on you to choose the fruit had some influence, but it did not determine your choice. You were free to ignore the inner voice of caution if you chose. Pressure is not constraint or determinant. Other pressures were present, of course. If you had been a diabetic, your choice would have been more predictable—your life and health would have been more important to you than your taste buds. Perhaps you are at the banquet with an attractive young woman, and you realize she might be critical of your choice if you bring back a big piece of fattening chocolate cake; potential embarrassment puts its thumb on the scale of decision, influential but not decisive.

Without a doubt science has established that we are under the influence of a myriad of forces in every situation, both external and internal pressures that affect our decisions, our will to act, and our behavior. Psychology has for over a century searched out these many factors that shape our personalities, our beliefs, and our actions. There is no argument with the psychological "laws" which are part of human nature and our culture. Our basic needs for food, water, shelter, companionship, and approval of others are important motivating forces on us all, and all these and dozens more put limits on our range of choices and decision-making. None of us is "free" of these influences. Does that mean preprogrammed responses determine what we do or decide? We know, for example, that genetics play a significant part in determining who we are and what we will do. Some choices are genetically excluded at birth, and some opportunities are enhanced by genetic factors beyond our control. One person inherits genes that influence physical strength and athleticism, and that child is usually swept by the genetic tide toward a particular kind of life; another child may be genetically doomed to blindness or some physical handicap that constrains her choices in life, narrowing the options for choice. Is that an argument against "free will"? No, for whatever the external limitations that are imposed, every conscious human being still has choice, still has "free will" in some domain and to some degree. Even Steven Hawkins, whose physical life was so cruelly and completely limited still had "free will" till his death. He became a marvelous human being by exercising his control, his will over his circumstances.

Science and Determinism

Determinism is the theory that everything that happens in the universe—including every thought, feeling, and action of man—is necessitated by previous factors, so that nothing could ever have happened differently from the way it did, and everything in the future is already pre-set and inevitable. Every aspect of man's life and character, on this view, is merely a product of factors that are ultimately outside his control. Ayn Rand, a radical and influential American philosopher describes this viewpoint in stark terms:

> Do not hide behind the cowardly evasion that man is born with free will, but with a "tendency" to evil. A free will saddled with a tendency is like a game with loaded dice. It forces man to struggle through the effort of playing, to bear responsibility and pay

for the game, but the decision is weighted in favor of a tendency that he had no power to escape. If the tendency is of his choice, he cannot possess it at birth; if it is not of his choice, his will is not free. It's true that there's no such thing as free will. We can't help what we are or what we do. It's not our fault. Nobody's to blame for anything. It's all in your background ... and your glands. If you're good, that's no achievement of yours - you were lucky in your glands. If you're rotten, nobody should punish you - you were unlucky, that's all.[122]

Another statement of this rejection of "free will" is even more stark and impressive since it comes from a scientist and educator, Professor Massimo Pigliucci (2007):

Free will is an illusion. Our amazingly, wonderfully complex brains are comprised of various cognitive systems cycling amongst themselves and generating our thoughts, consciousness, choices and behaviour. These systems and their effects all result from the mechanical, inorganic laws of physics, over which we have no control.[123]

Philosophers generally agree that if strict determinism is accepted as true, it must be considered a contingent matter: that is, determinism may be *true* but it also may be *false*. We don't have certainty about this critical subject. Philosophers for many centuries have argued for "free will" based on logic and reason, informed by introspection and self-examination. Because having no free will would release us all from *responsibility*, philosophers reasoned that such a world would collapse in chaos for there would be no "right" or "wrong," not even "good" or "bad." Such words are meaningless if human behavior is not chosen but is dictated. Civilization would not be possible, they reasoned, if no one could be held accountable or judged: they can't help themselves. Not only would we lose the effective tool of judgement or condemnation for actions we just happen to not like, but we also lose the privilege of praising or approving actions of others. If they did something you approve it was not because of some praiseworthy quality, it was just predetermined. "Besides," someone would say, "that's not your choice or it is none of your business." The subject can't help doing that deed, and you can't help either liking it or disliking it—it was what was "supposed to be."

Trust, But Verify

If "determinism" is true, as most scientists believe, then should it not be verified by empirical methods such as observation, comparisons, research and testing? Has determinism been "proven" by science? Is the theory of determinism supported by empirical evidence we now have? "Determinism" like many other ideas and concepts is difficult to test with the usual tools of science. We know that some aspects of the Universe are undoubtedly "determined" by the known laws of physics. There is no real question that the motion of stars, planets, meteors and even galaxies are following predictable paths and speeds which are determined by natural laws (gravity, ergonomics, trajectory, etc.) "as they are supposed to do" we could say. We can identify what forces **cause** their actions, and we can predict what their future positions and actions will be. Determinism definitely works for the physical world at the level of our observation and experience.

Even something as variable as the weather is determined by things we know about, and so we can make good guesses what the weather will do tomorrow if we have all the data about temperatures, humidity, wind direction and speed, and a dozen other knowable factors. We can even predict the future weather <u>accurately</u> on a small local scale (tomorrow or weekend, in Kansas or New York etc.) but we are better at long term, macro-cosmic predictions such as global climate change (warmer), sea levels, droughts and salinity of the oceans: we can measure the relevant factors and use historical data, and make on-site observations of glaciers and water temperatures and dozens of other such information, and make broad, dependable forecasts. Weathermen can't tell you with 100 percent accuracy about whether it will rain on the next holiday, but climatologists can be pretty certain of what kind of July we will have in 2087. The laws of nature determine the outcomes in the physical realm, and are dependable (unchanging). But it seems doubtful that laws of nature have such causal control over human thought and actions. Let's explore this difference further.

Certainty Is Uncertain

Logically we can posit that our world (Universe) is either deterministic or it is not deterministic. If everything is determined by the laws of nature then those laws of nature must not be variable or changeable because the long sequence of cause and effect, cause and effect, and so on would be broken. Science deals with "probability" in the case of some matters which cannot be measured in total, such as the voting patterns of women 35-50 in the USA. We cannot get an exact count of the voting behavior of every living US woman in that age group, so using math and statistical methods, we interview a random sample of that population (for example) 1000 women picked out of the 35 million such women. If the 1000 are truly random (not chosen by color or language or marital status, etc.) we can reasonably predict that the average results for those 1000 will accurately predict the voting of the entire 35 million, **with a degree of probability.** It is realized that perfect prediction is impossible because people change their minds, or don't always tell pollsters the truth, or other reason, and so we say the prediction about the 35 million is 95% probability, or 80% probability. Probability seems to accept the possibility that those 35 million votes were not caused, but were choices or decisions of will. Votes may have been *influenced* by TV ads or newspaper articles, but influence is not *cause*.

We have suggested that not everything in our universe is caused by something else, including almost every "nonphysical" or "immaterial" element or construct. Physical objects of any size obey the laws of nature quite readily, and if they don't on some occasion, we look for the unknown law controlling them. In the natural world, the laws of physics and geometry and genetics are predictable and we can usually detect a cause for every observed effect. This **does not apply** to that non-material thought that just went through your mind, or the idea for a new dish for dinner. These invisible "things" are coming from our brain, we believe, and they are not entirely predictable. We sometimes can look back in our memory and say "Ah Ha! I got that idea yesterday while watching Oprah!" Did the Oprah show cause you to think of that delicious dish? There is a connection, granted, but not a cause and effect. Almost everyone who watched that show did not think about that dish for tonight's supper—you did it on your own in some way. As a matter of fact, you may have already decided to adapt that Oprah recipe to some less fattening version—that came from you unbidden, it appears.

Thoughts, beliefs, preferences, wishes and hopes, love and loyalty are real, but not material and not determined by any natural laws of which we are aware. A sense of awe, an unexpected insight into life or the universe which inspires us, or the conviction that one is in contact with God or some spiritual power—all these and more are real, objective experiences but elude any known way to measure or quantify them. Psychology and Sociology and Economics are disciplines which study human behavior, and they look for ways to understand why people do as they do or think as they do, and try to make predictions about what individuals or populations might do. But, unlike physics, these are "inexact sciences" dealing with humans who are convinced they are independent and free, exercising their own judgment and will, none of whom want to give up that sense of freedom.

Quantum Science Challenges Determinism

The philosophical debate about determinism and free-will is not going to be settled by scientific study or experiments, and the questions will probably never be answered definitively. But hard science, on the other hand, may be able to settle some of the questions about free will and determinism. Two such scientific "breakthroughs" are mentioned below as representative of the kinds of "hard science" study and research is going on. It is probably a misnomer to call the "uncertainty principal" and quantum physics as recent breakthroughs for neither is actually new to science. But science is always playing the "long game" so things that proposed a hundred years ago are still being tested, and an amazing number of the ideas of the earlier great minds have been proven valid, but almost everything old is still subject to review. Quantum physics is much more in the "news" these days but is actually a century old idea, originating in the work of famous scientists *Albert Einstein, Werner Heisenberg, Neils Bohr* and *Max Planck*. Heisenberg won the Nobel Prize in Physics in 1932 "for the creation of quantum mechanics" though he insisted it should have been shared with Planck, Bohr and others. Quantum theory is extremely complex, and one of its creators, Niels Bohr, said *"If quantum mechanics hasn't profoundly shocked you, you haven't understood it yet."*[124]

Quantum physics is essentially a modern and more precise form of Newtonian physics which has been the gold standard of science for centuries. Newtonian Physics (or Classical Physics) was and still is sufficiently accurate for all the "big things" in physics (motion, velocity, mass, gravity, starts, galaxies, energy, etc.) Quantum physics deals with the subatomic world of matter, light, protons, prions, quarks, etc. where Classical Physics is not precisely applicable. At the micro level, scientists now know, matter does not behave predictably as it does on the macro level. Whereas Classical Physics can determine the exact location a satellite or rocket will be in 27 years, 3 days and 40 minutes, if they have data about speed, velocity, weight, etc., Quantum theory can only predict of a subatomic particle: "It will be either here, or there, at this time, or that time." Large matter is apparently totally dependable and constant, whereas very, very small particles of subatomic matter are random in behavior. Randomness allows probability about the location or speed of a neuron or a photon, but not certainty. At the smallest level of reality, determinism fails, and law and order are "fluid." The **Uncertainty Principle** was proposed by Werner Heisenberg in 1926, and that law of micro mass is accepted by almost all scientists today.

Science has simply discovered that the atomic world is in fact full of murkiness and chaos, and not the precision clockwork suggested by classical theory, and by "determinism." Everything is not caused by something else, at least at the very smallest, most fundamental level of reality. If we cannot predict the future action of a proton or a quark or other basic element, it is not unreasonable to challenge the idea that we can predict the mental activity and decision making of a living, sentient human being. People have "minds" and quarks do not (so far as we know). One of the principles of strict determinism which science advocates is uniformity: If a world is governed by determinism, then everything in that world or realm must be determined, without any exceptions. A world in which we suppose some things are set or determined and other things are not predetermined, then it is not determinism. Science has accepted that subatomic particles are not deterministic but are random or "free" and so the argument is fouled.

Neurological Experiments May Support Determinism

The neurologist Benjamin Libet performed a sequence of remarkable experiments in 1983 that were enthusiastically, if mistakenly, adopted by supporters of determinism to show that human free will does not exist. His first report on his experiments at science conferences stirred a flurry of similar studies in the next few years; he published his complete findings in his 2004 book *Mind Time: The Temporal Factor in Consciousness*. Using volunteers connected to an electroencephalogram he measured when they reported having a particular conscious thought about an action (raising a finger or moving wrist) and when the actual action started. Libet created a dot on the screen of an oscilloscope circulating like the hand of a clock, but more rapidly. The subject was asked to note the position of the moving dot when he/she was aware of the conscious decision to move a finger or wrist. Precise measurements in milliseconds were made of when the first brain activity started, when the subject reported having made a conscious decision, and the time the action was carried out. He found that although conscious awareness of the decision preceded the subject's finger motion by only 200 milliseconds, the rise in the Type II readiness potential (specific brain activity) was clearly visible at about 550 milliseconds before the flex of the wrist. The subject showed unconscious activity to flex about 350 milliseconds before reporting conscious awareness of the decision to flex. He noted an even earlier slow and very slight rise in the readiness potential by 1.5 seconds before the reported conscious awareness. It appeared that the subjects had actually made (unconsciously) the decision to act measurably earlier than when they became aware of it consciously. It was as if the **conscious brain was not the decider** but simply the spokesperson. This result seemed to cast doubt on the idea of a freely chosen action, the operation of free will leading to decision and action.[125]

Not surprisingly, many neurologists and other scientists have challenged these conclusions, and some have faulted Libet's research methods. Other studies have essentially confirmed Libet's findings, showing similar "time gaps" between the subject's brain "lights up" in anticipation of a need and the time when the subjects recognized they had made a conscious decision. The time between decision and action was no surprise to neurologists, but they had not expected neurons firing that indicated some unconscious preparation for the action 1 or 2 seconds in advance. Some other studies have detected the activation of neural activity as much as 10 seconds before the subject "thinks" he is making a decision, while others have found minor variations in the time for different test subjects. There seems to be "something" or "someone" thinking about the choice to be made even before the person has made up their mind. That "something" is naturally occurring neurological activity with neurons and synapses and nerves and white matter doing what they do, according to many scientists. This would negate the idea of a free and conscious choice made by the rational mind after thoughtful consideration of alternatives.

But Dr. Libet did not make that claim for his research. He felt that free will was still a valid possibility in the experiments he conducted. He described an optional **"conscious veto:"**

The finding that the volitional process is initiated unconsciously leads to the question: Is there then any role for conscious will in the performance of a voluntary act? The conscious will (W) does appear 150 msec before the motor act, even though it follows the onset of the cerebral action (1W) by at least 400 msec. That allows it, potentially, to affect or control the final outcome of the volitional process. An interval msec before a muscle is activated is the time for the primary motor cortex to activate the spinal motor nerve cells, and through them, the muscles. During this final 50 msec, the act goes to completion with no possibility of its being stopped by the rest of the cerebral cortex. The conscious will could decide to allow the volitional process to go to completion, resulting in the motor act itself. Or, the conscious will could block or "veto" the process, so that no motor act occurs[126].

Libet considered that "veto option" an act of free will, regardless of whether the original idea was conscious or unconscious. Everyone has experienced impulses to action which seem to come from nowhere, and most of us have learned to delay quick action of sudden impulses. It is possible that this type research explains only one kind of decision-generating that could have been formed through unconscious or forgotten thoughts. Perhaps most of our real exercise of free will involves more conscious thought, rational examination of options, and the other elements of good decision making. Measuring the point at which a subject decides to move a finger is a rather limited test of how and when decisions are made in more complex acts of will required every day in real life settings. It seems foolish to attribute some random neurological activity or unconscious motivation to a decision about joining the military, or accepting a job offer in another state or whether to vote for flawed politician A or deranged politician B (or not vote at all). Acts of will frequently are about very important matters, and our lives are only made more difficult and even meaningless if we are not really free. You are, of course, FREE TO DISAGREE, totally free to think and decide for yourself.

Jesus promised:

You shall know the truth and the truth will set you free."

Chapter 17

SIN, EVIL AND GUILT

"To be free from evil thoughts is God's best gift"
AESCHYLUS

SIN AND SALVATION ARE CONCEPTS WHICH ARE HALLmarks of the Abrahamic religions (Judaism, Christianity and Islam), though the specifics and significance vary widely, even within each faith. Most readers who have had any exposure to religion will have some familiarity with the concept of "sin," probably based on personal contact with some religious group, or perhaps on second hand information about such groups. The variations in the concept of "sin" among religious groups of all stripes is even more extreme than the variations in the concepts about "god." The subjects of "guilt" and "evil" are bound to the question of "sin" and will be addressed in this chapter as well. For Believers or those who are religiously informed non-believers this book will present a Christian understanding of "sin" based on a progressive biblical interpretation, with the addition of a fresh new brain-based theory. For Skeptics and other non-believers who are science enthusiasts, a more extensive sociological and psychological exploration will be pursued, based on scientific research, psychiatric studies and emerging neurological explanations.

Sin and Human Nature

For readers interested in serious study of God and religion, the concept of "sin" cannot be simply ignored: without some universal flaw or failing in all of human nature, there is no compelling need for a god or for "salvation." All the greatest playwrights and story tellers in history, from Aesculus to Shakespeare to Thomas Wolfe, have built their plots around some such human failing. This category of writing is aptly labeled "tragedy," and the main character is usually doomed by some fault, some personal character flaw. Whether it is greed, hatred, lust, hubris or one of the many other demons that plague humans, *"The fault, dear Brutus, is not in our stars, but in ourselves..."* Shakespeare noted. Apparently, there is something wrong with humans, something self-destructive and harmful, and **"sin"** is the label given this problem by most religions. In more modern times, in the life sciences such as psychology, sociology, philosophy, and ethics, the "problem" is simply called **The Human Condition.** It is apparently **the way we are.**

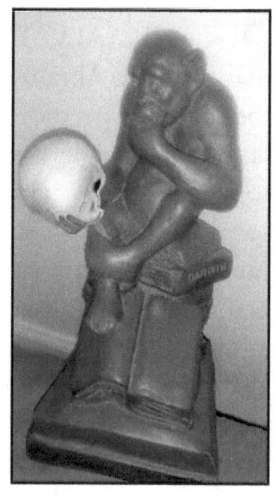

The "human condition" is viewed by philosophers, ancient and modern, as a struggle between *what is* and *what ought to be* in terms of our introspection. Those who look inward in self-evaluation, whether occasionally or frequently, are usually dissatisfied and disappointed with themselves. Sometimes it is just circumstantial disappointment with our performance on a particular job or assignment, realizing that we made a mistake or failed some challenge. Such specific shortcomings of our expectations are normal and positive, leading to efforts to improve and correct our mistakes on the next opportunity; we normally don't universalize our particular failure to considering ourselves a *total failure*, a *loser*. Such blanket condemnation of ourselves is not healthy and can spiral into depression or other mental illness. But we do sometimes ponder our condition; we are "thinkers."

We are *"Homo sapiens"* of course, a label we gave ourselves in vanity, meaning "thinking man" or "wise man." We are most human while thinking, seriously and persistently searching for answers to life's crucial questions. We present again an image of a chimpanzee pondering a human skull in his hand, sitting on a stack of books, including Darwin.

This is an interesting artistic commentary, like an editorial in stone, simulating Auguste Rodin's famous statue "The Thinker" into a contemplation of human life and evolution.

We **are** thinkers, whatever the quality of our individual thinking: we are capable of performing the mental activity in our wonderful brain, in the mysterious inner room we call the "mind." It is there, our inner sanctum, where we face a full-length mirror, where we privately view all the warts and wounds, all the quirks and ambiance of who we are. When we are psychologically healthy, we may be kind and gentle in our assessment: "Hey, I'm not perfect, but I'm doing pretty good for an old guy."

Unfortunately, many of us who look at ourselves in that mental examining room are not satisfied nor pleased with the image, and our "self-esteem" is in the basement or the toilet. We *don't like* ourselves very much, and are sometimes ashamed. Most of our "self-esteem" problems are not "sin" in the traditional religious sense, but are complicated results from being imperfect beings living with other imperfect beings. These self-doubts are trademarks of our humanness, possibly the inevitable result of having a composite evolutionary brain, our ancestral reptilian base overlaid and competing for control with our mammalian brain and our higher aspiring "human brain," the Neocortex of primates.

Most of us get pretty skilled in developing what the life sciences call "defense mechanisms" to protect our fragile "ego" or "self-image." These include such common strategies as denial, repression, projection, and sublimation among scores of such mechanisms scholars have named. Denial is simply trying to fool ourselves by refusing to accept the "truth" you can't face: "I'm not an alcoholic—I am just a social drinker. I can quit any time."

Repression is essentially trying to forget what is painful, to put it out of your mind, to hide it in your unconscious mind. You can have an "alarm system" which warns you when a painful thought drifts into your mind so you can quickly distract your thought to something else.

Sublimation is often seen as a positive way to protect our fragile ego, when we transform our unpleasant self-image or our unmet hopes into positive, productive alternative. For example, a young woman who thinks she is not attractive enough to marry and have children may devote her life to helping children as a teacher, caretaker or social worker, throwing all her energy into a different dream which nurtures her self-esteem. We all want to avoid the pain of our disappointment, shame or guilt. That is normal human nature, although the protective mechanisms we adopt may not be healthy or productive to a good life. Avoiding mental pain can give temporary relief from anxiety, but it may deny us the growth that comes only from an honest facing of reality—our personal reality.

What's It All About?

So far as we now know humans are the only species in the animal kingdom who ponder the great existential questions: What is the meaning of life? Why are we here? What is the purpose of life? What is the purpose of **my** life? Is this **all** there is? The search for answers to these deep existential questions is why we have so many philosophers in our past, and so many popular psychology books and articles in magazines, as well as TV gurus telling us how to achieve happiness or peace or some relief from our problems and anxieties. Lots of cartoons feature a climber reaching a guru atop a mountain, asking "What is the meaning of life?" Sometimes the cartoon guru answers something wise, such as "To love and be loved," and another cartoon may offer something silly like "*Pickles*," or maybe "*42* is the answer." Such answers, serious or in jest, usually do not satisfy the lonely longing of the human heart for some reassurance, some significance, some sense of worth. **"What is the meaning of life?"** can be a plea for help by someone contemplating giving up on life and ending it all at the end of a rope or a gun; thousands of people every year decide that life, their life, has no meaning, no purpose. Thousands, old and young, prefer the dark abyss to their own current existence, and so they kill themselves. **We all want to matter.**

As mentioned in an earlier chapter, humans apparently are the only animals who are aware of mortality, who know that someday they will die. Death is a certainty in a world of uncertainties, but we are not so comforted by this particular certainty. Some animals appear to realize when death is immanent, either by being very sick or seriously injured, and perhaps just accepting that old age is closing in ominously, and they are getting weaker and are suffering pain. Elephants in particular have been documented to withdraw from the herd and isolate themselves when death is approaching, and other elephants seem to exhibit "grief" at the death of one of their own, sometimes congregating around the deceased for hours or even days. But, so far as we know, elephants don't worry about their future death as humans do. It is likely they, like other animals, are spared the dread and fear that comes from being mortal.

In Social Psychology a concept called "terror management theory (TMT) has been proposed and gained credence in recent years. This is the idea that a mental or psychological conflict is created by having the normal "self-preservation" instinct which is common to all animals, *plus* the human awareness that death is inevitable and unpredictable. The theory was originally proposed by Jeff Greenberg, Sheldon Solomon, and Tom Pyszczynski, and codified in their 2015 book *The Worm at the Core: On the Role of Death in Life*.[127] These authors were influenced by anthropologist Ernest Becker's 1973 Pulitzer Prize-winning work of nonfiction *The Denial of Death*, in which Becker argues most human action is taken to ignore or avoid the inevitability of death. *The Worm at the Core* examined how this terror is then managed by embracing cultural values, or symbolic systems that act to provide life with enduring meaning and value.

The Hope for Immortality

The simplest examples of cultural values that manage the terror of death are those that offer spiritual immortality (e.g., belief in a conscious afterlife, religion, faith), and cultural values which offer <u>symbolic immortality</u> (such as heightened national or patriotic identity, or by producing a posterity through children and grandchildren, or by the achievement of fame and honor which endures beyond your life.) Symbolic immortality can provide a sense that one is part of something greater, some cause, that will outlive the individual. These buffers against dread attempt to offer hope that our symbolic identity is superior to our biological identity, that we are more than a random collection of cells and electro-chemical energy that just disappears, or that at least we will "live on" in the memories of our survivors, or maybe in the history books. Some desperate souls apparently even resort to some horrible notoriety such as a mass murder of school children in order to secure a place in history. To be remembered for evil may seem better than being forgotten forever, since death accompanies both.

It is not news that humans have always been troubled by the thought of an ultimate death and the prospect of "non-existence." This worry probably extends all the way back in time to our early Hominid ancestors, those who first became fully conscious and could recognize their own self as distinct from other selves. The dawn of awareness of identity was the dawn of inner anxiety. Their budding imagination, the ability to mentally envision some future event or condition, brought with it the knowledge of their mortality. *"Moog died; I will too."* Modern mortals try to keep fear of death at bay by repressing the thoughts, distracting themselves by frantic activity and by focusing on pleasure and mind-numbing pills and beverages.

The cultural values of a society determine what is meaningful and important, and our individual sense of self-esteem is greatly influenced by our subjective evaluation of how well we are living up to those cultural values. Society defines what is desirable in appearance (tall, thin, healthy skin, full head of hair, bright white teeth and smile, etc.). Society defines what abilities or talents are valued (music, art, fluent speech, intellect, monetary success, etc.). To some degree, our personal self-esteem is impacted by how well we fit (or think we fit) the societal mold. Our significance in life may be defined by what the crowd thinks (our reputation) rather than what we believe ourselves to be (our true self.)

What's WRONG with Us?

Those who do not buy this "flawed human condition" analysis may argue that there is so much human goodness and generosity in the world, so many heroes reported on the evening news for their sacrifice to help a homeless person, or to rescue an injured dog. That's true, but how can we explain the many historical examples of supremely EVIL INDIVIDUALS? In case the reader is fortunate enough to have never known an evil person or have not read about evil people, we will cite a few of the most evil people in history in our opinion. We will skip **Adolph Hitler, Josef Stalin, Saddam Hussein** and **Osama bin Laden** for this lineup of evil people because they are well known to most readers and their wickedness is uncontested. Other evil characters from other times and other cultures will round out our Hall of Evil. A hundred equally evil examples could be cited, some in our own time, some this year.

Pol Pot was a political leader/dictator who led the Khmer Rouge communist government in Cambodia from 1975 to 1979. During his reign of genocidal terror some 2 million Cambodians and Vietnamese were slaughtered or starved. The bodies of hundreds

"Killing Fields of Cambodia"

of thousands of victims were buried in mass graves which came to be known as "killing fields," which gave its name to a movie about this evil man. Before his evil atrocities he spent a year in a Buddhist monastery, attended a French Catholic school, and studied technology on a scholarship to Paris. He was 50 years old when his killing began.

Nero

Nero Claudius Caesar, the fifth emperor, ruled Rome from 54 A.D. until his death by suicide 14 years later. He burned entire cities (though probably did not "fiddle while Rome burned"). He had thousands murdered, including his aunt, stepsister, ex-wife, mother, wife and adoptive brother, systematically wiping out every member in his family. His killing technique included boiling baths, poison, burning, beheading, stabbing, crucifying and impaling. He is most famous for his persecution of the Christians in Rome and elsewhere, including the famous Colosseum public "shows" where Christians were eaten by lions, burned at the stake, and forced to kill each other as gladiators. He is reported to have raped and mutilated both men and women for his own pleasure. He killed himself at 31.

We leave untold the stories of the Nazi doctor *Josef Mengele, Genghis Khan, Ted Bundy, John Wayne Gacy, Jeffrey Dahmer, "Jack the Ripper,"* or the several other serial killers who will be famous by the time this book is published. There is no doubt that there are a lot of very bad, evil people among us, and something is horribly wrong with some people—people who seem normal on the outside, who live and work in our city, people who may be your neighbor until some terrible day when the evil erupts beyond their control. The question is, as it was asked of Jesus at the Last Supper: **"Could it be me?"**

Could It Be Me?

Carl Jung, the famous Swiss psychologist from the last century, pondered the connection of human nature with our species history, our ancestral past contained in our unconscious. According to Jung the human mind has innate characteristics imprinted from our "collective" memory. We are bothered not only by memories of our personal past, but also by faint hints of a past shared by all mankind. He cites fear of snakes and spiders as examples of "remembered" fears we inherited, but also regards our vague, shadowy fear of our own dark side, our tendency to violence, as such a collective memory: ***"When it (our shadow) appears...it is quite within the bounds of possibility for a man to recognize the relative evil of his nature, but it is a rare and shattering experience for him to gaze into the face of absolute evil."***[128] *A Socratic Perspective on the Nature of Human Evil* by Max Maxwell and Melete describes us in stark, perceptive terms:

> The most terrifying thing about contemplating the Nazis is not that they were some kind of inhuman monsters. **The most terrifying thing is that they were just like us.** They were ordinary human beings filled with the amazing human potential for virtue and beauty, and who were also capable of behaving like monsters. We all have this capacity. If we are human beings, remaining mindful about even the smallest wrongdoing in our attempts to live well is more important than many imagine, because the nature of human evil is the same in both small and large wrongdoing.[129] (Emphasis added)

What Is Evil and Who Did It?

One of the greatest arguments against God is the existence of **evil**. How could a "good God" create evil, or allow it to exist? One "cute" answer is to simply add a **D** to "evil," giving us **Devil**, the evil One who is God's nemesis, who "bedeviled" Jesus for 40 days in the wilderness, Satan the fallen angel, The Prince of Darkness, Beelzebub, aka: Lucifer. ***"The devil made me do it"*** Christine used to tell TV comedian Flip

Wilson, and this is still a popular excuse for the guilty. Skeptics use the Christian Bible to suggest that this so called "Devil" was created by God, so the blame cannot be so easily shifted. This volume will not devote much space to dealing with the Satan question, other than to acknowledge that orthodox Christianity holds the reality of the devil as a personified force of cosmic evil.

The idea of an evil force in the Universe seriously competing with Yahweh is not a Jewish creation, and their earliest theology seems to attribute both good and evil to the one God, Yahweh: *"I form the light and create darkness, I bring prosperity and create disaster; I, the LORD, do all these things."* (Isaiah 45:7). Some older translations have "*I make peace, and create evil.*" Before the Exile (586 B.C.) a character named "Satan" appears in the heavenly court of Yahweh, an antagonist but not a divine competitor. Satan appears to be an angel of God "gone bad," a rebel leader of an ancient angelic revolt. Satan has power, but must get Yahweh's permission to use it against the main character, Job. In Genesis it is a serpent that temps Eve to sin: *"Now the serpent was more cunning than any beast of the field which the Lord God had made."* (Genesis 3:1) The serpent is an opponent of the Creator, but is not identified as the "Devil" or "Satan." In later Jewish writings and in Christian thought, the serpent is the Devil in disguise, an eternal force of Evil from the beginning.

Almost all civilizations earlier than the Jewish state had a world view based on the battle of the ages and the Universe between Good and Evil, a dualistic theology. The Sumerians, Babylonians and Persians all had well-developed cosmology involving a mortal struggle between Good and Evil, usually portrayed as the personification of their god (e.g., Marduk, Ahura, Tiamat); other, lesser gods were sometimes the cosmic evil force, usually given a name as well. Their myths and legends centered on the battles these two dueling forces fought, with Mankind as the pawn in their struggle for control. The Old Testament does not have this dual concept until quite late in their history, after the Babylonian captivity and exile from 586 B.C. to 538 B.C. After the Exile, the Israelites appear to have adopted the idea of an eternal cosmic struggle between God and the "devil" as the personification of evil. During the seven decades Israel was kept in Babylon they were exposed to a very popular religion called Zoroastrianism, which featured an eternal struggle between good and evil as it's center piece, plus the vision of a future final battle when evil is defeated and the Good prevails in a wonderful new world.

The Eternal Battle

Judaism and Christianity accepted the idea of the eternal struggle, and the culmination in some future victory of God and a paradise of good will on earth. In the Abrahamic religions God is triumphant in the end, but is engaged in a daily struggle for the human soul against an evil force called *Satan*, the *Devil, Lucifer, Beelzebub, Mammon* and *Mephistopheles*. In popular culture the Devil is often portrayed as a horned and hoofed being, fiery red and usually with a long tail and an ominous pitchfork. He has access to our minds just as God does, he knows all our weaknesses, but does not have power over our will. He can control humans only if they permit him to do so, either by trickery or by acquiescence. Christians in the New Testament are given siren-like warnings about Satan: ***"Be alert and of sober mind. Your enemy the devil prowls around like a roaring lion looking for someone to devour."*** (I Peter 5:8)

In the dramatic book of Revelation, the final great battle with the Devil is spelled out in frightening word pictures, with the Devil ultimately vanquished and thrown into Hell, a bottomless pit: ***"And the devil, who deceived them, was thrown into the lake of burning sulfur, where the beast and the false prophet had been thrown. They will be tormented day and night for ever and ever."*** (Revelation 20:10)

Now let us connect the idea of wrongdoing to the term **evil**. In the West, the term evil is so overloaded with Christian theological content that it is difficult to separate the **force of evil** from the **doing of evil**. In Christian thought, evil is the abstract malevolent power of Satan and his minions in the world. ***"For our struggle is not against flesh and blood, but against the rulers, against the authorities, against the powers of this dark world and against the spiritual forces of evil in the heavenly realms."*** (Ephesians 6:12) Paul is attributing both external persecution and the sins of individuals as the effect of the Devil's evil work against God in real time. "Kill and destroy" is the mission of the demons infesting our world. Demonic forces figure prominently in the ministry of Jesus, and demon-possession is encountered and cured by Paul and Silas (see Acts 16).

In the Socratic perspective evil behavior is the same thing as wrongdoing. When we speak of human evil, we will use it solely in association with harmful human behavior (including the harmful neglect of withholding an action). Evil can even "hide" in "good deeds" if the motivation for doing good is foul. This is because it is only through intentional harmful behavior that any measure of human evil (no matter what your concept of evil) is recognizable. **Harmfulness is the only evaluative criterion used here for assessing the evil, or the wrong, of behaviors.** If a behavior is not harmful at all then there is no basis of defining the evil of that behavior. It may be bad, despicable or sinful, but it is not evil as used in this book. One could argue, as Socrates did, that any wrong doing is harmful, at least to the doer; violating one's own sense of right and wrong is a corrosive force in the personality, easing the slide into greater and deeper levels of moral decay. This is because it is only through harmful behavior that any measure of human evil (no matter what your concept of evil) is recognizable.

Is Evil in Me or In Us?

Another definition of evil involves a communal aspect rather than an individual deed. **When a corrupt and persuasive leader arises in a group, society or nation, the degree of harm possible is exponentially much greater.** A rabble-rouser stirs up hatred and anger among some acquaintances, raising the pitch of their discontent to verbal and then physical violence. The instigator, through oratory or peer pressure gets an angry mob of people who have surrendered their own rational thought to the group think mentality. The "I" becomes the "we" and the emotions are increased and the sense of individual responsibility fades to black. The mob becomes the movement and the movement becomes the de facto majority in control of the reins of power. Examples of this pattern are Adolph Hitler, Rev. Jim Jones in Guiana and David Koresh in Texas. A "bad" person plus great political or social power seems to be a reasonable definition of the difference between sin and evil. Individual wrong multiplied by tens of thousands can unleash unspeakable evil, and it has, over and over.

How such takeovers of political and militant power can occur is somewhat of a mystery to historians, psychologists, criminologists and sociologists. The conditions have to be just right (perhaps just "wrong") for such a mass mind-control to happen. There must be some discontent or dissent already present that can be exploited by a charismatic fear monger and hate baiter. The target population may be disenfranchised or isolated, apparently or in reality suffering some injustice or discrimination in their society. The new voice stirs up their outrage at their condition and points to the culprits causing their problem: it may be the Blacks, or the Rich, or the illegal immigrants or the Muslims, but it is always some "them" instead of "us." Anger and resentment grow into hatred and violence is soon started. Whence come such vile and thoughtless emotions?

The New Testament describes individual sin as arising from within a person when a germ of temptation is allowed to grow: "***God cannot be tempted by evil, nor does he tempt anyone; but each person is tempted when they are dragged away by their own evil desire and enticed. Then, after desire has conceived, it gives birth to sin; and sin, when it is full-grown, gives birth to death."*** (James 1:13-15). This amazing Biblical insight has been verified by numerous scientific studies, charting how a cascade of bad feelings fester and erupt in some individuals, with a negative thought creating an unpleasant emotion, and that emotion fostering a desire to hurt the person or group being blamed. Sometimes such arousal to violence is so swift and the action taken so harmful that the Prosecutor may not be able to prove "Premeditation" for the crime. Seemingly, no thought is involved. We may claim we were provoked to the violence, but the reality is just as the passage from James points out: it came from within ourselves, something was already there waiting to be awakened. As we proposed earlier in **Chapter 4, The Brain Game**, it may just be our older Reptilian Brain raising its ugly head, but doing what it was "designed" by evolution to do: fight for our survival. It seems possible that sometimes the Devil is in our brain stem instead of our neighborhood.

Evil as the Absence of Good

The great Christian leader, Augustine of Hippo (AD 354-430), viewed God as omniscient, omnipotent, omnipresent, morally good, the creator (*ex nihilo*) and sustainer of the universe. Despite these multiple descriptors, God is uniquely simple, according to Augustine. Being entirely free, He did not have to create, but did so as an act of love. As His creation, we reflect His mind. Time and space began at creation, **and everything in creation is good.** On the other hand, **Evil is un-created, being a lack of good and without positive existence.** For example, God created Light, and light expelled Darkness; darkness was not created, it is simply the absence of light. God didn't create darkness but darkness occupies any space lacking light. Darkness is not a "thing" just as "cold" is not a "thing." Both are natural consequences of some positive, light and heat respectively. So, **evil is some natural force, a kind of spiritual "anti-matter"** whose purpose is to oppose, to thwart a positive element or action. The Bible certainly proclaims the reality of this evil force, personifying it and naming it as Lucifer, Satan, the Devil, Beelzebub, Mephistopheles, the Prince of Darkness and The Evil One. Paul describes the Devil as a hungry, roaring, stalking lion. (1 Peter 5:8) In the desert encounter with Jesus, Satan is a wily trickster, the "Tempter in chief" who seems to be an actual being of some kind. Virtually every culture in the past has their version of the evil force, and scores of their names are known from archaeological finds.

Some Christians believe that God created the angel "Lucifer" who at some point led an angel revolt against God. According to interpretation of some scattered Bible verses many Believers say Lucifer was expelled from heaven, and subsequently has made earth his evil battleground against Mankind in an ongoing attempt to thwart God's redemption of His erring children. Here is the Biblical account from Revelation:

> *Then war broke out in heaven. Michael and his angels fought against the dragon, and the dragon and his angels fought back. But he was not strong enough, and they lost their place in heaven. The great dragon was hurled down—that ancient serpent called the devil, or Satan, who leads the whole world astray. He was hurled to the earth, and his angels with him. Then I heard a loud voice in heaven say: 'Now have come the salva-*

> *tion and the power and the kingdom of our God, and the authority of his Messiah.*
>
> *For the accuser of our brothers and sisters, who accuses them before our God, day and night, has been hurled down. They triumphed over him by the blood of the Lamb and by the word of their testimony they did not love their lives so much as to shrink from death. Therefore rejoice, you heavens and you who dwell in them! But woe to the earth and the sea, because the devil has gone down to you! He is filled with fury, because he knows that his time is short."* (Revelation 12: 7-13)

Many consider the story of Job in the Old Testament as a portrait of the devil, or Satan as he is called there. He appears to be a part of a council in God's court, and he acts as an "accuser," another name given this Evil One in the New Testament. The evidence and the metaphors are mixed, at best. It is possible that God created an angel who "went bad" but that leads to some tricky and sticky theology. It seems that the best metaphor for sin and evil is the light-darkness one mentioned above. In our movies Light almost always is Good, and Darkness is usually Bad.

Are We Really THAT Awful?

It is expected that many readers will discount this section, believing that "sin" is not a problem for themselves. Many will say, sincerely, that they are not plagued with guilt or remorse for the way they live. "I am doing quite well without religion, thank you; I am a 'good' person, and I am satisfied with who I am, morally." Influential atheists such as Richard Dawkins, Christopher Hitchens and Stephen Hawking are scholars who actively promote atheism, and are effective apologists for atheism. These three and dozens of other scholarly atheists, almost to a person, claim a high level of morality with no help from religion. They live a good life, they are responsible citizens, they are kind and generous, and treat others fairly and with respect. "What more does religion offer?" In fact, almost all the scholarly atheists view religion as not only unnecessary, but actually as a dangerous and destructive force in the world. "Sin and guilt" some say, "Are religions' make-believe tools for controlling the masses." Another group of influential atheists includes Neil deGrasse Tyson,

Bill Maher, Mark Zuckerberg, Lance Armstrong, and Jodie Foster. These are famous celebrities, even super-stars, and while they make their belief (or non-belief) clear, they are not activists or advocates promoting atheism. Each of these has expressed satisfaction with their lives without a "god" or a religion, and they are widely admired and respected. They are "good people", and at least for now, no serious charges of immorality or gross misconduct have been publicly levied against any of them. It is agreed that atheists are not, as a group, a threat to society, not the forerunners of a "godless" society governed by heartless, self-centered narcissists bent on rooting out every superstition and ignorant fable. Atheists probably have a very low crime record, likely are below average in spouse abuse and child neglect or bank robbery, or tax evasion, or religious terrorism. In fact, because atheists are more likely to be educated than the average person in society, they are more likely to be financially secure in significant careers, and thus, are more shielded from the psychologically and morally corrupting influence of poverty and social stress.

Let us grant without question that atheists and agnostics and religious skeptics can and do live lives that are upright, positive, and satisfying; that they can, without religion's influence, live good, moral lives. Does that mean that the idea of "sin", or "flawed human nature" is only an ancient myth, a superstitious tradition handed down generation to generation? Is a sense of sin, an inner experience of guilt, really a mental health issue, rather than a religion question? Is the struggle of the New Testament's Apostle Paul a sign of mental illness rather than a troubled conscience? *I do not understand what I do. For what I want to do I do not do, but what I hate I do.* (Romans 7:15)

For many people, these words of Paul ring true and familiar and many of us, maybe the majority of us, have times when we are in moral conflict, knowing what is right but not eager to do it. It may not be something of great import like murder or robbery, but there is a nagging inner argument, perhaps our conscience pushing us to do something but our conscious mind throwing up excuses and roadblocks. Perhaps a colleague has falsified some data on an office report, and you are the only one who knows about the cheating. Do you report him to your boss, or do you "mind your own business?" Do you sympathize with the culprit and hate to cause him to be fired? "What good would that do?" your inner voice whispers. Do you confront him in private and try to persuade him to correct the problem? Would he welcome your intervention? Probably not. What is it that makes you "want to do right?" and what is it that pushes back and resists any action? Is your conscience overactive? Is it just the way you were raised, what your parents or church taught? Is your conscience an outdated vestige of trying to please your parents? Down deep down in your psyche, is there "good" you and a "bad" you, struggling for control?

How Did We Get This Way?

Is there such a thing as "human nature," something inherent in being a human being, something we were destined to become? Are all humans alike in our capacity to be good or bad? Are we basically good by nature, but subject to some slips? Are we basically animals in our makeup, driven by self-protection and survival, but capable of overlaying it with a thin veneer of civilized humanity?

The ancient Greek philosopher Socrates turned philosophy from the study of the heavens (science) to the study of human beings (philosophy). Socrates, like other philosophers of that era was concerned about how life should be lived, what constituted a "good life", and how to achieve it. He knew well from his keen observations of Athenian leaders and heroes that humans have both the capacity for great good and for great evil. Using a questioning method with his students, Socrates sought to tease out human nature, what is innate and what is learned. He is famous for his statement at his trial, in which he chose death rather than exile from his pursuit of wisdom: **"The unexamined life is not worth living."** His overall philosophy is captured in his dictum: *"Know thyself."* Socrates believed and died for the belief that philosophy—the love of wisdom—was the most important reason to live, perhaps the only reason to live.

It was in the fearless examination of himself and his "Socratic questioning" of his followers that Socrates sought to understand human nature. Wisdom for him was honest self-knowledge, freed of hubris and ego protection and inflation. Unfortunately, this great man left no written account of his philosophy and teachings, perhaps considering the preservation of his life-work to be an act of the self-righteousness and self-aggrandizement he sought to expose in human nature. Fortunately, much of Socrates' teaching and his methodology were preserved in the many dialogues written by his greatest student, Plato. In these dozens of documents, we have access to the rich treasures of the most profound thinking ever produced by mankind.

The Evolution of Guilt

The idea of sin and the need for salvation did not arise in the earliest primitive human mind because the idea of morality is a higher level of consciousness and reasoning than their developing brain was capable of achieving. Animals can be trained to obey commands, and like humans, they sometimes disobey or displease their master. Domesticated animals seem to show guilt, or shame when they are chastised by their human owner. Many dog owners swear that their pet knows they have done wrong and the pitiful look in their eyes is clearly repentance, certainly a plea for forgiveness. "How could you stay mad at that furry brown spaniel with such huge, teary eyes?" In spite of this "human like" behavior, science disagrees: animals cannot "feel" guilt because their cognitive capacity is limited, and they cannot understand concepts or symbolic ideas. They can learn and respond habitually, but so far as we know, cannot think or ponder their behavior. **Right** and **wrong** are categories for more highly developed brains, the sentient, conscious mind; animals probably only know the learned categories of **reward** and **punishment.** Animals, therefore cannot "sin" because they are not mentally capable or morally aware.

At some point in hominid evolution, the human brain passed the other animals in cognitive capacity, becoming self-aware and introspective, and eventually morally aware. The birth of "guilt" was a significant development for humankind, one that has troubled us mercilessly ever since. And yet, it may also be argued that "guilt" is such a strong motivator that some societal advances have happened only because of a "guilt trip." Where would we get so many doctors and lawyers and preachers without at least some guilt-inducing mothers? Of course, we know that "guilt" is often a mental health problem rather than a moral problem. Feeling guilty can be a symptom of neurosis, totally unrelated to some actual "sin" or heinous conduct. However, such false guilt inevitably leads to unhappy and unhealthy lives, whereas appropriate guilt often leads to restitution, an effort to make amends for one's harmful behavior, to pay one's debt. Appropriate guilt can be relieved by correction, penance and forgiveness, and thus has great potential for producing better human beings, raising the standards for "fully human."

From a semantics perspective the words "guilt" and "shame" are quite different, though in common usage we often interchange them. "Guilt" is a familiar term in courts of law and to all TV watchers. "Guilty" is a legal judgment, a finding that the facts presented support the conclusion that the person accused actually **did it.** So, guilt is an official status in the legal world. But not everyone found legally guilty is remorseful, sorry for their crime; some may actually be innocent, but probably most of the unrepentant are guilty but don't care. They show no contrition, offer no apology, and experience no **shame**. Shame is a painful feeling of humiliation or distress caused by the consciousness of one's wrong or foolish behavior. It is similar to "embarrassment" only a hundred times stronger. For our purposes here let us consider **"Guilt" as an external judgment and disapproval** of our actions—what others think about us. **"Shame" is an internal emotion aroused by our own self-judgment**—what we think about ourselves. We speak of people who are troubled by "guilt" but it is more accurate in this book's context and semantics to describe them as troubled by "shame." The distinction is important in the discussion of sin and evil, as well as forgiveness and redemption (Next Chapter).

"Shame" is emotionally painful, but like other pain, it is a warning of danger; if you feel the pain from touching a hot stove you don't enjoy it, but it saves you from death. Shame is the mind's way of telling us we need to change our position (get away from the heat) or change our conduct. It is facilitated by our fear of what others think about us, for rejection or condemnation by our peers is devastating to our self-esteem and our physical health. Shame is real and effective in helping humans become more fully human, more like the ideal, or "more like Jesus" for the Believer.

Early humans and "pre-human" hominids certainly experienced fear of things not understood and not controlled, things such as predatory animals, thunder and lightning, forest fires and earthquakes. These were threats to their existence that they had come to fear by experience, either their own or experiences communicated by their family or clan. Consciousness, and the emergence of what we would call the mind, gave our human ancestors the ability to form actual social relationships with the larger group or clan, beyond the kinship and parental relationships. These social ties were more portentous than the mutual cooperation observed in groups of apes or chimpanzees or other animals. Many species act together in searching for food or in the face of an external threat, but only the developing mind of these early humans produced individuals with such awareness and appreciation for the "other" corresponding to the "myself." By way of comparison, modern human children individually develop mentally within their first four or five years to a degree which probably took evolution fifty thousand years or more to produce in our hominid species, a **moral conscience. (Chapter 15: Being Fully Human** has an extended discussion of conscience and of children's stages of moral development.)

Our Inner Supervisor: The Conscience

What is the conscience? Is there even such a thing? Does everyone have a conscience? In common discourse the conscience is seen as an alarm system alerting us to right or wrong actions or behaviors, an inner voice or an uneasy "feeling" about our choices. Some experience it as an "inner light" or an internal coach or guide, and most people experience some regret or remorse if they violate that inner guidance system. Conscience seems to serve to remind us of our moral values, the things we believe or the standards we have already set. We are sometimes discomfited by a "guilty conscience" when we occasionally fail to listen to that inner voice. We outlined in **Chapter 13** the theory that humans are born with a built-in sensitivity which can distinguish "right" and "wrong" as categories in our mind, preset containers for the rules, values, mores, or norms we learn from our society. We compared "conscience" to the eye in being sensitive to particular impulses: the conscience senses **right** as the eye senses **light**.

The capacity to distinguish the categories of RIGHT and WRONG is an innate ability present at birth in all normal humans, probably empty but quickly filled by "lessons" in the child's environment. Almost everything one considers "right" probably comes from culture—beginning with parents or family, and continuing input from schools, groups, laws and religious teaching. C.S. Lewis has a marvelous treatise in **Chapter 12** which demonstrates the existence of "moral law" built into humans as much as the Law of Gravity is built into the Universe. Jean-Jacques Rousseau, the great Swiss-born philosopher, writer, and political theorist, part of the Great Enlightenment, *"There is therefore at the bottom of our hearts an innate principle of justice and virtue, by which, in spite of our maxims, we judge our own actions or those of others to be good or evil; and it is this principle that I call conscience."*[30]

It is acknowledged for clarity that some few people do not seem to have this basic moral equipment in their brain structure—the rare individuals who seem to have no conscience, who feel no remorse and cannot experience empathy; these are people we call "psychopaths" which is a mental illness term often applied to serial killers and to political monsters such as Hitler and Stalin.

Socrates, the prince of Greek philosophers, taught reliance on what he called his "daimōnic sign," an inner voice he heard when he was about to make a mistake or do a moral wrong. Interestingly Socrates used the Greek word meaning "demons" or "angels" to describe his inner moral guide; this reminds one of the cartoon depictions of a conflicted person having a little angel on one shoulder whispering in the right ear, and a little devil on the other shoulder whispering wicked advice. It was similar to the phrase used by Lincoln about making moral decisions by listening to *"our better angels."*

Our Better Angels

Conscience can cut both ways, it seems, warning us not to do wrong and violate our operational values or rules, but our conscience can also press us to act in accordance with even higher moral values than we have learned from society, and to "seek the highest good" or some Universal value beyond all moral requirements, to even sacrifice one's life for a higher purpose. Some people apparently develop such "over-active" moral consciences that drive them toward the good rather than deterring them from the bad. Most of us "feel guilty" if we go against our conscience on minor follies, but some people—heroes and saints, perhaps—feel a guilty conscience if they fail to live up to the super high goals that only they can see.

Is Our Conscience Our Guide?

As acknowledged before, the conscience is not an infallible guide because it is formed and shaped in an imperfect world, and its content may include abominable rules and values (as might be the case of a child raised in a family and culture of criminals). The Godfather families in the two movies taught the children a very strict Roman Catholic religion, but also the Mafia values and standards required for the success in the Mob. So, a mobster might feel guilty about missing the Sunday Mass, but have no guilty feelings about shooting to death a *stoolie* he considered a "rat" because he talked to the cops. Socrates taught that having beliefs was an admirable thing, but beliefs must be **right beliefs** to have value, with "right" being defined as holding up to rational scrutiny. This is part of what Socrates was referring to in his famous maxim: ***An unexamined life is not worth living***. As another, probably less-wise man said: "An easy conscience may just be a bad memory." Only the well examined conscience is trustworthy.

The term "conscience" comes from the Latin "conscientia" which mean **knowledge** *(scientia)* **shared** *(con)*, which implies a conversation within, an internal discussion between ourselves and WHO? We all engage in this inner conversation at times but who are we talking to? Sometimes it seems the other voice is a trusted older brother we bounce ideas off of and expect only mild criticism. Regarding the conscience it may seem that we are the defendant or subject, and God is the examiner. Another view is that our **subjective self** is being examined and challenged by our **rational, objective self**. Those in the Freudian tradition see the inner companion as the Super-Ego, the parental voice trying to control the passions and impulses. Attending to our conscience is always introspection, an inward-looking exercise, a subjective look at who we are and what we believe, and since it implies a judgment about ourselves our conscience certainly has an influence on our self-image and self-esteem.

Our Conscience Versus Other's

Conscience is subjective and internal, and applies to you and your life and behavior. Whether your values and rules applied by your conscience are objectively true or not, they are the rules which guide the judgment your conscience renders. Your conscience may be based on entirely different beliefs than those of your neighbor or relatives. Your conscience may be bothered immensely by abortion because you believe it involves killing a child—which is wrong, while another person may not believe that abortion is wrong because they do not see the unborn fetus as a person, and so their conscience is quiet.

Perhaps you are deeply troubled by poor people, homeless or street people, and you feel compelled to help the panhandler who stands on the street corner, giving whatever you have or can afford without question. Yet you know that your friends and most of society seem to think you are foolish to pay attention to those people: "You know they'll just take your dollar and go get some beer!" Some cities have posted warning signs discouraging people making contributions to the beggars, suggesting that your dollar or two only encourages the poor to continue to publicly beg rather than seek the official help from the organizations equipped to give professional help. Your conscience usually won't let you look the other way or carefully avoid eye contact with the destitute person with the crayon sign on cardboard. It may be true that your little help may be "enabling" as professionals call it, helping the afflicted continue with patchwork help rather than submit to "official helpers." Whose conscience do you follow? The more fully human we become, the more persistent our conscience becomes, guided by rational thought and self-examination so that our conscience is true to our deepest values.

Peace of Mind and Soul

One of the marks of "happiness" which always shows up in research projects and national polls of a great number of people is "peace with myself." Though reported in different ways and using different terms the fundamental idea is **being satisfied with who you are and how you have lived**. Though this stage of comfort with your identity as a person is more common in older people than young, it is not just the domain of the elderly. Many elderly people are sad and angry and dissatisfied, and many idealistic younger people enjoy their lives and are pleased with their life and their future. It is not the number of years one has lived but how the stresses and conflicts attendant to life have been resolved. As poets describe it, "Being true to yourself," being able to look the guy in the mirror in the eye every day, without wincing. To repeat an old adage "*A clear conscience might be just a bad memory*," and so we must not fool ourselves by putting our failures out of mind. Fooling one's self is being the biggest kind of fool of all, though it is actually hard to fool yourself in your solitary moments. As Socrates did in his life the person who is fully human will be one who honestly examines himself. But it is definitely true for most people, that after sober reflection, being comfortable with yourself is a very pleasant and healthy condition, a feeling which might very well be called "Happiness."

For Believers, the approval of the "man in the mirror" is not enough, and the more mature and healthier minded of Believers find satisfaction and peace in the spiritual mirror which reassures them that they are loved and accepted completely by God. The spiritual mirror may show flaws and blemishes and scars and even smudges on our nose, but the God who is looking back at us is smiling and welcoming, apparently pleased to see us. It is one of the audacious assumptions of happy Christians that when they read of God saying "This is my beloved son with whom I am well pleased" they imagine that God is also saying it to them ("son" or "daughter" or just "child.") God doesn't just love us in an abstract way, He is pleased with us, even knowing our faults. **Jesus loves me, this I know, for the Bible tells me so."** To be at peace with one's self and at peace with God is the working definition of Happiness here. There may be more to happiness than this, but nothing less can be true happiness. It is comforting to believe as song writer Bill Gaither wrote:

"The One who knows me best loves me most"[131]

Chapter 18

SALVATION AND REDEMPTION

"I'd rather laugh with the sinners than cry with the saints."
BILLY JOEL

ONE OF THE ODDITIES THAT SKEPTICS FIND AMUSing about Protestant Christians, especially those groups labeled *Evangelical*, is the quaint notion of "getting saved" or "being saved." Even the most unlettered true believer will quickly and unashamedly approach strangers on the street and ask "Are you saved?" This is of course, an intrusive and touchy question for most people, and many more of these strangers quickly head for the exit than decide to head for heaven. While most Christian groups agree that sinners need a Savior, they don't personally, aggressively "push" their religion on strangers. But for the broad evangelical Christian groups, "getting sinners saved" is their dominant driving impulse. Telling people about salvation through Jesus is their mission in life, for they believe that being "lost" is the natural and normal condition of all mankind. *"For all have sinned and fall short of the glory of God,"* their Bible warns them (Romans 3:23).

SALVATION AND REDEMPTION

Hard Sell Christians

Evangelical Christians sincerely believe they individually are responsible for rescuing the "lost", "spreading the Gospel," "soul winning", carrying out the Great Commission: ***"Therefore go and make disciples of all nations, baptizing them in the name of the Father and of the Son and of the Holy Spirit..."*** (Matthew 28:9). For some Christians, failing to spread the Gospel is to disobey Jesus, and therefore to risk one's own salvation. With this mindset, it is not hard to understand the passion of Evangelicals, why they can't simply let people alone to find God, ***or not***, on their own time and in their own way. It is that ***or not*** that haunts evangelical Christians: "if they go to hell, it will be my fault if I don't tell them about Jesus."

A seminary class was discussing the fate of people in darkest Africa who have never heard the Gospel. "Will they go to Hell if they have not heard about Jesus?" "No," most of the class agreed, "They are innocent in God's eyes, like little children who can't understand." One student raised his hand, "If we don't '***go into all the world and preach the Gospel***," won't we be condemned for not obeying the Great Commission?" Most agreed, including the Professor. The troubled student continued: "But if we go tell them, and they **don't believe**, then **they** are guilty, and so are lost. Right?" Most nodded their head. The class is silent for a minute, and then the same student spoke up again: "If we don't go tell, we will probably go to Hell; if we go and they don't believe, they'll go to Hell." He pauses to let that sink in. "It looks like somebody's going to Hell, doesn't it? **It's either us or them.**"

Witness is an important word for Believers, describing the process of sharing the Gospel, trying to let the world know about Jesus and the Gospel. Jesus used the word at the end of His earthly stay, His very last recorded words to the disciples, reported in all four Gospels and Acts:

> *"**Then he** (Jesus) **opened their minds so they could understand the Scriptures. He told them, "This is what is written: The Messiah will suffer and rise from the dead on the third day, and repentance for the forgiveness of sins will be preached in his name to all nations, beginning at Jerusalem. You***

are witnesses of these things. I am going to send you what my Father has promised; but stay in the city until you have been clothed with power from on high." (Luke 24:45-49) (Emphasis added)

The Greek word translated "witness" is μάρτυς, or transliterated: "martyr." Most of the time "martyr" means one who dies for his faith, or faces severe persecution for his religious beliefs. Being Jesus' "witnesses" into all the world was a dangerous mission and all the disciples were martyred, except John, who was severely persecuted and tortured, but died in old age. To be a Christian was to be a "witness," a martyr, one who tells the truth, shares the Jesus story at any cost. That first generation of Christians was very good at it, spreading Christianity to the whole Roman Empire within 60 years, even in the face of unspeakable torture and death for Roman public entertainment. Thus, the slogan of the Church came to be **"The blood of Martyrs is the seed of the Church,"** thanks to Tertullian, a second century Christian apologist.

The Marching Orders

Christianity has traditionally considered ***The Great Commission*** (Matthew 28:9) the "marching orders" for the church, for every Believer, and not just clerics and missionaries. "Go make disciples" Jesus said. Thus, those who follow traditional Christianity feel compelled to share their faith in all their world of work, home, friends, neighborhoods, nation and world. "Personal witnessing" means letting people you associate with know that you are a follower of Christ, and sharing your religious experience with all who are interested. Some "witnesses" are more driven and bolder, going further than their associates want to go, pushing their religion to the point of intrusion and rudeness.

Perhaps it may help Skeptics and other targets of evangelism to understand the urgency displayed by "pushy" Christians if you hear some more words of Jesus that disturb Believers: *"If anyone is ashamed of me and my words in this adulterous and sinful generation, the Son of Man will be ashamed of them when he comes in his Father's glory with the holy angels."* (Mark 8:38) And this: *"But whoever disowns me before others, I will disown before my Father in heaven."* (Matthew 10:33) Some overzealous, so-called "pushy" Christians fear

SALVATION AND REDEMPTION

that silence about their faith is being ashamed of Jesus, or that keeping their religion hidden is the same as denying it. Discretion is not denial.

Fortunately, most Christians have learned how to let their love for Jesus shine out in normal life experiences and normal conversations, with occasional opportunities to express their faith in words appropriate to the time and circumstances, and the interest of the person listening. Believers reading this may be conflicted, for the command to witness for Christ is compelling, but many "witnesses" feel uncomfortable and ill-equipped to "share the Gospel." We know we should, but it is awkward and even embarrassing to initiate such a discussion with a non-believer; it is so hard to do it right! And if I mess up it will drive that person even further away from God! There are classes on effective witnessing for Believers who want to learn how to be better witnesses, and this book does not pretend to make the Great Commission easy. However, a bit of wisdom from Dr. D. T. Niles may help Believers who are uneasy with this assignment. **"EVANGELISM IS JUST ONE BEGGAR TELLING ANOTHER BEGGAR WHERE TO FIND BREAD."**

Beggars helping other beggars

Just as a hungry beggar will not resent you telling them where to get some food, neither will most people you know resent it if you care about whatever troubles them, whatever empty spot they may have. Most non-believers aren't interesting in "saving their souls" —they first want help "saving their job" or "saving their home" or "saving their empty stomach." Friendship comes before Discipleship, Caring beats Preaching. To act in kindness IS preaching Christ. The words will come later if needed.

Who's A Sinner?

As discussed in the previous chapter, most skeptics don't see themselves as "sinners", or in some way "lost." For many, living a good moral life, obeying laws and practicing good citizenship seems to be attainable by most people without resorting to some supernatural religion. Maybe the poor, the down and out, the reprobate, the addicted, or the criminal class need a "savior", but not the well-educated and successful lawyer, doctor, physicist, business owner or others like themselves. Even if these good, upright people go to a church, synagogue or mosque, it is not for the cleansing their personal sins. Perhaps they enjoy the pageantry or the rituals, and may even contribute financially; but they are largely immune to the occasional clerical calls to repent or to seek divine forgiveness. They don't feel "lost" in some metaphysical sense and so "getting saved" is usually meaningless to them.

Perhaps the Believers have inadvertently allowed widespread caricatures of sin to multiply as they allowed God to be caricatured as "policeman," "butler," "doting grandfather," or "disapproving father." If you ask a varied group of people on the street, "What is sin?" you would probably get a list instead of a definition. Most people probably think in terms of "ten commandments" items: lying, stealing, adultery, cheating, bullying, murder, and maybe a few "softer sins" such as gossip, rudeness, bigotry, or greed. Except in a few religious circles, most people probably don't connect God to such "softer sins," but view them as offenses against other people, or society in general *(By the way, the Bible doesn't "soften" such behavior)*. The public vaguely understands that some bad acts are **illegal** and other "sins" are **legal** but are "bad" or "immoral" or "impolite." A phrase recently came into usage for such questionable behavior: "*Lawful but Awful*." Even religious groups sometimes distinguish between "sins" by labeling some lesser sins as "venal" and other terrible sins as "mortal sins," with drastically different consequences in the afterlife. But does God categorize sins? Are there "soft sins" like "white lies? Are there "venal sins" and "mortal sins" as some believe?

Theologians tend to pass up the lists of **sins** and focus on the concept of **Sin.** To be sure the Bible has its own long list of sins which are prohibited, especially in the earlier part, the Old Testament. The New Testament presents a more evolved understanding of Sin as being an offense against God, a matter of attitude or the "heart" more than a matter of deeds. Jesus explained it this way after being accused of sin for violating some Jewish ritual: *"For out of the heart come evil thoughts, murders, adulteries, fornications, thefts, false witness, slanders. These are what defile a person; but eating with unwashed hands does not defile them."* (Matthew 15:19-20). For Jesus, sins are just a symptom of Sin, a wrong attitude or mind-set which eventually manifests itself in external behaviors, words or deeds. This "heart disease" view permeates the New Testament, such as James described in an earlier quote (James 1:14-15), with our own "evil desires" entice us and we think about it and then act upon the desire—committing the act of sin, willingly and with gusto.

It is also clear that the New Testament theology does not attribute **any** sin or evil to God. In fact, sin is often personified, seen as a thing or entity in itself, frequently identified with the Devil or his deceitful machinations. Jesus had harsh words for the hypocritical Pharisees: *"You belong to your father, the devil, and you want to carry out your father's desires. He was a murderer from the beginning, not holding to the truth, for there is no truth in him. When he lies, he speaks his native language, for he is a liar and the father of lies."* (John 8:44) The New Testament couches the life of Jesus as a battle with the Devil: *"The one who does what is sinful is of the devil, because the devil has been sinning from the beginning. The reason the Son of God appeared was to destroy the devil's work."* (I John 3:8) Paul describes the struggle between good and evil as a *spiritual war:*

"Put on the full armor of God, so that you can take your stand against the devil's schemes. For our struggle is not against flesh and blood, but against the rulers, against the authorities, against the

powers of this dark world and against the spiritual forces of evil in the heavenly realms. Therefore, put on the full armor of God, so that when the day of evil comes, you may be able to stand your ground, and after you have done everything, to stand" (Ephesians 6:11-13)

The New Testament views Sin as a mortal enemy in a cosmic battle with God to lay claim to Humanity; a Holy God against a powerful Satan, with satanic powers potent and pernicious, but not supreme. God does not tempt us to sin, but the devil can and does tempt us mercilessly, but **cannot make us sin**. We have a choice because God gave us "free will," including the freedom to sin, which is to choose Satan instead of God. (See again **Chapter 16** for further discussion of "free will.")

Christian theology over centuries has come to define sin as a moral defect in mankind, not so much like the traditional "original sin" connected with Adam, but something fundamentally wrong in human nature, something dark and disturbing. Acts of sin of various kinds are not seen as the problem, but rather as the symptom. A person is not a sinner because he sins, but rather he sins because he is a sinner. In earlier discussions about **human nature** a great deal was written about the tragedy of the "human condition," the subject of famous Greek dramas 2500 years ago and of many modern novels, plays and movies. A fatal character flaw eventually destroys the hero in a tragic ending, ruined by greed, hubris, selfishness, hatred or some other deadly defect. Christian theology fixes the blame for this universal spoiling of God's original creation, the creation of man in God's image. Whether there ever was a time when humans bore the "image of God" unblemished or not, there seems to be a universal longing for some lost perfection, some "Garden of Eden" in the distant past of mankind, a cultural memory. We sense what we could be, realize what we should be, and finally acknowledge that we are not what we long to be (again). Perhaps this disappointed longing is an illusionary memory of a time in our life when we were good, when we were pure and worthy, maybe in our innocent childhood or in our high esteem days at 19 or 21, a time when we were invulnerable, and had the magical life ahead of us. Our human nature sooner or later breaks through for most of us, and we come to terms with the fact that we are imperfect creatures, a mixture of good and evil, a hybrid angel/devil when we face our truth. We recognize our moral frailty and then we have to recognize and anticipate our physical expiration date. Mankind is a sad creature as many authors have described. Shakespeare's Macbeth (Act 5, scene 5, lines 16–27) says it well:

> Life's but a walking shadow, a poor player
> That struts and frets his hour upon the stage
> And then is heard no more. It is a tale
> Told by an idiot, full of sound and fury,
> Signifying nothing.[132]

If, perchance, this gruesome description of our human condition has depressed the Reader to the point of either a stiff drink or a bridge jump, do not despair. The Good News of Christianity is that human nature can be redeemed, our rotten center can be repaired and our image of God can be restored. We are not promised angelic status, but we have been offered "sainthood." The New Testament calls Christians "saints" in a number of places. ***"Paul, an apostle of Jesus Christ by the will of God, to the saints which are at Ephesus, and to the faithful in Christ Jesus."*** (Ephesians 1:1 **KJV**) ***"Now therefore you [Gentiles] are no more strangers and foreigners, but fellow citizens with the saints, and of the household of God;*** (Ephesians 2:19 KJV) ***"Paul and Timotheus, the servants of Jesus Christ, to all the saints in Christ Jesus which are at Philippi*** (Philippians 1:1 KJV) Newer translations use "holy people" instead of "saints," for "saints" is not culturally appreciated today.

These first century people referred to as "saints" are not to be confused with the later Roman Catholic beatification of saints such as St. Thomas, St. Patrick or St. Elizabeth. The Roman Catholic saints are considered extraordinarily holy people, far above the run of the mill Christian; these hundreds of recognized Saints were granted sainthood after their death, and after verified miracles done in response to those who prayed for their help. They had to have a sterling resume, as well, usually a life of service and good deeds. The "saints" Paul wrote to in these and other passages were not dead and were not particularly "holy." Some of these Christians about 60 A.D. were former heathens, prostitutes and idol worshipers who had believed on Christ and had been forgiven and accepted by God, but some of them were still just "baby Christians," learning to live like Jesus but still a work in progress.

Reading Second Corinthians will confirm that Paul had to correct and chastise some of the new "saints" and even had to threaten one or two; but still, they were labeled as "saints" because they had accepted both their sinfulness and God's salvation in Jesus Christ. Their "condition" was not yet "perfect" but their "position" with God was changed completely: they belonged to Him, not the Devil or their animal nature. Paul describes the process as "reconciliation with God," (2 Corinthians 5:18) returning to a relationship with God, being counted as "children of God," treated as "righteous" as a gift from God, not a position they had earned by being good (or anything else). Like the Prodigal Son in Jesus' parable (Luke 15:11-32), when they turned to the Father, the Father embraced them and enfolded them in His arms of love. They were somebody now, somebody "new." They were not perfected, but were made new. That is **Salvation**.

In the Old Testament the concept of "salvation" largely centers on the rescue and preservation of the nation, the Hebrew people. From the entrance of Joshua and the tribes of Israel into the land we now know as Palestine, the wandering Hebrews settled into their new homeland only after decades of war and conflict with the existing population—the Philistines, Moabites, etc., Naturally, these previous occupants did not welcome the invaders, and time after time the loose federation of Hebrew tribes was in danger of extinction. Miracle after miracle is recounted in the Israelite conquest legends—God came unexpectedly and cleverly rescued the tribal armies, "snatching victory from the jaws of defeat." Their times of "salvation" brought peace and prosperity to these "chosen people" for a while. But repeatedly, about every forty years, the memories of miraculous rescues faded, their trust in God was diluted, and they turned to other gods, idols popular with their neighbors. Thus, it was largely idol worship that was their recurring national sin, a sin punished by renewed oppression from enemies. The prophets told them clearly:

> *"Oh, that salvation for Israel would come out of Zion! When the LORD restores his people, let Jacob rejoice and Israel be glad."* (Psalm 14:7)

SALVATION AND REDEMPTION

"Save us, Lord our God, and gather us from the nations, that we may give thanks to your holy name and glory in your praise." (Psalm 106:47) *"But the Israelites said to the Lord, "We have sinned. Do with us whatever you think best, but please rescue us now." * (Judges 10:15) ***Then the sons of Israel said to Samuel, "Do not stop crying out to the Lord our God for us, that he may rescue us from the hand of the Philistines."*** (1 Samuel 7:8)

But the Old Testament also reveals the evolution of sin, a changing understanding of the nature of sin and redemption. The recognition of sin in the first few hundred years of Israel in the Promised Land was almost exclusively group disobedience, the sins of the nation. The annual high Day of Atonement was the once-a-year entry of the High Priest into the Holy of Holies in the Temple, there to make sacrifices and pray for the forgiveness of the sins of Israel. The sin of individuals was reported and condemned harshly, often with a penalty of death, but even these were almost always tied to the idea of the corporate sin of the whole nation. When Joshua led the Hebrews in the destruction of Jericho, God forbade taking any of the booty—jewels, gold, silver. ***"But the Israelites were unfaithful in regard to the devoted things; Achan son of Karmi, the son of Zimri, the son of Zerah, of the tribe of Judah, took some of them. So, the Lord's anger burned against Israel."*** (Joshua 7:1)

Achan could not resist the temptation of all the riches left in Jericho, so he secretly hid some of the loot under his tent (bars of gold and silver, brass bowls, a beautiful robe). No one saw his skullduggery. When Joshua led the Israelites into the next battle, they suffered a great defeat. Joshua discovered that God had punished the nation because of Achan's sin, which was soon uncovered. Achan and all his family and livestock were slaughtered for his sin, and God's blessing returned to Joshua and the tribes.

This group punishment for sin is explicit in Exodus 20:5 ***"You shall not bow down to them or worship them; for I, the Lord your God, am a jealous God, punishing the children for the sin of the*** *parents to the third and fourth generation of those who hate me."* Of course, we consider that theology as an early stage of evolution in understanding God, and later books in the Bible counter this mistaken view. It is true that the sin or failings of parents often have a lasting negative effect on their children and grandchildren—sin has its consequences. This is one of the laws of nature, a law of psychology—**we reap what we sow**, (Galatians 6:7) both in our lives and in those who follow us. This law of God may seem slow or delayed, but it is relentless. God eventually brings justice.

Moral Laws

As C. S. Lewis explained so completely in **Chapter 15**, just as there are physical laws governing the material world there are also moral laws governing the Universe, though we have not systematically cataloged these moral laws. "Karma" is the popular name given for the original Hindu belief, the idea that there are always consequences from our actions, and that what we do, good or ill, will eventually come back upon us. "What goes around, comes around" is another popularization of this law in modern culture. There is a fairly widespread belief in our society that the "bad" gets punished and the "good" gets rewarded. This is a "faith statement" that often is left unsubstantiated and often seems contradicted by what we observe (e.g., "***Why do bad things happen to good people?***") Joshua and the Hebrew tribes followed the Old Testament version of this law of God, implementing harsh justice (death) on Achan and his kin, punishing the many for the sins of one. They believed that facilitating God's law was obeying God's law, administering God's justice immediately rather than wait for God's later punishment of Achan and his family. Based on their "tribal god" view, their early theology, they believed God blessed the faithful tribes and rewarded the group because sin (sinners) was eradicated from their midst. "Get rid of the Bad Apples" was their theory of salvation. Readers may find that this view of justice seems remarkably similar to modern theories of law and order, with penalties and punishments sometimes reflecting class status, race or ethnic origin. Jails and prisons are filled with "bad apples" who just happen to be predominantly darker, poorer and less educated.

However, with a more mature understanding of God's nature, the Semite tribes eventually modified their views on justice, and put more trust in God's timing and balance. We now accept the blame for creating a toxic family environment rather than blaming God for creating this natural law. Sin, we now realize, is a personal matter between each individual and God, a betrayal of the spiritual bond, valuing something more than our love for God. In a fundamental way, all sin is idolatry—worshiping another god. The original commandment was "***You shall have no other gods before Me***" (Exodus 20:2-3). After some 1500 years of Jewish teachers refining this theology into over 600 specific religious laws, Jesus condensed the whole Old Testament Law into two beautiful sentences: ***"'Love the Lord your God with all your heart and with all your soul and with all your mind.' This is the first and greatest commandment. And the second is like it: 'Love your neighbor as yourself.' All the Law and the Prophets depend on these two commandments."*** (Matthew 22:37-40) The <u>First Commandment</u>, given to Moses, had evolved over time, to become the <u>Great Commandment</u>. To **love Go**d and **Love Others** is the ultimate requirement—a mutual love relationship between the Creator and the Created, rather than a perfect performance in keeping all of the added rules and commandments. **Faith, not works.**

The Exodus as Creation

The Exodus was the central event of the Old Testament, the Act of God that created Israel and made them the People of God. Through Abraham and the other Patriarchs God had become increasingly a real and identifiable God to the Semite wandering sheep herders, who eventually ended up in Egypt during a regional drought and shortage of food. From their high point of being the family of Joseph the Deputy Pharaoh, the twelve tribes who had descended from Jacob now fell into their final state of slavery in Egyptian brick yards. They still had their tribal and familial identity and some of their old religious rituals and traditions but they were leaderless for over 300 years. Without priest or prophet or sacred texts they were "lost in the desert" as a people. But God was still with them, still honoring His covenant with Abraham some 500 years earlier. Moses was born to a Hebrew mother in a time of great crisis and disruption.

Over the centuries, the Israelites had to come to an understanding of both parts of that concept. What does it mean for God to be God? And what does it mean to be his people? The exodus provided the Israelites the most basic understanding of the nature of God. He was the kind of God who heard the cries of oppressed slaves, and entered human history to bring deliverance and freedom. "I will be your God" was an idea defined by the exodus (Exodus 6:7, Leviticus 26:12-13). It would take many years, even centuries for them to understand all the implications of that act of grace. But their understanding of a God of love and grace and mercy began on the banks of the Sea of Reeds (the Red Sea) as recounted in Exodus 14. They learned that this God was concerned with the helpless and hopeless of humanity, with those who had no power to affect their own future. The Israelites were reminded frequently through their prophets and leaders: "Remember, you once were slaves, you once were strangers in another land" (Exodus 22:21) "I am the Lord your God, who brought you out of the land of Egypt, out of the house of slavery." (Exodus 20:2)

The Exodus told about God and His self-revelation in history. The Sinai narratives are rooted in that historical deliverance and encounter, but focus on how the people are to respond to that revelation. They must always remember that all of Abraham's descendants were "lost" in Egyptian slavery, and they were rescued by the will and power of Yahweh. The tribes of Jacob were rescued from oblivion, and they belong to the God who saved them. The introductory speech to the Sinai narratives helps us understand this relationship between God's grace and the people's response to grace (Exodus19:4-6).

> *You yourselves have seen what I did to Egypt, and how I carried you on eagles' wings and brought you to myself. Now if you obey me fully and keep my covenant, then out of all nations you will be my treasured possession. Although the whole earth is mine, you will be for me a kingdom of priests and a holy nation.' These are the words you are to speak to the Israelites.* (Exodus 19:4-6)

Poets and Prophets Enlarge Vision of Sin and Salvation

The Old Testament presents two major understandings about sin. Early on sin was primarily thought to be the disobedience of the nation of Israel or transgression of God's many detailed rules (legalism). The solution to taking away sin and guilt was participation in the temple rituals of offerings and animal sacrifice. Many believers today believe, as most Old Testament writers did, that sin is violation of God's laws (legalism), so sin is still understood as offense against God. Many also believe that the only sufficient solution to sin and guilt is blood sacrifice, though the sacrifice is not that of temple ritual but is the blood sacrifice of Jesus on the cross. Some church groups such as The Roman Catholic Church have a ritual sacrifice in every official Mass, believing that the symbolic bread and wine miraculously become the actual body and blood of Jesus (a doctrine called "transubstantiation").

While much of the Old Testament is taken with legalism, punishment for disobeying God and solving sin through ritual temple sacrifice, some of the prophets take an entirely different view toward law, sin, and temple ritual. For example, the author of Isaiah 1 decries the condition of the state of Judah and includes these lines:

> *"The multitude of your sacrifices—what are they to me?" says the Lord.*
> *"I have more than enough of burnt offerings, of rams and the fat of fattened animals;*
> *I have no pleasure in the blood of bulls and lambs and goats."* (Isaiah 1:1)

> *"Wash and make yourselves clean.*
> *Take your evil deeds out of my sight; stop doing wrong.*
> *Learn to do right; seek justice.*
> *Defend the oppressed. Take up the cause of the fatherless;*
> *plead the case of the widow."* (Isaiah 1:11, 16)

Amos 5;21-24 says this,

> *"I hate, I despise your religious festivals; your assemblies are a stench to me.*
> *Even though you bring me burnt offerings and grain offerings, I will not accept them. Though you bring choice fellowship offerings,*
> *I will have no regard for them.*
> *Away with the noise of your songs!*
> *I will not listen to the music of your harps.*
> *But let justice roll on like a river, righteousness like a never-failing stream!*

Sin is still understood as relationship, but it is no longer exclusively a relationship between people and God. Now it is a relationship among people based on a right relationship with God, treating others as God has treated you. The emphasis is on social justice as well as moral behavior to please God.

The Old Testament is filled throughout with concern for the marginalized, such as Deuteronomy 27:19 "**Do not deprive the alien or the fatherless of justice, or take the cloak of the widow as a pledge**; or Proverbs 22:22: "**Do not exploit the poor because they are poor and do not crush the needy in court.**" This concern for the marginalized is pervasive in Jesus' words, but it was up to Isaiah and Amos to introduce a new orientation: justice for people INSTEAD OF ritual sacrifice, a new heart not a new law.

And the poet of Psalm 40:6-8 chimes in: "***Sacrifice and offering you did not desire—but my ears you have opened—burnt offerings and sin offerings you did not require. Then I said, "Here I am, I have come—it is written about me in the scroll. I desire to do your will, my God; your law is within my heart.*** Here and elsewhere the expanding understanding of God leads to an expanding idea of what a relationship with God means: no longer is it a "spot" cleaning through sacrifice and then living life as always. Now the vision is establishing a personal relationship with God, including forgiveness, and then living all of life in a way pleasing to God, a way that maintains "salvation." Until Jesus made it so abundantly clear several hundred years later, this radical idea of a "new heart," God's "laws written on our hearts" and a completely "changed life" was only partially understood and implemented. Moving from a sporadic and episodic "forgiveness" to a permanent, growing and continuing love relationship with God is the essential idea of redemption. An object in modern life can be lost or stolen, or given as a pawn to a lender; getting that possession back is called "redeeming" or "buying back." Metaphorically, redemption is God buying us back after we were lost to God's enemy, "redeeming" and restoring that which God had made in the first place, and now and paid to recover.

The broad scope of the Old Testament is, in essence, a "salvation history" or "the Redemption Story," the overarching story of how God chose and saved the people of Israel and preserved at least a remnant of them for His purposes. It shows a growing or evolving recognition of sin as an individual matter, rather than a group or national affront to God. And the appreciation by the poets and prophets of Israel for the infinite patience and love of God for His children provided the groundwork for a more father-like God. Christians regard this act of God in preserving Israel as a necessary part of God's ultimate plan: the full revelation of God in Jesus Christ, "at the right time." The Apostle Paul is the primary apologist for the Jewish religion being the necessary and sufficient forerunner for the Gospel. He, long before others, saw the historic pattern of God's preparation in the Old Covenant as the fulfillment in the New Covenant by the sacrifice brought by Jesus. *"You see, at just the right time, when we were still powerless, Christ died for the ungodly."* (Romans 5:6) *But when the set time had fully come, God sent his Son, born of a woman, born under the law, to redeem those under the law, that we might receive adoption to sonship."* (Galatians 4:4-5) God's timing is impeccable, even if we don't figure it out for ourselves. Other authors have adequately addressed how the timing of the Incarnation was exactly perfect for God's plan, Roman legions notwithstanding.

Jesus Saves

Perhaps nothing taught in the New Testament is a clear as the popular but non-biblical slogan: **"Jesus Saves"**. Sometimes in popular culture this thought is converted into a *New Yorker* type cartoon extolling the virtue of some particular bank (e.g., JESUS SAVES—WHY DON'T

YOU?) or maybe as the punch line for some Saturday Night Live type comedy piece. This idea is a "hard sell" to a secular, non-Christian audience, difficult to explain or defend, perhaps the greatest challenges to an apologist. And yet "**Jesus Saves**" sums up the whole Christian Gospel, one of the most distinct and uncompromising doctrines of Christianity, perhaps THE central teaching. "*Salvation is found in no one else, for there is no other name under heaven given to mankind by which we must be saved.*" (Acts 4:12) It would be strange if a non-believer reading or hearing this claim **did not** get offended, or immediately write off Christianity as a narrow minded, rejecting and exclusionary cult. "**What a turn-off!**" (Emphasis added) Who wants to be associated with a religion that has such a rigid, divisive, and judgmental approach to rest of the world?

But it gets worse, dear non-believers: The New Testament hammers away at the centrality of Jesus Christ in God's *plan of salvation*. "*For there is one God and one mediator between God and men, the man Christ Jesus,* (1 Timothy 2:5) "*The Father loves the Son and has placed all things in His hands. Whoever believes in the Son has eternal life. Whoever rejects the Son will not see life. Instead, the wrath of God remains on him.*" (John 3:35-36) The harshness of this doctrine, threatening the wrath of God on non-believers, is made even more difficult to explain because of the preceding verses. "*For God so loved the world that he gave his one and only Son, that whoever believes in him shall not perish but have eternal life. For God did not send his Son into the world to condemn the world, but to save the world through him.*" (John 3:16-17) Now, that's more like it—love and eternal life, no condemnation from this God of love! But then, there it is again in the next verse: *Jesus or else*: "*Whoever believes in him is not condemned, but whoever does not believe stands condemned already because they have not believed in the name of God's one and only Son.*" (John 3:18) How can this God be so willing to love everyone (the "world") and yet so quick to condemn those who do not believe in Jesus? Why didn't this Almighty God simply grant blanket forgiveness for everyone, and "save" the world, condemning no one? If **Jesus saves**, **who** does He save and **how**?

SALVATION AND REDEMPTION

Jesus Saves: But How?

Let us begin an attempt to explain and defend this key article of the Christian faith, referencing other sections of this book, some preceding and some following later. The difficulty for religious skeptics in accepting a "Jesus Only" answer lies in understanding and appreciating the central focus of this book: a word-portrait of a particular God, the *Jesus-like God*, who has progressively revealed Himself to an evolving humanity. That detailed description of that particular kind of God is presented in the earlier **Chapter 10, God Is Great, God Is Good.** Based on that extensive discourse about the nature and character of God the Father, three collateral premises are suggested as keys to understanding the seemingly rigid Christian doctrines of sin and salvation. **First**, SIN is a lot more serious and important to God than we thought. **Second**, SIN is a broken *relationship* with God, rather than the breaking of some *rules or laws*. **Third**, God hates SIN, not because it hurts Him, but because sin is a pernicious, destructive morally *fatal sickness that harms the people God created and loves unconditionally.*

God hates sin the way a good earthly father hates cancer or drunken drivers—they are life threatening to his child or his grandchildren. Sin is not sin because God made a list of "don't", but rather God opposes anything harmful or dangerous that we do to ourselves or others. Our Heavenly Father does not forbid something because we enjoy it at the time, but forbids something the way good earthly fathers forbid their 5-year old to play in the street, or to go to the pool alone. Familiar named sins such as greed, lying, stealing, cheating, adultery or taking drugs offer us pleasure but all sins harm us in deep and deceptive ways, corroding our character and our soul, damaging the person we were created to be. God hates sin, but still loves sinners: if He didn't, we would all be doomed, for "all have sinned and come short of the glory of God." (Romans 3:23)

Rather than having a single idea of atonement Christianity has many **"theories of atonement,"** a series of metaphors that seek to explain how the transaction is achieved. Notice that we have "theories" about how the salvation work is accomplished, but not a binding doctrine required for salvation. Skeptics may accept the concept that Jesus somehow made a relationship with God possible, without choosing one of these proposals. All of these theories of atonement are based on the observations and reports that have been handed down by the eyewitnesses and early apologists: what changes are seen. This is not science, but resembles the scientific method in many ways: observing phenomena, considering the cause for the phenomena, forming a tentative hypothesis that seems to fit the available evidence, and then the hard-headed testing of the proposed explanation in evangelistic outreach. Pushing this comparison further, the observed phenomena would be random cases of people claiming Christian "salvation" and manifesting some observable changes in behavior and character over time that they attribute to Jesus. Did they objectively change for the better? Was it religion, or something else?

A Simple Overview of Atonement by CS Lewis

> The central Christian belief is that **Christ's death has somehow put us right with God and given us a fresh start**. Theories as to how it did this are another matter. A good many different theories have been held as to how it works; what all Christians are agreed on is that it does work. I will tell you what I think it is like...But I think they will all agree that the thing itself is infinitely more important than any explanations that theologians have produced. I think they would probably admit that no explanation will ever be quite adequate to the reality.[132] (Emphasis added)

Jesus Saves: But Who?

Christians almost universally believe that the crucifixion death of Jesus of Nazareth, and His subsequent resurrection and ascension provided the means of salvation and the reconciliation of **all** sinners to right relationship with God. *"Believe on the Lord Jesus Christ, and you will be saved."* (Acts 16:31) was the stock answer given by the early evangelists who took the Gospel of Jesus to the whole Roman world. Then, as now, some religious leaders have added other requirements (such as being baptized, living a holy life, forsaking pagan lifestyles, etc.), but the core belief has always been that what Jesus did is sufficient to change sinners into "saved," regardless of any external conditions such as racial or religious heritage, the magnitude of sinfulness, or any other characteristic. **Any, all, everyone**: God's gracious salvation is available to all who seek it. Exactly HOW the life, death and resurrection perform this spiritual change is not precisely explained. What follows are "theories of atonement", a series of metaphors that seek to show how the transaction is achieved. **Atonement** is the name theologians use for this doctrine of the reconciliation of humans with God through Jesus Christ, the restoration of a right relationship between God and man. The word itself originated in Old English from "*At one*" (or "in harmony") coupled with "*ment*," thus the process of "being made at one with God, or put at peace with God." There have been dozens of ideas about how God "saves" people from their sins, and frankly, many of them sound a bit "wacky" to modern seekers. Most of these less respected explanations of atonement also fall far short of a "theory", lacking rational connecting arguments and citing few, if any, accepted facts or even scriptures in support. There are, however, five traditional and historical versions which have been proposed and debated over for hundreds of years; these five have gained wide "acceptance" by theologians and Bible scholars, though none has gained universal consensus. Most of these theories of atonement are considered as "plausible" explanations by theologians, but none commands anything near universal agreement as complete and compelling. The "accepted but not certain" handling of this important article of faith resembles the scientific process, whereby competing theories often may seem "promising" but still requiring further research and thought. The science of the "Big Bang" has been in this tentative position for many years, and yet still has some competitors in cosmology.

The atonement theories which follow have proved themselves useful to those sincerely seeking to understand God and His relationship to humans, trying to explain in human terms what may be yet beyond our limited understanding. No one theory may totally satisfy the reader, but each seeker is free to pick whatever rings true, in part or the whole, or may find none of them convincing explanations of God's "salvation plan." The most prominent Atonement

Theories are **Ransom** Theory, **Substitution** Theory, **Satisfaction** Theory, **Penal Substitution** Model. Some new ideas have emerged in our time: **Christus Victor** Theory, **Recapitulation** Theory, and **Moral Influence** Theory. For our purposes here only the first three will be explained in this section in detail, since they are the oldest and most dominant views of Christian theologians.

The Ransom Theory

This theory of atonement is one of the oldest explanations in Western Christian theology, articulated by Origen of Alexandra, a remarkable second century Christian theologian. He argued that the death of Christ was a payment, a ransom, given to Satan, buying the release of the souls of humans from the bondage and slavery to the devil because of original sin (Adam's fallen race). The Bible seems to support this theory in Mark 10:45: *"For even the Son of Man did not come to be served, but to serve, and to give his life as a ransom for many."* Matthew 20:28 is a parallel verse: *"Just as the Son of man came, not to be ministered to, but to minister and to give his life as a ransom in exchange for many."* Paul presents the idea of Jesus being the intermediary, somewhat like a hostage negotiator: *"For there is one God and one mediator between God and men, the man Christ Jesus, who gave Himself as a ransom for all..."* (I Timothy 2:5-6) The emphasis is on Jesus serving us not excluding us.

This theory argues that Satan was holding sinful Mankind hostage since he deceived them in the Garden of Eden. In order to secure the release of sinners from the enslavement to the Devil, Jesus' sacrificial death was demanded and delivered. Others modify this theory by proposing that it is Death, not the Devil, holding the hostages, and Death (or The Grave), is paid the ransom. Jesus' death then acts as a payment to satisfy the debt on the souls of the human race, the same debt we inherited from Adam's original sin. Note that "satisfaction" here does not mean that God is pleased or appeased, but that a spiritual obligation has been fulfilled, a deficit erased, a debt has been paid in full. Further biblical support for this theory includes *"For the wages of sin is death, but the gift of God is eternal life in Christ Jesus our Lord."* (Romans 6:23)

The Substitution Theory

Several versions of atonement theory involve the idea of substitution to some degree; the Ransom theory described above could be seen as Jesus substituting Himself for the hostages, and the Satisfaction theory which follows could be seen as Jesus taking our place on the Cross. We will try to distinguish the theories as clearly as possible, while acknowledging the similarities. Since these are proposed "explanations", they will, like all multiple witness descriptions of an event, have some variations and some similarities. Considered together, multiple reports can often provide greater truth and insight than any single account.

The earliest and simplest description of Atonement is found the New Testament, of course. *"He himself bore our sins in his body on the cross, so that we might die to sins and live for righteousness; "by his wounds you have been healed."* (1 Peter 2:24) and *"For Christ also suffered once for sins, the righteous for the unrighteous, to bring you to God. He was put to death in the body but made alive in the Spirit."* (1 Pet. 3:18) The writings of Paul contain many references to this idea of Jesus dying as a substitute for us, taking our place to pay the price we could not pay ourselves. *"For Christ's love compels us, because we are convinced that One died for all, therefore all died. And He died for all, that those who live should no longer live for themselves, but for Him who died for them and was raised again.* (2 Corinthians 5:14-15)

The Satisfaction Theory

This explanation of the atonement is that Jesus Christ suffered crucifixion as a stand-in or proxy for all human sin, past and future. God is Just and justice requires the guilty to pay for their sins; to excuse or overlook the wrong doing would be unjust, and therefore God cannot simply overlook the guilt or just dismiss the charges. There is a moral law in God's Universe, Justice, and like the laws of physics, the law of justice cannot be broken with impunity. Sinful humans have nothing in themselves to pay the price justice demands, they have no merit to offset their transgressions nothing to offer to the Judge except their life—the death penalty. But the just God maintains justice by allowing the infinitely pure goodness of the perfect Jesus to be used to satisfy justice. His righteousness is to be counted as our righteousness; our unrighteousness placed on Jesus. *"God made him who had no sin to be sin for us, so that in him we might become the righteousness of God."* (2 Corinthians 5:21) Somebody must pay, and since we can't, Jesus pays it for us, with His life satisfying the just demands of the moral law. The beauty of this Satisfaction Theory is revealed when we move the scene to an American courtroom. The Judge is clearly the ruling authority, the symbol of Justice itself. The defendant (us) is proved to be guilty, and the Judge must pronounce judgment—what penalty does Justice demand? The Law says that small offenses may be paid by a monetary fine, and greater crimes may require that we pay with years of our life in prisons. But some crimes, heinous crimes may require our life—our death as the only satisfactory penalty. But Jesus proclaimed that He did not come to condemn the world, but He came to give us Life—true life, abundant life. So, dying for our own sins is a losing proposition. In this theory, Jesus steps up to the Bench and asks the Judge to let Him take the guilty persons' place—to offer to take the punishment meant for the guilty sinner. Jesus becomes the "scapegoat" as described in Exodus: a goat was chosen and through prayers and ritual the "sins" of the people are transferred to the goat, and the goat is then put out of the camp to roam helpless in the dangerous wilderness. Jesus became our "scapegoat" so that we might be free from sin and free from the punishment for sin. In many ways this Satisfaction model is quite similar to the "Penal Substitution" theory which puts more emphasis on the punishment—the suffering and violent death Jesus endured: **Jesus paid it all**.

Briefly, two other more modern theories of atonement deserve mention for their unique twist. The ***Christus Victor*** theory posits the idea that Satan was tricked into believing that he had won the battle for control of the world because Jesus was killed. While Satan and his demons were rejoicing and having a victory party, God raised Jesus from the dead, overcoming sin, Death and Hell. Jesus was the Victor! The other theory, ***Moral Influence Theory***, says that people are changed and redeemed because of the amazing example of Jesus in sacrificing Himself because of His love for us. His moral influence was convincing to the sinner and that influence continued to reshape and redeem their lives. This latter theory has the virtue of having no blood or torture involved in our salvation. However, there is no substantial Biblical support for this theory, while the other, perhaps more "gruesome" theories are clearly presented in the New Testament.

Notice that we have "theories" about how the salvation work is accomplished, based on observations and reports that have been handed down by the eyewitnesses and early apologists, and interpretations of a handful of New Testament verses. People who experience some type of religious conversion in a revival or church service are the witnesses to the reality of "being saved." When an alcoholic, abusive husband "suddenly" gives up the booze, sobers up and begins repairing his damaged family relationships, people in the community notice. When a hardened prisoner "gets religion" under the care of a visiting Christian, the other prisoners, the guards and even the warden notice the difference. Such anecdotal cases may not qualify as scientific evidence, but they suggest that "something" happened, that the "before and after" pictures are genuine. There is plenty of data documenting, or at least narrating, changes in subjects' life following some religious experience (some which are radical). Nineteenth century psychologist William James' did extensive research on American religion, documented in his famous book, *Varieties of Religious Experience*.[133]

In science, the process of research uses observations and measurements to form a hypothesis that might explain some phenomenon, then constructs predictions based on the hypothesis. Testing the hypothesis yields "proof" of the validity or falseness of the original theory. Religion is not science and so hypothetical metaphors are not usually translated into a prediction, to see if the proposed answer can be tested and repeated. The "proof" in Christianity is mostly the anecdotal type: preachers and evangelists deliver sermons to audiences promoting faith in Jesus, and then push for a "decision," a public acceptance of forgiveness and salvation. The ministers are convinced by the audience response that the "Gospel" works, that believing in the atoning power of Jesus changes sinners into Christians, instantly. The number of seekers at the altar is counted and the believers are encouraged in the effectiveness of their personal evangelism for Christ.

Does It Make Any Difference?

The above excursion into comparing science with religion is meant only to entertain and amuse both the Skeptic and the Believer, to illustrate that methodology might be transferable, but the underlying phenomena are irrevocably different. A hybrid "religious-science" would be foolish, it seems clear, although this book is advocating what might be called "*science-friendly religion.*" Measuring velocity is easy for science, but no easy way exists for measuring spiritual realities. For science to accept a friendly coexistence with religion in the culture requires acceptance of some form of measurement other than what science uses. If not verifiable by microscope or micrometers or Bunsen burners, what would count for "measuring" religion or other spiritual entities?

There are available multitudes of credible data documenting dramatic changes in people following some religious experience. William James' famous book, *Varieties of Religious Experiences* focused a great deal of attention on "conversion" stories of people whose whole psychological and behavioral life dramatically, instantly changed after some religious encounter. Many such first-hand stories offer very powerful anecdotal evidence of a permanent reorganization, a total change labeled "conversion." The most spectacular conversion story in history, of course, is recounted in the New Testament (Acts 9:3-6). Saul of Tarsus, a violent Jewish opponent of the early Christians was on his way to Damascus to arrest and punish some Christians reported there. Suddenly a bright light from the sky knocked Saul off his horse, and blinded him. He heard the voice of Jesus rebuking him, and then he was commissioned by that Jesus voice to become His servant. Saul, who then adopted his Roman name, Paul, went from being a persecutor of Christians to being the greatest proclaimer of the faith. A BIG change!

Many Christian denominations consider the "Damascus Road" path to salvation is the only valid one: "conversion" is always dramatic, sudden, and emotional. It's probably not "real", you are told, if you didn't experience a profound sense of overwhelming sorrow and guilt, followed by a climactic emotional release, a sudden sense of joy and peace, a certainty that you have been set free. In such groups, the person who cannot give the exact day and hour when they were "saved", is viewed with some suspicion. The person who makes a decision to believe in the quiet of their home, or perhaps gradually over several months is sometimes envious of the dramatic, convulsive experience claimed by other believers. They may mistakenly think they didn't get it right and doubt their salvation.

Thoughtful Skeptics, please don't be troubled by this type of narrow view of what God does in the process of atonement—it is an inadequate, distorted image of God. *It is God who atones, and He can do it any way He likes.* Choosing to believe is a private, personal act of will, and each person is affected in a different way by that decision. Some may grow gradually in comfort and confidence in the decision to believe, and some may be quickly certain and have an "ah ha" moment, a light turned on. Some who come to believe may experience great, overwhelming emotion comparable to receiving wonderful news by phone. Some may tell their friends about the experience, and some may quietly ponder it for several months, tentatively taking a step at a time. The variety of religious experience is why there are a half-dozen or so theories of atonement. It is hoped that one of these "theories of atonement" appeals to the Skeptic, one or a combination that make sense of a very deep philosophical problem. It is also OK with God if you aren't moved by <u>any</u> of these explanations and want to just leave it unknown. If you believe and you experience some newfound connection to God, it doesn't matter what the method or means is that accomplishes this. God does it and we can believe it, while not having our curiosity totally satisfied about how He did it. Uncertainty is not all bad: trusting God more than your own intellect or feeling is good theologically and psychologically.

Does Redemption Include Everyone?

The question needs to be asked, "For whom did Christ die?" Evangelical Christians are split on this bit of theology, and so two answers are possible. Both answers have some support in scripture but without an extended dealing with the question. Both answers have traditionally enjoyed a substantial support in Church history. **For whom did Christ die?** The first answer is *"everyone,"* Jesus died on the cross for the redemption of all men (humans). Paul seems to include all sinners: *"Here is a trustworthy saying that deserves full acceptance: Christ Jesus came into the world to save sinners—of whom I am the worst."* (I Timothy 1:15) That suggests the "general redemption" view. The alternate answer is this: "Jesus died only for the *elect*," the so called "limited" or "particular redemption" view. Almost no modern Christian leader teaches that the sacrificial death of Christ on the cross means that everyone is, or will be, saved, and that no human will go to Hell. That view is held by some, called "Universalism" but it is soundly rejected by most Christians and is contradicted by the Bible itself. Jesus told stories and referred to specific people who were in Hell after a sinful life. And the scripture cited before clearly is not universalistic: *"God is not willing that any should perish but that all would come to repentance."* (II Peter 3:9). God doesn't wish it to happen, but men are free to choose, and that choice seems to be the determining factor, for Peter warns: *"Therefore, beloved, since you already know these things, be on your guard so that you will not be carried away by the error of the lawless and fall from your secure standing."* (2 Peter 3:17).

Universal Redemption is a hopeful, optimistic theology, espoused by relatively few who cannot bear the idea that God would send anyone to Hell or allow anyone to ultimately go to Hell. While this is a pretty, rosy picture, it **is not taught in the Bible** and is not taught by Jesus. Period. While there is not time or space for a full exposition of this doctrine, we must address some of the crucial issues raised. Certainly, you have noticed that we promote here the image of a good God, a Father God, a God like Jesus, and so the challenge is how can God let any of his creation end up in Hell if He is the God of love? There are several good answers to this tough question, and a few will be presented briefly.

First, there is that pesky "free will" thing discussed earlier. For God to be God and for us to be humans, God had to let us think and decide, to make choices free of His direct control; only "free will" allows us to voluntarily love God, and it would not be love if we lacked the choice to "not love." God didn't want the artificial "love of puppets" or robots, and so He set us free. Having been set free, we therefore must be able to choose "God or Self" or "Love or Ignore" or "Heaven or Hell." **The God described in this book will fight to the very edges of the pit** of Hell, reaching out dangerously and desperately just in case you reach for His outstretched hand. This is metaphorical, of course, but it seems to capture the tenacity of God. You may go to Hell, but this Jesus/God will weep for you, not taunt nor cheer your slide into doom.

A second answer to the God and Hell dilemma is similar: suppose God forced you to go to Heaven even though your will and your life made it clear you had other plans. Would you enjoy Heaven if you had been dragged there kicking and screaming? Would you ruin Heaven for the zillions of God-loving humans who were there rejoicing and praising their Savior? If you were not really that comfortable in Heaven, would you be at risk of stirring up trouble? Here we go again on that "fallen angel" story.

A third reason is based on the **rest** of the nature of God: sure, He is love, but He is **also** just, righteous and fair. If it turned out that God's moral universe was more smoke and mirrors than substance, not real, then the whole idea of morality and right and wrong in life would be only "dust in the wind" with no substance or reality. The standards are fluid, and being fully human is like being a "shape shifter," with no fixed pattern or form. The universe would go off its axle if laws are meaningless.

Who Are the Elect, the Chosen Ones?

Are some of us chosen by God before we were born to be Believers, and others were selected to be Sinners? Scientific determinism would say "yes" if it accepted the God part of the equation. Scientific determinism says everything is caused by some previous event, in physics and humans. There are substantial groups of Christians (followers of Reformation leader John Calvin, 1509-1564) who also say "Yes, some are Elected by God to be saved, and some are not selected or elected." These groups emphasize the **sovereignty of God** as His dominant quality, His power more than His love and mercy. In their theology the idea that God could surrender His will and control over our lives is unthinkable, reducing God to a weak caretaker role. The proponents of this "predestination" theology fall into two camps: first, those who say God predestines the fate of both the Saved and the Lost (charmingly called "Double Predestination.") The other camp agrees that God predestines some to be the Elect, chosen to be saved regardless of what, but God does not finally predetermine who will be lost or damned. This second group is a bit vague about whether the "un-Elected" can be saved if they meet some conditions, but that little bit of hope is probably helpful in trying to get converts: you **may** be Elected but we can't know, but at least you have a chance in the Holy lottery. Both sides in this dispute agree that the gospel can and should be genuinely offered to all men, that it is sufficient for the salvation of every man, **but that not all men will be saved.**

Obviously, the view presented in this book is in conflict with the Calvinist tradition in Christianity; we present a God who loves every person equally and extravagantly, sparing nothing in His pursuit of His wandering creatures, working within the limits of human free will. This is the doctrinal position of the Reformer Jacobus Arminius (1560-1609), called "Arminianism." It is hard to reconcile the Jesus/God image with a Creator who marks us each for redemption or rejection before we are created. Some earthly fathers in the past have exercised such power over their unborn children that they choose which one will live and which one will be placed on a flat rock in the hot sun to die. Roman nobles did such a thing, a God who is like Jesus cannot be twisted enough to allow such predetermination. It must be candidly admitted that the concept of God's sovereignty and His power of "predestination" is found in the New Testament, especially in Paul's letters. A couple of examples will be reviewed among many.

> *"Praise be to the God and Father of our Lord Jesus Christ, who has blessed us in the heavenly realms with every spiritual blessing in Christ. For he chose us in him before the creation of the world to be holy and blameless in his sight. In love he predestined us for adoption to sonship through Jesus Christ, in accordance with his pleasure and will."* (Ephesians 1:3-4)

> *"For those whom he [God] foreknew he also predestined to be conformed to the image of his Son, in order that he might be the first-born among many brethren. And those whom he predestined he also called; and those whom he called he also*

justified; and those whom he justified he also glorified." (Rom. 8:29–30).

All the references to "predestination" (4 total) are by Paul, so his views are the ones to be examined. In the Ephesians 1 passage above writes about God "In love he predestined us for adoption to sonship...in accordance with his pleasure and will." He is writing to the Christians in Ephesus where he had established a congregation and with whom he corresponded as an overseer and guide. He is writing about the new Christians there, probably mostly Gentiles, not Jews. He says that God planned ahead of time for us (Paul and the Ephesians) to be adopted by God, making "us" sons of God. This adoption status is God's pleasure and will, he asserts. Notice this predestination is not to salvation or damnation, but to "sonship" or Christian living.

The Pauline passage from Romans 8 is to Gentile Christians in Rome, and he is including them in this statement above: **"For those (of us) whom God foreknew he also predestined..."** Notice that foreknowledge is not automatically "predestined." God foreknows us, as explained in **Chapter 10**, because He is outside of time, so all things past and future are present to Him. Still, he does say that God **"predestined *us*** (Paul and the Romans) **to be conformed to the image of His son...**" (Romans 8:29) This is the *intentional* will of God for all His creatures as we have earlier discussed, helping humans to become more and more like Jesus in their lives on earth—a process of "conforming" or "fitting" the model. This does not mention either Heaven or Hell as being chosen for us, but centers on shaping us into the image of His son. The work of God on these Roman Christians had a purpose, Paul points out, "**that He** (Jesus) **might be the first born among many brethren...**" (Romans 8:29) that they follow in Jesus steps. He the "first born" but they Christians are to be the many, many brothers in Christ's image who are added in the future. And then he clearly outlines the process: **predestined – called – justified – glorified.** That is the sequence: God plans for all to be saved—He *predestines* it without forcing it; He "*called*" or invited all those predestined (everybody).

Those who said "yes" when called (surrendered their will to God's will) were *justified* (declared to be righteous, holy, in harmony with God, freed of sin) An old Sunday School lesson used this word play:

"**Just** as **If I'd** never sinned." And having been set right in their relationship with God, the believers were *glorified*. This may mean going to heaven, but more likely means being honored and praised by God for their service to Him. Those who have lived a life of Christian service do not often get "glory" in their life time or by the world they serve, but to be <u>allowed</u> to work for the Creator of the Universe, to use His name, is honor and glory enough. The other passage where Paul mentions predestination is Ephesians 1:11-14, he is clearly thinking back to his Jewish heritage, and his belief in Israel being God's chosen people. Notice that he is talking to Jews like himself who are wrestling with how to honor Judaism while accepting the fulfillment of God's great plan in Jesus and the Church. He uses "we" to include himself in this unfolding plan that did have God *choose* Israel in the past (predestined) but has now ordained a New Testament/Covenant for redemption through Jesus:

> ***In him*** (Jesus) ***we*** (Jews) ***were also chosen, having been predestined according to the plan of him who works out everything in conformity with the purpose of his will, in order that we, who were the first to put our hope in Christ, might be for the praise of his glory. And you*** (Gentiles) ***also were included in Christ when you heard the message of truth, the gospel of your salvation. When you believed, you were marked in him with a seal, the promised Holy Spirit, who is a deposit guaranteeing our inheritance until the redemption of those who are God's possession—to the praise of his glory.*** (Ephesians 1:11)
> (Three notes inserted by Author for clarity about subjects)

Though Paul used the word "predestination" in these verses, he is nowhere teaching the Calvinist doctrine of God pre-selecting who will ultimately be saved, preordaining some chosen humans to attain a heavenly home, or "predestining" all Mankind to have no free will of their own. He makes it abundantly clear that God has **chosen everyone,** not just a select few, and that everyone has a choice, a free will, by which they validate or reject the choice God made for them. *It is said that "Election" means God votes YES, the Devil votes NO, and we each have the deciding vote on our salvation: YES or NO. And there is no interference in this important election.*

Jesus does not mention "predestination" at all in our Gospel account, though He refers a time or two "being chosen." His references all are to a future time of terrible persecution (though some interpret it to be about the End of Time):

> "(B)ecause those will be days of distress unequaled from the beginning, when God created the world, until now—and never to be equaled again. If the Lord had not cut short those days, no one would survive. But for the sake of the elect, whom he has chosen, he has shortened them. At that time if anyone says to you, 'Look, here is the Messiah!' or, 'Look, there he is!' do not believe it." (Mark 13:19-21)

The Good News is found in that last New Testament book: *Whosoever will may come. And whosoever will, let him take the water of life freely.* (Rev. 22:17)

The invitation has been delivered:

Whosoever Will... come!

Chapter 19

WHAT IS REAL?

> *"A man should never be ashamed to own he has been in the wrong, which is but saying, in other words, that he is wiser today than he was yesterday"*
> ALEXANDER POPE

WHAT IS REAL IS BOTH A PHILOSOPHICAL AND A SCIentific question which is to be expected since science was the off-shoot of philosophy and the first philosophers we know about considered this question as the first step to defining knowledge and truth. In spite of the passage of twenty-five centuries since Socrates and his successors first debated "reality" in the forums of Athens, the most far-sighted scientists of our time, the "cutting edge" thinkers, are still contemplating that old question. The discoveries arising from Quantum theory in our lifetime has unsettled the old questions and answers in science. The orderly world of Newtonian physics is now regarded as a "test run" in explaining the ultimate nature of reality, working quite predictably for large realities, such as planets, stars, galaxies, and other astronomic wonders, but not nearly as helpful in understanding the microscopic or subatomic realities of our universe. The fundamental divisions between science and philosophy remain essentially the same (a material world only versus a more complex material and non-material reality). The question is whether there is only what we see, hear, smell, taste and touch, things that can be measured, or if there is also another world or realm of reality that is above or beyond the physical universe. The theories and the names ever expand and change, but the answer is still as unsettled in the 21st Century A.D. as it was in the 4th Century B.C.

Bridge Building

The primary purpose of this book is to construct a rational bridge between those who are religious Skeptics because of their scientific knowledge and mindset, and those who believe in God, but doubt Darwin and other scientists who seem to oppose religion or to challenge biblical precepts. It seems essential to explain the nature of science and the claims it can rightfully make so that the disaffected Believer can find an intellectually satisfying way to make peace with science. Likewise, this task involves explaining to scientists the actual nature and scope of religious beliefs (specifically about God), and carving out a space of rational dubiety and modest receptivity on questions in the domain of supernatural (or non-material) reality. Religious Believers can rest easier if they can reconcile the realm of science with their own spiritual beliefs (giving up neither their intellectual nor spiritual integrity). It is hoped that scientists, many of whose historical predecessors were also believers, can relieve any cognitive dissonance they may have by finding here an intellectually satisfying way to reconcile the idea of faith with the idea of science.

By "idea of science" we mean the fundamental approach, **the scientific method**, which governs all branches of modern science *(discussed in detail below and also in **Chapter 3**)* and the basic premises and assumptions on which the discipline of Science is built. There is, unfortunately, no such widely recognized corresponding **idea of faith** for a point-by-point method of research or objective study of theology comparable to that used in science. There is no recognized discipline "Science of Theology" or "Science of Faith" though many articles and books are being written about the general ideas, and some works by neurologists are focusing on the effect on the brain of religious practices, such as prayer and meditation. *(Perhaps in a future book sequel.)* For our purposes here we use the term *faith* to denote basic principles rather than specific beliefs which identify a specific religion. These core principles, believed to be original in this formulation, are listed as examples of what defines **faith,** its markers or indicators. Note well, this is not about religion (group phenomenon) but about the deeply personal mental experience of an individual which we call "faith." These characteristics might be theistic or not. These are not research findings, though recent neurological imaging studies suggest a reality that may be measurable. Obviously, some of these markers will be hard to measure or quantify.

1. The existence of a "non-material" reality is one such religious fundamental.
2. All humans are both physical and non-physical, with both a body and a "spirit" or "soul."
3. Normal humans are conscious moral agents with "free will" and self-determination.
4. The human **Mind** is a non-material entity, arising in the physical brain, biologically dependent on the brain, but distinct from it.
5. Humans as a species have an innate and often insatiable curiosity, a drive for finding "meaning" or "patterns" or "causes," for "understanding" their environment.
6. All normal humans internalize their interpretations of their experiences as a set of beliefs or opinions; these inner convictions are firmly held and resilient, but can, with effort, change or develop within an emergent environment and social influences.
7. It appears that humans have a universal and innate brain-based capacity to experience episodes of awe and wonder in which they perceive that there is a greater, more powerful "other" force or being in nature, a sense of humility, respect, fear and vulnerability.
8. This "awakening" awareness of a "non-material" invisible reality almost inevitably becomes an object of "worship" -or at least an acknowledgment of a "superior" power to their own "inferior" position, a sense of impotence or neediness. Ironically such "visions" usually leave the subject "satisfied" or "fulfilled." (Etymologically **worship** means attributing worth, value, or reverence" to an object or person.)

These eight aspects of faith are only tentative suggestions based on many other works in many fields; these are not established theories, but might be possible subjects for future research and study. It is argued here that these or similar steps or stages of human development apply to our prehistoric human ancestors and to modern humans of our day. They serve our purpose for now, allowing some basis for comparing, and/or contrasting, Science and Faith. This general subject is also extensively addressed in **Chapters 7 and 13**.

The Place for Humility

It behooves both the convinced science believer and the religious believer to recognize the limits of human enterprise and the long record we have in all fields of "missing the target" on first try or on the first dozen tries. We in science and we in religion have had to retract some of our "truths" because we got ahead of the "facts," or stopped searching a bit too soon, or we simply went off on some side road that led us astray, or we let some human bias or self-interest blind us to the "truth" in front of us. We call it "human error" because it is so common among us. We followed the faulty science of eugenics in the early twentieth century, and gave scientific backing to forced sterilizations of 64,000 people in the US before some other scientists said "**Whoop! Our bad!**" We fervently followed Bible-quoting religious leaders on several occasions to abandon homes and jobs and wait together for the return of Jesus Christ to bring the end of time; some even fooled us twice or thrice, but eventually sanity returned to most Christians, but probably not permanently.

In studying the history of religion both scientists and theologians had long regarded the mythology and legends of primitive people as pure "fiction," tales made up to control and amuse the superstitious population. We have since come to appreciate that the myths, legends and folk-tales were vital elements of the religion of primitive people, giving them hope, comfort and some sense of belonging. Modern men may not find inspiration in the ancient stories but the people who lived in those time certainly did. Joseph Campbell pioneered this understanding of myth:

Mythology is not a lie, mythology is poetry, it is metaphorical. **It has been well said that mythology is the penultimate truth—penultimate because the ultimate cannot be put into words.** It is beyond words. Beyond images, beyond that bounding rim of the Buddhist Wheel of Becoming. Mythology pitches the mind beyond that rim, to what can be known but not told.[134] (Emphasis added)

The Golden Bough by James George Frazer, published in 1890, introduced the disputed results of his study of comparative religions, from the most primitive back through ancient legends and myths. He concluded that all of mankind's religions evolved from superstition, to magic, to religious beliefs, to scientific beliefs. Frazer's writings stirred much public debate largely because he considered the story of Christ's death and resurrection as similar to, and comparable to, other ancient myths of incarnate gods and the ritualistic death of one special god. He modified this "dying god" view in later editions. But Frazer's research and theories about the origin of religion have had lasting influence on scholars, especially his understanding of myth as more than fanciful tales from ancient people, to actually being containers for deeper truths that carried meaning to the believers. Frazer himself accepted that his theories were speculative and that the associations he made were circumstantial and usually based only on resemblance. He wrote:

> **Books like mine, merely speculation, will be superseded sooner or later (the sooner the better for the sake of truth) by better induction based on fuller knowledge**...It is my earnest wish that the lectureship should be used solely for the disinterested pursuit of truth, and not for the dissemination and propagation of any theories or opinions of mine.[135] (Emphasis added)

We will draw some ideas from his 800-page magnum opus in later sections, but for now it is useful to attend to the reservations and the humility he demonstrated in presenting his controversial ideas. The current Author is attempting to emulate that attitude: *We are like heirs to a fortune which has been handed down for so many ages that the memory of those who built it up is lost, and its possessors for the time being regard it as having been an original and unalterable possession of their race since the beginning of the world.* But reflection and enquiry should satisfy us that to our predecessors we are indebted for much of what we thought most our own, and that their errors were not willful extravagances or the ravings of insanity, but simply hypotheses, justifiable as such at the time when they were propounded, but which a fuller experience has proved to be inadequate. Frazer said

> It is only by the successive testing of hypotheses and rejection of the false that truth is at last elicited. After all, what we call truth is only the hypothesis which is found to work best. ***Therefore, in reviewing the opinions and practices of ruder ages and races we shall do well to look with leniency upon their errors as inevitable slips made in the search for truth, and to give them the benefit of that indulgence which we ourselves may one day stand in need of.***[136] (emphasis added*)*

The mission of reconciliation involves opening and exposing rigid stereotypes and misunderstandings on both sides. It means reminding scientists of their principled skepticism, the value of maintaining openness to the possibility of premature or erroneous conclusions, always questioning. It also involves showing believers another way to view and understand revelation and the Bible, preserving their belief in its sacredness, while largely eliminating, or at least softening, most of the criticism and attacks which non-believers make on their holy scriptures. Not all Skeptics will be persuaded by the ideas and arguments given here, and not all Believers will accept the proposed pathway to integrating the Bible with the world of science. But perhaps some will reconsider, and a slight opening of closed doors will let in some light, and as light drives out darkness, so does truth drive out error.

When Two World Views Collide

The beginning of a productive discussion between the scientifically minded person and the religiously minded person seems almost doomed at the first contact. The world view of science is exclusively based in the "reality" of the empirical, the measurable, the natural, to the exclusion of the supernatural; the religious world view is grounded in the "reality" of the supernatural, non-material, non-physical world beyond our five senses. Scientists doubt the claims of supernatural experience, and the religious are very skeptical about the certainty of many scientific claims. Science generally argues that only that which can be measured, weighed, observed or calculated mathematically is real. So, to the skeptical scientist, gods are not real in the way that a frog is real. We can see, touch, and dissect a frog, but we cannot observe, measure, or otherwise perceive of gods in empirical terms. The skeptical religious person knows that science is obviously right about a lot of empirical things (gravity, light, germs, molecules, even such mysterious ideas as relativity), but they cannot blindly accept it for many of its other claims (radio carbon dating, skulls and bones dug up and pieced together, evolution, and fantastic estimates of time and distances in the cosmos). Proof means something different to the scientist and the non-scientist. Truth is viewed in entirely incompatible ways between these two big world views. Discussion is difficult between people with different languages *but having competing world views is even more challenging.*

What Is Real? What Is Truth?

Any discussion of religion or God necessarily involves questions about what is "real" and this has been the great philosophical question since ancient times. Does what we perceive (see, hear, feel) actually exist, or is it all an illusion, a product of our imagination. Broadly speaking, this leads to the two most prominent schools of philosophy: **Realism** and **Idealism**. Realism asserts that the objects of our perception are indeed "real" and not illusions, things materially and physically existing in our external environment. The Idealism philosophy argues that the only reality that exists is in our minds, and that what we perceive externally

WHAT IS REAL?

is only an illusion, a projection of our thoughts. Both science and religion are strongly in the Realism camp; both believe that "what we see, hear, feel, etc. is REAL, physical and material. Science operates on the belief that whatever "reality" exists must be measurable and whatever cannot be measured is **not real.** Though most religious people agree the material world is real, their focus is primarily on the non-material, the "spiritual" realm, a realm not recognized by most scientists. For materialists, such as most scientists, things that cannot be seen, measured or counted are simply **"not real"** and are "imaginary, illusionary, wishful thinking, or superstition." Philosophy has developed many schools of thought about the nature of reality, of which "Materialism," favored by science, is just one within the broader philosophy of Realism. The basic philosophy of mainstream biology and other hard sciences, the philosophy of materialist realism, *assumes the existence of a material world independent of human observation and cognition.*

Another credible school of thought, Idealism, holds the opposite view: "there is **no material world**, for everything we experience is created in our mind; reality is a projection or a perception." Many young students taking their first philosophy class have been startled to hear this assertion, since it is so out of sync with their own experience. That philosophy, called "Idealism," has deep historical roots with famous advocates such as Plato, Immanuel Kant, Friedrich Hegel, Arthur Schopenhauer and George Berkley. It has many variations and schools, and many fine, intelligent current followers, but all share the basic idea that what we perceive by our senses is just a projection of our mind. Some, like Plato, argue that what we think we see in the material world is *not a creation* of our minds, but a *re-creation* or a partial duplication of some reality that exists outside our material realm. Some Christian philosophers have adapted Plato's idea of an original perfect "form" for everything, arguing that God is the Creator and Originator, that all that exists is a projection of God's mind. Extreme "Idealists" go so far as to suggest that we all may be merely chess players on some cosmic game board, or even just pixels in a sophisticated video game played by one or more unseen powers (usually some malevolent powers.) Several popular Hollywood movies, such as *Matrix*, have used this "not-real" theme and plot, with a kind of cosmic computer game challenged by human heroes to outmaneuver the evil gaming force.

Christianity, like most formal religions, is based on the Realism view of the universe, and in many ways has been overly "materialistic," some would say. "This is my Father's world" the upbeat hymn proclaims, and God wants good things for His beloved children. But religion is also clearly **dualist**, that is, firmly believing in a material reality **and a** non-material reality, operating simultaneously. **Dualism** is not new nor limited to religions, for as far back as men have been creating stories, they have envisioned their universe as cosmically divided, with Heaven and Earth, good and evil, light and darkness, or sacred and profane, often with dueling deities or spirit powers waging eternal war for dominance and control of Earth.

The ancient Sumerians, by 3700 B.C., wrote epic stories on clay tablets about the catastrophic struggle between Marduk and Tiamat, between moral man and immortal fickle gods. In the basic theology of Hinduism, Vishnu is cast as the principle of creation and the sustenance of life with Shiva as the opposing principle of destruction and death. Christianity has carried over that theme with a view that the Devil is waging eternal war against God, fighting for the souls of humans. Whether populated with demons or angels, there is a very strong intuition in Mankind that this world is preparation for another world, a spiritual world. "*This world is not my home, I'm just a' passing through….*" a favorite song of hope for many people of faith. **Science sees one world, Christianity sees two.** Which is true?

So, **what is reality?** Is reality simply the material world we can sense with our eyes, ears, tongue, noses or fingers? Or is reality an ethereal, invisible realm beyond our physical senses, but knowable by mental perception, thoughts, reasoning and intuitions, the place of soul and spirit, *experiential* rather than *experimental?* Or, a third choice: is reality a figment of our imagination, an illusion we created in our minds and project on life, a reality that exists only as we think it? Or, are **none** of these ideas of reality true? Orthodox (traditional) Christianity is *"dualist,"* believing in **both** of the first two options, **a material reality** and **a non-material reality**, operating simultaneously. The third option, "idealism," has far too many unanswered and unanswerable questions for most scientists and religious people to follow. There is not much to discuss if everyone's illusion of reality is theirs alone. So, for the purposes of this book, we will argue that **reality actually exists independently of our thoughts**, and that **it functions in two different and distinct realms** integrated by the whole person, a body with sensory perception, and a mind or spirit perceiving the metaphysical world occupied by God.

All in The Family

How did we get to the point where science and religion seem to be adversaries? It has not always been so. Looking back in history as far as the Greek and Roman centuries the distinctions between them are not as clear or as separate as they are at present. In fact, both science and religion began as parts of another discipline, both the off-spring of a common ancestor. It may be offensive to professionals in both fields to hear, but *science and theology are brothers*, not twins, certainly, but inherently siblings. They are descended from a common ancient parent: **Philosophy.** Historically, religion is the elder brother in the philosophy family, but science eventually dominated the family. "Philosophy" derives from the Greek word, φιλοσοφία, ("philo" meaning brotherly love, and "sophia" meaning wisdom or knowledge.) Socrates, Plato, Aristotle, Euripides, Euclid, Pythagoras, Democritus, Hippocrates, and scores of others of our intellectual forefathers were first of all philosophers—lovers of knowledge and wisdom, searchers for the truth. *These early philosophers were dualist*, accepting the idea that truth is found in both the observed physical world, but also in the unseen world of ideas, causes, forms, and supernatural forces. Plato, for example, argued that everything in the material world is a copy of the perfect original somewhere in the unseen world. This was not posited as a religious theory, but it seems clearly to envision an "Other" who creates the original "form", and what humans can know here has some supernatural, perhaps "heavenly" counterpart of reality. These ancient Greek philosophers and teachers from 2500 years ago *were also becoming scientists*, exploring the whole breadth of human thought, developing ideas and models about reality, truth, morality, beauty, justice, and all aspects of nature. The Nature of Man inevitably dealt with our origins, our values and purposes in life; the Nature of Matter dealt with physics, geometry, astronomy, mathematics and all the other aspects of the physical world. These titans of thinkers are sometimes labeled as "natural philosophers", for it was their keen observation of nature, and the nature of men, that inspired their voluminous writings, dialogues, and treatises. It is reasonable to recognize that "science" probably would not exist at all without philosophy. What we now call "science" was originally known as *"the natural sciences"* —a loosely defined subset of the fields of knowledge about the physical world (of which there are now scores (e.g.: astronomy, biology, cosmology, demography, ecology, forensics, and so on to zoology.) Bertrand Russell, famed critic of religion, had a keen insight about the way in which science arises from philosophy; though Russell intended these words as a put-down of philosophy, they actually are complimentary and **complementary**:

> Philosophy, like all other studies, aims primarily at knowledge. The knowledge it aims at is the kind of knowledge which gives unity and system to the body of the sciences, and the kind which results from a critical examination of the grounds of our convictions, prejudices, and beliefs. But it cannot be maintained that philosophy has had any very great measure of success in its attempts to provide definite answers to its questions.
>
> **Thus, to a great extent, the uncertainty of philosophy is more apparent than real**: those questions which are already capable of definite answers are placed in the sciences, while those only to which, at present, no definite answer can be given, remain to form the residue which is called philosophy.[137] (emphasis added)

Socrates, arguably the greatest philosopher of them all, apparently did not put his amazing ideas in written form, but he was immortalized and his teachings preserved by his disciple, Plato. Aristotle, Plato's greatest student, carried the intellectual revolution forward to impact all of Western civilization for a thousand years, even into our own time. Reading and discussing these giants of the mind is the curriculum for much modern college study. The highest and most prestigious academic degree traditionally awarded by American universities is the Ph.D., the "doctor of philosophy." More than other, more specific doctorates, the Ph.D. represents the broadest and more comprehensive mastery of human knowledge. Even famous physicists and rocket scientists are likely to have the *Doctor of Philosophy* in their credentials.

Philosopher Scientists

Philosophy is regarded by a portion of the modern general public as too "ivory tower" or "out of touch" with the real world. Philosophers, it says, debate each other, write and sell books to other philosophers, and usually inhabit universities to teach distracted sophomores the mysteries of the "Mother of All Knowledge". But the facts are with the philosophers: all current branches of human knowledge are descendants of this original "Mother" or "Father." In Classical antiquity, and up through the Middle Ages, philosophy was traditionally divided into two major branches at the universities: **Natural Science** and **Metaphysics**. Natural philosophy ("*physics*") was the study of the physical world (*physis*, literally: nature); Metaphysical philosophy was the study of existence, causation, God, logic, forms and other abstract objects (*metaphysika* – Greek for "what comes after physics", or "beyond physics"). This classical division is based on the monumental, prolific work of Aristotle (384–322B.C.), the intellectual descendant of Plato and Socrates. (*Incidentally, Aristotle was the tutor for Alexander the Great.*) Aristotle's works were later compiled into two large collections by his followers. The first group, dealing with what we call math and science, was called **Physics**; the second collection, dealing with what we now call philosophy, was simply labeled **Metaphysics**, meaning "after physics". "Metaphysics" eventually came to mean "beyond the physical" or "above the mere material world." This division was not Aristotle's plan, but it became the standard way of looking at philosophy until modern times—Natural Science and all the other fields of philosophy.

Theology, a metaphysical subject, was a respected major branch of higher education for hundreds of years, the so-called "Queen of Sciences," reigning unchallenged until the explosion of science and scientific methods in the 19th century. Natural philosophy has split into the various natural sciences, including astronomy, physics, chemistry, biology, medicine, cosmology and many more. Moral philosophy has birthed the social sciences such as psychology, sociology, history and economics, but also includes value theory, aesthetics, ethics, and political philosophy. Metaphysical philosophy has branched into such formal sciences as logic, mathematics, philosophy of science, religion or theology, epistemology, cosmology, and others still emerging.

Relatives don't always get along in real life, and the same affliction troubles professions and disciplines. As introduced above, in terms of heritage and origins, Religion and Science are actually brothers, branches growing out of the original root of philosophy. Perhaps these two "intellectual brothers" are modeled on the biblical twin brothers, Esau and Jacob, opposites in nature and obsessed with out-doing the other. But eventually Jacob and Esau reconciled, and thus we can perhaps hope for some restoration of brotherhood, at least conversation, between science and theology. Scientists may not consider themselves philosophers, but they certainly are, ever reaching out beyond the known to the unknown, pushing the boundaries of our human knowledge to the farthermost frontiers, testing and challenging every idea, open to anything that can possibly be true.

The Peril of Certainty

Some scientists, like some religious believers, may become arrogant and so impressed with their knowledge that they lose their skepticism and make boasts of certainty. Total certainty is the enemy of thinking, whether the subject is theological or scientific content. Professional scientists **know** this risk of jumping to conclusions, or the danger of so much personal identification with one's own ideas that rational judgment may be tainted. It is easier to practice scientific skepticism in the laboratory or in field experiments, for there are usually several or many possible explanations (theories) to explain observations or findings.

But once a strong case is built up, and initial objections are dismissed, the idea, theory, hypothesis or explanation can take on a life of its own. True science has built in a correction for hasty or premature conclusions in the form of competition. Once a new theory or hypothesis is published or made public, every other scientist on the planet is invited to try to prove it wrong. This self-correction in science often takes place in a much smaller, more intimate setting—conversations with one's colleagues or mentors. The interchange of ideas and objections can sharpen and improve such a new idea, or it can shoot it down in a blaze of disappointment.

Even with the most rigorous peer review, however, some ideas become theories and gain wide acceptance, only to later (even much later) be challenged and refuted. Almost every scientific theory was wrong or partially wrong for a while, but the grinding wheels of academia and the world of hungry scientists will trim and polish and refine the proposal until it can withstand any present challenge or viable contradiction. Many are simply refuted and rejected.

It Seemed Like a Good Idea at the Time

Modern science is not embarrassed to admit that some things that they once believed have proved to be wrong or at least incomplete. The most obvious case the "flat earth" theory, which prevailed for most of human history. Early Greek scientists and philosophers theorized that all matter consisted of four basic elements (most famously air, earth, fire, and water). This was finally refuted by Antoine Lavoisier's publication of Elements of Chemistry, which contained the first modern list of chemical elements, in 1789. Another well-known example is the "geocentric model" associated with Ptolemy, a second century A.D. Greek astronomer, but actually universally believed since Babylonian times. In this theory, the Earth is the center of the universe, and all celestial bodies orbit our stationary planet. This was the prevailing view until 1543 when Nicolaus Copernicus published his "Heliocentric" theory that the Sun was the fixed center of our solar system, and that Earth and other planets orbited around our own star/Sun. Religious leaders opposed this change in cosmology, but scientists accepted the research and evidence Copernicus presented. The famous laws of physics formulated by Isaac Newton ruled the science world for centuries, and still are used with some reservations: Newton's laws hold up under normal conditions, but are not accurate when applied to velocities that are very fast, where relativistic mechanics apply.

In the fields of biology and medicine "Spontaneous generation" of complex life from inanimate matter rather than sexual reproduction was the accepted theory until Louis Pasteur's experiments proved this wrong. A principle called "Preformation" was accepted by science and in folklore– the theory that all organisms have existed since the beginning of life, and that gametes contain a miniature but complete preformed individual, in the case of humans, a *homunculus*. This was debunked when microscopes became available. A related false science theory held that sperm alone were responsible for producing offspring, with each of the millions of sperm being tiny humans waiting to be nurtured by the womb of the female. An extreme version of this myth argued that each "homunculus" sperm also contained a supply of other miniature humans—regressing all the way back to Adam! Better microscopes doomed this theory. Hundreds of other examples could be cited of scientific theories once believed and later rejected over time; such self-correction is the strength of science, and healthy skepticism is it's "fail safe" system. In science, "certainty" is almost certain to fail.

It can be argued that much in science is a matter of interpretation. We can observe the effect of objects in cosmic space, phenomena whose nature we cannot directly observe. We cannot yet directly observe a "black hole" for example; we can only observe the effects it has on visible parts surrounding it. We can be sure that black holes exist, and we have theorized a great deal about them, but without a more direct way to observe and measure, our black hole theories are interpretations. Two of our major frameworks in science, **General Relativity** and **Quantum Mechanics,** which are currently the dominant models for understanding reality, are in conflict in describing black holes. Based on the fundamental premises of the two competing models it is reasonable that scientists arrive at different interpretations or explanations. We don't just reject the reality of black holes because we can't yet see one, and so we operate on *tentative answers*.

We know from past scientific discoveries that sooner or later most "effects" have turned out to be the clue that eventually reveals the material, empirical proof we can see. For example, Neptune was first "discovered" by mathematical calculations from observing Uranus. Something was causing a strange deviation from its predicted orbit. This deviation was interpreted to be the effect of another unseen planet, and Neptune was found at its mathematically predicted location. An effect, correctly interpreted, led to the observable reality: a "non-material" force revealed a "material" reality. Interpretation in science and interpretation in Biblical studies are similar "guesses" though scientific interpretations are usually verified or denied, while Biblical interpretation has no final, uncontested answer other than the degree of acceptance by scholars, or occasionally, as an archaeological find in Israel may shine new light and insights.

Citing the previous temporary mistakes or false starts which characterizes science historically is not an attempt to demean or downplay the value of science. **Science is true—eventually**, because it keeps on searching even after a supposed "answer" is found. In the material world, science is our wonderful and powerful servant, and no amount of religious doctrine or faith can successfully do what science does. A servant is not always right and is not always deferential to the master (society), and so we must always be vigilant and cautious. Technology, the product of science, is morally neutral but can be used for the greatest of evils as well as the greatest of good. **Religious people should not regard science as an enemy but would be wise to regard it as a vehicle.** Since science cannot find or invent something which would be a surprise to an adequate God worthy of worship, we have no need to fear that science or technology is going to damage our faith. A useful metaphor might be that religion sees science as a very beautiful and powerful new Mercedes (or a Ford F-150 truck). It can be useful to get us to places we need to go, and we need to know at least a little about how the vehicle works and how to operate it safely. We can use it for good, or we can smash into a group of children because we are incompetent or careless. We must know what our vehicle can and cannot do, and we must make sure to maintain it properly (being science savvy). It is a wonderful machine but it is man-made and so is imperfect, a work in progress (like Christians, who rightly can claim only to be "a work in progress.)

So, What Is the Conclusion?

The change of mind advocated in this book is directed to the scientists, skeptics and other materialists, as well as to the religionists. **Is a "non-material" realm of reality a possibility?** Can it be ruled out rationally and logically? Can it be considered skeptically, agnostically, with reservations, or in a word, can a metaphysical world be considered by the scientific method? If this were any other proposition or hypothesis, would we agree that without further "evidence" we can't say a definite "Yes" or "No"? In that same mental discipline, the idea of a metaphysical realm **could be true** or it **could be false**, and a definite "Yes" or "No" is not logical. **Do we have a maybe? "Maybe" is a good place to start.**

For the Believers the mind-change advocated in this book is "fear not," and "open your mind." If you already have faith in a "big enough" God like the One advocated in this book, then science is not going to damage that faith. Whatever is true can withstand examination, for God is the Creator and sustainer of ALL THAT IS, so He's never going to be surprised nor bypassed. You might find **something** which you believed about God smells a bit suspicious when compared with Jesus, for a lot of things people have said about God are not true (like being vengeful and spiteful.) Under whatever crud people in your life have plastered on God will wash right off with a good application of Jesus. Science is not divine but neither is it the Devil. Worship God and enjoy science. If you have been serving a "too small God" or an "inadequate God" now is the time to trade the old "clunker" for a new Jesus-like model. You can face Reality, in the material world and the spirit world, for He is Lord of both.

Chapter 20

BELIEF VS KNOWING

"It's not what we don't know that gives us trouble, it's what we know that ain't so."
WILL ROGERS

FOR ANY TWO PEOPLE TO HAVE A RATIONAL CONVERsation, there must be some common ground, some *a priori* agreements about the conditions in which the interaction will take place. Shall we speak, or shall we write our ideas? Shall we use English, or shall we use Spanish? Shall we sit as we talk, or should we stand at podiums? Will we discuss in private, or will we have an audience? Will we have time-limits for each segment, without interruption, or shall we be informal, commenting or interrupting politely, going back and forth in a friendly give and take?

What are the rules of engagement that will keep us on track and facilitate honest discourse? Most of all, what is the subject we will consider?

In a previous chapter we have attempted to deal with the philosophical question "What is Real?" This is a question dealt with in the field of *Ontology*, a study of being or existence in general, reality, what actually exists, if anything. Ontology is the oldest school of philosophy; what Aristotle called the "first philosophy" in Book IV of his Metaphysics. Obviously, an agreement about the reality of everything is the key to further discussions about what is true, what is logical, what is believable, what can be known. This is the question we take up in this chapter, then, the question of knowledge, the philosophical field of "epistemology." Knowledge, as defined here, is the accurate perception and understanding of reality— "what is", and "what is can be," for either concrete reality or abstract reality. We can "know" about rocks (very concrete) and we can know about "freedom" (an abstract concept) and our "knowing" may be valid, or it may be incorrect. In this chapter our mission is to distinguish "believing" and "knowing" in a universe which actually IS, an objective universe which is accepted as "real."

Thinking Is the Precondition of Believing

The previous pages have explored (perhaps too long) the nature and varieties of thinking, contrasting "scientific thinking" with "religious thinking" among other topics in preparation for the intended focus on believing and knowing. We have avoided using "belief" and "knowledge" for comparison, because we emphasize here the active engagement of the mind in decision making; what is going on in the brain is more important that the "product" which results. Our knowledge is a "thing," an entity that has form and substance, has boundaries and limits, and remains relatively stable over time. We add to our store of knowledge almost every conscious moment, but the bulk of what we know changes very little. It is hard to replace something we "know" with something that is new and more accurate. The Will Rogers quote heading this chapter is a gem of truth: *It's not what we don't know that gives us trouble, it's what we know that ain't so.*" All humans seem to take comfort in what they already "know" and are not eager to disturbing our storehouse of knowledge with something contradictory. The same is true of our clinging to OUR BELIEFS, only more intensely possessive. We have our "belief compartment" all filled and kept in a protective place, and trying to change our beliefs is seen as a mortal attack. We may not have a well-organized or logically coherent system of belief in our lock box, but "By God, it's MY belief, and it's none of your business!" Such profane protestation is oddly ironic but anger is common when the beliefs challenged are *religious beliefs*. Religious beliefs are intensely personal.

How do people come to have their set of beliefs? Did we adopt the beliefs taught in our childhood? Did we go through a rebellion as we approached adulthood, rejecting almost everything our parents or our social milieu, and assert our independence by claiming radical beliefs? Or perhaps it was an influential college professor whose philosophy impressed you deeply. We may do some deep introspection and conclude that what we believe now "just happened," so far as we can recall, it did not come at some specific time in the way our knowledge often can be pin-pointed. What we "know" is often attained at a specific time. For example, if a third-grade child memorizes the multiplication table (or maybe the 1s through 5s), and finally he "has it." It is a block of knowledge that is dependable and useful, and we know when and how we obtained that knowledge. But what about my belief in democracy or honesty or Santa Claus or the Tooth Fairy? How do I come to believe or disbelieve any of these abstract ideas?

Knowing versus Believing

What do we mean by "belief" or "believing?" How does "believing" relate to "knowing?" In ordinary conversation "knowing" is a stronger claim than "believing." We may say "I believe tomorrow will be very cold." We may also say, "I know tomorrow is your birthday." The first statement is predicting the weather, which is often changeable and unpredictable; the second statement is data-based or evidence based because you have seen the subject's birth certificate, or you wrote the information in your calendar last year when you attended their birthday party. Either statement can be wrong, of course, for mistakes are part of life; you may have written the date on your July calendar page instead of the actual June date, or you may have been unaware that the birthday party was held *two days early* because of scheduling conflicts. Certainly, the weather prediction is subject to error, for several reasons: "very cold" is not a specific temperature, and you may consider 60 degrees "very cold," for July, but other people may have in mind 20 degrees as their definition of "very cold." Likewise, an atmospheric change in the Gulf Stream may push warm air north to produce an unusual balmy 80 degrees tomorrow. Thus, we have *Uncertainty possible versus Uncertainty probable*. Questions of "fact" are typically more definable, while questions of values, ideas or opinions are much more elusive and difficult to define. Another way *believing* and *knowing* differ: "Facts" are usually considered objective (external to the mind) and "beliefs" are seen as subjective (exist in the mind). Facts usually are verifiable by more than one person, whereas belief is unique and personal to the individual.

Believing and knowing also differ in the "degree of confidence." Knowing expresses a high level of confidence (or "certainty) while believing normally indicates a lower confidence level, a tentativeness open to revision. For example, we "know" that the Sun will appear again tomorrow, but we can only "believe" that your candidate will be elected tomorrow. You would be willing to wager as much as $100 about the Sun's dependability, but you probably would only bet $20 on the outcome of a free election.

Standards of Proof

In the American legal system, there are three different levels of "proof" which are commonly used in determining the truth of an accusation or claim. For criminal cases such as murder, rape, bank robbery and other such felonies the standard of proof which the jury or the judge is obligated to follow is "beyond a reasonable doubt." This means that the certainty of the truth is very, very high—perhaps having a 95% confidence that the accusations are true, for the defendant faces loss of liberty or even life in the decision. The courts don't use percentages such as this, but it is helpful here in order to distinguish the other levels. Judges will usually explain to the jury that "beyond a reasonable doubt" doesn't mean "beyond ANY doubt." Jurors sometimes struggle to decide that distinction.

The second level of proof in our justice system is "clear and convincing evidence," a less demanding standard approximating 75% of certainty. This standard is used in less serious cases in civil or family court trials, where the potential loss is not liberty or life, but such things as custody of a child in divorce, loss of custody due to abuse or neglect, paternity, or probate of wills. Until the 1970's the "clear and convincing standard" was used in Juvenile Court for alleged "delinquency" but the US Supreme Court ruled that depriving a youth of liberty required the higher "Beyond a reasonable doubt." Other, non-criminal cases in Juvenile or Family Court usually involve lower standard of proof, and normally are decided by the judge rather than a jury, with "the best interest of the child" guiding.

The final and lowest level of proof in American courts is "preponderance of the evidence." the standard required in most civil cases and in family court determinations solely involving money, such as child support, alimony payments and in most civil lawsuits. "Preponderance of the evidence" means anything beyond 50% probability, slightly more likely than not. For example, a sick person may sue the tobacco company for causing his lung cancer, and the jury must determine how much evidence supports that claim and how much evidence disputes the claim. There is almost never real *certainty* as to how to affix the blame, to know the full truth.

Believing vs Guessing

Sometimes we use "believe" as an initial guess, a tentative guess which is more like a question. We risk a try at determining what someone thinks or feels. "I believe you are upset about what I just said," is such a question/ statement. Our "theory of mind" tells us that the other person has the same kind of thoughts and feelings as you do, and we can sometimes detect clues to that inner sanctum by body language, facial expression or intuition. We are essentially asking "Are you upset?" rather than stating an opinion. The foolhardy boyfriend may say "I know you are upset!" to his girlfriend, and pay a penalty for his audacity: "YOU DON'T KNOW ANYTHING! (Bursting into tears) YOU ARE SO INSENSITIVE!" In his own style George Bernard Shaw reminds us "Beware of false knowledge; it is more dangerous than ignorance."[138]

Sometimes we use "believe" when we are proposing an answer, making an *educated guess*. "I believe that 32 is the answer to question four, Teacher." Or, "I believe we are going to have some rain later today." These "beliefs" are not binding, and we don't have much investment in them; being wrong in your belief in these cases is not very consequential. On the other hand, the public wants members of the Press to report hard, solid facts, and are not interested in hearing a reporter say "I believe the President is going to resign," or "The network is convinced that the casualties are much larger than originally reported." Audiences scorn such weak statements, perhaps labeling them as "fake news." This weaker form of "believing" does not make much of a commitment, and does not change anything substantial. Oh, you may believe it is going to rain soon, and you take your umbrella to work, all for nothing if you guessed wrong. But no penalty is extracted for your mistaken belief, and no one remembers the next day, including yourself. But "belief" has a stronger, more serious connotation in real life. At some deeper level, what you really believe defines who you are, and how you live your life. Believing is serious stuff.

Do We Ever Really Know?

We have emphasized the scientific principle that absolute certainty is impossible in empirical science. Science has learned from centuries of experience that we make mistakes, draw the wrong conclusions, or simply do not have all the information we need. In normal life, apart from scientific endeavors, it is obvious that humans "think" they know something, something which turns out later to be false. We are prone to state things with certainty—we "KNOW this is true because I saw it with my own eyes!" It is almost a natural law to humans: "Seeing is believing." There are a thousand ways we can be wrong, no matter how CERTAIN we are. We can be fooled by con men, politicians, gossip, propaganda, liars, card sharks, and even trusted relatives. We can be deceived by optical illusions, magicians (illusionists), our hearing, and all our other sensory equipment under the right conditions. Still, we have the utmost faith in our perceptions, what we experience for ourselves.

All humans, and not just scientists, are natural *materialists* in that we believe what we see, hear, smell, taste or feel more than information that comes from someone else; we trust our own senses even when confronted with conflicting reports. It probably is a healthy habit to trust our bodies and our senses for life would be chaotic if we suddenly began to see things that were not real, or hear sounds or voices no one else can hear, or if our sense of smell began interpreting the scent of pizza as dog dropping, or the aroma of fresh coffee as a gasoline odor. Such confusions do exist, medically, as well as cases of cross/sensory confusion, whereby a patient "hears" colors or "sees" smells. Fortunately, most of us have a normal set of senses and we trust them implicitly.

Is Reality Only an Illusion?

Let us take one other brief side excursion into the question of "knowing." There are a great many well educated and thoughtful people who believe that "everything is an illusion," and thus we cannot know anything objectively. This is the position of the branch of philosophy generally known as "Idealism." Don't confuse this with the quality of having high ideals, following noble moral principles, or seeking perfection rather than accepting lesser goals. The philosophical Idealism is not a single, unified theory, but is a strain of thought that has appeared many times and in many forms in philosophy's long history. Plato provides one of the earliest and most famous versions of Idealism, with the view that everything we perceive in the material world is but an imperfect copy or reflection of an ideal, perfect form, the only true reality. Thus, a chair we see or touch is not *real* but is a poor copy or version of the Ideal Chair in an alternate reality.

Plato, one of the most influential philosophers of all time, in *Allegory of the Cave* invites us to imagine a cavern in which there are people who have been imprisoned and chained and can only observe a blank wall. They can see, because of a bonfire, the shadows of themselves and of whatever is happening behind them. The voices echo in the cave while the shadows dance on the wall thus making the shadows appear real and talking. One of the prisoners escapes and outside the cave he experiences reality and not just shadows. He returns to the cave to free the others from their shadowy reality, but they refuse to believe him. Plato compares mankind to those who are chained to the "cave wall" (materialism), believing falsely that we see reality in the "shadows" of our minds, whereas another world lies beyond our perceived reality, a world of perfect forms or universals.

According to Idealism we see shades, imitations of how things truly are in Ultimate Reality, a copy of what actually exists in a "Metaphysical Reality" we might interpret as "heaven" or God. Bishop George Berkeley, known as the "Father of Idealism", claimed that the entire world is contained in the mind of God. In the early 18th century, he argued that our knowledge must be based on our perceptions and that there was indeed no "real" knowable object behind one's perception (in effect, what was "real" was the perception itself). Rene Descartes, quoted earlier, was one of the first modern philosophers to claim that all we really know is what is in our own consciousness, and that the whole external world is merely an idea or picture in our minds. Therefore, he claimed, it is possible to doubt the reality of the external world as consisting of real objects, and "I think, therefore I am" is the only assertion that cannot be doubted. The basic premise of Idealism is found in several branches of philosophy, identified with one particular advocate usually, and each variation with a unique name.

Even Science Has Its Uncertainties

Modern science is also "toying" with the idea that reality may include illusion, or at least "illusionary" substances. Quantum mechanics suggests that particles do not assume a specific location or velocity until they are observed, and that observation alters the reality. This apparent strange behavior of tiny bits of matter has been verified by numerous experiments since the 1900's, wherein a particle may appear to be in two places at once, or be unpredictable by normal physics. Science has even adopted a formal "uncertainty principle" known as the "Heisenberg Uncertainty Principle." First articulated back in 1927 by the German physicist Werner Heisenberg, it states that the position and the velocity of an atomic particle cannot both be measured exactly, at the same time, even in theory. At the molecular level the exact location of a single particle is always uncertain. Quantum theory is extremely complex and full of surprises, but it is the dominant paradigm in today's science, and though it seems there is much yet to learn it also holds much promise for future applications.

Finally, to end this "brief" side excursion, popular culture sometimes ventures into this "alternate reality" philosophy. *The Matrix* is a 1999 science fiction action film depicting an evil future world government in which reality as perceived by most humans is actually a simulated reality called "the Matrix." *The Truman Show* (1998) has an insurance salesman living a simulated or "staged" life that unknown to him is actually a TV program. Kurt Vonnegut Jr.'s 1973 *Breakfast of Champions* involved a science fiction writer who creates a story suggesting that reality is only one human being and one God, and everyone else is actually robots used for testing man's reactions, a sort of Genesis simulation. Such science fiction films and novels are usually very successful, for apparently ordinary people like to contemplate what is real, and what is a dream. If nothing we experience is real, except our thoughts, it leaves a lot of questions. For the purpose of this book let us presume that reality is objective and knowable, a material world perceived by our senses, but also the possibility that this material world has a companion world, a non-material world of mind and spirit which is real, and is knowable, but not perceived by sensory perceptions. We don't have to deny materialism in order to consider the idea of a non-material realm of reality accessed by our mind and not by our microscopes or test tubes.

Does Science "Know" but Faith just "Believes?"

As cited several times previously, scientific statements are widely respected in modern Western Culture as "truth" or "fact." Careful scientists usually avoid using the terms "truth" or "facts," opting instead most often to discuss "evidence" and "proof," and even "proof" is used a tentative way to mean that several findings supporting the same answer are given substantial weight, and many confirmations may add up to "strong proof." Science has gained respect and acceptance because it has produced such an abundance of benefits to society, it has shown results. Science has certainly brought about revolutions in agriculture, engineering, medicine, transportation, communication, and hundreds of other practical applications that have made life better for millions of people. (Sadly, science also gave us weapons of mass destruction and war.) It is hard to argue with success. Science has been successful to such a great degree that it is viewed by many as the hope and salvation of Mankind, perhaps replacing the need for a religious Messiah.

Science can tell us a lot about reality, at least about the physical, material observable reality. The scientific method observes, quantifies and codifies relationships of cause and effect, bringing order and predictability out of a world that once seemed to be filled with chaos, randomness and mystery. Science has given us confidence that there is law and order in nature that can be understood and harnessed. Science doesn't have everything cataloged and explained yet, but there is much optimism about future progress. The greatest scientists are looking for the grand design, the "theory of everything" which will tie together Newtonian physics, quantum theory, relativity, string theory, and all the other promising "loose ends" of the universe. Science certainly seems to be "knowing" rather than "believing."

The Whole Truth and Nothing but the Truth

In spite of its admirable track record in understanding the material world, science is incomplete as a means of discovering the truth about all of reality. As discussed before, science is empirical, in fact it is exclusively empirical. *(Relying on or derived from sensory observation or experiment rather than on theory or logic.)* Because the empirical sciences are by definition limited to the study of physical, material reality, only that which can be reduced to matter and energy can be observed and quantified. Science operates by the "materialistic paradigm," a formal way of looking at everything, a world view about reality. If everything in reality is material then science has all the answers.

But there is another respected paradigm going all the way back to Socrates, Plato and other Greek philosopher/scientists: the metaphysical paradigm. Some very important and meaningful facets of human experience do not have physical, material form, and so can't be measured by the empirical means of materialistic science. Materialists, including scientists, may acknowledge the possibility of some non-material reality, but they insist such an unseen world is perceived by faith or intuition, not by evidence or proof. "Faith," to the scientist, is a very weak instrument, associated with superstition, magic and imagination, and so, they often assert, beliefs have no existence outside the Believer's mind.

For many thoughtful people, "the best things in life are not things." We crave "things," and 'things' are necessary, but material things are not sufficient. Mankind also has non-material needs and desires, from our first fully conscious primate relative to the billions of humans living today. Curiosity is not a material thing, but the curiosity that leads to searching for knowledge is universal in mankind; the need for finding "rhyme or reason" in nature and life and the drive to find patterns has been with us always. Fear of the unknown, especially about death, is built into us all, and fear is very real, but we cannot see or touch it; the hunger for meaning and purpose for our individual lives is part of being human. Love is an empty, hollow place in every person ever born, an innate urge to value, to treasure others, and an innate, pressing need for being important and valued by someone or some others. These realities are not "survival" needs that have material solutions, but such things which cannot be seen, heard or weighed are, never-the-less, absolutely critical to our "humanness." Survival makes us living animals, but these metaphysical ingredients make us truly alive as Humans and they nourish our "soul." Regardless of how important such things are (and we argue that they are supremely valuable) they are not detectable by science and they cannot be "proved" by physical measurements. So, are they real?

Science Begins with Belief

It may be a startling assertion to some scientists and science fans, but "beliefs" are a vital part of the scientific way of thinking and searching for truth. Scientific discovery often begins with a question or a "hunch," an idea arising from some observation. Fleming noticed his careful experiment with bacteria had been spoiled by an accident, upsetting his plans. But he began to question, to wonder: "Could that mold be what killed my bacteria? Probably not, but still, maybe so. Who knows? It's possible." He did not know that the penicillin mold was the culprit, but he believed it was worth setting up more tests and experiments to find out. The history of science is the history of puzzled people wondering if something might be possible, looking further without much evidence or support from other people. Whether it is called "hunch," "guess," or "intuition," the scientific mind takes a chance on an idea, believing for the time that it might be worthwhile. Some of these beliefs are quickly dispelled by empirical experiments, and some gain greater believability the more they are tested. In science, unproven beliefs can become knowledge after thorough study and confirmation in laboratory or field. Unfortunately, sometimes science has embarrassing "knowledge" that later proves to be false. Less than 1000 years ago everyone "knew" that the sun and moon and all the stars rotated around the earth, and our earth was the center of the universe. Until about 500 years ago everyone "knew" that the earth was flat. Just a decade ago, the US President, the Congress, many scientists, and almost everyone else "knew" that Iraq had a cache of weapons of mass destruction. "Knowing" is stronger than "believing," and has the power to halt questioning and generate unwise actions, as in the case of the Iraq War.

As discussed earlier, "beliefs" can also mean a whole set of convictions deeply held and emotionally dynamic. Theism is one such set of beliefs, Communism is another, and yet another is Conservatism as a political view. These kinds of belief packages are internal mental commitments to a particular world view or a way of organizing our lives around a set of principles and values. These established beliefs may be carefully and rationally constructed, or they may be second handed answers accepted from some authority figure without serious, rational reflections. The followers of Jim Jones and David Koresh and other such false prophets demonstrate the effect of powerful beliefs inculcated into vulnerable minds, defying all logical, rational challenges literally "to the death." It may come as a surprise to some, but even Science has a belief system: the reverence for the "scientific method" and confidence in the Laws of Nature (Laws of Physics, Laws of Thermodynamics", etc.) are orthodox beliefs to which all true scientists ascribe and follow faithfully ("religiously, we might even say.) These packages of time-tested beliefs give stability to our mental life, not just for religious believers, but also for science or technology believers. We trust in our belief systems, even "betting our lives on them" by the way we behave or by the career we pursue. We all accept *"Pascal's Wager"* in one way or another, betting our destiny on what we believe. (See Chapter 21 for more on "Pascal's Wager")

Beliefs Are Resistant to Change

To say that beliefs are firm is an intentional understatement to emphasize how stable and permanent our deeply held beliefs are for almost everyone. To say that our beliefs are "carved in stone" has a religious connotation to it, and it is true that some people have such a strong conviction about their set of beliefs that it is nearly hopeless to try to change their minds. For most adults, our set of beliefs may not be rationally spelled out and carefully thought out, but we are apparently "hard-wired" to hold on to them as if our life depended on it.

Whether referring to our political beliefs such as Democrat or Republican, or liberal versus conservative, or social beliefs such as universal healthcare or racial equality, our beliefs are very resistant to any challenge or change. The certainty and confidence demonstrated by talk radio hosts or the various cable "talking heads" is legendary, and their fervor attracts and stirs up strong support for their particular truth: for Rush Limbaugh or Ann Coulter to "change their minds" or admit they were wrong is as impossible as "Hades freezing over" or "Pigs to fly." Debates between political candidates, activists, or religious zealots almost always yield more heat than light; such contests almost never have winners and almost never does a debater or listener change their minds.

Change is Hard

Scientists have studied and researched the concept of "change" for many decades, mostly those in the human sciences such as psychology and sociology. Kurt Lewin was one of the pioneers in the 1940's trying to learn how organizations changed or resisted change. He studied change in large organizations rather than individual change, having found that organizations take on a life and "mind" of their own, not always controlled by individual group members. His cornerstone model for organizational change was labeled for the three-stage process he discovered: Unfreeze – Change – Refreeze. Lewin was a physicist as well as a social scientist, and so he compared the social change process metaphorically to the physical changing of the shape of a block of ice. To reshape a 50-pound block of ice, he argued, we must first unfreeze it, thaw it until its rigidity was softened, and then cutting and shaping the large block of ice was easier. But, he cautioned, change will not be permanent unless you follow up the change with a "refreezing" step: with the ice we cool the object below 32 degrees, the freezing point; with organizations undergoing change must be consolidated and reinforced with social pressure or they will revert back to their previous condition (unchanged).[139]

By looking at change as a process with distinct stages, we can anticipate the resistance and obstacles to change and plan to carefully manage the transition from comfortable, settled ideas and ways of doing things into the period of fear, trepidation and outright oppositions. "Look before you leap" is a good motto for most endeavors, and changing social environments can create unnecessary turmoil and even chaos if done too quickly or without sufficient preparations. Announcing change and reorganization in an agency or company is always upsetting to the group, and attempting major change without adequate preparation is almost always doom to failure. Groups and individuals are naturally inclined to oppose change—changing schedules or work sites or supervisory structure is almost always disliked by those being changed; individuals whose beliefs or habits or world view are challenged inevitably harden their positions and become defiant rather than compliant. Resisting change is part of our human nature.

To begin any successful change process, one must define accurately why change must take place. If the proposed change seems to be only the "brain child" of some new executive or manager, "change for change's sake" we say, the organization and individuals will certainly be "cool" toward the idea (cool to the freezing point.) If there is a good, rational reason why the change is necessary, and if it is clearly and transparently explained, some people will start to warm up to the idea. Perhaps a new law requires the change, or keeping the company solvent requires some drastic action, or some new product or design requiring changes in production, but will increase the profit of the company and compensation to the employees. Good, believable explanations can melt much of the resistance, and make the change tolerable or acceptable. Lewin [140] recognized that motivation for change must come first, must be generated, reexamining previous views and beliefs, challenging hidden assumptions, loosening the hold of the status quo. This is the unfreezing stage from which any change begins.

Promoting Change

This is a book promoting change, an "apology" seeking to convince Skeptics to consider belief in a God like Jesus, and persuade Believers to accept the reality of science as a fact of life and reality without fear that science will destroy their religious faith. Skeptics (atheists and agnostics) are already set in their beliefs about God and to ask them to change those beliefs is audacious and presumptive, at the very least. Perhaps the even greater challenge is to soften up the Believers who so firmly oppose and fear scientific ideas such as evolution and creation by chance, and a thousand other assaults on their traditional beliefs. Changing one's mind or beliefs is a gradual process, in some cases taking years and years to make the transition complete. What we already believe has such a firm hold on us that we find it almost impossible to flush it out and make room in our minds for its replacement. Nobody wants to change their beliefs.... Not Yet.

What Difference Does It Make?

What is the difference between believing and knowing? Does knowing evolve from believing? Is knowing just a stronger form of believing? It is not hard to accept the proposition that *religion relies on "believing"* —acceptance of ideas or concepts as "true" though they cannot be proven empirically. But what about science? Does science rely on "believing" in some way? In addition to believing and knowing two other related words must also be considered: Opinion and Faith. There are common, dictionary definitions for the four words under consideration, though common usage has changed these "official" definitions in society. It may seem to be just semantics, and other definitions may be better, but for purposes of this work we will try to clarify what these words mean here in this context:

> **Opinion**: a view or judgment formed and held, not necessarily based on fact or knowledge
>
> **Knowing**: being aware of, or directly perceiving something by sensory input and/or experience
>
> **Believing**: to accept something as true, genuine, or real with or without empirical evidence; a firm conviction
>
> **Faith**: complete trust or confidence in someone or something; a firm belief in something for which there is no proof

One way of looking at these **four key words** is "degree of active choice." Previously we have explained why "believing" is chosen instead of "belief," and "knowing" used instead of "knowledge": the emphasis here is on action, mental activity involved rather than the result of that activity. Once the process of believing is concluded our minds have created an entity, we call a belief (along with other previously created beliefs held in our consciousness). The same is true of knowing, which implies a process by which we obtain and consolidate what we think are true representations of reality—that is, knowledge. Beliefs and knowledge are static products, finished results which are operational and functional until reopened by our minds for reexamination at some later date. Likewise, our knowledge (which we have accepted because of our personal experience or perception) is stored safely and confidently in our memory, that is until something in our constant, ongoing "knowing" and learning causes us to doubt or question what we had thought was true and factual knowledge. Both **knowing** and **believing** are mental processes for **deciding,** and deciding is the mental activity of choosing one out of several options. Believing, even more than knowing, is an exercise of a free will, with free will as the essential human characteristic previously argued in **Chapter 16.**

Believing Is a Choice Made by Our Mind

The claim made here is that believing is a mental activity, a choice between alternatives that is decided one way or another. "Is there a God?" becomes: Either **"There is a God"** or **"There is no God."** There can only be one answer logically and so a choice is required. One can take the agnostic option and say "We can't know for sure, maybe there is a god, and maybe not." But in such a basic choice as this neutrality does not work, for whatever we tell ourselves about our "non-choice" in fact we live our lives according to one world view or the other, and we act upon our *de facto* decision in all our life spheres.

Another way in which the four key words above are distinguished is "degree of certainty." **Opinion** is a tentative belief that something is true, such as "I believe the Patriots will win the Superbowl next year." You may have formed that opinion based on previous performance, or by studying player statistics, or you are just making a wild guess. Opinions are essentially weak, unverified beliefs, and opinions are subject to change relatively easily and often. **Knowing** implies a greater degree of certainty because it is based on personal experience or sensory input. Knowing is relatively stable and not easily changed: "I saw it with my own eyes, so I know for sure that he did it." **Believing** usually is strongly held and resistant to change, but it is not empirically provable; it is personal and individual, and may be based on personal experience (such as a spiritual encounter), or based on views of authority figures or trusted sources, such as "I believe the scientists about climate change, that we humans are damaging the environment." **Faith** is a firm and confident **trust** in something or someone, taking a risk by acting on that belief, a belief which cannot be proven. For example, "I have faith that God will provide for my needs, and therefore I will give my rent money to the homeless shelter. I believe the shelter is doing God's work for needy people, and I know (*my own personal experience*) God helped me last year when I needed food."

Tight Wire

A story is told of a stunt man who announced he was going to cross Niagara Falls walking on a tight wire. The wire was in place and to the astonishment of the gathered crowd, he stepped out on that tiny wire and gingerly walked to the middle of the falls, a hundred feet above certain death. He made one complete trip, and then shouted to the crowd: "Who thinks I can walk across again pushing this wheel barrel?" Many expressed doubts, but several said, "Yes, I believe you can." The stunt man pushed the empty wheel barrel a few feet and then yelled to the crowd: "Who will volunteer to ride across the Falls in my wheel barrel? What about you, sir? You said that you believed I could push it safely across, didn't you? Why don't you come up here?" Embarrassed, some in the crowd started to move away, and some were heard to say, "I believe the guy can do it, but I don't trust anybody enough to go with him! I may believe it, but I don't have enough faith to risk my life. I may be gullible, but I'm not insane."

The crowd knew the stunt man could walk the wire, for they had **seen** him do it. But that knowledge did not translate into taking a chance for themselves; they "believed" but not enough to put their faith in him. Scott Atran is anthropologist at the National Center for Scientific Research in Paris, and also teaches science at the University of Michigan and the John Jay College of Criminal Justice in New York. His research interests include cognitive science and evolutionary biology, and he often presents students with a wooden box that he pretends is an African relic. He tells them with all seriousness and pomp of the magic powers of the box: "If you have negative sentiments toward religion," he tells them, "The box will destroy whatever you put inside it." Many of his students had said they doubt the existence of God but in this demonstration, they act as if they believe in something. "Put your pencil into the magic box" he tells them, and the nonbelievers do so blithely. "Now, put in your driver's license" he says, and most do, but only after significant hesitation. As they gather around the box, he tells them "Now, put in your hand." With embarrassed giggles they all drew back, and no one would risk their hand." Then professor Atran picks up his box and asks the students solemnly, "If you don't believe in God or gods, what exactly are you afraid of?" Though these bright students knew there was no magic in this box, their knowing was uncertainty, and they weren't sure enough to trust the professor.[141]

Believing Changes Things

Knowing is the state of mind where we have first-hand awareness of an event, something that we have personally experienced through any of our five senses or through our own personal participation. Belief is not certainty for the thoughtful, "rational religionist." Beliefs grow and change and evolve over time based on cumulative experience or evidence. One may believe in God in a very satisfying way, and yet one cannot prove God in any scientific way. Our beliefs may be strongly supported by what we learn and new ideas and experience we have, or our beliefs may be weakened by contradictory experiences or encounter with competing views and arguments. Religion and science both depend on "faith," the variable degree of confidence in a belief or a theory, always somewhat short of absolute certainty.

Anything accepted as true is subject to some risk, some possibility that our conclusions are wrong. Such uncertainty, while uncomfortable to humans, is the necessary condition for learning, growth and change. Certainty closes our mind, or at least a door of our mind. Challenging your certainty, asking tough questions about your beliefs, taking a risky closer look—opens the mind for new ideas or new possibilities. Agnostics are often at this point or near it; not certain that God is an illusion, but not yet ready to buy into the belief. "Maybe" is a logical position on such questions as this. Looking at some evidence which could support this "maybe" might be reading from the Gospel of John, or slipping into a church service anonymously to see how it "feels," or questioning some wholesome, low-key Believer about what their life is like. The central premise of this Apology is this: "Get to know the real Jesus and you might just like Him." If this Jesus is the kind of person portrayed in this book, you might want to get to know Him better—test to see if He is available to you in some fashion.

For the Atheist reader the same challenge to certainty is proposed as a logical, scientific thing to do. We cannot "prove" there is no God with scientific methods, and the Believer cannot prove belief in God is true with scientific evidence, so swinging a little toward the middle ground of neutrality seems to be the justifiable and logical position. There really is **no loss to you** if you become a little less certain of your atheism: **God either is** or **is not** regardless of what you or anyone else believes. Unless you regard it as your duty to rescue misguided theistic believers to freedom, or perhaps you are angry at some Believers who use their religion to hurt other people, your crusade is not against God but against some or all of those bad people who claim to serve this God. If it is not about God but about "god pushers" then you might take another look at your beliefs and dial back the "certainty button." For you, perhaps a good review might lead you to this new stage: "**IF THERE WERE** A GOD (*which I doubt*) **A GOD LIKE JESUS WOULDN'T BE TOO BAD.**" Maybe you will take another look at what has been said about Jesus in this book or some other positive account. It's worth thinking about, isn't it?

Good Theology Clarifies Life

Chapter 21

DECISIONS AND CHOICES

*A decision is the product of choosing,
and an ability to choose is what makes us human."*
A.A. ALEBRAHEEM
Islamic Philosopher

AND SO, THE CASE IS MADE. PERSUASIVE OR NOT THE evidence and ideas have been presented and the result is in the readers' hand (or Mind). For this final chapter, the author will come from behind the academic curtain which prescribes scholarly work to be presented impersonally, avoiding any direct reference to the individual person writing or reporting. Occasionally a "we" has sneaked into the narrative, in the traditional mode of the "imperial we" used by queens and emperors to maintain decorum and dignity. In this final chapter of this apologetic for both Christianity and Science, I will seek to replicate a kind of dialogue, seeking to respond to imagined objections or questions through rehearsal of the original arguments presented in the previous chapters. Like a secular salesman, I will try to answer unresolved dissent or doubts which are anticipated, and then I will encourage a decision of some degree. The goal, as stated in the Preface, is not to completely convert anyone but to induce a thoughtful consideration of the propositions presented, to foster an honest reevaluation of preconceptions, and a mind open to the possibilities of exploring a fresh world view. This goal is the same for both intended audiences, the

Skeptic and the Believer: **relax your grip** on your old "certainties" and **take a good look** at these new possibilities intended. In Shakespeare's play, *Julius Caesar*, Cassius faces a decision, whether to attack Marc Anthony's growing army now, or wait for a more advantageous battle field. He mulls the consequences of this fateful decision:

> There is a tide in the affairs of men,
> Which, taken at the flood, leads on to fortune;
> Omitted, all the voyage of their life
> Is bound in shallows and in miseries[142]

Decisions are hard for most of us, especially some major choice that could alter the course of our life: whether to marry, where to live, what career or profession to pursue are such examples. Our daily lives are filled with such decision points, mostly minor and routine, but sometimes more serious or profound. Sometimes the pressure to decide on a course of action is time limited, as Cassius observes: the tide of events moves on and if we miss our opportunity to choose, the opportunity may be lost forever. It is a cosmic truth in the proverb: "To not decide is to decide." If we fail to decide, the decision will be made for us.

The Islamic philosopher A.A. Alebraheem, quoted above as a chapter heading, perceptively connects choices and decision making in the broadest context: it is part of our evolved Homo sapiens identity, a gift and a burden. Choosing is a decision, and decision making is a key skill human need. *"A decision is the product of choosing, and an ability to choose is what makes us human."*[143] We humans are "blessed" with the ability to choose (and the necessity), because we possess "free will." Without this "free will" we humans are puppets or robots.

As discussed in an earlier chapter the philosophical and religious concept of "free will" is controversial, and many people of Science consider such "freedom" as an illusion. To those who deny "free will," the nature of reality is determined by physical laws and forces, all that happens is caused by the irresistible influences shaping our lives. That argument was fully vetted in **Chapter 16 "Freedom and Free Will"** and will not be rehearsed here, but suffice it to say that *this book is grounded in the premise of "free will" in normal humans*. If everything we do is predetermined, by definition our decisions are moot: we only imagine that we have decided on Plan A, when in fact natural law (or

God) imposed that choice. We emphatically deny here both the "*predestination*" theology of some Christians, and the "*deterministic*" world view of some philosophers and scientists. If your decision is already settled about the God described and espoused in this book, and have reviewed whatever you had believed about some of these "big" issues, thoughtfully and rationally considered the "pros and cons," you probably are ready to move on to some other topic or book. **BE BLESSED!** However, if you believe your decision is fluid, (a decision yours and yours alone), but you really **do want to decide** something, please read on: even keeping on is a decision, an act of will, isn't it? It's sort of like a growing intent: "I will…**will…to WILL!**"

Choices and Decisions

Though there is normally not much difference between a "**choice**" and a "**decision**," we are impressed with the insight provided by A.A. Alebraheem quote cited above. For our discussion we **have decided** to follow his idea that decisions are the end products of choosing. In this model, we consider a range of choices (if there are any options), weighing the pros and cons of each option, and then, based on some kind of judgment, we select the choice we believe to be the best: that selection is a decision if we then implement it or take action on it. This may seem like mere semantic trivia but for our purposes here it is the implementation or the action that counts. Some decisions may require immediate steps, such as the decision to quickly exit a room filled with smoke, or to abandon a ship that is sinking. We make some such emergency decisions "instinctively," absent the internal discussion of the pros and cons of several options, and move quickly to act out a plan as if we had prepared ahead of time, had perhaps thought of such situations previously and had a quick decision ready at hand. This kind of emergency action may not be "instinct" in the traditional scientific definition usually applied to animals. Our quick reaction may be just another learned behavior rather than some primitive automatic response from our reptilian brain. The little green lizard may not mull over options for escape when you frighten him, but for humans the decision making we are considering is a higher-level function, using the more advanced abilities of our mammalian brain and our Neocortex. Quickly or at leisure, all humans consider the options, weigh the alternative choices, and make judgments that lead to a decision to act. The process may take only milliseconds but it is detectable on brain scan equipment.

Perhaps an example will clarify this proposed distinction between choices and decisions. Suppose you are driving happily down Main Street and a red Ford truck in the lane beside you suddenly comes over into your lane to get ahead of you. Like most normal human beings, you immediately hit your horn and say some naughty words questioning the offending driver's ancestry (probably an equine relative), and you slam on the brakes to avoid hitting the red truck. (Did you momentarily consider allowing the crash?). Your face probably turns red and your blood pressure and heart rate go up: you are angry. Here begins that discussion in your mind. The Reptilian Brain urges attack: "Don't let that fool get away with that! It's your lane! Yell at him and sit on your horn." Your Mammalian Brain, concerned with emotions, offers soothing advice: "Don't let that warped driver upset you...just shake it off, he's not worth having a stroke. Don't embarrass yourself this way—what will the other people think? Just calm down." Your fists are clinched and you are feeling pretty pumped up now, you are ready to fight. Your Neocortex, your Higher Brain, brings up logic and reason: "Heh, no harm was done, there was no accident, so let's not pick a fight with this guy. Besides, look at him. He looks pretty big and strong, a real "bruiser." Think about what will happen if the police come, maybe blame you for starting a fight? It doesn't make sense. Just go on your way without looking at the guy. Some people are just like that but you don't have to be like them. You are lucky and OK., be thankful, nobody hurt, nothing lost." From a list of quick possible choices, you decide to take a deep breath and drive away. Probably a good, reasonable decision, listening to your "better angel."

Some Decisions Are Bigger and Harder

Decisions about giving in to road rage are easy when compared to deciding many of the other questions life presents us. Deciding on getting married is undoubtedly different from deciding whether to buy a Buick or a Toyota, and deciding which job offer to accept is infinitely more important than choosing to wear a tie or not. The "big" questions have major consequences that have long term effects. If you make a marital mistake, you are very likely to have a miserable life. You may escape that bad decision, but not painlessly. On the other hand, if you make a bad decision about an automobile, you can correct a buying mistake by trading vehicles; you may lose some money, but with no lasting damage. Another way the "big" decisions differ from routine decisions is the **evidence** you consider. What evidence do you use to decide if this potential spouse the one for you, is he or she as great as they seem? What scientific measures will help you decide on a spouse? You gather data on the prospect's finances, height and weight, skin condition, education level, maybe even intellect. But data won't tell you what you **really** want to know in this decision. What evidence can tell you this person will love you and uplift you? What measurement will prove they are emotionally mature, a strong character, one who will be your friend and partner for life, through both good and bad times? What evidence do you accept for any of these desirable qualities? Is it just your "gut" feeling, or do you have reliable evidence about what marriage to this person would be like? Plato advised us: "A good decision is based on knowledge and not on numbers." Where do you get that knowledge about the big decisions in life if numbers fail you?

If your decision is about which car to purchase you have good, solid, empirical evidence (though it may be exaggerated by the salesman). You know the MPG, the safety ratings, the horsepower, the warranty terms and hundreds of other data-based details. You consider the individual features and consider which are more important to you, and which package will suit your driving for years to come. You may even be persuaded by the projected "trade-in" value touted by the dealer. You can use the material evidence to make a rational, sound decision. Still, it may be the color of the beautiful vehicle that sells you, or the fancy wheels and upholstery might influence the decision. Deciding by the numbers is the most rational, logical way, right? Maybe for cars, but not for spouses and not for such bigger questions such as "What am I going to do with my life?" or "How can I find happiness?" or "Is this life all that there is?" or "Does it make any difference what I believe?" or "Is there a God of some kind behind all this?"

The Truly Important Questions Are Not Empirical

Questions about the meaning and purpose of life are not answerable by any mathematical formula or sensory measurement. Such big questions are the purview of philosophy rather than natural science for science must have observational, measurable evidence to function. To say that science cannot actually tell you "What is the meaning of life," or "Is there a God?" is not to disparage science but simply to recognize that as non-material, non-physical matter is involved, such issues are invisible to sensory-fed science. Can we prove that **God does exist**? Not with empirical evidence, not by using measurable data from sensory observation. Neither can we prove **God does not exist** for the same reason—lack of evidence. As argued in **Chapter 1 and 3**, absolute proof and certainty are elusive and probably impossible in science and philosophy.

Considerable evidence indicates that our cognitive system consists of (at least) two subsystems, one **rational-scientific** and the other **intuitive-spiritual**. Since these subsystems work on overlapping data bases, it seems reasonable that sometimes they come up with comparable results as briefly mentioned above. However, these separate results are experienced consciously in widely different ways. Although the two subsystems are working in parallel, they probably influence each other, because the human person appears to function as a self-organizing system. We are *ourselves*, whether considering our unconscious decision-making processes or focusing on our conscious, rational evidence-examining thinking: we are *one*, all the parts and pieces that make up the "Us." Even our habits and biases and our personality quirks are us, complicated and confused sometimes, but still one person. Sometimes we are in the intuitive, spiritual mode and ideas and thoughts come to us subjectively, maybe a bit vague but compelling, and sometimes very detailed and complete, such as a song or poem or an "invention." Other times we are intensely conscious and focused on a question, and we martial objective facts or knowledge to be scrutinized and evaluated with logic and reason. These two modes actually interplay, with the intuition/spiritual "inspiration" leading to a rational/scientific testing of the new idea and drawing conclusions. Likewise, our study and research for objective facts and generate intuition or "hunches" which seem possible and believable, even without "evidence." We are "thinkers" and it appears that every part of our physical and mental machinery gets into the act.

Intuition is the ability to acquire knowledge without proof, evidence, or conscious reasoning, or without understanding how the knowledge was acquired, by the standard definition. It is common to think of intuition as a magical phenomenon—but hunches are actually formed on the basis of past experience and cumulative knowledge. Gut feelings have their value, but they do not always lead to good decisions. Intuition is essentially the brain on autopilot, performing the actions of processing information without the person's conscious awareness that it is operating. It is nonconscious thinking. How much to trust intuition? More than most rationalists would guess. The automatic information processing that underlies intuition can be seen in something people experience daily, the phenomenon known as "highway hypnosis." It occurs when a driver travels for miles without a conscious thought about the activity of driving the car. Pedestrians walk down a street, get lost in thought, and find themselves at their destination without awareness of the processes that got them there.

Nonconscious processes operate in our complex decision-making as well as the routine day-to-day kind of activities. We often cite rational sounding reasons for our decisions, without revealing (or realizing) the subjective preferences, biases or prior experiences not only in routine activities by also in complex decision-making—often enough, without due credit. People typically cite rational-sounding criteria for their actions and do not disclose the subjective preferences of feelings that arise spontaneously. There is no substitute for devoting time to gathering information about any task or situation. But neither should people be afraid of not consciously knowing every reason for feeling the way they do in every situation. Self-examination is good and introspection is a valid research tool, especially when it is then examined with cold-eyed objective knowledge. Balance between the intuitive and the rational modes is crucial for good decisions. "Gut feeling" and hunches and first impressions are often well-founded even if we can't know exactly why we know. But our feelings can fool us, and so some decisions with serious consequences may require further study, more reflection, even seeking advice from others. The questions about religion, ethics, mortality and God are examples of decision-making that is informed by both our intuition and our scientific method, not in competition but in collaboration. Just because we cannot "prove" God's existence with empirical data does not mean we cannot make a rational decision.

The Quest for The Whole Truth

Ernest Rutherford (who discovered the "nucleus" in a famous experiment with alpha particles and gold foil and thus set the stage for the atomic theory of matter) famously noted: "*All science is either physics or stamp collecting.*"[144] While many will take offense at this, there is an important truth here. Ultimately physics is a search for a grand unified theory of everything based on the principle that the natural world is comprehensible and describable. In a real sense it encompasses all other subfields of science unless we tack on a restrictive definition of physics. Chemistry, biology, and psychology, as examples, are aiming for coherent unified truth, not simply classification and local truth. In any event, science is not simply a collection of disjointed facts, the practice of science involves a quest for real intelligibility in the material world, "making sense" of the whole and not just parts.

In Christian circles the analog to Rutherford's quote is the idea that theology is the queen of the sciences. If science involves a quest for knowledge, a grand theory of everything, then theology is at the pinnacle as God is the source and center of everything that exists. More broadly, one's worldview provides a grand unified theory of everything – thus the quest for knowledge must include or even begin with a metaphysical worldview. Thus, in some sense, theology is the queen of the sciences whether one is theist, spiritual, or atheist. We are in a quest for truth, the Whole truth, the structure of thought that is able to fit all we know and believe into a logical and satisfying pattern—a world view is another term for this goal. It is not satisfying to the inquiring mind to have a coherent pattern for what science tells us if we don't have a world view large enough to accommodate our religious or spiritual beliefs. Accepting them as mutually exclusive options is emotionally uncomfortable, and so we have hope that the "Big Picture" can fit all that we know and believe in a rational schema.

The thesis of this book is that the Christian God, rightly understood as being like Jesus, is the basis for a coherent, rational and comprehensive belief system which satisfies both our intellect and our human emotional need for harmony and oneness with the whole of life. We want a world view that comforts us in our inner self that we are "OK" in this Universe, we are accepted and important to the Creator or the unseen spiritual force operating above and beyond what is scientifically measurable, at the same time letting us be confident that the laws of nature or physics are understandable and sensible, making sense to the degree we have so far defined them. We want peace with God (or Nature) and peace with the physical realities of living on this planet, at this time, and with these companions. It takes a "Big God" to be adequate for the task. It takes a "Big Believer" to accept a multipurpose world view which allows new ideas and new discoveries to find a place in their existing mental structure. And of course, it takes a "Big Scientist" to accept the possibility of a non-physical reality and to find room in their current world view to accommodate some kind of supernatural truth. Small minds are dangerous for both the religious and the non-religious. Having an intellectual "blind spot" (or a closed dark mental room) is an unnecessary handicap for fully functioning humans.

Living with Inference

Inference is a mental exercise for drawing a conclusion on the basis of evidence and reasoning. Some of our commonly used synonyms are more familiar: deduction, conclusion, reasoning, conjecture, speculation, surmise, thesis, theorizing, hypothesizing, presumption, assumption, supposition, reckoning, extrapolation, reading between the lines and more. Generally, science is wary of this idea, regardless of the word used inferences are not proof, not fact, and therefore, are suspicious. But in the real world and real minds inference is a useful and frequent help in thinking. Harvard Professor Chris Argyris has studied inference for years and has developed a model to illustrate how the process works in real life. He has presented a "Ladder of Inference" to show how we tend to confuse objective facts with our interpretation; he argues that our assumptions (pre/*sumptions*) shape the way we see the world and how we form conclusions greatly influenced by our pre-existing assumptions. Argyris' model (a ladder leading up step by step from the pool of data through assumptions and biases, etc.) shows our beliefs, assumptions and cultural environment may shape what we see or attend to, and thus can bias our conclusions.[145] It suggests that we always begin with a set of data (to what we are exposed), but we then narrow the choice to what we actually observe, and then select those facts or ideas which fit our prior beliefs or convictions, and then begin to interpret those observations and facts based on assumptions (usually not conscious or examined.) Thus, according to this model, our eventual decisions and actions are highly filtered and far from objective in the scientific or rational sense.

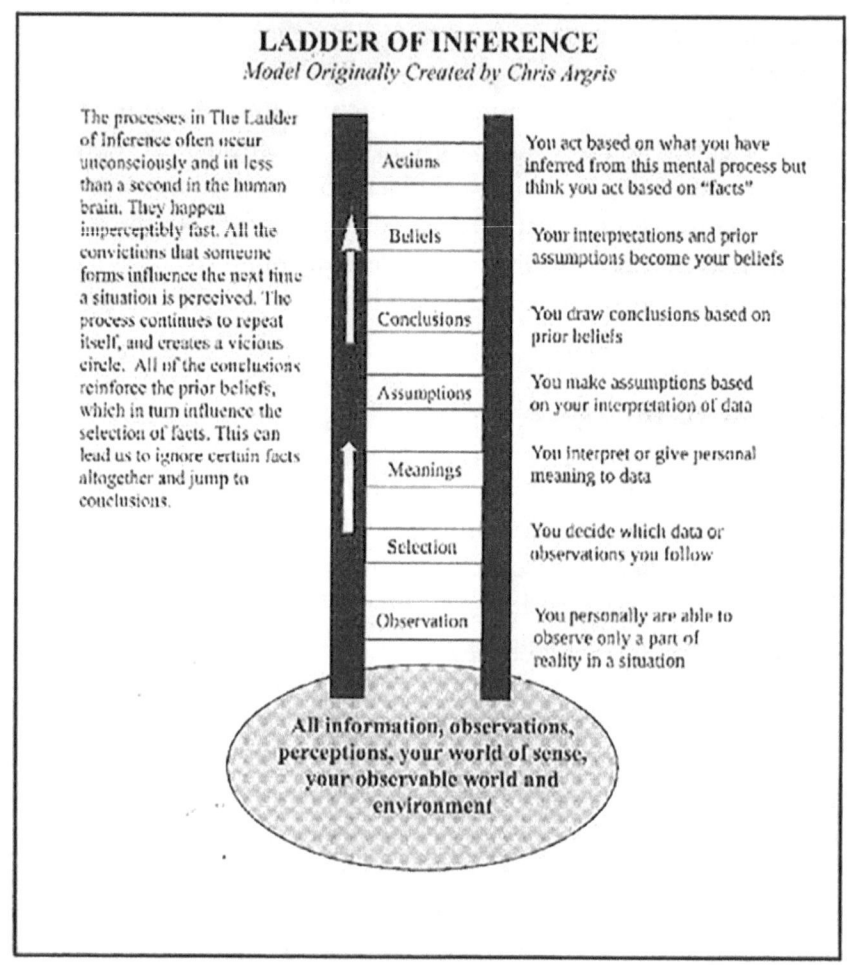

DECISIONS AND CHOICES

We already know that we don't pay real attention to some of the thousands of impressions and inputs we receive every day, and what we think we are looking for often blinds us to what is in front of us. We don't take in all the data available to our brains but we select out or filter some things (such as background noise, or opinions we dislike). We might see the unkempt appearance of a speaker and not actually hear what he is saying, or we may be distracted by the defective sound system in the auditorium and let irritation block our attention.

Even if we observe and select some data or events to consider, we still put it through an "interpretation machine" in our mind, attaching the meanings familiar to us, the ways we had been taught or influenced by our culture. Professor Argyris discusses assumptions in great detail, for the previous decisions and beliefs we have formed are a strong influence on what we conclude from the new circumstances. Assumptions are often hidden from others and from ourselves, operating at the unconscious level where they are usually not rationally challenged.

How often have we each made the mistake of "jumping to conclusions" without thorough thinking and reflection? Jumping to conclusions suggests it is a dangerous enterprise, for jumping can lead to a great downfall, literally. We pass judgment too soon or without adequate information, and make unwarranted inferences from the data, either because we already "knew" what we would find and were looking for support rather than facts. Once we make our inference or conclusion, it is likely to be our precious belief quickly set in concrete, difficult to change or challenge. We tend to have instant confidence in our very own decisions. Considering the two primary audiences this book is written for, the Skeptics and the Believers, let us briefly review how this inference ladder might apply to those who have been on opposite sides of the science/religion question.

Reality and Facts: It is likely that Skeptics have observed a number of religious Believers, perhaps even been close friends with some. The sample you observed is critical in determining what you see as facts: some Believers are arrogant, pushy, close-minded, argumentative, and believe in a God who likes to kill little children to punish their parents. That sample of reality is skewed horribly, and certainly would lead a Skeptic to have a negative opinion of "religious people" or Believers.

Obviously, starting with that portion of reality, your interpretation of that "reality" is going to be negative: "I certainly don't want the *religion* they have! They are a hateful, narrow-minded bunch of prudes!" The sample reality determines the interpretation of the facts, but the sample is already distorted. Ask yourself, dear Skeptic "Are there any good Christians, any kind and compassionate religious people who don't pass moral judgment on the rest of us?" You may have to go to different sites than customarily visited, but if you look around, you probably can find some good Believers, decent and kind people you will like. It doesn't have to be church, though that should be where you find good believers, but you can find them in all parts of your work world, or your social circle, or in civic groups. If you find and get acquainted with some good people, involved people, they will likely be Believers of some kind, serious thinkers, not necessarily religious, but committed to something or idea. If you get to know them, your view of reality will be better informed.

Believers, you too are probably making inferences and conclusions based on a selected view of reality. You may think all scientists are atheists, are profligate and even a little arrogant, for you probably learned most about scientists from TV or movies. Sure, there are some attractive TV scientists such as Neil deGrasse Tyson and Carl Sagan and even Bill Nye, "the science guy." But most likely you have not had a big sample of "scientists" in real life, and probably have never had a serious conversation with one. It is easy to forget that medical doctors, nurses, pharmacists and lab technicians are all practicing science, and they tend to be "nice" don't they? Scientists are actually very hard working, dedicated people who are trying to make the world better (maybe not everyone, but most). They are usually smart, have had decades of education, and are just like the rest of us when it comes to living, loving, worrying, grieving and dying; they most often are married and raising children for free in their own homes, just like most of us. Some of them are very religious and some are strident atheists, but not much different from the whole society according to surveys and research. So, if your argument with science is based on a very small and select sample, you are in danger of "jumping to the wrong conclusion."

Biases Are Bad! Most of us think of "bias" as a prejudice, a predetermined opinion about someone or some group, being "unfair" and partial toward one side against another. Those are true definitions, and we know we should be unbiased, fair and honest. But another definition of "bias" is quite revealing: the same word is used to describe a <u>diagonal</u> cut across the grain of a fiber, a cut of meat, or a diagonal cut of carrots. The underlying meaning seems to be "crooked" or going against the grain (of normal). Wood and other natural things have patterns of fibers and growth, and it is easier to make a clean cut when you are going with the grain. Assuming the way nature builds things as the "truth" then a bias is cutting crooked or distorted in our thinking. Bias misleads us.

Belief in God Is Not Religion

Contrary to what many secular people assume, **Christianity is not a religion**; it is a one-on-one, **personal relationship** with God, a relationship initiated and nurtured by the Creator with His children. Though there are thousands of groups of Christians, and there are common doctrines and teachings in congregate Christianity, God only deals with the singular, the individual "lost sheep" in the world. God does not "save" a group, a Nation, a People, or a Race, though all these groups of humans are under his grace and concern. The grace-based relationship between God and man is the foundation of the Gospel of Christianity and is the antithesis of religion. Established religion in Judea was one of the staunchest opponents of Jesus during His earthly ministry. They rejected "God in the flesh" in favor of their rule keeping structured religion, Judaism. Therefore, Skeptics reading this are not being asked to accept "Christianity" *per se*, but simply to consider accepting the reality of a God, a God like Jesus. This God wants to be your Heavenly Father, with all that has packaged with it. God loves you, as you are, and has moved heaven and earth to win your heart. He never gives up on you. Like the "Hound of Heaven" in Francis Thompson's epic poem, "The Hound of Heaven," He is pursuing you, not to harm you but to embrace you. Read again a brief selection about the enthralling words of God's chase:

> I FLED Him, down the nights and down the days;
> I fled Him, down the arches of the years;
> I fled Him, down the labyrinthine ways

Of my own mind; and in the mist of tears
I hid from Him, and under running laughter.
Up vistaed hopes I sped;
And shot, precipitated,
Adown Titanic glooms of chasmèd fears,
From those strong Feet that followed, followed after.
    But with unhurrying chase,
    And unperturbèd pace,
Deliberate speed, majestic instancy,
They beat—and a Voice beat
More instant than the Feet—
'All things betray thee, who betrayest Me.'[146]

Caught by Surprise

One of the most ardent atheists of modern times was C.S. Lewis, the famous British author of *The Screwtape Letters, Chronicles of Narnia, Mere Christianity* and dozens of other popular books. Lewis was exceptionally brilliant, Oxford educated, and a struggling atheist/agnostic until age 32. He regarded religion as non-sense, and Christianity the worst of the bunch. He later described his struggle as an intellectual and philosophical scoffer, but with a nagging inner questioning and doubt. **"Really, a young Atheist cannot guard his faith too carefully"** Lewis wrote; it seemed that he was being pursued and hounded by something, Someone. He described the chase: *"The fox had now been dislodged from the wood and was running in the open, bedraggled and weary, the hounds barely a field behind."*[147] Like the "Hound of Heaven" by Francis Thompson, Lewis felt that God was chasing him, hounding him. *"You must picture me alone in that room at Magdalen, night after night, feeling, whenever my mind lifted even for a second from my work, the steady, unrelenting approach of Him whom I so earnestly desired not to meet. That which I greatly feared had at last come upon me. In the Trinity Term of 1929 I gave in, and admitted that God was God, and knelt and prayed: perhaps, that night, the most dejected and reluctant convert in all England".*[148] The agnostic became a theist that night, somehow coming to simple belief in God, though not Christianity, not belief in Jesus as God incarnate.

It was two years later, September 19, 1931, that the persistent intellectual and philological struggle suddenly ended, while riding in a motorcycle side car: *"I know very well **when** but hardly **how** the final step was taken. I went with my brother to have a picnic at Whipsnade Zoo. We started in fog, but by the end of our journey the sun was shining. When we set out, I did not believe that Jesus Christ is the Son of God and when we reached the zoo I did.*[149] Lewis attributes that life-altering change of mind and heart to the long and deep discussions with two Christian friends at the college. He became, in a moment, the greatest advocate for Christianity since Paul of Tarsus.

A God who pursues us in love is radically different from the gods of myth and legend of ancient people and radically different from the popular images of today, either a weakling "wuss" or a monstrous chess player watching us squirm. Ancient gods indeed chased people, but it was a malevolent hunt for the helpless prey who had offended the gods. In Jesus' stories we see a father longing for his prodigal son to come back home, to return to his place in the family, a father who runs recklessly to his beloved son, arms open wide, and an embrace that surrounds the repentant child. That was a story about God, a God who recklessly lavishes His love and forgiveness upon us, who wipes out the pig-stained old garments and bestows a royal robe to our shoulders. That's some kinda' God!

What Do YOU Think Now?

Readers have been presented with a portrait of God who is reflected in the person of Jesus of Nazareth, a Jewish teacher of First Century Palestine. We have tried to persuade readers that Jesus embodies the very nature and character of the God Jesus called "Father," and we can understand the invisible, holy and loving "Father" by looking at what Jesus did and taught. The Creator of the Universe has involved Himself in human life and destiny, and has demonstrated His unrestricted love for Mankind throughout all time, and finally in the death and resurrection of Jesus that God has "redeemed" humanity from our flawed human, animal-like, selfish nature. We have argued that "If there **was** a God, this Jesus-God is as good as we could ever dream of." A quaint phrase coined by St. Anselm, Archbishop of Canterbury (1033-1109 is used in philosophy to define God as **"That than which no greater can**

be conceived." The argument is a bit convoluted but the basic idea is helpful here: **Who can we conceive of that which is better or greater than Jesus?** Obviously, we mean "Jesus as reported." The evidence for the factual reality of an historical Jesus was presented in **Chapter 11** and is quite solid, empirical evidence, we believe. Even though many modern people are not sure about whether Jesus was God, or that He did all the miracles attributed to Him, virtually no one denies that Jesus was superbly great and good man. It is hard for anyone to conceive of a person who could be as great or as good as Jesus apparently was. Again from St. Anselm "If there is a being who is greater than all others, there being none greater, that Being must be God." Even atheists tend to admire Jesus and regard Him as "He than which no greater or better can be conceived." What more would we want in a Savior? To be sure, we believe Jesus was more than a good, great man, as C.S. Lewis so clearly explained in **Chapter 12.** *He was God in human skin.* Jesus is the ultimate description of God. As Jesus explained, to know Him is to know God.

We have urged readers to strip away the false, distorted, cruel and vengeful ideas about this God that have accrued over the centuries, based on primitive thinking, misunderstandings and bad theology of ancient worshipers. We have argued that the Old Testament is a record of the **search for God** by many sincere seekers, each adding to the fuller picture as their understanding evolved and the truth was revealed to them gradually and partially due to their limited capacity for reason and a limited world perspective. The wicked, petulant, genocidal Yahweh they wrongly imagined was like an early, preliminary sketch, with lots of inaccuracies and mistakes that eventually are noticed and revised. The revisions are related to that early sketch, but with lots of erasures and red pen notes, a better, more accurate picture emerges. With input from many others the image is cleaned up and made more detailed, until it is finally considered "OK." Someone may modify it and improve it later, almost certainly, but it is infinitely better than that first rough drawing. So too has our picture of the God of the Universe undergone many changes over the centuries, improvements in this section for now, and some new insight about another section next week. Such a drawing may never be FINAL, unless we get to see the **real thing** right before our eyes. Our sketch may still look pretty good, but it is a crude representation of the **real thing**. The claim here is that Jesus was the **real thing:** God in person.

Pascal's Wager

Blaise Pascal (1623–1662) was a seventeenth-century French philosopher, mathematician and physicist who created a famous argument for God.[150] His philosophic proposition is that humans bet with their lives that God either exists or does not. Life is a game of chance, he says, and logically there are only two theological choices: either God exists or God does not exist. Like the toss of a coin, it may land tails or it may be heads—it is a gamble. Lacking certainty, one must choose to believe or choose not to believe, as each has an equal chance of being correct. But, Pascal argues, it is logically better to bet on God than to bet against Him, to wager your life on a belief in God because the consequences of the two betting options are not equal. His calculation is a math problem, an issue of probabilities. Here is his thesis in a chart form:

	God exists	God does not exist
You believe in God	Eternal happiness (=Heaven) A1	Nothing happens A2
You don't believe in God	Eternal damnation (=Hell) B1	Nothing happens B2

Pascal argues that a rational person should live as though God exists and seek to believe in God. If God does actually exist, such a person will have only a finite loss (perhaps some temporary physical pleasures, great luxury, attending boring sermons, etc.), whereas they stand to receive infinite gains (as represented by eternity in Heaven) and avoid infinite losses (eternity in Hell).

If you choose (A) <u>Believe in God</u> then your possible consequences are **(A1)** *Eternal Happiness* or **(A2)** *Nothing Happens*-no loss, no gain.

If you choose (B) <u>Don't Believe in God</u> then your possible outcome is (**B1**) *Eternal Damnation* or (**B2**) *Nothing Happens*-no loss, no gain.

Given that reason alone cannot determine whether God exists, Pascal concluded that this question functions like a coin toss or drawing straws: one chance out of two. We all know that chance or luck is random, it has no preset preferences (unless you're dealing with a crooked gambler.) We have one life and two choices; we must decide whether to live as though God exists, or to live as though God does not exist, even though we may be mistaken in either case. The choice is a gamble. However, even if we do not know the outcome of this coin toss, we must base our actions on some expectation about the outcome: if "heads" I win a new car; if it comes up "tails" I will lose my old car. In that kind of gamble, you might be able to say "I don't want decide, so I don't want to participate." When it is your life and future involved, however, we can't just say "I won't decide!" You are going to live your life, expend your one lifetime, and the binary choice is forced; to **not decide** the existence of God is automatically a vote for the negative **"God does not exist."** Unalterably, our lives are shaped one way or the other on the basis of this belief, for better or worse, but never neutral.

You Bet Your Life

Pascal argued that the wise decision is to wager that God exists, since "If you gain, you gain all; if you lose, you lose nothing, meaning "one can gain eternal life if God exists, but if not, one will be no worse off in death than if one had not believed. On the other hand, if you bet against God, win or lose, you either gain nothing or lose everything. You are either punished forever, or you are annihilated (in which case, nothing matters one way or the other). For Pascal and many others, the logic is persuasive. Betting on God has more ways to win, and fewer ways to lose. Some have argued that living as if God exists is not a "win" for you have to behave and please God (and maybe follow some rules). They say "It costs you something, maybe more than the atheist choice." Many million Christians living and billions not now living would claim that is an unfortunate and untrue supposition, probably based in the defective image of God one has accepted. In fact, those who live their lives as if God exists and matters, are demonstratively more healthy, happy and satisfied in life. Many studies have shown that religious people live longer, survive diseases better, claim to be happier, and are more productive and satisfied human beings.

These are people, on average at least, who make a positive difference in their world. Most of us are seeking meaning and purpose in life, perhaps calling it "happiness." A.A. Alebraheem is a wise Islamic philosopher and writer has put this issue clearly in a thoughtful article:

> Although life offers many pleasures, the people who purvey these pleasures conveniently forget to warn us that they are temporary pleasures. The sweetness of food fades in moments. The pleasure may be intense, but by the time the food has been swallowed, the pleasure has ended. All life's vanities are short-lived. Yet somehow in our minds we transform these fleeting moments into something more enduring. When in fact, pleasure is just a series of short-lived moments. It is these false memories that trick us into believing that we should strive for enduring happiness, when we ought to know that such happiness does not exist.
>
> If you are seeking happiness, here is news that will not make you happy. Everlasting joy does not exist on earth; anyone searching for it will be disappointed, and anyone who claims it is either bragging or trying to sell something. *Seeking endless happiness leads to frustration and discontent, because it is reaching for the impossible, whereas seeking tranquility is a much more realistic goal. Tranquility is peace of mind, emotional stability and inner satisfaction.*[151]

Belief in God does not guarantee health or happiness, for as Jesus reminded us **"*your Father in heaven... causes his sun to rise on the evil and the good, and sends rain on the righteous and the unrighteous.*"** (Matthew 5:45) Nature treats us all the same, the natural laws apply equally to the saint and the sinner. The difference is not how wet or how hot we get but the person who believes God is his friend and guide has an inner confidence that "Everything is going to be OK. Not that what happens is always good, but whatever happens, God will help me through it." Ultimately that means that the Believer will come to life's end as we all do, and can accept it as "OK! I had other plans, but I've had a good, happy life, a meaningful and worthwhile life, and I am soon to be with my loving God forever. *Not a bad ending.*" Non-believers certainly can face mortality courageously and calmly, as many do, but resoluteness, grit and guts facing death is not the same as the confidence and assurance that Believers normally enjoy.

The Payoff: Pain or Pleasure

If you don't believe in God then you probably don't believe in Hell (or Heaven either); many non-believers argue that a good God would not punish people in the pit of Hell for eternity, burning and sizzling forever and forever. Hell doesn't really make a difference in this equation, I would argue, and it doesn't really matter if the "punishment" is fire or ice or whether the temperature is 98 degrees or 98,000 degrees. The punishment is not the heat, it is the separation from the Creator, the source of life and love and happiness. Whoever else may be there (your friends or enemies, maybe?) **God will not be there.** That is Hell for the mind and spirit and the memories and all the regrets of a life wasted and lost.

Hell seems to me to be more like the lone astronaut who is lost out into empty space, drifting forever further and further from home, maybe still hearing the radio crackling "This is Houston. Can you hear me?" with no way to answer "I'm here!" Separated forever...drifting, lost in space or nothingness. Dying out there would be release and relief—but what if it was forever, never-ending separation, loneliness and lostness. Hell, if there is one, would just be a warmer version of such an eternal capsule in an endless universe. Heaven, whatever it may be (gold streets and crystal cathedrals are not the attraction), is **Home with God.** Whatever it is like it will feel like love and peace and oneness with the Universe, for we will be with the Creator and our Father. **Whatever vision you have of Heaven, you won't be disappointed!**

A Choice Not an Echo

In 1964 Phyllis Schlafly self-published *A Choice, Not an Echo,* a book which many credit for giving conservatism control of the Republican Party. She argued that the Republican Party had become just an echo of liberals or moderates in the Democratic Party, giving voters no real choice. Like Barry Goldwater, she urged her party and candidates "think for yourself." That is still a good bit of advice, for the pressure of "group think" is a well-known detriment to creative and honest thinking. As we end this argument for belief in **a God who is like Jesus and a Christianity that accepts that God is a Scientist**, the decisions the readers make is their own to claim and implement. You may have been raised in a conservative Evangelical church that abhorred modern science and higher education as well, and it is likely you think somewhat the way you were raised. Or you may have grown up in a home of atheistic or agnostic scientists for whom religion was a foolish illusion foisted on the ignorant by the Clerical Elites. To think differently from your background is not easy, even if you think you have long ago rejected the "indoctrination." As shown in the earlier "Ladder of Inference" we all are subtly influenced in what we observe, trained to select some things and deselect other things based on our culture and background. You are not your past, behaviorally or intellectual. You are now.

To make a rational choice about God or no-God is to think for yourself and not being an "echo." You may be an echo of your current colleagues and circle of friends, where it is uncomfortable and even risky to stand out from the herd. It is our hope that here at the end of your reading of this book your mind is stirred and inquisitive about your beliefs: they are yours and no one else is authorized to criticize them. "Your decisions are honorable because they are your own" someone has said, anonymously. "**Once you make a decision, the universe conspires to make it happen**" is a profound thought often attributed to Ralph Waldo Emerson."[152] Whether Emerson said it or not, it seems to be a moral or spiritual law. Deciding is destiny. Both Skeptic and Believer have been asked to examine yourselves, look inside and consider what might keep you from free will choices.

We end with this repeated argument in the face of being unable to prove or disprove the existence of any god: <u>If there was a Creator God who was exactly like Jesus, that would be a Good God</u>. Jesus is the only evidence presented which really counts. If you like Jesus (admire Him, respect His teachings, etc.) then you're going to love His Father. **He's some kinda' God.**

BLESSINGS!

End Notes

1. Grant, Allen the Evolution of the Idea of God, (1909) by the Rational Press Association
2. Wilson, Robert Anton quoted: in *Stargazer Magazine* (1980) "Searching for Cosmic Intelligence", interview with Jeffrey Elliot
3. Drost, Steve, Quora (Jan 7, 2018) an American question-and-answer sharing website
4. Burgon, John William Inspiration and Interpretation 1861, Oxford & London, preface
5. Brennan Manning, The Signature of Jesus, 1996, pp. 174-175
6. Benjamin Warfield, The Bible, The Book of Mankind A paper read at the World's Bible Congress held at the Panama-Pacific Exposition, San Francisco, California, August 1-4, 1915. Reprinted by Forgotten Books 2018
7. Artemesia, Mary (died 1913) "Break Thou the Bread of Life" Public Domain, Published in multiple hymnals
8. Gould, Steven. J. (1997). "Nonoverlapping Magisteria." *Natural History* 106 (March): 16–22 & 60-62
9. Ibid
10. Yaconelli, Mike, The Core Realities of Youth Ministry (2003) Zondervan. P. 5ff
11. Green, William Batchelder, The Blazing Star, (1872) A. Williams, Boston, Hath Trust Digital Library
12. Darwin, Charles, (1958), in Barlow, Nora (ed.), The Autobiography of Charles Darwin 1809–1882. *Edited and with appendix and notes by his granddaughter Nora Barlow*, London: Collins
13. Darwin, C. R., "Letter 12041". to Fordyce, John, 7 May 1879. Darwin Correspondence Project.
14. Guilford, J.P. (1967). The nature of human intelligence. McGraw-Hill

15. Kahneman, Danny, (2011) Thinking, Fast and Slow, 7th (seventh) Impression edition by Kahneman, Daniel (Author) published by Doubleday Canada
16. Shermer, Michael, "Is Religion Harmful?" in The Edge of Reason, Alex Bentley editor, 2008, Continuum International Publishing, p. 110.
17. MacLean, Paul, "A Triune Concept of the Brain and Behaviour" The Clarence M. Hincks Memorial Lectures (January,1973)
18. Swanson LW, Petrovich GD (August 1998). "What is the amygdala?". *Trends in Neurosciences.* 21 (8): 323–31
19. Frackowiak, Richard, "Chapter 16: Human Brain Function" in The Neural Correlates of Consciousness (2004) p. 269
20. Nagel, Thomas, first published in *The Philosophical Review* (October 1974), later in Nagel, Thomas, Mortal Questions (1979. Cambridge University Press.
21. Francis Crick & Koch, Christof, "A Neurobiological Framework for Consciousness. - 2007 - In Max Velmans & Susan Schneider (eds.), The Blackwell Companion to Consciousness. Blackwell. pp. 567—579.
22. Stern, Daniel The Interpersonal World of the Infant, London (1985). Pp. 165
23. Doherty, Martin J. Theory of mind: How children understand others' thoughts and feelings (2009) Psychology Press
24. Plato, The Republic (601d) and (105c)
25. Egnor, Michael, "The brain is not a meat computer," in *Mind Matters News* (August 2018) published by the Walter Bradley Center for Natural and Artificial Intelligence.
26. Aristotle's De Anima "On the Soul", Book III, Chapter 4, subsection (1)
27. Harlow John Martyn, (1868). Recovery after Severe Injury to the Head. Bulletin of the Massachusetts Medical Society. Reprinted in *History of Psychiatry, 4(14),* 274-281 (1993)
28. Ibid., p. 276
29. Ibid., p. 280
30. Ibid., p. 281

31. Muckli, Lars, et. al., "Bilateral visual field maps in a patient with only one hemisphere" <u>Procedures of the National Academy of Sciences, USA</u>, August 2009, pp. 13034-13039
32. Sacks, Oliver <u>Musicophilia: Tales of Music and the Brain</u> (2007) Random House, pp. 162-164
33. Treffert, Darold <u>Extraordinary People: Understanding Savant Syndrome</u>, Ballantine Books, 2000.
34. From interview by Maureen Seaberg with Billy Joel <u>Psychology Today</u> (May 2012) [31] p. 89
35. Brentano Frans, *1874, Psychology from an Empirical Standpoint (Duncker & Humblot, in German)* p. 68
36. Grandin, Temple; Scariano, Margaret M. (1996). <u>Emergence: Labeled Autistic</u>. Grand Central Publishing. p. 91
37. Grandin, Temple (1995). <u>Thinking in Pictures: And Other Reports from My Life with Autism</u>. New York: Doubleday
38. Grandin, Temple (2009). "How does visual thinking work in the mind of a person with autism? A personal account". *Philosophical Transactions of the Royal Society B*. 364 (1522): 1437–1442
39. Ibid.
40. Chomsky, Noam Syntactic Structures (1957) Ph.D. Thesis
41. Humphrey, Nicholas, "Cave Art, Autism, and the Evolution of the Human Mind" Cambridge Archaeological Journal 8:2 (1998), pp. 165-91
42. Chomsky, Noam, 1996. *Powers and Prospects. Reflections on human nature and the social order.* London: Pluto Press, p 30.
43. Darwin, Charles, 1871. <u>The Descent of Man, and Selection in Relation to Sex</u>
44. Chen, Keith, "The Effect of Language on Economic Behavior: Evidence from Savings Rates, Health Behaviors, and Retirement Assets" <u>American Economic Review</u> 103 (2), 690-731
45. Saxe, John Godfrey, (1816–1887) The Poems of John Godfrey Saxe (1872) "The Blind Men of Indostan", p. 260 ff. ***(in public domain)***
46. Sprong, John Shelby, A New Christianity for a New World: Why Traditional Faith is Dying & How a New Faith is Being Born, Harper, San Francisco, (2001), Pages 37 & 38
47. Ibid, Page 40 & 41

48 Mithen, Steven, (1988). To Hunt or to Paint: Animals and Art in the Upper Paleolithic. *Man, 23*(4), new series, 671-695.
49 Rainey, Anson F. (2008). "Who Were the Early Israelites?" (PDF). *Biblical Archaeology Review*. 34:06, (Nov/Dec 2008): 51–55
50 Schweitzer, Albert (1922) The Quest for the Historical Jesus, A & C Black, Ltd. Page 401
51 Carlisle, Clare, Part 4, "Bertrand Russell the agnostic" in The Guardian, 9 Dec 2013
52 Sagan, Carl, Billions & Billions: Thoughts on Life and Death at the Brink of the Millennium, (1998) Ballantine Books
53 Freberg, Stan, "Freberg to "Sell" Religion on Radio" New York Times (7/3/64)
54 Xenophane,"1*KR, fr. 169. All fragments from the pre-Socratics are as trans. in G. S. Kirk and J. E. Raven: The Pre-Socratic Philosophers (Cambridge, 1957).*
55 Young, William P., The Shack (2007) Windblown Media, CA
56 Curtinger, Curt God-Views, (2001) Video, and God-view Teaching Guide with Gary W. Moon, Life Springs Church Resources, Franklin Springs, GA
57 Phillips, J.B., Your God Is Too Small (1953) The MacMillan Company Ny
58 Ibid., Phillips "Introduction", p. v.
59 Ibid.
60 Meyer, Joyce, (popular Christian evangelist) Internet Blog, February 2, 2010
61 Lyrics by Harriet E. Buell, Music by John B. Summer, 1877
62 St. Athanasius, De inc., 54, 3: PG 25, 192B
63 of Time", incorporated into A Brief History of Time Bantam Books, 1998; it is reported that the book was based on the scientific paper J. B. Hartle; S. W. Hawking (1983*)*. "Wave function of the Universe". Physical Review D. **28** (12): 2960.
64 Khayyam, Omar (1048-1131) The Rubaiyat of Omar Khayyam - Rubai 51, translation by Fitzgerald, Edward, 1859 Public Domain
65 Sagan, Carl, with Druyan, Ann, Pale Blue Dot: A Vision of the Human Future in Space (1994) Random House, p. 52.
66 Lyrics for "How Great Thou Art" were penned by Swedish editor Carl Boberg in 1885; originally titled "O Store Gud" ("O

Might God"); it was sung to several tunes and eventually translated (loosely) into English by Stuart K. Hine, an English missionary, and in 1949 it was published as "How Great Thou Art." It is copyright by © Sony/ATV Music Publishing LLC, BMG Rights Management, Downtown Music

67 "God of Wonders" (2000) Songwriters: Marc Byrd, Steve Hindalong, © Capitol Christian Music Group

68 Heisenberg, Werner <u>The Heisenberg Uncertainty Principle</u> (1927) Published in German: Heisenberg, W. (1927), "Über den anschaulichen Inhalt der quantentheoretischen Kinematik und Mechanik", <u>Zeitschrift für Physik</u> (in German), **43** (3–4): 172–198, Bibcode:1927 Z Phy...43. 172H, doi:<u>10.1007/ BF01397280</u>.D

69 Olson, Roger E., "An Example of Unwarranted Theological Speculation: Divine Timelessness", Patheos, on line blog, February 19, 2015

70 Lewis, C.S. The Problem of Pain (first published 1940) Published by HarperOne (2001), p. 18

71 Richardson, Don, Eternity in Their Hearts (2006) Baker Books, 21-22

72 Brightman, Edgar S., <u>The Problem of God</u>, New York, (1930) p. 113

73 Augustine of Hippo, (2012) <u>The Confessions of St. Augustine</u>, Edward Bouverie Pusey (Translator), (Lib 1,1-2,2.5,5: CSEL 33, 1-5)

74 Paschal, Blaise, <u>Pensées</u> (1966). Penguin Books, New York, p. 75

75 Peck, Scott, <u>The Road Less Traveled: A New Psychology of Love, Traditional Values and Spiritual Growth</u> (1978) Simon & Schuster, and <u>People of the Lie: The Hope for Healing Human Evil</u> (1983) Simon & Schuster

76 Kennedy, John F., 1961, Presidential Inaugural Address

77 Weatherhead, Leslie, <u>The Will of God</u> (1947) Abingdon Press, pp 9-12 *Much of the content in this section is inspired and informed by Weatherhead's book and other works of his. Many other authors have presented similar approaches to God's will, though Weatherhead's was seminal and still regarded as the best explanation.*

78 Ibid. pp. 9-12

79 Ibid. p. 13,

80 Ibid., pp. 46-47
81 Tacitus, *Annals* 15.44, in Tacitus V: Annals Books 13–16, translated by John Jackson, Loeb Classical Library, Harvard University Press, (1937), p. 283.
82 Pliny The Younger (61-113 AD), full name *Gaius Plinius Caecilius Secundus* Letters (*Epistulae* X.96), cited in Pagan Rome and the Early Christians by Stephen Benko (1984), Indiana University Press, pages 5-7
83 Suetonius, Gaius Tranquillus, Nero 16 in Lives of the Twelve Caesars translated in Catharine Edwards. Lives of the Caesars (2001) pp. 184, 203
84 Josephus, Titus Flavius, The Antiquities of the Jews translated in Josephus, Judaism and Christianity, edited by Louis Harry Feldman, Gōhei Hata, (1987) Brill Society, pp. 54-57
85 Ibid.
86 Uncertain: sometimes attributed to James Allen Francis (1864-1928) It is quite similar to a sermon by Rev. Francis included in The Real Jesus and Other Sermons (1926) by Judson Press, pp. 123-124. It is in the Public Domain due to date of last copyright
87 Lewis, C. S., Mere Christianity, London: Collins, 1952, pp. 54–56. (In all editions, this is Bk. II, Ch. 3, "The Shocking Alternative.")
88 Maher, Bill, "Real Time" TV program, May 13, 2011, copyright HBO, Fair Use Claimed
89 Jersak, Bradley A More Christlike God: *A More Beautiful Gospel*, 2016, CWR Press
90 Wesley, Charles, Hymns and Sacred Poems, (1742) Bristol England, Felix Farley, Publisher, pp. 194–95.
91 Lyrics from "Only the Good Die Young" (1977) in the album, The Stranger, Columbia Records.
92 Yancy, Philip, What's So Amazing About Grace? (1997) Zondervan, pp. 54-55
93 Fugelsang, John, "Jesus Was a Radical Nonviolent Revolutionary' Post by John Fugelsang Is Spot On" Huffington Post (12/28/2013). This American actor and comedian posted this statement on his personal Twitter posting and the Huffington Post publicized it nation-wide.
94 Augustine of Hippo, Gen. ad lit. vi.

95. Jeeves, Malcolm, (2011) Rethinking Human Nature: A Multidisciplinary Approach edited by Malcolm Jeeves Wm. B. Eerdmans Publishing. p. 191
96. Kennedy, John F., 1961, Presidential Inaugural Address (Ibid.)
97. Koko: A Talking Gorilla (1978) Documentary by Barbet Schroder, USA, *(original title: Koko, le gorille qui parle)*
98. FaceBook post by Dr. Jane Goodall from Aug 26, 2016, subsequently widely published as posters and in her speeches
99. Stromberg, Joseph, "Seven of the most impressive feats of animal intelligence" in VOX (an on-line magazine) November 16, 2014
100. Howard, Scarlett R, et.al. *"Numerical ordering of zero in honey bees,* Science 08 Jun 2018: Vol. 360, Issue 6393, pp. 1124-1126
101. Sheldrick Daphne, Love, Life, and Elephants: An African Love Story (2012) Farrar, Straus and Giroux, p.145
102. Beckoff, Marc, "A fox, a cougar, and a funeral", Psychology Today (July 2009), p. 12
103. Census of Marine Life. "How many species on Earth? About 8.7 million, new estimate says." ScienceDaily, 24 August 2011
104. Fletcher, Joseph, Humanhood: Essays in Biomedical Ethics (1979) Buffalo, New York: Prometheus Books,) pp. 7-19
105. Rowlands, Mark (2016) "Are animals persons?". Animal Sentience 10(1)
106. Ibid.
107. Chandroo, KP, Duncan, I and Moccia, *RD (2004) Can fish suffer? perspectives on sentience, pain, fear and stress,* Applied Animal Behaviour Science, *pg. 225-250*
108. Composed by Adolphe Adam in 1847 to the French poem Minuit, *"Chretien"* (Midnight, Christians) written by wine merchant and poet Placide Cappea in Public Domain
109. Attributed to Marie de France. Coined by George Weinberg. First appeared in print in an article written for the May 23, 1969, edition of the American tabloid Screw.
110. Tolle, Eckhart, A New Earth: Awakening to Your Life's Purpose (2005, 2016), Penguin Books, p. 15
111. Dawkins, Richard, The Selfish Gene, (1976) Oxford University Press

[112] Dawkins, Richard, The Extended Phenotype: The Long Reach of the Gene (1972, 1999) Oxford University Press
[113] Sumner, William Graham (1914). The Challenge of Facts and Other Essays. Yale University. p. 233-234.
[114] Harris, Thomas A., I'm OK—You're OK (2004) HarperCollins, Quill edition, p. 233.
[115] Lewis, Clive.S., Mere Christianity (1960) The MacMillan Company, pp. 3-5 (Permission Received)
[116] The Universal Declaration of Human Rights was adopted by the third General Assembly of the United Nations on 10 December 1948 in Paris.
[117] Maslow, Abraham H., (2013, [first published 1968, Toward a Psychology of Being. Simon and Schuster. Maslow's hierarchy of needs is a theory in psychology proposed by Abraham Maslow in his 1943 paper "A Theory of Human Motivation" in Psychological Review.
[118] Kohlberg, Lawrence (1984). Essays on Moral Development: Vol. II. The Psychology of Moral Development: The Nature and Validity of Moral Stages. San Francisco, Harper & Row, also Kohlberg, L. (1963). "The development of children's orientations toward a moral order: I. Sequence in the development of moral thought." Vita Humana, 6 (1–2), 11–33.
[119] Kohlberg, Lawrence (1981). Essays on Moral Development, Vol l. I: The Philosophy of Moral Development. San Francisco, CA: Harper & Row.
[120] Berne, Eric, Games People Play (1964) Grove Press
[121] Harris, Thomas Anthony, I'm OK, You're OK (1967) Harper
[122] Rand, Ann (1961) For the New Intellectual: The Philosophy of Ayn Rand, Penguin, p 136
[123] Pigliucci, Massimo in Skeptical Inquirer (2007) May/June) p. 26-7
[124] Heisenberg, Werner. (1971) Physics and Beyond, New York: Harper & Row. p. 206
[125] Libet, Benjamin Mind Time: The Temporal Factor in Consciousness (2004) More to add
[126] Libet, Benjamin, "Unconscious cerebral initiative and the role of conscious will in voluntary action" The Behavioral and Brain Sciences (1985) 8:4, p. 536

127. Greenberg, Jeff, Solomon, Sheldon, and Pyszczynski, Tom The Worm at the Core: On the Role of Death in Life. (2015)
128. Aion: "Researches into the Phenomenology of the Self" (1959), tr. R.F.C. Hull; in The Collected Works of C.G. Jung, Vol. 9/2, p.10
129. Maxwell, Max and Melete (pseudonym) Essay "A Socratic Perspective on the Nature of Human Evil", Online Philosophy Club (Oct 7, 2014) accessed at *OnlinePhilosophyClub.com*
130. Rousseau, Jean-Jacques. Emile, or On Education, first published 1762, Trans. Allan Bloom. New York: Basic Books (1979), p. 301
131. Gaither, William, (1979) Lyric in song, "I Am Loved" in album by same name, featuring Gaither Trio, publisher, Indiana
132. Shakespeare, William, Macbeth (Act 5, scene 5, lines 16–27)
133. James, William (1902) The Varieties of Religious Experience: A Study in Human Nature, Longmans, Green & Co.
134. Campbell, Joseph (1991). The Power of Myth. New York: Anchor. pp. 64-65. The book is based on a PBS six-part series with Bill Moyers, broadcast June 21-26, 1988.
135. Frazer, Sir James George, 1921, on establishment of Frazer Lectureship in Social Anthropology in his honor, Universities Oxford, Cambridge, Glasgow and Liverpool.
136. Frazer, J. G., 2001, in Slow Cures and Bad Philosophers: Essays on Wittgenstein, Medicine, and Bioethics, Carl Elliott, editor, Duke University Press, p. 22.
137. Russell, Bertrand, 1912, The Problems of Philosophy, New York, Henry Holt and Company, pp. 239-240
138. Shaw, George Bernard, Man and Superman: A Comedy and a Philosophy, (1905) Brentano's, New York, p. 230
139. Lewin, Kurt, (1951) Field Theory in Social Science: Selected Theoretical Papers (ed. Cartwright D). New York: Harper & Row
140. Ibid.
141. Atran, Scott, (2002) In Gods We Trust: The Evolutionary Landscape of Religion (Evolution and Cognition) Oxford University Press
142. Shakespeare, William, Julius Caesar, Act 4, scene 3, lines 218–224
143. Alebraheem, A.A. (2016) 5 Essential Dimensions: How to Balance Your Life for Health, Success and Contentment, CreateSpace Independent Publishing Platform

144 Rutherford, Sir Ernest, Attributed but uncertain, "A Preview of Biophysics" by A. G. Bogle, (1952 October) <u>New Zealand Science Review: Official Journal of the New Zealand Association of Scientific Workers</u>, p.158

145 Argyris, Chris and Senge, Peter M. (1990, 1996) <u>The Fifth Discipline</u>, Doubleday

146 Thompson, John Francis, *(1912)*. <u>Francis Thompson, the Preston-Born Poet, with Notes on Some of His Works</u>. Read Books.

147 Lewis, C.S., <u>Surprised by Joy</u>, 1955, Harcourt Brace (US) p. 217

148 Ibid.

149 Ibid., 218

150 Pascal, Blaise, <u>Pensées</u> ("Thoughts") composed in 1600s, first published in 1800s, section 343; The Project Gutenberg E-Book of Pascal's <u>Pensées,</u> by Blaise Pascal (a free public domain edition) was published in 2006. Several other editions have been translated & reprinted by Penguin and many others.

151 A.A. Alebraheem is a column writer for Kuwait's bestselling newspaper, published in <u>ALQABAS.</u> July 9, 2017

152 Attributed to Emerson in The Gift of Depression (2001) by John F. Brown, p. 56; no prior occurrence of this statement has been located; it seems to be derived from one that occurs in The Alchemist (1988) by Paulo Coelho, p. 22: **"When you want something all the universe conspires to helping you achieve it."**

Sources for Chapter Epigrams

Preface

"There is a God-shaped vacuum in every heart" Blaise Pascal (1623 - 1662) Pensées *(New York), Penguin Books, 1966) page 75. Some translations of this sentence vary and are less elegant; some editing of the original may be suspected*

Introduction – No epigram

Chapter 1

"Uncertainty is an uncomfortable position. But certainty is an absurd one"
Voltaire
French philosopher in Letter to Frederick II of Prussia (6 April 1767).

Chapter 2

"Most people are bothered by those passages of Scripture they do not understand, but the passages that bother me are those I do understand" Mark Twain (1835-1910) This quote is not found in any of Twain's books, but the earliest attribution was the "Watertown Daily Times" of Watertown, New York in 1915. Twain probably spoke the words in one of his humorous speeches and may not have kept a written record.

Chapter 3

"Science is a way of thinking. It is more than a body of knowledge" Carl Sagan
(1934 –1996) Sagan's last TV interview on May 27, 1996, with Charlie Rose, PBS

Chapter 4

"The chief function of the body is to carry the brain around" **Thomas** A. Edison
As quoted in The Romance and Drama of the Rubber Industry (1936) by Harvey Firestone

Chapter 5

"I simply believe that some part of the human Self or Soul is not subject to the laws of space and time" Carl Jung in Modern man in search of his soul. (1933).

Chapter 6

"Too often we enjoy the comfort of opinion without the discomfort of thought"
John F. Kennedy, 35th US President (1917-1963), Inaugural Address 1961

Chapter 7

"That's one small step for a man, one giant leap for mankind" **Neil** Armstrong
Broadcast from moon July 20, 1969

Chapter 8

"Whatever you think God is, know he is more than that" Ibn Ata Allah (1215-1298)

(13th Century Sufi scholar) Ibn 'Ata' Allah. The Book of Wisdom. Translated by Victor Danner. Ramsey, NJ: Paulist Press, 1978

Chapter 9

"God don't make no mistakes, that's how He got to be God" **Archie** Bunker Character on "All in The Family" TV program (1971-1979) Created by Norman Lear

Chapter 10

God is Great, God is Good; Let us thank Him for our food.
By His hands we all are fed, Give us Lord our Daily Bread.
Amen Traditional American folk lore, original author unknown; used as lyrics for song composed by Asahel Abbott (1852) published in several hymnals

Chapter 11

As the print of the seal on the wax is the express image of the seal itself, so Christ is the express image – the perfect representation of God"
St. Ambrose (aka Aurelius Ambrosius 340-397 A.D.) Sermon based on Hebrews 1:3 ("express image")

Chapter 12

"God loves each of us as if there were only one of us" Augustine of Hippo (354-430)
Some translations less elegant, Confessions, trans. Henry Chadwick (Oxford: Oxford University Press, 2009), 3.11.19, p. 50.

Chapter 13

"I like your Christ, I do not like your Christians. Your Christians are so unlike your Christ" Mahatma Gandhi (1869-1948) Disputed quote: A similar quote appears to be from an Indian philosopher named Bara Dada, brother of Rabindranath Tagore.

Chapter 14

"All animals are equal, but some animals are more equal than others" George Orwell
In the George Orwell novel <u>Animal Farm</u> (1945) *(Chapter 10, pg. 3-4)*

Chapter 15

"There is so much good in the worst of us, and so much bad in the best of us, that it ill behooves any of us to find fault with the rest of us."
James Truslow Adams 1878-1949) Disputed quote, also attributed to Edgar Cayce or Robert Louis Stevenson

Chapter 16

"I have noticed even people who claim everything is predestined, and that we can do nothing to change it, look before they cross the road" Stephen Hawking In an essay *"Is Everything Determined"* from his book <u>Black Holes and Baby Universes and Other Essays</u>, first published in 1993. Interestingly, his next line was "Maybe it's just that those who don't look don't survive to tell the tale."

Chapter 17

"To be free from evil thoughts is God's best gift" Aeschylus (525 -456 B.C.) From <u>Prometheus Bound</u>, 459 B.C., disputed but usually attributed to Aeschylus

Chapter 18

"I'd rather laugh with the sinners than cry with the saints" Billy Joel Lyrics from "Only the Good Die Young" (1977) in the album, **The Stranger**, Columbia Records.

Chapter 19

"A man should never be ashamed to own he has been in the wrong, which is but saying, in other words, that he is wiser today than he was yesterday" Alexander Pope (1688 –1744) from Thoughts on Various Subjects (1727)

Chapter 20

"It's not what we don't know that gives us trouble, it's what we know that ain't so"
Will Rogers (1879-1935) American comedian; this quote is in dispute, also being attributed in somewhat similar words to Mark Twain and Artemus Ward. The quoted version here was likely part of Will Rogers' many Vaudeville Shows.

Chapter 21

"A decision is the product of choosing, and an ability to choose is what makes us human"
A.A. Alebraheem from <u>5 Essential Dimensions</u>: <u>How to balance your life</u> <u>for health, success and contentment</u>, published by author, 2016 on Kindle e-book format

www.ingramcontent.com/pod-product-compliance
Lightning Source LLC
Chambersburg PA
CBHW020246010526
44107CB00002B/115